MW01026186

THE
LIFE

Hugh OF *Showcraft*,

POPE SIXTUS the Fifth.

(One of the moſt Remarkable and Entertaining LIVES that is
to be met with in Ancient or Modern Hiſtory.)

IN WHICH IS INCLUDED

The State of England, France, Spain, Italy, theSwiſs
Cantons, Germany, Poland, Ruſſia, Sweden,
and the Low Countries, at that TIME.

WITH AN ACCOUNT OF

St. PETER's, the Conclave, and Manner of chuſing a POPE;
the Vatican Library, (the many Grand Obeliſks, Aqueducts, Bridges, Hoſpitals, Palaces, Streets, Towns, and
other Noble Edifices, Begun or Finiſhed by him.

The Whole interſperſed with ſeveral Curious Incidents and Anec-
dotes, not to be met with in any other AUTHOR.

Tranſlated from the Italian of GREGORIO LETI,

WITH A PREFACE AND NOTES.

By ELLIS FARNEWORTH, M.A.

Some time of JESUS COLLEGE in Cambridge,

And Chaplain to ſeveral of his Majeſty's Ships, during the late War.

ORATIONI ET CARMINI EST PARVA GRATIA, NISII
ELOQUENTIA EST SUMMA: HISTORIA, QUOQUOMODO
SCRIPTA, DELECTAT.   PLIN.

DUBLIN:

PRINTED FOR W. COLLES, DAME-STREET; AND
L. FLIN, CASTLE-STREET.

M DCC LXXIX.

C 4516.8

1863. Mar. 26
Gray Fund
.75

HARVARD
UNIVERSITY
LIBRARY

―――――――――――――――――

TO

WILLIAM FITZHERBERT, Esq;

Of Tissington in Derbyshire.

SIR,

THE long experience I have had of your candour and friendſhip, encourages me to aſk the favour of your countenance to the following perform-ance: And it gives me, I aſſure you, a very ſincere pleaſure, that I now have an opportunity of making a public ac-knowledgement of the many great obli-gations I lie under to you: Obligations kindly and generouſly conferred, at a time chiefly when almoſt every body elſe was ſtriving who ſhould get the far-theſt from me.

The ſtings and arrows of outrageous Fortune,
Th' oppreſſor's wrongs.—The law's delay,

are bugbears, I know, that too often fright away our beſt and deareſt friends,

A 2   and

and leave but a very fmall remnant of fuch as have either the courage or humanity to ftand by us *on a raw and gufty day.*

Yet Adverfity, with all its whips and fcorns, has this advantage attending it, that it not only teaches us to know ourfelves, but other people, as it fhews them to us under their true colours, and fuch as they really are. The tiger and the bear then appear in their native ferocity; the familiar ape, and the petulant jack-afs, will leap upon our fhoulders, or kick up their heels in our face. For to what purpofe fhould they lay any reftraint upon their nature, or put on a painful difguife, and endeavour to conceal their brutality by a ufelefs and unprofitable civility, to perfons from whom they have nothing to hope and but little to fear?

I have feen the fame animals proftrate themfelves in the moft abject manner before a man in power, and come in humble guife, creeping and fawning, and licking his fpittle, to court a fmile or deprecate his frowns. Profperity
hides

hides thefe things from our eyes, like a film,

Quæ nunc obducta tuenti
Mortales bebetat vifus,

and tempts men to think all their adoration is a tribute due to their virtue, when in reality, it is only a homage paid to their greatnefs.

Hence it is, that, I freely own, I have made a great alteration in my eftimate both of men and things, and at prefent entertain but a very low opinion of the generality of mankind, tho' I fet out into the world with far different fentiments, which yet upon long experience (the beft guide) I have found, for the moft part, chimerical and falacious.

However, in all the various changes and viciffitudes of my life, in every ebb and flow of fortune, amidft the perfecution of caufelefs enemies, and the unkind defection of fummer friends, under the fevereft and moft poignant afflictions that could wound the heart of man, you have always been the

firm

firm and steady friend, and your character still uniform and confiftent.----
Delineation I forbear; it might perhaps, to fome, make this addrefs appear
more like a piece of mean adulation
(which I know you abhor) than a grateful acknowledgment of paft favours. Indeed, I think it would be paying a very
bad compliment to a kind and benefi-
cent patron, always affable and eafy of
accefs, to treat him like an Indian pa-
god, or a peevifh and mercenary tyrant,
never to be approached without incenfe
and oblations.

Surely there is a great affinity betwixt
the fin of fome modern dedicators, and
that of the Ifraelites worfhiping a golden calf. For my own part, I ftill
preferve a fpirit fo far unbroken by the
frowns of Fortune, that whenever I
fee thofe vile proftrations, I cannot help
equally defpifing both the idol that ac-
cepts, and the idolator that offers them.

Thus much, however, I hope I may
be allowed to fay, without any imputation of flattery, that whatever deftiny
is referved for me, or to what fhore fo-

ever

ever it fhall pleafe Heaven to conduct
my fhattered bark, after having been
toffed about by adverfe winds, I fhall
never ceafe to remember how much I
am, and ever ought to be,

S I R,

Your moft obliged

and moft obedient

Humble Servant,

ELLIS FARNEWORTH.

PREFACE.

IN the autumn of the the year 1752, I went to spend a few days at a [1] friend's house in the country, where I accidentally met with a French version of the following life, and read it over with a good deal of pleasure; tho' I perceived it was but an abridgment of a much larger work in Italian, which, after long enquiry, I at last procured, with a design to translate it, at the request and by the encouragement of several of my acquaintance. If I came to it with a degree of eagerness and expectation, my courage began to fail me, upon taking a view of the outworks; for tho' there was much good matter, I found such a chaos of trash and rubbish to be cleared away, such a want of coherence, so little regard to time and order, and the method (if indeed there was any method) so confused and inverted, that I was obliged in many places to transpose it (a difficulty that seldom occurs in any translation) and grew so sick of the undertaking, that I heartily repented of my engagement.

But afterwards, when I saw, that amongst all this dross, there was a considerable quantity of very valuable metal, and recollected the promise I had made to my friends, I not only thought it shameful to recede,

[1] The Rev. Mr. Pilkington's prebendary of Litchfield, author of several valuable performances in the defence and support of the Christian religion.

a

but

but a duty in some measure incumbent upon me, as far as I was able, to rescue a shining character from that cloud of obscurity in which it was eclipsed and almost extinguished. Encouraged by these considerations, I determined to persist, tho' besides the above-mentioned difficulties, I met with many gross mistakes in point of history and inscriptions, and more false pointings, than in any book I ever read; which cost me infinite pains to rectify, by consulting other authors. Though very likely there may be still some uncorrected, which might either escape my notice, or exceed my abilities [2]. Indeed I believe I should never have been able to go thro' with it, at any rate, if it had not been for the free access that was indulged me by my ever honoured friend Brooke Boothby, Esq; to a large collection of books in his possession at Ashbourn Hall, where I met with Thuanus, Schraderus, Roma Antiqua Figurata, Relation de la Cour de Rome, Platina, Sir Paul Ricaut, Il Cardinalismo di Santa Chiesa, and many other writers that were of great service to me.

Leti himself, was an Italian of a considerable family, born at Milan, in the year 1630. After he had travelled thro' Savoy and France, he came into England, where he was well received by K. Charles II, and had a promise of being made his historiographer; but meeting with some disappointment, he went to Amsterdam in 1682, and was chosen historian for that city. His works are very numerous, as may be seen in the account given of them by Moreri. When he wrote this

[2] I apprehend there may be some error, at least deficiency, in what the author says in his description of the vatican library, p. 519, concerning the letter F, said to be invented by the emperor Claudius, and the Y of Pythagoras, p. 518, for farther satisfaction in that matter, the reader is desired to consult Tacit. Annal. xi. 14. Aulus Gellius v. 4. Chishul's Antiquitates Asiaticæ, Dr. Taylor's Marmor Sandvicense, and the Historia Græcarum et Latinarum literarum, by Dr. Reynolds.

history

hiftory he feems to have been far advanced in years, or at leaft in the decline of life, and got into his talkative ftage; for tho' I believe moft, or all of the facts that he recites are true, becaufe I find them generally attefted by other hiftorians of thofe times, yet it is certain they are related in an old woman like manner, full of tautology and repetition: He often forgets himfelf, and tells the fame ftory over and over again, with little variation, in the compafs of a few pages, without any regard to connection, eafinefs of tranfition, or that lucidus ordo which is neceffary, not only to make a hiftory entertaining, but even intelligible and confiftent with the accounts of other nations. He likewife abounds with puerilities, low puns, quaint fayings, ufus verbborum, and what the Italians call concetti, or nice conceits (as an old friend of mine ufed to ftile them) which is a fault that hardly the very beft of either the Italian or Spanifh authors, with all their gravity, are quite free from.

As to the tranflation, it is very far from being a literal one: I own myfelf entirely indebted to Leti for the marrow and fubftance of the hiftory, but have, in a great meafure, taken the relation of the facts out of his hands, tho' with a ftrict regard to the truth of the whole, and every particular circumftance. Whether I have reduced it to a clearer method, or told the old man's ftory in a better manner, or how I have fucceeded, I can't tell, nor will I take upon myfelf to determine whether this is an allowable way of tranflating or not.

If, as Pliny fays [3], "It is a generous and praife-
"worthy undertaking to prevent the memory of thofe
"that have merited eternity by their actions, from

[3] "Pulchrum imprimis videtur non pati occidere quibus æternitas debeatur." *Plin.*

"finking

a 2

xii PREFACE.

" finking into oblivion;" without doubt, Sixtus V. has
a very juft claim to our utmoft edeavours to fet his
actions in a fairer light, and wipe off the mould and
duft which either the hand of time, or the pen of a
doting hiftorian, has contributed to fcatter over his
fame. For if we examine his character from his infancy to the grave, it is indeed a very extraordinary
one, and fuch as highly deferves to be tranfmitted to
future times.

His morals and behaviour, in private life, were unexceptionable, if we can excufe his reftlefs ambition
and thirft of power, fo vifible in the continual fquabbles and contentions he was engaged in for fuperiority :
He was remarkably affiduous in the labours of his
calling, or ftrict juftice and honefty, charitable, be-
neficent, grateful, temperate, and chafte. But if
ambition be a crime, without queftion he may juftly
be numbered amongft the greateft tranfgreffors.

It is certain he had fixed his eyes upon the tiara
very early, and purfued his defign with an unwearied
conftancy thro' all the various fcenes of his life,
triumphing over the infirmities of flefh and blood,
bringing into captivity every appetite and emotion of
nature, and keeping all his paffions in the ftricteft and
moft flavifh fubjection. If he fteered a different
courfe to his port from the generality of mankind, and
feemed to defpife what he moft ardently wifhed for,
failing one way whilft he looked another, he did no
more than feveral other great perfonages (whofe
names, perhaps, it might be invidious to mention,
tho' they will be handed down to immortality with
glory and applaufe) have done both before and after
him.

So complete a victory had he gained over himfelf,
that tho' he was a man of the ftrongeft and moft furious

ous paffions, naturally vindictive, turbulent, and proud, he feemed the moft forgiving, meekeft, and humbleft, of all human kind.

During the courfe of 15 years that he was cardinal, and found it neceffary to wear this difguife, he never made one flip, or fuffered any of his failings to peep out.

From hence we may learn, that it is not only impious and unreafonable, but highly ridiculous, to accufe Providence of having dealt unkindly with us, in implanting paffions in our breafts that we cannot govern, and to lament our conftitutional infirmities as incurable, when we plainly fee, it is in our power not only to correct, but almoft, if not totally, to change and alter our nature. Strange it is, that when *every kind of beafts, and birds, and ferpents, and things in the fea have been tamed,* (Ja. iii. 7.) man alone, the nobleft work of God's hands in this world, endued with reafon, and animated with the hope of a future reward, fhould be deemed a favage and untameable animal, incapable of being ever thoroughly broke, or unable to fubdue his inordinate defires and inclinations.

It muft be owned, indeed, to the reproach of our fpecies, that we every day fee inftances of men hurried away headlong by their paffions, and guilty of the moft abfurd and irrational actions: This, however, is no juft impeachment of the creator's goodnefs, but a lamentable debauch and vitiation of our nature, originally perfect and without blemifh. Our appetites naturally grow ftronger and more importunate by indulgence, like a fpark of fire in combuftible matter, which, if not timely extinguifhed, burfts out into a flame, and threatens every thing round it with ruin and defolation. Upon which account it behoves us, if we expect any fatisfaction, or peace of mind in this world, to be conftantly upon our guard, to rein them

hard

hard down, and carry a strict command over them ; except we have a mind to enter volunteers into their service (for there is no medium) and become of all slaves the most abject and contemptible ; which would be a conduct highly unworthy of a man, and a sure indication not only of a mean and pusillanimous disposition, but the lowest and last degree of stupefaction.

Some, perhaps, may be apt to find fault with the unrelenting rigour of his justice, as proceeding from a cruel and blood-thirsty nature ; but the amazing licentiousness of the age he lived in, will, I think, be a very justifiable apology for him in this respect.

He has been charged by others with hypocrisy, which is indeed a very odious vice, both in the sight of God and man ; what reason there is for such an accusation I know not, except his having gained an absolute conquest over his passions, and pretending to be older and more infirm than he really was, in which I cannot see any great harm, as nobody was injured or prejudiced by it.

In the pursuit of dominion (which is of all others the most eager chace) men are too apt to think every thing lawful that is any way expedient, or conducible to their ends: So that Sixtus will appear innocent at least, if not praise-worthy, when compared with those that have opened their way to empire by the sword, or laid the foundation of their greatness in all manner of fraud, injustice, murder, poisonings, assassinations ; nay, sometimes in the utter subversion of the laws and liberty of their country : Of which it would be easy to quote many examples, if there were occasion, both from our own history and that of other nations.

Julius

Julius Cæsar openly avowed this principle, and had (as Tully informs us) the two following lines of Euripides conftantly in his mouth :

Nam fi violandum eft jus, regnandi gratiâ
Violandum eft ; aliis rebus pietatem colas.

Be ever ftrictly juft, except a throne
Come in thy reach, then---Juftice, get thee
    gone [3].

His raifing the immenfe fums of money that enabled him to perform fuch wonderful things, in fo fhort time, is a remarkable proof how much a wife and attentive man, may avail himfelf of the foibles and extravagancies of mankind, efpecially in diffolute times.

In fhort, when we confider that from a poor, half-ftarved, ragged boy, attending hogs in the field, he arrived at the higheft dignity in the Romifh church (indeed a monarchy, and a very refpectable one too) paffing in regular fucceffion thro' the feveral functions of lay-brother, profeffed-religious, preacher, regent-procurator, inquifitor, till he came to be general of

[4] "Ipfe autem, i. e. Julius Cæfar, in ore femper Græcos "verfus de phœniffis habebat, quos dicam ut potero, incondite "fortaffe, fed tamen ut res poffit intelligi." "He, viz. Julius "Cæfar was always repeating thefe two verfes out of the Phœ-"niffæ of Euripides, which I will tranflate as well as I can, badly "enough, perhaps, yet fo, I hope, as to be underftood." Tull. de Offic. l. iii. Which muft likewife ferve as an apology for my tranflation of them.
The lines in the original

" Ειπερ γαρ αδικειν χρη, τυραννιδος περι
" Καλλιςον αδικειν, τ αλλα δ' ευσεβειν χρεων.

are the anfwers of Eteocles to his mother, who is perfuading him to reftore the kingdom to his brother Polynices, whom he had defrauded of it.

his

his order, bifhop, cardinal, and at laft, one of the
greateft pontiffs that ever reigned, we muft acknowledge that much was owing to his own prudence and
good conduct, which generally command fuccefs, and
are attended with the blefling of God, who *raifeth the
poor out of the duft, and lifteth the needy from the dunghill, to fit amongft the princes of his people.* Pfalm
cxiii. 7, 8. Old verfion.

Machiavel indeed feems to reafon after a different
manner in his life of Caftruccio, where he has the following reflection:

" E pare, a quelli che la confiderano, cofa maravig-
" liofa, che tutti coloro, ò la maggior parte d' efſi,
" che hanno in quefto mondo operate grandiffime cofe,
" è tra gl' altri della loro età, fiano ftati excellenti,
" habbiano havuto il Principio è Nafcimento loro baf-
" fo et obfcuro, òvero della Fortuna fuora di ogni mo-
" do travagliato; Perche tutti, ò ei fono ftati expofti
" alle fiere, ò eglino hanno havuto fi vile padre, che
" vergognatifi di quello, fi fono fatti figliuoli di Giove,
" ò di qualche altro Dio: Quali fiano ftati quefti Sen-
" done a ciafcuno noti molti, farebbe cofa a replicare
" faftidiofa et poco accetta a chi legeffe: Percio come
" fuperflua poftporremo. Credo bene che quefto nafca,
" che volendo la Fortuna dimoftrare al mondo d' ef-
" fere quella che faccia gl' huomini grandi è non la
" Prudenza, comminicia a dimoftrare le fue forze in
" tempo che la Prudenza, non ei poffa haver alcuna
" parte, anzi da lei fi habbia a ricognofcere il tutto."
" It is worthy of notice, that they who have performed
" the moft heroic actions, and fhone with the great-
" eft fplendor in their paffage thro' the world, have
" generally either been born of very mean and ob-
" fcure parents, or fuch as have been remarkably per-
" fecuted by Fortune: Some of them having been in
" their infancy expofed to wild beafts, and others fo
                                          " afhamed

" afhamed of their nativity, that they have pretended
" to be the fons of Jupiter, or fome other deity : Of
" which it is needlefs to recite inftances, as many will
" naturally occur to every one's memory. It feems
" by this as if Fortune had a mind to fhew the world,
" that it is fhe alone, and not Prudence, that makes
" men great, by exerting her power at a time when
" Prudence cannot poffibly be faid to have any fhare
" in it."

The fiercenefs and impetuofity of temper that we
meet with in the firft part of his life, muft be imputed to the little care that was taken of his education,
whilft his paffions were yet ductile and flexible, and
the want of more early culture and difcipline, which
has fo remarkable an effect upon the fubfequent part of
all men's lives, and as the Poet very truly fays,

Emollit mores, nec finit effe feros.

However it is certain, that with all his foibles and infirmities, from which alas! the very beft of men are
not wholly exempt, he was a moft extraordinary per-
fonage, *a burning and a fhining light*, and as Cotton
fays of another great man, " Had there not been a
" little mixture of human frailty amongft fo many
" excellent qualities that he was mafter of, the ftory
" would have looked like the idea of a pope only, and
" rather a character of what a great pontiff fhould be,
" than what any one ever truly was. There are in-
" deed fome paffages in his hiftory that are not alto-
" gether to be juftified, tho' none that may not (me-
" thinks) be flipped over amongft fo many better pages
" of his life, like one counterfeit piece in a great fum
" of current gold."

After I had made fome progrefs in this work, I
heard it had been tranflated formerly, but by what
hand I could not learn, nor by any means obtain a
                                                    fight

fight of the book, till I had begun to write my copy fair over for the prefs, when my very worthy and learned friend, Tho. Bonfoy of Afhbourn, Efq; procured me one out of his brother's library at Abbot's Ripton, in Huntingtonfhire, tranflated in 1704, by one Dr. Salmon, a licentiate of the college of phyficians (a writer of very moderate reputation) and I have fince met with another of the fame impreffion; but, upon perufal, found it was only an epitome of the French verfion, which itfelf is an abridgement of the Italian. It is a fmall octavo, and if it had been ftill lefs, it would have faved me many a yawn, for it is a very crude, indigefted, and, according to the phrafe now in vogue, an immenfely ftupid performance: So that my wonder at its being fcarce immediately ceafed; for, I dare fay, the far greater part, if not the whole of the impreffion, except the two copies I have juft now mentioned, has long ago paffed into the grocers and tobaconifts fhops.

Tranflators, I know, are generally looked upon but as fecond-hand writers at beft; yet they have their merit, and may boaft of being countenanced by Dryden, Pope, Addifon, Melmoth, Cotton, Orrery, and many others of great diftinction in the literary world: But if there be more honour in appearing as an original author, I have fome reafon to be forry for the lofs of a work that had coft me a good deal of time and pains when I was abroad, and which I defigned, fome time or other, to have fent into day-light. It contained an account of what paffed at Jamaica, and other parts of the Weft Indies, from the year 1742 to 1747, the cuftoms and polity of the inhabitants, with all the remarkable tranfactions, both at fea and land, in that period. The fecond part was a fort of a natural hiftory, defcribing moft of the plants, animals, minerals, &c. that are to be met with in the Torrid Zone, with fome charts and draughts of them, given

me

me by a friend. But happening, unluckily, in the
course of my peregrinations, to fall into the hands of
the honeft monfieurs de Bayonne, they fairly ftripped
me of that and every thing elfe.

In pouring off one language into another, a good
deal of the ftrength and fpirit muft naturally evaporate,
and it is hardly poffible for any tranflation to appear
wholly free from an air of ftiffnefs and conftraint, except great care is taken to avoid too literal a verfion.
It is full as eafy to compofe; for when a man is writing upon his own bottom, he may ufe a latitude of
expreffion and variation of fentiment, which he muft
not often make bold with when he comes to tranflate.

In either cafe it is extremely difficult to write with
purity; for fo vague and undetermined is the fenfe of
many words and phrafes, in our tongue (which, I fuppofe, is the misfortune of all living languages) that,
when an author comes to examine them, he often
finds (though perhaps he did not expect it) that feveral
expreffions, which yet are paffable enough in common
converfation, are in truth either very ungrammatical
and improper, or abfolute nonfenfe: for inftance, *All
manner of perfons, Let me recommend* it *to you to do
this, To make a man welcome, To fend word of fuch a
thing, &c.*

There has been much altercation about ufing the
word hopes in the plural number; but chiefly amongft
fuch, I have obferved, as were no very cunning clerks,
fince it is adopted by Milton, Tillotfon, the prefent
bifhop of Clogher, Mr. Johnfon, and feveral other
authors of great name. For my own part I can fee
no abfurdity or impropriety in it. For why not hopes,
as well as fears, or doubts, or expectations? It is objected, it feems, that the word fpes, in the Latin, has
no

no plural; but this is futile and frivolous; if we are to be such servile imitators of the Latins, why don't we, like them, use angers, and strengths? which last especially, I think hardly any one will contend for, as there are already other consonants enough, in that word, almost to smother one poor solitary vowel, without tagging another to them, the frequent return of which is the opprobrium of our language, and gives foreigners occasion to reproach us with hissing like snakes.

I might mention a thousand other expressions, if it was necessary, which seem short of weight when put into the grammatical balance: but if we look upon them as downright Anglicisms (every known language claiming a right to its idioms and peculiarities of speech) there can no longer subsist any reason for cavil about them, as in all disputes of this kind, we must ultimately have recourse to the decision of custom. A Derbyshire man writes according to the idiom of his county; he that has been educated, or lived the greatest part of his life in Yorkshire, does the same; so did the Ionians, Dories, and Æolians amongst the Greeks; the different provinces of Italy, in former times, the Siennese and Florentines at this day. But it is generally supposed (how truly I can't say) that a greater degree of elegance and propriety has reigned at London, Rome and Athens.

I think then it is almost an impossibility to write with absolute and unsinning purity, in any living language, considering the continual flux and reflux that is in every one: many words that were never heard of before are daily introduced, some falling like leaves, and by slow degrees, whilst others that have been thought long since dead, have suddenly revived, and

sprouted

fprouted out again with frefh vigour, as Horace long
ago prophefied,

Multa renafcentur quæ jam recidere, cadentque
Que nunc funt in honore vocabula, fi volet ufus,
Quem penes arbitrium eft, et jus et norma loquendi.

The Italian is commonly reckoned the eafieft of all
the modern languages, and it is often faid, that every
one underftands it that can read Latin. I own I am
not of that opinion, for I think the knowledge of both
the Spanifh and French tongues is much fooner to be
acquired. It is true there are feveral words in it immediately derived from, and indeed the very fame
with the Latin, as there are in moft others. But
if we confider the many Gothic words that are Italianized,
and the many Itatlan, or rather Latin words that are
Gothicized, with the poetical licences, the frequent ufe
of one mood and tenfe for another, the whimfical
tranfpofition of particles and pronouns, and other
idioms, it will be fufficient to juftify my affertion. It
is certainly very foft and mufical; but yet there is
fomething in the return of, very often, the fame vowel
at the end of many words together, that rather palls
and jades an ear that delights in variety ; for inftance,
fono, ftato, molto, obligato, &c. Perhaps I may be
fingular in my opinion, or over partial to our own language, which, though not tuneful enough for the pipe
of an eunuch, or thofe dying ftrains that are warbled out
at our operas, cannot now be looked upon, as either
beggarly or defective, fince the naturalization of fo
many polyfyllables, which, as far as I can find, are
altogether of foreign extraction, and unknown to our
anceftors. It is not only fufficiently copious and ex-
preffive, but, I may venture to fay, a ftrong, nervous,
and, in the main, a very noble and luxuriant language :
though it muft be confeffed, there is ftill room for a little polifh and melioration.

It

It is much to be wished some able hand would undertake that task, and publish a dictionary to ascertain the true sterling value of every word and expression, with references (like Cooper's Latin dictionary) to the particular places where and in what sense they are used by such authors as may be accounted the classics of the English tongue for the last 50 or 60 years, which, if I prophesy right, will hereafter be reckoned the Augustan age of the English nation. A work earnestly longed for by the public, but more particularly by all such as have occasion to launch into print. I have been informed the learned and ingenious Mr. Johnson (to whom the world is much obliged for his excellent writings) has a thing of this kind under his consideration, and dare say, from the many specimens we have already had of his abilities, it will be executed in a very masterly manner, in which I heartily wish him success, as it is an undertaking highly worthy of a patriot, in the true sense of the word; and such as deserves encouragement from every friend of his country.

I hope what I have said concerning our language, will not be looked upon as tedious, or impertinent and superfluous, when we remember how attentive other nations were to this point, what qualms and scruples some of the greatest genius's of antient Rome formerly had about writing *In Piraea* or *Piraeeum*, *consul tertium* or *consul tertio* [5], and then consider whether purity

[3] Pompey was preparing an inscription for the front of a temple which he had built to Venus the conqueress, containing as usual, the recital of all his titles: but in drawing it up, a doubt arose concerning the manner of expressing his third consulship, whether it should be by *consul tertium*, or *consul tertio*; this was referred to the principal critics of Rome; who could not, it seems, agree about it; some of them contending for the one, and some for the other: so that Pompey left it to Cicero to decide the matter, and inscribe what he thought best. But Cicero being unwilling to give judgment on either side, when there were great
authorities

rity is a matter indifferent, and of small concern, or whether it does not merit our serious regard and attention.

Some of my friends were apprehensive Mr. Bower's work would be of prejudice to this, though I cannot see for what reason. Far from depreciating his performance, I, on the contrary, think it deserves great applause; but hope I may be allowed to say, that I have as good a title to write (at least to translate) the life of a pope, or all the popes, if I pleased, as Mr. Bower or any other man; and dare engage he is of that opinion himself: why else has he ventured upon a task that has been executed by Onuphrius, Platina, Sir Paul Ricaut, Marianna, Volaterran, and many others long before him? Besides his history at present only comes down to the year 757, 800 years short of the period that mine includes, which it is much to be feared he will never be able to reach, at least in the space of a great many years, and, if ever he should, it must likewise be considered, that a person who undertakes to write the lives of all the popes (which must amount to some hundreds, and is a labour, if properly executed, that the life of man is not equal to) cannot be supposed to be either so accurate, or copious, or circumstantial as another, who has made one life only the care and subject of his study. He must necessarily omit several very material transactions, at least relate them in a cursory and imperfect manner; which is inexcusable, when we reflect that there are several even minute circumstances and occurrences in the lives of

great

---

authorities on both and Varro amongst them, like a good lawyer, advised Pompey to abbreviate the word in question, and order ᴛ ᴇ ᴀ ᴛ. only to be inscribed; which fully declared the thing without determining the dispute. From this, we may observe, how nicely exact they were in that age, in preserving a propriety of language in their public monuments and inscriptions. See Middleton's life of Cicero, vol. ii. p. 162. and Aulus Gellius, lib x. 1.

great men, which are entertaining and agreeable to all readers, and confequently fuch as they would regret being left untold: whereas the prefent hiftory takes in every ftage and period of this pope's life, from his keeping hogs in a field, when a child, till through a very uncommon variety of the moft remarkable events, he arrived at the papacy; with the whole of his reign, and the ftate of all Chriftendom, and many other parts of the world, during his life.

Such as it is, O world, I here deliver it up to thee, to be treated as fhall feem beft to thy great wifdom: if it has the good fortune to meet with the approbation of the candid and ingenious, I fhall not give myfelf much trouble about the opinion of others.

T H E

THE

L I F E

O F

POPE SIXTUS the FIFTH.

BOOK THE FIRST.

O F all the monarchies that have ever exifted, from the creation of the world to this day, the Roman Pontificate is certainly the moft admirable in its frame and conftitution, and indeed every other way the moft refpectable.

Few princes, either Chriftian or Pagan, have reigned more defpotically than the Pontiffs; none had the glory of feeing fo many Kings and Emperors proftrate at their feet.

That union of temporal and fpiritual power, the complication of fecular and religious interefts, that alliance betwixt the fword and crucifix, that authority which they claim not only upon earth, but in heaven, have eftablifhed a dominion that has been revered by almoft all the nations in the world.

Governments founded upon authority purely temporal, have feldom fubfifted long, fome falling to decay foon after their firft inftitution, whilft others, that have been carried up to a more confiderable height, have melted away, in the courfe of a few centuries, like fnow upon the mountain tops.

But by whatfoever ftorms and tempefts this monarchy has been affailed, from its infancy to the prefent time, it has conftantly maintained, nay often extended, its power and influence; a power fo wifely

B   founded

founded upon the *rock* of spiritual authority, that *neither winds, nor rain, nor floods,* nor a long succession of *ages, nor the gates of hell, have been able to prevail against it.* ~~til the reign of the Emperor Bonaparte.~~

The election of a Pontiff has always been attended to, with the greatest care and circumspection, by the clergy and princes of Christendom, as both spiritual and temporal authority, are intimately and indissolubly united in his person.

In the first ages of the church, spiritual concerns were much more regarded than temporal, and the clergy applied themselves with greater assiduity to direct the consciences of the faithful, than to acquire civil empire and dominion : they chose persons of exemplary piety, long practised in meditation and prayer, who by the holiness of their lives, and indefatigable labours in their calling, converted whole provinces and kingdoms to the faith of Jesus Christ.

But in succeeding times, the church being enriched by the liberality and devotion of several Christian princes, and in possession of considerable territories, thought proper to fix upon such persons, as were not only devout and zealous in matters of religion, but of great experience in the management of secular affairs.

This conduct, of choosing persons equally versed in politics, and eminent for their virtue and learning, has been more strictly observed by the clergy during these two or three last hundred years; so that when other states have been upon the brink of ruin (as it has often happened) by the errors of young and unexperienced princes that governed them; the see of Rome has grown stronger and more vigorous, by the care that has been always taken, to intrust the reins of government in the hands of none, but those that were far advanced in years, of the maturest wisdom and prudence, as well as distinguish'd learning and piety.

Now of all the successors of St. Peter, if we select those who have filled his chair most worthily, and with the greatest applause, we shall find very few, or none, whose merit and virtues exceed those of Sixtus the
fifth :

fifth: as his life abounds with examples highly worthy
of imitation, and affords a great variety of remarkable
incidents, we hope the history of it, may not only serve
as a present entertainment, but be of use to the reader
hereafter, and heartily wish our poor endeavours may
any way contribute to preserve the memory of so illustrious a personage from darkness and oblivion.

He was born in the province of La Marca d'Ancona,
at a village call'd Le Grotte in the Signiory of Montalto, containing about seven or eight hundred inhabitants, from which he took his title, when he was afterwards made cardinal: his father, Francis Peretti a native of Castello di Farnese was obliged to leave his country for some crime he had been guilty of, which he
did without much reluctance, and he had nothing to
live upon but the sweat of his brow.

The night after he left Castello di Farnese, he came
to Le Grotte to advise with his uncle, who lived there,
what course he should take; and was recommended by
him to a rich country gentleman in that neighbourhood, who was so pleased with his diligence and fidelity, that at the end of six years, which he served him
as gardener, he gave him a favourite servant-maid to
wife, whose name was Gabana, from which he was
called sometimes, in banter the Gabanese.

They had three children, two sons and a daughter;
the daughter's name was Camilla, whom we shall have
occasion to mention again in the course of this history.

The eldest son, Felix, was born the 13th of December 1521, at a time when all Italy was in arms; Pope
Leo the tenth having, in the last year of his pontificate,
joined with the Emperor, to drive the French out of
Italy, as they actually did, before the end of that year,
recovering the duchy of Milan, with Parma and Placentia, the former of which was restored to Francis Sforza,
the latter to the church. About this time flourished
Peter Bembo, Nicholas Massa, Augustine Stenchius,
James Sadoleto, William Budæus, and John Fabri, afterwards bishop of Vienna, all men of great learning;

B 2   the

the laſt was fixed upon to diſpute at Zurich with Zuin-glius and Oecolampadius, who oppoſed the doctrines of the Roman church, in the diſcharge of which office he acquired great reputation.

During his infancy, he was twice in ſo much dan-ger, that his life was deſpaired of; the firſt time, when he was but four years old, by the ſmall-pox, a diſeaſe often fatal to infants, and which then raged with great violence all over Italy : his parents were not able to procure him the common remedies that are neceſſary in ſuch circumſtances, and gave up their child for loſt; but God, who deſigned him to be one day the leader of his people, reſtored him to his health, and he eſ-caped without any other damage than a few trifling marks upon his face : the extremity to which he was then reduced, made ſo deep an impreſſion upon him, though a child, that, when ever he ſpoke of it he uſed to ſay, he was born in the Holy Year : the year 1525, in which the grand jubilee was celebrated, being the ſame with that of his recovery.

The archers, who came in purſuit of his father, were the occaſion of the ſecond diſaſter that befel him : he was ſo terrified at the ſight of theſe gentry, that he ran to hide himſelf in the garret of an old ruinous houſe, the floor of which giving way under him, he fell headlong above twenty feet upon a rough pave-ment : a poor woman that ſaw him fall, thinking him dead, took him up and carried him to a neighbour's houſe, where, perceiving that he ſtill breathed, they ſent for a ſurgeon to dreſs the wounds he had received upon his head, and to ſet his legs and and arms, which were all broke : the misfortune of the ſon, ſaved the life of the father, who made his eſcape, whilſt the archers ran to ſee what occaſioned the crowd, that was by this time gathered about the houſe, to which Fe-lix was carried.

It was feared a long time he would have been lame all his life, but in a while he got quite well again, to the great joy of his father and mother.

He would ſpeak ſometimes of this fall, when men-tion

tion was made of the taking of Rome, by the Emperor's army, contrary to the promife he had given the
Pope: Charles of Bourbon, who commanded, was the
firft that mounted the breach, and thought to have entered in a triumphant manner, but was, killed by a
mufket ball.   The city, however, was plundered with
a barbarity beyond example, not the leaft regard being had to the modefty of women, or any thing elfe,
however facred : they made a prifoner of Clement the
feventh in the caftle of St. Angelo, where he had taken fhelter with moft of the cardinals, and thought
himfelf fecure from the rage and infolence of the Germans ; nor was he fet at liberty till he had paid a very
large ranfom [1] : when this ever happened to be the
fubject of converfation, Felix ufed to fay, " I remem-
" ber our houfe was rifled by the archers that very
" year, however our lofs was inconfiderable, having
" but little to lofe :" and when the difcourfe turned
upon the Pope's confinement in the caftle of St. Angelo, he faid, " If his holinefs could have leaped as
" well as I, he would have had no occafion to pay
" any ranfom to his enemies."

His father and mother would gladly have given him
fome education, if they had been able, and their acquaintance, who faw the quicknefs of his apprehenfion,
faid, " It was a pity they could not, as he had parts

---

[1] Four hundred thoufand ducats to raife which, all the veffels of gold and filver, belonging to the churches, that had efcaped
the hands of the enemy, were melted down and coined : the vacant
cardinals hats were fold, by publick outcry, to thofe that would
give the moft : the perfons that purchafed at that time were, Marino Grimani, and Francis Cornaro, both Venetians ; St. Severino,
Caraffa, and Parmerio, Neapolitans ; and Cardina, a Spaniard.
It was further agreed, that the Pope fhould deliver to the Emperor,
the caftles of St. Angelo, Oftia, Civitia Vecchia, Caftellano, with
the cities of Parma and Placentia, to hold them as long as he
pleafed : that his Holinefs and 13 cardinals with him fhould remain
prifoners in the caftle of St. Angelo, till the money was paid, and
afterwards go to Naples or Gaieta, till his further pleafure was
known. Platina continued by Sir Paul Ricaut. It was faid of
this Pope when he was in prifon. *Papa non poteft errare.*

" that

" that might fome time or other make him a great
" man." When he was nine years old, his father
hired him to an inhabitant of the fame town, to look
after his fheep ; and, though the child, even at that
age, had a fpirit above fuch an employment, he would
not difobey his father in refufing it. But his mafter,
being angry at him, for fome little mifbehaviour, took
from him the care of his fheep, and fet him to prefide
over his hogs : fo difagreeable a change would have
thrown him into defpair, if it had continued long, but
he was foon delivered from this vile occupation, by an
accident wholly unforefeen, and that looks fomething
like a miracle [2].

He always loved to be in the company of his betters,
and was fo fond of thofe that belonged to religious
houfes, that, whenever he faw any of them at a diftance, he would run to meet and falute them with all
the civility and complaifance he was mafter of ; which,
happily, by the favour of Providence, was the foundation of all his future greatnefs : to fuch minute and,
feemingly, accidental circumftances, is often owing
that continual ftream of fuccefs or adverfity, which fo
remarkably attends fome men through the whole
courfe of their lives.

Father Michael Angelo Selleri, a Francifcan friar,
going, in the beginning of February, 1531, to preach
during the Lent feafon, at Afcoli, a confiderable town
in that province, loft his way near Le Grotte, and coming to four lane ends, could not tell which to take,
but was looking round for fomebody to direct him :
when little Felix, who was attending his hogs, juft by,
faw father Michael in diftrefs, he ran to falute him,
making him, at the fame time, a tender of his fervice :
the friar chearfully accepted it, and afked him the road
to Afcoli; " I'll foon fhew you the way thither," faid
he, and immediately began to run before him : as they

[2] The reader muft remember the author was a *Roman Catho-lick*.

went

went along, the anfwers he gave to father Michael's queftions were fo fmart and pertinent, and accompanied with fo much good humour, that every time the boy turned his face to liften more attentively to what was faid, he was charmed with him, and could not conceive whence a child that had no higher employment than looking after hogs, fhould have fuch afhare of fenfe and good manners.

When father Michael had got into his road again, he thanked Felix for his trouble, and would have difmiffed him with an alms, but he kept running forwards, without feeming to take any notice of what he faid, which obliged the friar to afk him in a jocofe manner, whether "he defigned to go with him quite to " the town." " Yes," fays Felix, " not only to Af- " coli, but to the end of the world, with a great deal of pleafure," and upon this took occafion to tell him, that, " the poor circumftances of his parents would " not allow them to fend him to fchool as he defired, " that he earneftly wifhed that fomebody belonging " to a convent, would take him as a waiting boy, and " he would ferve him to the utmoft of his power, pro- " vided he would teach him to read."

To try the boy a little further, he afked him, if " he " would take upon him the habit of their order :" Felix, who was in very good earneft, immediately anfwered " he would ;" and though the other fet forth to him in a long detail, and very frightful colours, all the mortifications and aufterities he would be obliged to undergo in that courfe of life, he boldly replied, " He " would willingly fuffer the pains of purgatory itfelf, " if he would make him a fcholar :" the prieft, furprized at his courage and refolution, thought there muft be fomething extraordinary in fuch a call, and refolved to take him along with him, but told him, " He muft " firft conduct his hogs back to his mafter, and then " come to him at the convent in Afcoli." Felix, who would not leave him upon any account, faid, " The " hogs ufed to return home of themfelves, when they
" faw

" faw the night coming on," fo, continuing their journey, they arrived at Afcoli in the evening.

The fraternity received their preacher with great civility, but were furprized to fee him attended by a poor ragged boy : however, when he had told them by what accident he picked him up, and with what extraordinary zeal he had followed him hither, the warden had the curiofity to fend for and afk him feveral queftions, to which he made fuch replies, that he thought him ftill mcre extraordinary than father Michael had reprefented him : fuch an examination, before fo large a community, might very well have difconcerted a perfon of riper years, and more ufed to the world ; but Felix anfwered without any hefitation, and with an air of truth and fimplicity that could not be fufpected of any artifice or contrivance. Every thing he faid tended to perfuade them of his call, and the ardent defire he had to become a preacher of the Gofpel, if they would qualify him for it.

The whole brotherhood, convinced that the hand of God eminently appeared in this affair, conjured the warden " not to overlook fo remarkable an interpofi-
" tion of Providence, when his attention to it might
" be the means of raifing up a man that would be per-
" haps hereafter an honour to their order." The warden was of the fame opinion, and fent out a friar, the next day, to Le Grotte, to enquire who he was.

This was the firft account his parents had of him fince his elopement : they had been almoft diftracted at the lofs of him, but were overjoyed when they heard into what hands he was fallen, and willingly confented to his defire of confecrating himfelf to God : as they now faw themfelves difcharged of the care of his education, they were very eafy about him, having another fon named Anthony about four or five years old.

The warden being fatisfied of his parent's confent, put on him the habit of a [3] lay brother, with the approbation of the whole community.

As

[3] Fratre converfo, or lay brother, is a perfon that is employed
as

As father Michael had been at the expence of clothing him and other necessaries, he asked the favour of the warden to let Felix wait upon him, which was readily granted on account of the obligations this new brother lay under to him.

He served him all Lent with great diligence and gratitude, and father Angelo employed what spare time he had, in teaching him to read: his memory was so prodigious, that at night he could repeat a sermon, which he had heard in the morning, word for word, without omitting the least action or gesticulation of the preacher: his master now and then entertained some others of the society, with the pleasure of hearing these repetitions, who were astonished at his apprehension and memory, and prognosticated great things of him.

His desire to learn was equally remarkable; for, even before he knew his letters, he would sometimes open one of the books that lay upon his master's reading desk, and look at it with that stedfastness and attention, that any one would have imagined he understood it : he made so surprizing a progress, that towards the end of Lent, he could easily read any book in the vulgar tongue, and whenever he met with one, would run to some of the society and desire them to hear him his lesson.

Father Angelo, at his return to Rome after Easter, designed to have taken his pupil with him, and the warden consented to it, but upon consideration he thought it better to leave him at Ascoli, that he might further recommend himself to the warden and superiors of the society.

After his departure, the warden ordered Felix to assist the [4] sacristan in sweeping the church, lighting the candles, and such little offices, who, in return for his services, was to teach him the responses and rudiments of Grammar : when the sacristan had taught him as far as he was able, he frankly told the warden

as a menial servant in the convent, as gardener, cook, or porter, and wears a different habit from the professed ·

[4] Sexton.

" He

" He muft provide a better mafter for him :" fuch a
perfon was enquired for, and one of the fociety, who
was a very good grammarian offering his fervice, he
was immediately put under his care.

The chapter having appointed a new warden to the
convent at Afcoli, called Father Fabricius of Ancona,
a morofe kind of man, he changed all the officers of
the convent, obliging many to leave it, and amongft
the reft poor Felix, whom he ordered to be fent home
again to his parents.' The whole convent expreffed
their concern at it, and earneftly intreated the new
warden to let him ftay, affuring him, " They were
" edified by his behaviour, that he was of great fer-
" vice to the houfe, and at the fame time recounted
" to him the adventure that brought him thither :"
but he was inexorable, and infifted upon his leaving
the convent in eight days,

Before the expiration of that term, the provincial
luckily came to vifit them, and the fociety reprefented
to him the refolution of their fuperior, to difcharge a
young lay brother of uncommon hope, and told him
the furprizing hiftory of his call.

The provincial gave them a favourable hearing, and
having feen Felix, was fo pleafed with the anfwers he
made to what was afked him, that from that time he
conceived a tender friendfhip for him, and not only ordered the warden to retain him as a lay brother, but
forbade him likewife to put him upon any dirty or
flavifh offices, and gave a bachelor of arts the charge
of inftructing him in the Latin tongue.

The warden, who durft not difobey the provincial,
as to letting him ftay amongft them, found out other
means however to exercife his patience, and make his
life uneafy. But when the time of his going out of
office drew near, he began to reflect how hardly he
had ufed Felix, and being charmed with his patience,
neglected no opportunity of making him amends for
his paft feverities.

In the month of May, 1553, there was held another
provincial

provincial chapter, in which father Auguſtine de Fermo, doctor in divinity, was choſen warden of the Fran-
ciſcan convent at Aſcoli, in the room of Fabricius. He
was a great encourager of ſuch as were fond of letters,
and eſpecially thoſe in whom he obſerved a promiſing
genius and good natural parts : As father Angelo, who
was his particular acquaintance, had given him the
hiſtory of Felix at Macerata, where they chanced to
meet at the holding of the chapter, he immediately,
upon his arrival at Aſcoli, declared he would take the
care of his ſtudies into his own hands, to ſhew the regard he had for that father's recommendation, as well
as the merit of Felix, who, by this time had gained the
affection of the whole ſociety, the ſevereſt and moſt rigid of thoſe fathers not being able to find any fault in
him, except that he had rather too much fire and vivacity.

He had now been two years in the convent, which
he had employed ſo well, that he could not only read
any Latin author, but immediately explain it in the
ſame tongue, and often put the other ſcholars to the
bluſh by his ſuperior diligence and quickneſs of underſtanding.

The warden, who had a mind to conſecrate him
wholly to religion, determined to give him the cowl,
and make him a profeſſed brother ; for this purpoſe he
opened his deſign to the whole community, repreſenting to them, in the ſtrongeſt terms, the expediency of
admitting ſo promiſing a youth to the noviciate [5].
The whole convent approved of it, and were of opinion it ſhould be done without delay, in order to incite him, by this mark of their favour, to double his
application to ſtudy.

Upon this reſolution, the ſeniors having ſummoned
him before them, and aſking him, " If it was agreeable
" to his inclination," he ſaid, " He thought there
" could be no true happineſs in this world, except in

[5] The noviciate is a year's trial, or probation, which the religious are obliged to go through before they are admitted into any
order.

" wearing

" wearing the habit of St. Francis," and thanked the warden and whole affembly, for " the great honour " they defigned to confer upon him". The leave of the provincial being neceffary upon this occafion, the warden acquainted them he had already obtained it, and a day was fixed for his putting on the habit : to give him every poffible demonftration of his affection, he likewife permitted him to go firft and fee his father and mother, to receive their benediction : a few days afterwards, the warden gave him the habit, with his own hands, in the prefence of the whole fociety, and leave to perform his noviciate in his own convent, as he thought it would be more agreeable to him than that of Macerata, which the provincial had given him the choice of : he was accordingly received into the order of the religious conventuals, the 25th of September, 1534.

The intention of the warden was, that he fhould be a creature of his own hands, and bear the name of Auguftine, according to the ufual practice of the religious. who generally change their baptifmal name, except they have any material objection to it. Some advifed him to take the name of Michael Angelo, in gratitude to his old benefactor ; others would have him called Francis, out of devotion to to the faint who was the founder of their order : but he intreated the warden to let him retain his own, and be called brother Felix, a name very well fuited to the good fortune that con-ftantly attended him to the laft moment of his life [6] : he took the habit upon him, the day that Clement VII. died. When that news arrived at Afcoli, the warden faid to him, " You are born to religion, the fame day " that the Pope is dead to the world :" to which Felix anfwering, " That he had rather wear the habit of St. " Francis, than that of the fovereign Pontiff;" the warden replyed, " Perhaps you may live to wear both."

[6] " Poftea apud Afculi, quæ civitas haud longe à monte alto " abeft, in Sancti Francifci monafterio vitam religiofam profeffus, " nomen Felicis, a parentibus inditum, mutare, ut fieri folet, noluit, " jam tum fortunæ fuæ profperæ præfagus." Thuan. in initio, lib. lxxxii.

During

During the year of his noviciate, he applyed himfelf fo clofely to learn the Latin tongue, that he both
fpoke and wrote it with the fame eafe that he did his
own. With this great and uncommon turn to ftudy,
it muft be confeffed he had one failing, which he found
it very difficult to get the better of, that was, a fiery,
impetuous difpofition, and too quick a refentment of
injuries, which gave occafion to his fellow ftudents to
call him, fpirit [7].

As jealoufy fometimes creeps into cloyfters, his acquaintance had uttered fome expreffions that touched
him to the quick ; but his good friend the warden, privately admonifhed him of the neceffity of bearing fuch
trifling affronts with patience, in order to conciliate
to himfelf the affection and intereft of the fociety, on
which his being admitted to make his profeffion, entirely depended : he made fo good a ufe of this advice, and
behaved himfelf fo well afterwards, that he was admitted to it at 14 years of age, on the firft of November,
1535, with the confent of whole community.

This year was remarkable for the feparation of England from the church : K. Henry VIII. having tryed
in vain to obtain a brief from Pope Paul III. (who fucceeded Clement VII.) to repudiate his wife Catharine
of Arragon, daughter of K. Ferdinand, and to efpoufe
Anne of Bullen, whom he loved to diftraction, was fo
piqued at the denial, that he caufed himfelf to be di-
vorced from the one, and marry'd to the other : he
likewife put feveral of the Englifh nobility to death ;
amongft whom was [8] Cardinal Wolfey, becaufe he
would not abandon the interefts of the Pope, and having publifhed very fevere edicts againft all thofe that

[7] The Italian word, il folletto ; and the French, l'efprit follet,
fignify a fairy, or familiar fpirit.
[8] This is a palpable miftake in the author, as it is well known
Cardinal Wolfey either poifoned himfelf, or died a natural death at
Leicefter Abbey, in his road to London, where indeed he might poffibly have fuffered death, from the temper Henry VIII. was then in.

profeffed

profeffed the Roman Catholick religion, he declared himfelf head of the Englifh church.

During this cruel perfecution in England, the Emperor Charles V. laid fiege to Tunis, and having made himfelf mafter of it in a few days, fet at liberty 20,000 Chriftian flaves, and returned in great triumph to Italy, where this fuccefs was celebrated with folemn proceffions and thanfgivings through the whole ecclefiaftical ftate. The religious of Afcoli were not willing to be behind hand with the reft of their brethren, and begun their rejoicings with a proceffion from the cathedral of St. Francis, which was magnificently decorated upon this occafion; brother Felix, whilft he was affifting the facriftan to put up a piece of fine tapeftry, fell from the top of a very high ladder to the ground, without being in the leaft hurt: when he got upon his legs again, he could not forbear faying, " The devil take " him that was the occafion of this; truly it's pleafant " enough to fee his Holinefs, fo mightily overjoyed at " another perfon's taking a little piratical town, that " he won't be a pin the better for, whilft he does not " fhew any fign of concern at the lofs of a rich and " opulent kingdom, that ufed to acknowledge him as " head of the church."

His acquaintance ufed to treafure up thefe fayings, and looked upon them as the fallies of a luxuriant genius, which, in its proper time, would diftinguifh itfelf in matters of greater confequence; but the poignancy of his wit afterwards coft him dear, and created him many enemies amongft his brethren.

This year the Anabaptifts made themfelves mafters of Munfter, a very ftrong city in the circle of Weftphalia: the bifhop, juftly incenfed at the behaviour of thefe hereticks, laid fiege to the place, and after feveral affaults, fo ftraitly inclofed them on every fide, that having been obliged to live fome time upon dogs and cats, and the hides of cattle, they were forced at laft to furrender at difcretion. The bifhop did not fpare one of them, and caufed the city to be facked to the

very

very foundations ; the inhabitants, who looked more like ſkeletons than living men, not being able to op-poſe ſo rigorous a chaſtiſement.   They had made their ringleader, John of Leyden, governor of the city : he was a Hollander of very low birth, and had formerly been a hog-keeper in France.   Notwithſtanding the meaneſs of his extraction, he had vaſt talents, and a courage that prompted him to undertakings which made him famous all over Europe : his name would have been as glorious as his memory is now deteſtable, if he had made a proper uſe of the great endowments with which God had bleſſed him.   This news, becom-ing the common topic of converſation throughout Ita-ly, furniſhed the ſtudents of Aſcoli with matter of much banter upon Felix : one of them, who was glad of any opportunity to upbraid him with the obſcurity of his family, ſaid to him, as he was walking in the cloyſters one day, " Hark'ee, pray let us have a little talk with " you, about your relation, John of Leyden, who, it " ſeems, has been a hog-keeper as well as you :" Felix, nettled at the compariſon, replyed, " If John of Leyden " and I are relations, only becauſe we were both of us " formerly hog-keepers, I think the conformity of your " vile opinions with his, makes you much nearer a kin " to him than I am.

In the year 1536, the provincial intending to reduce the number of the Franciſcans at Aſcoli, by the requeſt of the warden, who found the convent not able to ſupport them all, ſent an order, for three ſtudents to quit it, one of whom was Felix, who was directed to go to Macerata, and continue his ſtudies there. He left Aſcoli in the month of April, at the time when the Emperor, returning from the conqueſt of Tunis, was magnificently received at Rome by the Pope, and though the people, who remembered the grievous ha-vock and devaſtation that had been made by his army in their city, could not take any very ſincere pleaſure in ſeeing him within their walls, yet political reaſons
made

made it neceſſary for both them and the Pope to make a ſhew of it.

Felix did not ſtay long at Macerata, for father Angelo being appointed warden of the convent at Fermo, requeſted the provincial that he might have him near his perſon. As ſoon as this favour was obtained, he immediately left Macerata to live under a warden, of whoſe friendſhip and protection he had long had the ſtrongeſt aſſurances.

This created a ſort of jealouſy amongſt his brethren, who could not bear to ſee him in ſuch a degree of favour, eſpecially as he grew inſolent, and carried himſelf towards them with as high a hand as if he had been warden. Provoked at this manner of proceeding, they wrote letters of complaint to the provincial againſt them both, in which they acquainted him with " the " remiſs behaviour of their warden, and that he truſt- " ed the care of their revenue, with the entire diſpoſal " of all offices, ſolely to the management of Felix, " who was an idle fellow, ſeldom appeared at the pub- " lic ſervices of the houſe, deſpiſed the advice which " the ſenior fathers had given him, in relation to his " conduct, and, ſtudying only to oblige the warden, " entirely neglected all other concerns belonging to " the convent." Upon theſe complaints, he was or- dered to depart the convent in three days, and go to Recanati.

The warden, who was acquainted with the contents of theſe letters, thought himſelf ill uſed by the provincial's orders, and immediately went to wait upon him at Urbino, in hope of clearing up the matter to his ſatisfaction, and to demand juſtice upon them that had aſperſed him in ſo flagrant a manner: but the provincial having ſome reaſon to believe what had been alledg- ed againſt them to be true, was deaf to all his remon- ſtrances, and the poor warden returned to Fermo mor- tified with a ſecond order, to ſend his pupil away directly to Recanati.

Felix affected a diſdainful ſort of a behaviour towards

wards thofe that he imagined were the caufe of his removal, and giving way to his refentment, dropped fome
warm expreffions, which were immediately carried to
the warden of Recanati, with a defign to prejudice
him againft Felix ; and indeed it had in fome meafure, the intended effect, for he received him very coolly, and looked upon him with a fufpicious eye for fome
days. But Felix fet himfelf to pleafe him with fo much
diligence and obfequioufnefs, that he foon got the better of the bad opinion he had conceived of him.

Towards the end of May, 1538, the Cardinal legates having fettled an interview betwixt the Pope,
the Emperor, and Francis I, at Nice, a town in Provence, they agreed to leffen the ufual number of their
attendants, out of regard to the ftraightnefs of the
place. The Pope, who had undertaken this long and
troublefome journey, notwithftanding his great age,
with all his endeavours, could never bring thefe two
princes together in his prefence. They came to pay
their obeifance to him, feparately, at a neighbouring
village ; fo that having laboured, for fome days, in vain,
to fet on foot a negotiation betwixt them, he returned,
very much difpleafed with them both to Genoa, where
he embarked, and taking his route thro' Tufcany, arrived at Sienna the 15th of July.

The towns of Italy, upon this occafion, were forfaken
by their inhabitants, who ran in crouds to fee him upon his journey : the warden of Recanati, moved with
the fame curiofity, went three days Journey, with fome
of his convent to meet him, and ordered [8] the fteward, who likewife attended him, to leave the keys of
his office with brother Felix, of whofe honefty and
œconomy he entertained a higher opinion than of any
other perfons in the houfe. It will appear, from a trifling inftance which occurs here, that he liked to command much better than to obey : the monks thought

[8] Il difpenfiere, is an officer that furnifhes the convent with victuals, and may be called a fteward or caterer: proveditore, is not a
proper word, as it bears a different fenfe.

C   they

they might take a little more liberty, and regale themselves now and then in the warden's abfence, and that Felix would make them a more liberal allowance for that purpofe : but they found themfelves miftaken ; the new fteward, inftead of giving them any thing for extraordinaries, fhortened their ufual commons, and faved the houfe ten crowns in the three weeks, which the warden was abfent : a piece of frugality that pleafed him as much at his return, as it difgufted the monks, who called him mifer and niggard, and all the opprobrious names they could think of. The prefident, who governed in the warden's abfence, ordered him to give up the keys of the office into his hands, and to keep his apartment, but he refufed to obey ; as he had received them from the hands of his fuperior, he would not deliver them up again to any perfon but him, and defended his proceeding with fo many other good reafons, that they could not confine him. This affront fharpened him fo much againft the prefident, that whenever he met him afterwards, he ufed to fay, " I'll remember you, my friend, when I come to be Pope." To which the the other replyed with a laugh ; "I wifh my head may never ach till that day."

After a year and a half's ftay at Recanati, the provincial fent him to Ancona, towards the end of November, 1539. The regent, who was to have the fuperintendence of his ftudies, had known him at Macerata, and was no ftranger to his capacity : upon which account, he fhewed him a great deal of friendfhip, and prepared him to refpond publickly in philofophy, for which he was ready in three months, and performed his exercife in their own chapel, before feveral perfons of learning and diftinction in all the religious orders : a bachelor of great note amongft the Dominicans oppofed, and was fo taken with his acute manner of difputation, that, when it was over, he tenderly embraced him, and faid, " I am very much miftaken, if this " youth does not one day make a great man :" his be-
                                                                    haviour

haviour in this difputation was rumoured all over the city, and gained him much reputation.

As he frequently went with others of the religious to attend proceffions, funerals, &c. he would often enter into a difpute with them upon fome controverted point in philofophy, in which he acquitted himfelf fo well, that even the doctors in divinity, who feldom trouble themfelves with arguments of that nature, fometimes vouchfafed to take up the cudgels, and give him an opportunity of difplay his abilities. His fellow-ftudents feeing his reputation daily increafe, did every thing in their power to hurt him, fometimes whifpering it about, " That he was an empty, conceited fellow," at others running to the warden or regent, with complaints, that he was always teazing them to difpute. This however feldom anfwered their expectation, as the fuperiors regarded it as nothing but envy : and whilft he was in poffeffion of their efteem, he did not much care what opinion the others had of him : indeed they never came into his company, if they could avoid it, as they generally had little or nothing to fay when he was prefent.

Thefe little jealoufies increafing every day, engaged him in feveral broils with the other ftudents. As he held them in the higheft contempt, he could not help fhewing it fometimes, and when he met any of them, ufed to fay with an air of derifion, " Vifne difputare mecum ?" " Will you difpute with me ?" which put them upon feeking all opportunities of revenge.

They were continually giving him fome marks of their refentment, and would fometimes throw the door in his face, when he offered to come into any room where they were, putting him in mind of his mean parentage, and telling him, " He was not fit company " for them," with a thoufand other affronts of this kind. Though Felix did not think much worfe of himfelf for the lownefs of his birth, he could not help being ftung a little fometimes by thefe reproaches, and made his complaint to the warden, who forbade them, on pain of his pleafure, to ufe fuch opprobrious lan-

guage

guage for the future. This reprimand had its proper effect upon them for a while, but they began to revive the old story again towards the end of the year, 1540, at which time the provincial coming, in the course of his visitations, to Ancona; the warden, in giving him an account of the state of his convent, acquainted him with the heart-burnings and animosities that reigned amongst the juniors: when he came to examine strictly into the matter, and found it impossible to preserve the peace of the society, without proceeding to severities, he ordered Felix and two others to leave it, and sent them to finish their studies at Osmo.

    Though the order was express for three days, he found means to put off his departure above a month, to the great mortification of the other two, who were obliged to march off exactly at the time appointed. The desire he had of staying to distinguish himself in the public disputations, that were to come on in a short time, put him upon soliciting this delay by the warden's interest with the provincial. These exercises were to be performed in the convent of the Jesuits, an order established by Ignatius Loyola, a Spaniard, and confirmed this year by Pope Paul III, which ceremony occasioned a sort of a public act to be celebrated at Ancona, upon the account of two eminent professors of their order residing at that place, one of whom was acquainted with the merits and learning of Felix, and desired him to be an opponent to some of his pupils, in the disputations that were to be in the Christmas holidays, time the fixed for the confirmation of their society.

    When the month was near expiring, he obtained letters of recommendation to the provincial, desiring leave to stay at Ancona till the end of the winter, but he granted him only eight days, so that he was obliged to go away the beginning of January 1541.

    The warden of Osmo, who was his countryman, received him with great civility, and recommended him to his new regent, who examined him strictly concerning the many stories he had heard of him; for at the

same

fame time that he was reprefented to him as a very promifing youth, he was told, that he was of a wrangling and perverfe difpofition ; but he cleared himfelf fo well of thefe afperfions, that he foon gained the efteem, not only of the regent, but of every one elfe that had conceived any prejudice againft him.

Amongft many other things that made this convent agreeable to him, an accident happened, that gave him an opportunity of feeing the Pope and the Emperor : after the diet of Ratifbon had broke up, the Emperor determined upon an expedition to Algiers ; the neceffity of paffing through Italy occafioned an interview betwixt him and the Pope at Lucca, where they were to concert meafures for the execution of feveral important defigns ; efpecially the calling a general council, which his Holinefs had fo much at heart, that he left Cardinal Rodolphus Pius di Carpi, protector of the Francifcan order, in quality of legate at Rome, and went to Lucca, contrary to the moft preffing inftances of his phyficians, and the major part of the Cardinals, who would by no means have had him undertake fo hazardous a journey, upon the account of his great age and infirmities : but the Pope, who preferred the public good to his own health and repofe, immediatelly fet out and arrived there five days after the Emperor, who came out to meet him, and returned him three vifits for one only which his Holinefs paid him.

The warden of Ofmo having been inform'd of the Pope's journey, by his brother, who attend'd his Holinefs, and wifhed, if it was poffible, to fee him at Lucca, was equally defirous of giving him the meeting there. As foon as he had made publick his defign, though there was not a member of the convent, but employed his utmoft intereft to be taken along with him, Felix had the preference. The good opinion which the warden entertained of him, had already decided in his favour, and nothing more defirable could have happened to him, as he had from his infancy always taken a particular pleafure in feeing perfons of high quality.

The

The spleen of those that were disappointed by the warden, vented itself upon Felix : when any of them met him, they used to say with a sort of a sneer, " A " fine fellow indeed to go and see the Pope," to which he would answer merrily, " I am going to look at him, " that I may learn how to behave when I am Pope " myself."

Their accommodations at Lucca were so bad, that they stayed there but three days, during which short space, a person of Felix's penetration, could not help making several useful observations upon the conduct and behaviour of the prelates and courtiers that were there assembled ; and when he came to speak of them, he made such pertinent remarks, as gave strong indications of what he afterwards proved to be.

Dining one day at the warden's table with some other company, he asked so many questions concerning the Pope, that one of them smiled and said, " I fancy " you have a mind to be Pope yourself : I am not old " enough yet," answered he, " to be Pope ; but if God " should be pleased at any time hereafter to put it in " my power to be so, I think I should have courage " enough to accept of that high dignity, in hope that " he would never forsake me in the discharge of an of- " fice that he himself had called me to." Another time, one of his brethren meeting him in the warden's apartment, made him a very low bow, and said, in a scoffing manner, " Since you have had the honour of " seeing his Holiness, you seem to look upon yourself " as a person of no small consequence ;" to which he answered in the same tone, " If you are so angry at my " having only seen his Holiness, what will you be when " I am Pope myself." These circumstances, though otherwise trifling, serve to shew that he was not void of ambition, even at that age, and that he had fixed his mark very high, and never lost sight of it, as will appear, from many other of his sayings, and the whole tenor of his behaviour in the subsequent part of his history.

This year the infidels made themselves masters of
all

all the territories that the Christians had left in Hungary, after the death of King John, which was followed
by a bloody war betwixt the Emperor and the grand
Signior Soliman : on the other side, Francis I. renewed
the rigorous edicts that had been published against the
Protestants in 1534. These events were the more sen-
sibly felt in Europe, at this time, as the Emperor had
just miscarried in his grand enterprise upon Algiers,
which he had undertaken in the most dangerous and
tempestuous season of the year, contrary to the advice
and persuasions of the Pope; his fleet which had struck
a terror into the Algerines, was wrecked in a storm
upon the Barbary shore; all those that escaped the
fury of the waves, being cruelly murdered by the inhabitants of the coast ; and the Emperor forced to return, in a manner very different from the magnificent
expectations he had conceived.

From these public disasters, we must turn our eyes
to transactions of a more private nature in the convent
at Osmo, where we left brother Felix.

There was a monk of the Servite order, who, being disgusted at his superior, upon some frivolous account or other, was not content with eloping himself,
but endeavoured to persuade others of the religious, to
run away with him to France. He had a brother-in-
law, who was a bachelor in divinity, belonging to the
convent of Cordeliers, or Franciscans, at Osmo, of a
disorderly life and dangerous example in such a community, to whom he no sooner opened his design of
escaping into France, than he heartily entered into it,
and agreed to go with him. As this bachelor used
sometimes to go out of the convent with Felix, he one
day asked him to take a walk to a garden a little way
out of the town, where the other had appointed to
meet him, and whither he actually came at the time
fixed, The bachelor, as they went along, entertained
him with extravagant panegyricks upon the French
nation, and lamented, very pathetically, the misera-
ble condition of ecclesiastics in Italy, where merit was

so shamefully overlooked ; and a man of worth and
learning could find no patron or friend to espouse him.
By discourses of this kind, he endeavoured to mould
Felix to his purpose, without communicating to him
the whole of his scheme, which he did not enter into,
till he joined his brother, who was punctually at the
place of rendezvous.

Felix, at the sight of him, and a bundle of cloaths,
which the bachelor had caused to be conveyed thither, began to suspect something. and imagined the
pretence of a walk was only to cover some design of
greater consequence.

After the two brothers had talked together apart
some time, they came to Felix, and turning the conversation again upon France, with the happiness of living in so free a country, at last disclosed their intention, and invited him to make one of the party, telling
him, " That a person of his extraordinary parts and
" merit could not fail of raising himself in the church,
" where there was so much encouragement given to
" learning and virtue."

He was at first a little staggered with their propo-
sals, but calling reason and religion to his assistance,
he told them, " He could not but wonder whence
" they had conceived so vile an opinion of him, as to
" think him capable of such an action," and not only
refused to have any concern in it himself, but used his
utmost endeavours to dissuade them both, especially
his companion, from so dangerous and wicked an undertaking.   But they were hardened beyond the reach
of argument : when he found that, he made what haste
he could back to the convent, lest he should be suspected of being privy to their design.   The other two
travelled night and day through by roads, and took such
other precautions as were necessary to cover their
flight : without which they had certainly been taken,
as Felix immediately informed the warden of their de-
sertion, who sent a party after them ; but they had laid
their scheme so well, that it was to no purpose.

They

They received an account some months after, that
they both got safe into France, with four others, whom
they had seduced, where they not only renounced
their orders, but the church of Rome, and embracing
the proteftant religion, were married, contrary to the
folemn vows they had made to God, at their profeffion.
As it was reported, the bachelor had met with very
good fortune ; Felix feemed to repent fometimes that
he had not gone with them, and when he was out of
humour, at any ill ufage from his fuperiors, often faid,
" What a fool was I for not going to France, when
" I had fo fine an opportunity of delivering myfelf
" out of this houfe of bondage :" which made many
fufpect that he really had fome fuch defign, but it was
found to be rather the effect of choler, than any
fettled intention.

James V, King of Scotland, died this year without
male iffue, and left his daughter Mary, then but eight
days old, heir to his crown : fhe was afterwards efpoufed to Francis II. King of France, which occafioned
great troubles in England. Felix ufed to lament the
miferies of that poor kingdom, and was often heard to
fay, even after he was Pope, that " he never expected
" any good under the government of a princefs in
" leading ftrings."

Whether he was tired of Ofmo, or had not time
enough to follow his ftudies fo clofely as he defired, he
wrote to one of his friends, before the chapter was to
meet, defiring he would ufe his intereft with the provincial to remove him either to Ancona, Urbini, or
Afcoli. His friend ferved hin fo effectually, that they
fent him an order, with a blank left in it, to be filled
up with the name of that place which he liked beft.
He was fo fenfibly touched with it, that he remembered
it all his life, and ufed to fpeak of it, as the greateft,
nay almoft the only favour he had ever received during
the courfe of 40 years that he lived amongft the conventuals. He chofe Ancona, a place he had always
loved, and to let the world fee it was in his power to
come back, after fo much pains had been taken to
drive

drive him away from thence. He returned thither, about the end of October, to the great satisfaction of his friends, and mortification of his enemies.

Soon after, he had a second opportunity of seeing the Pope. His Holiness, having resolved to visit the whole ecclesiastical state, left Rome the beginning of March 1543, and came to Ancona, where he stayed eight days, and was entertained with the utmost splendor and magnificence.

Felix, who was now in deacon's orders, and had been preparing himself some time to preach upon the day of the Annunciation, was advised by the warden, not to venture upon it, as it was the first time, " For, " besides the usual concourse of town's people, there " would be many prelates at church, whose presence, " perhaps, might disconcert and put him out of coun- " tenance." But he (conscious of his own abilities) returned for answer, that " he was rather glad of it, " than otherwise, and should be so far from being " daunted at their presence, that he did not care if " his Holiness himself was to be there." He acquitted himself so well, that nobody would have suspected it was his first essay. One of the most eminent prelates that was at church that morning, sent for him after dinner, and entering into a long conversation upon the subject of his sermon, was so pleased with him, that he said at his going away, " If I was Pope, you " should soon be a Cardinal."

The warden was so charmed with it, that he ordered him a double portion of commons in the [10] refec- tory, and drank his health before the whole community.

Felix gratefully acknowledged the honour that had been done him, and the praises they had so liberally be- stowed, not only upon this, but his former exercises, and said, " He should for ever have the highest regard " for the society in general, and particularly for those

[1] The refectory, is the common hall in the convent, where the religious dine and sup, from the Latin word, reficere, to refresh or recreate.

" persons

" perfons in it, that had taught him the way to fame
" and glory."

He had now acquired the higheft reputation in Ancona for learning and eloquence.   But as the old fore
began to break out afrefh. the provincial fent him to
Urbini in the beginning of the year 1544.

This convent proved more agreeable to him than
he expected, as it afforded him fome opportunities of
diftinguifhing himfelf, which he always thirfted after.
At the provincial chapter of the Auguftines, they
maintain publick thefes in philofophy and divinity.
He engaged in one of thefe exercifes with a bachelor,
who had the fame of being the moft accute and fubtle
difputant of the whole order ;' though the warden was
unwilling to give his confent to it, upon the account
of the great character and reputation of his antagonift.
But he handled the poor bachelor in fuch a manner,
that the warden was afhamed of the diftruft he had
expreffed of his abilities.

After this, he wrote to the provincial for permiffion
to go into prieft's orders, as there was a want of preachers in the convent.   But he ordered him to continue
his ftudies, and faid, " He would call upon him in his
" vifitation, to fee whether he was qualified for that of-
" fice," which he did foon after, and having thoroughly examined him as to his learning, and made a ftrict
enquiry into his morals, he gave him a teftimonial to
the bifhop, by whom he was ordained prieft, in June
1545, and affumed the name of father Montalto.   He
took his bachelor's degree the fame year, and faid mafs
for the firft time, upon the day of the Vifitation of the
Virgin ; after which, having got the bifhop's licence,
he began his firft courfe of Lent fermons.   He was
no fooner in poffeffion of his bachelor's degree, than
he fell into a difpute with fome fathers of the convent,
who pretended to take place of bachelors by virtue of
certain privileges they were invefted with.   But he
was obftinate, and would not give up a right which he
proved by feveral decrees and conftitutions, and having

ing reprefented the affair to the general at Rome, obtained an order from him in favour of the bachelors.
The provincial however, who rather leaned to the
fide of the other fathers, fent him away from Urbini
(but in an honourable manner) appointing him preacher at Jefi.

His ufual prudence and forefight feem to have failed
him a little in an affair that happened whilft he refided
at this place.   Preaching there one day, in the year
1546, when all Europe rung with the news of Luther's
death, after he had occafioned fo fatal a fchifm in
Chriftendom,   he fuffered himfelf to be fo transported
with anger againft him, that he launched into bitter
invectives againft the whole order of Auguftines, of
which Luther had formerly been a member.   An Auguftine doctor, who was prefent, took fuch offence at
his difcourfe, that he went to Rome on purpofe to
complain of it to the bifhop of the diocefe, who ordered
Montalto to explain himfelf in another fermon, which
he did in fuch a manner as gave full fatisfaction to the
Auguftines, without any prejudice to his own honour.

The provincial came about this time to Jefi, and, his
fecretary falling ill, took Montalto to write for him; in
this employment he continued two months at Macerata, from whence he went to Fermo to make intereft
for a doctor's degree.   He had folicited the provincial's licence for this purpofe, by feveral perfons of diftinction, at whofe requeft he fent him to that place,
where there is an univerfity, in the year 1547.   During
the fpace of five months that he ftaid there, he performed feveral public exercifes, both in the fchools and
in the pulpit, which fhewed him to be fully qualified
for that honour.   However, the provincial coming thither, about the end of October, to create doctors, poor
Montalto had not the good fortune to be of that number, but was fet afide till another time, though he had
paffed a better examination than any of the other candidates.   He was much affected with it, and could not
help fhewing his fpleen not only to the new doctors,
but him that created them, and was determined to go
himfelf

himself to Rome, and make his complaint against him there. But considering that he could not go, except the provincial gave him leave (without which the general would have looked upon him as a vagabond and a deserter) he was advised to bear it patiently ; and being told, that the provincial had acted entirely according to the general's order, he comforted himself with the hope, that what was now so unjustly refused, would be conferred upon him in a short time.

The bishop of Fermo had granted him a licence to be lent preacher in a town near that city, though some of his brethren had been endeavouring to do him ill offices with this prelate ; but he behaved himself so well in his station, that, when he came to wait upon him at his return, he ordered him to preach in his own cathedral the Lent following.

Soon after his arrival at Fermo, he received a letter from the provincial, with orders to prepare himself to keep a divinity act before the whole chapter, which was soon to be assembled at Assise. His acquaintance sent him word, that the committee of the chapter had cast their eyes upon him, as the fittest person for that purpose ; that such a preference was a great honour to him, especially as it was much dreaded and declined by all the other divines. Though he felt a secret satisfaction at this distinction, he could not help shewing a little resentment, at what had passed, and signified to the provincial, that " as he was not thought worthy " of a doctor's degree, he doubted he should but ill " maintain the cause and interests of religion before so " numerous and learned an assembly;" The provincial understood the hint, and wrote back to him, that he should have his degree very soon, desiring him, in the mean time, to qualify himself for the act. Soon after he accordingly came, with necessary powers, to Fermo, and having examined Montalto, only for form's sake, gave him the doctorial ring in the presence of the whole university, and an infinite multitude of others that were assembled from all parts to hear his thesis, in which he far exceeded the expectations they

had

had conceived of him, from the fame of his other performances. As foon as he was invefted with this dignity, which is reckoned a mark of great diftinction amongft the religious, he immediately printed all his thefes, with a defign to dedicate them to the Cardinal, protector of the order, who was to prefide in that quality at the general chapter. This was Rodolphus Pius di Carpi, a perfon, the moft efteemed of any in the whole college of cardinals, as appeared by his being appointed to reprefent the Pope during his abfence from Rome.

As he knew him to be a man of fingular modefty, without ambition of oftentation, he avoided the common track of dedications, and addreffed him in a plain and honeft manner ; with which the Cardinal was fo well pleafed, that he ever after honoured him with his patronage and protection.

When the chapter was fummoned, Montalto fet out with feveral other ecclefiafticks of diftinction, and arriving there the fame day that the cardinal did, thought it his duty to wait upon him immediately with his thefes. To fecure himfelf a favourable reception, he firft applied to his fecretary Sigifmond Boffius, to introduce him, who received him with great courtefy, and did him all the good offices he could in this audience.

The chapter was hardly met, when they fell to quarrelling about precedence and fuperiority ; the difputants likewife entered into thefe wrangles : Montalto infifted upon refponding before another doctor, who faid, " It was his right, as he was in his own diocefe," and looked upon Montalto as a ftranger and intruder. He replied, " That in a general chapter, where people " of all countries belonging to the order, were affem- " bled, no regard was to be had to the place of one's " birth, and that being his fenior, he would either " have the honour of opening the difputations, or re- " turn directly to his convent."

The affembly was divided into two parties, and Montalto feeing (notwithftanding whatever he could urge to the contrary) that the majority was like to go againft him,

him, said, " He thought the respect that was due to
" his patron, if there had been no other reason, was
" sufficient to decide the matter, in his favour." The
other submitted to this last argument, provided the
Cardinal would say, " It was agreeable to him that it
" should be so." But he modestly gave it against
Montalto, and desired he would be content with the
second post of honour.

He got infinitely more reputation however, by his
behaviour in these disputations, than he could ever
have acquired from any degree of rank or precedence.
When he responded in the presence of the Cardinal,
the schools were crowded with people of all sorts and
conditions, that came from far and near to hear him,
and returned with the highest admiration of his wit, vivacity, prodigious memory, and judgment, it being
easily seen then, who ought to have had the preference.

He one day engaged with a Calabrian, called father
Mark Anthony, first lecturer in divinity to the convent of Perugia, a very famous disputant, with whom
every body was afraid to enter the lists. But Montalto was so far from avoiding, that he took the first opportunity of attacking him, and pushed him so vigorously, that he was very glad to get quit of him.

The Cardinal, to shew that he took notice of his
merit, admitted him to sup at his table that night ;
and all the while the chapter lasted, was continually
giving him some mark or other of his esteem and approbation. He likewise, at the same time, cultivated
a strict acquaintance with Bossius ; they both of them
ever afterwards, were his steady friends, in all the various turns of his fortune.

After the chapter was over, he begged as a favour
that he might go and reside at Ascoli, to gratify the ambition he had, of being a doctor in the same house
where he had learned to read. When he came thither,
he sent for his relations, and instead of being ashamed
of their poverty, thought it an honor to him. One day,
talking

talking of the moſt illuſtrious families in Italy, he ſaid
(playing upon the word) " For my part I don't know
" any houſe more illuſtrious than my own : ˙for if that
" houſe is the moſt illuſtrious which has the moſt light
" in it, I think ours has a very good title to be ſo eſ-
" teemed, as one might conſtantly ſee the daylight
" through a hundred chinks in the roof and ſides of
" it [1]."

This was no bad way of diſcountenancing that family pride, which is too often found even among the
Religious, who, whilſt they ought to look upon all the
honours of this world with contempt, are rather apt to
glory in the rank their friends and relations, and they
themſelves once held in it, than of the holineſs of their
profeſſion, to which they think they have done great
honour, by ſacrificing to it the falſe ſplendor of their
birth and parentage.

Montalto on the contrary, even after he was Pope,
made no ſcruple of publiſhing what many others would
ſtudiouſly have endeavoured to conceal, and is a rare
inſtance of a man in his exalted ſtation, that was not
aſhamed of his mean original. He could not, however, upon ſome occaſions (as we have ſeen) refrain
from ſhewing his reſentment, when he was bantered
by his fellow-ſtudents upon that account, which may
very well be imputed to the natural fervour and ebul-
liency of youth.

Whilſt he reſided at Aſcoli, an affair happened, that
embroiled him not a little, with his provincial. Father
Charles Contini, profeſſor of divinity in the convent,
dying the beginning of the year, Montalto read lectures in his ſtead, with the warden's approbation, who
promiſed to get him confirmed in that office by the
provincial, in the firſt chapter that he ſhould be con-
vened. The provincial accordingly ſent him this con-

[1] " Is Cryptis pago, qui Montis alti caſtro, ſubjectus eſt, in
" Piceno, natus pauperrimis parentibus, quod et ipſe gloriabatur,
" cum ſe illuſtri domo natum diceret, quippe quæ ſine tecto a ſole,
" ex omni parte illuſtraretur. Thuan. lib. lxxxii."

firmation,

firmation, but referved to himfelf a power of revoking
it whenever he pleafed, which he actually did, about
two months after, in favour of another perfon, whom
he appointed to fucceed Montalto as regent, without
any fort of reftriction in his patent. After he had fignified his refentment of this affront to the provincial,
with fome afperity, he joined with a fet of difaffected
people in the convent, and wrote a letter of complaint
againft him to the general. The provincial being
acquainted with this by the general himfelf, who
fent him the letter, immediately concluded Montalto
had been the promoter of it, as he knew he was provoked at being fuperfeded in his profefforfhip, and
taxed him roundly with it in the prefence of feveral
others. Montalto made but a weak defence, and, when
he found he was fufpected, if not difcovered, began to
wifh he had not been guilty of fo indifcreet a ftep.
He faw it behoved him to look well to his conduct for
the future ; but this precaution was of little fervice to
him : as it is always in the fuperior's power to harafs
their inferiors when they have a mind.

His behaviour to the provincial gave fo much offence to his brethren, that they drew up feveral accu-
fations againft him : at firft, " That he had flandered
" the provincial in divers companies; that he had
" often gone out of the convent without the leave of
" his fuperior ; that he never made any refponfes
" when he was at divine fervice, which was but fel-
" dom ; that he had fecreted fome part of the obla-
" tions, was guilty of indecent and obfcene conver-
" fation in the company of laicks ; that he did not
" keep faft upon faints eves ;" and many other things
of that nature, which were fufficient to authorize the
provincial's fending a commiffary the next day to take
informations, and begin a procefs againft him. But
when he came to be interrogated, he found fo many
ways of invalidating thefe depofitions, fometimes by
impeaching the credit of the teftimony, at others by
calling his friends to bear witnefs to the truth of what
he afferted, that the whole charge was looked upon as

D   frivolous

frivolous and malicious. He further publifhed fo ftrong a vindication of himfelf in writing, that the commif-fary was thoroughly convinced of his innocence in the main, and would not proceed to fentence.

But as he had been guilty of difobedience to the provincial, upon fome other occafions, he commanded him to go in two days times to Reeanati, and keep his room there, till the provincial and his affeffors had re-vifed the procefs, and given fentence.

Montalto thinking himfelf hardly ufed, protefted againft this order in the commiffary's prefence, and faid he would go to Rome himfelf, and appeal to the ge=neral [2]. But after fome confideration, he fubmitted to it, imagining that (as Pope Paul III. was but juft dead) it would not be for his intereft to have his caufe heard during the vacancy of the fee, in which interval affairs are generally in confufion.

After having continued about two months in a fort of imprifonment, without any further notice taken of him, he wrote a fubmiffive letter to the provincial, who fent him for anfwer, " That the procefs would be " laid before a congregation of the province," and in the mean time, made a ftrict enquiry into his conduct and manner of life in the religious houfes where he had ever refided ; Montalto, on his fide was ufing all the in-tereft he had at Rome. to obtain a regency, imagin-ing that would be a means of reconciling him to the provincial, and putting an end to the procefs, though he did not feem much to apprehend the confequence of it ; as he thought the worfe that could happen would be fome flight penance, and a few months fufpenfion.

He had recourfe, upon this occafion, to his friend Boffius, who immediately applied to his mafter. The Cardinal ordered him to go in his name, to the gene-ral of the Cordeliers, and tell him the efteem he had for

[2] General, in a monaftick fenfe is the chief of the order, or of all the houfes or congregations eftablifhed under the fame rule, and refides at Rome, to take care of their intereft and affairs.

Montalto,

Montalto, defired he might have the firft regency that was vacant: Boffius exerted himfelf fo effectually in his behalf, and was fo diligent in his attendance upon the general, that he foon obtained that of Maccrata for him, which was the beft in the province. The general gave it him to fhew his regard for the Cardinal his patron; and the defire he had of obliging his fecretary, by whom he fent the proper inftruments to Montalto. He received them in May, 1550: but as he could not get into poffeffion, without the confent of the provincial, he employed one of his friends to deliver him a petition, and try all means to obtain this favour.

The provincial however, inftead of granting it, abfolutely forbade him to go to Maccrata, and fent word to the general, " That as Montalto had a procefs carrying on againft him for matters of a criminal nature, he was incapable of holding fuch an office." So that notwithftanding all his intereft at Rome, and the interceffion of many powerful friends, he could make no impreffion upon him.

Seeing this way barred up, he attempted to get leave to go to the jubilee, which was to be celebrated this year at Rome, by order of the new Pope, Julius III; but that being likewife refufed him, he went away without it; and, by this ftep, put it into the provincial's power to proclaim him difobedient and a deferter. He accordingly wrote in thefe terms to the general, who would certainly have had him apprehended and fent to prifon, if Boffius had not interfered. All means were thought of to bring about a reconciliation, but to little purpofe; the general being highly exafperated at Montalto, whilft the Cardinal was refolved to protect him.

The general, however, at laft, tired out with the importunities of Boffius, and not willing to do any thing that fhould be difagreeable to the provincial, for whom he had a great refpect, determined to feparate them, by putting Montalto into fome employment in another province, and foon after gave him the divinity chair at Sienna, with licence to preach there, an office

of

of much more confideration than that of Macerata.
He went thither towards the end of Auguft, with letters of recommendation, from Cardinal Carpi to the
provincial of Tufcany, who having a brother in his
eminence's fervice, received him with a great deal of civility and friendfhip, and defired him to preach upon
St. Francis's day, which he would willingly have declined at that time. But there was a neceffity for it, to
fatisfy the curiofity of many who longed to hear him,
not only from the character they had received of his
fermons, but becaufe he was to be their preacher during Lent. The very fame reafons made him rather
fearful of hazarding his reputation upon the fuccefs of
his firft performance, before an audience, whofe tafte
and difpofition he was wholly unacquainted. However
he ventured, and the congregation was fo charmed
with his eloquence, that they waited for lent with impatience, and when it came, the church was fo crowded
every day, that there was hardly room to fit down.

The chapter of La Marca, was to be held the year
following, in order to chufe new officers; and Montalto, had now a right to affift at it. As he could not
leave his chair without the permiffion of the general,
he afked and obtained it, with licence to preach the
next Lent feafon at Camerino. During the fitting of
the chapter, he could not forbear making fome complaints againft the provincial; but the prefident, being acquainted with the animofity that fubfifted betwixt them, did all that was in his power to make
them friends, that the election might be carried on with
peace and unanimity.

When Lent was over, the magiftracy of Camerino
came in a body to return him thanks for the honour he
had done them, affuring him, "They were much more
" edified by his preaching, than they ever had been by
" that of any other perfon:" as he had in his fermon
particularly recommended a poor family at Le Grotte
to their charity, they made him a prefent of 40 crowns,
befides the ufual collection, which they faid, were for
the ufe of the poor family he had mentioned in the
pulpit.

pulpit. Montalto thanked them, and said, "It was "his own family, whom he was not afhamed to call "poor, as poverty was no fin.".

From thence he went to Afcoli and Le Grotte, to fee his old friends and relations, where he found his fifter Camilla, bufy wafhing and ironing linen, which occupation, fhe had been obliged to take up for her daily fupport: at the particular defire of his parents, he preached one Sunday at the parifh church, and took for his text, 1 Cor. i. 27. *God hath chofen the foolifh things of the world to confound the wife, and the weak things to confound the mighty*; to the inexpreffible fatisfaction of his whole family. As the [3] curate of the parifh had lodged him in his houfe (his father having no convenience for him) he left the alms, that had been collected at his fermon, which amounted to 50 crowns, in his hands, and told him, "He thought it no harm "to fupply the wants of his poor parents, after that "manner." The magiftrates likewife prefented him with 20 crowns (as he did honour to their country) which he gave his fifter Camilla, as he faid, "for part of her portion; and afterwards having taken his leave of the curate, and defired him to give his father and mother fome of that money from time to time as they fhould want it, he returned to Sienna, which he found all in an uproar and confufion, and there was guilty of an error that had like to have been fatal to him.

Though this city pretends to be a free ftate, Diego Urtado de Mendoza, who was the governor of it, under Charles V. treated the inhabitants with a rigour, that approached very near to downright tyranny. He had begun to build a citadel, pretending an order for it from the Emperor, to prevent the popular tumults and feditions that often happened there. The principal inhabitants, frighted with the profpect of a yoke, they faw was going to be rivitted upon their 'necks, with the affiftance of the French minifter, the Count de

[3] Il curato in Italian, and le cure in French, fignify the rector or vicar of a parifh.

Petillan,

Petillan, and the Farnefe family, who, by their intereft and authority in the country, had got together a body of troops in hafte, under a colour of fending them upon fome other expedition, furprized the Spanifh garrifon, put one part of it to the fword, and drove the other out of the city and fortrefs

Montalto, who lived in great friendfhip with Mendoza, happening to be in company with feveral of the chief citizens, that made loud complaints of the Spanifh government, was fo imprudent to enter into a defence of his adminiftration; which enraged them to fuch a degree, that if the refpect due to his function and character, had not in fome meafure reftrained their fury, they had certainly torn him limb from limb: a piece of mifconduct, that he afterwards endeavoured to rectify, by declaiming in all companies, againft the Spaniards. As he perceived however, that the Siennefe, ever after, looked upon him with an evil eye, he cautioufly avoided meddling in their affairs. The Pope employed Fabius Mignatelli, Cardinal of Sienna, as his legate to prevail upon the people to fubmit; but finding his endeavours to no purpofe, he recalled him foon after. Montalto, who was apprehenfive that, if the Emperor fhould call the city to an account for their rebellious behaviour, he was liable to be involved in the general ruin, defired Cardinal Carpi to procure him fome honourable excufe for leaving the place, which he did, by appointing him preacher to the convent of the Holy Apoftles in Rome, for the Lent following, whither he drew an infinite concourfe of people after him. The Cardinal himfelf, ufed to go hear him at leaft twice a week, and take fome of his brethren with him: one day five cardinals, befides many other great prelates, honoured his congregation with their prefence.

There happened an odd adventure this Lent, which was the fubject of much converfation in Rome, and proved a lucky one to him, as it was very inftrumental in advancing his fortune. He had one Sunday chofen

for

for his text this paffage in St. John's Gofpel, *I am the good fhepherd, and know my fheep, and am known of mine,* defigning to enter into the article of predeftination. This difcourfe contained the moft learning and eloquence, of any that he had preached that feafon. As he had given public notice the Sunday before, that he defigned to preach upon that fubject, in the numerous auditory that was affembled that day, there happened to be a Lutheran, who came out of curiofity. After the fermon was over, he went home, and looking over fome minutes that he had taken of it, to the end of every propofition, which the preacher had laid down, he fubjoined in great letters, This is a lie, and folding the paper up in the form of a letter, gave it to one of Montalto's friends, as if it came by the poft from Sienna. When Montalto opened it, he was exceedingly furprized at the contents, and enquired ftrictly of his friend, what fort of a man he was that gave him the letter ; but as he received it in the dufk of the evening, he could give no fatisfactory defcription of the bearer. Upon this he immediately fent it to the prior of the Dominicans at the convent [4] Sopra la Minerva, where the tribunal of the Inquifition was held. The prior having perufed it, fent it to Cardinal Carpi, as he was a principal officer in it, and protector of the Francifcan order ; and the Cardinal ordered a commiffary to go directly, and concert proper meafures with Montalto, for an examination into this affair, as it required fome notice and confideration.

Cardinal Caraffa, the inquifitor general, had juft made father Michael Ghifilieri commiffary of the holy office. He was born at a little village called Bois, about fix miles from Alexandria, of very mean parents. But having taken the habit of St. Dominick, he had been a Lent preacher many years, and governed feveral houfes of that order, in quality of prior. He was

[4] So called from being founded upon the ruins of a temple, formerly dedicated to Minerva by Pompey the Great. Vid. Relation de la Cour de Rome. p. 474.

made

made inquifitor of Rome, at the time when there was a great rumour of a herefy fpringing up in Lombardy, and behaved himfelf, at that juncture, with fo much prudence and zeal, that he acquired the good opinion of all the Cardinal inquifitors. But having been accufed of mal-practice in the execution of his office by fome of the Milanefe, he was cited to Rome; where he gave fo fatisfactory an account of his conduct, that they fent him again into the Swifs cantons, to commence a procefs againft one of the canons of Coire, who was accufed of being a heretick. He was afterwards fent to Bergamo; and the court of Rome was fo pleafed with his behaviour in thefe employments, that he was made commiffary at his return, which is one of the moft honourable pofts in that office. He was fo taken with the behaviour and penetration of Montalto, that from his firft vifit, he entertained a great opinion of his abilities, and faid, "He never "before had received fo much pleafure in any man's "converfation." By the many fignal fervices he did him, he attached him clofely to his intereft, and at laft made him Cardinal when he himfelf came to be Pope Pius V.

There happened another event this year, which occafioned his firft diflike to the French and Spanifh nations. Charles V. had concluded a peace, with the Proteftants in Germany, the laft fpring, not at all to the advantage of the church, and confequently difagreeable to Julius III. Pope; being indeed in a manner compelled to it, by fome advantages they had gained over him. But the court of Rome makes little account of the maxims that oblige princes to accommodate difputes, in which religion is concerned, for reafons of ftate. What made the name of Charles ftill more odious at Rome, was the murder of Cardinal Martinufius, who had been promoted to that dignity by the earneft folicitation of King Ferdinand, and whofe brother was his ambaffador extraordinary in Hungary; but having the misfortune to lofe his favour by neglecting, or, as he alledged, acting contrary to his
interefts,

interefts, he caufed him to be affaffinated by fome Italian bravoes ; upon which, the Pope not being able to put up fo outrageous an affront to the facred college, after feveral monitories and exhortations to humble himfelf before him, at laft excommunicated Ferdinand as the author of it.

Some years before this, Henry II. fucceeded to the crown of France, upon the death of his father Francis I. and Octavius Farnefe could not prevail upon Charles V. to reftore Placentia to him ; though he had a grant of it from Paul III. he was determined, if poffible, to recover it by force of arms ; for which purpofe, he put himfelf under the protection of the new King of France, who furnifhed him with fupplies for the undertaking : fo that all Italy was involved in war; and Julius thinking the intereft of the Holy See concerned, as Placentia was a fief of the church, threatened to excommunicate, not only Octavius, but Henry alfo, if he fhould dare to give him any affiftance in this enterprize. Henry, in return, commanded his fubject not to fend money to Rome for bulls, difpenfations, or indulgences, ordering his metropolitans to grant them according to the antient privileges of the Gallican church.

To thefe heavy misfortunes was added the entire defection of England. For Henry VIII. (who gave the firft blow to the Roman Catholic religion in that kingdom) being now dead, his fon Edward VI. fucceeded him at the age of ten years, whofe guardians and counfellors being all appointed by his father, and declared enemies to the Catholick faith, entirely finifhed what he had begun, to the utter extirpation of the popifh religion. Julius, upon this occafion, difpatched nuncios, briefs, and letters to every court in Europe, and ufed all poffible means to remedy the evil, holding frequent conferences and confultations both in the confiftory and in private ; but finding all human endeavours vain, he ordered the hoft to be expofed for forty hours at every church in Rome, with continual prayers and interceffions for three days, commanding the moft celebrated preachers to exert their utmoft eloquence

quence in exciting the people to join in earnest petitions to implore the assistance of heaven.

Montalto was appointed to preach in the convent of the Holy Apostles, Cardinal Carpi and father Ghisilieri, both zealous asserters of the pontifical rights, and grandeur of the church, being present at his sermon. He took his text out of the second Psalm, *The kings of the earth stand up, and the rulers take counsel together against the Lord, and against his anointed,* and, either as it was his own opinion, or he thought it would be agreeable to the audience, run into great encomiums upon the zeal of the Pope, inveighing bitterly, at the same time, against Charles, Ferdinand, and Henry, calling them hereticks, apostates, as bad as Edward, and worse than Luther himself. The French and Spaniards resented this extremely, and made heavy complaints of it to the Pope, who acquainted Cardinal Carpi, as he was protector of the Franciscan order, and present at the sermon. As the Cardinal did by no means approve of Montalto's licentious and unbridled manner of speaking, and the great liberties he took with crowned heads, though he thought he had spoke nothing but truth, and what was almost necessary in such times, he sent for him, and told him, what disgust it had given, adding, that " he had behaved like a good divine, but " a bad politician ; and that in the pulpit it was neces- " sary to mix prudence with zeal ; the age being now " such, as would not allow prophets to rebuke princes " for their faults in so publick a manner : that it was " highly impolitick in private ecclesiasticks to do any " thing that might draw the resentment of the King of " Spain upon them, as his Holiness was continually " sending such numbers of them into his dominions ; " that he would advise him to make some sort of satis- " faction, to those that were offended at a behaviour " which yet perhaps, strictly speaking, could not be " termed criminal."

After he had given him this gentle reprimand, he sent him with a letter to the Spanish ambassador, Don Diego Guzman di Silva (whom he had already pre-

(pared)

pared to make a fubmiffion for his fault. The ambaffador infifted upon a writing under his hand, in which
he fhould not only acknowledge that he had no intention to affront the Emperor or the King of Spain, or
either of the nations in general ; but promife to be
cautious for the future, and ufe more refpect and moderation, when at any time he fhould have occafion to
fpeak of the houfe of Auftria ; which he at laft complied with, though much againft the grain. Little
notice was taken of the complaint made by the French,
as they were not then in any great degree of favour, or
in a capacity to do much prejudice to the court of
Rome.

Soon after this [1553] he was fent to preach at Perugia, though it was his defire to have gone to Afcoli. But another Perfon had already obtained a promife of that church. He did not anfwer the expectation of his new audience there, and, whether it was
owing to his indifference for them after he had been
difappointed of Afcoli, or that the Perugians were
wanting in their tafte, he was not fo much followed as
another preacher in the fame town. Upon fome difference with the fuperior he left that place and returned
to Rome, in hope of obtaining a regency [5], at a
time when feveral were to be difpofed of. He applied
to Cardinal Carpi, who had already thought of him,
and faid, " The general had given him his word, he
" fhould have one of the moft beneficial that was va-
" cant," which happened to be that of St. Lawrence in
Naples; and though great intereft had been made for
it, the Cardinal's recommendation prevailed, and he
fet out immediately for Naples, in company with his
provincial. The fociety having heard fo many ftories of his fpirit and temper, entertained him very
coolly, though he did all that lay in his power to gain
their affections.

A few months before, Don Pedro di Toledo, vice-

[5] A regent, is a mafter of arts, and fometimes a doctor of divinity, whofe office it is to preach and read lectures to pupils in colleges and religious houfes.

roy of Naples, had marched from thence, by the Emperor's order, at the head of a confiderable army, compofed of Spaniards, Italians, and Germans, to chaftife the Siennefe for their late rebellion ; and left Cardinal Paceco, a Spaniard, as his lieutenant there. Montalto, feeing the little refpect he had fhewn him in the convent, thought it no bad policy to ftrengthen his intereft by a recommendatory letter from his patron Cardinal Carpi to Paceco ; but proved rather a differvice to him than otherwife. For relying too much upon his favour and fupport, he treated his fuperiors with great contempt ; efpecially father Caracciolo, who was nearly allied to all the beft and moft antient families in Naples : a mifbehaviour, that he repented of afterwards.

Not long after, he was fent by the general to Orvieto, at the defire of the bifhop of that place, to open the fynod, that was fummoned there, with a fermon, which he willingly undertook, as he neglected no opportunity of doing any thing that he thought would increafe his reputation, and diftinguifh him among the ecclefiafticks.

The general's anfwer to the bifhop, as it happened, had mifcarried, and the bifhop being afraid the preacher would not arrive in time, as it was then the 20th of December, and the fynod was to be opened on Chriftmay-day, fent to father Maoli, an eminent divine, to perform that office. On the 22d, Montalto arrived, and hearing what had been done, faid he would with pleafure give up the pulpit to fo worthy a man as father Maoli, who returned the compliment to Montalto. But the bifhop interfering, faid, " One of them " fhould open, and the other clofe the feffion with a " fermon." The firft being the more honourable, and their merits fo equal, that he could not determine who ought to have the preference, efpecially as they both modeftly declined it, he thought it was the beft way to caft lots, faying in joke, that " whoever was favoured " by fortune in this affair, might look upon it as a fure " omen of his being Pope hereafter." The lot falling
upon

upon Montalto, the bifhop cried out, " Behold his
" his Holinefs ;" and Maoli turning to him, faid to
him, " Remember me when thou comeft into thy
" kingdom.

On Chriftmas-day he preached in the cathedral, upon
the following text, *And there were in the fame country
fhepherds abiding in the field, and keeping watch over their
flocks by night*, a fubject very well adapted to the time
and occafion; from which he took an opportunity of
difcourfing largely upon the nature and duties of the
paftoral office, to the great fatisfaction of his audience,
which was a very learned and numerous one. He
printed this fermon with much applaufe, and dedicated it to the bifhop of Orvieto.

This year died Edward VI. King of England ; and
Mary, his fifter, no fooner was in poffeffion of his crown,
than fhe re-eftablifhed the Roman Catholic religion in
that kingdom by the counfel and affiftance of Cardinal
Pole, and then married Philip, fon to Charles V. As
there were great rejoicings upon this occafion in the
kingdom of Naples, which the Emperor had given
his fon at his marriage, the convent of St. Lawrence,
being a royal foundation, had a mind to fhew their
loyalty, by a magnificent feftival which lafted nine
days. Montalto opened it with a very eloquent oration ; which fo pleafed the citizens, that they wrote to
the general in his favour, and defired he would give
him the chief pulpit in the city at the return of Lent.
He immediately fent him his licence ; and though there
was another very famous preacher that drew a great
concourfe of people after him, to a church near his, he
had always a much larger.

The warden advifed him not to preach his fermon
upon predeftination again, which had made fo much
noife at Rome, but he anfwered, " That ; in that mat-
" ter he fhould follow the impulfe of the Holy Spirit,"
which, it feems, moved him to preach a fecond time
upon the fame fubject, but with much more vehemence than before ; for he ran into fuch invectives
againft Cranmer archbifhop of Canterbury, who was
afterwards

afterwards burnt at a stake for his close attachment to the Proteſtant religion, that it gave great difguſt to many ſenſible and moderate people.

The warden, angry at his preaching again upon that ſubjeċt contrary to his advice, gave him a reprimand, which occaſioned a quarrel betwixt them; and put Montalto upon writing to Rome, that he ſuſpeċted the warden's principles; the other hearing of this, was thoroughly nettled at it, and ſought an opportunity of revenge with much eagerneſs.

Amongſt many others that had their particular merit, he preached two ſermons here, that were extremely admired, and was daily importuned to print them; which he was unwilling to do at firſt, but afterwards gave his conſent, and dedicated them to his friend and patron Antony Simoncelli. Theſe two pieces, though full of learning and eloquence, were not ſo well liked when they came to be read, as when he delivered them from the pulpit.

There was now a ſort of a perſecution raiſed againſt him in the convent; his brethren would ſcarce condeſcend to ſalute him as they paſſed by. The warden made ſome complaints againſt him to the general, but as he found they proceeded from paſſion and malice, he gave little attention to them. It did not ſeem to give Montalto much uneaſineſs; yet he publiſhed a defence, which he preſented to the community in the refeċtory. This ſort of uſage he ſupported for the ſpace of two years, and bore the daily inſults which he received with a tolerable degree of patience; but being at laſt quite tired out, after he had both ſpoke and written ſeveral bitter things againſt the ſociety, the warden, and the provincial himſelf, he left them without either leave or ceremony, and went to Rome; where the general, who was thoroughly offended at his behaviour, treated him like a deſerter, and was determined to ſend him immediately back to Naples.

This hurt his reputation in the convent of the Holy Apoſtles, where Cardinal Carpi at laſt got leave for him to reſide; and the brotherhood gave him ſuch continual
al

al marks of their difesteem, that he entreated his eminence to deliver him out of that uncomfortable situation, and to obtain him a brief from the Pope, that he
might extricate himself out of these broils in an honourable manner, by leaving the cloyster. This request displeased the Cardinal to such a degree, that he
threatened him with the loss of his friendship and protection, if he heard any more of it, and told him, that
" such thoughts never found entertainment in the hears
" of any but those of rebellious and ungovernable spi-
" rits." Upon this rebuke he resolved to sit down quietly, and arm himself with patience, according to the
advice of father Ghisilieri, to whom he had communicated his design, in hope of his approbation and af-
sistance.

When this came to the ears of the general and his
brethren, they were so provoked, that when they spoke
the most favourably of him, they said, " He was fit-
" ter to return to his hogs, than to live in a religious
" society." But Cardinal Carpi made use of his authority with the general, to put an end to these animosities, exhorting Montalto at the same timo, with much
kindness, to bridle his passions, and behave with more
moderation for the future, telling him, that " such a
" conduct was not to be suffered in a cloyster, where
" every one ought to mortify himself in order to ob-
" lige his brother."

On the other had, Montalto, willing to justify himself, said, " If there had been uneasinesses in the con-
" vent, he was sorry for it, though conscious that it
" was not any way owing to him, but the envy and
" ill nature of his brethren."

" This ill nature that you complain of," replied the
" Cardinal, " is probably occasioned by yourself; if
" your enemies were few, there would be some colour
" of truth in what you say, but as there is hardly one
" person in the convent, that does not speak ill of you,
" it has a bad aspect:" for which reason, it " highly
" concerns you to alter your conduct: as it would be
" very

" very unreasonable to expect, that a whole commu-
" nity should submit to the humours and extravagan-
" cies of one person." His friend Bossius likewise, by
the Cardinal's order, gave him some advice of the same
nature, though he had conceived so great an opinion
of him, that he thought the fault proceeded wholly
from the monks.

When Montalto was last at Le Grotte, he desired the
favour of his friend John Baptist Mancone, the curate,
to send him an account sometimes of the health and
welfare of his family; and, if possible, to provide a
husband for his sister, a circumstance he passionately
wished for. As an opportunity offered soon after, that
was agreeable to her parents, the curate wrote him
the following letter, which came to his hands just at
the time of his disgrace.

REVEREND FATHER,

" AFTER many enquiries where to direct a letter
" to you, I am informed by a gentleman of my
" parish, who has lately been at Rome, that you are just
" arrived there, to complain of some ill usage you have
" received from the conventuals at Naples, amongst
" whom merit is always sure to meet with persecution.
" As it is uncertain, into what hands this might other-
" wise fall, I enclose it in a cover to Signior Bossius, ac-
" cording to your direction, when I had the happiness
" of seeing you last, being assured it will give you a
" sincere pleasure (as it is a great comfort to your pa-
" rents in their old age) to hear, that we have a fair
" opportunity of marrying both your brother Antony
" and your sister Camilla. Your brother, who is a
" mason, gets a very good livelihood; and is in a man-
" ner engaged to Mary daughter of John Tabotto the
" taylor, who has a good house, with a pretty garden,
" and no other child to leave it to. So that I think it
" a good match for him, and only wait for your con-
" sent and approbation, which they desire, and make
" no doubt of.

" Your

" Your fifter is courted by Andrew Botero, a car-
" penter, who is at leaft twenty years older than fhe ;
" but well thought of both by her and your parents,
" as he is a very honeft man, and in good bufinefs,
" but the love and refpect which fhe has, and always
" had, for fo worthy a brother, will not fuffer her to
" make any promife (though nothing elfe is wanting)
" till fhe is affured it is not difagreeable to you. Her
" lover often comes to me, and expreffes the utmoft
" impatience to hear his doom. Be pleafed therefore to
" let me know, whether you have any objection to
" make, and if not, what I can do further to ferve
" them or you in this matter. Camilla hopes, if you
" confent to the match, as you have always expreffed
" fo much affection for her, that you will give fome-
" thing towards her fortune, out of the charitable col-
" lections made at your fermons, fhe having already
" faved 30 or 40 crowns, got by her own labour. All
" your friends are well, and defire to be remembered
" to you. Let me have your anfwer as foon as you
" can, and it will much oblige

" Your affectionate friend,

Le Grotte,
    May 8, 1554. " and humble fervant,

' J. MANCONE.

When he had read this letter, he fhewed it in confidence to Boffius, and he carried it to the Cardinal his
patron, who expreffed much fatisfaction in reading it,
and was fo pleafed with Montalto's honefty and humility, in not being afhamed at all times to confefs the
meannefs of his family, or taking any pains to conceal
it according to the cuftom of monks ; that he ordered
40 crowns to be given him for the ufe of his fifter,
which, with 20 more that were added by Montalto,
and ten by Boffius, he fent with the following letter to
his friend the curate.

.E   Sir,

Sir,

" I Received a double pleasure from your letter, as
" is gave me, at the same time, an account of my
" poor family, and an affectionate proof of the conti-
" nuance of your friendship. The kind concern you
" exprefs for the welfare of my relations, and the high
" opinion I have of your prudence, juftly demand my
" ready confent to whatever you advife or think will
" be for their advantage. Nothing further remains to
" be done on my part, but to return you hearty thanks
" for the favours you have already beſtowed upon us,
" and to defire a continuance of your good offices till
" the affair you mention is brought to a conclufion. I
" could wifh fortune, or, to fpeak more properly, the
" divine providence, had put it in my power to fhew
" the affection I ever had for my family in a better
" manner; and to convince you by fomething more
" fubftantial than mere thanks and acknowledgments
" of the grateful fenfe I entertain of your kindneffes.
" But what can I do?" *Wherewith fhall I fave* Ifrael ?
" *Behold my family is poor in* Manaffeh, *and I am the*
" *leaſt in my father's houfe.* Yet I have great reafon to
" be thankful and adore the goodnefs of almighty
" God in raifing me out of the duft, to ferve at his
" altar. I here fend you inclofed three letters, one for
" my dear parents, another for my brother Anthony,
" and the third for my fifter, which I defire you to pe-
" rufe : as they will ferve in fome meafure to fhew
" (whilft I rejoice with them upon the approaching
" marriages) how much we think ourfelves obliged to
" you. With this you will receive 70 crowns, ten of
" which you will be pleafed to give my poor mother,
" to make fome little entertainment upon this occa-
" fion, and the other fixty to my fifter, as an addition
" to her fortune; with which fhe ought to think her-
" felf not a little honoured, as it is chiefly the benevo-
" lence and generofity of the Cardinal protector of
" our order. In my letter to her I have made ufe of a
                                    " quotation

" quotation out of the Acts of the Apostles, viz. *Au-*
" *rum et argentum non est mihi, quod autem habeo, hoc tibi*
" *do* [6], which I must beg you will be so kind to ex-
" plain to her.   Perhaps heaven may hereafter enable
" me to do a more material service to both them and
" you.   In the mean time believe me

Your truly affectionate friend and servant,

" FELIX PERETTI."

At this time cardinal Pole was detained in a sort of
honourable confinement by the Emperor in Flanders,
who would not suffer him to proceed in his voyage to
England, whither he was sent by the Pope, at Queen
Mary's request, to confer with her upon proper means
for a thorough re-establishment of the Roman Catholick religion in her dominions.   It was reported, the
Emperor was afraid he might put a stop to the marriage between his son and that princess, notwithstanding they were already contracted, and rejoicings had
been made in both kingdoms upon that occasion ; for
which reason he would not let him pass the seas till it
was consummated, detaining him first on one pretence,
and then on another. The Pope was highly displeased
at this, being impatient to see heresy extirpated, and
the true religion restored in England (as he expresses it
in his letter to him).   For the effecting of which, he
thought the Cardinal's presence altogether necessary ;
as he was not only an Englishman, but cousin to the
Queen, and nearly related to most of the nobility in
that kingdom.   Upon which account he made heavy
complaints to the Emperor, accusing him of being
lukewarm in the R. C. religion, and repeating the old
grievance of having made peace with the Protestants.

To give the Cardinal a greater degree of authority,
and to engage the Emperor more effectually to dismiss

[6] Acts iii. 6. Silver and gold have I none, but such as I have
give I to thee.

him,

him, he declared him legate a latere [7]. imagining the Emperor would not prefume to detain him any longer, when he was invefted with that high character, for any private reafons of his own, to the prejudice of the holy fee.

Before Pole was acquainted with the refolution of the Pope, he had fent Ormaneto, his auditor to Rome, to acquaint his Holinefs with feveral particulars relating to the ftate of England, and to complain not only of the affront that was offered to himfelf by the Emperor, but the manifeft injury that was done to the interefts of religion in general, and the inftances he had fo often in vain repeated to be fet at liberty ; which determined the Pope to fend an inftrument, appointing him legate by the return of Ormaneto.

Boffius thought this a good opportunity of delivering his friend Montalto from the confinement of a cloyfter, which he knew had been a long time very irkfome to him ; and for that purpofe, applied to Cardinal Carpi, telling him, " That as Pole was to be " foon declared legate a latere to the court of England, " and muft confequently take two religious with him, " one as a preacher, the other as his confeffor, he

[7] A legate is a prelate, whom the Pope fends as ambaffador to any foreign prince, from the Latin word legare. Wicquefort.

There are three kinds of legates, viz. Legates a latere, legates de latere, and legates by office, or legati nati : of thefe the moft confiderable are the legates a latere, whom the Pope commiffions to take his place in councils, they are fo called from the Pope's never giving this office to any but his greateft favourites and confidants, who are always at his fide, a latere, that is, to the Cardinals. Du Cange, in his Gloffary, fays, there were antiently, counts a latere and monitors a latere. A legate a latere may confer benefices, without a mandate, legitimate baftards to hold offices, and has a crofs carried before him as the enfign of his office. The legates de latere, are thofe who are not cardinals, but yet entrufted with an apoftolical legation. Legates by office, or legati nati, are thofe who have not any particular legation given them, but by virtue of their dignity and place in the church become legates. Such are the archbifhops of Rheims and Arles. But the authority of thefe is much inferior to that of the legates a latere.

The power of a legate is fometimes alfo given without the title : fome of the Nuncio's are invefted with it.

" thought

" thought Montalto was a perfon very well qualified
" for either of thofe functions."

The Cardinal was by no means averfe from the propofal, but faid, " If Montalto could not govern his
" temper in a convent, he was afraid he would find it
" much more difficult to do it amongft courtiers : and
" that it was firft neceffary to afk him, whether he lik-
" ed that ftation, and thought he could behave in it with
" more decency, than he had done heretofore amongft
" the Cordeliers." Boffius anfwered, " That as foon
" as the defign came into his head, he had communi-
" cated it to him, that he feemed highly pleafed with
" the thoughts of it," and faid, " Nothing could be
" more agreeable to him :" promifing, if this favour
was granted, to demean himfelf in fuch a manner,
as he hoped would give fatisfaction to the legate,
and his Eminence no reafon to be afhamed of his
recommendation.

Upon this, he refolved to try his intereft with the
legate in behalf of Montalto ; but thought, though he
was pretty well acquainted with him himfelf, it would
be more proper to recommend him firft to Cardinal Sadoleto, as he was very intimate with Pole, and had the
care of expediting the briefs that were to be fent him by
Ormaneto, who lodged in his houfe. He knew Cardinal Pole had been twice to hear Montalto during the
Lent, in which he preached at the convent of the Holy
Apoftles, and had fpoke of him with fome approbation, feeming much pleafed with his fermons, which he
looked upon as no inconfiderable circumftance in his favour, and therefore the more willingly recommended
him to Sadoleto, who he knew had the appointment of
the legate's train ; Boffius did the fame to Ormaneto,
with whom he had a very ftrict acquaintance.

Sadoleto immediately promifed to reprefent him in a
favourable light to the legate, but defired to be excufed
from fending him to Flanders, till he knew his Eminence's pleafure in that refpect, and faid there would
be time enough for his voyage to England, where the
legate was to ftay at leaft two years. Befides, Ormaneto

neto travelling poſt, might think it inconvenient to take Montalto along with him, as the Cardinal and Boſſius requeſted.

However, to recommend him the more effectually to the legate's notice, he employed him to compoſe two bulls, that were to be diſpatched to him, giving him minutes of the Pope's order in Italian, which he modelled an drew up in Latin. Theſe were the Cardinal's legantine powers or commiſſion, in which he was ſtrictly charged, amongſt many other things of importance, that he was to negociate in England, to take particular care that all the abbey lands, and other poſſeſſions, that had been violently torn away from the church in the two proceeding reigns, were punctually reſtored.

Sadoleto was extremely pleaſed with the Latin, and wondered how it was poſſible for him to be ſo well acquainted with the ſtyle and terms of the [8] Datary, without any practice or knowledge of it, except what he had accidentally gathered from meeting with a bull now and then in the courſe of his reading. When he preſented them to his Holineſs to be ſigned, he aſked him how he liked the ſtyle. The Pope commending it very much, and deſiring to know the reaſon of that queſtion, " Becauſe," replied he, " they were drawn by " a monk." The ſame day he read them to Cardinal Carpi, whilſt Montalto was in the ſame apartment, and turning to him ſaid, " Young man, if you had been a " a ſecular inſtead of a monk, you might have made " your fortune at court," and was ſo deſirous of ſending him to England in the legate's ſervice, that he wrote a letter to Pole himſelf in his favour, with the two bulls: which, being ſeconded by the kind offices of Ormaneto, had ſo good an effect, that he deſigned to have ſent him orders ſoon after, to ſet out for Flanders, at leaſt to meet him in England. But when this came to be known by Montalto's enemies at Rome, they ſent let-

[8] The Datary, is an office at the court of Rome, in which all briefs, bulls, preſentations to benefices, &c. and other publick inſtruments are expedited, ſo called from the date being put to them there in theſe words, Datum Romæ, &c.

ters to the legate, giving a moſt vile character of him, with a terrible narative of his proceedings and behaviour amongſt the religious. Upon which he wrote back to Sadoleto, that though he had received a very different account of Montalto, from that, which he had given him, and was afraid of a man of his temper could not behave with that complaiſance and politeneſs that is always expected in courts, yet he would leave the matter wholly to him and Cardinal Carpi, and to oblige them, would take him if they deſired it. When Sadoleto communicated the contents of this letter to Carpi, they both concluded his merit muſt be very extraordinary, that could raiſe ſuch a ſpirit of detraction and perſecution againſt him; and though he was not free from failings, yet they were not ſufficient to overbalance his virtues, and agreed to ſend him away. But when he came to know how he had been miſrepreſented to the legate, he entirely gave up the matter, and would not go upon any conſideration. With this reſolution he waited upon the two Cardinals, to thank them for their recommendation, and kind endeavours to ſerve him, which had been fruſtrated by the malice of his enemies, and ſaid, he hoped, " they would ex- " cuſe him, if he now declined going, as he had " ſome reaſon to think he ſhould ſoon be taken notice " of by the Colonna family," into whoſe good graces he had inſinuated himſelf in the following manner.

Their palace, where the Abbe Mark Anthony Colonna then reſided, joins cloſe to the convent of the Holy Apoſtles. As that noble family had always honoured the order of St. Francis with their protection, and the Abbe wanted a tutor to inſtruct him in the philoſophy of Scotus [9]: Montalto made him an offer of his ſervice (in hope of procuring the favour and

[9] J. Duns Scotus, a Scotch or as ſome ſay, an Iriſh Cordelier. He was a famous ſchoolman in his day, i. e. about the end of the 13th century, and went by the name of the ſubtile doctor. He maintained the immaculate conception of the Virgin, and that ſhe was born without original ſin, in oppoſition to Thomas Aquinas, and the Thomiſts; as to philoſophy, the Scotiſts were, like the Thomiſts, Peripateticks..

patronage

patronage of one of the greateſt and moſt conſiderable
families in Italy) which the Abbe ſaid, " He would
" gladly accept of, as he had the character of being
" the beſt philoſopher in Rome, provided he would
" give him leave to wait upon him at his convent."
He was not, however, ſo unpolite as to ſuffer that,
but daily attended him at the palace ; and by his great
aſſiduity and obſequiouſneſs, acquired ſuch a degree
of eſteem, not only with the Abbe, but whole family,
that they were his friends and patrons ever after.

  As he was ambitious of being a confeſſor, which is
eſteemed a great honour amongſt the monks, he procured a licence for that purpoſe, by the intereſt of Boſſius, with the cardinal-vicar ; and was ſcarcely in poſſeſſion of his new office, when he went and ſeated
himſelf in a confeſſional chair, in the church of the
Holy Apoſtles, without ever acquainting the general
or warden of the convent that he had a licence.

  The latter, who was an imperious ſort of a man,
and expected a great deal of reſpect to be ſhewn him,
being informed that Montalto had taken upon him to
ſit and hear confeſſions in a chair belonging to a father
of his convent, immediately made a complaint of it to
the general of the order. The general, knowing Montalto was ſo ſtrongly ſupported by Cardinal Carpi, and
now by the Colonna family, did not care to interfere in
the matter ; but endeavoured to ſoften the warden by
mild and gentle meaſures, without, however, depriving him of his privileges: for though a faculty to hear
confeſſions, is granted by the cardinal vicar, or ordinary
of the place, it is further neceſſary to have a licence
from the curate of the pariſh amongſt the feculars, or
the ſuperior of the convent, amongſt the regulars.
the warden, to maintain his privilege, forbade him to
hear confeſſions any more in that convent. Montalto
provoked at this anſwered with ſome warmth, " That
" he was doctor in divinity, and had a licence from the
" general, to hear the confeſſions of regulars, and ano-
" ther from the cardinal-vicar, to confeſs feculars; and
                                        " his

" his refidence being appointed in the convent of the
" Holy Apoftles, there was no occafion for any fur-
" ther ceremony that he knew of." But the warden,
who was well affured he had right on his fide, confirmed his prohibition, and told him, that " if he pre-
" fumed to do the like again, he would inftantly ex-
" communicate him."

The breach growing wider and wider, Montalto
complained to the cardinal-vicar and protector.   But
the general fupported the warden, and not only feverely reprimanded Montalto, but fent two monks on
purpofe to acquaint Boffius, " That he grew fo info-
" lent, his behaviour was no longer to be borne with."
Upon which Boffius came to the convent, and, by his
mediation put an end to the quarrel, prevailing upon
Montalto to make fome little fubmiffion.

As he had then a great deal of leifure time upon his
hands, and but little employment, except reading lectures to the Abbe an hour or two in the day, he applied himfelf to ftudy cafes of confcience, and wrote a
book, intitled, Inftructions neceffary for confeffors and
penitents, with a long preface or introduction to the
work, concerning the nature of true contrition, the excellency and neceffity of confeffion, the antiquity and
reafons of its inftitution, and the right manner of preparing for it, with many other articles of that kind,
for the ufe of penitents.   He further explained the duty and office of confeffors, fhewing what kind of ftudies
they ought chiefly to apply themfelves to, and the
qualifications they fhould be mafters of.   Confirming
his pofitions by the authority of feverals bulls and quo-
tations from doctors of the church.   The body of the
work confifted of twenty-two dialogues between confeffors and penitents [1].

[1] The author mentions the title of them all, and gives a fpeci-
men of two ; which the Italian reader may fee, if he pleafes, in
the Appendix, under the numbers I, and II. as they are not fit to be
tranflated,

When

When it was finished, he shewed it to father Cavana, an old man, who had been confessor near forty years, and one of these who were appointed by the cardinal-vicar, to examine the candidates for that office, desiring his opinion of the book, as he designed to publish it.

But Cavana (whom Montalto thought his friend) being much offended at the manuscript, instead of returning it to the author, with his opinion, carried it to the general, who, having perused it, and finding, that it not only did not seem likely to be of any edification, but was scandalous, obscene, and profane, sent for Montalto, and gave him a severe rebuke, threatening to put him into the Inquisition; the manuscript, as he said, deserving to be burnt, and the author made an example of. As he had long wanted an opportunity of doing Montalto a prejudice, he thought this was a very good one to ruin his credit with the cardinal-protector; for otherwise, he was not desirous of making the affair publick, much less of representing it to the Inquisition, knowing it would not only bring a scandal upon his convent, but the whole order. Upon which consideration, he thought it would be a sufficient punishment, at present, to put his patron out of conceit with him; and that when he had lost his favour and protection, he might afterwards treat him as he pleased, or at least get rid of a person, that was a continual thorn in his side. With this view, he went to the Cardinal, and gave him the manuscript, making such a report of it, as he thought would effectually do his business.

Montalto, in the mean time, instead of endeavouring to close the breach, by humbling himself before the general, and, by good words and submissive behaviour, to get the manuscript out of his hands, still added fuel to the flame, reproaching Cavana with breach of confidence, and threatening revenge, of which Cavana complaining to the general made him resolve to acquaint the Cardinal with the whole.

It happened, luckily for Montalto, that when the general gave his manuscript to the protector, he was wholly

wholly taken up with matters of great importance; and not being at leisure to give much attention to what the other said, referred it to his secretary Boffius, with orders to read it over, and give him an account of the contents. Eight days passed before Montalto knew of this, and as he thought the manuscript still in the general's hands, he was endeavouring, through the interest of a friend, to get it back again; but when he was informed by him, that it was delivered to the Cardinal, he began to be terrified, being convinced from the rebuke he had received both from Cavana and the general, that it was a very exceptionable performance, and, as such, had resolved to revise and correct it.

There was no remedy left, but to apply to his never failing friend Boffius; to him he had recourse, and happily found him with the manuscript in his hand. Boffius received him with his usual courtesy, and after he had shut the door, gave him a friendly admonition, " Not being able to conceive," as he said, " how a " man of his prudence and discretion could be guilty " of such an inconsiderate action, which he could ne- " ver have suspected him of, if he had not been con- " vinced of it by unquestionable proof:" pointing out, at the same time, several very obscene and indecent passages, and by no means to be justified by one in his station. Upon this, Montalto gave up all for lost, and imagined he had now nothing more to hope for from Cardinal Carpi; but he soon recovered his spirits, when Boffius embraced him, and said, " My " dear Montalto, as I believe you had no bad design " in what you have done, it has not made any ill im- " pression upon me, nor hurt you in my esteem. I " love you too well to be easily put out of conceit with " you : my friendship you may depend upon as long " as I live". and immediately gave him back the manuscript, with a caution not to shew it to any body else; telling him, he would use his utmost endeavours to pacify the general, who seemed much enraged, and give a favourable account of the whole affair to the

Cardinal,

Cardinal, which he did in such a manner as put a stop to all further proceedings.

The chapter of La Marca was to meet soon after, to chuse a new provincial, Montalto was not without hope, that the election might fall upon him, and made use of all his interest to obtain that dignity. The Colonna family spoke to Cardinal Carpi, who, out of regard to their recommendation, and the esteem which, he himself always had for him, asked it of the general as protector of the order, assuring him, this favour would make him forget all the injuries and ill treatment he conceived he had met with amongst them.

The general, who hated Montalto, and had already promised his interest to another, said, " It was not " possible to oblige him at that time, that the mem- " bers of the chapter were not at all inclined to chuse " him, and would rather give their votes for any other " person whatsoever. Besides, as he had not resided " in the province for three years, he could not expect " to be preferred to those who had made themselves " worthy of that honour, by their constant residence " and long services to the order." When he saw the Cardinal would not give him up, he declared, " He " could not in conscience do such a piece of injustice, " to so many elder persons of at least equal merit and " desert." After this answer, there being no room for the Cardinal to say any thing further, he exhorted Montalto to bear his disappointment with patience, and assured him, he should not be long without preferment. The general, that he might not absolutely break with the Cardinal, soon after gave him a chair at Genoa, whither he went, in February to preach during the next Lent.

At his arrival there, they brought him the keys of the strangers apartment [2], and received him with a great deal of civility at first. As the Genoese are a fru-

[2] A room in all convents, set apart for the lodging of travelling brothers and strangers.

gal

gal people, and their generofity feldom lafts longer than
two or three meals, they gave Montalto to underftand,
" They could not afford to be at the expence of en-
" tertaining his companion, that came with him from
" Rome [3], in the fame manner as they did him, and
" that it was but reafonable he fhould take up with the
" common provifions of the houfe, as others had done
" in the fame circumftances, before him." Montalto
had fo great a value for his companion, that he rather
chofe to maintain him at his own charge, than fend
him home again.

This was not the only affront he met with there.
The preachers commonly lodge in the apartment that
belongs to the general or provincial, when they come
to refide at Genoa. When Montalto was informed of
this, he made heavy complaints of being thruft into
the ftrangers chamber, and threatened to leave them
directly ; but the warden acquainting him, " That he
" expected the provincial in a few days, and thought
" that putting him into his apartment, would rather
" be an inconvenience to him than otherwife ; as he
" would be obliged to remove out of it; when the pro-
" vincial came, he was pretty well fatisfied."

For fome time after his coming to Genoa, he was
not much followed. The other conventuals of that
city fet up a preacher of their own of great reputation,
in oppofition to him, who drew a multitude of people
after him. But by degrees this prejudice fubfided,
and the other's audience grew lefs and lefs every day,
tho' he ufed every artifice to keep them together. On
the contrary, Montalto's fermons began to be fo
much talked of, that the Cordeliers church, which is
one of the largeft in Genoa, not being able to contain
the numbers that flock'd to hear him, they were forced
to erect fcaffolds for them.

Julius III. dying the 23d of March, this year, the
news

[3] When the religious go out of their convent, they are generally attended by a lay brother, or fome other companion of their
order, as a check upon their behaviour.

news of his death arrived at Genoa the evening before
the fourth Sunday in Lent. The Gofpel for that Sunday, relates the miracle of our Saviour's feeding the
multitude with five loaves and two fifhes, which he
took for the fubject of his difcourfe, and fo happily
applied to the concern which the whole church muft
feel upon the lofs of their common paftor, that his audience confeffed he had, upon this oecafion, exceeded
all that could be expected from the greateft preachers.
Some of the fenators, and chief inhabitants, were defirous of feeing it in print; but he remembered the
fate of thofe which he publifhed at Naples, and would
not run that rifque a fecond time. He preached another on Eafter Sunday, that was no lefs applauded,
upon the words, *This is the day which the Lord hath
made, we will rejoice and be glad in it.* Marcellus Cer-
vinus, a Tufcan by birth, was elected Pope in the
room of Julius, and retained his baptifmal name. It
was known at Genoa on Saturday in Paffion week. In
this performance he compared the joy, that they now
experienced, in having a new head of the church, with
that which all true Chriftians feel, when they meditate
upon the refurrection of Chrift. It gave fo much fatisfaction to the Genoefe, that they petitioned the general to let him preach there again the next Lent; and
the Cordeliers, feeing their church fo crouded every
day, willingly confented to defray the expences of his
companion, which they refufed at firft, made him a
handfomer allowance than they had ever done to any
preacher before, and vyed with each other, who fhould
fhew him the greateft civilities.

When Lent was over, they preffed him to ftay a few
days longer with them, to repofe himfelf after his labours; but he took his leave of them, and fet out for
Rome, where a general chapter of the order was to be
held in a fhort time. As he was very defirous of a
regency, he thought it beft to go and follicit one himfelf, left the general, who had affured Cardinal Carpi
he would remember his friend in the diftribution of his
preferments,

preferments, should evade the promise, by giving him
an inconsiderable and perhaps disagreeable one.

Though he was determined, for these reasons, to
make what haste he could to Rome, he had a mind to
take Le Grotte, in his way, that he might have an opportunity of seeing his relations. Father Caputi, a
religious, who was of a good family, and seemed to
value himself much upon it, agreed to go with him,
and would have stopped at Montalto, which is the nearest great town to Le Grotte, but was desired by his
friend to go on further with him, and honour the place
of his nativity, with his presence. Upon which a lay-
brother, that accompanied them, and was a sensible
fellow (though no great scholar) and Montalto's countryman, called him aside, and told him, "He could
" not but wonder at his inviting any person to go with
" him, to see the nakedness of the land, especially one
" of Caputi's turn, who would not fail to make a
" joke of it afterwards in all companies." At which
Montalto only laughed and said, " You simpleton,
" this is the best way of mortifying such people as are
" continually bragging of their descent; for what can
" be more galling to this poor vain creature, who
" boasts of so many noble relations, and such an estate
" in his family, than to see himself every where oblig-
" ed to give place to, and acknowledge me his superi-
" or, who am born of so mean a parentage?"

When they arrived at Le Grotte, they took up their
lodging at the house of Mancone, and dined the next
day, by Montalto's particular request, at his father's
cottage; Montalto making a very hearty meal of such
homely fare as he found there; whilst Caputi, who said,
" He had not been used to that kind of diet," could
not be prevailed upon to sit down with such a collection of beggarly people, or to eat upon earthen platters
and trenchers as they did.

He staid there two days, and when he took his leave
of them, his old friend Mancone said merrily to him,
" Father Peretti, make haste to be Pope, you'll soon
" have nephews and nieces enough to fill all the apart-
" ments

" ments in the Vatican:" hinting to him, that there was likely to be an addition to his family in a short time, at which he expressed much satisfaction, and gave 12 crowns to his father and mother, 6 to his sister, and 6 more to his brother's wife. At their departure, his father and mother, with near forty more of his relati ons, attended them above a mile, according to the cuftom of country people, some carrying children in their arms, and others leading them by the hand.

When Caputi saw this ragged troop following them, he asked Montalto, " How he proposed to provide for " such a number of poor relations?" Montalto answered, " He should be able to do it very well " when he was Pope." " If that be the case," replied Caputi, " St. Peter will be left very poor at your death." " Quite otherwise," said Montalto, " If you are alive, " when I die Pope, you shall see I will leave the " church richer than ever it was before;" which actually came to pass afterwards.

When they got within two days journey of Rome, he heard of the death of Pope Marcellus, who died the first of May, twelve days after his election ; upon which he said to his companions, " If the Popes take " it into their heads to die so fast, surely it will come " to my turn to be Pope in a short time."

During the vacancy of the see, he preached in the church of the Holy Apostles by the general's order, who was as good as his word, and performed the pro-mise he made to his patron, by giving him the option of all the regencies in Italy. Montalto, who always hated restraint, chose that of Venice, upon the account of the great liberty that every body enjoys there, having likewise strong recommendations from the Colonna family to several noble Venetians.

A little before he obtained this regency, John Peter Caraffa, Cardinal of Ostia, was elected Pope, and took the name of Paul IV. He was Carpi's intimate friend, and honoured father Ghisilieri with so great a degree of
his

his efteem, that he made him a Cardinal foon after his exaltation to the Pontificate.

When Montalto went to take his leave of the two laft mentioned, they defired him, "Not to be uneafy "in his abfence, for they would take care of his inte- "reft." It happened, fortunately for him, that the Pope, being determined to fend a commiffary of the Inquifition to Venice, afked them to recommend a proper perfon; which gave them an opportunity of faying, "They did not know any body fo fit as Montalto."

As his Holinefs already entertained a favourable opinion of his abilities, from fome fermons; which he had heard him preach not long before at the convent of the Holy Apoftles, he approved of their recommendation, and immediately appointed him Iniquifitor General at Venice, to the inconceivable furprize and mortification of his enemies.

End of the First Book.

BOOK THE SECOND.

MONTALTO having now received his patent, with orders to fet out for Venice as foon as poffible, was introduced by Cardinal Carpi to the Pope, who, after he had exhorted him to zeal and firmnefs in the execution of his Office, admitted him to the honour of kiffing his feet, and then difmiffed him with his benediction.

When he went to take leave of the Cardinal, his friend Boffius, by his mafter's order, made him a prefent of 40 crowns, towards the expence of his journey, advifing him, "To exercife his authority with " prudence and moderation, and to be very circum- " fpect in his behaviour; as the Venetians were a " ftiff-necked fort of people, and not fo conformable

F   to

" to the will and pleafure of the Holy See, in all ref-
" pects, as could be wifhed.

Father Ghifilieri likewife, who had been many years
Inquifitor, and was thoroughly acquainted with the
duty and nature of that employment, not only gave
him fome good advice by word of mouth, but inftructions in writing for his conduct, which we fhall fet
down at large hereafter; and as he knew he muft be
at a great expence in his journey, buying books, and
other neceffaries, at his firft coming to Venice, he procured him 2000 crowns from the Congregation [1] of
the Holy Office, with a pretty large fum, befides his
falary, to be paid him immediately upon his arrival at
Venice, by the tribunal of the Inquifition in that city.

It is cuftomary for every Inquifitor to have a Vicar
under him; and as that poft was already filled by one
Piazzi, a Venetian, Montalto was defirous of having.
him removed, and one of his particular friends, whofe
name was Mendoia, appointed in his room : to obtain
which favour, Father Ghifilieri, at his requeft, applied
to the Congregation of the Holy Office, who directed
him to confult Soranzo the Venetian Embaffador, upon it.

The Embaffador advifed him, " Not to attempt it
" by any means, as he was very well convinced, the
" Senate would not fuffer fuch an indignity to be put
" upon a fubject of their's, who had likewife a confi-
" derable place in the Arfenal; and as he had not in
" the leaft mifbehaved himfelf, or been guilty of any
" fault, his friends, who were both numerous and
" powerful, would not fail to refent his difgrace
" in the higheft manner." Thefe objections feemed
fo reafonable, that the Congregation did not think it
prudent to make any alteration at prefent to the great
dif-

[1] A Congregation, is an affembly or committee of feveral Ecclefiafticks united, fo as to conftitute a body. The term is chiefly
ufed for affemblies of Cardinals and prelates appointed by the Pope,
and diftributed into different chambers, for the difcharge of particular
functions and jurifdictions, after the manner of our offices and
courts.

difappointment of Montalto, who was very follicitous for the promotion of his friend, and faid, "He did "not like fuch a fetting out."

When the general, who had taken fo much pleafure in mortifying him, whenever an opportunity offered, faw him fo ftrongly fupported, not only by Cardinal Carpi and Ghifilieri, but the whole Colonna family, advanced to fo honourable a poft, and in a fair way to rife ftill higher, he thought it the beft way, to make him his friend; fo that when he went to take his leave, he received him with great civility and complaifance, giving him a patent for the regency of the Cordeliers convent in Venice, with promifes of doing him all the fervice that lay in his power, if he would apply to him upon any occafion; and to fhew him ftill higher refpect, he invited him twice to dine with him in his own apartment, a favour never fhewn by the generals to any but very great favourites. He further defired him to make Bologna his road, and try if he could, by his prudence and addrefs, compofe fome differences that had lately happened betwixt the Warden and other members of the Francifcan convent; and to give him fufficient authority (in cafe gentle methods fhould not fucceed) he appointed him Commiffary General, ad bene placitum, " during his plealure."

He left Rome towards the end of September, and taking Afcoli, in his way, arrived at Bologna on the eve of St. Francis's day; where he at firft endeavoured by fair means, as the general had advifed him, to put an end to their animofities; but the parties were fo thoroughly embittered againft each other, that they would hear of no accommodation.

When Montalto found there was no other way left, he made ufe of the power given him by his commiffion, and fufpended the warden, fending feveral of the religious to other houfes, and two of them to prifon, till he could have further inftructions from the general. One of them that was imprifoned, wrote to his patron Count Pepoli, a man of great power and intereft in Bo-

logna,

logna, to acquaint him with his misfortune. Upon
which he came immediately to afk the favour of Montalto to releafe him ; but he told him, in a very rough
manner, " That the laity had no bufinefs to concern
" themfelves in affairs of that nature." The Count,
who was naturally of a warm difpofition, and piqued
himfelf upon his family and intereft, was fo enraged
at this rude behaviour, that he threatened " to remem-
" ber him the firft opportunity." But Montalto feemed
to laugh at him, though one might perceive it ftung
him inwardly, and he did not forget it afterwards.

When he had compofed thefe differences in the beft
manner he could at Bologna, and taken proper meafures to eftablifh peace amongft them for the future,
he left that place with the character of a rigid and fevere man, and arrived at Venice in November. They
had already received accounts of him from Rome, Bologna, and La Marca, not much to his advantage. As
the Venetians are remarkably jealous of any attempts
upon their liberty, the whole city was alarmed. Even
the religious, who pretend to freedom there, thought
themfelves in danger, and implored the protection of
the Senate.

The Commonwealth, at this time, watched the
Pope's proceedings very narrowly, apprehending, that
under a pretence of the Inquifition, he was endeavouring to eftablifh a temporal authority over the Italian
Princes. For as they had made fome difcoveries of
this kind in the year 1551, under the Pontificate of
Julius II. they ordered all their Judges to attend at
whatfoever proceffes fhould be fet on foot by the Inquifition againft any of their fubjects. As foon as the
Pope was accquainted with it, he fent Achilles Graffi,
as his Nuncio, to complain of the injuftice of this proceeding to the Senate, but he was forced to give the
point up at laft, and confent that fome of their Judges
fhould always be called in upon fuch occafions.

The Senate was aware, from the very firft year of
this

this Pope's reign, that they had a refolute man to deal with, and were upon that account very cautious of entering into any conteft or difpute with him. They knew he had been all his life a great promoter of the Inquifition, that by his advice, Paul III. firft eftablifh it in Chriftendom, and were apprehenfive, now he was Pope himfelf, that he would take the moft vigorous meafures to extend it's power and influence ; for thefe reafons the arrival of an Inquifitor was very ill relifhed at Venice, efpecially of fuch a temper and character as they had heard of Montalto. By the inftructions which Ghifilieri gave him at his departure, it feems as if that Father expected what afterwards came to pafs ; they were as follow :

" I. Y O U muft in the firft place remember, that
" your office reprefents the tribunal of divine juftice ;
" for which reafon, you are to erect a large Crucifix
" over your gate, with this infcription upon it,
Afpicite in me, fi vultis recte judicare.
" and under it,
Terribilis eft locus hic, fed Domus Dei, et Porta cæli.
" which will be fufficient to let people know, that it is
" the office of the Inquifition.
" II. You muft never forget, that it is the principal
" duty of your office, to defend the caufe and honour
" of God againft the attacks of impious and profane
" men, againft herefy and fchifm, and to be particu-
" larly careful at all times, to maintain and affert the
" privileges of the Church, and the rights of the Holy
" See.
" III. You are to communicate thefe inftructions to
" your Vicar (not to him that you afked for, but him
" that was appointed by the Holy Office at Rome)
" who is to reprefent you in cafe of ficknefs or ab-
" fence, and be careful to live in harmony, and upon
" good terms with him.
" IV. You are to have under you twelve Confultors,
" of whom fix are to be divines of different orders,
" the

" the other fix, doctors of law, a Secretary a Notary,
" two Affeffors, a Jailor, two Beadles, a Marfhal, fix
" Archers, Sergeants, Tipftaves, and Familiars [2],
" and thefe lower officers will be paid out of the trea-
" fury of the Inquifition.

" V. When you have taken poffeffion of your em-
" ployment, you will have feveral candidates for thefe
" offices, into whofe merit and characters you muft
" make a ftrict enquiry, and prefer them accordingly.
" Their names and quality muft be immediately re-
" turned to Rome, for the approbation of the Holy
" Office, and then the Senate and the Apoftolick
" Nuncio muft be informed of it.

" VI. The form of the oath that is to be admini-
" ftered to them, muft be as follows ;

*I A. B. Confultor of the Holy Office, do folemnly promife
and fwear, in the prefence of Almighty God, his Son our
Saviour Jefus Chrift, the bleffed Apoftles St. Peter and St.
Paul, our Holy Father the Pope, and the High Court of
Inqu:fition at Rome, here reprefented by your Reverence,
to be always faithful to the Holy Church, and that facred
tribunal, to be diligent in finding out, difcovering, and
making known, all fuch perfons as are any ways guilty, or
fufpected to be guilty, of Herefy, to defend the privileges
of the Church, and to fupport the interefts of the Inquifition. So help me God.*

" VII. You muft from time to time remind your
" officers of their duty, charging them frequently to
" vifit the Churches, to report any abufes, indecencies,
" or innovations, they fhall obferve in the celebration
" of divine fervice, and to inform you if they hear of
" any mifrule or irregularities in religious houfes.

" VIII. But above all things, It is neceffary to have
" a number of Spies, whofe veracity you can depend
" upon; to inform you if they hear of any enormities
" that are committed in the city, either by the clergy
" or

[2] Familiars are fpies, or inferior imps of juftice.

" or laity, especially of blasphemy, or the profanation
" of holy ordinances.

"IX. Though you do not depend upon the Nuncio,
" but upon the high court of Inquisition at Rome, and,
" in a more particular manner, upon his holiness, you
" must however, out of respect to his dignity, confer
" with him in all cases of importance, especially in any
" affair that may tend to the advantage of the holy
" fee.

" X. You must be very cautious not to be too inti-
" mate or familiar with any person whatsoever, either
" laick or ecclesiastick, as it may tend to make your
" person cheap, and so diminish the respect due to the
" holy fee. Let it be your endeavour to be beloved,
" but with reverence, and to be feared without horror.
" For which purpose, you must maintain a decent re-
" serve both in your words and actions, and set a good
" example in every thing.

" XI. As the Venetians look with an evil eye upon
" the Inquisition, pretending to an authority over the
" persons of ecclesiasticks, which is not consistent with
" the jurisdiction of that tribunal; and, out of the
" excess of liberty, or rather licentiousness, which
" reigns in that city, often treat religion with inde-
" cency and contempt, living as if they were strang-
" ers to christianity, it will require your utmost dex-
" terity and prudence, to apply a remedy to that evil,
" and to behave in such a manner as not to enflame a
" sore, which you are sent to heal.

" XII. Though no body can be so wicked or void
" of sense, as to imagine, the Almighty is not suffici-
" ently able to defend his own cause, yet he is pleased
" in the course of this world, to make use of minis-
" ters to support it against the attemps of profane and
" irreligious men; for which reason, it behoves them
" to shew the greatest zeal, where there is the highest
" degree of corruption, which (God knows) is the case
" at present in Venice.

" XIII. As to the jurisdiction, which the Senate
                                        " claims

" claims over ecclefiafticks, it is prudent, in fome ca-
" fes, to wink at it, till it fhall pleafe God, in his ap-
" pointed feafon, to furnifh the holy fee with power
" to fupprefs and eradicate that evil. However, if it
" is not poffible at prefent, to find an effectual cure,
" every expedient muft be tried to palliate and pre-
" vent it from increafing, and whenever there offers
" any opportunity of breaking through this jurifdicti-
" on, you muft be fure, if you value his holinefs's fa-
" vour, or dread his difpleafure, not to let it flip, but
" labour with all your might to accomplifh it, yet in
" in fuch a manner, as is confiftent with prudence.

" XIV. Many are the abufes which prevail amongft
" the clergy, efpecially the Monks, who take upon
" them to live like Seculars, to the great fcandal and
" difgrace of their profeffion. A ftop muft be put to
" this, by admonifhing the fuperiors, threatning and
" even punifhing fome of the inferiors, for an example
" to others. As for the irregularities of the laity,
" you muft complain of them to the Magiftrates, and
" exhort them, at leaft to attempt a reformation.

" XV. You muft give a diftinct and particular ac-
" count of all your proceedings to the tribunal at
" Rome, and have recourfe to it for advice in any cafe
" of difficulty and importance, acting, in the mean
" time, in fuch a manner as becomes a wife and dif-
" creet man.

" XVI. When it is neceffary to pafs fentence, you
" muft always give notice to the Patriarchal-Vicar, and
" acquaint him with the nature of the procefs, as he
" has a right to be prefent and affift upon fuch occafi-
" ons. Let this fuffice at prefent; when any new mat-
" ter occurs, we fhall fend you frefh inftructions."

The Vicar Piazzi having received advice from Rome,
what pains Montalto had taken to get him removed
from his office, and finding himfelf pretty well fupported by his friends, determined to take his revenge the
following manner. Whilft Montalto was upon the road,
he wrote to defire Piazzi would meet him, with fome

of

of his brethren, half a day's journey from Venice, that they might settle the ceremonial of his entry, but Piazzi, to shew his resentment, would not stir an inch, nor so much as make an excuse of indisposition; so that he was obliged to come almost alone to the convent, and, considering the humiliation he underwent, we may suppose in no very good humour.

The Vicar being informed of his arrival, received him upon the stair-case of the gallery, and conducted him to his apartment, where he was waited upon by the warden and the rest of the society. Though he was ordered in his instructions, to live in harmony and upon good terms with the Vicar, and to consider him as a brother, he could not forbear asking him, in a sharp manner, the very first moment he saw him, " What was the reason he did not come out to him, " as it was a compliment always paid to persons in his " station, upon such occasions:" and the other making some trifling excuse, he rightly judged there was no reason to expect any great degree of civility from him afterwards; for, in the same letters that gave the Vicar an account of Montalto's endeavours to supersede him at Rome, he was represented as a quarrelsome, factious, hot-headed, domineering fellow, which Piazzi took sufficient care to shew, not only to his brethren the ecclesiasticks but all the senators and nobles of his acquaintance. Upon some words that happened betwixt them one day soon after, Piazzi told him, " He should not care a straw for him; though he was " Pope, much less as he was only a little petty inqui- " sitor :" a saying, that sufficiently moved his choler, though he could not tell how to help himself.

He was hardly arrived at Venice, when, by his own authority, he nominated a Doctor of Trevise to be consultor and assistant of the Inquisition. This was the first bone of contention betwixt him and the Senate. For as soon as they were informed of it, they sent to acquaint him, that he must not exercise his function, without their consent, nor till he was acknowledged

knowledged by them in due form, which was not yet done. Montalto at firſt deſigned to acquaint the court of Rome with this impediment, as it ſeemed to be purpoſely thrown in his way. But conſidering what they demanded, was a reſpect due to all ſtates, he went to the ſenate with his credentials, which he thought it was ſufficient barely to exhibit. But being given to underſtand, by one of the ſecretaries, that " he muſt " leave them with him, till the Signiors had time to " examine them ;" he anſwered " That a commiſſion " from the Pope was not ſubject to the examination " of any inferior power." When the ſecretary had reported this anſwer to the ſenate, they ſent word to Montalto, that " as they did not concern themſelves " about the rights and privileges of the Holy See, " they expected to be left free and undiſturbed in the " poſſeſſion of their own." At laſt the Nuncio interfered, and put an end to the diſpute, but Montalto could not get himſelf acknowledged Inquiſitor, by the ſenate, till the beginning of January [1556].

Though theſe were but trifles in the main, the heat and obſtinacy with which he aſſerted his authority, and the intereſt of the Pope, ſerved to confirm the Venetians in the bad opinion they had conceived of him.

The ſenate began to treat him with little reſpect, the religious had an eye upon his conduct in ſpiritual affairs, and the nobles watched him ſo narrowly in his political capacity, that it was impoſſible for him to conceal the minuteſt of his actions. But as he had been uſed to contradiction, he made light of his enemies, and proceeded boldly in the execution of his office, without fear or apprehenſion of any thing they could do to annoy him. They complained in the convent of his harſh and ungentlemanlike behaviour to his pupils ; and the citizens who regard liberty as their deareſt and moſt valuable poſſeſſion, began to look upon him with great jealouſy and diſtruſt, curſing them that had no more ſenſe than to give two employments, of ſo different a nature, to the ſame perſon, one of which

required

required the utmoſt patience and affability, the other a degree of rigour and auſterity.

For how adroit ſoever Montalto might be upon other occaſions, he found it impracticable here to join the ſeverity of an inquiſitor with that douceur and ſoftneſs of temper, which is abſolutely neceſſary in a Tutor to inſpire his pupils with a love of virtue and learning. They forgot he was, their preceptor, regarding him only as inquiſitor, and, as much as they could, avoided his company and converſation, which provoked him again on his ſide. to treat them in a rough and churliſh manner.

This ſort of behaviour drew upon him the odium of all the religious, whom he was continually perſecuting and tormenting by virtue of his office. But he had like to have paid dear for his treatment of father Julio, (an eccleſiaſtick of great reputation, who had done conſiderable ſervices to the ſtate) againſt whom he had begun a proceſs upon ſome trifling accuſation; and Julio, coming to juſtify himſelf before him, had ſo little regard to his quality of inquiſitor, that he treated him with a ſort of contempt, and reproached him with ſome actions of his former life, which he did not much care to hear of at that time. Montalto, who thought himſelf protected, by his authority, from ſuch ſorts of inſults, was ſo provoked at this, that he accuſed him of hereſy, and would have proceeded to examine witneſſes againſt him directly, but could get no body in the convent to make any depoſitions ; upon which he was going to excommunicate the whole ſociety, if the Nuncio had not put a ſtop to ſuch violent proceedings. The ſenate wanted an opportunity of falling upon him, and would have ſhewn him no favour, if he had preſumed to exerciſe ſuch an act of juriſdiction in the city, without the concurrence and aſſiſtance of their judges, as he certainly would have done, but for the timely interpoſition of the Nuncio.

The Plague [3] raged at this time in Venice to ſuch a degree

_____

[3] " Cum ea lues qua Tridentum ad ſolitudinem pene reduc-
" tum

a degree, that it put a ſtop to all manner of commerce, the ſhops were ſhut up, the markets prohibited, and the courts of judicature ſuſpended. Poor Montalto was reduced to ſuch an extremity, that being a ſtranger in the country, and having treated his brethren in ſo imperious a manner, he did not know whom to have recourſe to, though he wanted the common neceſſaries of life. The convents were locked up by an order of the Senate, and none but ſome few religious were ſuffered to go out, who had courage and charity enough to viſit the ſick. Montalto was abandoned by every body, and ready to die with hunger. Some people were fooliſh enough to ſay, this calamity was a judgment upon the city, for their behaviour to him.

In the midſt of theſe misfortunes, [1557] he received an account that father Ghiſilieri was made Cardinal by Paul IV. and had taken the name of Alexandrino, being born near Alexandria. He had great reaſon to rejoice at this promotion, not only on account of favours already received, but the expectation he now had of others ſtill more conſiderable, which was far from being a vain one, as we ſhall ſee hereafter. The news he immediately communicated to the Prior of the Dominicans, who he knew was Ghiſilieri's friend, and would rejoice with him upon it. Not long after, he ſent the new Cardinal a congratulatory letter, and received an anſwer to it written with his own hand, in which after he had thanked him for the pleaſure he expreſſed at his exaltation, and promiſed him his protection upon all occaſions, he concluded with aſſuring him, " That he ſincerely wiſhed for an opportunity of " giving the moſt convincing proof of the general

---

" tum eſt, ſuperiore anno Veronæ in Italia cœpiſſet, et multos mortales abſumpſiſſet, contage etiam per reliquam ditionem Venetam ſerpente, hoc anno cum vis morbi reſediſſe videretur, ſtatim Venetiis recruduit ; ita ut a Decembri proximo, ad Maium uſque, ingraveſcente malo, numerus quotidie morientium, ad 36 excurreret, et menſe ſequenti etiam ad 100 uſque excreverit, totoque illo anno in urbe ad ſeptuaginta millia hominum abſumpta memorant. Thuan. lib. lxii.

eſteem

" esteem he had for him." Montalto kept this obliging letter a great while, and was fond of shewing it. He had so great a dependance upon his word, that he often used to say, " If ever Ghisilieri comes to be Pope, " I shall certainly be a Cardinal." This looked like a rhodomontade at that time, but proved true afterwards.

Seeing himself thus supported by two such patrons as Carpi and Alexandrino, he began to hold his enemies in contempt, and could not forbear saying to some of his brethren, " That he was strong enough now to " cope with an hundred princes." This was immediately spread abroad by some of the company, with a design to have it taken notice of by the Senators, whom, they would have it thought, he pointed at by the hundred princes. In short, he was guilty of many other indiscretions, that were sufficient to have set the Pope and the Republick together by the ears (the consequence of which might have been fatal to both) if the Nuncio had not always found means to close those breaches.

The Emperor Charles V. died this year, [1558] after he had resigned his crown to his brother Ferdinand, and the Pope having made a peace with the King of Spain, set himself in earnest to extend the power of the Inquisition. He designed it should not only take cognisance of heresy, but many other crimes, that more properly came before secular courts, and chose sixteen cardinals to be judges in this tribunal, setting Alexandrino to preside over them, with the title of Inquisitor Major, charging him to write to all the commissaries in christendom, to use more than ordinary diligence in their functions. He wrote to Montalto the first, not only upon account of the friendship that subsisted between them, but to shew the distinction that was due to so celebrated a state as that of Venice, and which, he thought, stood in need of a thorough reformation, from certain heresies that had lately sprung up there. Amongst other things he charged him to prohibit the Bookfellers printing or publishing any book without his licence and approbation, and sent him a
long

long catalogue of thofe that were cenfured by the Inquifition, as tending to promote heretical doctrines,
further enjoining all perfons not to read, or even keep,
them in their poffeffion on pain of excommunication.

Montalto, who was impatient to fhew his authority,
had no fooner received thefe orders, than he began to
put them in execution. He fent for all the Bookfellers,
and examined them feparately, concerning the lift that
was come from Rome, and commanded them, on the
feverest penalties, to bring him a catalogue of the
books they had in their fhops and warehoufes. This
put the whole city in a confternation, which was much
increafed, whan one of the bookfellers, that did not
appear when he was fummoned, but faid, " He knew
" no other fovereign than the figniory," was immediately put under an excommunication, and the fentence fixed to his door.

The fenate looked upon this, as a violent attack upon their liberty, and ordered one of their officers to
pull it down, and tear it to pieces, and to arreft the
perfon that had ftuck it up; but he had withdrawn
himfelf in time to the Nuncio's palace, who was heartily mortified at thefe proceedings, which he forefaw
would bring no credit to the holy fee. As he was a
prelate of wonderful moderation and good fenfe, he
advifed Montalto " to have regard to the publick peace,
" and not to carry things with fo high a hand ;" but
received for anfwer, " That he had the Pope's orders
" for what he did," to which the Nuncio replied,
" That the Pope's authority was one thing at Rome,
" and another at Venice."

This good advice of the Nuncio was fo ill taken by
the Inquifitor, that he wrote to Cardinal Alexandrino,
" That he feemed to have but little zeal for the inte-
" refts of the holy office." The Nuncio was reproached with this in fome private letters from his friends at
Rome ; and though they endeavoured to conceal the
perfon, who had done him this ill office, he eafily
gueffed at him, and refolved for the future to leave

Montalto

Montalto to manage his quarrels with the senate as he thought proper; foreseeing they were not likely to come to a speedy conclusion, as that body grew more and more tenacious of their privileges, and he every day more infolent and incroaching. They were so provoked at laft with his intolerable behaviour, that they once determined to fend him to prifon, if the Nuncio had not thought himself obliged to use his utmost endeavours to prevent the honour of the holy fee from being wounded in so fenfible a manner. ·

The next quarrel he was engaged in, was with the Spanifh ambaffador, Don Francifco de Vargas. This gentleman had refided at Venice fome years as ambaffador from Charles V. by whom he was recalled a few months before he refigned the crown, with a defign to have tricked the French out of their right to precedence. For he thought, if he firft recalled, and then fent him back again, after his refignation, with frefh powers from his fon Philip, he would remain in poffeffion of his precedence, without the French ambaffador's being aware of the fineffe, as he would ftill imagine Vargas was the imperial minifter, which conceffion he might afterwards plead at at a proper opportunity, as a proof of the Spaniard's right to that honour, by fhewing that he was ambaffador from the King of Spain, and not from the Emperor.

When Vargas arrived at Venice the fecond time, King Philip had declared war againft the Pope; and the duke of Alva, who commanded his forces, was making terrible havock in the ecclefiaftical ftate, advancing almoft to the very walls of Rome. The bifhop of Laon was then ambaffador from the crown of France at Venice, and had entered into a ftrict friendfhip with Montalto, of whofe qualifications and abilities he had fo great an opinion, that he chofe him for his confeffor extraordinary, and often honoured him with his vifits. They grew more intimate every day, after the breaking out of this war, efpecially as the King of France had entered into an engagement to fupport and defend his Holinefs. For the fame reafon, Graffi, the

the Nuncio, paid much court to the French ambaffador, and got him to join in a memorial with them, in
which they prayed the Senate not to acknowledge
Vargas as ambaffador, " It being," as they faid, " in-
" confiftent with that zeal for true religion, and the
" honour of the holy fee, which the republick had al-
" ways profeffed, to receive a minifter from a prince,
" who was at open war with the church."

As the Nuncio was confined by the gout, he left
Montalto to concert proper meafures with the bifhop
for that purpofe, who exerted himfelf vigoroufly in
the affair, thinking it a good opportunity of recommending himfelf to the favour of his Holinefs, as a
ftrenuous champion for the caufe of religion and the
holy fee. With this view he drew up a memorial, conceived in very bitter terms, accufing the houfe of Auftria, particularly the King of Spain, of downright herefy, and reprefenting him as unworthy of remaining
in communion with the holy Catholick church.

The French ambaffador was much pleafed with it.
But when it was fhewn to the Nuncio, who was a cool,
difpaffionate man, he would have had it new modelled, the afperity of the ftile mitigated, and the charge
of herefy entirely left out, as there were topicks fufficient of another nature, to found their memorial upon.

Montalto however, with his ufual vehemence, infifted, " That the behaviour of the Spaniards, had
" been to the laft degree, wicked, audacious, and fa-
" crilegious, in prefuming to take up arms againft the
" holy church and the vicar of Chrift, that they
" ought to be excommunicated without further cere-
" mony, as guilty of the moft flagrant herefy, and
" wondered how the Nuncio could offer to fay any
" thing in extenuation of their crimes."

As the French ambaffador declared himfelf of the
fame opinion, it was at laft refolved, that Montalto,
who feemed to defire it, fhould deliver the memorial,
without any alteration, fubfcribed by himfelf as Inquifitor,

fitor, which he accordingly did into the fecretary's own hand.

When the Senate had deliberated upon it, they fent him word by the fame fecretary. " They could not " fufficiently exprefs their furprize, that a perfon, who " pretended to no higher character than that of Inqui- " fitor, fhould dare to ftigmatize fo auguft a houfe as " that of Auftria, with the odious appellation of He- " retick ; that they did not apprehend either the " caufe of religion, or the honour of the holy fee, " were any way concerned in their receiving, or not " receiving the Spanifh ambaffador, which was entire- " ly left to their option by the law of nations.   That " his holinefs was miftaken, if they imagined they " were to be tutored or directed in their proceedings " by an Inquifitor, and that they could not help think- " ing him very impertinent to thruft himfelf into af- " fairs, that he had no manner of concern with, " which was all they had to fay to him at prefent."

There is no ftate that weighs things more maturely, or executes their refolutions with greater fecrecy and refolution, that the republick of Venice,   At the time when thefe difputes happened, they behaved with more refpect to the holy fee, than they do now, for after the miferies they were fo long expofed to, by the excommunication which Julius II. put them under, till the pontificate of Paul V. they were very cautious of doing any thing that might give offence to the Pope ; and though they would not even then fuffer any attack upon, or infringment of their liberty in material points, yet they thought it prudent to wink at fuch things, as were not likely to be attended with any dangerous confequence.   But after their conteft with Paul V. in which they came of with fo much ho- nour, they proceeded in a very different manner, and would not brook the leaft attempt of any kind upon their privileges.   So that it is not improbable, that if any one had been fent thither in the character of In- quifitor, after his pontificate, and behaved as Mon-

G   talto

talto did, they would have tied him up in a fack, and thrown him into the fea.

The Senate fhewed fo little regard to the memorial, that they fent for the Spanifh ambaffador, and gave him a copy of it. When he was informed that Montalto was the author, at leaft had the principal hand in drawing it up, he ordered his fecretary to write a letter to him, in which he gave the lie to every thing he had advanced concerning the houfe of Auftria, and told him, " The name of heretick more properly be-" longed to himfelf, who daily converfed with peo-" ple fufpected of herefy, as he was ready to prove."

Montalto was highly enraged at this, and fhewed the letter to the French ambaffador, who ftill blew up the flame, by telling him his perfon was pointed at, by the expreffions in the latter part of it ; upon which he threatened to excommunicate Vargas, or at leaft his fecretary, if he did not prove what he had afferted. But in a ftep of fo much importance, he thought it proper to confult the Nuncio, who told him, " It was " ridiculous to be in fuch a fury, at an affront which he had drawn upon himfelf, and might have eafily forefeen, that for his own part, confidering the nature of the memorial, he expected both the Senate and the Spanifh ambaffador would behave to him as they have done, and advifed him to take up with the treatment he had met with for fear of worfe."

Montalto faid, " That fuppofing he had been " guilty of an error, the ambaffador ought not, how-" ever, to have accufed him of herefy ;" the Nuncio anfwered, " That fince he had treated the houfe of " Auftria as hereticks, out of a tranfport of zeal, as " he fuppofed, for the holy fee ; the ambaffador had " a right to ufe him in the fame manner, as it might " be reafonably fuppofed, one was as zealous for the " honour of his mafter as the other ; and faid, he " thought it would be the beft way to tear the letter " and behave as if he had not received it." Montalto replied, " That if he fuffered himfelf to be accufed of " herefy, and converfing with hereticks, without
— " taking

" taking any notice of it, it would not only be an ac-
" knowledgment of his guilt, but putting up an in-
" dignity offered to his holiness, which it was his duty
" to resent, no less than himself."

When the Senate was informed of the clamour that
Montalto raised about it, and that the ambassador
threatened to take a further revenge, they sent to the
latter desiring him, " To keep within the bounds of
" decency and moderation, and not to disturb the
" peace, which the Republick was ever desirous of
" maintaining, or to engage them in any quarrel ;"
letting Montalto know at the same time, " That it
" would be good for him, not to exceed the limits of
" his office ; that as his authority did not extend to
" the persons of ambassadors, who depended upon no
" body but their masters, and were under the protec-
" tion of the Senate (whilst they resided at Venice)
" which alone had a right to call them to an account,
" for any error or misbehaviour, they were highly of-
" fended, that a monk, under the pretence of execut-
" ing the office of Inquisitor (which was a very ques-
" tionable authority with them) should have the inso-
" lence to enter into disputes concerning matters of
" government, with the ambassador of so great a
" prince; and that if he did not think proper, of him-
" self, to behave with more modesty for the future,
" they would make use of such means, as the nature
" of their government furnished them with, to com-
" pel him to it."

This did but irritate Montalto still more, and it is
likely he would have obliged the Senate to proceed to
extremities, if the general rejoicings, which were celebrated soon after, upon the conclusion of a peace betwixt the Pope and King Philip, had not put an end to
this dispute, though he could not forget it.

These differences were hardly composed, when there
happened another betwix Vargas and the French Mi-
nister, the former still pretending to the precedence
he enjoyed, when he was the imperial ambassador,
which the latter would by no means admit of, as his

master

Mafter had a right to take place of all the Kings in
Europe. Montalto, who loved the French ambaffador, and hated Vargas from the bottom of his heart,
took part in this quarrel likewife, without being defired, though he had no manner of concern in it, any
further than as he thought it a proper opportunity of
revenging himfelf upon the one, and fhewing his regard to the other. Inftead of attending to the duties
of his own employment, he was conftantly at the
French ambaffador's houfe, drawing up memorials,
publifhing precedents, and doing every thing in his
power, that he thought could any way contribute (as
he faid) to humble the pride of Spain, to the great mortification of Vargas; efpecially as the Senate decided
the matter in favour of the French, and for this time
feemed to countenance Montalto's proceedings.

Henry II. finding himfelf diftreffed by the arms of
Spain, folicited the affiftance of the Venetians by his
ambaffador, who was joined in his inftances by Montalto, and fecretly by the Nuncio. For as the court of
Rome was not at all fatisfied with the peace which they
had been obliged to make with the Spaniards, they
would have been glad to fet any other more powerful
enemy upon their back. But the Senate would not by
any means liften to their propofals, and wifely preferred the friendfhip of King Philip, to a hazardous and
expenfive war. So that the King of France being without allies, and not able to ftand alone againft Spain,
now grown fo formidable by the acceffion of England,
joined himfelf with the Turk, who, at his requeft, made
a defcent in the kingdom of Naples, with a confiderable force, where he took Reggio, Maffa, and Surento.

Though this ftep of calling in the Turk was the effect of mere neceffity, it was loudly exclaimed againft
every where, efpecially at the court of Rome, as they
were in terrible apprehenfion of the Turkifh general's
penetrating into the ecclefiaftical ftate, which occafioned fuch a panick amongft the inhabitants, who expected the Janizaries at their heels every moment,
that

that they fled to Rome. which the Pope immediately ordered to be put in a posture of defence.

No body was more affected with this invasion, than Cardinal Alexandrino, who, being a subject of Spain, i. e. a Neapolitan, and having had the chief hand in making the peace betwixt the Pope and his master, inveighed most bitterly against the French: of which Montalto being informed, and fearing he would disoblige him by acting so furiously against the Spaniards, in favour of France, he began to alter his conduct, and detaching himself, upon some trifling excuse, from the acquaintance of the French ambassador, insinuated himself by degrees into the favour of Don Vargas.

Father Narpeo, his intimate friend. who was uncle to the ambassador's chaplain, undertook to bring about a reconciliation betwixt them, for this purpose it was thought necessary for Montalto to write a submissive letter to his excellency, which his pride would not suffer him to do, though he offered to make a verbal acknowledgment of his fault; but the ambassador said, " as he had reflected so severely upon the whole house " of Austria, and more particularly his master, the " King of Spain, in a publick writing, it was not con- " sistent with his character, to accept of a private ac- " knowledgment, which he could not think by any " means a proper satisfaction."

This terribly embarrassed Montalto, as he was very loath to make any condescension, that might give people occasion to reproach him with meanness of spirit; and on the other hand, if he did not, he was afraid of losing the favour of Alexandrino, from whom he had great expectations, which Narpeo represented to him, as the inevitable consequence of the ambassador's writing to that Cardinal, as he certainly would, when he came to know, what dependence Montalto had upon him, and advised him by all means to comply with so reasonable a demand. After a long struggle, interest got the better of his pride,, and he wrote a very humble letter to Vargas, in which, " He expressed his con- " cern for his late imprudent behaviour, and hoped he " would

" would impute it only to his zeal for the honour of
" the holy fee, and not to any ill will or difaffection
" to the houfe of Auftria, in general, much lefs his
" mafter, whom he loved and revered, and defired his
" excellency to do him the juftice to believe, there was
" not a perfon in the Pope's dominions, better difpof-
" ed, or more inclinable, to ferve him, if it lay is his
" power.. Don Vargas was fatisfied with this, and
" they were afterwards good friends.

Towards the end of this year, the Pope publifhed a
very fevere edict, commanding all the monks that had
left their convents, let their excufe be what it would,
to return immediately to them. Many chofe rather to
go ever the mountains to Geneva and other proteftant
ftates, than obey it, as the fuperiors of their refpective houfes, had orders to punifh them, when they returned, for their defertion. About 200 of thefe poor
creatures, terrified with the thoughts of a prifon, and
the aufterities of a cloifter, with which they were fo
well acquainted, entirely abandoned the church of
Rome ; others, that returned to juftify their proceedings, were treated with the utmoft rigour, many
being condemned to perpetual imprifonment, and fome
to the galleys.

The Pope was not fatisfied with publifhing this
edict in the ecclefiaftical ftate ; it was difperfed throughout all Italy, with orders to the Inquifitors to profecute
every one, without refpect of perfons, that did not
conform to it, as if they had incurred the greater excommunication.

Montalto was particularly enjoined to exert himfelf
ftrenuoufly in the execution of this order, and no fooner received it, than he applied to the Senate to have it
regiftered. But they took fome time to examine it,
and at laft told him, " It was not confiftent with the
" lenity of their government, which, in the punifh-
" ment of criminals, always more willingly inclined
" to the fide of mercy, than ftrict juftice, that he
" ought to be content with the publication of the
" edict, and muft take care (at his peril) how he pre-
" fumed

" fumed to inflict punishments upon any subject of
" the commonwealth, without calling in their judges
" to act in concert with him."

There was, at this time, a great number of these va-
grant Monks (some of whom were Francifcans) strol-
ling about Venice; many of them, abusing the protection that was given them by the senators, led very
diforderly and irregular lives, and despised both the
Inquisitor and Pope; Montalto took all the methods
he could think of to lay hold of them, excommunicating several, and causing their sentences to be stuck up
in the most publick places of the city, which were
constantly pulled down again by order of the Senate.
But these violent proceedings served rather to exafperate his brethren, than to reduce them to obedience,
and he had the mortification to see them laugh at his
impotent menaces, and ridicule an authority, which
he had not power to execute.

The General, either to do him an honour, or to
embroil him still more with the ecclefiafticks, sent him
a commission to preside at the chapter that was to be
held the next June [1559], at Venice, and desired him
to use his utmost endeavours to get father Anthony di
Trevife chofen provincial, who had a pretty strong
party in the chapter, besides the General's letter, and
very pressing recommendations from cardinal Carpi
and Alexandrino to Montalto. There were many warm
debates at the opening of the chapter, upon some regulations that Montalto had a mind to establish by virtue of his office; most of the religious opposed them,
as derogatory to the privileges they enjoyed under the
fanction and protection of the Senate. The conteft
was carried on with so much heat, that it had like to
have broke up the assembly; but Montalto seeing it
impossible to carry his point, fairly gave it up. This
defeat put it out of his power to gain a majority for
Trevife, and ruined his interest amongst his brethren,
who chofe father Cornelius Divo, a Venetian, notwithstanding all his efforts to the contrary.

Divo was a man of merit, in much esteem with the
chapter,

chapter, and the more fo, for being no friend to Montalto. Indeed, as the Senate had folicited the chapter
in his favour, it was almoft in vain to oppofe him, the
religious of Venice fhewing more regard to the recommendations of the loweft fenator, than that of a dozen
cardinals.

When the chapter was over, Montalto began to renew his perfecutions againft the monks that had not
returned to their convents. But they ftood up ftoutly
in defence of the liberty which God had bleffed them
with, and took fhelter again under the wing of the Senate. The Doge was fo out of patience with his proceedings at laft, that he ordered a fecretary to tell him,
in his name, " That he gave both them and himfelf a
" great deal of trouble :" to which he anfwered, that
" if the court of Rome would be fo good to excufe
" him, he would not trouble any body."

The death of the Pope [4] happened this year, foon
after that of Henry II. King of France [5], who was
unfortunately killed at a tournament, during the rejoicings that were made upon the conclufion of a peace
with Spain.

It was faid his Holinefs died with grief, occafioned by
the untimely end of his brother, who was ftrangled,

---

[4] See an account of his death Thaun. lib. xxlii.

[5] " The King runing againft Gabriel earl of Montgomery,
captain of the Scotch guards, was wounded in his eye with a fplin-
ter of the lance, of which he died, after having languifhed eleven
days in the greateft agonies. Collier.

The earl fuffered death for this, fifteen years after; the reafon
affigned for it is whimfical enough. " Hic exitus fuit Gabrielis Co-
" mitis Montgomerii, multis expeditionibus, fumma, celeritate con-
" fectis, clari, qui, ante xv annos, Henricum fecundum in Ludicro
" certamine imprudens lethali vulnere læferat; ob id calamitatis
" puplicæ invidia, potius quam proprio crimine, onerati. Nam
" quod illi perduellionis affictum eft, aut fuperioribus edictis, aut
" data nuper fide, remiffum fuerat : fed hoc impotenti Regentis
" defiderio condonatum, quæ hominem regia morte piacularem
" qua yis ratione, pœnæ dedi poftulabat, ut hoc infigni exemplo om-
" nes difcant, folo cafu, non tantum confilio, nocentes effici, qui-
" cunque vel imprudentes perniciem principibus attuliffent."
Thuan. lib. lviii.

or,

or, as some say, slain in an adulterous amour, the August before. He was not much lamented either at
Rome or Venice, for having been so active in establishing the Inquisition, and was rather feared than beloved
whilst he was alive. The Venetians always looked
upon his endeavours to erect a tribunal in their city,
as a snare laid for their liberty, and were fully convinced that his design in it, was to cramp their power
and authority.

But Montalto was very much alarmed at the news
of his death, and afraid of the Venetians resentment,
as they were now no longer held in awe by a Pope so
resolute and determin'd as Paul IV, who they knew
would have protected him whilst he lived. As he saw
he should be exposed to their Resentment, he thought
it would be the best way to retire as soon as he could,
since it was not possible for him alone to stem the
rage of the Venetians, during the vacancy of the see,
which interval the Italian States and Princes generally
lay hold on to revenge the the affronts they have received from the Court of Rome. He communicated
his design to the Nuncio, who approved of it, especially as he had just entered into a fresh quarrel with
the Senate, which must have proved fatal to him in
the consequences.

For these reasons he left Venice with a firm resolution never to return to a place, where the officers of the
court of Rome must either live in a continual subjecti-
on to the privileges of the state, or the fear of a prison.

All the officers of the Inquisition, especially Carpi
and Alexandrino, were much displeased at his return,
as they thought it would be not only prejudicial to his
own interest and reputation, but that of the Holy
Office. It was reported he was driven out of Venice,
by the contempt which they had there for his function,
and that he had behaved himself so ill to his ecclesiastical superiors, that they would not be at any pains to
countenance or assist him in the execution of it. This
seemed to be confirmed by the shuffling excuses, which
he made, when he was called upon to give an account

of

of his conduct, sometimes laying the blame on the re-
fractory disposition of the Senate, at others, upon the
ungovernable temper of his brethren, and the confusion which was occasioned in affairs, by the vacancy of
the fee. As these reasons did not appear satisfactory
to the Holy Office, they upbraided him with cowardice,
and having deserted his post, at a time when his Prefence was most necessary to support the Inquisition at
Venice, which could not be fo well expected from a
Vicar.

But the very arguments they made ufe of against
him, ferved for his justification; for the populace of
Rome having born the yoke of this tribunal a long
time with much impatience, grew fo outrageous at last,
that they fired their palace, and carried their refentment fo high, as to cut off the head and right-hand of
a marble statue of the deceafed Pope, which had been
erected in his life-time, and was reckoned a most curious piece of art, being the work of the best statuary
of that age. Not content with this, they dragged it
three days together through all the streets of Rome,
with every mark of contempt and indignation [6].

Montalto, upon the news of this fedition, faid to
one of his acquaintance, " I find it is better to be a
" fimple monk at Rome, than commissary of the In-
" quifition at Venice. If I was there now, I fhould be
" treated in the fame manner as the Pope's Statue is
" here." And talking one day with Cardinal Carpi
upon the fame fubject; he faid, " How could I have
" defended myfelf against the rage of the Venetians
" who are fovereign Princes, when the whole Col-
" lege of Cardinals together, could not fave the
                                                    Pope's

[6] " A furente populo, qui per urbem, quasi lymphata mente,
" difcurfabat, incenfus eft carcer novus inquifitionis, iis qui eo at-
" tinebantur emiffis; vixque cohiberi plebs potuit, quin incendi-
" um in Dominicanorum ædem, ad Minervam, intentaret, odio In-
" quifitionis, cui exercendæ illi a Pontifice præpofiti fuerant. Nec
" fatiatum ea re odium; nam ftatim, a quorundam impulfu, in Ca-
" pitolium impetu facto caput cum dextra manu ejus ftatuæ, quæ
" in palatio, e marmore Pario, nobilis artificis manu, S. P. Q. R.
" magno fumptu, pofita ei fuerat, præcifum, ac toto triduo per ur-
" bis vias fummo ludibrio provolutum eft." Thuan. lix. xxiii.

" Pope's ſtatue from the fury of people, that are their
" ſlaves and vaſſals ?"

He had ſome expectation of being choſen provincial
by the chapter of La Marca, which was to meet ſoon,
and thought the influence of his friends, and the conſideration that was due to the employments he had
held, would inſure him better ſucceſs than he had met
with there before, as they could now no longer object
to him his want of years and experience. Alexandrino (though he would gladly have ſent him back to Venice) did all he could to ſerve him in the affair ; but
aſked him at the ſame time, " Whether he had not
rather be Inquiſitor at Venice for life, than Provincial
of La Marca for three years ; at which Montalto
ſhrugged up his ſhoulders, and gave no other anſwer,
than Dulcis amor patriæ, " Dear is our native ſoil.

Cardinal Carpi likewiſe, as protector of the order,
wrote to the general and other principal members of
the chapter, recommending Montalto in the ſtrongeſt
terms, telling them, " He thought they ought in juſtice
" to chuſe him this time, to make him ſome amends
" for his former excluſion." They all engaged to
ſerve him to the utmoſt of their power. But the
monks are like courtiers, who generally promiſe every
thing, and perform nothing ; for when the election
came on, they gave their votes for another perſon ; upon which Montalto, who came to the chapter in full
expectation of being choſe, immediately left them, and
returned to Rome, without ſtaying to ſee the event of
the ſcrutiny.

The only perſon that exerted himſelf in Montalto's
intereſt, was father Conſtantius Saliga. This eccleſiaſtick was born of very mean parents at the caſtle of
Sarnano, and from thence commonly called Father
Sarnano, which name he retained when he was afterwards made Cardinal by Sixtus V. He had always
been one of his faſt friends and followers, and came to
the chapter on purpoſe to aſſiſt him with his vote and
intereſt. As he perceived the election was likely to go
againſt him, he drew up a writing and preſented it to
the

the General, in which he gave many ſtrong reaſons, why they ought to chuſe Montalto, but it had no effect, nor was ever anſwered by any body, the cabal being already determined in their choice. When he was convinced of that, he did not think it prudent to ſtay there any longer, but went way with Montalto, without ſaying any thing to the General, who was ſo provoked at his behaviour, that he intended to have puniſhed him ſeverely for it. Montalto, however found means, not only to prevent that, by his intereſt with Alexandrino, but to obtain a regency for him in another province, not thinking it ſafe to leave him at the mercy of a provincial, whom he had endeavoured to exclude from that office by voting againſt him.

Theſe things happened during the vacancy of the ſee, which laſted four months ; at laſt, ſome days after the return of Montalto, Cardinal John Angelo di Medicis, a Milaneſe, of a different family from the Medici's of Florence, was choſen Pope the 26th of December, and took the name of Pius IV.

He was at firſt determined to carry on the affairs of the Inquiſition in a gentler manner than his predeceſſor had done ; but Alexandrino and the other officers perſuaded him to ſend Montalto back to Venice, contrary to the opinion of ſome, who would have that power lodged in milder hands. The Cardinal however, who knew the man, and had a mind he ſhould return in triumph to a place, from which his brethren had given out that he was driven away in a diſgraceful manner, was very preſſing with the Pope, and at laſt prevailed.

This year was ſo remarkable for the deaths of ſo many illuſtrious perſons, that it could not be paralleled in any man's memory. There died in the ſpace of fifteen months, a Pope, an Emperor, two Kings of France, a King of England, a King of Portugal, a King of Denmark, a Queen dowager of Poland, a Queen of England, Queen Mary of Hungary, Queen Eleanor, the Doge and Patriarch of Venice, the duke of Ferrara, thirteen Cardinals, and ſeveral other perſons of great diſtinction.

Montalto

Montalto having received his difpatches, left Rome the beginning of January [1560] with a promife from Cardinal Alexandrino, when he took leave of him, " That he fhould foon have a more confiderable em= " ployment if he behaved himfelf well." A Modenefe doctor, who was going to Venice, defiring to accompany him, Montalto thought it a piece of good fortune to meet with fo worthy a companion; but after all, they could not agree to go the fame road. The doctor had a mind to pafs by Loretto, which Montalto would not confent to, " It going againft the grain," as he faid, " to travel through a province in a private " character, that had twice refufed him for their pro= " vincial." The Modenefe happening to mention this in fome of the religious houfes, where he called in his journey, it raifed fuch a fpirit of refentment amongft the ecclefiafticks that he was almoft afhamed of his acquaintance, when he heard them in every place thanking God that he was not fet over them.

Montalto took a different rout and paffing thro' Florence and Bologna, arrived at Venice, after a journey of three weeks, where he was received very coldly; and finding the affairs of the Inquifition in a much worfe condition than he left them, he immediately applied himfelf with all his power to put them in better order : by which he drew upon himfelf a frefh perfecution. The whole body of the religious, not only made complaints againft him to the Senate, but joined in a petition to the Cardinal Protector, and the fovereign tribunal of the Inquifition, intreating them to recal him, in order to prevent the fcandal he would infallibly bring upon the holy office. Some of the Senators wrote at the fame time, by the direction of the Magiftrates, to their ambaffador at Rome, defiring, " He would ufe his utmoft intereft to have him re= " moved, for that, if he ftayed there, his violent pro= " ceedings would certainly in a fhort time not only " create great animofities and heart-burnings among " the religious, but likewife in the Senate, and per=
" haps

" haps might at laft occafion a rupture betwixt his
" Holinefs and the Republick."

Montalto was acquainted with the contents of thefe
petitions, and for fome time feemed to make light of
them; but confidering, they might hurt him in the
end, and that the leaft he could expect upon any new
difturbance, was to be driven fhamefully out of the
city, he feconded his enemies letters to Alexandrino,
and defired, " If he had any regard for his welfare and
" peace of mind, that he would give him leave to re-
" turn to Rome, where he would acquaint him, by
" word of mouth, with the reafon that induced him to
" afk that favour." The Cardinal, feeing how things
were circumftanced, gave his confent.

Before he left the Venetians, he took all opportunities of fhewing the extreme contempt he held them in,
continually carrying on vexatious profecutions againft
both laicks and ecclefiafticks, and facrificing his own
repofe, to trouble and difturb that of others. As he
faw the term of his authority near at at end, a time
which both he and his enemies wifhed for, he made ufe
of what was left, in proceffes and excommunications,
and went on in fo furious a manner, that the Senate
again interpofed their authority, and forbade him to
take cognizance of affairs, that did not fall under his
jurifdiction, declaring, that, " if he prefumed to make
" any further incroachments upon their jurifdiction,
" they would make him dearly repent it."

Montalto, nettled at this, caufed a monitory to be
hung up on the door of St. Mark's church, in which he
cited fome of the Senate's officers to appear before him,
and anfwer to fuch things as fhould be alledged againft
them. As foon as it was hung up, which was in the
middle of the night, Montalto, who had a [6] Gondola
in readinefs, immediately left the city. This was a very wife ftep, for it is certain he had never been Pope,
if he had fallen into the hands of the Senate, who, when
they heard of it, and that he had left the city, immediately fent a party in purfuit of him, but he had taken pretty good care to get out of their reach.

From

[6] A paffage-boat ufed at Venice.

From Venice he came directly to Rome, to the great joy of his friends, who had waited for him with much impatience and anxiety, and were doubtful of his safety till his arrival, upon which they congratulated him as one that had made his escape from the Corsairs.

An intimate acquaintance, that had been his fellow-student, said to him one day, " My Friend, if you had " not shewn them a light pair of heels, the Pantaloons " [7] would certainly have tucked you up ;" to which Montalto answered, " That as he had some design of " being Pope, he thought it would utterly spoil his " scheme, if he staid to be hanged at Venice."

Five days after his return to Rome, when he had given an account of his conduct, he was made one of the Consultors of the Inquisition, by the interest of the two Cardinals his patrons, and ordered to reside in the convent of the holy Apostles. As he was not much beloved there, they declared, " They were not able to " maintain him," and refused to give him a supper the first night he came thither ; which the officers of the Inquisition hearing of, they allowed him a pension to defray his expences. This first difficulty being got over, another was started about lodging. The general ordered him to provide himself with one in the town in three days time ; but Carpi and Alexandrino having a mind he should lodge in the convent, obtained an order from the Pope himself for that purpose.

There happened some events about this time at Rome, that had a very tragical conclusion, and such as may serve for a warning to people in the most exalted stations to behave themselves with decency and moderation. As Montalto was consulted about the punishment of the criminals, it will be in some measure necessary to give an account of them.

Upon the exaltation of Pius IV. to the pontifical
throne,

[7] Pantaloon is a Merry Andrew, Harlequin, Scaramouch, or Morris Dancer, from the French word Pantalon, a sort of a Garment, or Breeches and Stockings of the same stuff (generally particoloured fastened together, and worn by such people.

throne, he was determined to put a ftop to the feveral
irregularities and debaucheries, that had been introduced by the nephews of his predeceffor, who was not
able to do it himfelf whilft he lived.   For this purpofe
he ordered the Cardinals, Charles, who was nephew,
and Alfonfo Caraffa, grand-nephew to the late Pope,
to be arrefted, one morning as they came out of the
confiftory.

John, brother of Charles Count di Montorio, who
had arrived but a few days before, was likewife fecured.   He then bore the title of Duke di Palliano, his
uncle having given him the inveftiture of that duchy,
which he had unjuftly taken from the Colonne, notwithftanding the many great and important fervices
they had done to the Holy See.   He alfo imprifoned
the Count di' Alis, his brother-in-law, and Leonard dî
Cardini, their near relation.

As they had not the leaft fufpicion of any fuch defign, they were extremely furprized, when they faw
themfeles arrefted and carried to Prifon, with a great
number of domefticks and creatures of the Caraffa
family.   Thefe orders were fo carefully executed, that
the provoft-marfhal [8], who had them in charge,
did not let one efcape that was upon his lift; and the
Pope was fo well fatisfied with his diligence and fidelity, that he gave him 100 Piftoles.

As his holinefs had a mind to fhew the publick, that
he defigned to act in a cool and difpaffionate manner,
he ordered their procefs to be carried on by other Cardinals, the chief of whom was Carpi, and referred the
cognifance of the whole affair to Fredrick Jerome, Bifhop of Sagona, and governor of Rome, in commiffion with Alexander Palentero, Advocate of the exchequer.   Montalto arrived at Rome whilft this profecution was carrying on, and was chofen one of the fix fecret Confultors, by whom the Cardinals were to be directed in conducting the procefs.   Carpi having a great
opinion of him, not only as a perfon very well verfed in affairs of that nature, but an able divine, and
                                        throroughly

[8] Bargelli, or Barigelli, is a Provoft-Marfhal or Captain of the
Archers.

thoroughly qualified to folve any doubts or fcruples that might arife in the courfe of the trial, had feveral private conferences with him upon that fubject. Frederick, who was of a fevere difpofition, likewife chofe him for his fecret confultor, which, being known amongft the monks, they could not forbear faying, " Lord have mercy upon the poor prifoners, they are " fure to fuffer now Montalto is concerned."

After the procefs had lafted nine months, it was laid before a full confiftory, and Cardinal Caraffa was convicted of felony ; the counts Montorio, D' Alis, and Leonard di Cardini of murder, and many other crimes. They were all four condemned to die, and orders given to the judge-criminal, to fee the execution performed according to the cuftom and laws of the country. The Cardinal was ftrangled in prifon, and the other three publickly beheaded upon a fcaffold at the common place of execution. Montalto being called in to affift one of them at the hour of death, was afked, after the execution, " Whether he had treated him, " in the affair of his Salvation, with the fame rigour " with which he advifed the Cardinals to proceed in " his trial ;" to which he anfwered, " That the only " rigour that had been fhewn them, was the keeping " them in prifon nine months, whereas, if he had been " Pope, he would have releafed them in nine days."

The council of Trent was at this time affembled, where his Holinefs kept feveral prelates and other ecclefiafticks of diftinguifhed learning and piety at his own expence. As the convent of the holy Apoftles did not like, or were afraid, of Montalto, they ufed their utmoft efforts with the Cardinal-protector to have him fent thither ; but he thought it an employment neither proper for, nor agreeable to him, and, for that reafon, abfolutely refufed to comply with their requeft. Befides, Montalto was not willing to be out of the way, when they were going to chufe a new Procurator of the order, as he had fome thoughts of being candidate for that office.

This confideration made his enemies, who dreaded

H   feeing

seeing him procurator, redouble their endeavours to get him out of Rome; but he was chosen about Whitsuntide [1561], in the room of father Gaspard of Naples, by Cardinal Carpi's recommendation, much against the inclination of many that had votes in the chapter.

Soon after his election, the General died at Rome, and was succeeded in that office by father Avosto, the vicar-general, a haughty, supercilious man, and one that had, upon all occasions constantly thwarted and opposed Montalto, especially in the election to his last dignity, which provoked him so much, that he wished for an opportunity of revenge. It was not long before one happened. The late General, who was an avaricious man, had heaped up a great sum of money, contrary to his vow of poverty; and as there was a constitution, ordaining that the goods and effects, which a general dies possessed of, should devolve to his successor, Avosto laid claim to it. But Montalto said it belonged to the church, and represented the matter in such a light to Cardinal Borromeo, the Pope's nephew, who then had the management of all affairs belonging to the church, that he obtained a brief, directing that whatsoever belonged to the late General, should be laid out in building a handsome apartment for the Generals [1562], repairing the vestry, erecting an organ in the church of the Holy Apostles, and other pius uses.

Soon after this, Cardinal Carpi died, extremely lamented by his Holiness and the whole college. He was a person of rare virtue and merit, and had done many important services to the church.

It is not possible to describe the affliction of Montalto at this event, as he lost in him a very powerful friend and protector, from whose patronage he had reason to hope for still greater favours.

He never left him during his illness; and when he saw him expire, said, with much vehemence, " I wish " to God I could die with him." The concern he expressed upon this occasion, was not displeasing to
　　　　　　　　　　　　　　　　　Alexandrino,

Alexandrino, who faid to him, " Without doubt,
" Montalto, you have loft a very good friend, and one
" who loved you dearly, but you have another left
" that loves you as well ;" to which he anfwered, " My
" Lord Cardinal, I fhall never ceafe to pray that the
" Almighty will blefs your eminence with profperity
" and length of days, as nothing elfe can repair this
" lofs." He was interred with great funeral pomp in
the church of the Holy Apoftles. But the General,
who had the direction of the ceremony, would not fuffer
Montalto to be invited, though he had a right to be
there by virtue of his office. He complained of this
affront to the Pope, and demanded fatisfaction ; but
as it appeared a thing of trifling confequence to his Holinefs, he gave himfelf no trouble about it. However,
it was the occafion of another wrangle betwixt them :
Montalto, as Procurator of the order, notified the
Cardinal's death to the feveral Provincial's, enjoining
them to order a mafs in every convent, for the repofe
of his foul. The General, pretending this was his
right, and that Montalto had broke in upon his privileges, ordered one of the monks to tell him, " That
" he defired he would be pleafed to mind his own bufi-
" nefs for the future, and not trouble himfelf with
" that of other people ;" which provoked Montalto
to fend him word back by the fame perfon, " That he
" knew his own bufinefs fo well, that he did not want
" to be inftructed in it by him."

Cardinal Borromeo at laft interfered, and endeavoured to put an end to their differences.

About this time, providence raifed Montalto another very great friend, in the perfon of Mark Anthony
Colonna, who was made Archbifhop of Tarentum,
and fent to the council of Trent, where he fo well anfwered the expectations that had been entertained of
him (not to mention the nobility of his extraction, and
the great fervices he had already done to the holy fee)
that the Pope thought proper to exalt him to the purple, with the title of Cardinal of the Holy Apoftles.
This promotion was agreeable to the whole city, and

Montalto

Montalto was overjoyed at it. As he had been his pupil, he had fome reafon to expect his favour and patronage ; when he went to congratulate him upon his
new dignity, the Cardinal received him very affectionately, and remembering he had ftudied under him,
faid, " Father Montalto I have not forgot that I was
" once your fcholar, and I hope you will always make
" ufe of my endeavours to ferve you, with the fame
" freedom, as if you, were ftill my mafter ;" to which
Montalto anfwered very refpectfully, " That perfons
" of his high quality were always to be regarded as
" mafters, that he looked upon it as a very great ho-
" nour to have been in his fervice."   The Cardinal,
who inherited the generofity and other princely virtues
that feem entailed upon that noble family, was not a
little inftrumental afterwards in his exaltation.

A general chapter was to be held foon, at Florence,
by the Pope's order, though many laboured to have it
at Rome, efpecially Montalto. who knew it would not
be at all for his intereft to have it meet there. Not that
he entertained any hope of being made prefident, from
from which he knew he fhould be excluded by Avofto,
who had already fecured a majority of the votes ; but
thought it would be more for the good of the order,
upon feveral accounts, as Avofto durft not abufe his
authority, when he was fo immediately under the eye
of his Holinefs.

His beft friends, efpecially Cardinal Alexandrino,
advifed him carefully to avoid all fubjects of difpute,
and, if it was poffible, to find out fome honourable excufe, for not going to a place fo far from Rome, where
in cafe of any quarrel, he could not defend himfelf
againft the General's authority. This good advice had
but little effect upon him, for notwithftanding the deference he ought to have fhewn to the Cardinal's opinion, he pretended, " That his going thither, was of
" the utmoft confequence to his character, that, if he
" did not, his enemies would take an opportunity of
" branding him as a pitiful and pufillanimous fellow,
" who had abandoned the intereft of his order, for fear
" of

" of the General, at a time when it moſt of all ſtood in
" need of ſupport ; that he had many things to lay
" before the chapter, which it was not poſſible to do
" by letter, or memorials : that moreover, the Gene-
" ral would take the advantage of his abſence to de-
" clare his office vacant."

As he continued firm and poſitive in this reſolution,
he left Rome in company with only one eccleſiaſtick,
and arrived at Florence two days before the opening
of the chapter.

As ſoon as the General heard of his arrival, he ſent
to let him know, " That he was ſurpriſed at his leaving
" Rome in ſuch a hurry, when his commiſſion requir-
" ed him to ſtay for the good of his brethren ; that
" he cught by no means to have come thither to in-
" commode the convent contrary to the eſtabliſhed
" rules, which forbade the Procurator io come before
" the chapter is opened." This affront was ſoon followed by another ; for at the firſt meeting of the chapter, which is generally employed in the diſpoſal of offices, Avoſta pretended that Montalto had no right to
ſit there, though the Procurators had always been ac-
cuſtomed to aſſiſt at thoſe aſſemblies. Montalto complained heavily of this piece of injuſtice, and entered a
proteſt againſt their proceedings, which the General
took little or no notice of. At the ſecond ſeſſion, he
was abſolutely refuſed admiſſion, though his preſence
was altogether neceſſary, and treated with many other
marks of ſcorn and contempt.

Tired out with theſe continual mortifications, he
drew up another proteſt, and, ſticking it upon the
door of the refectory, immediately left the city, without ſo much as taking leave, or any ſort of notice, of
the chapter. Avoſta, who wanted to get rid of him,
was not a little pleaſed at his going away after that
manner, and having thoroughly examined the the terms
of his proteſt, immediately diſpatched meſſengers to all
the wardens of the houſes of that order, by which he was
to paſs, commanding them to apprehend and confine
him till further orders. But Montalto was too cunning
for

for him, and avoided the houfes of his own order, calling only at thofe of the Dominicans and Auguftines.

He met with two adventures upon the road, that are
not altogether unworthy of being mentioned. The firft
was at an inn, about a day's journey from Rome, where
he lay down upon a bed to refresh himfelf a little with
a nap after dinner. He had fcarce clofed his eyes, when
he was awaked by a great uproar in the yard, upon
which he ran to the window to fee what was the occafion
of it; and perceiving the houfe was befet by a company
of Archers, fome of whom were coming in to fearch it,
he at firft took it into his head, that they were in purfuit
of him, by the General's order, and was looking for a
place to hide himfelf in. As the noife began to grow
louder and louder, fome body knocked violently at his
chamber-door, and threatened to break it down, if he
did not immediately open it, which he was forced to comply with, but was informed to his great fatisfaction, that
they were in purfuit of one of the Banditti [9], who as their
fpies acquainted them, was feen to go into that houfe.

The other happened upon the road. He chanced, as
he went along, to lofe his cloak, which, it feems, was
not well faftened behind him. As it was a good while
before he miffed it, he thought it in vain to turn back
again to look for it. The next day he was overtaken
upon the road by a merchant, who kept him company.
As they went on, it began to rain, upon which the
merchant unfolded a cloak that was behind him, and
threw it over his fhoulders. Montalto looking earneftly
at it, perceived it was his, and, without any ceremony,
plucked it of his back, and put it upon his own.

In the mean time Avofta, who determined to fhew
him no favour, was very bufy in collecting materials to
found a procefs upon, and drew up a charge, in which
he fet forth, " The little refpect Montalto had fhewn
" him as Prefident of the chapter; the manifeft violation
" of the antient rules and eftablifhments of the order,

[9] This word, I obferve, is always tranflated Banditti, with a
double t ; but ought to be fpelled Banditi, with a fingle one, as it is
a participle from the Italian verb. Bandire, to banifh.

he

" he had been guilty of, by bufying himfelf in affairs
" that did not belong to him; the premeditated defign,
" with which he came to embarrafs the proceedings of
" the affembly; and the threats he had made ufe of
" to influence feveral of the members :" To thefe were
added, the informations that had formerly been laid
againft him at Rome. All which articles together made
up a charge of fo heinous a nature in Avofta's opinion,
that, without giving Montalto an opportunity of
making any defence, he declared his office vacant.
Some of the members expreffed their diflike at fo violent a manner of proceeding, and advifed him to
act with more deliberation, reprefenting to him,
" That as Montalto had very powerful friends, he
" might affure himfelf, he would not fubmit to it; that
" he was like enough to demand juftice of the Pope
" himfelf; that when an office of fuch importance was
" to be declared void, it ought not to be done without
" the matureft advice and confideration."

The General paid but little regard to thefe remonftrances, and faid, " He neither could nor would let
" fuch enormities go unpunifhed; that he deferved
" not only to lofe his office, but to be expelled the
" order; that he was very certain the Pope would in-
" flict a ftill more heavy punifhment upon him, if he
" prefumed to trouble him with his complaint; in
" fhort, that he would take the whole affair upon
" himfelf, and engage to give a fatisfactory account
" of his proceedings to his Holinefs."

After this manner was poor Montalto deprived of his
office, though moft of the chapter were of opinion, that
he ought to have been fufpended firft, and then cited to
make his defence. The General propofed to the chapter, at the fame time, to chufe another Procurator in
his room, and recommended father Thomas di Varafa,
who was no friend to Montalto. The major part of the
affembly was furprized to fee with what vehemence he
laboured to get Varafa chofen, though there were many that deferved that honour much better than he.

This Varafa had formerly read lectures in logick to
Cardinal

Cardinal Borromeo, and hearing of his promotion and great interest with his uncle the Pope, immediately came to Rome, hoping to obtain great preferment by his favour and patronage. He had already got letters of recommendation from this Cardinal to Avosta, which laid him under a necessity (though he did not otherwise much like the man) of doing every thing that lay in his power to serve him, thinking it a favourable opportunity of obliging the Cardinal nephew, and of getting quite clear of Montalto, by filling his place with a person, whose interest with the Pope, would hinder him from declaring the deprivation unjust.

As soon as Montalto was informed of these proceedings he acquainted Cardinal Alexandrino with them, who having upbraided him a little with going to the chapter contrary to his advice, endeavoured to procure him some redress from the Pope, and interested Colonna likewise in the affair: For this purpose they presented a petition from him to his Holiness, but soon found there was no remedy to be had. Varasa was beforehand with him, and by the Advice of Avosta, had come post to Rome, and got his election confirmed by the Pope, who, without any regard to the complaints and remonstrances of Montalto, approved of the chapter's whole proceedings against him.

This threw him into so deep a melancholy, that his friends began to fear it would endanger his life, though Alexandrino did every thing that lay in his power to alleviate his concern.

But when he saw that Borromeo was made Protector of the order, he looked upon himself as undone, and despaired of ever obtaining any other preferment. For though this Cardinal had the character of a very worthy and good man, he was apprehensive his enemies would abuse the confidence he reposed in them, to his disadvantage, by misrepresentations and lies.

Whilst he was in this situation, the news of Calvin's death arrived at Rome from Geneva, where he had been held in as great veneration as if he had been a Pope (which he was in effect amongst the Protestants.) The

court

court was not a little rejoiced at this event as many were of opinion that the Genevese had long repented of their apoſtaſy, and only waited for a convenient opportunity of returning into the boſom of the church, but were deterred from it by the rigour with which he treated thoſe that ventured to expreſs any ſuch inclination ; ſo that it was generally believed now he was dead, they would eaſily be prevailed upon to renounce their errors.

This opinion was confirmed by a letter from the biſhop of Aneci (who was alſo titular biſhop of Geneva) to Cardinal Borromeo, in which he acquainted him with the good diſpoſition of the Geneveſe, and ſaid he made no doubt of their being brought back to the ſheepfold, if his holineſs would be pleaſed to ſend ſome good preachers amongſt them, with a man of prudence and experience at their head. Cardinal Alexandrino, who had been conſulted by Borromeo in this affair, ſaid he thought Montalto would be a very proper perſon to be employed in ſuch a miſſion, which the other approved of, and ordered ſix religious of different orders to hold themſelves in readineſs to attend him to Geneva.   But an old crafty prelate of long experience and great knowledge in the affairs of the world, diſſuaded the Cardinals from this reſolution, by telling them, " It would be a very impolitick meaſure " to ſend a diſguſted monk, eſpecially one of Mon- " talto's caſt, upon ſuch an errand as he might, proba- " bly, ſet up for himſelf, and become a ſecond Cal- " vin, and ſo continue a hereſy that would, perhaps, " otherwiſe drop of itſelf in a little time, if it was " treated with contempt and diſregard."

Borromeo was convinced after a while, that Montalto was not ſo much in fault, as he had been made to believe, and that, though ſome parts of his behaviour were hardly to be juſtified, he had not deſerved the treatment he met with ; but being unwilling to retract what he had done, he endeavoured to ſoften the matter, and, ſending for him, exhorted him to patience, and promiſed to procure him ſuch preferment as ſhould

make

make him ample satisfaction. He told the Cardinal he
designed to leave Rome, but he ordered him to stay,
assuring him, " That he would provide for him in a
little time." These fine words raised his drooping
spirits again, and encouraged him to wait with patience the fulfilling his promises. But there unluckily
happened in the mean time, two affairs of such importance, as entirely took up Borromeo's attention, and
made him for a while totally forget both Montalto and
his incidents.

One Benedict Acolti conspired with three other villains to assassinate the Pope whilst he was at audience.
This wretch desired the honour of giving him the first
stab, as he was reading a memorial that was to be presented to him ; but when it came to the point of execution, he was so dismayed with the horror of the action, that he could not perpetrate it. One of them discovered the whole conspiracy, and impeached his accomplices in hope of saving his own life. They died
in the midst of torments that were due to so execrable
a design, without accusing any other person as the author or abettor of it, and, tho' they were separately
examined, all positively declared they were impelled
to so desperate an undertaking, only by a persuasion,
" That after the death of the present Pope, there
" would be another chosen by the unanimous consent
" and approbation of all Christendom, who would be
" like an Angel or a God, and reign over the whole
" earth [1]." Some were of opinion, that the protestant

[1] The Italian Edition says, *Un certo Benedetto Accolti* ; the French
version, *Un certain Moine Benedictin d' Ascoli* ; Thuanus sets the
matter right in the following passage of his history, lib xxxvi. " Inter
" hæc Romæ detecta est conjuratio, a Fanaticis quibusdam contra
" Pontificem structa, cujus dux erat Benedictus Accoltius, Accoltii,
" qui olim purpurei galeri decus meruit, filius. Qui complices ha-
" buit Petrum Accoltium, gentilem suum, Antonium Canossæ Co-
" mitem, Pellicionem Equitem, Prosperum Hectoreum, et Thad-
" dæum Manfredum, ære oppressos alieno, nec satis sanæ mentis.
" Ille, aut spe prædæ, aut etiam emendationis Ecclesiæ obtentu,
" tantum facinus iis persuaserat ; aiebat enim, Pium quartum non
" verum Pontificem esse, ac, eo sublato, alterum suffectum iri, qui
Papa

tant powers were at the bottom of this; but others thought, more juftly, it was entirely owing to fanaticifm, or perhaps the defire of being famous to pofterity. Whatever was the caufe, it gave Borromeo a great deal of inquietude, and made him redouble his care for the fafety of the Pope's perfon.

The other event was a very warm conteft for Precedence, betwixt the French and Spanifh ambaffadors, which engroffed the application of the court to that degree, that all other concerns gave way to it. The ambaffador of France was ftrenuous for a decifion in favour of his mafter; the Spaniard was no lefs folicitous for the honour of his nation; and the Pope, who had a mind to carry fair with both parties, did not care to give the preference to either.

The French, provoked at his dilatory proceedings, threatened to appeal to the council of Trent. But the difference was at laft compromifed by the prudence and good offices of Cardinal Borromeo, who applied himfelf to this matter with fo much earneftnefs and affiduity, that it put all thoughts of Montalto quite out of his head.

In the mean time, the Pope was determined to fend a Legate a latere, with a great retinue, into Spain, to put an end to fome difputes that had happened concerning the Archbifhoprick of Toledo, as it was an affair of the utmoft confequence to the holy fee. So fplendid an embaffy

" Papa Angelicus diceretur, fub quo Ecclefiæ concordia, caftigatis
" erroribus, farciretur; additis vaticiniis de potentia ejus in om-
" nem terrarum orbem: tum patrata cæde, gazam Pontificis, et
" Cardinalis Borromæi prædæ ceffuram oftendebat. Infuper
" arces, ditiones, et montes aureos fociis pollicebatur, et Antonio
" quidem Ficinum, Thaddæo Cremonam, Pellicioni Aquileiam,
" Profpero denique annuos reditus ad 5000 aureorum infana vanita-
" te daturum promiferat: fed cum femel utque iterum oblata oc-
" cafione, ipfi Benedicto et Pellicioni, qui cædem faciendam fufce-
" perant, animus defuiffet, petita toties audientia, Accoltius, alioqui
" Pontifici invifus, et qui Genevæ aliquandiu fuiffe infimulabatur,
" fufpectior effe cœpit, a quibufdam delatus, atque ob id cum fo-
" ciis noctu comprehenfus eft, qui tormentis fubjecti, cum rem faffi
" effent, temeritatis et infaniæ, ad hunc diem inauditæ, pœnas capite
" luerunt."

baffy would likewife, he thought, tend to footh the
King of Spain, who was a little piqued at the manner
in which the precedence of the ambaffadors had been
decided. After having thought of feveral very eminent
perfons for that purpofe, he at laft fixed upon Hugo
Buon Compagnon, a Bolognefe, who had lately been
made a Cardinal, with the title of St. Sixtus.

He was a man of great experience in ftate affairs,
and, by his important fervices, afterwards obtained the
Papacy, taking the name of Gregory XIII. As foon as
he was appointed Legate, he immediately made preparations for his journey; the affair of Toledo being of
fuch a nature, as would not admit of any delay.

It was thought neceffary, that he fhould have a Confultor of the Inquifition in his train, to promote the intereft and eftablifhment of that office. Many were very
defirous of and earneftly folicited that honour, to ingratiate themfelves with the Cardinal, and out of curiofity,
as it was a good opportunity of feeing Spain at little or
no expence. Montalto, who was heartily tired of ftaying amongft the monks, told Alexandrino, that he fhould
be extremely glad to attend the legate in that quality.
The Cardinal ufed his intereft to obtain this favour for
him, but at firft met with fome difficulty in it; his petulant behaviour to the Spanifh ambaffador at Venice
was remembered, and objected to him upon this occafion; of which imputation he cleared himfelf fo well, that
though an Auguftine had been already recommended,
and almoft obtained a promife, when he applied to Borromeo, and defired his affiftance in it, he, remembring
how hardly Montalto had been treated by Avofta, and
the promife he himfelf had given of making him
amends the firft opportunity, ferved him fo effectually,
that he had the preference, and being appointed both
chaplain to the legate, and confultor to the inquifition,
left Rome at the end of Auguft [1565].

The legate, who was no ftranger to his merit and
experience in the concerns of the Inquifition, feemed
very well pleafed with his being appointed to attend him.
It is remarkable, that there were three perfons in this
legation

legation, who immediately succeeded each other in the pontificate, viz. Buon Compagnon, who was afterwards Gregory XIII. Montalto, who succeeded him, and took the name of Sixtus V. and John Baptist Castagna, bishop of Rossano in Calabria (from whence he was sent for by the Pope to go nuncio into Spain, and took his opportunity of accompanying the legate) who succeeded Sixtus, and was called Urban VII.

The legate communicated every thing relating to his embassy to Castagna and Montalto, and admitted them to a very near familarity with him. Montalto, who neglected no opportunity of making his court to them both, said to them pleasantly one day, " When I " see you two, methinks I see two Popes. " You have " great reason to think of a Pope," says the nuncio, " when you see the legate, whose merit justly entitles " him to expect that high dignity some time or other; " but for my part, father Montalto, I have no more " chance ever to be Pope, than you." " I was made " Cardinal indeed," replied the legate, " before you; " but you may possibly be Pope before me, as the " words of the gospel may often be very well applied " to the dignitaries of the church," *The first shall be last, and the last shall be first.*

Another time Montalto taking the Cardinal's hat, which lay upon the table, in his hand, the legate said to him, " come, Montalto put it on, let us see how it " will become you." " It will be time enough for that," says Montalto, " when your eminence is Pope." I wish " I was," says he, " if it was only to satisfy your cu- " riosity, and reward your merit."

The nuncio coming in during this conversation, Montalto said to him, " I must beg your lordship to re- " member, that his eminence has promised to make " me a Cardinal when he is Pope." " Yes," says the le- gate, " I have promised him a hat, because he has pro- " mised me the Tiara." Well," says the nuncio, " If " ever you should call upon me as a witness to this " promise, I shall be ready to appear."

In a little time, the legate began to have a very high
opinion

opinion of Montalto's judgment and abilities, and did nothing without confulting him. But the officers of his houfhold looked upon him with another eye, either upon the account of his ftiff and auftere behaviour to them, or the averfion and contempt this fort of people generally have for thofe that are bred up in a cloyfter; or the jealoufy it gave them to fee how great a fhare he had of their mafter's favour. He hardly paffed a day without a quarrel with fome or other of them, particularly the Maitre de Chambre [2], who could not bear him, and was acquainted with all the tranfactions of his life. This fellow reproached him one day, before feveral others of the legate's domefticks, with the broils and difturbances he had occafioned in his convent, and faid, " He did not wonder at his quarrelling with other people, when he could not live in peace even with his brethren," with many other ill natured things of that kind.

This coming to the legate's ears, he was fo difpleafed, that he would have immediately difmiffed the Maitre de Chambre, if Montalto had not generoufly interceded for him, and defired the nuncio to join with him in entreating his mafter to forgive him, which he did at their requeft; and advifed Montalto at the fame time, for the fake of his character, to avoid as much as poffible thefe little feuds and animofities for the future.

This piece of good advice, given in fo kind a manner, made fuch an impreffion upon him, that he endeavoured, by a quite different behaviour, to gain the efteem and good will of all the legate's houfhold.

He had heard, that when he was nominated to go into Spain, fome of his brethren had been fo kind to fay, " If he was of fo infupportable a temper in a " cloyfter, what would he be when he was more at " liberty?" And that his good friend the general had told one of the legates principal domefticks, " That " if his mafter kept him a month, he would be bound " to refign his office to him."

Thefe

[2] The Italian is Un Camariere, which we have no word in Englifh to exprefs, except Chamberlain, and that, I think, does not come up to it; the French word Maitre de Chambre, is better.

Thefe things being repeated, when he had that quarrel with the Maitre de Chambre, made him refolve to behave to every body, in fo complaifant and civil a manner, that the world fhould be convinced it was not his fault, if there had been any mifunderftanding between him and his brethren.

They arrived in Spain after a journey of fix weeks, where he was fcon taken notice of as a man of great and uncommon abilities. The religious of his order fhewed him the higheft refpect, and paid their court to him with an affiduity, that was very agreeable to his vanity, and the natural defire he had of command and fuperiority.

He was defired to affift at a general chapter, and to prepare fome affairs of importance that were to be laid before the legate, who defigned to honour that affembly with his prefence. He likewife had feveral private conferences with the minifters of the Inquifition, concerning the interefts of that office, which wes not yet thoroughly eftablifhed in Spain; and the Legate, to whom the care of this affair had been particularly recommended, was very well pleafed to have the Spaniards confer with his confultor about it. Soon after he was called to affift at the trial of two delinquents and fenence of death was paffed on them both, as he advifed and directed.

Yet he did nothing which he could not give a very clear account of to the Legate, nor without both his and the Nuncio's advice.

The marquis of Bergues and the count de Montigny were come from Flanders to Madrid, by order, as it was faid, of the duchefs of Parma, governante of the Low Countries. But it was pretty well known, that feveral of the principal inhabitants and chiefs of the faction were more concerned in their journey, than that princefs; and that the motive that engaged them to undertake it, was to prevail upon the King to abolifh the Inquifition, to which their countrymen would never fubmit.

The King, however, not admitting them to an audience for fome time, they thought it was owing to the

Legate

Legate; as they imagined he muſt know what they came to ſolicit was prejudicial to the intereſts of the holy ſee, and the views that had engaged the Pope to ſend his Legate into Spain with inſtructions to preſs the King to uſe his endeavours to eſtabliſh the Inquiſition in Flanders, and to employ all his forces, if neceſſary, for that purpoſe. The Legate, indeed, had already diſpoſed the King and his council to do the church that ſervice; and as he was apprehenſive the arguments of theſe deputies might make ſome alteration in the King's reſolution, ſo they, on their ſide, likewiſe ſuſpected, that he had been the cauſe of deferring their audience.

Not long after their arrival, they came to wait upon the Legate, who received them with great politeneſs. But this viſit paſſed merely in compliments and civilities. He declined entering into any buſineſs of concern with them himſelf at preſent; but ordered Montalto to inſinuate himſelf by degrees into their acquaintance. Montalto was not a little proud of being charged with ſo important a negociation, and took all poſſible methods to gain their confidence; eſpecially that of Montigny, who ſpoke the Italian tongue perfectly well, was very eloquent, and maſter of ſeveral other valuable accompliſhments.

He ſeemed to take much pleaſure in Montalto's company, though his converſation always chiefly turned upon the eſtabliſhment of the Inquiſition in Flanders, declaring, that the Legate would not have permitted him to enter into ſo ſtrict an acquaintance with them, if it had not been to promote that end. They were both of them ſo well pleaſed to hear him talk upon that ſubject, like a good Chriſtian an an able politician, that Montigny ſaid one day, " A hundred ſuch eccleſiaſtics " would do good ſervice in the Low Countries.

He reported every thing that paſſed betwixt them to the Legate and Nuncio; which laſt had likewiſe ſome conferences with them, but with more reſerve and greater reſtraint than Montalto, whoſe ſtation admitted him to viſit them at any time without ceremony.

They one day invited him to a handſome entertainment,

ment, which they made on purpofe for him; but he would not go to it without the Legate's confent, which he freely gave him, knowing how agreeable he would make himfelf to them.   It is certain he had a very extraordinary faculty of ingratiating himfelf when he pleafed, with any perfon he converfed with.   As to his political abilities, he gave the Legate fuch an account of his proceedings with the two deputies, that he was aftonifhed to fee a man, who had been educated in a cloifter, fo ready and dextrous in the management of temporal affairs.

Towards the beginning of December, the Pope fent a brief to the Legate, granting the King of Spain a tenth of all the ecclefiaftical revenues in his dominions for the next year, to be applied to the affiftance of the Emperor, who was engaged in a bloody and expenfive war with the Turk; a favour that had been long and earneftly folicited by his ambaffador at Rome.   At the fame time his Catholick Majefty determined to fend a miffion into the Philippine iflands, and other parts of the Indies lately difcovered, for the converfion of the inhabitants of thofe places to the Chriftian faith.

For this purpofe, having confulted with the Legate, he appointed feventy-five Miffionaries, viz. twenty-five Jefuits, thirty Francifcans, fix Benedictines, three Auguftines, three Carmelites, five Seculars, and three Superiors over them, to be approved of by the Legate after they had been examined, which office was performed by Montalto, as his chaplain, in the prefence of the Cardinal, and father Gora, a Jefuit, the King's confeffor.

Whilft preparations were making for their departure and orders iffued out for the collecting the tenths, lately granted by his Holinefs, to carry on the war againft the Turk; his Majefty, by the advice of the Legate, ordered prayers to be offered up, and the Hoft expofed, for forty hours, in all the churches of Spain, to implore the Divine Bleffing upon the Chriftian arms, and to excite the people to liberality in their contributions to fo pius an undertaking.

I   To

To set his subjects an example of zeal and devotion, he ordered a solemn service to be performed, for nine days successively, in the royal chapel, with a sermon, every day, at which he himself, the Legate, with most of the grandees, and all the missionaries were present ; and, having been informed of Montalto's eloquence and great abilities in the pulpit, desired him to preach one of those sermons in the Italian language, which he did to a very numerous and splendid audience, upon the words of Isaiah xlix. 6 v. *I will give thee for a light to the Gentiles, that thou mayest be my Salvation unto the ends of the earth* ; applying them to his Majesty as the person appointed by Providence, " To destroy the Otto-
" man empire, to extirpate heresy, to convert the
" Gentiles, and to propogate the glad tidings of Sal-
" vation, to the uttermost parts of the earth."

His performance met with great applause from the nobility, as most of them understood the Italian tongue. At their desire, he printed it with a dedication to the King, which so pleased his Majesty, that he made him a present of a very large piece of plate, and a purse of 100 pistoles.

This mark of preference raised a spirit of envy amongst the other preachers; and so galled father Pangora, one of the King's chaplains, that he published a pamphlet with critical and very severe remarks, " Upon the stile
" and matter of a sermon, lately preached in the king's
" chapel, by an Italian friar ;" in which he pretended to shew, " That there were several passages not fit to
" come out of the mouth of any Christian, much less a
" preacher;" and though he did not mention Montalto's name, it was very evident he meant him, as what he said, could not be applied to any other person,

When this came to Montalto's hands, he shewed it to the Legate and Nuncio; and they immediately sent for Pangora, who, though he had not set his name to it, was not only suspected, but sufficiently known to be the author; several of his own order affirming they knew him to be so, by his stile and manner of writing, with which they were perfectly acquainted, and
ha

had heard him say the same things in public company, soon after the sermon was preached.

When he appeared, the Legate, though he thought he had great reason to complain of his treating a person with so much indecency and disrespect, who was his chaplain, consultor to the Inquisition, and a preacher of established reputation, only asked him, with his usual mildness, " What could induce him to make so flagrant " an attack upon Montalto's character, as he had ne- " ver injured or offended him ? and said, he hoped he " would ask his pardon, and make him satisfaction in " as public a manner as he had affronted him," But Pangora, being brother-in-law to Henriquez, Secretary of State, and expecting he should be supported by him, abused the Legate's good nature and lenity, said ; " He was not the author of the pamphlet ;" and called Montalto, " An impudent lying fellow." Upon which the Legate ordered the Inquisitor General to make a strict and diligent search for the Printer, who was soon found out, and averred that Pangora both brought the copy to his press, and came for it again. This being proof enough, Montalto would have proceeded against him as an heretick ; but when the book was coolly examined, it was thought sufficient to send him to the prison of the Inquisition, to be proceeded against as the author of a scandalous and defamatory libel.

This was done by the King's immediate order, who was highly offended at it, and struck him out of the list of his chaplains ; but, by the intercession of Henriquez, his sentence was afterwards changed into three months close confinement in his own convent.

Montalto expressed much satisfaction upon this occasion, and said to his friends, that " if justice was as " duly administered in Italy, as it was in Spain, Avosta " would have no great reason to rejoice ot the injury " he had done him in the chapter at Florence ; that he, " hoped, from this specimen, fortune was beginning " to smile upon him, and would soon put it in his " power to triumph over his enemies." It is certain, that this event was fo far from doing him any prejudice, that it contributed much to his fame and credit at the court of Spain. His fermon being printed in the Italian tongue, and foon after tranflated into Spanifh, was every where read with the higheft applaufe; and fo liked by the King, that he made him his Chaplain in the room of Pangora, and fent him a patent, offering him a table and an apartment in the palace, with a ftipend of 100 piftoles per annum, if he would ftay in Spain.

But Providence defigned him to fhine in a higher fphere, and infpired him with a refolution of going back to Rome, where he thought he ftood a fairer chance to make his fortune, confidering the many fudden downfalls and viciffitudes that attend thofe that live in courts: for which reafon he defired the Legate to return his thanks to the King in the moft refpectful manner, and let him know the concern he was under, that the circumftances of his affairs would not permit him to refide in Spain, humbly befeeching his Majefty to give him leave to bear the honourable title of his Chaplain wherever he went; which requeft the King readily complied with.

END OF THE SECOND BOOK.

BOOK THE THIRD.

WHILST things were in this fituation at Madrid, the Legate and Nuncio received an account, that the Pope died at Rome the 10th of December [1565], which put an end to their negociations at that court. Montalto did not feem much affected at this news, as he was not without hope that Cardinal Alexandrino from whom he expected every thing, would fucceed him; which yet he was prudent enough to conceal him from from the Legate, who he knew did not defire that fhould ever happen. Not that he thought him unworthy of it, for he had often
said

said in private conversation, " That he did not know
" a better or more deserving man, but that he would
" never give his vote for him, as he had shewn him-
" self of a severe and unrelenting nature when he was
" employed by the Inquisition." Much about the
same time, Montalto had advice of the General Avosta's death, at the news of which he could not dissem-
ble his joy, and said to one of his friends, " That no-
" thing was now wanting to compleat his happiness,
" but the exaltation of Cardinal Alexandrino to the
" Papacy ;" upon which his friend asked him, " If the
" death of an enemy gave him as much pleasure as
" the promotion of a friend ;" he answered, " That
" the extinction of an evil, might very well be ac-
" counted equal to the acquisition of a positive good."

All the Legate's domesticks offered their most ardent
petitions to Heaven for the success of their master,
and Montalto seemed to join with them, but in reality
wished for nothing so much as to see his old and faithful friend Alexandrino invested with that dignity ; and
indeed, if the Legate had known the bottom of his
heart, he was of so humane and candid a disposition,
that it is much to be questioned, whether he would
have taken it ill, as he must likewise know, it was but
natural and reasonable for every man to wish well to
his friend or patron, and that the suffrages of private
persons had no manner of influence or effect in the
conclave.

The Legate, though he was so far from Rome, had
a great number of voices ; and Borromeo, who was
at the head of a very considerable party, used his utmost efforts to get him chosen, as he had always been
firmly attached to the interests of his late uncle, and
was possessed of abilities and merit not inferior to the
very best of those who were his competitors in the election. But, it seems, his hour was not yet come. Providence thought fit to postpone him at this time. For
Borromeo finding he could not obtain a sufficient majority in his favour, joined interests with Farnese (who
likewise had a great number of Cardinals at his devotion)

tion) and chofe Alexandrino the 7th of January [1566].
It is hard to fay, whether the great fecrecy and addrefs with which the election was conducted by thefe
two Cardinals, or the fecurity and negligence of the
oppofite faction, was more to be wondered at.

A courier was difpatched the next day, to give the
Legate an account of this election, with orders to return immediately to Rome. Though we may imagine he was not exceedingly pleafed with this news,
he put on an appearance of joy, and made a magnificent entertainment at his palace, where nothing was
heard but repeated acclamations of Long live Pope
Pius V. which name he had taken ; but he never was
in any great degree of favour with him after his return
to Italy, which was occafioned chiefly by his endeavour to foften and mitigate that extreme rigour with
which he adminiftered juftice.

Montalto, however, was fo tranfported, that he
could hardly contain himfelf within any bounds. As
foon as he heard the news, he went to congratulate
the Dominicans, and ftaid to fup at their convent. At
his return, the Legate's houfhold complimented him
upon it, as if he had been a relation of the Pope.

It was not without reafon, that he was fo overjoyed,
for the Pope gave him fome extraordinary marks of his
favour in the very firft week of his Pontificate. The
death of Avofta happening, as we have obferved, about
the fame time with the late Pope's, put Varafa, the Procurator of the order, upon intriguing to fucceed him in
his office ; when he received advice, that there was little or no hope of his recovery, he immediately applied
to Borromeo, and, by his favour, obtained a Brief for it.

As Avofta did not die till after the deceafe of Pius
IV. it was neceffary to eftablifh Varafa in his new office, that his Brief fhould be confirmed by the fucceeding Pope : For which reafon, immediately, upon the
election of Alexandrino, he prefented a petition himfelf;
in which he fet forth, " That it was the antient cuf-
" tom of the order, for the Procurator to fucceed the
　　　　　　　　　　　　　　　　" General,

" General, especially when his office became vacant by
" death," and to several instances and examples, which
he quoted of the same nature, he added many other arguments to prove, that " what he petitioned for, was
" nothing but his strict right and due, as he had a
" brief for it from the late Pope."

After Pius had read it with great patience and attention, he said, " He was mighty glad to hear it was al-
" ways customary to be preferred from the office of
" Procurator to the Generalship, and that as he would
" not, upon any consideration, break in upon old cus-
" toms, he thought himself obliged to confer that of-
" fice upon Montalto, who was the lawful Procurator,
" though unjustly dispossessed of his post, by the
" Brigue and cabals of his General."

Varafa, thunderstruck at this unexpected declaration, went directly to advise with Borromeo, how to
support the brief that had been obtained by his favour,
which the Pope said, was " null in itself, as it was
" granted without hearing the defence of the deposed
" party." The Cardinal told him, " The thing would
" bear a dispute, but that, unluckily for him, the Pope.
" who was to be judge, had openly declared in Mon-
" talto's favour." Varafa, who saw that it was in vain
to contend any longer with an adversary that was so
powerfully supported, was forced not only to give up
his brief, but thought himself well off in being continued Procurator ; for the Pope had certainly declared
his office void, if Borromeo had not requested the confirmation of it as a particular favour.

His Holiness ordered another brief to be immediately drawn up for Montalto, in which he declared,
" That he made him general of his order unasked and
" without any application from him," and to heighten
the compliment, sent it by an express who was charged with another pacquet for the Legate, and orders to
return by Genoa, where he was to adjust some matters
of importance.

The courier met the Legate at Asti, a City in Pied-
mont, and delivered him the pacquet, in which Montalto's brief was inclosed.   As

As foon as he had read the difpatches, he called
Montalto into his apartment, and giving him the brief,
faid, " You fee how early his Holinefs begins to heap
" favours upon you." " Yes," anfwered he, " and
" they are infinitely the more dear to me, as I owe
" them folely to his goodnefs and generofity, without
" an y kind of folicitation." " He does you but juf-
" tice," replied the Legate, " in fhewing a greater re-
" gard to your merit, than the petitions and recom-
" mendations of others." After this, the Legate
took him with him to the Cordelier's church in Afti,
where they fung the Te Deum ; and afterwards invited him to a fumptuous entertainment, and drank the
new General's health to the company. When fupper
was over, the Cardinal faid to him in a complimentary
manner, " Well, father Montalto, you and I muft foon
" part, you will henceforward be courted and followed
" as a man in authority, and I fhall retire to privacy
" and obfcurity ;" to which Montalto anfwered, " My
" Lord, I fhall ever think myfelf more honoured by
" having been in your fervice, than by the higheft
" poft that is to be obtained in our order."
The Legate preffed him to enter immediately upon
his office, but he declined it, by faying, " that he would
" not give up the honour of ferving him, till they ar-
" rived at Rome ; and that he ought by no means to
" exercife any function of his office, before he had kiffed
" his Holinefs's feet." This modeft behaviour did not
hinder him from receiving the honours that were due
to him. Wherever he went, the wardens and Provincials came from all parts to wait upon him. entertaining him at every convent, in thofe apartments that
were appropriated to the ufe of the General.
After he had kiffed the Pope's feet at his arrival, his
Holinefs embraced him tenderly, and entered into a
long converfation with him upon feveral topicks. The
brotherhood of the holy Apoftles, that had formerly
given him fo much uneafinefs, endeavoured to wipe
out the remembrance of their paft behaviour, by vy-
ing

ing with each other, who fhould fhew him the greateft honours. Their entertainments and rejoicings were profufe, beyond any that had ever been feen before him in that convent. They walked in folemn procef-fion, and the pulpits were filled with panegyricks. Several pieces of mufick were purpofely compofed on this occafion; verfes and poems, without number, ftuck upon the walls of every cloyfter, with bonfires, illuminations, and ringing of bells. In fhort, his entry into Rome had the air of a triumph, and fhoals of people flocked in from the country to fee it. All the generals of the other religious orders, and moft of the prelates that were then in Rome, came to vifit him out of refpect to his new dignity, and the great degree of favour he was in with the pope. Montalto was not backward in returning their compliments and civilities, and went in the firft place to wait upon the general of the Dominicans, to rejoice in private with him upon the exaltation of his holinefs. He always had a great efteem for the religious of this order, and paid more regard to their recommendation, than that of any other.

Not long after his promotion, he received a letter from his old friend the curate Mancone, with an account of his mother's death, and the ftate of his family, congratulating him at the fame time, upon his new preferment, and recommending his nephew James to him, who had been brought up in a cloyfter by Montalto's advice. With an anfwer to this letter, he returned 50 crowns, which he defired Mancone to lay out for the ufe of his father, thanking him for his early compliment, and the great kindnefs he had always fhewn to his relations; and, to let him fee the regard he paid to his recommendation, he fent his nephew James a diploma for a bachelor's degree, with affurances that he would not only provide for him, but, if he would fend another nephew that he had to Rome, he would take care of of his education, and do him any other fervice that lay in his power.

He

He began to exercife his authority with a reformation of fome abufes and irregularities, that had been introduced, through negligence, into the religious houfes
of his order, and, for that purpofe, fent circular in-
ftruſtions to be diligently obferved by the fuperiors of
them. After he had done this, he prepared to vifit all
the provinces of the ecclefiaftical ftate of Tufcany and
Naples.

When he went to take his leave of the Pope, his holinefs expreffed a great deal of fatisfaction, in feeing
that he had the care of his order fo much at heart, and
defired he would not ftay any longer upon his vifitati-
ons than was abfolutely neceffary, " For that he was
" defirous of having him near his perfon." He was fo
affected with the latter part of the Pope's fpeech, that
he would gladly have been excufed from his journey;
but as he had taken his leave, he thought he could not
in honour now decline it, and fet off in fuch a manner,
as fhewed how impatient he fhould be to return.

He firft of all vifited the province of La Marca, and
was fo ftrict in the execution of his office, that he
fpread a terror wherever he came, having no refpect
to perfons, and moft feverely punifhing fuch religious
as had any property of their own. Amongft others,
he depofed the warden of Fermo, having found fome
money in his poffeffion, of which he had not given in
an account to the chapter, and threatened him with
the galleys, for fome other faults that were of too frivolous a nature for fuch a chaftifement. He punifhed
nine others after the fame manner, in the fpace of
two years that he was general; which ftruck fuch a
panic into the whole order, that few would accept of
any office in it, They chofe rather to live as private
monks, than expofe themfelves to the lafh of a general,
who was more particularly fevere upon fuch as were
in any poft or employment, which he thought they
had not difcharged with fidelity and integrity.

It is worthy of notice, that a man of his warm difpofition, did not ufe the leaft endeavours to revenge
himfelf

himfelf upon any of his enemies, not even of thofe
that had taken the moft pains to ruin and difgrace him.
On the contrary, he feemed to wink at their failings,
and fhewed greater exactnefs and feverity to thofe who
had rather been his friends than otherwife, at leaft had
never done him any injury. He thought it his duty to
do fo, that he might fhew the world, it was not revenge,
but juftice that moved him to proceed in fo rigorous a
manner. In fhort, if he retained any fort of refentment,
it was with regard to his predeceffor, whofe memory
he endeavoured to extinguifh, by undoing every thing
that he had done, and invalidating all his decrees by
the new ones which he made. He ordered all thofe,
even the provincials, that had held any office under
Avofta, to give an account of their adminiftration ;
and fufpended father William, a Florentine, that was
accufed of bribing the late general to get him made a
provincial ; but reftored him to his power foon after,
at the interceffion of Cofmo, grand duke of Florence,
who preffed it very earneftly. Montalto could not refufe him, as he was a Prince of great merit, and had
entertained him at his Palace, in his return, with a regal magnificence.

He fpent but five months in vifiting the provinces of
La Marca, Umbria, Tufcany, and that of Rome, fearing a longer abfence might diminifh the value and efteem the Pope had for him, which made him lay afide
his defign of going through all Italy, and return to
Rome, where he thought his good genius refided, in
April, 1567, not a little pleafed with the refpect he had
every where met with, and feeing himfelf general over
thofe that would not let him be their provincial.

As foon as he arrived at Rome, he went to kifs the
Pope's feet, and gave him an account of his vifitation.
His holinefs received him very affectionately, and highly commended his zeal and diligence, though the Cardinal-Protector had done him fome ill offices in his abfence, and endeavoured to perfuade the Pope, that
Montalto had treated the conventuals in fo harfh and
imperious a manner, that many of them had made
                                        complaints

complaints againſt him, producing, at the ſame time, a great bundle of letters, which he ſaid he had received from different houſes. But Montalto juſtified himſelf ſo well, that the Pope was perfectly ſatisfied with his conduct, and declared, "His preſence was ſo neceſſary "to him, that he could not part with him any more."

As this mark af his confidence gave freſh hopes to Montalto, he entruſted the care of thoſe provinces, which he had not viſited, to commiſſaries, with a ſtrict charge to give him a true and ſpeedy account of the ſtate and condition in which they found them ; though he had a particular deſire to have gone to Naples in perſon, perhaps to ſhew the religious there, that it was not in their power to interrupt the courſe of his good fortune, nor ſo much as excite in him a deſire of revenge, by their former ill uſage and indignities.

The concerns of his office now took up moſt of his time ; yet he found opportunities of ſpending ſome of it in writing a commentary upon St. Ambroſe, which he had begun before he went to Spain; and deſigned, when it was finiſhed, to publiſh it with a dedication to the Pope ; but he was prevented by the multiplicity of buſineſs, which now ruſhed in upon him from every ſide. For beſides the cares of his generalſhip, which were numerous and weighty, the Pope referred many other affairs of great importance to his cognizance, which he was to report to him, being appointed conſultor to ſeveral congregations.

His holineſs had alſo given orders to Bonello, his ſiſter's ſon, whom he had taken from amongſt to Dominicans, and promoted to the purple, with the title of St. Maria ſopra la Minerva (tho' he took the name of Alexandrino, which his uncle had borne whilſt he was Cardinal) to viſit Montalto as often as he could, hoping he would improve himſelf by his converſation and acquaintance.

Theſe engagements and avocations interrupted the ſtudies he had dedicated to Ambroſe, and he had not time to put a finiſhing hand to that work, till after he
was

was made Cardinal, when he dedicated it to Gregory XIII. but it did not meet with such a reception from that Pontiff, as he exepected.

He paid great respect to Cardinal Bonello, whom we shall henceforth call Alexandrino, and applied himself with so much assiduity to gain his affections, by every sort of service that lay in his power.

He took frequent opportunities of commending him in his uncle'e presence, and spoke of his conduct with the highest approbation. The Pope was transported to hear such encomiums upon his nephew, from so penetrating, as well as sincere and disinterested, a person as he thought Montalto, and spoke largely in his praise to Alexandrino, giving him a hint of what he designed to do for him. The Cardinal, likewise, endeavoured to cultivate a friendship with Montalto, by shewing him all manner of respect and civility, and often speaking in his behalf to his uncle, who was, above measure, delighted to see the harmony that subsisted betwixt them. So great was his affection for him, that he at last made him his Confessor extraordinary, which every body looked upon as a sure presage of his elevation to the Purple.

Father Varasa, who still aspired to the generalship, wished for this event most heartily, as it would occasion a vacancy, and spared no pains that he thought might contribute to bring it about. He had been reconciled to him some time, and seeing how large a share he enjoyed of the Pope's favour, endeavouring to make him his friend, by consulting him upon all occasions, and following his direction with the most implicit submission.

They happened to meet one day in the Pope's presence, about some affairs that concerned the order, upon which the Pope said to Montalto as he was taking his leave, " Father Montalto, Varasa still seems to be " as desirous of the generalship, as when I gave it to " you ; are you content to part with it ?" I lay both " my office and my heart," replied Montalto, " at " your holiness's feet ; and as I hold it entirely by
" your

" your bounty, I fhall moft willingly refign it to
" whomfoever your holinefs fhall be pleafed to appoint
" my fucceffor." Varafa concluded from hence, that
Montalto would foon have a hat, and that he fhould
be made general in his room.

About the end of this year, [1568] the Pope gave
him the bifhoprick of St. Agatha, of no very confiderable value; the court expected to have feen him made
Cardinal, and was furprized at the fmallnefs of the
preferment, in comparifon of what they thought his
holinefs would have done for a perfon, that had long
had fo great an efteem for, which feemed to have been
increafing ever fince he was Pope; every body looking
upon him, as on the point of entering the Sacred College, rather than a general of the Cordeliers. He himfelf began to be apprehenfive his magnificent hopes
would end at laft in a fmall bifhoprick, which he accepted, however, with much feeming thankfulnefs;
though the generals of all the orders are, for the moft
part, made bifhops at leaft. So that in this promotion, there appeared but little diftinction in Montalto's
favour.

The fame day that he was made bifhop, he had the
news of his father's death from Mancone, who was
come to Rome, with his two nephews, to wait upon
Montalto. They were received by him with great affection and courtefy, lodged in his own apartments,
and entertained at his table. A canonry in the cathedral of Afcoli, and the office of treafurer to the chapter,
being vacant, he procured them both for Mancone,
appointed his nephew James, curate of Le Grotte,
and the other, provincial of La Marca.

The Pope's intention in making him a bifhop, was
to oblige Borromeo and his nephew Alexandrino, who
both earneftly recommended Varafa to the generalfhip.
He likewife defigned to employ him in fome Nuncia-
ture, knowing he had abilities equal to the moft arduous negociations; though he had not yet been concerned in any affairs, but fuch as immediately related
to the church or the holy office. He had deftined him

to

to treat with fome of the Italian princes, with a view of bringing about a league amongft all the powers of Chriftendom ; and as it had been a common obfervati-on, that the monkifh habit is not fo well looked upon in the courts of princes, his holinefs rightly judged that a bifhop would be more acceptable to them.

As the Queen of England detained a Spanifh fhip that had been lately taken, with 400,000 crowns on board, for the payment of the troops in Flanders, and was car-rying on a rigorous perfecution againft the Roman Ca-tholics in her dominions ; the King of Spain was conti-nually foliciting the Pope to excommunicate that prin-cefs, for which purpofe, his holinefs appointed a fort of a committee of four Cardinals and three bifhops, who were to meet in his apartment, three times a week, to confider of the ftate of affairs in England ; and having a great opinion of Montalto's abilities, was defirous he fhould affift at thofe deliberations, which was another reafon of his raifing him to the epifcopal dignity.

When the King of Spain, who was thoroughly em-bittered againft Queen Elizabeth, was informed of this committee, he wrote to congratulate Montalto upon his promotion, and defire he would make ufe of his favour with the Pope to get her fpeedily excommunicated, and to ftir up the other princes of Europe againft her. His holinefs, who did not want much inftigation, or-dered Montalto to draw up a fketch of a Bull for that purpofe, which he did firft in Italian, and then in La-tin, and brought it with him to the next meeting of the committee, where it was fo well approved of, that they refolved to make ufe of it without any alteration. It was as follows [1] :

[1] It is in Leti, as it was originally wrote in Italian, by Mon-talto ; but I fhall give the reader his Latin tranflation of it, as I found it in Speed, which, confefs, is not fo elegant as one would expect, from the applaufe it is faid to have met with, from a Pope, four Cardinals, and three Bifhops.

PII Papæ Pontificis Maximi sententia declaratoria, contra Elizabetham, prætensam Angliæ Reginam, et ei adhærentes Hæreticos. Qua etiam declarantur adsoluti omnes Subditi a juramento Fidelitatis et quocunque alio debito, et deinceps obedientes anathemate illaqueantur.

" PIUS Episcopus, servus servorum Dei, ad futu-
" ram rei memoriam.
    " Regnans in excelsis, cui data est omnis in cœlo et
" in terra potestas, unam sanctam Catholicam et Apo-
" stolicam Ecclesiam, extra quam nulla est salus, uni
" soli in terris, videlicet Apostolorum Principi Petro,
" Petrique successori, Romano Pontifici, in potestatis
" plenitudine, tradidit gubernandam. Hunc unum,
" super omnes gentes, et omnia regna principem con-
" stituit, qui evellat, destruat, dissipet, disperdat, plan-
" tet, et ædificet, ut fidelem populum mutuæ charita-
" tis nexu constrictum, in unitate Spiritus contineat,
" salvumque et incolumem suo exhibeat Salvatori.
" Quo quidem in munere obeundo, nos, ad prædictæ
" ecclesiæ gubernacula Dei benignitate vocati, nullum
" laborem intermittimus, omni opera contendentes,
" ut ipsa unitas et Catholica religio (quam illius auctor,
" ad probandam suorum fidem, et correctionem nos-
" tram, tantis procellis conflictari permisit) integra
" conservetur. Sed impiorum numerus tantum poten-
" tia invaluit, ut nullus jam in orbe locus sit relictus,
" quem illi pessima doctrina corrumpere non tenta-
" verit : adnitente inter cæteros, flagitiorum serva,
" prætensa Angliæ Regina, ad quam, veluti ad asy-
" lum omnium infestissimi profugerunt. Hæc eadem,
" regno occupato, supremi ecclesiæ capitis locum in
" omni Anglia, ejusque præcipuam auctoritatem at-
" que jurisdictionem, monstruose sibi usurpans, reg-
" num ipsum, jam tunc ad fidem Catholicam, et bo-
" nam frugem reductum, rursus in miserum exitium
" revocavit : usu namque veræ religionis, quam ab il-
" lius desertore, Henrico octavo, olim eversam claræ
" memoriæ Maria regina legitima hujus sedis præ-
                                                " -sidio

" fidio reparaverat, potenti manu inhibito, fecutifque
" et amplexis Hæreticorum erroribus, regium concili-
" um, ex Anglica nobilitate confectum, diremit, il-
" ludque obfcuris hominibus hæreticis, complevit,
" Catholicæ fidei cultores oppreffit, improbos concio-
" natores, atque impietatum miniftros repofuit, Mif-
" fæque facrificium, preces, jejunia, ciborum delectus,
" cœlibatum, ritufque Catholicos abolevit.

" Libros, manifeftam hærefin continentes, toto reg-
" no proponi, impia myfteria, et inftituta ad Calvini
" præfcriptum, a fe fufcepta et obfervata, a fubditis
" fervari mandavit.

" Epifcopos ecclefiarum, rectores, et alios facerdotes
" Catholicos, fuis ecclefiis et beneficiis ejicere, ac de
" illis et aliis rebus ecclefiafticis in hæreticos homines
" difponere, deque ecclefiæ caufis, decernere aufa,
" Prælatis, Clero, et Populo, ne Romanam ecclefiam
" agnofcerent, neve ejus præceptis, fanctionibufque
" canonicis obtemperarent, interdixit ; plerofque in
" nefarias fuas leges venire, et Romani Pontificis auc-
" toritatem atque obedientiam abjurare, feque folam
" in temporalibus et fpiritualibus dominam agnofcere,
" jurejurando coegit ; pœnas et fupplicia in eos qui
" dicto non effent audientes, imponens, eafdem ab iis,
" qui in unitate fidei et predicta obedientia perfevera-
" verunt, exegit ; Catholicos antiftites, et ecclefiarum
" rectores in vincula conjecit, ubi multi diuturno lan-
" guore et triftitia confecti extremum vitæ diem mife-
" re finierunt. Quæ omnia cum apud omnes nationes
" perfpicua et notoria fint, et graviffimo complurimo-
" rum teftimonio ita comprobata, ut nullus omnino
" locus excufationis, defenfionis, aut tergiverfationis,
" relinquatur, Nos (multiplicantibus aliis atque aliis
" fuper alias impietatibus et facinoribus, et præterea
" fidelium perfecutione, religionifque afflictione, im-
" pulfu et opera dictæ Elizabethæ, quotidie magis in-
" gravefcente) quoniam illius animum ita obfirmatum
" atque induratum intelligimus, ut non modo pias Ca-
" tholicorum principum de lenitate et converfione

K   preces

" preces monitionesque contempserit, sed ne hujus
" quidem sedis ad ipsam hac de causa Nuncios in An-
" gliam trajicere permiserit ; ad arma justitiæ contra
" eam denecessitate conversi, dolorem lenire non pos-
" sumus, quod adducamur in unam animadvertere,
" cujus majores de republica Christiana tantopere me-
" ruère.

" Illius itaque auctoritate suffulti, qui nos in hoc su-
" premæ justitiæ throno, licet tanto oneri impares, vo-
" luit collacare, de apostolicæ potestatis plenitudine,
" declaramus prædictam Elizabethem Hæreticam, et
" Hæreticorum fautricem, eique adhærentes in præ-
" dictis, anathematis sententiam incurrisse, et a Christi
" corporis unitate excisos ; quinetiam ipsam prætenso
" regni prædicti jure, necnon omni et quocunque do-
" minio, dignitate, privilegioque privatam ; item pro-
" ceres, subditos. populos dicti regni, ac cæteros om-
" nes, qui illi quomodocunque juraverunt, a juramenti
" hujusmodi, ac omni prorsus dominii, fidelitatis, et
" obsequii debito, perpetuo absolutos ; prout nos illos
" præsentium authoritate absolvimus, et privamus ean-
" dem Elizabetham, prætenso jure regni, aliisque om-
" nibus supradictis ; præcipimusque et interdicimus
" universis et singulis proceribus, subditis, populis, et
" aliis prædictis, ne illi ejusve monitis, mandatis, et
" legibus audeant obedire. Qui secus egerint, eos si-
" mili anathematis sententia innodamus. Quia vero
" difficile nimis esset, præsentes quocunque illis opus
" erit perferre, volumus ut eorum exempla, Notarii
" Publici manu, et Prælati ecclesiastici, ejusve curiæ
" sigillo obsignata, eandem illis prorsus fidem, in judi-
" cio et extra illud, ubique gentium faciant, quam
" ipsæ præsentes facerent, si essent exhibitæ vel osten-
" sæ. Datum Romæ apud S. Petrum, sub annulo
" Piscatoris, anno incarnationis Domini 1569. quinto
" Calend. Mar. Pontificatus nostri anno quinto.

When it was read, his Holiness, though very learned
in things of that kind, was so pleased with the style
and form of it, that he let drop some expressions, from
which it was conjectured, that it would not be long
before he made him a Cardinal. Hi

His affection for him seem'd to redouble, after he came to be Prelate, for he changed the design he had of employing him as a Nuncio, and ordered him to reside at Rome, where he entrusted the most honourable and important commiffions to his care. When he went to ask his bleffing, and leave to go and take poffeffion of his bifhoprick, the Pope told him, "It was neceffary " he fhould ftay where he was, that he fulfilled his du- " ty by doing fervice to the Church there, and would " find his account in it." From thefe words Montalto flattered himfelf, that he was one of thofe that the Pope defigned to raife to the Purple in a fhort time.

This promotion had been long expected, and, five or fix days before it happened, his Holinefs declared, "That " he intended one of the vacant hats for Montalto," thinking it an honour due to his merit; and that he fhould likewife thereby add a member to the College, that would always gratefully acknowledge the obliga- tion by his attachment to the interefts of his nephew.

He gave Alexandrino leave to hint this to him, but not to explain himfelf fully upon it, which he did by faying, the firft time he met him, "My dear Montalto, " both his Holinefs and I are defirous of doing you " fome material fervice, and I hope, in a few days, " you and I fhall embrace each other like brothers."

There had already been two promotions, and feveral confiderable wagers laid, that Montalto would be made Cardinal in the fecond; when it came to be known that he was not, it occafioned much furprize amongft the people, and gave him an opportunity of faying one day to his friend Alexandrino, "That the public, however, " had been fo kind to make him one;" to which the Cardinal anfwered, "You are really fo in the Pope's " intention, and have much more reafon to be pleafed " with that than the idle fpeculations of the town."

His Holinefs, this year, beftowed the title of Grand Duke of Tufcany upon Cofmo di Medicis [February, 1570] Duke of Florence, upon the account of his un- common merit and the great fervices he had done the

K 2 Church.

Church. He was crowned by the Pope himself [2], with the utmost splendour and magnificence. As the festival lasted several days, the populace were entertained with all manner of diversions and spectacles, such as plays, horse-races, tournaments, and triumphal arches, erected in honour of that Prince. Montalto was pitched upon to assist Alexandrino, who officiated in this ceremony, and conducted the Grand Duke back in one of the Pope's chariots.

The April following, his Holiness received an account of the great progress Christianity had made in the Indies, many Kings and their kingdoms being converted to the true faith. Upon this, there were solemn processions and thankfgivings; and, as an addition to the common joy, the Pope determined to make another promotion. He communicated this design to the sacred College in a full confiftory, and said, " It was " neceffary to augment the number of Cardinals in " proportion to the increafe of the Chriftian religion " in the world."

Montalto was one of thofe that were honoured with a hat in this promotion, which was upon the 17th of May. His brethren rejoiced heartily at it, not fo much upon his own account, perhaps, as the honour that accrued to the Order of St. Francis.

Many were the motives that induced the Pope to call Montalto into the facred College. The firft was, the great friendfhip and affection he always had for him, having faid feveral times, fince his exaltation, " That he found a ftrange propenfity in himfelf to do " Montalto good." He one day, before he was Pope, argued fo ftrenuoufly in his favour, when his conduct was called in queftion; that Borromeo faid, " I think " your Eminence could not be much warmer, if the " character of any of your near relations lay at ftake." " I own," anfwered he, " it gives me a very fenfible " pleafure, when I meet with an opportunity of fhew- " ing the great friendfhip I have for him."

His

[2] He put a Ducal crown upon his head, with this infcription on it: Pius Quintus Pont. Max. ob eximiam dilectionem, ac Catholicæ Religionis zelum, præcipuumque juftitiæ ftudium, donavit.

His fecond reafon, for making him a Cardinal, was, the regard he conftantly had for virtue and extraordinary merit in any perfon whatfoever, which he always honoured and rewarded when it was in his power. Indeed, he alledged this as a reafon in the confiftory, when fpeaking of Montalto, he faid, "He was going "to beftow a Hat upon a fubject of known worth, "whofe learning and experience would be of great "fervice to the Church."

In the third place, he thought it a refpect due to the memory of his deceafed friend Cardinal Carpi, who had often faid, in his hearing, "That he only wifhed "to be Pope, that he might make Montalto a Cardinal, "for he declared to his fecretary Rufticucci di Fano, "That he had received fo many favours from Cardinal "Carpi, whilft he was yet but in a very private ftati- "on, that he thought himfelf bound, in gratitude, to "honour his neareft friend with the purple."

The devotion he had for the habit of St. Francis, was another reafon of Montalto's elevation. His Holinefs had a mind, in his perfon, to fhew the great refpect he had for fo worthy and celebrated an order. On the day of the promotion, he faid to one of his domeftics, "As St. Dominick and St. Francis always lived "together in perfect friendfhip, I have given Hats to "the two Generals of their orders, to engage all thofe "who wear their habits, by this example, to live to- "gether in the fame harmony."

He likewife faid to the Procurator of the Cordeliers, and the Warden of the holy Apoftles, who came to kifs his feet, and to return him thanks for the honour he had done their order, "That the leaft thing he could do, to fhew the true veneration he had for St. Francis, was to make one of his fons a Cardinal."

The Pope feeing the new Cardinal was not rich enough to fupport his dignity in a proper manner, affigned him a penfion, and gave him a fum of ready money to buy houfhold furniture and an equipage. His friend Alexandrino, likewife, behaved very generoufly to him upon this occafion; the convent of the holy

holy Apostles, many of the Roman nobility, and several rich cardinals, made him handsome presents.

Not long after, his Holiness, animated with zeal and concern for the welfare of Christendom, sent his nephew Alexandrino Legate into France, Spain, and Portugal, to engage those crowns in a league against the common enemy. As soon as he was departed, the Pope charged Montalto with the care of some affairs that belonged to his nephew, with orders, to examine and correct the prayers contained in the breviary for saints days, &c. establishing a congregation of divines for that purpose. He took the opportunity of Alexandrino's absence, to insinuate himself still further into the Pope's favour: and, as he saw him resolutely bent to extend the ecclesiastical privileges and immunities, neglected nothing, that he thought might any way contribute to that end. Measures had already been taken to erect a tribunal in Spain, that should be entirely dependant upon the Pope, and several bulls published, empowering his officers to confiscate the goods of the laiety there, for any crime that fell under the cognizance of the Inquisition, and to cite the Bishops to Rome, without either acquainting the King, or asking his leave; who now at last perceiving that his zeal for the holy see, was likely to be of great prejudice to the liberty of his subjects, and the rights of his crown, began seriously to think of a remedy before the evil grew inveterate.

The Pope's reason for endeavouring to introduce the Inquisition into Spain before any other kingdom, was, that he thought a King, so zealous for religion and the holy see, would not make any opposition to it, and, that of consequence, all the other states of Europe, following the example of so potent a monarch, would admit it without any scruple or objection. Indeed King Philip, tho' in other respects a very wise prince, was so blinded with bigotry and superstition, that he was not aware that, by this step, the court of Rome had established a sovereignty in his dominions, independent on his own; till some of his ministers, who had a greater regard for the liberty of their country,

try, than the interefts of his Holinefs, acquainted his Majefty with the dangerous tendency of this new tribunal ; to prevent which he fent the Commendator, or Lord Lieutenant of Caftile, ambaffador extraordinary to Rome.

As Montalto had been acquainted with the Commendator in Spain, he was ordered, by his Holinefs, to confer with him upon the fubject of his embaffy ; which he did, and behaved with fo much addrefs in the courfe of this negociation, that the ambaffador left Rome, very well contented with the Agnus Dei's, and other reliques and trumpery of that kind, which Pius had beftowed upon him in great abundance, without gaining the leaft point in favour of his mafter, having, on the contrary, made feveral conceffions to his prejudice, and the great advantage of the holy fee ; with which the Pope was fo pleafed, that he embraced Montalto, in the prefence of feveral Cardinals, and faid, " That exclufive of his other deferts, which were " very great, the merit of this fervice alone gave him " a fufficient right to expect that his brethren would " exalt him to the chair of St. Peter, whenever it " became vacant."

He, not long after, did the Church another piece of fervice, greater, as the Pope himfelf acknowledged, than that which we have juft now related, in advifing the publication of the bull in Cœna Domini (fo called from being publifhed on Holy Thurfday) which he drew up and prefented to the Pope ; and though it was oppofed, by many in the confiftory, he argued fo ftrenuoufly in its defence, that it was approved of by his Holinefs, and publifhed with the ufual folemnities. In this Bull, all ftates and princes are forbid, on pain of excommunication, to lay any tax, gabel, or impoft of any kind whatfoever, upon the ecclefiaftics in their dominions, or to punifh, or even take cognizance of their offences.

Several ambaffadors remonftrated loudly againft it ; but the example of King Philip, who accepted and caufed it to be read in Spain, at laft induced all the
other

other Roman Catholic powers to do the fame, except the French and Venetians, who could not be prevailed upon, by any means, to receive it.

A league againſt the Turk being entered into, by the moſt conſiderable of the Chriſtian princes, Alexandrino returned home with great reputation, and Montalto reſigned into his hands the care of thoſe things that had been committed to his charge during his abſence, and was deſirous of retiring from affairs a while, to repoſe himſelf, and take a little breath ; but they would not let him enjoy this leiſure, continually calling him to ſome congregation, or other buſineſs.

Being now in poſſeſſion of the purple, he began to entertain ſtill more ambitious deſigns, and aſpire to the papacy. With this view, he became humble, patient, and affable, ſo artfully concealing the natural impetuoſity of his temper, that one would have ſworn this gentleneſs and moderation were born with him. There was ſuch a change in his dreſs, his air, his words, and all his actions, that his neareſt friends and acquaintance ſaid, " He was not the ſame man." A greater alteration, or a more abſolute victory over his paſſions, was never ſeen in any one, nor is there an inſtance, perhaps in the whole current of hiſtory, of a perſon ſupporting a fictitious character in ſo uniform and conſiſtent a manner, or ſo artfully diſguiſing his foibles and imperfections, for ſuch a number of years. Yet there were ſome, who, notwithſtanding his utmoſt care and diſſimulation, ſuſpected (which they afterwards found to be true) that he, all that time, had his eye upon the Triple Crown.

His confeſſor told him one day, after he came to be Pope, " That the whole court was aſtoniſhed, at his " having been guilty of ſo much hypocriſy whilſt he " was Cardinal ;" to which he anſwered, " That his " conſcience did not at all reproach him upon that ac- " count ; as what he did, was by the inſpiration of the " Almighty, who knew his virtues, and how proper an " inſtrument he was to ſave his Church, and reſtore " the declining glory and ſplendor of the holy ſee."

Before

Before he was Cardinal, he had always shewn great tenderness to his relations; but when he was invested with that dignity, he began to behave to them in a quite different manner, knowing that difinterestedness in that point, was one of the keys to the papacy; so that when his brother Anthony came to see him at Rome, he lodged him at an inn, and sent him back again the next day, with only a present of 60 crowns, strictly charging him to return immediately to the care of his family, and tell them, " That his spiritual cares " increased upon him, and he is now dead to his re- " lations and the world; but as he found old age and " infirmities began to approach, he might, perhaps, in " a while send for one of his nephews to wait upon " him."

His sister Camilla, thinking it a good opportunity, sent the following letter by Anthony; the stile and matter of which the reader will not think strange, when he considers that it came from a poor ignorant peasant.

LORD CARDINAL, MY DEAR BROTHER,

" THE sacristan of our church, who is a very ho-
" nest man, and one that I can trust with any
" thing, writes this letter for me. If all your relations
" and friends were glad to hear of your first being made
" General and then Bishop, you may be sure they
" were overjoyed at the news of your being Cardinal,
" for which I humbly thank God with all my heart,
" and don't doubt but the other Lord Cardinals will in
" time make you Pope. My son, who is now twelve
" years old, is grown a great boy, and is shortly to be
" apprentice to his father, but we make him learn to
" read and write. Anthony's son goes to school, and
" is fond of learning, as you used to be; it would do
" you good to hear him talk of you; poor child, he
" often says, If his uncle should ever come to be Pope,
" he shall be a Lord Cardinal, which makes him mind
" his book, and behave like a good boy. If you will
" give us leave to come to Rome, we will set out im-
" mediately

" mediately ; my hufband fhall do what he can for
" you in his bufinefs, and I will wafh and take care
" of your linen.　My daughter is about fourteen ; it
" is in your power, I fuppofe, to put her a fervant
" into fome nunnery, or get her a marriage portion
" out of the money that is given away every year to
" poor maids [3].　All our neighbours fay, you may
" now do us a great deal of good. if you pleafe, as we
" dare fay you will ; my hufband would have come
" to Rome with brother Anthony, but I would not
" let him, as I expect you will foon fend for us, and
" then I will come with them.　If you keep Anthony
" with you, let us know by a letter, whether you
" would have us bring the whole family with us ; and
" if fo, I hope, dear brother, you will fend us fome
" money, that we may come on horfe-back. We long
" to hear from you, and not only I, but my hufband
" and children die with impatience to embrace you.
" I can't tell whether you love me as you ufed to do,
" but this I know, that there is no alteration in the
" affection of,

　　　　" Lord Cardinal, my dear Brother,

　　　　　　" Your dutiful and loving Sifter,

　　　　　　　　" CAMILLA PERETTI."

HIS ANSWER.

Sifter CAMILLA,

" I HAD an account of our family by brother An-
" thony, who, at the fame time, delivered your let-
" ter to me.　If it was in my power, and I had no
" other cares of infinitely more confequence to attend
" to, than that of enriching my relations, I would en-
" deavour to make at leaft a competent provifion for
" them. But as God has been pleafed to call me to his
" fervice alone, I fhall ufe my utmoft efforts to diveft
" myfelf of all partiality to my kindred, and every
" other wordly affection.

[3] Moft of the religious houfes in Rome give large fums every
year for this laudable purpofe.

　　　　　　　　　　　　　　" The

" The fight of Anthony, was a fatisfaction to me,
" but I fhould have been much better pleafed, if he
" had ftaid at Le Grotte, whither I have ordered him
" to return. His Holinefs did not honour me with
" the purple only that I might have an opportunity
" of agrandizing my relations, but to attach me
" wholly to his fervice, and that of the church. Though
" I am now a Cardinal, I fhall lead a monaftic life,
" altogether retired from the noife and tumult of fe-
" cular affairs. I told Anthony, he did well in fend-
" ing his fon to fchool, and approve of your doing the
" fame ; if it is poffible, I will procure them fome-
" thing out of the charitable collections that are made
" here, and remit it to your curate for their ufe. At
" prefent I fend you 60 crowns by Anthony, to whom
" I have given the like fum. As for your daughter,
" I will endeavour to get her fome part of the alms
" that is given to difpofe of poor maids in marriage ;
" and, if any other opportunity offers of doing them
" a fervice, I will not neglect it : but don't fail to
" keeping them at fchool. I can't help pitying your
" fimplicity in defiring to come to Rome. You feem
" to forget who you are, at leaft not to know that you
" are not a proper perfon to be feen there, efpecially
" under my roof, as ecclefiaftics are not allowed to
" entertain any woman in their houfes. Let me ad-
" vife you to be content with your condition, and be-
" lieve me when I tell you, that a fmall pittance, ac-
" quired by honeft labour and induftry, is infinitely
" preferable to all the fears and cares that are the con-
" ftant attendants of riches. In fhort, this is all you
" muft ever expect from me, except my prayers to
" God for your health and welfare. You may affure
" yourfelf my tendernefs for you is not in the leaft di-
" minifhed, and that I fhall never be afhamed of cal-
" ling myfelf.

" Your affectionate Brother,

" Cardinal MONTALTO."

A₃

As he was known to be the author and adviser of the bull in Cœna Domini, and, for that reason, looked upon with an evil eye by most of the ambassadors, he went to visit them separately in a very humble manner; and gave so good an account of his behaviour, and such strong reasons for acting as he did in that affair, that he entirely wiped of the bad opinion they had conceived of him. He took great care, however, from that time, not to do any thing that might draw upon him the ill will and resentment of either princes or their ambassadors. The papacy being now the object of his wishes and designs, he laid down certain maxims, which (if he was not the author of them) he observed with so undeviating a perseverance, that he far exceeded every one that had gone before him in that respect, and at last, by their assistance, opened to himself the gates of the Vatican.

Soon after his exaltation to the purple, he received a congratulatory letter from his old friend Bossius, who, after the death of Cardinal Carpi, left Rome, and led a very retired life in the country; where he died in a short time after, to the inexpressible concern of Montalto, who had so great an affection for him (and indeed with very good reason) that, if he had lived till Montalto was Pope, he would certainly have made him a Cardinal.

Much about the same time, the Doge of Venice died, and was succeeded by Mocenigo, who was one of the Senators that Montalto had been recommended to when he went Inquisitor to that city, and had done him many important services, constantly supporting and siding with him in the squabbles that he had with the Conventuals there; but when he began to enter into disputes with the Senate, he turned his back upon him, and became as much his enemy as ever he had been his friend. The hurry and commotion that was occasioned by this election prevented the Venetians from sending their compliments to the new created Cardinals so early as they used to do; upon which Montalto, who now resolved to carry his cup even

with

with the Republic, where he was senfible he had many
enemies, thought it would be the beft way to be beforehand with them in his civilities, as it would fhew
he had quite forgot the quarrels that had happened
when he was amongft them; and ferve to obliterate
the bad opinion they formerly entertained of him ; for
which purpofe, he wrote to congratulate the Doge
upon his election, and the league which the Republic
had lately entered into with other Chriftian powers
againft the Turk.

The Doge, who was extremely pleafed with this
piece of complaifance, ordered public rejoicings and
bonfires to be made over-againft the convent of the
Francifcans, in Venice; the Te Deum to be fung at
St. Mark's, at which the whole Senate was prefent,
and an anfwer to be delivered to him, by their ambaffador at Rome, who was alfo to make him an offer of
his freedom at Venice, which would entitle him to
hold any abbey, bifhopric, or other ecclefiaftical preferment in that ftate: But as this would, in fome
meafure, make him dependent upon the Republic,
and oblige him, upon particular occafions, to vote
with the cardinals that efpoufed their interefts, he civilly declined it, defiring the ambaffador to return his
thanks to the Senate, and let them know how fenfible
he was of the great honour they had done him ; For
it was one of his maxims not to attach himfelf to the
fervice of any one particular power, but to obferve a
perfect neutrality and indifference to all, left he fhould
create himfelf many enemies, whilft he endeavoured to
gain one friend.

He retained, however, a grateful impreffion of this
favour ever after, both whilft he was Cardinal, and
when he came to be Pope.

The Senate of Genoa fent, likewife, to felicitate him
upon this occafion ; and the grand duke of Tufcany,
who had always expreffed a particular regard for Montalto, and entertained him like a prince when he vifited
that province as General, ordered his ambaffador to wait

upon him, not only with his compliments, but a present of 500 crowns, and several fine pieces of plate.

Amongst many others, of all ranks and degrees, that sent their congratulations, we must not forget father Sarnano, who was almost the only Monk that had constantly stuck close to him in all his troubles and persecutions from the conventuals, sometimes to the imminent hazard of his own person and interest.

The affairs of this world seem to be ruled by a sort of fatality or predestination. When Providence designs to exalt a person to any eminent degree of honour, it not only inspires him with courage and resolution. but suggests a proper conduct and means to attain that end ; as may be seen in several occurrences of Montaito's life, and in this of Sarnano's. For what other reason can be assigned why he would never forsake Montalto, though he was not only tempted, by great rewards and promises, but even threatened with the General's displeasure and resentment, if he did not ; at a time too when there was not the least prospect of his ever arriving at the Papacy ? Without doubt Divine Providence designed to make Sarnano a Cardinal by these means, and for that purpose indued him with an invincible firmness and constancy in his friendship, and impelled him to seek the favour and esteem of Montalto by all other methods.

Pius V. died the March following [1572], and the church lost in him one of the best and most zealous Pontifs that ever governed it. The order of St. Dominick, that has been so remarkably serviceable to Christianity, by propagating the faith in the most distant religons, by the conversion of so many thousand heathens, by the blood of its martyrs, by its confessors and preachers, by its unlimited charity to the sick and distressed, never yet merited so much of the Christian church as in giving it this Pope.

When the Cardinals had performed their last duty to this holy man after the usual manner, they entered the Conclave. Montalto, who was one of the number, did not seem to give himself the least trouble or concern
about

about the election, and lived altogether in his apartment, like a monk in his cell, without ever stirring out, except to his devotions. He affected privacy and a total ignorance of all the cabals and intrigues of the several factions. When any Cardinal asked him to enter into his party, he answered with the greatest appearance of simplicity and indifference, " That for his " part, he was of no manner of consequence; that as he " had never been in the Conclave before, he was afraid " of making some false step, and should, therefore, leave " the affair to be conducted wholly by people of great- " er knowledge and experience." By these means he avoided engaging himself to any party.

A behaviour so contrary to what it was before he put on the purple, gave reason for suspicion to some quick-sighted people ; and Cardinal Gambara, who wanted to draw him into his interest, seeing he could not prevail upon him, and that he was determined to have no concern with any side or faction, said to him with some sharpness, " I would advise you to let this " method of proceeding alone till another time, for " you have no chance at present."

It was matter of surprize to most people, that a man who had spirit and resolution enough to oppose the whole Senate of Venice, at the peril of his life, and had so many broils and fierce contentions with his superiors about trifles, should become, on a sudden, so calm and temperate, as to sit altogether inactive and supine in so important a concern as the election of a Pope. But he did not much trouble himself about what the public thought, and left them to give their opinions of his conduct as they pleased. When any one asked him, who he thought was the fittest person to be Pope? He said, " They were all so worthy men, and so thorough- " ly well qualified to govern the Church, that, upon " his conscience, he could not tell, but wished he had " as many voices as there were Cardinals, that he " might vote for every one of them."

As he was canting one day in this strain to Cardinal Farnese,, the Cardinal said smartly to him, " Other
" people

" people may fwallow this, Sir, but it won't go down
" with me."

It was very remarkable in this Conclave, that the
election of Cardinal Buon Compagnon was begun and
finifhed in five hours time, without any oppofition, or
the tedious formality of examinations and fcrutinies [4]
which are generally enter'd into by the heads of oppofite parties. It happened the 13th of May, 1572.
Montalto had heard nothing of the matter, till they
were conducting him to the chapel to be adored;
when Cardinal Alexandrino, knocking at the door of
his apartment as they went by, faid, " Come along
" with us, we have chofen a Pope," upon which he
followed them to the chapel where the adoration was
performed; and Buon Compagnon took the name of
Gregory XIII; the college of Cardinals walking before
him in proceffion from the Conclave.

Montalto expreffed a great deal of joy. and told his
Holinefs, when he had an opportunity, in private,
" That he had never wifhed for any thing fo much in
" his life, and that he fhould always remember his
" goodnefs and the favours he had received from him
" in Spain."

The Pope feemed to believe what he faid, but did
not fhew him any particular regard, or employ him in
any fort of bufinefs during his pontificate, leaving him
to enjoy his privacy and retirement. He neverthelefs,
took all opportunities of making his court to the Pope's
family, efpecially Cardinal Buon Compagnon his nephew; and as he had now little elfe to do, betook
himfelf again to his ftudies; and finifhed his commentary upon St. Ambrofe, which he publifhed and dedicated to his Holinefs, who received it very civilly,
without, however, fhewing him any extraordinary
mark of favour or refpect: on the contrary, he treated him, all the while he was Pope, with a coolnefs that
approached very near to contempt.

Some were of opinion, that his clofe attachment to,

[4] The words fcrutiny, and adoration, fhall be explained, when
we come to Montalto's election.

and

and the uncommon favours he had received from the late Pope, who was no favourite with Gregory were the occasion of this neglect.   Besides, he still looked upon him as a rigid and severe man, though he had of late put on that appearance of candour and simplicity. Others imagined, that his Holiness, who had discovered in the course of his acquaintance with him in Spain, that he was of a bold and enterprizing spirit, would not trust him with any share in the management of affairs for that reason.   This coolness of the Pope confirmed Montalto in his resolution (as he said) not to trouble himself any more with the concerns of this world ; and he immediately bought a small house, near St. Maria Maggiore, where he lived a very private and retired life, with few domestics, seldom stirring out, except upon the most pressing occasions.   To amuse himself, he was constantly making some little addition to it ; and when he came afterwards to be Pope, raised it into a magnificent palace, with noble gardens, fountains, statues, groves, walks, &c. and called it the [1] Palace of Peretti.

The Pope having opened the Jubilee in the year 1575, Montalto spent in works of piety full as much as his small income would bear ; he was very charitable to pilgrims and strangers that had no where to lodge; but especially to the sick, and those of his order that came for indulgences, whom he took to his own house, and entertained at his table twice a day.   He used to pass most of his time in the confessional chairs, as if he was nothing more than a common Priest, which got him a wonderful reputation amongst the people. It is certain, no other Cardinal exerted himself with so much zeal and piety, as he did upon this occasion.

The year after this [1576], the plague being in Italy, a Congregation was appointed to concert proper measures for preventing the infection from being brought to Rome, and somebody proposing Montalto as a very fit person to assist at it ; the Pope objected to him, as an indolent, dreaming fellow, when there was the greatest necessity for vigilance and activity.

L   About

[1] La Vigna di Peretti.

About the same time, the affairs of Poland being in extreme confusion, by the retreat of Henry III, who had abandoned that kingdom, to go and take possession of the crown of France, left him by his brother Charles IX, at his death; a consistory was called to deliberate upon what was necessary to be done to maintain the peace and tranquillity of that nation, and somebody observing that Montalto was not present, his Holiness said, "It did not much signify, for he was " of very little consequence wherever he was."

At the beginning of his Pontificate, Gregory diminished the pensions, which Pius V. had given to those Cardinals that had but a small revenue, either with a design to apply this money to the wants of the church, which he thought ought to be first considered, or to destroy what his predecessor had done; whatever might be the motive, Montalto was entirely deprived of his in the year 1557. Cardinal Alexandrino solicited the Pope to restore it; but he answered coolly, " If you will do any thing for him yourself, I will " give you my benediction for it."

Montalto did not express any sort of chagrin or resentment at this usage : on the contrary, happening to meet Philip Buon Compagnon, the Pope's nephew, who was made Cardinal with the title of St. Sixtus, he adroitly turned the conversation upon that subject, and said, " He would strip himself to his very shirt, to " second the zeal which the Pope so worthily mani- " fested for the good of Christendom; that he never " found himself so rich, as since he had no pension; " that he was sorry he had not resigned it voluntarily, " and thought he could not do better, than leave the " entire disposal of what he had to so pious and cha- " ritable a Pastor."

France and the Low Countries were in a deplorable condition at this time, by the great advantages which the Protestants had gained over the armies of France and Spain. This sect, for want of timely opposition, had established their new doctrine upon the ruins of the Romish Church; and the Pope, deeply afflicted at

fo

so dangerous a progress, ordered public prayers and supplications to be made ; and held several consistories to consider of a remedy for an evil that threatened the peace of all Christendom ; upon which Montalto said one day, " That, in so desperate a disease, there " was more occasion for something else, than Masses " and Consistories." This being carried to the Pope, he sent for Montalto to know what he meant by it ; but, after a long conference with him, he told his nephew St. Sixtus, " He could make nothing of him, " and that he was never the wiser.

Towards the end of this year, his brother Anthony died of grief, (occasioned, as it was said, by the disappointment and cool reception he met with at Rome from the Cardinal) at the age of 53, leaving behind him two sons and a daughter. Though he was much afflicted at this event, he endeavoured to conceal his sorrow ; and when the warden of the Holy Apostles, who had been one of his pupils and followers, came to let him know, they designed to make a magnificent funeral for his brother in their convent, he desired him to thank them for this demonstration of their respect, but said, " He could not help being surprized at their " intention, as he entirely renounced all ties of blood, " and was now dead to his relations, and they to him ; " that if they would, out of charity, say a private " Mass for the soul of his brother, he should be much " obliged to them ; but as for making a pompous fu- " neral for a poor rustic, he thought it would look " like a banter upon the meanness of his family ;" so that he would not suffer the least ceremony upon this occasion, nor receive any visits of condolence.

The plague still raging with great violence all over Lombardy, notwithstanding the rigour of the season ; the Pope appointed a fresh Congregation of Cardinals, not only to consider of means to keep it out of the ecclesiastical state, but to distribute the alms that had been collected at Rome amongst the poor people ; as this calamity was likewise attended with so severe a famine, that more died by hunger, than the pestilence.

Montalto

Montalto was fummoned to affift at it ; but as he was convinced, by feveral proofs, that the Pope did not much like him, and had neglected to call him to feveral others, when matters of great confequence were to be debated, he went to his Holinefs, and told him, " That his infirmities and bad ftate of health would " not give him leave to attend without manifeft dan- " ger of his life, and therefore hoped he would be fo " kind to excufe him." Upon which being afked by the Pope, " Whether he would not venture his life " for the good of the public ?" he anfwered, " That " he would not only venture, but moft willingly lay " down his life, if it would in any wife contribute to " the propagation of the true religion ; but upon fuch " an occafion as the prefent, he did not think himfelf " obliged to it, as there were fo many other wifer and " more worthy perfons than himfelf, who were able " to go through the fatigue of fuch functions with- " out the leaft peril or hazard."

Cardinal Farnefe, who was prefent, whifpering the Pope in the ear, " That fuch a poor filly old fellow " could be of no fervice to them ;" his Holinefs told him, " He was at liberty to attend, or not attend, juft " as he pleafed."

Alexandrino was piqued to fee a perfon that was fo much beloved, and had been created a Cardinal by his uncle, treated with that contempt, and took all opportunities of fupporting him, and fpeaking in his favour. As the Pope was not willing to difoblige this Cardinal, who had done him fome confiderable fervices, he gave Montalto the bifhoprick of Fermo at his requeft; which he thought would be very agreeable to him, as it was worth 1000 crowns per annum more than that of St. Agatha, and lay in the province where he was born. But Montalto, who was refolved to live in Rome, that he might be ready to take the advantage of any opportunity that favoured his defigns, after he had drawn the Cardinals into his net, feemed very indifferent about it, and did not exprefs fo much fatisfaction as was expected

pected. However, he went to wait upon the Pope to thank him for his great bounty and generosity to him.

Whilst he pretended to be thus ignorant and regardless of what passed in the world, nothing happened (how minute and inconsiderable soever) but he was informed of it. There was a Chaplain that lived with him, whom he had educated with as much care and tenderness, as if he had been his near relation. This man, who was of a cunning, subtile disposition, insinuated himself into different companies, picked up all the news, pryed into every secret, and related the whole to his Patron, who entered it into a little book to be made use of at a proper time.

As he had now acquired the character of great sanctity, and was esteemed a very learned Divine, many people had recourse to him for comfort or advice in their affliction or scruples of conscience, thinking themselves happy, if they could obtain his ear in confession. When he was aware of this, he gave them sufficient opportunities, going sometimes to one Church, and sometimes to another, especially to that of the Holy Apostles, where he sat hearing confessions two hours after morning, and as long after evening service : at which times he would artfully draw out of people, not only their own private sins, but every thing that was done in the houses of their acquaintance, with whatever else they knew of the public concerns.

The young and dissolute, the grave and sedate, the common people and magistrates, all resorted to him ; and as he affected an appearance of great modesty and simplicity, they unbosomed themselves to him without fear or reserve This made him so exact in the administration of justice, when he came to be Pope ; as there was no vice or scandal, or enormity of any kind, either in the Court or City, but he was acquainted with in all its circumstances.

Father Sarnano was likewise of service to him in this respect, and to furnish himself with another spy, that he could depend upon in ordinary occurrences, he sent

for

for Philip, one of his brother Anthony's fons, who was
taken away from fchool at his father's death, and had
no other relation that was either able or willing to give
him any further education.   When he came to Rome,
his Uncle bought him a fuit of coarfe clothes, without
the leaft finery or ornament about them ; fo that Cardinal Alexandrino, coming to vifit Montalto one day,
and feeing a country boy in the houfe, afked who he
was, and being told, he faid, " I fhould not have fuf-
" pected him to have been a Cardinal's nephew ; in-
" deed brother, you ought to cloath him in a better
" manner." But though he was fo carelefs of his drefs,
and in other refpects feemed to take no more notice of
him, than if he had not been his nephew, he fent him
to fchool to Father Migali, a Jefuit, to whom he gave
a ftrict charge not to neglect his education, and feemed
much pleafed when he found he had a genius for letters, often faying to him, " If you will endeavour to
" make yourfelf a fcholar, you may poffibly be the
" fupport of our poor family ; I have done what lies
" in my power, you muft now try what you can do."
But before he had been long under the tuition of Migali, he was unfortunately killed in a quarrel by fome of
his fchool-fellows, being only feventeen years old [5].

His uncle, who loved him tenderly, though he
feemed to have but little regard for him in public,
was fo fhocked at this unforfeen accident, that he had
much ado to difguife his grief ; however, as he found
it abfolutely neceffary, he put on an air of unconcern,
and did not appear to be much affected with it [6].
For when fome of his friends afked him, if he did not
design

[5] This ftory is related, in a manner fomething different by
Thuanus.

[6] The Reader may perhaps be at a lofs to know how this fort
of behaviour could any ways promote Montalto's defign upon the
Papacy ; for which reafon it is neceffary to acquaint him, that moft
of the Popes, after their advancement to that dignity, have brought
a parcel of poor, hungry nephews, and other relations, to Rome ;
and not only given them the beft places and preferments, but fometimes entrufted them with the fole power and management of affairs,
which

defign to apply to the Pope for juftice upon the murderers, he faid, "It would be affronting his Holinefs to
"prefs him to that which he was naturally inclined
"to;" and told another perfon, who came (as he faid)
to comfort him in his affliction, "That he was much
"obliged to him for being more concerned upon that
"occafion, than he was himfelf."

One of the Cardinals feeming furprized that he did
not profecute the authors of his nephew's death, he
faid, "That his affection to his relations ought not to
"make him offend God; that he could not revenge
"the death of his nephew, without wounding his con-
"fcience, and endangering his falvation, which he
"would not do upon any earthly confideration," at
which the Cardinal could hardly forbear fmiling, and
when he went away, faid, "Truly, Sir, you are a
"mighty good Chriftian!" and reporting it to Farnefe, who could not endure him, he faid, "Such is the
"penance that they muft undergo, who afpire to the
"Papacy."

He had two other nephews left, Alexander, the brother of him that was killed, not quite fifteen years old;
and Michael, the fon of Camilla, about the fame age,
whom he afterwards obliged to take the name of Peretti. Of thefe two youths, he began to take particular care, though in fecret, and fent one of them to be
educated at Bologna, the other at Afcoli, procuring
them fome little appointments, through the affiftance
of Sarnano, who often recommended them to Cardinal
Alexandrino, pretending to be furprifed, that Montalto
would take no notice of fo near relations, nor ever fuffer
them to come near him; and when Alexandrino fpoke
to Montalto of it, he faid, "That his age and infirmi-
"ties

which they have generally made ufe of to plunder the Church, often
alienating its dominions and revenues; fo that the Cardinals are
very cautious how they chufe a perfon that has a numerous family,
or is remarkably fond of his relations. This cuftom gave birth to
the word, il nepotifmo, or nephewifm (if I may be indulged the
fame liberty of expreffion that the Italians make ufe of) from
nipote. a nephew.

" ties admonifhed him to think no more of flefh and
" blood, or concern himfelf any longer about the
" things of this world, as his poor foul now demanded
" all his care."

In the year 1579, the Pope eftablifhed feveral hofpitals in Rome and other parts of Chriftendom, for the
reception of ftrangers that were forced out of their own
country by the Proteftants, and endowed them with
confiderable revenues. But this defign was not fpoke
of in the moft favourable manner, as it was thought a
mifapplication of the Church's treafure, and a means
to invite diforderly people to come and fettle there.
Montalto however, out of complaifance to the Pope,
fpoke highly in their praife to every body that came
to fee him.

Alexander Farnefe, Duke of Parma, gained feveral
confiderable advantages over the Proteftants this year,
and took from them many towns ; upon which great
rejoicings were made at Rome. The whole College
waited in form upon Cardinal Farnefe, to congratulate
him upon the fuccefs of his nephew, Montalto was
not one of the laft to pay his court to him ; and to
do it the more effectually, he made a florid fpeech in
the Confiftory, upon the great obligations the Church
lay under to his valour, for fo often and fo generoufly
expofing his life in its fervice ; and from thence took
occafion to make a long panegyric upon the whole
Houfe of the Farnefe.

About this time, the Grand Duke of Mufcovy [7]
fent an Ambaffador to Rome, befeeching his Holinefs,
" To interpofe, as the common Father of all Chrif-
" tians, and endeavour to make peace betwixt him
" and the King of Poland, as his dominions had been
" grievoufly laid wafte in the courfe of a long war by
" that Prince.

The Ambaffador was entertained in a very fplendid
manner at Rome, in the houfe of James Buon Compagnon, General of the Church, and received very
gracioufly by his Holinefs ; when he admitted him to
his

[7] They were not yet called Czars.

his firſt audience, he, for ſome time, refuſed to kiſs
the Pope's feet ; but was given to underſtand, that no
perſon of any quality whatſoever was ſuffered to appear in his preſence, without paying him this reſpect ;
that even the Emperor himſelf ſubmitted to it. As he
ſpoke Latin very fluently, Montalto, who underſtood
that language better than any of the other of the Cardinals, was ordered to explain the nature of that ceremony to him ; which he did with ſo much addreſs, that
he ſoon complied without waiting for an anſwer from
his maſter, to whom he had diſpatched a courier for
inſtructions how to behave in this difficulty.

The people that were in his train had ſome cuſtoms
ſo very odd, that it may not be amiſs, perhaps to mention one or two of them. They always put brandy into their wine, though it was never ſo ſtrong, and when
they were heated almoſt to a fever, plunged themſelves
over head in the coldeſt water they could find.

They went very often to Maſs, but would immediately run out of the Church, if they ſaw a dog there,
as " that holy place, they ſaid, " was not deſigned for
" ſuch filthy animals ;" for which reaſon, orders were
given to take particular care, that none came into the
Churches whilſt they ſtaid at Rome.

The Pope diſmiſſed the Ambaſſador in a very good
humour, wrote to the King of Poland, to deſire he
would liſten to an accommodation ; and ſent father
Poſſevini to his court to perſuade him the more effectually to it, who ſucceeded ſo well in his negotiation,
that peace was reſtored ſoon after betwixt Poland and
Muſcovy.

Before the Ambaſſador left Rome, he went to take
his leave of ſeveral Cardinals, and amongſt the reſt of
Montalto, with whoſe modeſty and frugality he was ſo
taken, that he ſaid to one of his attendants, " Surely
" this man muſt be a baſtard, for it is not poſſible to
" believe or think, conſidering the meanneſs of his houſe
" and furniture, that the other Cardinals ſhould be his
" brethren." The diſproportion that he ſaw betwixt
the pomp and magnificence of their palaces, and the
plainneſs

plainnefs and fimplicity of Montalto's little dwelling, where there was hardly furniture fufficient for a monk's cell, embarraffed him to that degree, that he was a long time before he could be brought to believe that people, amongft whom there was fo wide a difference in the diftribution of church preferments, fhould yet be of the fame rank and denomination.

The confufions that had long difturbed the peace of Malta, being at laft happily extinguifhed by the good offices of the Pope, and the grand mafter, who had been long detained in prifon, came to Rome, attended by an hundred of the principal Knights of his order, where he was received by a train of 8 or 900 horfe, and took up his refidence in the palace of Cardinal D'Efte. Soon after, he was admitted to an audience by the Pope, at which there were prefent twelve Cardinals; one of them was Montalto, near whom he took his place after he had kiffed his holinefs's feet, and was fo charmed with his humility, and the foftnefs of his behaviour, that, during a ftay of two months at Rome, he did not feem to relifh any thing fo much as his converfation. He would not part with him, though he was at laft taken dangeroufly ill; but defired him to ftay with him and prepare him for death, faying very often to his moft familiar friends, who came to vifit him, "That every time he faw Montal- "to, it put him in mind of the holy Bifhops of the " primitive church;" and at his deceafe, which happened foon after, he left him a legacy, as an acknow-ledgement of his friendfhip and fervices.

Montalto had been confidering many years of a proper method to reform the calendar, having formerly propofed it to Pius V. and had fome converfation with Gregory about it, when he was with him in Spain. But either not caring to be at the trouble of it, or making light of the propofal, as it came from Montalto, he put it off from time to time with an excufe, " That it " would not do for any long duration, and that in the " end, it might introduce diforder and confufion into " the eftablifhed rules and cuftoms of the church."

This

This year Antony Lilio, a Phyſician, by Montalto's advice, who had ſeen and approved of it, preſented a ſmall treatiſe to the Pope compoſed by his brother Lewis Lilio, which his holineſs ordered Montalto, who he concluded had put him upon it, to take into examination. This work contained a quite new ſyſtem, in which the epact was accommodated to the golden number, and the calculations ſo exact, that no confuſion or alteration cauld happen in it ever after. Montalto approved of the ſcheme, and preſſed the Pope to put it in execution as ſoon as poſſible. But he thought it proper to have a thing of ſo great conſequence laid before the conſiſtory ; and as Montalto had a conſiderable ſhare in this great undertaking, we ſhall give a more particular account of it.

Gregory, then, having communicated his deſign to the college of Cardinals, ſent copies of Lilio's letters ta all the Princes and Univerſities in Europe, for their opinion of à ſuch a reformation. As ſoon as he had received their anſwer, he ſubmitted it to the judgment of the moſt able mathematicians and aſtronomers of that age, whom he had purpoſely ſent for to Rome. After a thorough examination of the ſcheme in their meetings at Montalto's, who preſided over them, they found Lilio's computation ſo accurate, that they reſolved to make it a ſtanding and perpetual calendar for the future.

It was neceſſary in the firſt place to aſcertain the exact time of the vernal equinox ; ſecondly, to find out the 14th day of that moon, which happens upon, or immediately after it ; and thirdly, to fix Eaſter-day for ever, on the firſt Sunday after that 14th days, as had been done by the ancient fathers, the Popes Pius, Victor, and the firſt general council of Nice.

Now to reduce the vernal equinox to the 21ſt of March (the day it was fixt upon by that council) they ſtruck off, once for all, ten days from the month of October, 1581 : and to prevent any error or alteration for the future it was determined, that every 4th year ſhould be a Biſſextile, or Leap Year, except the year
that

that concluded a century, which always before had
been a Biffextile, and fhould be fo again at the end of
that, viz. the year 1600. But after that, only every
4th centefimal fhould be a Biffextile, e. g. the years
1700, 1800, 1900, fhould be common years, and
the year 2000, a Biffextile.

In this manner, a remedy was provided for the errors and irregularities that had crept into the computation of time, by folar years, and the vernal equinox,
and Eafter-day exactly afcertained.

The ftyle, or calendar, being thus corrected, was
called the Gregorian, out of compliment to the then
reigning Pope ; for the obfervation of which, he publifhed the Bull, Inter graviffimas officii noftri Paftoralis
curas, ea poftrema non eft, &c. ordering that it fhould
take place throughout Chriftendom the next year [8].

The city of Rome was vifited, at this time, by a terrible famine ; and Montalto having neither money nor
provifions, was obliged to have recourfe to Cardinal
Colonna, who generoufly furnifhed him with both; out
of which he again fupplied the wants of the poor people in his neighbourhood, who were grievoufly diftreffed. But it continuing a long time, and to fuch a
degree, that at laft a man could but barely fupport
himfelf with bread, for a crown a day ; he was fo reduced himfelf, that he was obliged to the charity of
others. He got fo great a character amongft the poor,
by his behaviour in this calamitous feafon, that they
faid publickly in the ftreets, " That Cardinal Montal-
" to, who lived upon charity himfelf, gave them with
" one hand, what he received with the other ; whilft
" the reft of the Cardinals, who wallowed in abun-
" dance, contented themfelves with fhewing them the
" way to the hofpital."

The rapacity and avarice of the Pope's relations increafed

[8] The French edition fays, not till the year 1585, which I
fancy is an error. " Mais comme cette reformation, ne fe pouvoit
" faire meme temps par toute la Chretienté, afin de prevenir le
" defordre, que ce retardement pourroit caufer ; on fit un inftruc-
" tion pour l'etablir dans l'annee 1585, et les fuivantes.

creafed this dearth : for as they knew the harveft had failed, and there was but little corn in the country about Rome, they not only fent all that was in the public magazines to be fold there, at four times the price they could get for it in Rome, but bought up all that was in private hands, forbidding every body elfe to fell any out of the city, by which means they brought on a remedilefs famine. Many of the Cardinals complained to the Pope; but Montalto, who, for his own intereft, was cautious of doing any thing that might difoblige the Cardinal nephew, made the beft excufes he could for it in all companies.

There happened, about the fame time, a quarrel betwixt fome Roman gentlemen and the archers, in which there was a great deal of bloodfhed. As Montalto was in fome danger of his life, one of the parties being dangeroufly wounded clofe by his fide, it is, in fome meafure neceffary to give a fhort account of this tragical accident.

The Provoft-marfhal, attended by a party of his people, went into the Piazza di Sienna, to take one of the banditi that he was in purfuit of, and apprehended him very near the palace of the Urfini. As he was taking him to prifon, he happened to meet the Signiors Raymond Urfini, Sylla Savelli, Octavio Rufticucci, with fome others of their friends, and feveral officers, who had been out on horfe-back to take the air. Urfini, when he was acquainted with the affair, ordered the Marfhal to releafe his prifoner, whom he had no right to arreft in the precincts of his palace, which he refufing to do, Rufticucci was fo provoked, that he ftruck him with his cane. The Marfhal, enraged to fee himfelf treated after that manner, called out to his attendants to fire upon them ; which they immediately did, and mortally wounded the three noblemen. Rufticucci died immediately, and was dragged along, by his horfe, after he was dead. The other two were carried off, their wounds ftreaming with blood, and only lived till the next day.

Montalto

Montalto happening to come that way on foot, juft as the fray began, drew near to them, thinking, perhaps, they would have fome refpect for his habit ; but when he heard the balls whiftle about his ears, he got off as faft as he could, and ran into a houfe with his fervant, who received a large wound in his arm.

This rencounter caufed a great uproar, and filled the city with confternation. The friends and relations of the Urfini, to glut their revenge, purfued and killed all the archers they could find in the ftreets for two days after, even clofe to the gates of the Pope's palace. They killed four all together in a narrow alley, and it was dreadful to fee with what a fpirit of rage and blood-thirftinefs, they chafed thefe poor wretches about the city. His Holinefs, who knew how dangerous it was to oppofe the firft emotions of an enraged populace, for fear of provoking them to a higher degree of madnefs, let them fpend their firft fire ; but, in a little time after, caufed the ringleaders of this fedition to be publicly executed, on pretence of having been guilty of other crimes. The Marfhal faw the danger he was in. and fled, in difguife, the night after this happened; but the Pope, who thought it proper to punifh him in an exemplary manner, made fo diligent a fearch after him, that he was foon taken and brought to Rome, where he had his head cut off. His death, in fome degree, appeafed the Urfini, and fatiated the fury of the people, who loudly exclaimed againft his infolence, in daring to fire upon perfons of fuch quality.

As it gave the Pope a great deal of concern and un-eafinefs to fee the city in fuch a ferment, to put it in good humour again, and efface the remembrance of what had lately happened, he refolved to make a promotion of Cardinals, and prefer fuch people only as were truly worthy of that honour. The whole city expreffed an extraordinary degree of joy upon this occafion; and it gave his Holinefs no fmall fatisfaction to hear the people fay, " That never any Pope had " given the Hat to fo many deferving men at one
time,

" time, and that not only the Holy College, but all
" Chriftendom, was obliged to him for it."

It is not unworthy of notice, that four Cardinals of
this promotion became Popes, viz. John Baptift Caftagna, a Roman, of Genoefe parents, Cardinal of St.
Marcellus, who was Urban VII ; Nicholas Sfondrata,
a Milanefe, Cardinal of St. Cæcilia, afterwards Gregory XIV ; John Anthony Facquinetti, a Bolognefe ;
Cardinal Santiquattro, who took the name of Innocent
IX ; and Alexander di Medicis, Archbifhop of Florence, with the title of St. Cyriack (though he was
generally called the Cardinal of Florence) afterwards
Leo XI. The fhortnefs of their Pontificates is no lefs
remarkable ; for Urban was Pope only 13 days ;
Gregory 10 months ; Innocent not quite two ; and
Leo but 25 days ; fo that they all four reigned but a
little above a year : and there has not been an example of fo quick a fucceffion, fince the days of St. Peter.

Immediately after this promotion, the ftreets were
crouded with Prelates and Cardinals, going to vifit,
and returning from, thofe that had been lately created.
But Montalto, who pretended to be infirm, and almoft
dying for the three laft years, was very flow in paying
his compliments, and took almoft two months to wait
upon them : As there were at leaft three days betwixt
every vifit, he ufed to make apologies for being fo tar-
dy in performing his duty, and faid, " His infirmities
" and great age would not permit him to be fo early in
" his congratulations as he could wifh, but that his
" inclination was good, though his body was weak."
They could not guefs at his motive for affecting to
feem old and infirm ; for if any one enquired of his
age, he told them he was many years older than he
really was. To act confiftently, he very feldom went
to Confiftories ; and when he did, would lean upon
fome body's arm, as if he was not able to fupport himfelf. In coming out from any Congregation, he never
troubled himfelf about order or precedence, but ufed
to ftay behind the reft ; and if there was any ftair-cafe

to

to afcend or defcend, would be a quarter of an hour
betwixt going up or down every five or fix fteps, to
take breath, as if he was almoft fpent ; fo that he was
often faluted in a manner that would not be very
agreeable to any body elfe, " God help you, poor old
" man, you have almoft run your race."

When he went one day to wait upon the Cardinal
of Auftria, who was come to Rome upon affairs of gr^ ^ ^
importance, the Cardinal, vexed and out of humour to
be troubled with his trifling and impertinent vifit, faid
angrily to the perfon who told him he was coming in,
" What bufinefs can this old Lazar poffibly have with
" me ?" However, that he might not entirely mifpend
his time, he endeavoured to draw him into the Spanifh
faction, by faying, " He hoped he fhould have the fa-
" vour of his fuffrage, at any time when the intereft of
" his nation was concerned." But Montalto who was
notwilling to lay himfelf under any engagement, nor
yet to difoblige the King of Spain, after he had made
many excufes, faid, " That a man of his great age had
" nothing more to do in this world, but to think how
" to go well out of it." Many Cardinals of the laft
promotion defired him, " Not to give himfelf the trou-
" ble and fatigue of vifiting them, as they would glad-
" ly excufe him upon the account of his infirmities."
Cardinal della Torre, meeting him one day at a vifit,
he fell into fuch a fit of coughing, that the Cardinal
thought he would have been choked, and faid to him,
" Indeed, Sir, your complaifance will coft you your
" life, you had better fpare yourfelf a little more."

One time, when he was in company with Caftagna,
for whom he had a great friendfhip and efteem ; the
converfation turning upon fome things that happened
when they were together in Spain, Caftagna faid to
him, " Your Eminence is much altered fince that
" time." " Yes," fays Montalto, " old age preffes
" upon me very faft." Caftagna, who had feveral
times heard him fay, that they were both of an age,
told him, " He had no great reafon to complain of that
                                    " yet."

" yet." " Ah, Sir," replied Montalto, " ten years
" make a great alteration in so weak a constitution as
" has fallen to my share."

The Lutherans having tried in vain to proselyte Jeremy, the Patriarch of Constantinople, accused him of
having conspired with the Pope against the Grand Signior Amurath III. which so enraged Amurath, that he
~~~~~~ into exile, and filled up his See with another
~~~~~. The Pope fearing this affair might in the end,
be of prejudice to the Holy See, established a congre-
gregation to consider of a proper remedy for this evil.
Montalto, as a man of great experience and abilities in
such things, was desired to preside at their deliberations. But he excusing himself upon account of the ill
state of his health, his Holiness ordered the Commissaries to meet at his house, who seeing he was not in a
condition to give them any assistance, but desired to be
governed by them, determined to come no more to
him upon that errand, as he likewise pretended to have
a violent fever.

Several Protestants returned this year into the bosom
of the Church, which was owing chiefly to the labours
of some missionaries that were sent into France and
Germany for that purpose. The merit and quality of
some of the new converts was so considerable, that it
occasioned publick thanksgivings to be returned in all
the Churches. Montalto, who had taken great pains,
in concert with the warden of the Holy Apostles, to
convert a Lutheran Baron that resided in Rome, had a
mind himself to introduce him to kiss the Pope's feet,
which he did ; and St. Sixtus inviting him to stay dinner, he would have declined it, and said, " He was not
" in a condition to come to feasts." However, being
much pressed to stay, he sat down to table : but fainted away twice before dinner was over. As he seemed
to have but little appetite to his meat, St. Sixtus said
to him, " If you don't eat, Sir, you'll never live to be
Pope." " Alas !" replied Montalto, " I should make
" a fine Pope indeed, with one foot in the Grave. I

M   " expect

" expect every moment to be fuffocated with the
" Phthific ;" and the Cardinal recommending fome
medicines, that he thought would be of fervice to him ;
he anfwered, " They may perhaps give me a little ref-
" pite from my pains, but it is not poffible they fhould
" cure me of old age."

He paffed eight days, during Lent [1585], in the
convent of the Holy Apoftles, to perform his devotions, and hear a celebrated preacher that was one of
his particular friends, perhaps to let the world fee, that
all the ill ufage he had met with in that convent, was
not able to make him behave otherwife than became
a good Chriftian ; which occafioned fome of his friends
to fay, " Poor man ! now he is going to the Monks
" again ; he has but a fhort time to live, and full of
mifery." They that had known him there whilft he
was a monk, and afterwards when he was General of
the Order, could not, by any means, account for the
wonderful alteration they faw in his temper ; and a
great Prelate, who was the warden's intimate acquaintance, afking him one day, " How Montalto behaved
" amongft them, and whether they were altogether by
" the ears as they ufed to be ;" the warden replied,
" That he hardly knew he lived in the convent."

Soon after he returned to his own houfe, the Pope
died. He had heard private Mafs, on Sunday the 7th
of April, at his own Chapel, and had a mind to go from
thence to high Mafs, that was to be celebrated in the
chapel of St. Sixtus IV. whither Cardinal Caftagna had
dragged Montalto much againft his will, though he
would not come to a Confiftory that was held the next
day, in which notice was given, that there would be a
Signature, [9] the day following, where the Pope defigned to have been prefent ; but being taken fick,
Blanchetti, the Chamberlain, countermanded it, which
occafioned the report of his illnefs to be fpread all over
Rome.

Gregory,

[9] A day appointed for figning all publick Inftruments in the
Confiftory, fuch as Bulls, Briefs, Difpenfations, Edicts, prefenting
Petitions, &c.

Gregory, who found himself but slightly indisposed at first, had a desire to have dispatched some things of great consequence, and was displeased that they put off the Signature. He got up late on Wednesday morning, and after he had walked some time, supported by the Cardinals St. Sixtus and James Buon Compagnon, his nephews, went to breakfast with them: As he did not seem then in any immediate danger, they took leave of him and returned home; but Blanchetti, about two hours after, perceiving him pale and much altered, sent for his physicians, who, finding his pulse very feeble and irregular, were of opinion he had not long to live, and immediately ordered him to be put to bed again, acquainting him with the danger he was in, which he did not seem to be apprehensive of, as he was not very ill at that time, though in a weak and languid condition. Upon this he sent for Farnese, Dean of the Holy College, to attend him, with most of the other Cardinals, and earnestly exhorted them to chuse a person worthy to fill St. Peter's chair. Amongst the others, Montalto was sent for, and immediately set out for the Vatican; but hearing, before he arrived there, that the Pope was dead, he was returning; when another Cardinal meeting him, would have persuaded him to go back with him, and said, " Come along, bro- " ther, if we don't find his Holiness alive, we shall at " least have the consolation of seeing him, though he " is dead;" Montalto replied, " It is much more pro- " per for me to go home again, for I'm sure I shall " soon follow him." The Pope did not live to see any of the Cardinals he had sent for; nor could his nephews arrive time enough to speak with him. For soon after his physicians came, the disorder being a quinsey, his throat began to swell to such a degree, that one could scarce understand him when he spoke. Being now convinced that he was in great danger, he asked one of the physicians, " How long he thought he might " live;" who told him frankly, " He could not in- " sure him two hours. Upon which he turned him- self on the other side, and said to the people that at-

tended

tended him, " I have now no more time to lose in
" thinking upon the things of this world ; give me
" my Crucifix, that I may meditate wholly upon
" Chrift." When he had finished thefe words, he
croffed himfelf feveral times, and recommended his
foul to God, praying with great fervency. After that,
he defired the holy facrament ; but as his phyficians
did not think him in a condition to receive it, his confeffor gave him the extreme Unction, and he foon after
expired.

This Pope had a very ftrong and athletic conftitution, which he had improved by his remarkable tempe-
rance. Towards the end of his life, his phyficians ordered him to drink out of a cup of maffy gold, for the
prefervation of his health. Montalto was advifed to
do the fame ; but he made a joke of it, and faid,
" He believed it was a very good thing to keep peo-
" ple well when they were fo, but that it was not pof-
" fible for it to reftore health, when it was once gone ;
" that he was convinced there was no remedy for his
" diftempers but death."

Gregory ufed to be very often troubled with a flux,
which was of fervice to him in one refpect, as it carried off what other diftempers he was fubject to, except an afthma, or oppreffion in the breaft, that he laboured under, for which he could find no relief, but
frequently taking the frefh air ; for the benefit of which
he went fometimes to refide at Frefcati [1]. He took
pleafure in riding on horfe-back now and then about
the adjacent country, and could have mounted or dif-
mounted without any advantage, and with fo much
agility, that Montalto feeing him one day, could not
forbear faying, " I wifh to God I was able to do fo ;"
not

[1] A moft delightful villa, near a fmall town of the fame name,
in the Campagna di Roma. It was the ancient Tufculum of Cicero,
and now belongs to the Borghefe family. It is the feat of a bifhop,
who ftill retains the name of Tufculanus Epifcopus. The town
was deftroyed in the time of Celeftine III. becaufe the inhabitants
fided with the Imperialifts ; and Frefcati built upon its ruins above
500 years ago. There are a great number of palaces and houfes of
pleafure in and about it.

not that he took any great pleasure in that exercise, for he seldom or ever got on the back of his mule, but at solemn processions and cavalcades, and then would be an hour or two in making preparations for it, and could not do it at last, without a great deal of assistance from his servants, to whom he would say, with a deep sigh, " God help me, I have more occasion for a bier, than a mule."

Some were of opinion, that the Pope, when he saw himself near his end, repented of having taken away the pensions from the poorer Cardinals, and had sent for the whole College to declare his intention of restoring them, with the arrears. This, however, was given out by his nephew, St. Sixtus, after his death. It is a great pity he did not think of it sooner, to undeceive those that thought it was owing to pique and revenge, without hearkening to the arguments of others, who said, " It was not probable that a person of his exten- " sive goodness and charity to all the world, could be " induced, by such mean considerations, to destroy " the generosity of his predecessor."

He always shewed a great affection for his country and countrymen, several of whom he made prelates, and some Cardinals, for no other reason or merit. Montalto followed his example in this respect, when he came to fill his place, as we shall see hereafter, and used to say, " He had not observed any thing more " commendable in Gregory's conduct, than the great " love he always bore to his country.

After this manner died Pope Gregory, when he had reigned thirteen years, leaving immense riches to his relations, though he often declared, " That he never " would gratify the desire he had of aggrandizing " them, by unjustly taking away what belonged to " other people, or dissipating the possessions of the Church." He did not erect Principalities at the ex- pence of the holy See, as some of his predecessors had done, who would willingly have given away the whole city and ecclesiastical state to their nephews, if it had been in their power.

Though

Though he had been extremely beloved by the people, the refpect which they had for his memory, could not prevent thofe diforders that ufually happen when the See is vacant ; for the very day after his death, there were not only grievous riots and feditions, but many affaffinations and murders committed by the rabble. Thefe enormities and outrages were carried to a ftill greater height in the ecclefiaftical ftate ; the death of the Pope was no fooner known there, than every one without the leaft regard to the memory of his virtues, and the clemency with which he had reigned over them, threw off all manner of reftraint and regard to the laws. The licentioufnefs of the people was fo great and unbridled, that they entirely laid afide all fort of refpect for the magiftrates, and paid not the leaft obedience to any authority ; acknowledging no fuperior, and fearing neither God nor man, Every one did what feemed right in his own eyes, as in the days when there was no King in Ifrael.

This made the government of Sixtus V. who fucceeded Gregory, feem the more fevere ; for the fubjects of the Church, when they changed their mafter, faw their joy turned into fadnefs ; their debaucheries into fafting and mortification ; their liberty, or rather licentioufnefs, into the moft flavifh and abject fubmiffion ; their idle and diforderly way of living into hard labour and ftrict difcipline, as no Pope ever governed with fo high a hand, or kept his people in greater awe and fubjection.

The Governors and Vice-Legates, the Lieutenants, and Auditors, and all other officers of the ecclefiaftical ftate, committed the moft audacious robberies during this interval. They took money from all parties, fet prifoners at liberty, and granted pardons, which they took care to be well paid for ; many people being releafed in the evening from their confinement, for crimes they had committed in the morning. The banditi, who were provoked at Gregory's having ordered fome parties of foldiers to harafs and purfue them towards the latter end of his days, began to appear again with

great

great boldneſs; and what was ſtill more melancholy they, whoſe particular office it was to purge the eccleſiaſtical ſtate of theſe nuiſances, not only connived at them, but were ſtrongly ſuſpected of encouraging and indeed of being in confederacy with the authors.

Theſe villains, not content with plundering all the neighbouring country and villages, when they heard of the Pope's death, entered into the towns and cities, where they lived with the greateſt ſecurity, in a continued ſcene of rapine and debauchery; no woman being ſafe in the houſe of her parents or relations; whilſt the governors and magiſtrates publicly aſſiſted and ſupported them in theſe outrages.

The very Monks, following the example of the Seculars ſhook off all obedience to their Superiors. Eight Fathers of the convent del Popolo introduced as many whores into their cells, whom they maintained at the expence of the houſe, and lived with them as if they had been their wives. The Prior, who was a very religious and worthy man, being grievouſly offended, often admoniſhed them to leave this abandoned and ſhameful way of life; but finding them above the power of reproof, and that his exhortations had no effect upon them, he ſent for ſome archers to aſſiſt him in impriſoning them; which ſo enraged theſe pious brothers and their ladies, that they rebelled, and with the help of ſome banditi (whom they called into their aſſiſtance) killed two of the archers, and a lay brother, plundered the convent and made their eſcape. But three of them were taken in the reign of Sixtus, and condemned to the gallies.

Father Sargo, a Dominican, belonging to the convent ſopra la Minerva, who was a man of learning, and a celebrated preacher, had collected money at his ſermons to beautify an altar that he had built, with the general's leave, at his own expence, and dedicated to St. James; which he did in a very handſome manner, with ſilver lamps and candleſticks, a large crucifix, two fine chalices of the ſame metal, an embroidered altar-cloth, and ſeveral other rich ornaments, which

he

he always kept in his chamber when they were not in ufe.

One day during the vacancy of the See, two monks, a lay brother, and a fecular, that were acquainted with him, broke into his chamber, whilft he was at Church, and ftripped it ; which affected him in fo violent a manner, that he died in a few days.

The Abbe Ficarelli, of a noble family in Venice, who refided at Rome for the fake of the diverfions that are always to be met with there, falling defperately in love with an apothecary's daughter ; and having in vain tried all methods to debauch her, at laft determined to carry her off by force. For this purpnfe he fent for one of the banditi, with whom he was acquainted, defiring him to bring three others to affift him in puting his fcheme in execution. The young woman had a brother that was banifhed five or fix years before for murder, and had fince that time changed his name to Titta, and lived amongft the banditti. Him the banditti brought, and three more to Ficarelli's houfe the evening before the rape was to be committed, where they ftaid drinking and revelling till the dead of the night ; at which time, Titta faid he would go and reconnoitre the houfe, and fee if the attempt was practicable ; but inftead of that, he went and acquainted his father with the whole affair, defiring him to fend immediately for fome of his friends, to give the Abbe a proper reception when he came, which would be in lefs than an hour, All things being properly agreed on betwixt them, he returned to Ficarelli's, and telling him, the coaft was clear, they all fallied out together, and attempting to get into the houfe through a window, which Titta told them was the beft place to enter at ; the people, that his father had ftationed near it, rufhed upon them, and killed the three banditti, carrying the Abbe into the houfe, where they made him write a note to his aunt, who lived with him, ordering him to fend all his jewels to him immediately. But fhe, being a prudent woman, refufed it ; and faid, It was a very improper time of the night, to fend things
of

of that value, through the ſtreet, by the hands of one perſon only ; which ſo provoked Titta, who carried the note, that he murdered her and the two ſervants, rifled the houſe, and then, returing to the abbe, cut his throat.

The palaces of five Cardinals were robb'd whilſt the ſee was vacant ; that of Farneſe, where there were above 30 ſervants, and guards patrolling round it day and night, was plundered, not ſecretly, or in a private manner, but publicly, in the middle of the day ; ſeveral of the nobility, having formed gangs of Banditi, ſome of them conſiſting of 60, others of 70, 80, and 100 men; with which they went about committing rapes, murders, robberies, and all manner of villainy and outrage.

Whilſt Farneſe was giving an account one day of his palace being robbed, to ſome other Cardinals ; Montalto, who happened to be by, ſaid, " I hope God will " give us a Pope ſoon that will put an end to theſe diſ- " orders." If you ſhould be the perſon," anſwered Farneſe, " I dare ſay, there would be no cutting off " heads, or ſtretching of necks, in your reign." " God " forbid," replied Montalto. " that I, who expect to " die every day, ſhould think of taking away any other " perſon's life." Some people who were preſent at this converſation, ſaid, as they came away, " There was " more occaſion for a Pope of iron, like Farneſe, than " one of wax, like Montalto." In ſhort, the prodigous and unparalleled degree of wickedneſs that reigned during this interval, and the enormity of thoſe crimes that were daily committed, loudly called for a ſpeedy and ſevere reformation, and will fully ſerve to juſtify the conduct of Sixtus V. whoſe reign, ſome authors have been very liberal in branding with the hateful epithets of Cruel and Sanguinary.

It is certain that it would have been the utter deſtruction of Rome and the eccleſiaſtical ſtate, if another Pope had ſucceeded like Gregory, though his only fault was an exceſs of tenderneſs and indulgence: ſo fatal ſometimes are the effects of ill-timed and unlimited mercy.

When

When Sixtus at any time paſſed by his ſtatue, which the Romans had erected whilſt he was yet alive (notwithſtanding the bull publiſhed by Pius IV. after the indignity offered to the memory of his predeceſſor) he uſed to point at it with his finger, and ſay, " That man, " by his fooliſh good-nature, baniſhed virtue and juſtice " out of Rome, and introduced all manner of vice and " wickedneſs, which occaſions us endleſs trouble."

Upon the pedeſtal of the ſtatue, are the two following inſcriptions:

GREGORIO XIII. PONT. MAX.
OB FARINAE VECTICAL SVBLATVM,
VRBEM TEMPLIS ET OPERIBVS MAGNIFICEN
TISSIMIS EXORNATAM,,
H. S. [2] OCTINGENTIES, SINGVLARI BENE-
FICENTIA IN EGENOS DISTRIBVTVM;
OB SEMINARIA.
EXTERARVM NATIONVM IN VERBE,
AC TOTO TERRARVM ORBE,
RELIGIONIS PROPAGANDAE CAVSA INSTI-
TVTA,,
OB PATERNAM IN OMNES GENTES CHARI-
TATEM,
QVA. EX VLTIMIS NOVI ORBIS INSVLIS,
IAPONIENSIVM REGVM LEGATOS,
TRIENNI NAVIGATIONE,
AD OBEDIENTIAM SEDI APOSTOLICAE EX-
HIBENDAM
PRIMVM VENIENTES ROMAM
PRO PONTIFICIA DIGNITATE, ACCEPIT
S. P. Q. R.

[2] " Octingenties mille ſeſtertium, 800,000 Seſterces." The great Seſterce is 7 l. 16s. 3d. ſterling, the leſs about 7 farthings ; I ſuppoſe the leſs is here meant. See Danet,

The

The Second:

GREGORIO XIII. PONT. MAX.
OPTIMO PRINCIPI
HVGONI BVON. COMPAGNON BONONIENSI,
QVI
PER ROMANOS MAGITRATVS, ET ECCLE-
SIASTICAS DIGNITATES,
IVSTITIAM ET PIETATEM COLENS,
AD PONTIFICIS SEDEM EVECTVS,
VNIVERSAM REMP. CHRISTIANAM,
SVMMA PROVIDENTIA ET CHARITATE MO-
DERATVR.
S. P. Q. R,

End of the THIRD BOOK.

BOOK THE FOURTH.

THE Cardinals held a confiftory the fame night
that Gregory died, to give orders for the care
and well government of the city, They affembled
again upon the Thurfday and Friday following, to
adjuft the ceremonies that are ufually obferved at the
celebration of the Pope's obfequies, Cardinal Gambara fung mafs, after which they gave audience to
count Olivarez, ambaffador from the King of Spain,
who delivered himfelf in a manner that was much approved of by the whole affembly.

Cardinal di Como [5] fung mafs the next day, after
which they held a confiftory, where the Emperor's
ambaffador was admitted, and Cardinal D'Efte; in the
name of his moft Chriftian Majefty. The Cardinal of
Arragon arrived from Naples the next day, which,
being Palm Sunday, paffed without any confiftory.

On Monday, mafs was fung by Cardinal Alexan-

[5] The French fays de Cofmo.

drino,

drino, and a confiftory held ; as there was upon the three following days, on the laft of which they gave audience to the French ambaffador, who arrived the evening before.

The Cardinals [6] Gefualdo and Medicis came the fame day ; the firft from Naples, the other from his archbifhoprick of Florence.

On Saturday, the Spanifh ambaffador had another audience, and made a very pathetic and eloquent fpeech. The Cardinals Paleotto archbifhop of Bologna, and Caftagna Legate at that city, arrived together the fame day.

During the ten days, that the funeral ceremonies of the deceafed Pope lafted, they that had any pretenfions to the papacy, were carrying on their fchemes and intrigues, running about to folicit the fuffrages and intereft of their friends ; whilft Montalto did not feem to give himfelf the leaft trouble or concern. He took fo uncommon a road to it, that no body fufpected he had any defign at all of that kind. Some of the Cardinals, out of contempt, ufed to call him, The Afs of La Marca (which he pretended not to hear, or take notice of) looking upon his faculties and intellects as entirely gone ; and others feeing him bent down with difeafe and old age, did not in the leaft dream of his ever being elected. But we muft take notice, by the by, that he was the youngeft of all thofe that afpired to the pontificate, and though he often ufed to fay, " That an old fellow, of threefcore and ten, was fit " for nothing in the world," it is certain he was, as that time, but in his 64th year.

Indeed, hardly any one could have imagined, that the Cardinals would turn their eyes upon a perfon that could fcarcely ftand upon his legs, whom they thought little better than a dotard and a driveller ; as the government of the holy fee requires a man of found and ftrong faculties, both of body and mind. Yet it was to thefe very failings, that Montalto owed his exaltation.

His proceedings were dark and fecret; he alone, if

[6] The French fays, Guife.

we

we may ufe the expreffion, lay at anchor, when all the other candidates were under full fail. Taking a quite different courfe from them in all refpects; he fpoke well of every body, and feemed to have a very low and mean opinion of himfelf.

Amongft other vifits that he made before they entered the conclave, he went to Cardinal Farnefe, who was at the head of a very potent faction, though he knew he could hardly bear to fee him with any fort of patience, and told him, "He thought it his duty to "wait upon him, as dean of the holy college, to de-"fire, if he thought the conclave would laft a long "time, that he would be pleafed to difpenfe with his "going into it ; for he verily believed he fhould not "live many days." Farnefe exhorting him, "Not to "abandon the interefts of the church in an affair of fo "great importance to all Chriftendom ;" Montalto anfwered, "That the hope of his fuffrage being not "altogether ufelefs to his eminence, was the only con-"fideration that could induce him to go and meet his "death there ;" to which Farnefe replied, "I would "advife you to go and try your own intereft, for I dare "fay you would be as glad to be Pope as any one "elfe." Montalto, furprifed at the repartee, faid, "That the Cardinals muft be very wrong-headed in-"deed, to think of fo poor an object as him, who had "it not in his power to do any one thing, but wifh "well to his patrons and friends." He talked in the fame ftile to every one of the Cardinals that he thought ftood any chance of being Pope ; efpecially to the chiefs of factions, continually fpeaking in their praife, acknowledging the obligations he lay under to them, telling them, How ardently he wifhed he was able to "do them a fervice ; and what a prejudice he thought "it would be to the church, if the government of it "was intrufted in any other hands."

In the diftribution of their apartments in the conclave, which is always done by lot, he happened to be fituated in the midft of the principal officers; Cardinal Farnefe, dean of the holy college, and vice-chancellor

of

of the church, lodged on his left hand ; Contarelli, the datary, on his right ; and Guaſtavillano, the great chamberlain, next to Contarelli. As ſoon as the maſter of the ceremonies had made this diſtribution, he came to congratulate Montalto, as if, what was nothing but the effect of chance, had been a lucky omen, or preſage of his election.

Upon Eaſter Sunday, the 21ſt of April, the ſolemn maſs of the Holy Ghoſt was ſung, every one of the Cardinal Prieſts having before ſaid maſs in private : Montalto got up very early that morning to perform his devotions in the church of the holy Apoſtles; after which he came to St. Peter's, attended by the whole convent.

Muretus, who was one of the moſt eloquent men of his time, made an oration when maſs was over, and read the bull, concerning the election of a Pope ; but the noiſe and tumult, occaſioned by ſo great a concourſe of people, hindered it from being heard. After this, all the Cardinals that were then in Rome, to the number of 39, went in proceſſion to the conclave. The Cardinals of Auſtria, Mandrucci. and Vercelli, arrived the ſame day, and entered the conclave in the evening, which made the number 42.

We muſt take notice of two incidents that happened upon the Cardinal of Auſtria's going into the Conclave, which occaſioned a good deal of tumult and confuſion, for the ſpace of two hours. Juſt as he preſented himſelf to enter, the Cardinals were going to count voices in their firſt ſcrutiny, and ſent a maſter of the ceremonies to him, deſiring he would defer his entry till the afternoon, " As it was neceſſary to read ſeveral bulls " to every freſh member that entered; and this delay " would interrupt the ſcrutiny, and break in upon the " rules laid down by the Cardinals ; " his friends in the conclave gave their conſent to it, as they ſaw there would be no election the firſt ſcrutiny. But he, who did not know what ſchemes were carrying on, was afraid of being excluded from the honour of having any ſhare in the election; and that they ſhould
chuſe

chuse some body that would be disagreeable to the court of Spain. This made him continue knocking at the gate, to prevent them from proceeding any further, protesting against the scrutiny as void and null, if he was not admitted to assist in it. The Cardinals, who were glad to shew their respect for a person of his power and merit, and to take away all cause of altercation that might arise from his protest, unanimously agreed to defer the scrutiny, till he had made his entrance. After this manner the first difficulty was got over.

Cardinal Gambara, a person in great credit and esteem, was the occasion of the second : For, as soon as it was resolved that the Cardinal of Austria should be admitted, he said, " It was necessary to be first inform-
" ed, whether he, who was styled a Cardinal Deacon,
" had ever taken Deacon's Orders, as enjoined by the
" Bull of Pius IV. which forbids all Cardinals to enter
" the conclave, or to have any suffrage, except they
" have taken the respective orders that are expressed
" by their titles." Gambara only raised this objecti-
on, to prevent any scandal that might arise from evil disposed persons, saying after the election was over,
" That it was an illegal one ; the forms established by
" that Bull not having been duly observed." The
The Cardinal Santa Croce got up, and said, " That
" the Cardinals were not obliged to exhibit their letters
" of ordination ; that it was sufficient they had been
" proclaimed Bishops, Priests, or Deacons, according
" to their title." This answer did not seem satisfacto-
ry, as the Bull above-mentioned had been approved of by the whole consistory ; it rather encreased the embarrassment, and obliged the Cardinal Dean to submit the affair to a formal deliberation.

Whilst it was under consideration, the Cardinal of Austria, who still kept thundering at the gate, having been informed of the objection, soon put an end to the debate, by sending in a dispensation, that had been granted him by Gregory XIII. which he had luckily brought with him. This instrument being read, before all the Cardinals, by which his taking Deacon's Orders

was

was difpenfed with, and he declared capable of voting in any future conclave; his friends went to receive him a the gate, and conducted him into the chapel, where a mafter of the ceremonies read three Bulls to him; the two firft prohibiting the alienation of the church's poffeffions; and the third againft fimony, which put an end to all cavils.

The Cardinals took an oath the fame day, that who-ever was chofen Pope fhould obferve certain rules agreed upon amongft themfelves, that would be for the honour of the college, and the intereft of the Holy See, and the advantage of Chriftendom in general. This cuftom had been eftablifhed above 200 years, but not in the fame form, nor the things fworn to, al-was punctually obferved.

Here follows the purport of the rules and injuncti-ons that were made and fworn to in this conclave:

" I. That whofoever fhould be exalted to the throne
" of St. Peter, fhould endeavour, with all his might,
" to maintain peace amongft the Chriftian powers, and
" encourage them and their fubjects to unite their for-
" ces againft infidels, hereticks, fchifmaticks, and all
" other enemies of the Chriftian name.

" II. That he fhould never refide any where but at
" Rome, unlefs forced thereto by the moft preffing ne-
" ceffity, or other reafon that would be of the higheft
" advantage to the church, according to a law ap-
" proved of and confirmed by a majority of Cardinals
" in the confiftory.

" III. That he fhould oblige all Judges Magiftrates,
" &c. in the ecclefiaftical State, to give a ftrict ac-
" count of their conduct, at the expiration of their ref-
" pective offices, in the fame place that they executed
" them, where there fhould be a commiffion opened
" for fome days (of which publick notice fhould be gi-
" ven to the inhabitants) to receive the complaints
" of thofe that had been any way injured or oppreffed.

" IV.

" IV. That he fhould not promote any perfon to the
" dignity of Cardinal, but of the moft exemplary life
" and converfation, as well as eminent learning and
" erudition ; and that, according to a decree of Ju-
" lius III, the Hat fhould never be given to two bro-
" thers, upon any motive whatfoever, either fpiritual
" or temporal.

" V. That he fhould take efpecial care, not to alie-
" nate the treafures and poffeffions of the Church,
" upon any confideration, without the confent and
" approbation of the confiftory ; and that the furplus,
" after the ordinary expences of the Church are de-
" frayed, fhall be laid up in a place, appointed for that
" purpofe, againft any fudden emergency.

" VI. That he fhould not declare war againft any
" power, tho' upon never fo juft an occafion, without
" firft propofing it to the Confiftory, and afterwards
" taking the opinion of every Cardinal, and not even
" then, except there be a majority of voices for it, and
" upon condition that he fhould not make peace
" without obferving the fame method.

" VII. That he fhould engage himfelf to maintain
" the dignity, privileges, and immunities of the fa-
" cred College, without being permitted to degrade,
" or put to death, any Cardinal ; and that the Procefs
" fhould be conducted by the Confiftory, in which
" alone fhould be lodged the power of paffing fentence
" upon them.

The 42 Cardinals, of which the Conclave confifted,
were divided into 5 factions ; Farnefe was at the head
of the firft ; d'Efte of the fecond ; Alexandrino of the
third ; Altemps of the fourth ; and the fifth, which
was almoft equal in number to all the reft, was conducted by Buon Compagnon, Cardinal of St. Sixtus,
nephew to the late Pope.

There were 14 that afpired to the Papacy, viz. Farnefe and Savelli, created by Paul III ; Santa Croce,
Paleotto, St. George, and Sirletti, by Pius IV. Mon-

N   talto,

talto, Cefis, St. Severini, and Albano, by Pius V. Fachinetti, or Facquinetti, commonly called Cardinal di
Santiquattro, della Torre, a native of Udina, Mondovi,
and Caftagna, by Gregory XIII. and though they were
all palpable [1], there were not above half of them
propofed as candidates in the conclave. Thefe were
all, more or lefs, fupported by the heads of the feveral
factions, according to the opinion they had of them;
for though thefe chiefs pretended much zeal and concern for the intereft of all their creatures, left jealoufy
fhould detach them, and ruin their party; yet there is
generally one perfon, whom they favour more than
the reft, and with a greater degree of warmth and confidence.

The Cardinals Altemps, Medicis, and Alexandrino,
had joined their forces together at their entrance into
the conclave to chufe Peter Donatus Cefis, a Roman,
and laid their fcheme after this manner:

All the Cardinals have leave to go out of the conclave the firft day, after reading the bulls, but muft
return in the evening. Some of them made ufe of this
liberty, in going to take a turn in the city, thefe
three chiefs, with their party, refolved to lay hold of
this opportunity, and proceed immediately to adoration; which they thought might be eafily effected, as
they that were determined to exclude him, were gone
out of the conclave. But the defign, not being carried on with proper fecrecy, took air; and St. Sixtus,
who was the declared opponent of Cefis, hearing of it,
juft

[1] This term fignifies fuch as are not difqualified, by any incapacity, to be Pope. For many Cardinals, of unexceptionable merit,
are excluded from that dignity, upon particular confiderations, fuch
as original fin (as it is called at Rome) which is being born fubjects
of a crown or ftate that is out of favour, or having been made Cardinal at the inftance of France or Spain, or their adherents. Others,
upon the account of feveral accidental qualifications relating to their
rank or perfon: as having been already excluded, being born princes
or fovereigns of particular ftates, publicly efpoufing the interefts of
fuch a crown, akin to a very numerous family, remarkably fond of
their relations, unexperienced in ftate affairs, young or healthful, or
of a diffolute and irregular life.

just as he was going out to give some orders about his private affairs, immediately returned, and entering into a combination with those that were equally concerned to oppose him, destroyed this scheme in the embrio; for the heads of that party, seeing their measures entirely defeated, were forced to let it drop.

This attempt hurt Cesis so much, and caused so many people to declare against him, whom he thought firm and staunch in his interest, that his friends never durst mention him a second time whilst the conclave lasted.

The Cardinals assembled again, early on Monday morning, in the chapel, where, after they had all received the sacrament from the hands of Farnese, who officiated as Dean, they proceeded to a scrutiny, in which Cardinal Albano had 13 voices; but that number not being sufficient, they retired to dine in their respective cells; after which the interest and pretensions of several others were discussed, particularly that of Sirletti, a Calabrian, which was so warmly pushed by Altemps, joined by Medicis, and the Cardinals made by Pius IV. that they were in great expectation of succeeding. But D'Este, Farnese, and Sforza, objected to Sirletti. " That he had formerly been excluded;" for it is a maxim, generally observed in the conclave, not to chuse a man that has been once rejected.

Sirletti, it is true, was a wise and virtuous man, and, as he had but a few relations, likely enough to have made a very disinterested Pope; but he wanted some qualifications that were necessary to make a good governor of the Church in that critical juncture. They were besides afraid of his gloomy and reserved disposition, and the strict acquaintance he had with Cardinal Como, who was hated by the whole college, not only as he had been entrusted with the sole management of affairs, as premier secretary, for the space of 19 years, under the pontificates of Pius V. and Gregory XIII. but had likewise ill used and affronted almost every one of them. They had good reason, therefore, to oppose Sirletti, as they foresaw, if he was elected, the power

and

and influence of Como was likely to revive, and raife again to as high, or perhaps higher, pitch than before Altemps was blamed for chufing an improper time to propofe him, and his very beft friends highly difapproved of the boldnefs and precipitation with which it was carried on, fo foon after his coming into the conclave.

As all the competitors were impatient to know their deftiny, things were pufhed forward with great heat and animofity. But a variety of clafhing interefts, is often the bane of fchemes that would fucceed in peaceable conclaves, and obliges the electors to turn their eyes upon men that they had not the leaft inclination to ferve, or ever thought of before. Sometimes indeed it comes to pafs, though very rarely, that, when only one perfon is propofed, the Cardinals unanimoufly agree to chufe him, before factions and cabals have time to form themfelves; as happened to Gregory XIII. This example, however is by no means fufficient to juftify the conduct of Altemps; for if he had kept his defign fecret, and amufed his adverfaries with fair words, he would have gained time, and certainly carried the election for Sirletti. Whereas, by this ill-timed and premature attempt, he rendered the undertaking abortive, and extinguifhed his hopes for ever.

Farnefe, who earneftly wifhed to be chofen, thought Sirletti in his way, and, as he was working underhand for himfelf, broke out into invectives againft Altemp's faction, and faid aloud in the conclave, " He could " not conceive why any perfon took fo much pains for " Sirletti." Some people were of opinion, that Altemps was only endeavouring to impofe upon Sirletti, and make him believe he was labouring for him, whilft he ultimately defigned to give his whole intereft to Cardinal Ferrerio, a Piedmontefe, bifhop of Vercelli, his near relation and intimate friend, thinking that Farnefe and D'Efte, who had a great efteem for Ferrerio, would have joined him as foon as he was propofed, but as it proved, they had fixed upon another perfon.

After

After the defeat of Sirletti, St. Sixtus employed his credit in favour of Caftagna, preffed it ftrongly upon every one that he thought lay under any obligations to him. His great merit and reputation feemed to affure him of fuccefs ; yet, though there could be no reafonable objection made to him, the old Cardinals would not confent to his election, as he was created only at the laft promotion.

There were fome endeavours ufed in behalf of Savelli ; Medicis, in particular, laboured the point with much zeal and application, but this project likewife fell to the ground. Colonna and Cefis, his profeffed enemies, oppofed him vehemently ; and taking advantage of the jealoufies that fubfifted amongft the Roman Cardinals, threatened Medicis, if he perfifted in canvaffing for Savelli, immediately to join Farnefe. Upon which Medicis chofe rather to abandon his friend, than be the inftrument of exalting his inveterate and declared enemy ; though Savelli was much efteemed by · the college, and had given many proofs of his probity and good conduct whilft he was inquifitor-general and vicar to the Pope. He had indeed a fort of haughtinefs in his behaviour, that was very diftafteful to moft people, which made them afraid of feeing him Pope, as he behaved with fo much pride whilft he was only Cardinal. The fickly and unhealthful afpect he had worn a long time, gave fome occafion to fay, that he counterfeited it, to facilitate his exaltation to the Popedom. But what was the greateft obftacle in his way, was the prodigious number of baftards which he had.

Upon this, there were practices fet on foot for Della Torre, a perfon of extraordinary worth, and who would have been propofed the firft of any, if he had been there, at their entrance into the conclave. This delay was of infinite differvice to him : Farnefe, D'Efte, and Savelli, expected him impatiently every day, and endeavoured to protract matters as long as they could to give him an opportunity of arriving in time. But the defign being penetrated by Medicis, gave him a great

deal

deal of uneafinefs, and made him enter into confultations with his friends how he fhould exclude him. His
chagrin encreafed, when he reflected that if Torre
fhould be chofen, Farnefe would totally engrofs his
favour, and prevail upon him to make fuch, and fo
many people, Cardinals, as would be fufficient to
chufe him Pope, if he fhould furvive Torre, which
feemed very probable.

These chiefs, who fecretly fupported the intereft of
Torre, had refolved to chufe him Pope immediately
upon his entrance into the conclave, which they
thought would not be a difficult matter. When a
Cardinal enters the Conclave, all the reft of his brethren go to receive him at the gate, and they had
agreed amongft themfelves to take the opportunity,
whjlft he was receiving the compliments of the other
Cardinals, of crying out, Long live the Pope ; and carrying him to the chapel, inftantly perform the adoration, which none of the Cardinals, they thought, would
have the courage to oppofe.

There had been already fome fecret proceedings, in
favour of Montalto, begun by Alexandrino and D'Efte.
The former hoped to have a great fhare in the adminiftration, under a Pontiff, that had been made Cardinal by his uncle, to whom they lay under fo many
other obligations. D'Efte was drawn in with the fame
view, by the perfuafion of Rufticucci, who had a great
influence over him, and had been flattered by Montalto, till he began to grow fond of him.

Medicis and his friends, apprehenfive of Farnefe's
intrigues for Torre, went privately, and made an offer
of their fervice to d'Efte and Alexandrino, promifing to
affift Montalto. They were both highly pleafed at
this : As Medicis, who was in great credit at the court
of Spain, was affured of the Spanifh intereft ; and
D'Efte, as chief of the French faction, anfwered for
their concurrence ; fo that thefe two powerful, and
generally oppofite parties, for once joined in chufing
the fame perfon.

Thefe

These three Cardinals having engaged their word to each other, came secretly to Montalto's apartment in the night, and acquainted him with their design to make h m Pope. Alexandrino, who undertook to be spokesman, whispered to him, for fear of being overheard by Farnese, whose room was next to that of Montalto, "we are come to tell your Eminence a " piece of very good news, which is, that we are resolved to make you Pope."

Montalto had all this time kept himself close shut up in his little chamber, and was no more thought or spoke of, than if he had not been in the conclave. He very seldom stirred out, and when he went to mass, or any of the scrutinies, appeared so little concerned, that one would have thought he had no manner of interest in any thing that happened within those walls. But he was, nevertheless, advancing his interest at a great rate, whilst he seemed to give himself no trouble about it. When he met any Cardinal, that he knew wished well to the interest of St. Sixtus, he used to say, " The " Cardinals ought to chuse a person that would be " agreeable to him, out of regard to his own merit, " and the memory of his uncle Gregory XIII. who " had governed the Church with so much gentleness " and clemency." If he saw any of Farnese's friends, he seemed to wonder, " That he was not yet chosen."

Before the adherents of Medicis, he extoll'd their patron, " as the most worthy man in the conclave." In short, he spoke well of all the Cardinals, but particularly of such as he did not think his friends, or had the greatest credit and interest. As soon as he was acquainted with their intentions by Alexandrino, in the presence of Medicis, and D'Este, he fell into such a violent fit of coughing, that they thought he would have expired upon the spot, and said, as soon as he could speak, " That his reign would be but of a few days; " that, beside the continual difficulty with which he " drew his breath, he had not strength enough to sup- " port such a weight; and that his small experience

" in

" in affairs, made him altogether unfit for a charge of
" fo important a nature, except he could depend up-
" on the affiftance of others ;" they anfwered, " That
" God would give him ftrength fufficient to govern
" his church ;" to which he replied, " That he would
" never accept of it upon any terms whatfoever, ex-
" cept they would all three promife not to abandon
" him, but take the greateft part of the weight off his
" fhoulders, as he was neither able, nor could in con-
" fcience pretend, to take the whole of it upon him-
" felf." The other Cardinals affuring them they would;
he faid, " If you are refolved to make me Pope, it will
" only be placing yourfelves on the throne; we muft
" fhare the pontificate ; for my part, I fhall be con-
" tent with the bare title ; let them call me Pope, and
" you are heartily welcome to the power and authority."

Deluded by thefe infinuations, they fwallowed the
bait, and determined to chufe him. Thus he craftily
brought about his great defigns, by methods, in all appearance, the leaft probable. He had forefeen, that
at the death of the Pope, there would be great contefts
and divifions in the conclave; and very rightly judged,
as it proved, that if the chiefs of the parties met with
any difficulty in chufing the perfon they intended,
they would all willingly concur in the election of fome
very old and infirm Cardinal (as had been done more
than once in fuch cafes before) which would give them
time to lay their fchemes better againft another vacancy. This was the true reafon of his fhamming the
imbecile, affecting to appear like a dying man, and
endeavouring, by a harmlefs and inoffenfive behaviour,
not to difoblige any body.

The Cardinals were no fooner got out of his apartment, but they retired into a private place, to confer
amongft themfelves about the advantages that would
accrue to each of them from fuch an election. " What
" can we wifh for more," faid they, " than to have
" the entire difpofal of the Pope ? We fhould be
" egregious fools, indeed, and deferve to be foundly
" laughed

" laughed at, if we let such an opportunity flip out
" of our hands. Montalto has opened his heart to us
" very frankly, and in quite different terms from any
" of the other candidates; as he never had any govern-
" ment, but that of his own order for a little while, he
" will be altogether raw and inexperienced in that of
" the whole church, and must necessarily make use of
" us; there is no probability, nor indeed possibility, of
" his pretending to steer the vessel alone. He has no
" relations to call in, that are capable of assisting him.
" his nephews are fitter to hold a plough than rule a
" state. He is sensible, that we have been long em-
" ployed in the government of the state; that we are
" able to direct him with our counsel and advice; and,
" that as he owes his exhaltation entirely to us, he
" cannot, in conscience, lodge the power in any other
" hands. We may depend upon having the admini-
" stration wholly to ourselves: For if, whilst he was
" but Cardinal, he did not think himself able to ma-
" nage the few affairs that fell within that narrow cir-
" cle, the distrust of his abilities will naturally in-
" crease, in proportion to the weight and number, of
" the difficulties he will meet with when he comes to
" fit in the chair of St. Peter."

Having fully satisfied themselves with these arguments, they used all their endeavours to get him chosen,
and began with trying to bring over the Farnesian interest, artfully causing a report to be spread, that Torre would be there in two days; and Rusticucci, to
whom they had communicated their design, shewed
several letters which he said he had received to that
purpose. They gave it out, that if Farnese could not
procure him to be chosen, he would set up for himself.
To operate the more effectually upon the Cardinals
that opposed the election of Farnese, they further pretended, that he daily expected the return of two couriers, whom he had dispatched to the Kings of France
and Spain, who most probably, would bring with
them an account of the favourable disposition of those
two monarchs; especially that of France, to whom he
had

had reprefented, in the ftrongeft terms, the faithful attachment of his family, and the great fervices his anceftors had often done to the French nation.

Some of the Cardinals were exceedingly furprifed, when they heard Medicis had declared for Montalto, and could not comprehend the reafons that induced him to be fo ftrenuous for a perfon, that had been a profeffed enemy to his coufin Paul Urfini. But, it feems, his ambition, and the defire he had to exclude Farnefe and Della Torre, prevailed over all family refentments, for he exerted himfelf with more zeal than any other Cardinal, in the intereft of Montalto; though he was not without fufpicions that Farnefe, by fome artifice or other, would feduce Alexandrino, who was naturally fickle and irrefolute.

It was thought by fome, that Medicis would not have acted this part, if he had not been thoroughly convinced that Montalto, far from being an invalid, was ftrong and healthful enough, in all probability, to furvive Farnefe, and all his faction, by which he imagined, he fhould get rid of thofe that were likely to be the greateft obftacles to his ever being Pope himfelf. But this, I think, is fpinning the thread rather too fine: For, though Montalto was in reality, as we have faid, but 64 years old, yet, after he was Cardinal, he appeared much more aged than he was, by letting his beard grow, and neglecting his drefs (which makes a great alteration in a man's looks) feeming almoft bent double, and hardly able to fupport himfelf with a ftaff, which he conftantly made ufe of when he went abroad.

Many of the Cardinals were aftonifhed, that Alexandrino fhould prefer Montalto to Albano, who had done him fome fignal fervices, was more advanced in years than any of them, and had been particularly recommended to him, by his uncle, upon his death-bed; as he was likewife a perfon not only of diftinguifhed wifdom and experience, but uncommon patience and affability. Alexandrino had indeed given him fome hope that he would efpoufe his caufe, but it was only to attach

tach him the more ftrongly to his party; for he faid to thofe that propofed him, " Albano has too many near " relations. His family is very numerous, and he is, " beyond meafure fond of them. Befides, he is of " an enterprizing fpirit, capable of attempting great " things, which would fet the Spanifh faction againft " him, and the whole college feems more inclined to " Montalto than him."

Oppofition is no new thing in the conclave; the practices in favour of Montalto and Albano were daily traverfed. But time at laft, and vigorous efforts, got the better of every difficulty; Alexandrino broke all the meafures of Albano's party. Not that he loved Montalto better. or held him in greater efteem; for he often faid, " He thought himfelf much more obliged " to Albano." But intereft and ambition got the better of his gratitude. He thought he fhould be at the head of affairs, if Montalto was Pope; but that if Albano was elected, he fhould have no fhare at all in the adminiftration, knowing he was capable of reigning alone, and had many relations to affift him, if he fhould have occafion. On the contrary Montalto was almoft in his dotage, as he imagined, and had no family, that he cared for, to ftand in his way. Thefe confiderations determined him for Montalto. But he afterwards heartily repented it, when he faw Montalto had been too cunning for him, and that he had been duped by trufting to appearances.

People of judgment and experience, who entered into a nicer difcuffion of this matter, thought both Alexandrino and Albano deficient in their politics, and laughed at the firft, for depending too much upon an equal fhare of authority and power, which he expected under Montalto, with Rufticucci, whom he had decoyed into his net by the fame lure. Whereas (if they had reafoned like Cardinals) they ought not to have reckoned upon a thing as certain, which was, at moft, but probable; fince many Popes, even in their memory, had governed by maxims quite different from what they feemed to adopt whilft Cardinals. This alteration

teration was fo fudden in Montalto, that the perfons that had taken the moft pains to ferve him, repented of their forwardnefs, before they went out of the conclave.

Albano was thought in the wrong, for having neglected to gain the intereft of Alexandrino, and the other Chiefs; as he could not plead want of experience in the practices of the conclave, and the method of making friends upon fuch an occafion. Perhaps, after the manner of his countrymen the Bergamefe, he prefumed too much upon himfelf, and thought it below a Cardinal of his diftinction, to have recourfe to the common, little artifices that are generally practiced at thofe times, looking upon them, not only as nngenerous, but difhoneft, and of dangerous example. For when his friends advifed him to make ufe of the fame means, that the other candidates did; he faid, " No Cardinal " ought to be too folicitous about the Papacy, much " lefs to be guilty of any dirty or underhand wiles; " but to live and behave himfelf in fuch a manner, as " to let all good men fee he was worthy of it."

In the mean time, Alexandrino and Rufticucci, impatient to be at the helm, left no ftone unturned to get Montalto elected. To engage the other Cardinals in his favour, they reprefented him as a perfon that had all the qualificatious neceffary for a Pope. They faid, " He was of a quiet and gentle difpofition, grateful " without gall or refentment, had very few relations, " exceeding zealous for the good of the Church, a lo- " ver of peace and order, humane and benevolent to " the laft degree."

But though they were fure of Medicis and D'Efte, they could not bring their fcheme to bear, without the affiftance of thofe Cardinals, that were created by Gregory XIII. and particularly of St. Sixtus, who was at the head of them, and had always profeffed himfelf ftrongly attached to Farnefe, the known enemy of Montalto, though Montalto had, upon all occafions, behaved to him with the greateft deference and refpect.

After

After a long confultation, they refolved, if poffible, to draw off fome of St. Sixtus's friends. Medicis, who had a pretty good intereft in that party, firft endeavoured to fhew them, how much it would be for their intereft ; aud then threatened them with his difpleafure, if they did not comply. Cardinal Riacio, a Bolognefe, created by Gregory, and a friend to Montalto, perfuaded Guaftavillano, who was likewife a Bolognefe, to give him his vote, which he confented to the more willingly, as he had always a greater regard for Medicis than St. Sixtus, and was glad to go with a party, in which he faw his friend and countryman engaged. They alfo prevailed upon the Cardinals Spinola, a Genoefe ; Ganzaga, of the houfe of Mantua; Antonio Maria Salviati, a Roman ; Julius Cavanio, a Ferrarefe ; and John Baptift Caftagna ; who had all been made by the late Pope, and were the principals of St. Sixtus's party.

But they had the Cardinal of Florence, and Francis Sforza, who had both great influence in the Conclave, ftill againft them ; the firft was foon brought over, by the perfuafion of his relation Medicis; the fecond made fome difficulty, upon the account of the alliance which there was betwixt his family and that of Farnefe. However, they prevailed upon him, by telling him how great an efteem his uncle Alexander Sforza had for Montalto, " That he always honoured him with his " friendfhip upon every occafion ;" and that when fome of the Farnefians formerly upbraided him with deferting them in favour of Montalto, he only faid, " I fhall endeavour to ferve a perfon of worth ; other " people may do as they pleafe."

There was no other thing wanting to accomplifh their defign, which was to fecure Altemps, a man of great confideration, and at the head of the Cardinals created by Pius IV. That province was affigned to Medicis, and Gefualdo, a Neapolitan, promoted by the fame Pope, and in the intereft of Altemps. He had fuch a regard for them both, that he did not ftand in need of much folicitation, as he was likewife glad of an

opportunity

opportunity of revenging himself upon Farnese, for excluding his friend ; not forgetting that he had said publicly, when he proposed Sirletti, " That he could " not conceive what people meant by thinking of " making him Pope."

They carried on these intrigues chiefly in the night, in which both Alexandrino and Rusticucci shewed a great deal of management and addrefs. Medicis feconded their endeavours with the afliftance of Gefueldo and Simoncelli ; Cardinal D'Efte acted in concert with Gonzaga, Caffamo, Cefis, and Caraffa, all man of long experience, and thoroughly capable of conduct-ing an affair of that confequence. Rusticucci was bufy in every place, fometimes in getting a new vote, at others in confirming and keeping fteady thofe that they had already got. They were not, however, without ap-prehenfions, that the oppofite faction would corrupt D'Efte; and indeed there was fome reafon to fear that Farnese, who fpared no pains to penetrate into their de-figns, might get him over, when he was let into them.

But he did not think their party fo formidable as it really was, and exerted himfelf more to weaken D'Efte's intereft, than to exclude Montalto.

During thefe cabals, Montalto kept clofe in his cell, without expreffing the leaft defire or expectation of the Papacy; though there was not any of the Cardinals that had fo much reafon to hope for it. When the heads of the party called at his chamber-door, as they paffed by, to inform him; how the election went on, and who had declared for him ; he ufed to fay, " The difficulties " you meet with in the Conclave are not worth notice; " I doubt you'll find much greater in the Vatican. Let " me conjure you not to think of chufing me, except " you will be content to bear the whole burden of the " government yourfelves." This is what the game-fters call a Sweetner, to draw them on, and made them labour more earneftly for his exaltation.

After all, the chief difficulty yet remained to be con-quered, they had not gained St. Sixtus, who, with his party, ftill had it in his power to exclude him; as it was

moft

moſt likely he would, left, if he came to be Pope, he
ſhould remember his uncle Gregory's having taken
away his Penſion; though he had dedicated a Commentary upon St. Ambroſe to him, as we have obſerved,
which had coſt him a great deal of labour and time.

As St. Sixtus began to be a little ſtaggered, they
made uſe of the confidence they knew he repoſed in
Cardinal Riario, who, at that time, had a fit of the gout;
but cauſed himſelf to carried to his chamber, where he
told him, " That Montalto's party was ſo ſtrong, and
" things ſo far advanced, that he would infallibly be
" choſen; that it was in vain, and only loſt time, to
" to conteſt it with him, as he would ſucceed in ſpite
" of all oppoſition; which was the reaſon of his pay-
" ing him this viſit, to adviſe him to come in with a
" good grace, as it was not in his power to prevent it."
St. Sixtus was ſtrangely ſurprized at this diſcourſe,
and much more ſo, when Guaſtavillano entered the
room juſt when Riario was coming out, as had been
concerted, and told him the very ſame thing, earneſtly
exhorting him to join with them, " As it would be,"
he ſaid, " acting inconſiſtently with his uſual pru-
" dence, now to do otherwiſe."

There happened a thing which would have ruined
all their meaſures, if it had been known by the op-
poſite faction. Alexandrino had been ſeen one night
diſguiſed in the Conclave; but Providence, which favoured Montalto, did not ſuffer this irregularity to be
diſcovered, and, at the ſame time, lulled his enemies
into ſecurity; the chief of whom was Farneſe, who did
not dream of Montalto's friends being ſo numerous,
and only imagined he might poſſibly have a majority
of votes at the Scrutiny (whereas two thirds are required) eſpecially as St. Sixtus had given him his word,
that he would not conſent to any election, without firſt
conſulting with him about it,

As we have ſpoken only occaſionally, and at different
times, of Montalto's conduct both within and without the Conclave, it is neceſſary here to enter into a
fuller detail of it.

He

He had lived many years in a very obscure manner, at the house which he bought near St. Maria Maggiore, with an attendance suitable to the modesty and humility he made profession of. When he went to any consistory or congregation, he put on an air of mildness and submission, and never was obstinate in supporting his opinion in contradiction to any other Cardinal, but giving up his own sentiments, always suffered himself to be guided by some body else. He knew how to stifle his resentment, and bore all sorts of injuries and affronts in so patient a manner, that he would turn to those that had used him with contempt in the consistory, and " thank them heartily, for the great "·favours he had received from them ;" like some other Popes that had obtained the pontificate, only by returning good for evil.

Though his nephew had been killed but the night before, he went to the consistory, he did' not seem under the least concern, nor even demanded justice of the Pope for that murder ; so that people thought his death was very indifferent to him.

When the affairs of princes were treated of, he took particular care not to say any thing that might seem harsh or offensive to their ministers. He was always careful, however, that the interest of the holy fee receiv'd no prejudice ; the rights and privileges of which he constantly asserted with great zeal and spirit, and much more so, after he came to be Pope. He was courteous and complaisant to every body ; but especially to those among the Religious, that had formerly been the most bitter against him, whom he would embrace tenderly, when they came to see him, as if they had always been his steady friends ; so that many of them used to say, when they had taken leave of him, " certainly, Cardinal " Montalto is one of the best of Christians, that can so " easily forget we were once his inveterate enemies."

Both in public and private company, he was continually magnifying the obligations he lay under to Alexandrino, and said, " if he was master of a thousand " worlds, he should never be sufficiently able to return the

" the favours, that both he and his uncle Pius V, had
" heaped upon him." In this, he certainly fpoke truth;
and Alexandrino, who was deceived in him, as well as
others, very juftly thought he had great reafon to expect a confiderable fhare of his favour, if ever he was
Pope.   He always behaved with the higheft refpect to
the Spaniards, whofe politics inclined them rather to
wifh for a Pope of but moderate abilities, than of a
bold and enterprizing turn; being apprehenfive, that a
genius of that kind might difturb the peace of Italy,
which they were highly concerned to preferve, upon the
account of the large fhare of territory they had in it.

As Montalto's love of repofe and retirement had
made them believe he was a man for their purpofe, and
prepoffeffed them in his favour, they were amongft the
firft that declared for him, giving it out, " That the K.
" of Spain had a perfonal efteem for him, and the more
" fo, as he knew he was equally a lover of moderation
" and tranquillity, and an enemy to violent and arbi-
" trary proceedings."

In the Conclave, he did not fhew the leaft fign of
ambition, and was ready to make a tender of his fervice to any one that feemed to have occafion for it,
particularly the chiefs, and fuch as he knew had great
intereft.

The very morning they entered the Conclave, he
went to wait upon Altemps, and faid, " He had fo many
" obligations to him, that he fhould ever look upon
" himfelf as a creature of hands." It is faid, Altemps
thought him fo much in earneft, that when he found
there was no probability of fucceeding himfelf, he very
readily came into the meafures that were taken to ferve
him, and faid, " If it only depended upon my vote,
" you might be fure of being Pope;" to which Montalto anfwered, " God only knows how little defirous I am
" of that dignity; I am truly fenfible how unfit and
" unworthy I am of it. If any confideration could
" move me to wifh for that honour, it would be only
" to give my friends, and particularly your Eminence,

O   " a fubftantial

" a fubftantial proof of the great efteem I have for
" them." He faid the very fame thing to Madrucci
juft after. The king of Spain had entrufted this cardinal with his moft fecret intentions as to the election;
which was no fmall mortification to Medicis, who, as
protector of the Spanifh nation, expected to have had
the whole confidence of that crown. It was commonly
believed, Madrucci, according to inftructions, had encouraged the Brigues in favour of Sirletti, Montalto,
Caftagna, and Mondovi; and that in regard to Montalto, befides his own vote, he had made ufe of all his
credit and intereft, and heartily joined his particular
friend Altemps, to get him elected.

But to return to the Conclave. It is neceffary to acquaint the reader, that after the abovementioned Cardinals had declared for Montalto, and waited, with impatience for day-light to bring on the election; Peter
Francis Ferrerio, a Piedmontefe, bifhop of Vercelli,
arrived at Rome, and early next morning was admitted amongft his brethern.

This happened very fortunately for Montalto : For as
foon as he entered, Medicis and Gefualdo took him a-
fide, and preffed him vehemently to oblige them with
his vote, which he did. Prefently after, mafs was faid
in the chapel, to which the Cardinals generally go, before they proceed to a fcrutiny. When that was over,
the Dean ordered a mafter of the ceremonies to read the
three bulls to Vercelli.

The chiefs of Montalto's party thought this a proper
juncture to give the finifhing ftroke to their fcheme;
and as foon as he began to read them, D'Efte beckoned
Alexandrino, who fat over-againft him, to follow him
out of the chapel. Alexandrino, who underftood him,
got up, and leaned forward over his feat, as if he had
been writing his vote; but in reality, for an opportunity of fpeaking to St. Sixtus, whom he took out along
with him, and faid to him foftly, " Your Eminence
" may affure yourfelf, upon my word; that Altemps
" and Medicis have joined their ftrength with us, and
                                        defign

" defign to chufe Montalto immediately ; that Guftavil-
" lano and many others of the greateft power, are privy
" and confenting to it ; that in fhort, every thing is quite
" fettled and agreed upon.   However, out of the great
" regard we have ever had for your Eminence, we
" would not proceed to the election, till we had firft
" acquainted you with it ; that the new Pope might
" lye under fome obligations to you, as well as others.
" We, for our parts, have by this difcharged the duty
" of friends, it now lies upon you to chufe, whether
" you will come into it voluntarily, or have the morti-
" fication of feeing a Pope made whether you will or
" not."

As St. Sixtus had not forefeen or expected any thing
of this kind, he was fo difconcerted, that he quite loft
all refolution and prefence of mind.   It recalled to his
memory what Riario and Guaftavillano had faid before,
and made him entirely forget the engagement to Farnefe; he thought no more of the reafons, that ought to
have induced him to vote for nobody but one of his
own creatures, and feemed to be altogether deferted by
the prudence and conftancy, which are fo neceffary to
the head of a party, efpecially fo confiderable a one as
his, and of which he had given repeated proofs; though
it muft be owned, that, whilft he governed the church
under his uncle Gregory, he had in fome cafes behaved
like a man of a changeable and unfteady difpofition.

Thus much is certain, that if he had continued united with Farnefe, and taken proper meafures with their
party to ftand the firft fhock of this Brigue, they would
have ftrangely embarraffed, if not totally excluded,
Montalto ; but, God permitting their reafon and courage
to abandon them at that crifis, he fent for his followers, to the number of 12, into the hall, and told
them, " That he thought proper to call them together,
" to confult what fteps were further neceffary to be
" taken in the prefent fituation of affairs; and advife
" with them, what would be moft conducive to the
" glory of God, and the good of his church."

The Cardinals, who had before engaged themselves to Montalto, and were at the bottom of this, viz. Florence, Cananio, Gesualdo, Salviati, Spinola, Riario, Sforza, and Castagna, said, " They thought they could not " chuse a fitter person than Montalto, nor one that " would fill the throne more worthily." Nobody offering to contradict them ; Fachinetti, a person of great wisdom and singular goodness, said, " We shall be " wholly directed by your Eminence, and approve of " whatever measures you please to recommend to us."

Not one of them returned into the chapel, except the cardinal of Austria, who went back to ask Madrucci, " Whether he would consent to this election?" He said, " he would, to oblige St. Sixtus."

The going out of Alexandrino and St. Sixtus was without example, and put a stop for some time to the scrutiny. It was much wondered at, that Farnese, who had carried several elections before, to whom Pius IV, Pius V, and Gregory XIII, entirely owed the Pontificate, was not able at this time to exclude Montalto ; as he was dean of the H. College, leader of a considerable party, very quick-sighted, expert in such intrigues, and of excellent judgment. In short, it was thought exceeding strange, that he did not follow St. Sixtus out of the chapel (whom he knew to be of a fluctuating and unstable temper) to keep him steady, and try if it was not possible to defeat the measures of Montalto's party, by proposing a friend of his own, or joining with Altemps, in the election of Sirletti, Vercelli, or Paleotto, rather than a person, whom he had always openly despised, and expressed so mean an opinion of.

He was quite confounded, when he saw the chiefs of the parties all united against him ; and heard Cardinal D'Este who had beckoned to Alexandrino to go out of the chapel) say aloud, " There was no occasion to read " the bulls, for the Pope was chosen." Upon this, Alexandrino returning in haste to keep him in the chapel, came and told him, that Montalto was actually elected, advising him, at the same time, to make a show of
concurring

concurring with them in it; that he might find the fame degree of favour in this Pontificate, that he had done in that of Paul III.

It is imagined, that he was at laſt prevailed upon to come into their meaſures, by the conſideration of the infirmities Montalto had ſo long laboured under, and his ſeeming inſenſibility, from which he thought there was no cauſe to apprehend any reſentment of paſt injuries; it appeared to him a matter of little or no conſequence, whether a man, with one foot in the grave, and ſo ſtupid as Montalto, was made Pope, or ſtill continued cardinal. In ſhort, he only aſked St. Sixtus, " What were " his motives for this conduct;" to which he anſwered, " that he knew him to be of a gentle and ductile na- " ture, and was ſure they ſhould be very happy, and " enjoy a great deal of liberty, in this Pontificate." " I do not know but we may," replied Farneſe, " for he " has neither the ſpirit to do any miſchief, nor ſenſe " enough to do good."

It is not to be wondered at, that the ſuffrages of the cardinals did not concur with the voice of the people, who wiſhed to ſee Farneſe exalted to the Papacy. They looked with a ſuſpicious eye upon the grandeur of his houſe; the valour and good fortune of his nephew Alexander Farneſe (the greateſt and moſt ſucceſsful general of his age) who commanded the K. of Spain's armies in Flanders. Beſides, the college had not forgot what paſſed under Paul III. Farneſe was capable of undertaking great deſigns, eſpecially if ſeconded and aſſiſted by his nephew, who might diſturb the peace of Chriſtendom, and more particularly that of the eccleſiaſtical ſtate, by endeavouring to put them into execution, having already experienced to their coſt, that ſuch attempts are prejudicial, not only to the church, but the whole world, when the eaſineſs or affection of the Popes, have ſacrificed the good of the public to the ambition of their nephews, or other relations.

Some were of opinion, that the contempt in which he ſeemed to hold the poorer Cardinals, contributed not
a little

a little to Montalto's fuccefs. He was governed by a very peculiar fort of a maxim in this refpect, and thought the fureft way to arrive at the Papacy, was to appear morofe and fupercilious, and to have but little familiarity or intercourfe with them ; but he was deceived in this, as well as the great confidence he put in his intereft, without which he thought they could not make a Pope, and that all thofe that had any pretenfions of that kind, ought to make their court to, and live in a fort of dependence upon him.

It furprized every body, that was acquainted with the variety of fchemes that were carried on in this Conclave, that not one of the chiefs ever propofed, or fo much as named, the Cardinals St. George and Santa Croce, the laft a Roman, and both of them men of fome fame and reputation. This feemed more ftrange with regard to Santa Croce than St. George, as he was not only made Cardinal by Pius IV, but expected to have been propofed the very firft by D'Efte, upon the account of his having been Nuncio in France, and created at the requeft of that crown. He had likewife carried his cup very even with the K. of Spain, and always fupported his intereft, whenever that of France was not concerned, which gave room to fufpect that he fecretly afpired to the Papacy. But unluckily for him, he was obliged to fit down content, with the honour of having been only candidate for it.

People were at a lofs how to account for the flight that was put upon thefe two Cardinals. Many imputed it to the unexpected turn that affairs had taken, and fome unlucky accidents which human prudence could not forefee. Others thought the chiefs were unwilling to propofe fuch a thing, to fpare them the fhame and mortification of feeing themfelves difgracefully excluded. For there were objections to both one and the other, more than fufficient for that purpofe. St. George was reckoned an unexperienced felfifh man, and of a martial turn (which circumftance alone would have been a fufficient objection to him with the Spaniards) and

and not at all to be trusted, as he had no manner of regard to his word or promise.   Santa Croce, on the other
hand, though he had the reputation of a very sensible
and polite man, was accounted revengeful and ambitious.   France and Spain put no great confidence in him;
his very relations were afraid of him; and his own countrymen, the Roman Cardinals, would certainly have voted against him, if he had been named; so that he was,
like a prophet, *without honour in his own country.*

Though Paleotto had a good share of popular favour,
and both city and court were of opinion that his chance
was by no means a bad one, he was never proposed.
Not that there were any material objections that could
be made to him; but the College was tired of the last
Pope's reign, which had been a very long one, and determined not to chuse another Bolognese to succeed him.

The nephews of Gregory would not consent to chuse
him, though he was their countryman, lest he should obscure the splendor of their house.   Besides, he was not
very well liked by some of the Cardinals, upon the account of the shyness and little acquaintance there was
betwixt him and Farnese.   Fachinetti likewise was not
once mentioned, because he too was a Bolognese; and
so whimsical, and sometimes contrary, are the reason-
ings even of wise men, that whereas it had been urged
as an objection to Paleotto, that he had no good under-
standing with Farnese; Fachinetti was accused of being
too familiar and intimate with him.   As he was, nevertheless, a man of singular virtue, long experience in
ecclesiastical affairs, and very zealous for the good of
the H. See; his exaltation would, without doubt, have
been a great blessing to the whole Christian world.

Augustine Valerio, Cardinal and bishop of Verona, was
much talked of, during the vacancy of the H. See; and
though he was but 50 years old, or thereabout, it is
certain he would have been named at least, if not elected, though his being a noble Venetian prejudiced the
Spaniards against him.   Some people too were rather
afraid of seeing him Pope, as he led a very ascetic life,

and

and was a great friend to ſtrict diſcipline and reformation, though, in private, he was of a very ſweet and
amiable temper; but not being in the Conclave, there
was nothing ſaid of him.

Mondovi, who was a new Cardinal, was likewiſe abſent, and never mentioned. As he had a very conſiderable intereſt, it was thought, if he had been there, he
would certainly have been choſen; eſpecially if France
and Spain had joined in his favour, as it was ſaid they
deſigned.

Julius Santorio, called Cardinal St. Severino, was barely ſpoken of, and that was all. Ruſticucci, his particular
friend, waited for a proper opportunity of propoſing
him; but theſe intrigues, in favour of Montalto, put an
end to his expectations. He was much eſteemed by
every body, for his remarkable candour, piety, and con-
ſtant endeavours to ſerve the public. Spain was hearty in his intereſt; Farneſe repoſed an entire confidence
in him; and Alexandrino loved him tenderly.

As ſoon as St. Sixtus perceived his friends were inclined to give their ſuffrages for Montalto, he put himſelf
at their head, and led them back into the Chapel, with
a deſign to begin the adoration immediately, to the
great aſtoniſhment of many.

After they had taken their places, a ſcrutiny was propoſed. But St. Sixtus, either out of impatience, or for
fear any ſudden change might happen, or deſirous of
ſeeming to have the principal hand in this election,
ſtepped out of his place to Alexandrino, and taking him
by the hand, they both went up to Montalto, and cried
out, a Pope, a Pope; the greateſt part of the Cardinals following their example, and approving of what was done.

It is neceſſary here to give a general account of the
method obſerved in electing a Pope, which may not, perhaps, be diſagreeable to the reader. It is uſually performed by ſcrutiny, by acceſs, or adoration. There was
formerly another way, called compromiſe [2], made uſe
of.

[2] I remember an inſtance in *The Hiſtory of the Knights of Malta*, of the Conclave's leaving the choice of a Pope to a particular
Cardinal

of. When diffentions ran fo high in the Conclave (as it too often happens) that they could not, by any means, agree in their choice, they, by common confent, engaged themfelves to two or three Cardinals, and fometimes to one; that what perfon foever he or they fhould chufe, out of fuch a number as was propofed by them, fhould be their lawful Pope. But this is now out of ufe, and, in cafe of any difference in opinion, they have recourfe to one of the three ways above mentioned. The fcrutiny which is the principal and moft ufual way in the Conclave, is performed in this manner.

Every Cardinal orders his conclavift to bring him a ticket, made of a long, narrow piece of paper wrapped up in five folds. On the uppermoft he writes his name with his own hand, and then doubles it down, fo that it becomes the innermoft. After that, he doubles it down again to the third, which he feals at each end with two different feals. The two lowermoft being ftill vacant, the conclavift writes the name of the perfon, whom his mafter defigns to vote for, upon the fourth, in this form: " I give my vote to his Emi-" nence, Cardinal A. B." and covers all with the laft fold. On the outfide of the ticket is wrote a motto of the Cardinal's own chufing; as Faith, Hope, Charity, Peace, Juftice, Religion, or any other word or words, as he pleafes. So that if there fhould be an accefs (in which he muft not give his vote for the fame perfon, that he did in the fcrutiny) it may be eafily known whether any Cardinal has a right to accede or not, by having recourfe to his ticket, without opening them all, which might occafion infinite animofity and diftraction.

Thefe tickets are put into a golden chalice, that ftands upon the Altar in the Chapel, where the fcrutiny is made. But firft the three fenior Cardinals, who prefide at it to fee that every thing is done according to

Cardinal (his name I cannot recollect, as I have not now that book by me) who having taken fome time to confider of it, afked them, if they would all acquiefce in his choice, and they anfwering in the affirmative; he faid, *Ego fum Papa*, " Then I'll be Pope myfelf."

due

due form and order, go to the apartments of those that
are sick, to take their votes, which are sealed up in the
same manner, and put into the chalice with the others,
and then poured out upon a table placed before the
altar.   If it happens, that two thirds of the votes fall
upon one person, he is immediately declared Pope; and
the tickets opened, that he may know the names of
the persons that voted for him.   But this very rarely
comes to pass; it did indeed at the election of Adrian
VI, Preceptor to Charles V, and never since.

If the election cannot be decided by a scrutiny, they
proceed to the access, or approach in which a Person
is proposed by one of the Cardinals.   This is of very
ancient standing, and much like the custom of the Roman senators; who, in giving their votes, if they agreed
in opinion with any other senator that had voted before, rose from their seats, and going to the place where
he sat, said, *Accedo ad Fabium, Brutum Pompeium, Ci-
ceronem*, or whatever his name was; which gave rise
to the Latin phrase, *In sententiam ire.*

The Cardinal that accedes, says, " I accede to Cardi-
" nal D, and have a right to do so, as appears from
" my Ticket superscribed, *Peace, Justice, Religion*, or
" whatever the word may be."

The third way is by adoration, and is thus performed:
That Cardinal who is the candidate's chief friend, goes
up to him and making a low reverence, cries out, *a
Pope, a Pope*; when it happens that two thirds of them
do the same, he is then acknowledged as such; but if
there wants only one of that number the election is
void.   It has often happened, that persons have been
adored, who never came to the Papacy; because they
had not a sufficient number of Cardinals to complete
their adoration.   This way is usually tried by a Junto,
obstinate in the promotion of the person whom they
propose, lest some of those, that had promised them,
should fail in the scrutiny, which is sometimes the case.
It must be observed, that both access and adoration are
usually confirmed (for form sake) by a scrutiny, which
is of no prejudice to either; for the chief friends of
                                                      the

the new elected Pope, generally make a verbal proteſt to that effect, and ſometimes in writing, before a notary. This laſt way is accounted the moſt honourable, as the Cardinals are ſuppoſed to be then influenced by the immediate impulſe and inſpiration of the Holy Ghoſt : Though ſome think it a dangerous and violent method, as three or four young Cardinals may put themſelves at the head of a faction, and over-awe and intimidate others into a compliance with them.

This has obliged the Popes, from time to time, to make ſeveral new regulations, to preſerve the peace and quiet of the Conclave, by ordering the method of electing by ſcrutiny only to be obſerved ; in which there is no dependance of one Cardinal upon another, but every one diſpoſes of his vote according to conſcience.

Whilſt they were crowding towards Montalto to congratulate him, he ſat coughing and weeping, as if ſome great misfortune had befallen him. But when the Cardinal Dean ordered them to retire to their reſpective places, that they might proceed to a regular ſcrutiny ; he drew near to St. Sixtus, and whiſper'd in his ear, " Pray " take care that the ſcrutiny is of no prejudice to the " adoration;" which was the firſt diſcovery he made of his ambition.   St. Sixtus was extremely ſurprized to ſee a perſon, who had always pretended to be totally ignorant of all the forms and ceremonials that are practiſed in the Conclave, ſo well acquainted with the niceſt and moſt delicate circumſtance of the election ; and that he, who had hitherto ſeemed quite indifferent about, or rather afraid of the Papacy, ſhould, on a ſudden, be ſo apprehenſive of being diſappointed of it.   However, being now too late, as he thought, to recede, he ſpoke to Alexandrino; and when the Dean was beginning the ſcrutiny, they both got up and proteſted againſt its being any prejudice to the adoration.

It was obſerved, that after it was begun; Montalto walked backwards and forwards, and ſeemed to be in great agitation of ſpirit ; but when he perceived there was a ſufficient number of votes to ſecure his election,

he

he threw the ftaff, with which he ufed to fupport himfelf, into the middle of the Chapel, ftretched himfelf
up, and appeared taller, by almoft a foot, than he had
done for feveral years, hawking and fpitting with as
much ftrength as a man of 30 years old.

The Cardinals, aftonifhed at fo fudden an alteration,
looked at him with amazement, and Farnefe obferving
by fome figns that St. Sixtus and Alexandrino already
began to repent of their forwardnefs in this election,
faid aloud, " Stay a little, foftly, there is a miftake in
the fcrutiny;" But Montalto, with a ftern look, boldly
anfwer'd " There is no miftake; the fcrutiny is good,
" and in due form;" and immediately thundered out
the *Te Deum* himfelf, in a voice that made the Chapel
fhake. Of fuch confequence, fometimes, is courage
and prefence of mind: For if he had not acted in this
manner, there is no doubt but fo fudden a change of
behaviour, and the Dean's faying, " there was a miftake
" in the fcrutiny," would have overfet the whole, and
put a ftop to his election, if the Cardinals had feconded him. But they all ftood dumb and motionlefs, looking at each other and biting their lips. What feemed
moft ftrange was, that Farnefe, Dean of the College,
a man of long experience and great authority, of a
bold and refolute difpofition, haughty and difdainful
in his carriage to every body, fhould begin the attack
with fo much fpirit, endeavouring to fet afide the fcrutiny, by declaring there was a miftake in it, without
offering to proceed any farther, or fpeaking another
word, againft a man that he hated and defpifed. That
fo many heads of factions, fuch a number of papable
Cardinals who might have had an opportunity of advancing themfelves, or their friends, fhould, in an inftant become fo tame and fpiritlefs, that it looked like
an infatuation. It is certain that if the Dean, whofe
office it was to fing the *Te Deum*, had commanded
Montalto to defift, the other Cardinals would have
fupported him in it, and he had been for ever excluded.

When

When they came to that verfe in the *Te Deum, We therefore pray thee, help thy fervants whom thou haft redeemed with thy precious blood*; he threw himfelf upon his knees before the altar, and after it was finished, made a fhort prayer according to cuftom, which was purely mental; for it was remarked, that he never moved his lips, but kept his eyes attentively fixed upon a crucifix all the time.

Whilft he was in this pofture, Bombi, firft Mafter of the Ceremonies, came to him (as is ufual) and faid, " My Lord Cardinal Montalto, your Eminence is duly " elected Pope; the Holy College defires to know, whe- " ther you pleafe to accept the Papacy;" to which he replied fomewhat fharply, " It is trifling and imperti- " nent to afk, whether I will accept what I have alrea- " dy accepted, as I have fufficiently fhewn, by finging " the *Te Deum.* However, to fatisfy any fcruple that " may arife, I tell you, that I accept it with great plea- " fure, and would accept another, if I could get it; for " I find myfelf ftrong enough by the Divine affiftance, " to manage two Papacies."

Farnefe, who ftood near him, hearing this, faid to St. Severino, " The Gentlemen that took upon them " to conduct this election, thought to have engroffed " the whole adminiftration of affairs to themfelves, by " chufing a fool and an ideot; but I plainly fee, we " have got a Pope that will make fools and ideots both " of them and us;" St. Severino only fhrugged up his fhoulders, and faid, " the Lord have mercy upon us all."

When he was afked what name he would take; he anfwered, Sixtus V, which he did in honour of Pope Sixtus IV, who had likewife been a monk of the fame order. Some fay out of compliment to Cardinal St. Sixtus; but this does not feem probable, confidering the little refpect he fhewed him afterwards.

It was obferved, that whilft the Cardinals were putting on his pontifical robes, he ftretched out his arms with great vigour and activity; upon which Rufticucci, who was furprized at fo fudden a metamorphofis, faid to him in a familiar way, " I perceive, Holy Father, the Pon- " tificate

" tificate is a fovereign panacea; fince it can reftore
" youth and health to old, fick Cardinals;" to which
he replied in a grave and majeftic manner, "So I
" find it."

The very moment the fcrutiny was ended, he bid
adieu to that appearance of humility he had fo long
worn; and laying afide the civility and complaifance he
ufed to fhew to all manner of people, behaved with
great ftate and referve to every body; but more particularly to them, that he had been moft obliged to for
his exaltation.

This immediate change in the new Pope, was a
thunder-clap to D'Efte, Medicis and Alexandrino. One
might perceive evident figns of repentance in their fa-
ces before the election was well over. Cardinal Farnefe faid to Sforza, as they were going out of the Conclave, " Charles V. refigned his crown in the morning,
" and repented of it in the evening; but I fancy thefe
" Gentlemen (pointing to them) have began their re-
" pentance already. "It will be well for them," replied Sforza, " If their repentance does not laft longer
" than the Emperor's did."

After he was dreffed in his robes he afcended the
Pontifical Throne, that ftands over againft the Altar in
the Chapel, where he fat with fo much ftate, that any
one would have thought he had been Pope feveral years.
The Cardinals advancing, two by two, to adore him;
his Holinefs gave them feparately, the *Ofculum Chari-
tatis*, "the Kifs of Charity," upon both cheeks; and
then admitted every body, that was in the Conclave to
the honour of kiffing his feet. It is faid, when Farnefe came, amongft the reft to perform that ceremony,
he did it with great reluctance, and fhewed particular
figns of difguft, at proftrating himfelf before a perfon
of his mean birth, whom he ufed often to call in derifion, " The dregs of the Conclave, the Afs of La
" Marca, ftinking old Lazar," &c.

Some people thought he faid in his heart, *Non tibi
fed Petro*, " Not to thee, but St. Peter;" be that as it
will,

will, when he beheld him fitting fo erect, and with fo much Majefty, upon the Throne, he faid to him, " Your " Holinefs feems a quite different fort of a man from " what you were a few hours ago. " Yes, fays he, I was " then looking for the keys of Paradife, which obliged " me to ftoop a little; but now I have found them, it " is time to look upwards, as I am arrived at the fum- " mit of all human glory, and can climb no higher in " this world.

When the adoration was finifhed, the firft Cardinal Deacon affifted by a Mafter of the Ceremonies, took a crucifix in his hand, and proceeded into the Hall, at- tended by the Cardinals.   Laft of all came his Holinefs, the choir finging before him the Anthem, *Ecce Sacerdos magnus, qui in diebus fuis placuit Deo, et inventus eft juf- tus*, &c.   Whilft this was performing, the Cardinal Deacon caufed a window to be broke open, and fhewed a crucifix to the people, who now began to affemble, in great numbers, in the Piazza, of St. Peter [3]; and at the fame time proclaimed him after the accuftomed manner, *Annuncio vobis gaudium magnum*, &c.   *Behold I bring you tidings of great joy*; *the moft illuftrious Car- dinal* Montalto *is chofen Pope, and has taken the name of* Sixtus V.

This happened upon a Wednefday [April 24, 1585], a day that had often been propitious to him. The ftreets immediately echoed with acclamations of *Long live Six- tus* V. the guns from the Caftle of St. Angelo were fired, and the bells rang in every Church and Convent.

As it is cuftomary in Rome, at the proclamation of a new Pope, for the mob to run directly and plunder the houfe where he lived before ; the followers and domef- tics of every Cardinal, that is likely to be made a Pope, generally take care of that, by ftripping it themfelves beforehand ; and, if their patron does not fucceed, bring every thing back again.   But at this time the populace was not in any great hurry to go to Mon- talto,

[3] A vaft Area before St. Peter's.—This is the ufual fignal of a Pope being chofen.

talto, "expecting," as they said, "to find nothing there,
" but a few old broken chairs and tables."

In this interval, the cooks and confectioners of the
Conclave prepared a collation, at which the Pope pronounced a solemn blessing; and after he had eat a
mouthful or two, and drank a glass of citron water,
ordered the masons to unwall the doors of the conclave,
and let in the people.

He was then conducted to the chapel, and adored, a
second time, by the Cardinals. This adoration was
performed by kneeling upon the ground, and kiff ng his
left-hand only, whilst he gave his benediction with the .
right. When this was over, a master of the ceremonies
took up the crucifix, and walked before the choir, who
sang hymns and anthems; the Cardinals followed two
by two, the Pope coming last, carried upon men's
shoulders. As they came out of the Conclave in this
order, he gave his blessing, and distributed little cruci-
fixes to the citizens and strangers, who flocked, in great
crouds, to see the new Pontiff, crying out, " Where is
" he? Which is the Pope? This cannot be the poor old
" Cardinal, that used to faint away in the streets. Sure-
" ly, this cannot be father Montalto, who went tottering
" about with a staff."

In his passage from the Conclave, the people cried
out, *Long live the Pope*; and added, according to custom, "Plenty, Holy Father, Plenty and Justice; " to
which he replied, " Pray to God for plenty, and I will
" give you justice."

When he arrived at St. Peter's, all the Canons came
out, in procession, to meet him, singing an anthem; and,
being carried up to the great altar, he was adored, for
the last time, by the Cardinals kissing his feet, whilst
the Choir sang the Te Deum. When that was over, the
Cardinal Deacon read some prayers, the Pope sitting all
the while. After this, the Cardinal Deacon taking the
mitre off his head, he gave his benediction to the peo
ple, with a very strong, clear voice, stretched out his
arms, with all the appearance of great strength and
                                              vigour.

vigour. The Deacon then putting on his mitre again, he afcended the fteps of the altar with the Cardinals, and gave a benediction to them only; after which he put off fome of his pontifical habiliments, and getting into a clofe chair, was carried to the Vatican, attended by a guard of foldiers.

When he got thither, he was fo impatient to exercife the fovereignty, that he could hardly be prevailed upon to defer it, according to the cuftom of his predeceffors, till he was crowned (before which it is not ufual for the new Popes to ftir out of the palace upon any occafion whatfoever) telling the Cardinals, " he would be-" gin to reign that very evening, as there was great " need of immediate reformation," and ordered the crown to be brought directly. Nor was it without the utmoft difficulty, that they perfuaded him to put off his coronation a few days. Indeed he would not hear of it, till he was convinced it was not an effential point, and that he might exercife the pontificial authority in as full and ample a manner before, as after that ceremony; which gave occafion to one of the Cardinals to fay, " he never faw a Pope fo greedy of command " before."

After moft of the Cardinals had taken their leave, he eat a bifcuit or two, and drank a glafs of wine, to refrefh himfelf, and then was conducted into the Pope's apartment, whither he was attended by Alexandrino and Rufticucci, who preffed him, " to repofe himfelf a lit-" tle, after the fatigues of the day;" but he anfwered, " Labour fhould be his chief pleafure." Upon which Alexandrino took the liberty of faying to him, " your " Holinefs talked in a different ftrain yefterday, and " the day before." " It may be fo, replied he, but " I was not Pope then."

Rufticucci met with another rebuff, that chagrined him extremely. The Pope's robe happening to lie in a fold upon his fhoulders, that Cardinal was endeavouring to pull it ftraight; and the Pope thinking he handled him rather too freely, faid angrily, " Pray, Sir, not quite
P   " fo

" fo familiar if you pleafe." But what gave the finifhing ftroke to both their hopes, was, that having taken
upon them to give directions, " that nothing fhould be
" wanting in his apartments;" he faid very gravely to
them, " you need not put yourfelves to any trouble,
" gentlemen, I fhall give orders for what I want my-
" felf." Upon which Rufticucci whifpered to Alexandrino, " that's for you." " I think replied the other,
" it is for you too, if I am not miftaken."

Whilft he was walking very brifkly about his apartment, to the great aftonifhment of thofe that faw him
(as he ufed to go with a ftaff before, and that with
much difficulty) brandifhing his arms, and ufing other
geftures, as if he was revolving great defigns in his
mind, the fteward of the houfhold * came to afk him,
" what he would pleafe to have for fupper;" Sixtus,
looking fternly at him, faid, " Is that a ufual queftion
" to afk a fovereign Prince? prepare us a royal ban-
" quet, and we fhall choofe what we like beft; ordering
him to invite the Cardinals, Alexandrino, Medicis, Rufticucci, D'Efte, St. Sixtus and Altemps. D'Efte excufed
himfelf (upon a pretence of indifpofition) the others accepted of the invitation, and fupped with his Holinefs,
not much to their fatisfaction: For they were hardly
fat down to table, when he began to let them know after what manner he intended to govern; and expatiated
largely upon the power that Jefus Chrift had given to
St. Peter, in making him his Vicar upon earth, often
repeating to them, *thou art Peter, and upon this Rock I
will build my Church*; which he explained to them after
this manner, " how profound and incomprehenfible are
" the ways of God! Jefus Chrift has left upon earth but
" one Peter, but one Pontiff, but one Vicar, but one
" Head and Chief. To him alone he has committed
" the care of his flock. Thou art Peter: that is to
" fay, thou only art the fovereign Pontiff; to thee I
" give the keys of the Kingdom of Heaven; thou

---

* Italian, *Maeftro di Cafa.* French, *Maître d' Hôtel.*

" alone

" alone fhalt have the power to bind and loofe ; to
" thee I give authority to govern and conduct my
" church ; to thee (who art my Vicar) and not to o-
" thers, who are but the Minifters and Subordinates."

The Cardinals eafily perceived the drift and tenour of
his comment ; and that all the golden hopes they had
conceived of rule and authority, were dwindled into
phantoms and fhadows. He would not fo much as fuffer them to make the leaft anfwer ; and if any one offered to open his lips, he interrupted him with faying,
" that one head was fufficient for the church."   Rufticucci, however ventured to fay, that he could not but
wonder a little to hear his Holinefs now talk in that
manner ; when he had told them fo often in the Conclave, " it was not poffible for him to govern the church
" without their affiftance." " Very true, replied Sixtus,
" I believe I might fay fo, and I thought fo at that
" time ; but now I perceive myfelf ftrong enough by
" God's affiftance, to govern without any other help.
" If I told you a ftory, you muft even make the beft
" of it.   I fhall give my confeffor a power to abfolve
" me from that fin.   You made me Pope for your own
" interefts, and I accepted that honour to do the
" church a fervice."   With this compliment he difmiffed them. As they went home Medicis, who feemed
to be the moft chagrined faid to them, " It is high
" time to provide for our fafety, I forefee a great ftorm
" rifing."

The next morning there appeared two pafquinades
[4] : The firft was Pafquin, holding a fqueezed turnip
in his hand, and a label, with thefe words upon it,

[4] Italian. *Mi Sia rotto 'l Capa, come quefta Rapa,*
 Si mai più Frate farà Papa.

French. *Qu'on me rompe la Tête, comme a cette Rave,*
 Si jamais Moyne devient Pape.

Pafquin and Marforio are two old mutilated ftatues at Rome, on
which the wits generally in the night time hang their fatyrs and
lampoons, from thence called Pafquinades.

May

" May my head be mafhed like this turnip, if ever we
" chufe a monk again."

The fecond had more wit and fatyr in it. Pafquin
was reprefented with a plate full of tooth-picks in his
hand; and Marforio afking him, " Whither he was
" carrying them ;" he anfwered, " to Alexandrino, Me-
" dicis and Rufticucci," that the reader may perceive
the fting of this, it is neceffary to inform him, that
when the Italians have a mind to laugh at, or make a
joke of a perfon that has mifcarried in any enterprize,
it is ufual to fend him a tooth-pick, hinting that he
has nothing to do now, but pick his teeth. The fame
prefent is fent to people that have lately been turned
out of their offices ; this being explained, it is eafy to
make the application. When Farnefe heard of it, he
could not help laughing and faid, " I am afraid thefe
" Gentlemen will not be the only people that will have
" occafion for tooth-picks."

After they had been guilty of this error, inftead of
thinking of any redrefs, they only vented their gall by
laying the fault upon each other. One day, foon after
the election, Alexandrino, D'Efte and Medicis, lament-
ing their misfortune, and curfing their meannefs of fpirit and ftupidity, in fuffering themfelves to be duped
by the hypocrify of Montalto, and not daring to exert
themfelves when they difcovered it, and had yet time
enough to have baffled his fchemes ; Farnefe faid, " he
" had done his duty in founding the trumpet; but that
" no body would draw their fword." They on the contrary accufed him of cowardice, for proceeding no further and faid, " they were ready to have feconded
" him, if he had ordered Montalto to leave off, when
" he began to fing the *Te Deum*." Thefe fruitlefs complaints were all the confolation they had for their folly,
and rather ferved to make bad worfe; for Sixtus hearing of their murmurs and mutual upbraidings, fent for
them and faid fharply. " We are informed that you
" repent of your choice; and that you did not make
" a fchifm in the Conclave, by breaking off the fcrutiny.

" tiny. We would have you to know, that we don't
" think ourfelves in the leaft obliged to you for the Pa-
" pacy, but to Divine Providence alone, and our own
" prudent conduct."

End of the Fourth Book.

BOOK THE FIFTH.

THE firft days of his pontificate were taken up in
receiving the congratulations of the Roman nobility, and giving audience to the ambaffadors and minifters of foreign Princes, whom he received in a very
complaifant manner, and with a chearful countenance;
but foon difmiffed them, defiring to be excufed, " for
" he had fomething elfe to do than attend to compli-
" ments." It is true, he treated the ambaffadors from
Japan, who arrived at Rome in the time of his predeceffor, with fo uncommon diftinction and refpect, that it
is worth while to relate fome particulars of their embaffy and reception at Rome,

Japan contains 36 different iflands, and is computed
to be three times as large as Italy. It is diftant about
60 leagues from China, and divided into feveral kingdoms. The climate is very cold; and the north wind
which blows there almoft conftantly, occafions large
and frequent fnows; yet it is a very fruitful country,
and abounds with every thing but grain, of which there
is little, befides the rice that ferves them for bread.
The inhabitants have a great averfion to the flefh of all
tame and domeftic animals; but are fond of venifon,
and delight much in hunting. They are genèrally
ftrong and well made, and very ingenious (as one may
judge by the Art of Printing, which they were mafters
of,

of, before we knew any thing of it in Europe) of a
warlike and courageous difpofition, and bear all manner of toil and fatigue with incredible patience. Poverty is not looked upon as any difgrace amongft them;
theft and robbery are held in the greateft abhorrence,
and punifhed with the utmoft feverity. They are very
religious, pay much refpect to their nobility, and are
naturally inclined to truth and juftice.

Francis Xavier (who was afterwards canonized) a
friend and companion of Ignatius Loyola, being fent into this country to extirpate idolatry, and eftablifh the
Chriftian faith, arrived there in the year 1549; and
made fo confiderable and fwift a progrefs in that important miffion, that he converted vaft numbers to the Catholic religion, baptizing the king of Bungo, one of
the moft powerful Princes in thofe parts, and fo beloved
by his fubjects for his wifdom and clemency, that his
converfion contributed very much to the eftablifhment
of Chriftianity in his dominions.

The example of this Prince, who took the name of
Francis, was followed by the King of Arima, and the
Prince of Omura, the former was called Prothais, or
Profafius, the latter Bartholomew.

The Jefuits willing to reap the honour of converting
thefe kingdoms, and at the fame time to fhew their
gratitude to Pope Gregory XIII, who had built them a
magnificent college at Rome, thought it would give him
great pleafure to fee nations fo far diftant reduced to
the obedience of the Church; and for this purpofe,
ufed their utmoft endeavours with the Princes that
were lately converted, to fend a formal embaffy to the
Pope to notify their converfion, to affure him of their
obedience, and acknowledge him as head of the
Catholic church, and Vicar of Jefus Chrift. With this
view, they difpatched Father Alexander Valignan to Ja-
pon, in quality of Vifitor, who encouraged them to fend
this embaffy. But as the length of the voyage (which
was fome thoufand leagues) made it feem too perilous
an undertaking for any pefons that were advanced in
years,

years, thefe princes thought it better to fend over fuch
as were young and healthful, and nearly allied to them,
to do the more honour to the Holy See. The king of
Bungo pitched upon Don Mantio, his brother-in-law,
and nephew to the king of Fungo. The king of Arima, and the prince of Omura, chofe Don Michael Cin-
giva, coufin to the one, and nephew to the other.

Thefe two ambaffadors were about 16 years old, very genteel and fenfible, and had letters to the Pope
from their fovereigns, wrote with their own hands, in
which they acknowledged him as the only true and lawful vicar of Jefus Chrift upon earth, fwore perpetual
obedience to the Holy See, and humbly hoped he would
excufe them from waiting upon him in perfon, as their
age, and the neceffity there was for their prefence at
that time, would not allow them to be long abfent from
their kingdoms. Thefe letters were filled with profeffions of eternal and inviolable attachment to the church
of Rome, and dictated, very probably by father Valignan.

They fent, with their ambaffadors, two other young
noblemen, about 18 years of age, by way of companions; one of them was called Don Julian Nacaura, of
the beft and richeft family in the country ; the other
Don Martino Fara, a young gentleman of great hopes,
well read in the hiftory of foreign countries, and very
defirous of feeing Europe. Valignan charged himfelf
with the care of them, and their attendants, who were
not very numerous, upon the account of the length and
tedioufnefs of the voyage.

Every thing being ready for their departure, they fet
out the 20th of February, 1582, and were conducted
to the frontiers of their dominions, by a prodigious
number of the nobility, and other principal perfons of
the realm, having firft received the facrament from the
hands of father Valignan.

The reader may eafily judge of the many difafters
and perils they. met with in their voyage, when he is
informed, that it was above two years before they arrived

rived in Italy. They got to Spain in 1584, at a time
when that court was celebrating a high festival, upon
the account of the marriage of the Infanta Catherina,
second daughter to the K. of Spain, with Charles Emanuel Duke of Savoy, who came the next spring to espouse her in person. The King took care that they
should be provided at their departure, with every thing
necessary for their voyage both by sea and land, and
ordered all manner of respect to be shewn them in their
passage through his dominions.

The first port they came to in Italy, was Leghorn:
As soon as the Grand Duke had notice of their arrival
in his State, he wrote to the Governors of the places
through which they were to pass, to receive them with
all possible respect, and entertained them himself at
Florence, with the highest magnificence.

But nothing could be equal to the reception they met
with at Rome, where they no sooner arrived, but all the
Cardinals and Ambassadors that resided there at that
time, went to wait upon them in form, by the Pope's
particular desire, with tenders of their friendship and
service. His Holiness would not admit them to a private audience (though they did not expect any other)
but gave them a public one, as he received the Ambassadors of other crowned heads, in the presence of
the whole Court, and an infinite number of people; he
could not conceal his joy at so new and unusual a specta-
cle. When they kissed his feet, he raised them up;
and bursting out into tears embraced them tenderly,
and said aloud, *Lord now let thy servant depart in peace,
for mine eyes have seen thy salvation.*

After this they declared the cause of their embassy,
and received a most affectionate answer. The letters
that they brought addressed to his Holiness, were read
in public, and the usual compliment returned upon
that occasion. After the Audience was over, the Pope
retired into his apartment, and admitted them to the
honour of lifting up the hem of his garment; which
ceremony

ceremony they performed with fo good a grace, that (confidering whence they came) the fpectators could not help expreffing their furprize.

The Jefuits Convent was appointed for their refidence, and the Pope defrayed all their expences, ordering them to be cloathed after the Italian manner; and was fo folicitous for their welfare, that even when he lay upon his death-bed, he enquired after them, and particularly Don Julian, who was at that time dangeroufly ill.

The exaltation of Sixtus to the Pontifical throne, in fome degree confoled them for the lofs of Gregory, which happened foon after their arrival. The ftate which the new Pope took upon him, and the fplendour of his coronation. gave them a great idea of the Pontifical power. Three days after his election, they were admitted to kifs his feet in private, as he was not yet crowned, and told him, "They came to congratulate " him upon his exaltation, hoping they fhould meet " with the fame degree of favour and protection they " had received from his predeceffor;" to which he anfwered in very affectionate terms, affuring them he would take particular care of their perfons; and, at the fame time, gave directions to the heads of the Convent, to fee that they had every thing, not only neceffary, but becoming the dignity of princes. His behaviour to them was fo remarkably kind and familiar, that the Cardinals faid, "He behaves to thefe Japonefe, as if he " was ftill a Cardinal, and to us like a Pope."

It has been a ufual thing with moft Princes to begin their reign with an act of grace, and to releafe all criminals that were found in prifon at their coming to the throne; but this cuftom, for what reafon I cannot tell, was never obferved by the Popes, till the time of Paul III, who was a very oftentatious, vain-glorious man, and a great lover of ftate and ceremony. He firft introduced the Royal Robes, and the Tria Regna, or Triple Crown, which are ftill in ufe, together with the cuf-

tom

tom of releafing prifoners on the day of their coronation, which had been continued ever fince under fome
reftrictions ; though, for the moft part, the Popes have
granted a free pardon, and ordered the prifon-doors to
be fet open ; for which reafon, many of the banditi,
and other delinquents, ufed to come and furrender
themfelves after the Pope was chofen, efpecially, if he
was reckoned a merciful, good-natured man.

This induced great numbers, that had been encouraged by the mildnefs and indulgence of Gregory (who
could not bear to hear of even a malefactor being punifhed) to commit the moft attrocious crimes during his
reign, and the vacancy of the Holy See, to come voluntarily to the prifons, not making the leaft doubt of
a pardon, from the general character of Montalto's lenity and humane difpofition.

But never were poor people more fatally difappointed : For on the Monday before the coronation was to be,
the governor of Rome, and the Caftellan, or keeper of
St. Angelo's caftle [1], waited upon his Holinefs, to
know his intention as to releafing the prifoners, and
whether he would pleafe to grant a general pardon, or
to except any, and if thofe that were pardoned were to
pay any fees ; to which the Pope replied, in an angry
manner, " You certainly either do not know your proper
" diftance, or are very impertinent. What have you to
" do with Pardons and Acts of Grace, and releafing pri-
" foners? Do not you think it fufficient that our prede-

[1] Formerly the Moles Adriana, or burying place of the emperor Adrian, and the Antonini ; it took its prefent name from
Gregory the Great feeing an Angel there (as it is faid) returning a
drawn fword into the fcabbard, to fhew that the anger of Heaven
was appeafed, whilft he was walking in folemn proceffion with
all the clergy of Rome, to implore the Almighty to put a ftop to a
peftilence, that raged at that time with great violence all over the
Ecclefiaftical State. It was formerly beautified with a vaft number of pictures, ftatues, &c. of the moft exquifite workmanfhip,
which were deftroyed by the Goths. The Popes have now converted it into a very ftrong fortrefs, or Citadel, with a fine arfenal,
and public prifons in it.

" ceffor

" ceffor has fuffered the judges to lie idle and unem-
" ployed thefe 13 years? Would you likewife have us
" ftain our pontificate with the fame neglect of juftice?
" We have too long feen, with inexpreffible concern,
" the prodigious degree of wickednefs that reigns in
" the ecclefiaftical ftate to think of granting any par-
" don.   God forbid we fhould entertain fuch a defign.
" So far from releafing any prifoners, it is our exprefs
" command, that they be more clofely confined.   Let
" them be brought to a fpeedy trial, and punifhed as
" they deferve, that the prifons may be emptied, and
" room made for others; and that the world may fee,
" that Divine Providence has called us to the chair of
" St. Peter to reward the good, and to chaftife the
" wicked; *That we bear not the fword in vain, but are*
" *the minifter of God, and a revenger to execute wrath*
" *upon them that do evil.*   It is our pleafure, therefore,
" that four of the moft notorious of them be tryed to-
" morrow, and publicly executed at different places,
" two by the ax, and two by the halter, at the very
" time of our coronation; which will likewife take off
" moft of thofe diforderly people, that always occafion
" fo much tumult and difturbance at that ceremony."

Though the Governor [2], (who was grand-nephew
to the laft Pope was aware that Sixtus was of a fevere
difpofition, he was furprized, that, inftead of gratify-
ing the people in a favour they had been long ufed to,
he fhould think of exciting their horror by fo early an
execution; efpecially, upon the very day and hour of

[2] The Governor of Rome, has two lieutenants under him in
civil caufes.   He regulates falaries, wages, &c. and enquires into
the condition of poor people.   In criminal caufes, he has one lieutenant under him, and a general jurifdiction in Rome, with a power
over all the tribunals.   He has many affeffors, and a head notary, that has feveral clerks under him, all whofe emoluments go to
charitable ufes; fo that his office is called the notaryfhip of charity.   He has a provoft-marfhal, and 300 archers, or ferjeants,
When he goes through Rome, he is attended by a guard of halber-
diers, all cloathed in the fame livery, at the expence of the apoftolic chamber.

the

the coronation, which always ufed to be a time of
great joy and feftivity.   But his aftonifhment increafed,
when, about two hours after, the Pope fent him word
by Salviati, a mafter of the ceremonies, " That it be-
" hoved him and his officers to look well to the prifo-
" ners; for if any efcaped, they themfelves fhould be
" punifhed in their ftead; that he expected to hear of
" at leaft four of them being condemned the next day,
" and to have a particular account of all the reft as
" foon as poffible; that he ought now, by his diligence,
" to make amends for the fhameful neglect of his duty
" in the late reign, out of complaifance, as he fuppofed,
" to the childifh and ill-timed mercy of his predecef-
" for.

As many of the ambaffadors and nobles had either
relations, friends, or dependants, that had fled for
the commiffion of fome crime, or affociated with the
banditi (it having been an infamous cuftom amongft
the nobility to fupport and protect gangs of thefe wretches to execute any act of violence, and make themfelves formidable to their enemies) they immediately
fent to them, upon the election of Sixtus, advifing
them, by all means, to come and furrender themfelves,
" For as he was of a mild and forgiving temper, a-
" verfe to all manner of feverity, and naturally inclined
" to mercy, they might be certain there would be a
" full and ample pardon granted to all offenders."   So
that amongft an infinite number of others that had fled,
or been banifhed, for fmaller offences, there came in
above 200 that had been guilty of murder.

When the Cardinals, Ambaffadors, &c. that were
interefted in the prefervation of thefe people, amongft
whom were Farnefe, Medicis, and Colonna, were informed of the Pope's refolution by the Governor, they
immediately went to him, and demanded an audience,
in which they reprefented to him, in the name of the
whole College, " That it would be a great reflection
" upon him, as Vicar of Chrift, and common father of
" the faithful, if he began his reign in that fanguinary
" manner;

" manner; and efpecially upon the day of his corona-
" tion, which had always been confecrated to mirth
" and rejoicing.   That the heretics would juftly re-
" proach them with chufing a perfon that delighted in
" blood, and had no bowels of mercy or compaffion."
   Wherefore they befought his holinefs, " That he would
" be gracioufly pleafed, out of his great humanity and
" benevolence, to continue a cuftom that had been fo
" long obferved upon that day, as the honour of the
" H. See, and his own glory were highly concerned in
" it; and it was not only commanded by Jefus Chrift,
" who was the father of mercy, but the very laws
" themfelves exprefly faid, *Melius eft de mifericordiâ*
" *reddere rationem, quam de crudelitate.*"   The Pope replied, " He was above meafure furprized at the info-
" lence of their reprefentations; for that when Jefus
" Chrift committed the government of his church to
" St. Peter, he could not any where find in the gofpel,
" that he had appointed the Apoftles to be his tutors,
" or pædagogues; and that if they thought to be fo to
" him, who was called by Divine Providence to prefide
" over the faithful (as he hoped) for their good, they
" would find themfelves egregioufly miftaken; that
" the heretics could not juftly upbraid them with any
" crimes that were committed, except they let them
" go unpunifhed; that he wifhed to God the Popes had
" been more fevere for the laft 100 years, at leaft in
" punifhing the crimes of ecclefiaftics, which were
" the firft caufe of all herefy; that he thought it very
" ftrange that they, whofe peculiar province it was to
" difcountenance wickednefs and immorality of every
" kind, fhould come on purpofe to defire him to patro-
" nize it, under a pretence of advifing him to begin
" his reign with acts of clemency and indulgence,
" when the whole ftate was in a manner overwhelmed
" in a deluge of vice and licentioufnefs; that he was
" refolved to purge it effectually, by the help of God,
" notwithftanding the craft of fome perfons whofe de-
" figns he could eafily fee through; that he knew the
                                        " people

" people had much more occafion for juftice than mer-
" cy, neverthelefs when he had fatisfied one, he would
" let them fee he knew how to practice the other."

After he had faid this, he fuddenly withdrew into
another apartment, and left them fufficiently mortifyed
and difappointed ; efpecially, when one of the chamberlains followed them, as they were going down ftairs, and
told them, " His Holinefs had fomething more to fay
to them." For as foon as they returned into his prefence, he faid to them, in a threatning manner, " he
" had forgot to add, that he was determined, not only
" to punifh the criminals themfelves with the utmoft
" feverity, but to make a ftrict enquiry after all their
" encouragers, and treat them in the fame manner ;"
and then immediately difmiffed them, not one of them
daring to make the leaft reply, or utter a word, till
they got out of his fight ; when Gonzago faid to Farnefe, " Is this your afs of La Marca ? "

Great was the fear and confternation of the prifoners,
when they heard this, and faw themfelves double ironed,
and more clofely confined inftead of being fet at liberty,
as they had vainly hoped, expecting every hour to be
conducted to the fcaffold or gallows.

Among the reft was one Sebaftian Ciacci, who having been guilty of murder, had fled from Rome, and
been a long time abfent, but upon the expectation of
a pardon at the coronation of the new Pope, was one
of the firft that furrendered themfelves. When the
Pope's refolution came to be known, his wife, who
was a Roman lady, diftracted with grief and defpair,
went with her two fons and three daughters, the night
before the coronation, and having, with much difficulty, got admittance, threw herfelf at the Popes feet,
and prefented a very moving petition in favour of her
hufband ; when he had read it, he faid, " Indeed we
" are very forry for you, poor woman, and your chil-
" dren, as you are likely foon to become a widow, and
" they fatherlefs ; but you are come too late ; we have
                                        " made

" made a folemn promife to Juftice, that we will bring
" her back to Rome, from whence fhe has been fo long
" banifhed; and we muft not be worfe than our word."
This was all the comfort fhe had, for her hufband
was foon after put to death.

No lefs remarkable was his rigour to Cartelli, treafurer and canon of St. Maria Magiore. This perfon
had been formerly Majordomo to C. Carpi, Montalto's
great patron, and done him many fignal fervices, often
receiving and entertaining him in his chamber, when
he went to wait upon the Cardinal. He had a Nephew
whofe name was Peter, againft whom a procefs had
been commenced, for running away with and ravifhing
a young woman; though he afterwards found means to
appeafe her father, by marrying her. But as it was neceffary to go through fome formalities of law to put
an end to the matter, and ftop any further proceedings,
his uncle advifed him to furrender himfelf before the
coronation, not in the leaft doubting but there would
be a general act of grace; or, if there was not, he
imagined he could eafily obtain his pardon, upon the
merit of his former intimacy with Sixtus. But when
he was informed that the Pope not only defigned not to
releafe any prifoner, but to proceed againft them with
the utmoft rigour, he went to him to intercede for his
Nephew, and faid, " He humbly hoped his Holinefs
" would forgive him, as it was an extravagance of
" youth; which he thought he had made atonement for,
" by marrying the injured perfon, and fufficiently fhewn
" his repentance by a voluntary furrender of himfelf,
" entirely depending upon his clemency;" to which
Sixtus anfwered, " that he was much obliged to him,
" for his friendfhip, whilft he was in a lower ftation of
" life, and fhould not forget it now he was Pope. But
" that if he had a mind to intercede for his nephew, he
" would do well to pray to God for his foul, for it was
" in vain to afk him to fpare his life, as he was determined
" to adminifter ftrict Juftice without refpect to per-
" fons." In purfuance of this refolution, he ordered
him

him to be hanged foon after, before the houfe where the fact was committed; though the judges, who had revifed the procefs, examined frefh witneffes and took the depofition of the young woman and her father, who faid, that whatever had been done was by their own confent. But Sixtus either fufpecting or being informed of the contrary, ordered the Judges to appear before him, with the minutes of the firft procefs, where the fact was fully proved by the ftrongeft evidence. At which he was fo enraged, that he commanded the two judges to draw lots in his prefence, fentencing one of them to be publicly whipped in a Court of Juftice, whilft it was fitting, and the other to be banifhed the City for ever.

After the execution of his nephew, the Pope fent for Cartelli, and told him, " that as his kinfman de-" ferved punifhment for his crimes, fo he thought there " was recompence due to him for his former friendfhip " and good offices; and immediately appointed him " bifhop of Amentea in the kingdom of Nap es, giv-" ing his canonry to another nephew." In this manner he made full fatisfaction to juftice, fhewing the world, that no regard to gratitude or any private obligation, fhould ever prevail upon him to deviate from it; and that he knew how to return the kindneffes of his friends without facrificing the laws of his country.

We muft not here pafs by his behaviour to Cæfarino, a prelate of great revenues and intereft, but entirely abandoned to his pleafures, leading a moft profligate and debauched courfe of life, entertaining many of the banditi at his houfe to make himfelf feared; and up·on occafion to cut off a man's nofe or ears, or perhaps his throat. This perfon had been intimately acquainted with him, when he was general of the Francifcans, and often entertained him at his houfe. As the friendfhip continued after he came to be Cardinal, Cæfarino was continually fending him pieces of plate, furniture, wine, and whatever rarities or delicacies were to be procured. He had a fmall houfe and

garden

garden next to Montalto's at Rome, which he generoufly made him a prefent of, as foon as he heard of his intention to enlarge his own (though he had promifed it
to another) and did him fo many other fervices, that
he always fpoke of him with the greateft friendfhip and
regard; fo that every body concluded, when Montalto
was chofen Pope, that he would certainly make him a
cardinal. But it proved quite otherwife.

Cæfarino had a country-houfe not far from Rome,
which was called, by the neighbourhood, * *The den of*
thieves, as he conftantly harboured fome of the bravoes
there; amongft whom there happened to be at that
time three of the greateft and moft notorious villains
that infefted the country, or belonged to any gang, for
whom there was a very ftrict fearch made by the archers. Now, whilft the See was vacant, he had ordered
them to come fecretly to his houfe in Rome, hoping
they would obtain their pardon, without any difficulty,
by going voluntarily to prifon, and being difcharged as
ufual, at the coronation. So that when he heard Montalto was made Pope, he was overjoyed; as he not only
depended upon a pardon for his friends, but fully expected a cardinal's hat himfelf. For which reafon he
advifed them to go and furrender themfelves immediately, affuring them, " They fhould be the firft that
" came out of prifon." When he heard there was to
be no jail-delivery at this coronation, he determined to
go himfelf, and afk that favour of the Pope, upon the
ftrength of his former acquaintance, which he did; and
when he came into his prefence, after congratulating
him upon his exaltation, he intreated his holinefs " to
" pardon three unfortunate prifoners that had been guil-
" ty of fome fmall offences, during the late times of
" general diforder and confufion; as he was defired to
" ufe his intereft in their behalf, by fome friends of
" great diftinction that he could not refufe, which re-
" queft he made no doubt but his holinefs would gra-
" cioufly indulge him in, according to his wonted

Q   good-

* *Stanza di banditi.*

" goodnefs and generofity; that the world might fee,
" he was ftill pleafed to honour him with his favour
" and countenance, and to approve of the zeal with
" which he had ever ferved him." This he fpoke with
great freedom, imagining the Pope would treat him with
the fame refpect that he did whilft he was cardinal.

But Sixtus, who was thoroughly acquainted with his
diffolute way of living, and the conftant entertainment
and protection he gave to the banditi, after he had
heard him with much patience and attention, anfwered
him in this manner: " We always thought ourfelves
" highly honoured by your friendfhip, and wifhed for
" nothing more ardently, than a continuance of it,
" which indeed you were fo kind to favour us with
" whilft we remained cardinal. But now we are Pope,
" you feem to have withdrawn it, and no longer look
" upon us with the fame degree of efteem that you did
" formerly, which gives us great concern. You are fol-
" licited, as you fay, by thofe whom you call your
" friends, though in reality they are your enemies, to
" ufe your intereft with us in favour of fome of the
" moft abandoned of all mankind, whom, if we fhould
" pardon, it would turn to your own ruin, and our
" difhonour. But if you had indeed that refpect for
" us which you only profefs, you would endeavour to
" avoid doing any thing that fhould difquiet, or make
" us uneafy; and we can affure you, that nothing gives
" us greater uneafinefs, than to fee our dominions over-
" run with fuch a deteftable race of villains; nay, the
" very city and court itfelf polluted and contaminated
" with every kind of iniquity. We have long been ac-
" quainted, Cæfarino, with your fcandalous courfe of
" life; and all the world knows what fhelter and en-
" couragement you have given to thefe reprobates. As
" your infamy is become fo public and notorious, we
" are obliged (Heaven knows with what concern) to
" condemn you to die, to die a violent and ignominous
" death by the ax. There is no occafion for any pro-
" cefs, your own confcience, and the notoriety of your
" crimes, are fufficient witneffes againft you; and the
" ftrict

" ftrict regard we have for juftice, obliges us to be
" your judge.   We therefore pronounce that fentence
" upon you.   But the Divine Providence, who wills not
" that the fervices you have formerly done us fhould go
" unrewarded, infpires us with mercy, and a defire of
" pardoning you this time, that you may henceforth lead
" a new life.   From this you may learn how grateful a
" fenfe we retain of your paft kindneffes in forgiving
" you, when we had firmly refolved to fpare no man
" that deferved punifhment.   We already know enough,
" and too much of you ; we don't defire to rake any fur-
" ther into that fink of iniquity which is concealed in
" your heart, or to add to the punifhment which, we are
" affured, your own confcience muft daily and hourly
" inflict upon you.   We now look upon you as having
" fuffered the rigour of the law.   That Cæfarino, who
" was acquainted with Montalto is no longer alive ; that
" Montalto, who was a friend of Cæfarino, is long fince
" dead.   The prefent Cæfarino lives a life that was given
" him by Sixtus V; from this hour, from this moment,
" you muft begin to lead a new life ; for we proteft to
" you that we will not any more remember what you
" were before we were Pope ; and that we will punifh
" you for the crimes that you fhall hereafter be guilty
" of, with greater feverity than any other perfon ; as
" guilty of abufing a favour that we never yet fuffered
" to be extorted from us, nor ever will again."

The fear and confternation that feized upon all that
heard the conclufion of this fpeech, increafed, if poffible, when at the end of five days, being informed of
the nature and quality of the crimes thefe three wretches had been guilty of ; and that Cæfarino had encouraged them to furrender, by faying, " He would infure
" their pardon ;" he was fo exafperated to think that
any other perfon fhould prefume to difpofe of his favours, that he fent for the governor of Rome, and ordered him to try and condemn them immediately ; and,
left that fhould not be fufficient, wrote the following
billet to him before he was well got to his own houfe :

Q 2   " YOUR

" YOUR inexperience and foolish good-nature ren-
" der you unfit for the post you have the honour to
" fill, under a Pope who told you a few days ago, that
" he expected you to do justice, and not to shew mer-
" cy; it is our pleasure, that you pass the following
" sentence, *viz. That the country-house of* Cæsarino,
" *where the banditi have usually assembled to hatch their*
" *wicked designs, shall be demolished to the very foundati-*
" *ons; upon which a gallows shall be erected, and the*
" *three criminals hanged upon it.* Let this serve you
" for instructions how to behave upon the like occa-
" sions for the future."

Cæsarino was so dismayed at the execution (which indeed was such a one as had never been seen or heard of
at Rome in the memory of man) that he took a resolution of bidding adieu to the world. And having obtained the Popes consent, retired into a convent of Cer-
tosini (the strictest order of Monks) where he lived till
the death of Sixtus, to the great astonishment of all
people.

Soon after Pasquin appeared in the habit of that order, and being asked by Marforio, " Why he turned
" Monk?" answered, " It is rather better to live in a
" cloyster, than be hanged."

Every thing being now ready for the coronation, Sixtus would have it celebrated on the 1st of May, not only
as it was the festival of two * apostles for whom he had
a particular devotion, but because it happened on a
Wednesday, a day that (as we have taken notice) had
been often fortunate to him; and which he observed so
superstitiously, that when any election was to come on in
which he was a candidate, or any thing of consequence
to be attempted in his favour, he used to say, " I don't
" expect to succeed, because it is not Wednesday."

It gave him great pleasure to hear of the rejoicings
that were made every day in Rome since his election;
and when he was informed, that they exceeded all that
                                                    had

* *Philip and Jacob.*

had ever been seen before upon such occasions, he told the person that acquainted him, "That his subjects should have no reason to repent of it." Indeed all ranks of people seemed to vie with each other in their demonstrations of joy. But the convent of the H. Apostles far exceeded the rest. They made bonfires and illuminations; they erected statues and triumphal arches; and performed several solemn masses in their church, in which they were assisted by a choir of the finest voices, and the most exquisite music that could any where be procured.

The cardinals, nobility, prelates, generals, and chiefs of the principal orders, came to compliment them upon the honour that was reflected upon them, by a member of their convent being exalted to the Papacy. There was not a prince or state in Europe, that had any religious house of that order in their dominions, but sent to congratulate them. The Dominicans seemed to be transported at his exaltation, looking upon him as almost one of their own order, as he had been protected, supported and preferred, made General and Cardinal by Pius V, and always both professed and shewn the highest regard for them.

Early on Friday morning, the third day of his Pontificate, he sent to let Farnese know, as dean of the college, that he intended to hold a consistory the next day, having something of consequence to communicate to the cardinals. Upon this, Farnese immediately went to inform him, " That it was unprecedented, and had ne-
" ver been usual before the coronation ; and would not
" only give people occasion to suspect something extra-
" ordinary, but bring a reflection upon that august bo-
" dy of which he had the honour to be the head."
But Sixtus answered hastily, " That Providence had made
" him Pope to command, and not to obey ; that he did
" not want to be taught what would be for the service
" and advantage of the church, nor wherein consisted
" the honour and dignity of the H. College ; that it
" was his pleasure the consistory should meet the next
" morning,

" morning, without any more fcruples or objections."
Which Farnefe was obliged to notify to them.

When they were affembled, he made a long difcourfe
to them upon this text, *And the times of this ignorance
God winked at, but now commandeth all men, every where,
to repent, becaufe he hath appointed a day in which he will
judge the world in righteoufnefs, by the man whom he hath
ordained.* In which he told them, " That when he me-
" ditated upon the goodnefs and mercy of God, that
" had fo remarkably attended and affifted him in all
" the feveral ftages and periods of his life, and at laft,
" in a miraculous manner, exalted him to be the head
" of his church, he was perfuaded that he defigned him
" to accomplifh fome great work; and fince he did not
" know of any fo important, as the endeavouring to re-
" form the morals of his fubjects, and put a ftop to that
" unexampled degree of wickednefs and corruption
" that had infefted the whole ftate, he was determined
" to go through with it at all events, defiring their affif-
" tance in fo arduous, though neceffary an undertaking
" that they would not ever interfere in his adminiftra-
" tion of juftice, or intercede for criminals, as it would
" be in vain; and that if they fhould hereafter know
" or hear of any thing that would be of fervice to
" church or ftate, they would communicate it to
" him, and he would immediately put it into execu-
" tion; concluding with that paffage in the epiftle to
" the Romans, xiii. 12. *The night is far fpent, the day is
" at hand; let us therefore caft off the works of darknefs,
" and put on the armour of light,*" &c.

When he had finifhed his difcourfe, which he pronounced with great vehemence, and in a refolute manner, the cardinals were not a little terrified; efpecially
with the conclufion of it, in which he told them, " That
" it would be in vain to folicit him for any man's par-
" don; as they from thence prefaged, they fhould live
at beft but an uncomfortable life, under a Pontiff fo rigorous and determined as he feemed to be.

However,

However, the cardinal dean got up, and, in the name of the whole college, returned him thanks for the great zeal which he had expreſſed for the good of his people, promiſing not to interrupt his cares for the public good, with unſeaſonable petitions or applications; and that if they ſhould know of any thing that would be for the benefit of either church or ſtate, they would not fail to communicate it to him; after which he got into a ſedan chair, and returned to the Vatican.

To paſs away the time till the coronation, which he waited for with the utmoſt impatience, he entertained himſelf at nights with reading over an old journal, in which he had written down a particular account of all the tranſactions of his life, as we ſhall more fully relate hereafter.

But he applied himſelf with much greater application, in the day time, to a book in which he entered all the ſchemes he intended to put in execution, whether they were ſuch as related to the government of the church or ſtate, or matters of juſtice and OEconomy, or any way concerned the intereſt and juriſdiction of foreign powers, with plans of ſeveral very great deſigns. This book he conſtantly carried in his pocket, and would not ſhew it to any one. It employed his thoughts ſo much, that when he was at his devotions (which indeed was but very ſeldom, for as the affairs of government neceſſarily took up moſt of his time, he granted himſelf a diſpenſation to compound for ſome part of that duty by acts of charity) if any thing came into his mind, that he thought worth putting down in the book; he would break off, and ſay to his almoner, " It " is but reaſonable, that the intereſt of a particular per- " ſon, ſhould give way to that of the public. My de- " votions concern no body except myſelf; but theſe " notes are of ſervice to all Chriſtendom."

The Monday after he had harangued the cardinals, he ſent for the governor, and all the magiſtrates, to attend him in a body, and exhorted them to be ſtrictly vigilant

vigilant and impartial in the execution of their refpective offices; telling them, that, if they acted uprightly,
they fhould be properly rewarded and encouraged, but
to beware how he caught them tripping in the minuteft
article, for, in fuch cafe, he would fhew them no mercy. When they went away, he followed them to the
door of his apartment, and faid, *Remember, I come not
to fend peace, but a fword amongft you.*

He had obferved, that at former coronations, befides
the difputes and contefts that ufually happened amongft
ambaffadors, prelates, and nobles, concerning rank
and precedence, there had beed innumerable crimes
and enormities committed that day, and the door
thrown open to all manner of licentioufnefs, under a
pretence of mirth and rejoicing; and upon that account, once thought to have been crowned in private;
but being perfuaded not to deprive the people of a
pleafure they had been ufed to at the beginning of every Pontificate, and expected in his, he at laft confented,
but with a full refolution to prevent all riots, confufion,
and irregularities of every kind: For which purpofe he
fent for the governor, and having confulted with him
upon a proper remedy, he publifhed fome orders to be
obferved upon that day, which he caufed to be ftuck
up in all the public places of the city: After a
long preamble, the fubftance of them was as follows:

" In the firft place, notice is hereby given, that the
" cavalcade will begin at eight in the morning, for
" which reafon, all thofe that are obliged to be there,
" by the nature of their offices, or are otherwife defi-
" rous of that honour, are required to appear, at feven
" o'clock, in the church, or piazza of St. Maria Mag-
" giore, (from whence the proceffion will begin) that
" they may be marfhalled in due order, and proper
" places, according to their refpective rank.

" II. It is ordered, on pain of his Holinefs's higheft
" difpleafure, that no perfon prefume to enter into any
" difpute or debate with the mafters of the ceremo-
                                                    " nies,

" nies, about rank or precedence, but every one quietly
" take the place and march in the order appointed him
" by them : And if any one think himfelf aggrieved or
" injured, it is his Holinefs's pleafure, that his rights or
" privileges fhall not be in any wife prejudiced by that
" inftance : and that there be a proper time appointed
" to hear and determine all pretenfions of that kind.

" III. That every one appear in a decent, but not
" extravagant drefs, and rather fet an example of mo-
" defty than luxury, efpecially ecclefiaftics : His
" Holinefs being defirous that fome diftinction fhould
" be fhewn to the folemnity of the day; but in
" fuch a manner, that they may not put any one to an
" expence he cannot well fupport.

" IV. As it often happens in folemnities of this kind,
" that the people vie with each other in extravagance, to
" their great prejudice, his Holinefs declares he will
" punifh thofe that are guilty of fuch folly, after the
" ceremony is over, either with banifhment or depri-
" vation of their pofts or dignities, if in office.

" V. If any perfon fhall on that day, be guilty of
" quarreling, fighting, abufive language, or any kind
" of infolence, indignity, affront, unmannerly or tur-
" bulent behaviour, he fhall be imprifoned for three
" years if noble; fent to the Gallies for five, if a
" common perfon, or feverely whipped, if a woman ;
" and they that are privy to offences of this fort, and
" do not immediately inform of them, fhall fuffer one
" half of that punifhment."

He likewife ordered the governor to provide 12
executioners or hangmen, of different nations, to
let the people fee he was determined to fpare none (let
them be of what country foever) that dared to violate
the laws, it being his defign, that every criminal
fhould be put to death by an executioner of his own
nation.

He commanded thefe fellows to parade round the
city the day before, and the very morning of the coronation,

ronation, and once a week ever afterwards, two by two, with each of them an ax in one hand, and a halter in the other, to ſtrike a terror in the people. A baker happening to throw a ſtone, which hit one of them upon the head as they walked their rounds one day, Sixtus ordered him to be ſeverely whipped upon the ſpot, and ſent to the gallies: But afterwards remitted the latter part of the ſentence, at the interceſſion of Della Torre; not ſo much out of regard for that cardinal, as becauſe he thought the poor fellow had been already ſufficiently puniſhed for ſo ſlight an offence.

This with ſeveral other orders that were publiſhed at the ſame time, made the name of Sixtus ſo terrible, that the oldeſt perſon living never ſaw a coronation paſs with ſo much peace and order as this did : For tho' a thouſand enormities ſuch as rapes, murders, robberies, &c. had been uſually committed on that day, and nothing could be heard or ſeen in the public ſtreets, but ſwearing, execrations, quarrels, fighting, and all manner of other irregularities and diſorders, the guards continually beating back the preſs with their halberds: On the contrary, tho' the crowd was very great upon this occaſion, there was not the leaſt diſturbance or confuſion, or mobbing of any kind; not an oath or an abuſive word heard, nor a blow given. Many ſtaying at home, looked out of their windows, or ſtood at a diſtance, for fear of being inadvertently drawn into ſome riot or quarrel.

When the firſt of May came, all the cardinals in their robes, the princes, nobility, prelates and ambaſſadors aſſembled at the Vatican, amongſt whom were the Japaneſe, very richly dreſſed. As it is the cuſtom for the ambaſſadors of the greateſt powers, to ſupport the Pope's canopy at his coronation, he deſired the Japaneſe might have that honour, and take place of all the reſt, which was readily granted, the precedent not being likely to be of much prejudice to the others. They were likewiſe admitted to kiſs his feet, and

miniſtered

miniftered to him, when he washed before the celebration of mafs; one holding the ewer, another the bafon,
and a third the towel; which ceremony by the inftruction of the Jefuits, they performed in a very graceful
manner; and is a favour never granted to any but the
ambaffadors of crowned heads.

From thence they attended the Pope to the Pontifical Chapel, where he was received with great folemnity,
and faluted by all the cardinals, who went before for that
purpofe; and then a mafter of the ceremonies taking off
his ordinary habit, cloathed him in the royal robes,
the cardinal deacon putting a mitre of great value upon his head: When this was over, he was placed in the
Cathedra Geftatoria, (with the canopy of ftate over his
head) and carried to St. Peter's, upon the fhoulders of
eight men, the cardinals fubdeacon bearing a large
crucifix of maffy gold before him.

The proceffion, which was the largeft and moft
fplendid that had ever been feen, was graced by all the
cardinals, ambaffadors, princes, nobles, archbifhops,
bifhops, prelates and other perfons of diftinction that
were in Italy; nay, many came out of France, Spain,
and other countries, on purpofe to fee it. They were rank-
ed according to their quality and degree, by marfhals,
and heralds, and mafters of the ceremonies; the hal-
berdiers marching before, and the Swifs guards bringing up the rear, with their fwords drawn. When he arrived at the Portico of St. Peter's, he was feated on a
throne (erected upon three fteps) covered with a red velvet, under an embroidered canopy, upon which the
Papal arms were finely wrought in gold; the cardinals placing themfelves on his right and left, on feats
built for that purpofe, and enclofed with baluftrades, to
keep the populace at a diftance. Here the cardinal
arch-prieft, and the whole chapter, came to make their
obeifance to him, and were admitted to kifs his feet: after this he got into the Cathedra Geftatoria again, and was
carried as before (the Japanefe and other ambaffadors and

perfons

perfons of great diftinction going before him, with white
ftaffs in their hands) thro' the main gate up to the
high altar, where the firft cardinal prieft, holding the
Hoft in his hand, he defcended from the chair to adore
it; and falling on his knees upon a cloth of gold,
laid there for that purpofe, prayed for fome moments,
with his head uncovered.

The firft cardinal deacon having replaced the mitre
upon his head, he went to the chapel of St. Gregory
the Great, (in the fame church) where he was adored
by all the cardinals, bifhops, and other dignitaries,
one by one, according to their rank and feniority, the
cardinals kiffing his hand, the bifhops his knee, and
the others his foot; and then rifing out of his chair,
and ftanding upright, he gave them his bleffing in thefe
words: " The bleffing of God the Father be amongft
" you, and remain with you always." From thence, after he had read fome prayers, he went, attended by the
cardinals, with the mitre upon his head, and a crofier
in his hand, the Imperial and French ambaffadors holding up his train, to celebrate his firft folemn mafs at
the Grand Altar.

In this proceffion, that is, from Gregory's chapel to
the altar, which is about 150 paces, the ceremony of
burning flax, cuftomary at thefe times, was thrice performed after this manner: Some of the fineft flax is fet
on fire at the end of a ftaff, which is carried upright
before the Pope, by a mafter of the ceremonies, who
at the fame time fays to him, " Holy Father, fo paf-
" feth away the glory of this world;" at which it had
been ufual for the Popes to make a fhew of weeping:
But Sixtus, who was not of the tendereft difpofition, or
apt to melt at fmall things, inftead of fhedding any
tears upon this occafion, ordered the Japanefe to come
nearer his perfon, that they might fee this ceremony
the better; and faid to them, in a lofty and majeftic
voice, " The glory of my name fhall never pafs
" away; I will eftablifh it for ever, by truth and
" juftice;" and then turning to them faid, " My fons,
　　　　　　　　　　　　　　　　　　" take

" take notice of this, and relate it to your sovereigns."
After some other prayers were read, the cardinal deacon, putting the pall upon him, said, " Receive the
" Holy Pall, and with it the plentitude of the pontifi-
" cal power to the honour of Almighty God ; his Mo-
" ther the most glorious Virgin Mary ; the blessed apos-
" tles Peter and Paul, and the Holy Roman C. Church."

The litany, with several other hymns and psalms
were then sung ; after which, he was again adored, and
incense offered to him by the cardinal deacon : This
being over, Farnese as dean, read a particular collect,
composed upon the occasion.

When the service was finished, Medicis as first deacon, put the triple crown upon his head, and said,
" Receive the Tiara, and know that thou art from hence-
" forth king of kings, governor of the Universe, and
" the true and lawful vicar of our Saviour Jesus Christ
" upon earth, to whom be all honour and glory, both
" now and evermore."

The Pope then gave his benediction to the people,
with the crown upon his head, and pastoral staff in his
hand, and putting off the pontifical robes, got into a
chair, and was conducted to the Vatican ; the cardinals
following him to pay him the usual compliment of *Annos multos & felices*, " Many and happy years :" The
evening was concluded with all the outward demonstrations of mirth and rejoicing, tho' it is certain there
were great fears and apprehensions, and many aching
hearts under that appearance : As there never had been
any instance before of criminals being executed upon
the day of the coronation, the people looked upon it
as a melancholy omen, and from thence foreboded a
cruel and bloody reign : Some being terrified with the
consciousness of their own crimes, and others full of
concern, and anxious for the fate of their friends that
were in prison.

It is remarkable, that in going thro' all these long
and tedious ceremonies, he did not shew the least sign
of

of wearinefs or fatigue : The fpeẟators were furprized to fee an old decripit man, whom they thought dying every day for many years paſt, exert himſelf with
ſuch extraordinary vigour, and looked upon it as a fort
of miracle; in which opinion they were confirmed
when they heard him chant the *Dominus vobiſcum*, and
the *Gloria in excelſis*, in a voice that made the vaults of
St. Peter's echo.

On the Sunday following he went in cavalcade, to
take poſſeſſion of the church of St. John de Lateran,
which is the proper fee of the biſhop of Rome, and the
oldeſt in Chriſtendom. The canons of that church always ſhut their gates at this time, and tho' the Pope
knocks three times, they don't open them till he commands them to do ſo, as their biſhop. He was received
by the arch-prieſt, at the head of the Chapter, to
whom he faid, " I fuppoſe you are not a little glad to
" have the Pope for your biſhop, and truly it is a cir-
" cumſtance that we are not forry for ourfelves."

The Pope was very defirous the Japaneſe ſhould attend
in this cavalcade, as it is the moſt pompous that is made
at the coronation, his train being compoſed of all the
cardinals, ambaſſadors, prelates, nobility, and officers of the court: He ſet them upon the fineſt horfes that could be any where procured, very richly ca-
pariſoned, and furniſhed them with every thing that
could contribute to the ſplendor of the ceremony, ho-
nouring Don Mantio with the office of holding his ſtir-
rup, whilſt he mounted; which he did with ſo much
agility, that the Japaneſe was furprized, and could not
forbear faying, " I am fure I could not have done ſo my-
" felf:" Sixtus hearing him faid : " I am old and hea-
" vy now, but it is no wonder as I have the weight
" of the whole world upon my ſhoulders: At which
cardinal Farneſe, who was near him, could not help
fmiling, and faid, " Your Holineſs was not half ſo nim-
" ble, whilſt you were cardinal."

After the proceſſion was over, he regaled them at a
royal banquet, and faid to ſome of the cardinals, " I
" have

" have hitherto entertained the Japanese ambaſſadors
" like a Pope, but now I will entertain them like an
" emperor."

During the banquet, he did them the honour to
drink their maſter's health twice, and ſeated them where
they could moſt conveniently obſerve all the ceremonies, the order of the diſhes that were ſerved up (to
which he gave his benediction,) the reſpect that was
ſhewn him, by everybody riſing when he was going to
drink, and ſo many other formalities, that the Venetian
ambaſſador whiſpered to one that ſat next him, " To
" be ſure it is an honour to dine with his Holineſs, but
" really it is ſo great a fatigue, that I never deſire to
" do it again :" After dinner the Pope entered into a
long converſation with them, and aſked ſeveral queſti-
ons concerning the nature and cuſtoms of their country,
a piece of familarity that is ſeldom ſhewn to any perſon (let their rank be never ſo conſiderable at thoſe times,
when the Popes generally affect the utmoſt ſtate and
reſerve.

Beſides theſe perſonal honours that were paid to the
Japaneſe ambaſſadors, he gave them ſeveral marks of
his bounty and benevolence to the whole nation, and
granted them every favour they aſked for it.

They had obtained a yearly penſion of 4000 ducats
[3] from the late Pope, for the maintenance of their
ſeminaries, and when they deſired a confirmation of that
grant from Sixtus, he augmented it to 6000, for the
better eſtabliſhment of theſe new ſettlements.

His Holineſs having been informed that they were in
want of money (from the ſlow remittances, occaſioned
by the great diſtance of their country) made them a
preſent of 3000 crowns [4], and paid the Jeſuits all

[3] The ſilver ducat is worth about four ſhillings and ſixpence
ſterling, the gold one twice as much ; they are current in Venice,
Florence, Genoa, Germany, Hungary, Poland, Sweden, Denmark,
Flanders, Holland, and Zurick.
[4] The value of a Roman crown is about five ſhillings and ten
pence ſterling.

the

the money they had advanced them befides the expences they had been at in maintaining them three months
in their convent; moſt of the cardinals, and principal
nobility entertained them at their palaces with great
magnificence: Farneſe, D'Eſte, Medicis, Alexandrino and
St. Sixtus, all invited them, this laſt more than once,
and made them preſents of ſilks, embroidery, and dreſ-
ſes after the Italian manner; Alexandrino preſented them
with jewels and plate of the moſt curious workman-
ſhip, to a great value.

The Pope gave them two ſwords, with gold hilts ſet
with diamonds, after the German faſhion, and two velvet hats, with hatbands ſtrung with oriental pearls;
preſents hardly ever made by the Popes, to any but
the greateſt Princes, as particular marks of their
favour.

To crown all, he made them knights of the Golden
Spur [5], putting a chain of gold about their necks
himſelf, with a gold medal at it, on one ſide of which
was his Holineſs's head, and on the other his arms,
with the Golden Spur, which is the enſign of that
order.

The next day his Holineſs, at their deſire, celebrated the maſs that is appointed for travellers by ſea or
land, to beg that God would bleſs them with a happy
return to their country, and gave them the ſacrament
with his own hands: from thence they proceeded to the

-----

[5] Italian *Cavilieri dello ſprono d'oro:* French, *Chevaliers de
l'ordre de l'eperon d'or* Our learned countryman John Selden, in
his Titles of Honour (a very valuable book, and highly worth reading by every Engliſhman) gives a large account of this order, and
ſays it was firſt inſtituted in Spain, and the Knights called *Cavalli-
ros d'Eſpuella dorada*, Knights of the Golden, or Gilt Spur. I
ſuppoſe it was from thence transferred into Italy, where the Pope
is the head of it : They are likewiſe called Knights of St. Peter
and St Paul.

Guillim ſays the order of the knights of Loretto, was inſtituted
by Sixtus V. in the year 1587, whoſe enſign is the figure of our
Lady of Loretto, hanging on a golden chain : But of this Leti
takes no notice.

capitol,

capitol, where they were received by the senator [6], conversators [7], and most of the Roman nobility, who gave them a place in their senate, and made them and their posterity, wherever they should be born, citizens and patricians of Rome.

Thus loaded with honours and presents they went, for the last time, to kiss his holiness's feet, and take leave of him : He gave them his benediction, with several medals and relics, and embracing them affectionately, recommended them to the protection of the Almighty.

They left Rome the 3d of June, attended by a numerous train of chariots and horsemen, till they were out of the city, and his holiness ordered particular respect to be shewn them, and their expences defrayed, throughout the whole ecclesiastical state : After they had made a tour through Italy, they embarked at Genoa, with Spinola, nephew to the famous John Andrew Doria, who commanded a squadron of eighteen sail, that were bound for Spain.

The arrival and stay of these ambassadors occasioned various speculations at Rome ; some did not scruple to say, the whole was a trick of the Jesuits to advance the credit of their order, and that the world, seeing kings and nations converted to the Christian Faith, might

[6] This magistrate resides in the capitol, and has under him two judges in civil, and one in criminal concerns ; he always appears in court in a robe of gold cloth, with long sleeves down to the ground, lined with crimson silk, and a great chain of gold about his neck, after the manner of the ancient Roman Senators, and is for the most part a doctor of law : He holds his place (worth about 2000 crowns per annum) during the Pope's pleasure, to whom he gives an account of his duty every week, wearing at that time, a senatorial robe of black satin or velvet.

[7] Officers appointed to take care of the antiquities of Rome, and the observation of the statutes : They inspect the market, and punish the sellers of victuals, either for want of weight, or measure, or exorbitant price : They are also ordinary judges of all appeals made by the consuls of trade and husbandry, expedite grants of freedom and naturalization, take care of the walls and aqueducts, and depute officers over the lands that belong to the public.

admire

admire their zeal and indefatigable labours in their miffions: That the pretended ambaffadors were only the fons of mean perfons, hired and inftructed to perfonate that character by thefe fathers, who likewife forged their credentials, and being their interpreters, made them fpeak whatever beft fuited their purpofes: Others imagined their chief defign was to get a fum of money for the better eftablifhment of their feminaries at Japan, which they reprefented as the only method of confirming thofe that were already baptized in the true faith, and of making ftill farther converfions.

There happened, unluckily, to be fome Englifh and Spanifh merchants then at Rome, that had lately been in thofe parts; who being eye-witneffes of this folemn farce, could not forbear laughing heartily at it, and affirmed they had not heard a fyllable either of the embaffy, or converfion of any king, whilft they were at Japan.

The day after their departure, Pafquin appeared with a letter in his hand, directed, to the noble Japanefe youths, the worthy pupils of the Jefuits; and the people began to murmur, and faid " That the Englifh, Spani- " ards and Hollanders, went to the Indies to bring the " riches of thofe countries to Europe, but the Jefuits " carried away what money there was left at Rome to " the Indies."

When Sixtus heard of thefe reports, he fmiled, and faid, " They were to be commended, even if that was " true; for taking away from fools to give to wife " men." It muft be confeffed, that no people in the world are more fubtle than the Jefuits, or more fertile in expedients to accomplifh their defigns: They have made themfelves fo neceffary to princes by their great fkill in cafuiftry, and folving fcruples of confcience; but above all by their confummate addrefs in ftate intrigues, that they are generally defirous of having one or more of thefe fathers near their perfons, whom they admit to the higheft degree of favour and confidence,

often

often making ufe, at critical times, of the prodigious influence and authority they have acquired over the fpirits
of both fexes, to infinuate themfelves into the hearts
and affections of their fubjects, whilft their appearance
of humility and difintereftednefs, and the education of
youth, which they have almoft wholly engroffed to themfelves, for the moft part conciliate the efteem of the
common people to them.   The religious of other orders make too great an apparatus, are too eager and
follicitous in the purfuit of what they afpire to, which
is the reafon that they frequently mifcarry in their undertakings : The Jefuits, on the contrary, very feldom
fail in their defigns, working in a fecret and almoft im-
perceptible manner, under the garb of modefty and
felf-denial; and feeming to neglect or defpife what they
moft ardently wifh for.

Soon after the coronation, Camilla, the Pope's fifter,
came by his orders to Rome, with her daughter and two
grandfons (who were the fons of another daughter) and
a niece, the daughter of her brother Anthony.   The eldeft of her grandfons, Alexander Peretti, was made
cardinal a few days after his arrival, with the title of
St. Jerome degli Schiavoni (the name of his church) but
the Pope was defirous he fhould take his old name cardinal Montalto.   He was then about 18 years old, and
had been but indifferently educated, yet he made fuch
improvements under his uncle's inftruction, that he afterwards became a very able man, and was employed
in the management of the moft weighty and arduous
affairs.

Sixtus had fent to defire his fifter would take particular care to behave in a decent and modeft manner, at
her arrival ; but when fhe came near the city, the cardinals, Medicis, D'Efte, and Alexandrino, went out to
meet her, and conducted her to a neighbouring palace,
where they dreffed her up like a princefs, thinking
thereby to make their court to the Pope, who, they
knew, loved her tenderly, and had expreffed a great
deal of impatience to fee her at Rome.

R 2   · The

The cardinals took her, dreffed after this manner, to the Vatican ; and the Pope, being informed of her arrival, ordered her to be immediately introduced to him : But when he faw her in that tawdry habit, he pretended not to know her, and afked two or three times, who fhe was: upon which Alexandrino, who had handed her in, faid, "It is your fifter, Holy Father." My fifter ! " (replied Sixtus, with a frown) I have but one fifter, " and fhe is a poor woman at Le Grotte : If you have " introduced her in this difguife, I declare I don't know " her ; and yet I think I fhould know her again, if I " was to fee her in fuch clothes as fhe ufed to wear." After he had faid this, he immediately retired into another apartment, and left the cardinals in great confufion.

His two nephews that came with her, were likewife dreffed out like young noblemen, and attended by the nephew of cardinal D'Efte, who gave them the right hand, as he was inftructed by his uncle, imagining the Pope would be highly pleafed with it : But Sixtus could not forbear laughing when he heard of it, and gave ftrict orders to the centinels at the gates of the Vatican, not to fhew them the leaft honour or refpect ; and would not fuffer any of his officers to go out and meet them, which occafioned Rufticucci to fay to Alexandrino " He was fure fomething was amifs ; and that it was " well if they were not in a wrong box."

After they faw in what manner his nephews and nieces had been received, none of the cardinals, or thofe that came with them, offered to wait upon them back. It is true indeed, Alexandrino fent his Majordomo to fhew them the way to an Inn. Poor Camilla, who thought herfelf a princefs at leaft, was extremely mortifyed at this reception and public difgrace : And one of the boys, whilft they were ftripping off his fine clothes, faid, "Alas ! mother our reign has been a very fhort one."

This event occafioned much laughter n Rome, as all
difcerning

difcerning people perceived the reafon of the Pope's behaving after this manner was, that he did not chufe to lay himfelf under any obligation to thefe two cardinals, in an affair of fo little fervice to him. It feems, when they knew the Pope had not given any orders to equip them with money and clothes for their journey, they furnifhed them very liberally with both. The only perfon that was fent by him, to conduct them from Le Grotte to Rome, was Ceroli, a gentleman of La Marca, who had been a long time his fecretary, to whom he gave fecret orders to bring them away in the very drefs he found them in, and to pack up all their clothes in a ftrong box, which he was to fend immediately to Rome: This he had done, fufpecting how the cardinals would behave; fo that when he had difmiffed them, as we have juft now related, he ordered Ceroli to take their own clothes (which he had in his poffeffion) to their inn, and defired they would drefs themfelves as ufual in them even to the very fame fhoes and linen; and then to carry back their finery to Cardinal Alexandrino's houfe, with Camilla's thanks for the ufe of them. When this was done, he fent two of his ordinary coaches, to bring them to the Vatican, cloathed as they were, to the infinite diverfion of great numbers of people, that were affembled in the ftreets to fee that comedy. When they were introduced a fecond time to the Pope, he embraced them tenderly, and faid to Camilla, "Now "we fee it is our fifter indeed: No body fhall make "a princefs of you but ourfelves." After which he admitted them to kifs his feet; and placing them on each fide of him, afked them feveral queftions about their family; who had been their beft friends; and many other particulars relating to the village.

He had often fent money to his fifter, whilft he was cardinal, but by little at a time, conftantly exhorting her to give her children the beft education fhe could; and was not a little pleafed to hear them make fuch anfwers to fome queftions of grammar that he afked them,

them, as she... they did not want parts, and had not
...altogether neglected: But perceiving they were a
little ove-awed at the richnefs of his robes, and the
fplendor of the palace, he took them by the hand, and
encouraged them, bidding them " not be afraid, but
" behave themfelves well, and he would be their friend."
When he had difmiffed the reft of the company, he
fpoke to Camilla in this manner:

My dear SISTER,

" WHEN we confider the very near relationfhip,
" and the great tendernefs that has always fubfifted be-
" twixt us, we think ourfelves obliged to do every
" thing for you that natural affection requires, and is
" confiftent with the rules and maxims of good go-
" vernment; as it would be very unjuft (now God
" has put it in our power to do good to all men) to
" overlook our own flefh and blood; efpecially, as
" it is highly agreeable to our inclination; and we are
" affured that fuch a conduct is far from being difa-
" greeable in his fight; he being called *worfe than an*
" *infidel, that does not provide for thofe of his own boufe:*
" But in matters relating to our paftoral office, and
" the government of the ftate, it is our pleafure that
" you give neither us, nor yourfelf, any manner of
" trouble, as we are determined not to have any affo-
" ciate in our fovereignty: For fince we have refolved
" not to admit even thofe who feem to have fome pre-
" tenfions to a fhare in the adminiftration of govern-
" ment, it would occafion a grievous reproach to di-
" vide the rule with a woman.

" It is our defign, in the firft place, to make you
" a prefent of the palace where we formerly lived, which
" we have ordered to be fitted up and furnifhed for you,
" in a manner fuitable to the rank you now hold;
" and hope it will not be the lefs agreeable to you, for
" having been a place that we ourfelves once took
" much delight in; as it will give us, on our part, the
" greateft

" greateſt pleaſure to reflect, that it is now the reſi-
" dence and habitation of our dear ſiſter. We have
" in a great meaſure built it with our own hands; and
" deſign to make ſuch an addition of groves, gardens,
" ſtatues, fountains, and other embelliſhments to it,
" that it ſhall not yield to any palace in our domi-
" nions.

" It is not our intention, however, that in the midſt
" of your affluence and abundance of all things, you
" ſhould be ſo forgetful of the very mean and hum-
" ble condition you once lived in, as to make you be-
" have yourſelf in an inſolent or intemperate manner,
" as it would bring an indelible ſcandal upon your-
" ſelf, and give us the ſharpeſt and moſt exquiſite con-
" cern: for this reaſon, we ſhall appoint you a decent,
" but reſpectable court and retinue; ſuch a one as
" will procure you ſufficient regard, without the dan-
" ger of envy or jealouſy: This, we don't doubt, you
" will be prudent enough to regulate, according to
" the penſion we ſhall ſettle upon you, which will be
" a thouſand crowns per month; and we ſhall take
" care to ſecure it to you in ſuch a manner, that, if
" it ſhould pleaſe God to call for us to-morrow, you
" cannot be deprived of it after our deceaſe. We ſhall
" give immediate orders to the maſter of our hou-
" ſhold, to provide you with a proper attendance,
" horſes, mules, two coaches, one for journies, and
" another for common occaſions, with all other ac-
" commodations that you ſhall ſtand in need of. As
" for your grand-children, &c. we ſhall not be want-
" ing in our endeavours to make ſuch a proviſion for
" them, as is ſuitable to the nephews and nieces of
" a Pope.

" We have told you what you have to truſt to; far-
" ther than this you muſt not expect. We hope, the
" great change in your fortune, this ſudden and unex-
" pected elevation from a cottage to a palace, from a
" peaſant to a princeſs, will not occaſion any alteration
                                        " in

" in your difpofition, which we know is naturally meek
" and humble : For, in matters of government, if you
" are imprudent enough (as we truft you will not) to
" afk the leaft favour, or make any interceffion for
" criminals, or otherwife interfere in our adminiftra-
" tion of juftice, we tell you, once for all, we will not
" grant it ; and therefore defire you will never attempt
" a thing, that will bring the mortification of a repulfe
" upon yourfelf, and give us infinite uneafinefs in re-
" fufing you.

" This caution we thought neceffary to give you, as
" we are, from long experience, fully aaquainted with
" the artifice of courtiers, who generally have recourfe
" to women that are in favour, and practife upon their
" weaknefs, when they have any intereft to ferve ;
" which cuftom we are determined to break through, as
" it always, juftly, brings a fcandal upon any govern-
" ment, but more efpecially upon that of a fpiritual fo-
" vereign. There are, we know, many people that
" will endeavour to infinuate themfelves into your ac-
" quaintance, with a view only of making a tool of
" you, to bring about their purpofes. The only way
" to put an effectual ftop to this, is to give them a re-
" folute denial at the firft ; to put on a hard face, and
" tell them you have no intereft at all with us in fuch
" affairs, and that we have abfolutely forbid you to afk
" us any favour of that kind. When they are once
" convinced of this, they will ceafe to deafen you with
" their importunities for the future."

In the evening when fhe took her leave, he embraced
her again, and fent her, handfomely attended, in one of
his coaches, to his palace near St. Maria Maggiore,
where fhe lived a month incog. without receiving any
vifits : This fhe did for two reafons, firft, that fhe
might be at leifure to fettle her houfhold, which, befides women, confifted of eight footmen, two pages,
two gentlemen-ufhers, a majordomo, a chaplain, a fecretary, two chamberlains, a butler, a cook, and feveral

veral others. The other reason was, that she might be
a little polished, and instructed how to behave herself
in a proper manner.

During this interval, the Pope visited her three times
in private: After it was over, the whole court came to
pay their compliments to her, as the Pope's sister:
But Sixtus would by no means suffer her to take that
state upon herself, or to be worshipped and adored in such
a manner as other women had been, who were * relations of his predecessors. Her greatest pleasure seemed
to be in frequenting those Churches where there were
the most brilliant ceremonies, and the finest choirs.

As the Pope's temper came to be more known, all
were contriving how to make themselves acceptable to him. The Grand Duke, at the request of
his brother the Cardinal, offered to make Camilla a
Marchioness; a Marquisate being then vacant in his
dominions, by the death of the last possessor. But Sixtus civilly thanked him, and said, " She was not ambi-
" tious of any other title than that of the Pope's sister."
The ambassador of Spain, likewise, by his master's
order, offered her the title of Countess of some place
in his kingdom of Naples. To these last words, " His
" kingdom of Naples," he made some reply that gave
the Spaniards the first suspicion of his aversion to their
nation; and that he himself had some designs upon
that kingdom.

Amongst other states and Princes that vied with
each other, in shewing their zeal and forwardness in
sending extravagant compliments to him, the Venetians
were not the last in their congratulations, imagining,
perhaps, (as they thought he could never thoroughly
forgive their treatment of him when he was Inquisitor
amongst them) it was necessary to close the breach by
shewing him particular honours and marks of respect,
upon this occasion: For which reason as soon as they
heard of his exaltation, they ordered the bells of all

* Dame Papaline.

the

the churches and convents to ring; and the whole
senate went to St. Mark's, in their formalities, to sing
the Te Deum, sending two of their secretaries to compliment the superior of the Francifcans, and made bonfires and illuminations throughout the city, that, and
several succeeding nights: After which the senate, being assembled, came to a resolution of sending a pompous embassy, to congratulate him upon his accession
to the Papal throne; and, for this purpose, appointed
four ambassadors, persons of the richest and most noble families in Venice, viz. James Foscarini, and Mark
Anthony Barbaro, both of them procurators of St. Mark,
[8]; Marino Grimani, and Leonard Donato, who were
likewise afterwards successively procurators of St. Mark,
and doges [9] of Venice.

Whilst these nobles were preparing for their embaffy, Nicholas da Ponte, the doge, died, which retarded
their journey till another was elected, who was Paschal
Cicogna. The senate, in the mean time, being informed of the arrival of the Pope's relations at Rome,
that he received them after a very affectionate manner,
and seemed inclined to live upon good terms with the
republic, resolved to do every thing that might increase this good disposition in him, by shewing him all
manner of respect; and therefore, in a full house, admitted the family of Peretti to the honour of nobility in their state. Alexander, the elder of the nephews,
was already created Cardinal by his uncle, and Michael, the younger, took the stile of Don, and Camilla
that of Donna; titles of very great respect, that had
been introduced into Italy by the Spaniards.

[8] Administrators of St. Mark's, the principal church in Venice, and of the revenues belonging to it: They are the patrons
of orphans and executors of testaments. This office receives
more lustre from the merit of those that discharge it, than from its
authority. They are cloathed in black, or violet, with ducal
sleeves.
[9] The chief magistrate of the republic; the office is elective, and for life.

The

The ambaffadors fet out with a train of above 500 perfons, and were received by Sixtus, upon their arrival at Rome, with a degree of courtefy and regard, that occafioned a jealoufy amongst the minifters of other powers.

Camilla fo punctually obeyed the orders given her by her brother, not to afk him any favours, that during the whole time of his pontificate, (tho' fufficiently teazed and importuned) fhe never durft attempt it, but once, and then with the utmoft unwillingnefs and reluctance, in behalf of a convent at Naples, of which they had made her protectrefs, much againft her inclination; as it was only fome trifling privilege or indulgence fhe afked for, he granted it without much difficulty, but reminded her of his firft injunction, and told her it was the only favour fhe muft ever expect.

Soon after it was publicly known that Montalto was made Pope, great numbers of people flocked to the Vatican, defiring an audience, and to have the honour of kiffing his feet: Several of them had been his real friends, in the former part of his life, and others only common acquaintance, or fuch as had, perhaps, tranfacted fome trifling affairs with him, all expecting to make their fortune. Sixtus, who feldom forgot a perfon with whom he was once acquainted, or had any dealings with, ordered the porters to inform themfelves particularly of their names, with other circumftances relating to them; and when they had made their report to him of thefe particulars, he appointed them a day of audience. At the time fixed they came, to the number of 80, and being introduced, he fpoke to them in this manner:

My Sons,
" AS it is not our intention to be forgetful of the
" kindneffes we have formerly received, we muft en-
" quire into the nature of your feveral pretenfions; for
" we are not fo fimple or credulous to believe, that eve-
" ry one that has cafually fpoke to, or had a curfory
                                        " acquaintance

" acquaintance with Montalto, was Montalto's friend:
" This is not by any means a fufficient foundation to
" build a friendfhip upon; we fhall therefore make
" a particular inquiry into your refpective merits,
" and endeavour to find out who have been the
" real friends of Montalto, and who only tranfient ac-
" quaintance, that we may know how to proportion
" our gratitude to your deferts; but the weighty and
" important concerns of the high calling to which the
" Almighty has been pleafed to exalt us, will not per-
" mit us at prefent to enter into this affair, as it is ve-
" ry reafonable that the fervice of God and our coun-
" try, fhould take place of every private intereft, and
" that juftice fhould be preferred to gratitude : When
" we have fatisfied the demands of one, we will fhew
" that we are not regardlefs of the other."

As this could not be interpreted an abfolute denial,
they went away pretty well fatisfied, efpecially as they
thought what he faid of dedicating his firft cares to
the public, highly commendable.

Amongft the many great defigns, with which he entered upon the pontificate, his principal one was to fill
the treafury, and raife large fums of money, that he
might be enabled to carry on his vaft undertakings:
The means he took to accomplifh this, we fhall hereafter relate. His next endeavour was to find a remedy for
the poverty that had fo long reigned amongft the common people of the ecclefiaftical ftate ; as almoft all the
money and lands were engroffed by thofe that were relations of the preceding popes : He firft thought to have
banifhed all fuch families out of Rome as could not fupport themfelves, either upon their own eftates, or places,
or by merchandize, or learning, or the fword, or fome
occupation; and for this purpofe he called together
thofe prelates and fenators that were beft acquainted
with the nature of thefe things, and defired them, after three days confideration, to let him know which
they thought the moft likely method to bring about
that end.

When

When they had maturely weighed the matter, they returned to his holiness and told him, they thought "it would not only be a difficult thing, but to the last degree inhuman, and inconsistent with the compassion and mercy of a common father, to drive away so many innocent families from their native country, for no other crime but being poor; that it would likewise be very bad policy, and much weaken the state; and that if it was not, reasons of government ought not by any means to be weighed in the balance with Christian charity and benevolence." This made him alter his resolution, and proceed upon a more rational scheme, and such a one as, it is to be wished, all princes would endeavour to imitate.

He appointed four persons of great prudence and experience in matters of œconomy, to whom he gave a power of summoning before them all the families in Rome that were accounted poor, or had no visible way of getting their livelihood, and of either finding them some employment, and compelling them to work, or of banishing them out of the city. It is said, this first put him upon undertaking those wonderful fabrics, which he afterwards finished in such a manner, as excelled any thing that the ancient Romans had ever attempted: For tho' he had a head naturally formed for great designs, it is not improbable that he was excited to undertake them, with a view of providing bread and employment, at the same time, for so many thousands of idle and indigent people.

The more effectually to prevent the city from being filled with beggars, he would not suffer foreigners to come and live there, except they first brought a good certificate that they were able by some trade or profession to maintain a family; strictly forbidding the clergy to marry any one that had not a proper licence and testimonial to that effect from the magistrate; and the laity, on pain of being sent to the gallies, to promise marriage before they had presented themselves to such magistrates as were appointed to examine their circumstances, circumftances, who, if they found them in danger of falling into poverty, or not able to maintain children, were not only to prohibit their marrying, but, in cafe they perfifted in their defign, to banifh them out of the city. And when it was told Sixtus, that many thoufands had been already banifhed upon that account, he faid, " it was better to depopulate a city, than have it " inhabited by beggars :" An opinion very different from that of Plato, who would have a mark of infamy fet upon all thofe, that did not marry before they came to the age of thirty five.

Before he was crowned he paffed a fentence, that fhewed he was determined to protect the poor, and to have no refpect of perfons, where juftice was concerned: Francis Brettoni, who was in the fervice of the Urfini family, and had acquired a handfome fortune in trade, happened to die without children, and having no very near relation, tho' many diftant ones, that were poor, left Don Bertoldo Urfini, Count of Pitiglian, a gentleman of great power and intereft at Rome, heir to the whole, with this claufe in his will, " That all the rea-" dy money that might be found on his eftate, fhould " be divided amongft his poor relations, according to " their refpective neceffities, and the largenefs of their " families, as Cardinal Montalto fhould direct." This trouble he thought he had fome right to expect Montalto would take upon himfelf, as he was under many obligations to him, and particularly for lending him a fum of money in the time of the great famine : His death happened in the vacancy of the fee, but his will was made eight months before : So that Urfini immediately took poffeffion of the eftate, which amounted to, at leaft, 40,000 crowns, declaring there were but 200 in readymoney ; which feemed incredible to moft people, as it was well known, he ufed to have very large fums in the houfe : But Urfini, not thinking it proper, or perhaps worth while, to ftay for the advice and direction of Montalto, who was then in the conclave, diftributed

200 crowns

200 crowns amongſt Brettoni's poor relations, according to his own diſcretion.

Montalto had received an account of Brettoni's death,
in the conclave, and as he was pretty well acquainted
with his circumſtances, thought it very ſtrange there
ſhould be only 200 crowns found in ready money, being aſſured there muſt be ſeveral thouſands; and was
not a little provoked, that though the power was inveſ-
ted in him, Urſini had taken upon him to diſpoſe of
even that, without waiting for his coming out of the
conclave (not dreaming he would be choſen Pope;) and
thought it a piece of great contempt and diſreſpect,
tho' in a matter of no mighty importance: But as he
entered the vatican with a full reſolution to manifeſt the
ſtrict regard he had for juſtice, he was determined not
to neglect this opportunity, but immediately ſent for
Urſini, with all Brettoni's relations, and a notary to attend him, with a copy of the will: When they came
before him, he aſked Urſini, "Whether he had paid
" thoſe poor people the legacy that was left them in
" the will?" And he anſwering, "he had; and that
" tho' it was true there was a clauſe in the will, that
" left the diſtribution of the ready money to his emi-
" nence Cardinal Montalto, as he was now exalted to
" the pontificate, he did not think it proper to give his
" hli neſs any trouble in ſo trifling an affair, ſince the
" whole ſum did not amount to quite 200 crowns." To
which Sixtus anſwered, in great wrath, "You have been
" guilty of ſo notorious a falſity, that you well deſerve
" to loſe the whole: You have unjuſtly taken upon you
" to diſpoſe of what you had not the leaſt right to,
" whilſt we were employed about our lawful concerns
" in the conclave, and ridiculouſly pretend there were,
" only 200 crowns left: He that has the aſſurance to
" tell a lie to the Pope, deſerves never to be believed
" again: to the end therefore that others may be de-
" terred by your example, from playing tricks with us,
" and deſpiſing our authority, we impoſe a fine of
" 2000 crowns upon you, to be applied to ſome works
of

" of piety and charity, for the good of the public,
" which we intend to begin in a short time : A very
" slight punishment for so henious a crime : This is
" with regard to the offence committed against our-
" selves: We must now take notice of the fraud you
" have been guilty of to these poor people."

Ursini was struck dumb and motionless, not expecting any thing of this nature; and they that stood by
were above measure surprized, too see a person of one of
the most considerable families in Rome treated with so
little respect, by a man whom, but a few days before,
he would hardly have deigned to speak to; but their
amazement encreased, when, having first ordered the
will to be read, he said, " The will is a good one, but
" the misfortune is, that either the notary does not
" understand what he wrote, or you have bribed him to
" explain it in such a manner as best suits your interest:
" The intention of the testator is clear, viz. that all
" the money that may be found upon the estate (these
" you see are the express words) should be divided
" amongst his poor relations; but you and your nota-
" ry have wilfully mistaken the plain sense of them, to
" the prejudice of these poor people, and the will of
" the Testator: the Testator says (and to be sure he
" knew his own intention best) that his poor relations
" should have all the money that may be found upon his
" estate, not all the money that is found; and you
" have the conscience to give them no more than 200
" crowns, which we will be so complaisant as to sup-
" pose (tho' it seems by no means credible) is all the
" money that was found, but certainly not all that may
" be found. You, for your part, good Mr. Notary,
" are an ignorant blockhead, and we will make you
" know, that all the money that may be found upon
" the estate belongs to these people : Now we are very
" well convinced, that 15,000 crowns may easily be
" found upon it, which we will give to them and take
" the estate ourselves to see if any more may be found up-
" on it, if you don't think proper to pay them this sum of
                                                    " your

" your own accord: This is the plain meaning of the
" Teftator; this is in juftice due to thefe poor crea-
" tures; and this is our immutable fentence: If it is
" not done in eight days, we will pay them the mo-
" ney and take poffeffion of the eftate."

After he had faid this, and received a thoufand
bleffings from the relations, he fuddenly retired into
another apartment (according to his cuftom) leaving
Urfini, tho' he was a proud refolute fpirited man, in
fuch confufion, that he could not tell what to fay, or
think of it.

When he came back to his houfe, he fent for all his
relations and friends, and two of the moft eminent
lawyers in Rome, to confult with them what meafures
were to be taken in fuch an exigency: They differed at
firft in their opinion, but at laft concluded, " That as
" Sixtus had given fome famples of his temper in the
" very fhort time he had been Pope, it would be to no
" purpofe, if not dangerous, to contend with him; and
" thought it the moft advifeable way to fubmit to
" him." Upon which he, within the time limited, fent
him the will, and 15,000 crowns, to be difpofed of as
he thought proper: Sixtus was fo mollified with his
ready compliance, that he ordered him to come to him
again, and returned him both the money and the will;
telling him, " That he hoped he would, out of his ufual
" generofity, confider the Teftator's poor relations:"
Which he did, by making them a prefent of 6000
crowns, to their great fatisfaction.

Amongft thofe things that may be accounted worthy
of cenfure, in the conduct of Sixtus, we may juftly
reckon that of taking advantage of the fecrets he had
drawn from the people in confeffion (which ought always
to be efteemed facred and inviolable) to bring offenders to juftice: We have heretofore acquainted the
reader, that whilft he was cardinal he put on an appearance of great meeknefs and fanctity, affecting to
fit frequently in the confeffionals; and that the opinion
the world had of his candour and piety, occafioned

S   vaft

vaft numbers of people, whofe confciences were ftained with the blackeft crimes, to have recourfe to him, as they looked upon him to be a dying man; or one of fo much honour and fimplicity, that he would never reveal them, and from whom they had nothing to fear..

But the event fhewed they were widely miftaken in their man, and that they had pitched upon a perfon of all others the moft infidious and defigning, who *noted all their offences down in his book*, Ifaiah xxx. 8. with an intention to call them out into day-light at a proper feafon: For he was no fooner got into the Vatican, than he gave a lift of five perfons, three men and two women, to the Governor of Rome, ordering him to commit them to prifon directly, without acquainting him with what they had communicated to him in confeffion, only faying in general, " that they had been guilty " ty of very great crimes, which he would take care " to convict them of in a fhort time." The governor anfwering, " That it was not ufual to imprifon " people, without fome evidence of their guilt:" He replied, " That when he had fecured them, he might " fafely proceed to torture; for he was well affured they " would then confefs what fhould be laid to their " charge." Of thefe delinquents, three were apprehended, the others being dead.

The firft was Martha Bertha, a widow, near 40 years of age. She had confeffed to Montalto, about eight years before, that, in the firft year of her widowhood, fhe had been got with child by a canon (who, luckily for him, was dead) that often ufed to vifit her, being a relation, and appointed truftee in her hufband's will: Upon which account they both agreed, for the fake of their reputation, to procure an abortion, and for that purpofe had recourfe to a midwife, experienced in fuch wicked practices, who had likewife been ufeful to them in another capacity: This woman gave her drugs, that made her mifcarry of a male child. Bertha, ftung with remorfe of confcience, applied

plied to Montalto for abfolution, and afterwards retired from the world, and led a very devout and exemplary life. When fhe was committed to prifon, and
accufed of it, fhe immediately confeffed, and upon her
confeffion was condemned to be hanged, and the midwife to be beheaded ; which fentence was immediately
executed.

Not much different was the fate of Antonio Saviage:
He was one of thofe people that 'affect to live like
gentlemen, tho' they have little or no eftate. It
happened that a rich merchant's wife, of a libidinous
difpofition, fell fo violently in love with him, that fhe
was conftantly fending for him to her houfe, whenever her hufband was abfent, tho' for never fo fhort a
time, and admitted him to the fame familiarities with
her, as if they had been married : But he, not being
content with his neighbour's wife only, coveted his
eftate alfo : With this view, he perfuaded the woman
to confent to the death of her hufband, and afterwards
to marry him. To put this in execution, fhe pretended an obligation to go to Loretto, to difcharge fome
vows fhe had made, defiring her hufband to go with
her, and invite their friend Saviage to make one of
the party : As he willingly confented to it, they fet
out, and taking a very dark and intricate road, came
to a little obfcure village, in the dufk of the evening,
where they found means to give him poifon, of which
he died that night ; they giving out that his death was
occafioned by a furfeit of fruit : and, pretending to be
very ill themfelves, took each of them a ftrong vomit,
the better to cloak their wickednefs. When they had
buried the poor man, the adulterers returned to Rome;
and as in the pontificate of Gregory, the moft flagitious
crimes were daily committed with impunity, they were
never punifhed, nor fo much as called to any account in
that reign.

About fix months after, they wer married ; and to
exonerate their confciences, they went to confefs to Mon-

talto; who made a memorandum of their names and
crime in his diary, and immediately after his exaltation, ordered them both to prifon, to their great
furprize, as they had been now fome years unmoleft-
ed, had feveral children, and lived in good repute a-
mongft their neigbours. The governor, by the
Pope's inftructions, examined them feparately concerning the fact; and the woman being told by him, that
her hufband had owned himfelf guilty, prefently confeffed, and gave a particular account of the whole:
But the hufband ftiffly denied it, and being confronted
with his wife, and ftill perfifting in his denial, was put
to the torture; and being able to endure it but a few
minutes, made a full confeffion. They were both
condemned to be hanged; and tho' no body pitied
them, as their crime was of fo deep a dye, yet it
filled the city with terror, when people faw offences,
which they thought long ago pardoned, or buried in
oblivion, now not only brought to light, but punifhed
with a feverity beyond example, which occafioned thofe
that were confcious to themfelves of any guilt, either
to fly from Rome, or, if they ftaid there, to live in
continual fear and trembling.

There were many other inftances of this kind in the
reign of Sixtus, who, in turning over his diary,
often met with old offenders whom he brought to
juftice, tho' their crimes were of the moft fecret
nature, and committed long ago, which made people
look upon him as a wizard, or one that dealt in the
black art.

As he was determined to fupprefs all manner of vice,
to the utmoft of his power, he was not content with
the information which he himfelf had drawn from
penitents in confeffion, but often fent for the oldeft
confeffors, and fuch as were moft reforted to, telling
them they not only might, without doing violence to
their confciences, but were in duty bound to communicate to him whatfoever they were trufted with in
confeffion

confeſſion : eſpecially if it was any thing of conſequence to the church or ſtate, or a crime of a very
grievous nature, and that he would give them abſolution.   Several of them either over-awed by his authority, or prevailed upon by his arguments, made diſco-
veries of crimes that had lain long dormant, and
brought many poor wretches to juſtice, that thought
the memory of their offences had been totally oblite-
rated.

Tho' this conduct ſeems hardly juſtifiable, we muſt
conſider it was in ſome degree neceſſary to eradicate
thoſe ſeeds of iniquity, which had not only been ſown
and taken root in the reign of Gregory, but were
now full grown, and run up to an amazing height.
If in deſperate diſeaſes, deſperate remedies are to be
applied, as all phyſicians and politicians ſeem to agree,
there is no room to cenſure the means Sixtus took to
re-eſtabliſh juſtice, and curb the prodigious degree of
licentiouſneſs, that over-run the eccleſiaſtical ſtate at
that time, as the ſafety and well-being of the whole
was at ſtake.

Whilſt he was thus buſily employed in adminiſtring
ſtrict juſtice, he was not inattentive to his main ſcheme
of frugality, and raiſing money, having deputed proper perſons to take a ſurvey, and bring him an exact
account of the ſtrength and riches, not only of the
ſtate in general, but of every individual of any note
or conſequence.   When this was finiſhed, it was found,
that tho' there were ſome few families, relations, and
dependents of former popes, that had heaped up im-
menſe riches ; and that that the eccleſiaſtics for the moſt
part, lived in great luxury and abundance, the reſt of
the country laboured under the moſt pinching neceſſity,
and afforded little elſe but one continual ſcene of poverty and diſtreſs.

It was with great concern that he ſaw no manner of
trade or commerce going forward in the metropolis
of his dominions, nor any ſort of manufacture eſtabliſhed, except a few medals, pater noſter's, and
agnus

agnus dei's [10], as almoſt all the neceſſaries, but
eſpecially the conveniences of life, were imported from
other countries, particularly ſilk and woollen cloths (of
which there was ſo great a conſumption in Rome) that
were entirely furniſhed by Naples, Venice, Genoa, Lucca, and Florence, to the great profit and advantage of
thoſe places.

To this evil he applied a ſpeedy and effectual remedy, by encouraging trade and manufactures in Rome,
inviting foreigners and merchants from all parts to
come and reſide there, by great privileges and exemptions: He farther ordered a particular ſtate of the ordinary and extraordinary revenue of the Apoſtolic
chamber [11] to be laid before him, which at his ac-
ceſſion to the pontificate, amounted only to the yearly
ſum of 1,686,814 crowns: This, beſides the infinite
ſums which he expended in public works, the paying
off many heavy debts, contracted by his predeceſſors,
and laying up a million every year in the treaſury,
he augmented to 2,576,814 crowns in the five years
that he reigned, as we ſhall relate hereafter. Indeed
it has been much increaſed ſince by the addition of
the two opulent duchies of Ferrara and Urbino to the
eccleſiaſtical ſtate; the former in the year 1599, the
latter in 1630, which yield the annual ſum of 750,000
crowns; ſo that at preſent the whole amounts to
3,326,814 crowns, out of which, if things were managed with good œconomy, a third part might be laid
up with much leſs difficulty than it was in the time of
Sixtus: But we ſee quite the contrary.

[10] An agnus dei is a cake of wax, ſtamped with the figure
of a lamb, ſupporting the banner of the croſs, conſecrated, with
great ſolemnity by the Pope, to be diſtributed amongſt the people,
and ſuppoſed to have great virtues annexed to it, ſuch as, to drive
away devils, and preſerve them from ſtorms, tempeſts, poſſeſſion, faſcination, &c. They cover it with a piece of cloth, cut in
the form of a heart, and carry it devoutly in their proceſſions:
The prieſts make a good penny by ſelling them.
   [11] The Apoſtolic chamber is the treaſury, or office, where
the affairs, relating to the revenues of the church are tranſacted.

He

He likewife ordered an eftimate of the whole income of the fecular clergy to be given to him; that is, of the archbifhops, bifhops, abbots, chapters, confraternities, and other dignities, churches, and particular cures, which amounted to 1,827,345 crowns, a fum, as he thought, fufficient, tho' not fo great as he expected.

It was a great furprize to him to find that there were only 74 hofpitals in the ecclefiaftical ftate, the revenues of which, all together, amounted to no more than 80,000 crowns. This put him upon building a very large one himfelf, as he afterwards did, and endowed it with a confiderable revenue.

He next ordered a rent-roll to be made of the eftates belonging to the regulars, both monafteries and nunneries, which came to 134,710 crowns per ann. Thefe fearches and enquiries gave great uneafinefs to the clergy, who apprehended he defigned to deprive them of part of their revenues; which fufpicion was not altogether ill grounded, as he found means to fqueeze out of them, at feveral times, by granting privileges and indulgences, in lieu of tenths, and other fubfidies which he levied upon them, above 1,642,000 crowns.

End of the FIFTH BOOK.

BOOK THE SIXTH.

SOON after the coronation was over, the Pope proclaimed a Jubilee, and ordered public fupplications and prayers to be offered up, througout all Chriftendom, that God would blefs him with ftrength and wifdom to govern the church, and difcharge the duty of his high calling, like a good paftor. Tho' it
is

is plain he did not think he wanted ftrength, by what
he faid to Rufticucci : That Cardinal calling upon his
Holinefs one morning, as he went to his devotions, told
him, " That he was going to pray God to fend him
" health and ftrength to ftruggle thro' the labours and
" fatigues of his office." To which Sixtus replied, " If
" he pleafes to continue us in the health and vigour we
" now enjoy, we fhall be very well content."

He foon perceived that it was abfolutely neceffary to
proceed with the utmoft rigour, in order to effect a
reformation of manners, and to redrefs thofe diforders
that had been introduced in the pontificate of the late
Pope; whofe exceffive lenity inftead of reclaiming
the diffolute and licentious, rather gave encouragement
to their vices.

Sixtus took a quite different method to re-eftablifh
order and difcipline : He immediately laid afide that
mild and gentle behaviour he had fo long affected, and
put on a feverity not to be parallelled in the reign of
any former pontiff.

As he knew it was of the laft importance to all governments, to penetrate into the fecrets of other
princes, and to be truly informed of the opinion and
fentiments of his own fubjects, he chofe the moft a-
droit and infinuating people that he could find amongft
the lawyers, priefts, monks, or any other trade or profeffion, to ferve him as fpies, and allowed them confiderable penfions, which were punctually paid every fix
months; befides extraordinary rewards, to fuch as had
acquitted themfelves well in this employment, and given him intelligence of the moft fecret defigns.

He difperfed fifty of thefe fpies thro' the ecclefiaftical ftate, to infpect the conduct of the magiftrates; to
acquaint him with the opinion the people had of them,
and what they faid of himfelf: Two of thefe, who had
no knowledge of each other, were ftationed in every
confiderable town; and for greater fecrecy had each
of them a different cypher and addrefs, with proper inftructions how to convey their informations to
　　　　　　　　　　　　　　　　　　　　　Rome

Rome every day, without difcovery or fufpicion. Fifty more he employed in other parts of Italy, and foreign courts, where any of his nuncios refided, with a charge to keep a ftrict eye upon their conduct and to give him conftant advice of it: There were fifty more planted in Rome, who had each of them a diftinct province: One was ordered to watch the motions of two or three particular cardinals; another to obferve the words and actions of the nobility; a third to give him an account of all the ftrangers that came to Rome, with their name, quality, nation, bufinefs, and other circumftances that belonged to them: Others to inform him of the proceedings of the officers, and prelates that attended the court: He had fome that were to let him know all public news, and what the common people talked of in bakers' and barbers' fhops: Nay, his curiofity went fo far, as to oblige them to acquaint him with the manners and life of pages, and liverymen: He likewife inquired ftrictly into the foldiery that compofed his guards, of all the militia belonging to the church: As he knew, by long experience, that the monks pry into every thing, and talk pretty freely of whatever is tranfacted, either in the city or at court (not imagining that what they fay will ever go out of their cloyfter) and are generally the firft that know any fecret, either by confeffion, or otherwife; he had two or three religious in every convent, that gave him a faithful and minute account of all that was faid or done in their community.

By thefe means he had continual information of what happened in the city, the ecclefiaftical ftate, and all the courts of Chriftendom; and we may truely fay, that there never was any prince in Europe, that had quicker intelligence, or knew with greater certainty the moft fecret defigns of other ftates, whilft he had the art of keeping his own concealed and impenetrable.

For this purpofe he fent inftructions to all his legates and refidents at other courts, to fpare no expence to come at the knowledge of fuch things as were

kept

kept moſt private, and allowed them more, or leſs, according to the nature and importance of their ſervice:
He diſburſed the largeſt ſums to his ſpies in Spain (as
he had formed a deſign upon ſome of the dependencies of that crown) particularly enjoyning them to
take great care they had good authority for whatſoever intelligence they ſent him; to uſe their utmoſt application to find out what the miniſters moſt ſtudiouſly endeavoured to conceal; to penetrate into the in-
moſt receſſes of their hearts, and not to ſuffer themſelves to be amuſed, or deceived, by idle tittle-tattle,
or popular reports: In ſuch caſes, no bounds were pre-
ſcribed to their expences.

His injunctions upon this head were ſo ſtrict and peremptory, that the nuncios, for fear of incurring his
diſpleaſure, were continually at work, in debauching the officers and counſellors of princes, alluring
them by bribes, and all manner of temptations, to betray the ſecrets of their maſters.

He diſplaced many of the governors and judges, both
in the city and country, and reſtored none but ſuch
as were naturally more inclined to ſevere meaſures
than lenity and mercy; filling the places of the others
with men of his own turn, who he thought would
adminiſter ſtrict juſtice, without partiality, or regard
to any conſideration whatſoever. When he paſſed through
the city, he uſed to look people full in the face, and if he
ſaw a man of remarkably ſour aſpect, he immediately
ſent for him, and enquired of his condition and circumſtances; if he found him fit for his purpoſe, he made
him a judge, and gave him a ſtrict charge to act
uprightly, and with integrity; telling him, "That
" the true and only way to gain his favour, was to
" make a right uſe of that two-edged ſword with
" which our Saviour appeared to St. John; adding,
" that he himſelf would not have accepted of the
" ſovereignty, but with an intention literally to fulfill
" his words, *I am not come to ſend peace but a ſword a-*
" *mongſt you.*"

He

He ordered the governors of the towns and fig-
niories in the ecclefiaftical ftate to make a careful re-
view of all the criminal proceffes that had been carried on for the laft ten years, and to fend him an exact account of them, that he might inflict heavier penalties upon thofe that had not been punifhed as their
crimes deferved ; and actually laid fines upon the heirs
of fome, whofe perfons death had delivered from the
rigour of his juftice : Others he fent back to prifon,
who had been difcharged four or five years, at the fol-
licitation of friends, or upon a compromife with
the injured party, as he thought they had not made a
fufficient fatisfaction to the laws of their country.

He eftablifhed commiffaries to examine the conduct
of judges, for many years paft, and commanded every one that knew of any mal-adminiftration, whilft
they were in office, to declare it, on pain of excommunication; promifing rewards to thofe that could
convict them of corruption, or having denied juftice
to any one, at the inftance or requeft of men in power. The commiffaries proceeded with fo much rigour
in thefe enquiries, that many who were accufed, and
fome who were not, either abfconded· or fled out of
the ecclefiaftical ftate.

An advocate of Orvieto, who was privy to a piece
of injuftice, which the governor of that town had
been guilty of, for the fake of a fum of money, and
would not inform againft him, becaufe he was his particular friend, and had been out of office above five
years, was not only excommunicated, but fent to prifon and put in irons, where he lay a long time, and
was not releafed till he paid a confiderable fine.

This ftruck a great terror into all manner of people, efpecially thofe that had been magiftrates, and
were confcious to themfelves of any mifdemeanor of
this kind. One might daily fee fomebody or other
dragged to prifon, who was fo far from knowing the
caufe of it, that he could hardly remember he had

been

been in office; but they were foon made acquainted with their offence, and given to underftand, that they would never be fet at liberty, till they had made fatisfaction to the perfon they had injured.

Thefe meafures fo awed thofe that were then magiftrates, that they were afraid to ftir out of their houfes, or keep any company, left they fhould be prevailed upon by their friends to grant them fome favour, as they knew they fhould certainly be called to an account for it. All the nobilitity and perfons of the higheft quality were likewife ftrictly forbid, on pain of difpleafure, to afk the judges any thing in behalf of their neareft friends or dependents, being allowed only to recommend their intereft in general terms, and to requeft nothing but juftice.

He farther commanded every body, on pain of death, not to terrify witneffes with threats, or tempt them by hopes and promifes; or to affront and infult the bailiffs and tipftaves, and other inferior officers, threatning the judges with the fame punifhment, if they fuffered themfelves to be biaffed by any recommendation whatfoever: But finding that rather too fevere, he changed it into fine and lofs of their office, with a total incapacity of enjoying any other for the future.

It was not long before thefe ordinances, were put in execution, upon five delinquents, that had liftened to the folicitation of fome perfons of diftinction, in favour of their friends, who were likewife feverely punifhed for it.

A gentleman of the houfe of Vifconti (one of the moft illuftrious in Italy) was feen, by the Pope's fpies, in clofe converfation with a judge; and though they did not hear what paffed, they thought there was fufficient reafon for fufpicion (as one of the gentleman's fervants was in prifon for fome crime that he had been guilty of) and immediately reported it to the Pope. The governor of Rome was fent for in all hafte, and ordered to bring the fervant to his trial the very next day, which he did, and condemned him to the

l   gallies

gallies for five years; though his offence was of so trifling
a nature, that, if Gregory had been Pope, his punishment would have been but two or three months imprisonment.   The judge was turned out of his office, and
thought himself happy to escape so; the Pope content-
ing himself with telling him, "That he knew he was
" guilty, and deserved a greater punishment; but that
" he would be so favourable to excuse him this time,
" as he hoped it was his first fault."

He ordered the syndics and mayors of every town
and signiory, as well those that were actually in office,
as those who had been for the last ten years, to send
him a list of all the vagrants, common debauchees,
loose and disorderly people in their districts, threatning
them with the strapado, and imprisonment, if they o-
mitted or concealed any one of them.

The syndic of Albano leaving his nephew, who
was an incorrigible libertine, out of his list, underwent the strapado in the public market-place, though
the Spanish Ambassador interceded strongly for him.
Most of these people were so terrified at this rigid inquisition into their lives, that they fled the country;
some took to trades, and others turned lay-brothers in
the convents.   So great was the fear, that they who had
been guilty of the smallest faults, were under continual apprehensions of seeing the archers after them; and
it was no unusual thing to see them at their pater nos-
ters in the streets, left they should be put down in those
lists.

He gave express orders to have them sent directly to
him, and they were punctually obeyed by the syndics,
who knew they must otherwise expect no favour from
a man whose chief glory was to appear terrible and severe: This he affected to such a degree, that having
one day read the dedication of a book addressed to him,
in which there were great encomiums upon his mildness and clemency, he said, "These praises were due
" to him when he was cardinal, but that he gave
" up all title to them now he was Pope."   It was observed

ferved that, during his whole reign, he took much more
pleafure in repeating ftories of his rigorous juftice, than
thofe that had any appearance of mercy and compaffion, never forgetting to mention the too great [1] facility and indulgence of his predeceffor: Sometimes he
would be fo overjoyed when he read the lifts fent him
by the fyndics, that he ufed to cry out, "How happy
" we are to have crews ready for our gallies !" It is faid,
his fole defign in building them, was to clear his dominions of that fort of vermin.

He exhorted the legates and governors of the ecclefiaftical ftate, by letters, which might very well
pafs for orders, to be expeditious in carrying on their
proceffes; more particularly thofe of a criminal nature,
declaring, " That he had rather have the gibbets and
gallies full, than the prifons." He commanded all
the inferior judges not to keep any criminal in jail
above two months, but either to condemn or releafe
him in that time; and if there was any procefs that
required a longer term to finifh it, to remit it to him,
that he might judge of the reafons that retarded it.

In order to put an end to the immortality of law-
fuits, he intended to have eftablifhed a certain num-

[1] I think I may venture to ufe the word in this fenfe, viz. eafinefs, mildnefs, gentlenefs and good-nature, as it bears it in moft o-
ther languages.   The Greek πραος and πραοτης ; the Latin faci|
lis and facilitas ; the Spanifh, facil and facilitad ; the French facile and facilité ; the Italian facile and facilità, are all written with
much grace.   In the Latin tongue, which is the parent of all, or
moft of the modern languages, nothing is more frequent.   A-
mongft ten thoufand paffages that might be quoted from the clafficks,
I fhall only mention the following : " Deos faciles.— facilis ro-
" gantibus. — facilis parens veniæque paratus.   Ovid.   facilli-
" mus & liberaliffimus homo.   Lenis et facilis homo. — Ad con-
" cedendum facilis. — Abuti immoderate facilitate alicujus —
" Dignitate principibus, facilitate parem infinis. — Cicero. —
" facilis impetrandæ veniæ. Claudius. Livy. — Blandus facilifque
" maritus.   Silius Ital. — Facilis pater.   Terence." And what
is more common amongft the Englifh than to fay, an eafy good-
natured man.   Thus much, not out of vain parade, or a pædgo-
gical affection of difplaying my learing, for I pretend to very little, but to anfwer fome cavils that have been raifed againft the word
facility.

ber

ber of commiffaries, that were to be learned, experienced, and confcientious men, who fhould difpenfe with
the ufual formalities, and determine them in a fummary
way: But his great attention to criminal proceffes
made him abandon this good defign.

He prohibited the practice of judicial aftrology,
which was then in great vogue at Rome, and condemned feveral who continued to impofe upon the people by
it, in contempt of his edicts, though they were of good
families, and protected by fome of the cardinals.

He likewife threatned to punifh any one that fhould
cry out, "Long live the Pope," as he paffed along the
ftreets, tho' it had been a cuftom in the reigns of all his
predeceffors, and what the people took much pleafure in.

Several reafons moved him to this; the chief was, that
he often had a mind to go incog. and without being expected, to the tribunals of juftice, convents, and o-
ther public places: This he caufed to be fo ftrictly
obferved, that two perfons, who did not know of the
edict, fhouted out, "Long live Pope Sixtus," were
immediately fent to prifon, and continued there fome
days as an example to others: This occafioned the people, inftead of coming out of their houfes to line the
ftreets whilft he paffed by (as had been ufual) to make
hafte to hide themfelves, not being able to endure his
looks: So that he feldom met with any body but poor
old men and cripples, that could not get out of the way:
They ftood in fuch awe of him, that the mothers and
nurfes, to quiet their children, ufed to fay to them,
Hufh, Hufh, Pope Sixtus is paffing by: His name had
made fo deep an impreffion upon them, that during his
life and many years after his death, they never heard
it without trembling.

Whilft he refided in the convent of the H. Apoftles,
and afterwards, when he was cardinal, he had taken
notice of a great abufe in the confeffions relating to the
fin of adultery, which the penitents did not diftinguifh from fimple fornication. To remedy this, he
ordered

ordered that adulterers fhould be condemned to death, and forbad the judges to give them any quarter, hunting them out with great pains and diligence, and promifing rewards to thofe that would bring any of them to juftice.

The firft that was brought to his trial upon that account, was a near relation of the marquis of Altemps. The cardinal of that name ufed all his credit and favour with the Pope in his behalf; but he was inexorable, and the poor man was condemned to have his head cut off, which he fuffered foon after. He likewife caufed feveral courtezans, that were convicted of having been familiar with married men, to be publicly whipped at the fame time.

He was highly offended at voluntary or contented cuckolds; who, to live at eafe, and without labour, hired out their wives to others. As he had learned from auricular confeffion, whilft he was cardinal, that there was a confiderable trade of this kind carried on in Rome, he was determined to put a fpeedy ftop to it, and for that purpofe eftablifhed an edict, by found of trumpet, as was cuftomary in thofe times, in which he threatned to punifh this horrible profanation of the holy facrament of matrimony, and the open violation of fo folemn vows, in the fevereft manner, efpecially in them that fhould be guilty of voluntarily proftituting their wives; ftrictly enjoining all hufbands, that were privy to this infamous practice of their wives, and were not able to reftrain them, either upon the account of their being termagant, fhamelefs, or ungovernable women, or for fear of the adulterer, if he was a man in power, to make complaint of it to him; otherwife they fhould be treated as if they had confented to it, commanding all their neighbours and acquaintance, that fhould hear of any fuch thing, immediately to difcover it, on pain of being proceeded againft as encouragers and abettors of fuch crimes, if they fhould come to be otherways known. This, in a great meafure, put a ftop to a

scanda-

scandalous custom that was at that time much in fashion at Rome; many of the cardinals, prelates, and nobles, marrying their favourite women to some servant, or domestic, that was willing to wear horns for the sake of a maintenance, or perhaps some little reward, that they might carry on their amours with less notice and observation.

Some days before the election of Sixtus, Charles Tasca, a gentleman of Salerno, had married one of his mistresses to his steward, who was an easy, contented, good-natured man, and in years, and used to take a journey, or pretend business in the city, whenever his master was inclined to divert himself with his wife; upon the publication of this edict, some of the neighbours, who were acquainted with the affair, either out of fear of the Pope (who they saw was not to be trifled with) or hatred to the parties concerned, went and admonished them of their crime; telling them the danger they not only were in themselves, but were likely to bring their neighbours into, and advised them to retire out of the ecclesiastical dominions; but Tasca laughed at this good advice, imagining, that as he was only a sojourner, and no subject of the Pope's, he was not obliged to the observance of his laws.

When the governor was informed of this, he consulted the other judges and magistrates, and finding he was really a foreigner, residing in hired lodgings, he was strangely embarrassed; but as he stood in great awe of Sixtus, he thought it the best way to report the whole affair, as it was, to him; when he did, Sixtus was not a little displeased that he should make any scruple of punishing them, and, after a severe reprimand, told him, "It was his pleasure that Tasca, the husband, " and wife, should all be hanged; that he was sur- " prized to find him so ignorant of his duty, as not to " know, that all foreigners were bound (according to " the law of nations) to a local allegiance, that is " to observe the laws of the country they reside in; " and that he would not suffer either foreigners, or any

T

" other

"other perfon, to trample upon his authority, or vio-
"late his edicts." In fhort, Tafca, in confideration
of his being a foreigner, and a gentleman of good family, was only fent to the gallies for a few years; the
hufband and wife were both hanged; and three fervants, that were acquainted with the affair, and had
not difcovered it, feverely whipped.

There lived at Rome, in the pontificate of Gregory,
Agatella Pignaccia, a celebrated courtezan, who by her
charms and allurements had fo bewitched the whole
court (there being few of the nobility, cardinals, or
prelates, of any note, who were not numbered amongft
her admirers) that in lefs than ten years fhe had made
up a purfe of [2] 30,000 Piftoles, befides a great deal
of plate, jewels, a rich wardrobe, and lived in fo
much fplendor, that fhe was called, the Princefs: Befides all this, fhe had bought a delightful villa, which
fhe called Pigna, after her own name, whither fhe
ufed to retire fometimes to take the frefh air, and enjoy the pleafures of the country, with fome of her
inamoratos.

Sixtus was thoroughly informed of her way of life,
whilft he was cardinal; and of the fcandalous familiarity in which the Pope's nephews, and feveral of the
prelates had lived with her, though fuch things were
but little taken notice of in that pontificate, every one
efteemed it an honour to have it thought he was acquainted with the princefs.

This woman was originally a Neapolitan, and the
wife of a notary, but either taking a diflike to her
hufband, or led aftray by her immoderate love for the
Abbé Ciapoli, fhe ran away with that ecclefiaftic to
Rome; where, having in a fhort time fpent all that he
had, and reduced him to beggary, fhe took a handfome houfe, and turned courtezan, felling her favours
at a prodigious rate: The notary her hufband, who

[2] A Piftole is worth about 17s. or 17s. 6d. fterling, according to the weight.

wa

was much affected when he heard of her infamous
course of life, came to Rome after her, and she refusing
to see him, applied to a magistrate, from whom he was
so far from obtaining any redress, that he was publicly
assassinated one morning in the open street: and notwithstanding there was the strongest evidence, that this was
done by her directions and contrivance, or that of her
lovers, she had so much influence over those in the administration, that there was not the least notice taken
of it, or the woman so much as carried before a magistrate, and examined for form's sake: Indeed, assaf-
sinations were so frequent at that time, that they were
hardly reckoned criminal: but cardinal Montalto, who
pretended to see nothing, and knew every thing, did
not fail to write this transaction down in his journal,
with all the circumstances of it.

When Pignaccia heard of the rigorous edict that had
been published against adultery, being conscious of her
guilt, and terrified with the report of the Pope's extreme severity (having great reason to fear that a strict
examination would be made into her past conduct) she
formed a design of flying to Venice, there to enjoy in
peace, what she acquired at Rome, and perhaps with a
view of still increasing it, by getting acquainted with
the nobility and rich merchants of that city.

For this purpose she sent for some jews, and treated
with them for the sale of her goods, and furniture,
and the remittance of her treasure in as speedy and secret a manner as possible, to Venice; offering them likewise the refusal of her country-house, at a very small
price, provided they would pay her in ready-money,
or jewels: But Sixtus was too cunning for her: As he
came to the papacy with a firm resolution to administer
strict justice, and to neglect no means of raising money to accomplish the vast designs he had conceived, he
thought the making an example of Pignaccia, was a
proper opportunity of serving both these purposes; and
whether he had been informed, or suspected that she was
endeavouring to make her escape, upon the publication

T 2   of

of the above mentioned edict, he sent for the governor of Rome, and told him, " he was determined to
" make a thorough inquiry, not only into her life and
" conduct, but the death of her husband. and the
" manner how she came to be possessed of so great
" riches, and to have a particular account of the whole
" from her own mouth, or the information of those
" prelates, and nobles, that had been most familiar
" with her, either by voluntary confession, or torture."
In consequence of this intimation, the unfortunate princess was apprehended, and conducted to prison, and
seals fixed upon the doors of her villa and town-house:
She was then about twenty-five years of age, in the full
blow of her charms, of a ready, lively wit, and an expression not to be resisted; which so prevailed upon the
governor, that he, at her earnest request, obtained her
an audience from Sixtus, telling him, " she had several
" secrets to disclose, of the highest importance to his
" holiness, and the state." When she came into the
Pope's presence, she threw herself upon her knees, and
addressed him in the following manner:

MOST HOLY FATHER,

" THOU true and lawful vicar of our Saviour Je-
" sus Christ, who looks down upon the most sinful of
" his creatures with an eye of mercy and compassion:
" A consolation, that encourages me to prostrate my-
" self at your adorable feet, inspired with a ray of di-
" vine hope (though I ingenuously confess, my crimes
" deserve a thousand deaths) that you will be so com-
" passionate to behold the frailties and failings of a
" weak woman, with some degree of pity and tender-
" ness. I did not ask the favour of being admitted into
" your holy presence, with any expectation of obtain-
" ing a reprieve from the sentence I so justly merit;
" the only request I have to make, is that your holiness
" will be pleased to give credit to what I shall say,
" concerning

" concerning the immature death of my unfortunate
" hufband: I here folemnly proteft, before the Almigh-
" ty and Eternal God, whofe moft worthy reprefenta-
" tive you are upon earth, that I had not the leaft part
" or concern in that tragical event: For the reft, let it
" fuffice that I own myfelf unworthy of any mercy,
" and am content to fuffer the moft cruel and ignomi-
" nous punifhment, for fo fhamefully abandoning a
" man that dearly loved me, and giving myfelf up,
" without fcruple or referve, to my inordinate lufts and
" affections. It is with the utmoft horror, the fharpeft
" and moft intolerable compunction of fpirit, that I
" own I have proftituted myfelf to almoft all ranks and
" degrees of men; that I voluntarily, and without any
" provocation, forfook the bofom of the beft and moft
" affectionate hufband, to minifter to the lufts of a
" vile abbé (now dead); and have taken, the Almigh-
" ty knows, a wicked pleafure in feducing other huf-
" bands from the duties of the conjugal ftate; that I
" have exerted all my cunning, and practifed every
" fraud, to ftrip my gallants, and enrich myfelf, at
" the expence of their fouls and bodies.

" You have here, moft holy father, a full and am-
" ple, confeffion of all the offences of a wretched, def-
" ponding, and truely contrite penitent, now proftrate
" at your feet. I afk, I wifh, I moft ardently wifh for
" death; and hope that, through the mercies of Chrift,
" will be a fufficient facrifice and atonement for my
" great fins; humbly imploring your abfolution before
" I go hence, and be no more feen. As for my wordly
" goods, I leave them to be difpofed of in fuch a man-
" ner as your holinefs, in your great charity and wif-
" dom, fhall think moft proper."

Such a fpeech, delivered with all the pomp of grief,
and foftnefs of female eloquence, was enough, one
would imagine, to have moved a heart of flint: Sixtus,
however, did not feem much affected with it: He expected fhe had fome great difcoveries to make, but
when

when he found she had nothing farther to say, he answered, "We shall take care of your soul, and grant
" you a proper absolution, provided you give satisfac-
" tory answers to such questions as shall be asked by
" our judges, in the course of your trial, and speak the
" truth without prevarication." She was put to the torture, to see if they could draw any secrets of importance to the state, out of her; but having nothing
more to confess, she was strangled, sitting in a close
chair, at the foot of the gallows: Two old women, that
had been employed as instruments in her wicked occupation, being unmercifully whipped at the same time
and place. Many of those that had been most intimately acquainted with her, had heavy fines laid upon them;
and two prelates, that had lived with her in an open and
scandalous manner, were suspended from their benefices: Her estate was confiscated, and applied, together
with the fines, to the building a noble hospital for the
sick and poor of Rome.

The nobility of Rome, and the country round about
it, were arrived at the height of vice and insolence, in
the reign of Gregory XIII. that they had entirely given
up all pretensions to common justice and honesty.
Many of them, who had contracted large debts with
the merchants and tradesmen, without any design of
ever paying them, used to send them away with threats
and hard words, when they asked for their money; and
if they came a second time, to treat them with a good
bastonading, and tell them, "They would knock them
" on the head, if they gave them any further trou-
" ble;" which frightened them so, that they durst not
go to law with them, for fear of losing their lives, as
well as their money.

Sixtus, who had taken notice of these things before
he came to the papacy, and was resolved to put an end
to such arbitrary and unjust proceedings, sent for a
gentleman that had owed a large sum of money, for
a considerable time, to a draper, and always used to
shuffle him off, when he came to demand payment,
with

with faying, "That gentlemen never paid their debts,
"but when they pleafed." When he came before the
Pope, together with the draper, who was likewife fent
for, he not only made him pay the money down immediately, but fent him to prifon, and ordered a procefs againft him, for having unjuftly detained it fo long:
He, at the fame time, commanded all the merchants
and tradefmen to bring him in a lift of their debts,
with the names of the people that owed them, which
he paid off, and took upon himfelf. This gave fuch an
alarm, that many, who were indebted to the merchants,
went to pay them that very night, begging of them, for
God's fake, to crofs their names out of their books, and
give them fuch receipts, as might fhew as if they had
been paid long ago, left the Pope fhould come to know
it. This fear was not without reafon; for one of the
fpies having informed Sixtus, that a certain merchant
had concealed, or not delivered in a debt due to him,
from a gentleman of confiderable fortune, he fent for
his books, and finding it true, he, in vain, endeavoured
to clear himfelf, by faying, "He was paid, and had,
"forgot to take it out of his book;" for the Pope, declaring he had been guilty of difobeying his orders,
delivered him into the hands of juftice, to be punifhed
for his crime.

By a cuftom that had long prevailed at Rome, the
domeftics and menial fervants of a cardinal, or
other great officer of the court, were not fubject to be
arrefted for debt, which encouraged many to borrow
large fums, and then, by making a prefent to the relation or favourite of a great man, to obtain fome little
place in his houfhold, by which means they fkreened
themfelves from profecution, and quietly enjoyed what
they had thus fhamefully defrauded their creditors of.

Sixtus, who had long been aware of this knavifh practice, as it was a great detriment to the public, and
occafioned a ftagnation of credit, was refolved to break
through it: For which purpofe, he fent for the governor,
and ordered him to make it known by found of trumpet,

pet, " That it was his pleafure, the fervants of card-
" nals, and other great perfons, fhould no longer en-
" joy this privilege; and that if their creditors would
" apply to the civil magiftrate, for the recovery of
" their debts, and were not paid in eight days, he
" would oblige their mafters either to difcharge fuch
" perfons from their fervice, or to pay their debts them-
" felves, by confifcation of their goods." The cardinals in general, were not difpleafed at this order, as
they were fenfible how prejudicial fuch a practice was
to the public good; but were fo exceedingly mortified
that it fhould be publifhed by found of trumpet, which
was looked upon as a difgraceful circumftance, that ten
of them went to wait upon the Pope, and defire, " he
" would be pleafed to recall the order, or at leaft to
" publifh it in fome other manner :" To which they
received the following anfwer:

" As God has been pleafed to call us to the govern-
" ment of his people, by your fuffrages, at a time
" when there is the utmoft occafion for good regimen
" and wholefome feverity, you are grievoufly miftaken
" if you think we are obliged, in confideration of the
" votes you have given us, to connive at your own
" frauds and robberies, or thofe of your domeftics.

" As for your votes, we are not under the leaft obli-
" gation to any of you, but to the infpiration of the
" Holy Ghoft alone, which conftantly influences and
" directs the hearts of the conclave in the choice of a
" Pope; and if you are fo impious or prefumptuous,
" to imagine it is in your power to difpofe of your
" voice at that time, according to your own carnal will,
" without the interpofition of Heaven, ye not only
" greatly err, but are guilty of moft flagrant here-
" fy, from which we fhall endeavour to reclaim you,
" by ordering our officers of the holy inquifition, to in-
" ftruct you in the true ancient doctrine and difcipline
" of the church. If therefore we are indebted to fuch
" impulfes and fuggeftions, for our exaltation to the
" pontificate; we think ourfelves, in confcience, bound
                                                    " to

" to obey the dictates of the same holy spirit in our
" government of the church, more particularly as
" Christ himself had promised, that he will never fail
" to grant us his powerful aid and assistance; and of
" this it is our pleasure, that not only you, but all
" other persons, whom it may concern, take especial
" notice.

" We flatter ourselves, it will give you no common
" satisfaction, when we assure you, from the bottom of
" our heart, that we have the most profound and sin-
" cere regard, and shall exert ourselves with as much
" zeal for the dignity and privileges of the sacred pur-
" ple, as in our endeavours, to prevent those stains that
" would eclipse and tarnish its lustre. It is certain,
" most dear brethren, you ought, and we hope, will
" approve our resolution, to extinguish a scandal, that
" would leave an everlasting reproach upon your repu-
" tation, (and which I tremble to think of) expose
" your sacred character to contempt and derision. What
" will the Heretics say? How will they triumph, when
" they hear that cardinals (who ought to shine like
" stars of the first magnitude, and set the purest and
" most exalted pattern of holiness and an apostolic
" life) are become protectors of fraud and injustice, in
" open violation not only of all human laws but the
" express commands and precepts of the gospel, which
" enjoins us not to injure or oppress our neighbour, or
" invade a property that we have no right to?

" We confess it fills us with amazement and surprize,
" to see you offended at that which is the safety and
" preservation of all societies: However, let who will
" be displeased, we are determined no longer to suffer
" so infamous a practice to shelter itself under the wing
" of your authority; as it not only affords matter of
" scandal to the Heretics, but unjustly offends all good
" Catholics. We are very well assured, that, if any
" one should be bold and wicked enough to make an
" attack upon your rights, and then retire into some
" privileged place, to skreen himself from justice, you
" would

" would, lift up your voice like a trumpet and deafen
" us with complaints and importunities: Why therefore,
" should you endeavour to injure others in a manner
" that you would not bear yourselves? In short, we
" would have the world know, that we are not that
" light and defultory person, as to publish our edicts
" one day, and revoke them the next: it is our plea-
" fure they shall be immutable and perpetual; and we
" shall take proper care to enforce them, by the weight
" of that authority which God has committed to our
" hands, and trust we shall fee you the first and readi-
" est to obey them."

This being all the fatisfaction they could obtain, they
returned to their houfes, with a full determination never to meddle any more in matters relating to his government, and to avoid all occafion of difpute with a
perfon of his refolute and obftinate temper. Cardinal
Sforza, who was one of them that was moft affected
by it, as his fteward and majordomo had contracted
very confiderable debts, came back in the fame chariot
with Gonzage; and falling into converfation with him,
concerning the unreafonablenfs of obliging them to
pay debts in a few days, that had been, perhaps many
years in contracting, at laft, faid, " he would fell all he
" was worth, and pay what he owed, and either retire
" into a convent, or go miffionary to the Indies, as he
" plainly faw they muft expect to live as if they were
" in hell, at leaft in purgatory, whilft that pontificate
" lafted." Gonzage anfwered, " This is exactly what
" the Pope wants; it would give him the greateft plea-
" fure, if he could either make us live like monks in
" Rome, or drive us out of it."

Notwithftanding the rigour of his edicts, he was refolved to make the cardinals obey them, as well as o-
thers; and ufed to fay, " No body could complain that
" he made laws for others, and not for himfelf, or his fa-
" mily; for it was his intention to obferve them inviola-
" bly, and to punifh the leaft tranfgreffion of them in any
" other perfon; but with a greater degree of feverity,
" if

" if he was his relation or dependent." It is certain,
nevertheless, he always had the honour of the sacred
college much at heart; and tho' he would admit the
cardinals to very little share in the government, especially in the first year of his pontificate, he published several bulls in their favour; and often said, " That
" if he expected them to live like subjects in Rome,
" they were princes out of it.

As for the payment of debts which were contracted
in the reign of Gregory, or perhaps before, and had
been the ruin of several merchants, it was his pleasure
this order should be observed with so much rigour, that
after he had taken care to inform himself there was no
fraud or deceit in it, he generously paid the debts of
people who had met with misfortunes, and were not a-
ble to do it themselves: By which means he soon restored the public credit, and saved many families from
destruction: for the solemnity with which the order
was published, and the severe penalties that were annexed to it, had such an effect, that every one that was
in debt, exerted himself to the utmost, and used all
means and expedients to satisfy his creditors.

He further shewed his generosity to those cardinals,
whose small revenues would not suffer them to live as
became the dignity of the purple, without borrowing
money, ordering the master of his houshold to inform
himself of their wants, and the sums they owed, which
he immediately sent them : For, as he was fully pur-
posed to see his edict put in execution, he was not willing that those that were able to pay, should be excused
by the example of those that really were not. Tho'
this was, in the main, of very great service, and obliged every body to proportion their expences to their
income, and introduced an œconomy of which there
was much need at that time, in Rome, many were
forced to leave the city, and abandon their houses to
the utter ruin of their families: Of which Sixtus being
informed by the governor, said, it was no great mat-
" ter ;" and bade him go on to execute his orders, and
make

make every one pay his debts; telling him, " That it
" was neceffary, fometimes to cut off a limb, to fave
" the whole body; and if it was hard upon fome few,
" it would do good to thoufands; that every well re-
" gulated ftate ought to difcountenance thofe that lived
" upon the labour of other people, by running into debt,
" and to encourage fuch as maintained themfelves and
" their families, by honeft induftry and frugality ; that
" this law would foon produce very good effects, as it
" would in the firft place reftore good order and œco-
" nomy, reclaiming many from a loofe and diforderly
" way of living, or indulging themfelves in a degree
" of luxury, oftentation, and extravagance, which their
" incomes would not bear, in expectation of being fup-
" ported by others, whilft the treafury would be rich-
" er than it has been for many years.

Some were of opinion that, befide the confideration of
juftice, he had a political and felf-interefted view, in
proceeding after this manner ; and that his chief intention was to oblige them that owed money to the Apoftolic Chamber, to pay it in a fhort time, which he
thought he might do with a better grace, after he had
compelled private perfons to pay their creditors. Whatever might be his motive, the debtors of the Apoftolic Chamber, in a few months after, paid above
600,000 crowns into it, that had been owing 20
years.   By this method he put a ftop to other people's
eating the bread, and living upon the revenues of the
church.

He fent every fifteen days to let the governor know,
" he was furprized there were fo few examples of juftice
" made in the city; that if it had been his lot to have
" filled his poft, he fhould have taken another courfe
" with the offenders." This reproach fo terrified the
poor governor, that he was hunting about for malefactors from morning till night ; and often inflicted
very fevere punifhments upon them for trifling offences.

It

It had been the custom for the new Popes (as we have observed) to throw open the prison-doors, and set at liberty all those that were confined : But Sixtus would not, by any means, comply with this; and said to the cardinals, who advised him not to break any old customs, " That there were too many villains in the city alrea- " dy; that it would be very wrong to increase the num- " ber, by setting those at liberty that were now con- " fined; that he had taken upon him the government " of the church, with no other view than to chastise " the evil, and prevent them from corrupting those that " were good, by their contagious example.

Ne pars sincera trabatur. Ovid.

Before the rejoicings for his election were yet well over, he ordered four wretches to be hanged, early one morning, who had been seen about two days before with arms that he had forbid the use of. It was in vain that many persons of the first quality, or even the Japanese ambassadors, interceded for them.

A little time after, he ordered the judges to condemn a gentleman of Spoletto to have his head cut off, only for having drawn his sword, in a threatning manner, upon another person that he had a quarrel with, without paying the least regard to eight cardinals, who sued for his pardon; for he had him immediately executed, that he might not be plagued with any further importunities.

It is true he had forbid every one to draw a sword, on pain of death, or to carry arms that had been specified, and publicly declared, he would not spare any person that disobeyed this order: This kept men of hasty and quarrelsome tempers in so much awe, that they durst not even go to fifty cuffs; but were forced to content themselves with saying, Well! Sixtus can't live for ever. Most of the gentlemen left their swords at home; and they that could not be prevailed upon to do so, took great care not to make any use of them.

About

About this time there came out a pasquinade, in which Pasquin was reprefentented on horfeback, galloping off as faft as he could, and Marforio afking, *Why fo faft?* he anfwered, *It's time to get away, 'faith the Pope is in fuch a humour, that I believe he would fhew no favour to* Jefus Chrift *himfelf*.

He publifhed an edict in his firft confiftory, in which he enjoined all archbifhops and bifhops (without any exception) to repair to their diocefes, and not to leave them upon any account, for the fpace of fix months. It was faid, this was done to get rid of fome of the cardinals, whofe company he did not much care for.

The ecclefiaftical ftate, at this time, was grievoufly infefted with banditi, who were become fo infolent and audacious by impunity, that nobody's eftate, or life, was in fafety; and this, not only in the country, and little villages, but in the large towns, and even at Rome itfelf. It is hardly poffible to conceive the prodigious number of robberies and murders that were daily committed, for a confiderable time, which made ftrangers afraid of coming to Rome: Gregory had endeavoured to fupprefs thefe mifcreants, by fending parties of foldiers in purfuit of them, but to no purpofe: Heaven referved the glory of this for the prudence and refolution of Sixtus to accomplifh; which he did fo effectually in a few months, that he entirely cleared his dominions of them, fo that one might travel any hour of the day or night, in the city or country, without the leaft danger or apprehenfion.

Sixtus then being determined to purge the ftate of all nuifances, to reftore trade and commerce, and to eftablifh fafety and tranquility amongft his fubjects, and feeing the great feverity of his proceedings (tho' abfolutely neceffary) had obliged many people of loofe and diforderly lives to, to fly from the face of juftice, and to take refuge amongft the banditi, by which their numbers were fo increafed, that they threatened the ruin and fubverfion of the ftate, began to think in earneft of

an

an effectual remedy for this evil, especially as he was daily informed of some robbery or affaffination: Indeed their infolence was so great, that there was no place in the ecclefiaftical ftate, where any one could live with fafety to his perfon or fortune; nor could ftrangers travel without the greateft danger of being robbed, ill treated, or murdered. They were come to that height of impudence, that they would go and lodge publicly in towns, and take what they wanted, let it belong to whom it would, without any ceremony, or payment.

In the firft place, therefore, he orderered his nuncios to acquaint the neighbouring princes, particularly the grand duke, the viceroy of Naples, the duke of Ferrara, and the republic of Genoa, with his intentions to extirpate this race of vermin, earneftly defiring them to contribute their endeavours to fo laudable and neceffary an undertaking, and not to fuffer thofe that fhould be purfued by him, to take fhelter in their dominions, from whence they might return to infeft the ecclefiaftical ftate hereafter; and being affured by them, that they would give him all the affiftance that lay in their power; he in the next place eftablifhed a tribunal, confifting of three judges, Don Lælius Urfini, General Mutio, and Francis Maldoviti, men of rigid and inflexible tempers, of great induftry and application to bufinefs, and fkilful in military affairs, appointing them a body of 500 foldiers and archers, with a liberty to increafe the number if they thought neceffary, according to their difcretion: They had the title of Inquifitors General againft the Banditi, with an ample commiffion to proceed in fuch a manner as they fhould think moft proper to deftroy them, to refide at, or leave any place, either alone, or accompanied by a party, all together, or feparately, as they judged fit; in which the fubjects of the ecclefiaftical ftate were commanded, on pain of death, to give them all manner of affiftance that lay in their power. This they immediately publifhed, in the following form:

" WHEREAS

" Whereas our fovereign lord Sixtus V. has been
" gracioufly pleafed by a bull for that purpofe, dated
" the 27th of May laft, to conftitute and appoint us,
" inquifitors general againft the banditi, and all forts
" of wicked and diforderly perfons, who difturb the
" peace of the ecclefiaftical dominions, to which the
" Almighty Providence has vouchfafed to exalt his
" Holinefs; that we may not betray the confidence he
" has repofed in our zeal, fidelity and diligence, to
" extinguifh that vile and abominable fet of people
" (which we are refolved to accomplifh if poffible) we
" think it proper to publifh the following ordinance
" and declaration, according to the command of his
" Holinefs.

" I. Although his holinefs looks with horror upon
" the crimes of wicked men, efpecially of fuch as,
" throwing off all manner of obedience to the laws of
" God and their Prince, fupport themfelves by murder
" and rapine, to the great annoyance of our well difpofed
" fubjects, yet out of his infinite compaffion to their
" fouls, as vicar of Jefus Chrift, and paftor of his flock,
" being likewife defirous of proceeding like a generous
" and magnanimous Prince, he is willing to make ufe
" of clemency before he draws the fword of juftice,
" in hope they will thereby be prevailed upon to forfake
" their evil courfes, and return to their duty and obe-
" dience.

" II. We therefore declare, in the name of his Holi
" nefs, and by his exprefs command, that all thofe,
" that in the fpace of three months to commence from
" the publication of this, will voluntarily furrender
" themfelves, fhall be received and provided with em-
" ployment, according to their refpective conditions,
" by which they may fupport themfelves, and their fa-
" milies, and get an honeft livelihood: That they fhall
" likewife have their goods reftored, if they have been
" confifcated, and a full pardon for their paft offences,
" upon condition that they will truly repent, and pro-
" mife faithfully hereafter, to lead a new life: For this
                                              " purpofe

" purpofe we have his Holinefs's orders, to grant paff-
" ports, and fafe conducts, to all fuch as apply for
" them, and let us know how they will come to their
" hands, and to promife that all this fhall be punctually
" fulfilled, with good faith, upon the word of a Pope.

" III. But if any of them fhall be apprehended after,
" or during this term, without furrendering themfelves,
" or fuing for a fafe-conduct, they fhall be for ever ex-
" cluded from all favour, and punifhed as contumaci-
" ous, obftinate, and incorrigible rebels, with the moft
" exquifite tortures that the wit of man can invent: to
" render their memory infamous to pofterity, and to
" ferve as an example to others.

" IV. Whofoever (being either ftung with remorfe
" for his fins, or moved by our generous promifes, or
" willing to make fome recompence to the community
" he has fo grievoufly offended) fhall deliver up any of
" his companions into the hands of juftice, fhall receive
" a reward of 500 crowns, for every fuch perfon, if a-
" live, and 300 if he be dead, to be divided equally
" amongft them, if there be more than one of them
" concerned, or if not, that one perfon fhall receive
" the whole: And we further promife him, or them,
" in confideration of this fervice, not only a full and
" free pardon of all offences, but will provide them
" with fuch an employment as is fuitable to their rank,
" and fufficient to maintain them and their families in
" a reputable manner.

" V. If any of our fubjects, or thofe that refide in
" our dominions, fhall lend his affiftance towards the
" fuppreffion of the banditi, he fhall receive 400 crowns
" for every head he fhall bring, and 600 for every one
" that he fhall produce alive, with a pardon for any
" criminal they pleafe: If he is their relation, and is
" condemned to fuffer death, his fentence fhall be
" changed to ten years imprifonment; and if in the
" gallies, he fhall inftantly be fet at liberty.

" VI. His Holinefs, being informed that feveral of
" the nobility, and other perfons, have not only dared
U   " to

" to protect and defend the banditi, but even to enter
" into a friendship and correspondence with them, fur-
" nishing them with intelligence and neceſſaries, has
" ordered us to inform all perſons, of what rank ſoever,
" to deſiſt from ſuch practices, after the publication of
" this, and not to afford them the leaſt entertainment,
" encouragement, aſſiſtance, or information, either di-
" rectly or indirectly, upon pretence of friendſhip,
" kindred, or any other connexion, but to reveal ſuch
" friendſhip, or correſpondence, on pain of death, with-
" out mercy.

" VII. It is hereby further declared, that in caſe of
" diſobedience, no nobleman ſhall have the privilege
" of nobility, but ſuffer death upon the gallows, or
" wheel, as a rebel, if after this he ſhall be convicted
" of holding any ſuch correſpondence, or of not re-
" vealing what he formerly held; and if they freely
" and ingenuouſly confeſs we promiſe them a full par-
" don of all that is paſt: The ſame is to be under-
" ſtood of eccleſiaſtics, magiſtrates, judges, ſyndics,
" governors of cities, &c. who are likewiſe ſtrictly
" enjoined in his Holineſs's name, on pain of being
" treated in the ſevereſt manner, to uſe their utmoſt
" endeavours to diſcover all ſuch perſons as they ſuſ-
" pect of maintaining any correſpondence with the ban-
" diti, and to ſeize upon their perſons, and give us im-
" mediate notice of it."

Theſe orders being publiſhed, the inquiſitors went
through the whole ſtate, examining all perſons, and
puniſhing thoſe they had any ſuſpicion of, in the ſevereſt manner, without any ceremony or form of juſtice;
ſo that in leſs than ſix months all the banditi were
either taken, or diſappeared, and ſuch a terror ſtruck
into the people, that every one being afraid any little
particular quarrel might make him paſs for a diſturber
of the peace, *made haſte to agree with his adverſary*;
differences that had laſted many years, were compoſed in a moment; and people that had long been
the

the bitterest enemies, now lived in the greatest friendship and amity.

As Sixtus one day passed through the city, he saw
the captain of the archers, or country-marshal, walking carelessly about the streets, instead of being, as he
ought, in pursuit of the banditi, and called to him. As
soon as the marshal was aware of the Pope, he took to
his heels; but he was presently stopped, and brought
back to his Holiness, who asked him in an angry tone,
" Who he was ?" The poor fellow, half dead with fear,
finding he was known by Sixtus, fell upon his knees,
and said, " May it please your Holiness, I am the cap-
" tain of the country archers." " You rascal," says
he, in the same voice, " have you the impudence to tell
" the Pope a lie ? how can you, that are loitering about
" the city, be the country-marshal ?" And, as upon
this, he immediately sent him to prison, most people
thought he was in a fair way to be hanged: However,
he sent for him again in the evening, and told him,
" He gave him his life, upon condition that in eight
" days he brought him the heads of six banditi, other-
" wise he should be put to death." The marshal, who
did not expect to come off at so cheap a rate, transported with joy, fell down and kissed the Pope's feet, and
leaving Rome that moment, acquitted himself so well,
that before the eight days were expired, he presented
Sixtus with four of the banditi alive, and three heads ;
with which he was so well pleased, that he gave him a
chain of gold worth fifty pistoles.

He ordered the heads to be stuck upon the gates of
the city, and on both sides of St. Angelo's bridge, whither he often used to go on purpose to see them. The
number was so great, that the smell becoming offensive
to passengers, the cardinals sent the magistracy to desire his Holiness would give leave to let them be fixed
in some other place, where they would not be so great
a nuisance to the public: But he only said, " Truly,
" gentlemen, you must be very delicate, not to bear

" the

" the fmell of a few innocent heads, that can now of-
" fend no body; for my part, I think there are many
" living heads, that difturb the public peace, of a
" much worfe favour."

All the other princes of Italy, who could not hinder
thefe vagabonds, of which Sixtus had cleared his dominions, from entering into theirs, complained loudly,
that the quiet and repofe of the ecclefiaftical ftate, was
eftablifhed at the price of their fubjects lives and fortunes. Some of the ambaffadors having made reprefentations of this kind to him, he told them, " If their
" mafters would give him their dominions, he would
" foon fweep them as clean as his own: That if they
" would do as he had done, Italy would prefently be
" free from that peft; that fovereigns could do great
" things, when they fet about them heartily."

In the month of September there happened a ftrange
adventure, and indeed a very fatal one, to a young Florentine, not quite 17 years old, who was condemned
to die, and executed, for having made fome refiftance
to the archers, when they came to feize an afs, belonging to another perfon, that was in his mafter's
ftable (it was upon the account of a debt): But the
archers were miftaken, for the afs did not belong to
the perfon that owed the money, and for that reafon
the young man thought he had a right to oppofe its
being taken away. Some were of opinion, that the
Pope had been mifinformed in this matter; others faid,
it was to reftrain the licence which the people had
been fo long ufed to, and let them fee, he would not
have the officers of juftice molefted, or oppofed, even
when they were in the wrong. Whatever were his
reafons, the whole city was in tears, and murmured
at fo unreafonable a piece of feverity: The ambaffador of the grand duke, and Cardinal Medicis, ufed
their utmoft endeavours to fave him; and the governor of Rome ventured to remonftrate to him, " That
" the laws did not allow them to punifh fo young a
" perfon with death." But it was all to no purpofe;
                                                    Sixtus

Sixtus only faid, " If he is not old enough to be hanged,
" we can fpare ten years of our age." The confternation that was occafioned by this extreme rigour,
was increafed by the fate of another unfortunate youth,
no lefs worthy of compaffion than the former. An
artificer had fent his nephew to the houfe of correction,
for behaving in an undutiful manner to his mother,
with an intention only to keep him there a few days,
as he thought that was punifhment fufficient for his
crime: When he went to take him out, the keeper
faid, he durft not let him go, as he had the Pope's orders to the contrary. Upon this, the man went to
wait upon his Holinefs, to acquaint him with the caufe
of his nephew's imprifonment. Sixtus, having heard
him with patience, faid, " We pronounce his punifh-
" ment too fmall, and can't, in juftice, let him go off
" in this manner: If you, who are his uncle, think
" he deferves to be imprifoned, for his difobedient be-
" haviour to his mother, we, as his judge, think him
" worthy of death." In fhort, he was condemned to
be hanged, but his fentence was afterwards changed,
and he was fent to the gallies.

They who had feen the prodigious debauch and licentioufnefs that reigned in the days of Gregory, were
aftonifhed to find fo great a reformation, wrought by
thefe feverities, in the fpace of a few months, throughout the whole city and country: Greater regularity and
decorum could not be obferved in a convent, than there
was at this time in every private family; nor were the
religious houfes ever better governed, the Pope fending for their fuperiors once a month, to recommend to
them the keeping up ftrict difcipline and order.

The tragical end of Count John Baptifta Pepoli, head
of the richeft and moft flourifhing houfe in Bologna,
ftill more awakened people's fears. This nobleman was
accufed of keeping a fecret correfpondence with fome
of the banditi; and tho' there was no direct proof
againft him, the accufation being chiefly founded upon
circumftances, there came an order from Rome, to arreft

and

and bring him to his trial. As there was not sufficient
evidence of his guilt, the judges were for acquitting
him, when there arrived a messenger from the court, to
let them know, " it was his Holiness's pleasure he
" should be condemned, for an example." The judges
durst not disobey him, and passed sentence of death upon the poor Count, but delayed his execution to give
him an opportunity of soliciting a pardon, tho' they
were pretty well assured he would not be able to obtain
one. Indeed, his friends told him so; they wrote however, to his Holiness in the most suppliant terms, and
such as would have moved any heart but his, beseeching
him to spare his life; but he was deaf to their entreaties, and sent orders to have him speedily executed. This
ill-fated nobleman, who was exceedingly beloved by
all, for his Prince-like generosity, and had always lived
in the greatest magnificence, was publicly beheaded
on a scaffold in the face of his country.

It must be confessed, that the protection and encouragement given to the banditi, by the Bolognese gentlemen, demanded an example of justice, to deter them
from having any further correspondence with them
This consideration induced his Holiness to proceed in
so unrelenting a manner. Tho' some did not scruple to
say privately, it was a piece of revenge, as the Count
was son of that nobleman that had formerly threatened
Sixtus, for refusing to release his friend, when he went
thro' Bologna, in quality of inquisitor to Venice, and
was made commissary by the general, to hear and redress some grievances among the Cordeliers of that
place. But this does not seem probable or consistent
with the rest of his conduct.

He gave orders for a process to be commenced against
those that had assassinated his nephew, and charged
Cardinal St Sixtus with the care and superintendence
of it, as that event happened in the reign of his uncle.
The cardinal told him, " they should have been severe-
" ly punished at that time, if he had not seemed to dis-
" approve

" approve of it." " True, fays he, I forgave it then,
" as his uncle, becaufe the law of God requires us fo
" to do, but now the duty of a fovereign obliges us to
" take cognizance of it. If your uncle had punifhed
" them (as he ought to have done) he would have
" faved us this trouble, and the tears we can't help
" fhedding afrefh, at the remembrance of a nephew
" we fo dearly loved."

Sixtus did not behave with this rigour in matters of
reformation, and to private perfons only ; for he treated
the greateft princes with the fame degree of roughnefs.
Before he had been Pope two months, he quarrelled
with Philip II. of Spain, Henry III. of France, and Henry K. of Navarre ; the caufes of which we fhall relate
as briefly as we can.

It is cuftomary for the Spanifh ambaffador, every
year, upon St. Peter's day, to prefent his Holinefs with
a genet, or palfrey, and a purfe of 7000 crowns, as
holding the kingdom of Naples in vaffalage of the
Pope ; a tribute that had been paid many years, and
was confirmed by the emperor Charles V. after he became mafter of that kingdom, who charged his heirs
and fucceffors with it. This ceremony was to be performed before the great gate of St. Peter's, where the
Pope was feated in royal array, upon a throne placed
there for that purpofe, and attended by all the cardinals and minifters of foreign princes.

When all things were in readinefs, the ambaffador
of Spain advanced with his genet, and complimented
his Holinefs, upon the inftructions he had from his
mafter, to fay, " That it was by way of tribute for
" the kingdom of Naples, which was a fief of the·H.
" See." Sixtus, putting on a great deal of ftate and
majefty, received him with fuch a countenance, as
fhewed he was not much pleafed either with the prefent
or homage ; and rifing from his throne, faid, in a fneer-
ing manner, " Certainly our predeceffors were in a ve-
" ry complaifant mood, when they accepted of a poor
" pitiful hackney, in lieu of a rich and flourifhing
                                        " kingdom

" kingdom: But we fhall foon put an end to this fim-
" ple cuftom." Thefe laft words touched the ambaffador to the quick, as they gave room for fufpicion,
that he intended to unite the kingdom of Naples to
his dominions: He certainly had that defign at heart all
his pontificate, and neglected nothing that he thought
proper or neceffary to accomplifh it.   But the Spaniards
being aware of his defign, took meafures that effectually prevented it, as we fhall fee hereafter.   The ambaffador fent immediate advice of this tranfaction to
the K. of Spain, who did not think proper to fhew his refentment, or take any public notice of it at that time,
but fent orders to Don Pedro Girone, duke of Offuna,
viceroy of Naples, to keep a ftrict watch and good garrifon upon the frontiers, and to endeavour, if poffible,
to penetrate into the Pope's intentions.

At the time that the duke received thefe orders from
the court of Spain, there was a great infurrection at
Naples, the people having taken arms on pretence of
a famine and fcarcity of bread: Their fury was fo great,
that they cut Vincent Starace to pieces, tore out his
heart and bowels, and hung his limbs in feveral places,
upon the walls of the city.   This man was very rich,
and had been in great favour with the Neapolitans; but
the friendfhip and familarity which he lived in with
the viceroy, made him at laft odious to them, and the
viceroy began to think himfelf in danger after fuch an
outrage, looking upon it as a prelude only to fome
further defign of the Pope.   There were two reafons
that feemed to coroborate thefe fufpicions, the firft
was, the great number of banditi, and other vagrants,
that were continually flocking out of the ecclefiaftical
ftate, into the kingdom of Naples, which, he imagined,
was to promote fome attempt of that kind.   The fecond was, that the Pope had forbid any corn to be ex-
ported out of his dominions, tho' he knew how grievoufly they wanted it there: For notwithftanding the
duke had ufed very preffing inftances with him for
that purpofe, and fet forth their neceffity in the
                                    ftrongeft

ftrongeſt and moſt pathetic memorials, he took no
notice of them, but uſed to ſay, when he heard of the
tumults in that ſtate, " We ſhall have fine fiſhing in
" theſe troubled waters, preſently."

The quarrel which he had with the K. of France,
made ſtill more noiſe in the world : It happened after
this manner: He ſent word one morning, at break of
day, to Piſani, the French ambaſſador, who had reſided there in that character, ever ſince the death of Gregory, with great credit and reputation, that he muſt be
gone, not only out of Rome, but the eccleſiaſtical ſtate,
in two days. They ſay, the true reaſon of his being
treated after ſo rough a manner was this : Sixtus having
recalled Jerome Raggazoni, biſhop of Bergamo, who was
nuncio in France, deſigned to ſend Fabius Mirto Frangipane, a Neapolitan, archbiſhop of Nazareth, in his
room, a prelate of conſummate wiſdom and virtue,
who had acquired much experience, by having been
long and often employed in ſeveral important negociations; he had been twice nuncio before, and given
great ſatisfaction by his prudent behaviour, and was
therefore thought, in the preſent ſituation of affairs,
to be the propereſt perſon that could be ſent to that
court.

The K. of France being informed of his departure
from Rome, and having great reaſon to be ſatisfied with
the conduct of Ragazzoni, immediately diſpatched a
courier to him, with an order, " not to proceed any
" further than the place where they ſhould meet, till
" he had freſh inſtructions from his Holineſs, whom he
" had wrote to, entreating him not to recall the biſhop
." of Bergamo." The archbiſhop of Nazareth had already got as far as Lyons, and made a very magnificent
entry there, when the courier arrived at that city, and
delivered his maſters orders to him : As he was naturally of a warmiſh diſpoſition, he was a good deal
nettled at it, and ſaid, " It concerned his Holineſs,
" more than him, to reſent the affront; and they
" would find he was not of a temper to be played
" tricks

" tricks with; that he would go back the next day,
" according to his inftrudions, which enjoined him,
" if he met with the leaft difficulty to return im-
" mediately to Rome; that he was fure, as foon as the
" Pope was acquainted with it, he would recall the
" bifhop of Bergamo, and fend no other nuncio into
" France."

When Sixtus was informed of this, by the courier,
who was fent to Rome for that purpofe by the archbifhop, he was fo exceedingly enraged, that he faid,
" he would never forgive it;" and, without affembling
a confiftory, fent immediate orders to Pifani, to leave
his dominions, as we have related. The K. of France
was no lefs exafperated on his part, when he heard
how his ambaffador had been treated at Rome; and
could not help making ufe of fome very harfh expreffions in the prefence of his whole court.

He fent for all the ambaffadors of foreign princes,
and protefted againft the Pope's proceedings, as arbitrary, unprecedented, and contrary to the law of nations.
He reprefented at the fame time, to the Pope, " That
" he did not believe any court in the world would
" have offered fuch an indignity to his minifter, even
" in the time of war; efpecially, as he had wrote to
" his Holinefs, in the civileft and moft obliging terms,
" before he ftopped his nuncio, defiring he would be
" pleafed to fend a perfon that was more agreeable
" to him." Sixtus returned for anfwer, " That after he
" had received the king's letters, he acquainted his ma-
" jefty's ambaffador with the contents of them, who
" faid, his mafter would confent to receive the arch-
" bifhop of Nazareth; and that, before that prelate's
" departure he had declared to Pifani, in the hearing of
" cardinal D'Efte, that it was by his confent and ap-
" probation, that the archbifhop went into France,
" he expeded there fhould be no means ufed to
" fruftrate it, nor any obftacles or impediments
" thrown in his way; for if there was, he would
" oblige him to quit his dominions the moment
                                        " he

" he heard of it." The king replied, "That his am-
" baffador had not communicated this to him." It
feems, therefore, as if they had both reafons to complain of each other. People, at firft, were inclined to
think the ambaffador was in fault, but he excufed him-
fe.f, by faying, " That he judged it more prudent, for
" the fake of. peace, to conceal from his mafter what
" Sixtus had faid in his paffion, than to let them toge-
" ther by the ears, which would be inevitable, if he
" fhould acquaint him with it."

The Pope, in anfwer to the king, gave him an account of what he had faid to Pifani, with his reafons
for recalling the bifhop of Bergamo, and fending the
archbifhop in his place; defiring him, at the fame time,
to recall his ambaffador; for, " That he would have
" nothing more to do with him." This letter he caufed to be delivered by Horace Rucellay, a gentleman of
a good family, and a frank open temper, who had the
honour of being admitted by the king to a confiderable degree of friendfhip and confidence: He received
it in a very civil manner, and wrote an anfwer which
he charged Rucellay to deliver into the Pope's own
hand.

If the king was angry upon this occafion, Sixtus was
furious; he bullied and menaced, and vowed he would
be revenged for the affront which, he conceived, had
been offered to him. In the mean time, the minifters
that refided at Paris, endeavoured to perfuade the king
to give way a little to the Pope's choler; and D'Efte,
with fome other cardinals, ufing their good offices with
his Holinefs, the affair was at laft compromifed in fuch
a manner that the archbifhop was received as nuncio
by the king, and Pifani returned to his refidence at
the court of Rome.

It was faid, that Sixtus was prevailed upon to recall
his nuncio Ragazzoni, by the league, who complained
he was not warm enough in their intereft; and that it
was vifible he favoured the caufe of Henry III, the K.
of Navarre, and the Prince of Conde; the Spaniards,

likewife,

likewife, made loud clamours at Rome againſt his proceedings: Upon which account, he ſent Frangipane,
who, as a Neapolitan, and ſubject to the K. of Spain, was
firmly attached to that prince, and a zealou◼◼mpion
for the league, which was the true reaſon why Henry
did not care to receive him.

But theſe were trifles and bagatelles, in compariſon of
the extremities he proceeded to with the K. of Navarre.
In the pontificate of Gregory, not only many of the
higheſt birth and nobility in France, but the very citizens and ecclefiaſtics of Paris had entered into a folemn league and covenant againſt this prince, for being a proteſtant, which was preſented to Gregory for his
concurrence: But, tho' the Spaniards took great pains
to prevail upon him, he would never come into it.

Sixtus, however, moved, either by a real concern
for the intereſts of religion, or reaſons of a political nature, was eaſily perſuaded to confirm it; but proceeded very ſlowly in it during the two firſt months of his
pontificate, tho' he was daily teazed and importuned to
quicken his pace, not for the reaſons aſſigned by Cam-
piglia, in his civil wars of France, viz. that he thought
it ill policy to embark in an undertaking that would
involve him in endleſs expence, and divert his intention from the care of the church; for he had always
been a friend and abettor of the league, and a ſtre-
nuous aſſertor of the intereſts of the catholic religion: The true reaſon was, that he had a mind firſt to
eſtabliſh a good regimen at home, where indeed, there
was great need of it. When he had effectually done
this, and ſettled the tranquility of his own ſubjects,
upon a firm and laſting foundation, having no cauſe
to fear any inteſtine commotions, he began to look
round him and attend to what was carried on in o-
ther courts: He ſaid one day to Largni, a biſhop that
was employed by the chiefs of the league to ſollicit
their intereſts at Rome, " We have hitherto been ob-
" liged to employ our thoughts for the welfare of our
" own

' own dominions, we fhall now take the affairs of
' France into confideration."

He began with writing letters with his own hand to
he heads of the Guife faction, and made them large
promifes of men and money, whenever they wanted.
He likewife thundered out, firft in the confiftory, and
hen in public, a bull of excommunication, attend-
:d with the moft direful execrations that had ever been
remembered, againft K. Henry of Navarre, the prince
of Conde, and all their adherents, pronouncing them
heretics, and the chiefs, fauters, and protectors of
herefy, and, as fuch, juftly obnoxious to the cenfures
of the church, declaring their ftates and dominions
forfeited, and both them and their dependants for e-
ver incapable of fucceeding to any fovereignty, efpecially the crown of France, and abfolving their fubjects from their oath of allegiance, not only difpenfed
with their rendeing them any fort of obedience, but
charged them not to do it, upon any account whatfoever, on pain of the greater excommunication. He finally exhorted Henry III, K. of France, in the name, and
by the mercies of Jefus Chrift, that calling to mind his
coronation oath, and the undeviating attachment of
his anceftors to the true religion, he would exert his
whole authority, and the many royal virtues he was
poffeffed of, to the utter extirpation of herefy in his
kingdoms, and enjoin all his archbifhops to take care
that this bull was publifhed in all the churches of
France, upon every Sunday and holiday. It was fubfcribed by only twenty-five cardinals, many going out
of the city, and others making excufes, amongft whom
was Farnefe, who retired to his villa, and ftayed there
fome days on pretence of indifpofition.

It was thought Sixtus had further views in proceeding after this manner, and that his intention was not
only to fatisfy the heads of the league, and thruft
himfelf into the affairs of France, but to lull the fears
and apprehenfions of the Spaniards, who, he perceived,
began

began to be very jealous of his machinations, and secret defigns upon their dominions; he thought therefore, as it was faid, to amufe them by a fhew of zeal for
the interefts of religion, which generally takes much
with that bigotted and fuperftitious nation; his fcheme
fucceeded fo far, that they entirely, for that time, laid
afide the fufpicions they had entertained of him, and
were overjoyed to fee him bending all the cares to the
protection of the league, and daily iffuing out his thun-
ders and excommunications againft the Proteftants.

The K. of Navarre, at that time, refided in Gaf-
cony, where he had abandoned himfelf to a moft volup-
tuous courfe of life; but upon the news of his excommunication, he fuddenly rouzed himfelf out of his lethargy, fhook off the foft chains of pleafure, and calling together his fcattered fpirits, exerted many noble
qualities and virtues, which the world, till then, did
not know he was in poffeffion of. He often faid afterwards, to thofe whom he honoured with the greateft intimacy, " That he could never fufficiently acknowledge
" the obligations he lay under to his enemies; fince,
" if it had not been for them, he fhould have lived,
" perhaps, in perpetual obfcurity and oblivion, in a
" private corner of the world, without ever being
" known or thought of; and been actually unqualified
" to wear the crown of France, in cafe Henry III.
" fhould die without male iffue."

He opened the fcene with two actions of great eclat;
the firft was the order he gave to the Sieur de Pleffis
Mornay, a gentleman of great learning and eloquence
(to whom nothing could be objected by his enemies,
except that he was a Hugonot) to draw up an anfwer
to a manifefto, that had been lately publifhed by the
league; in which he moft humbly befought his majefty, as his lawful fovereign, " to give him leave to
" confute the lies and malicious reports, that had
" been fpread abroad concerning him." To put an
end to the quarrel, and prevent the great effufion of
blood,

blood, both of nobles and private people, with the desolation and havock that are the usual consequences of war, he likewise challenged the duke of Guise to a single combat, or to fight with him two against two, ten against ten, or any other number he should fix upon ; entreating his majesty to appoint a field of battle in his own dominions, in case the duke did not chuse to fight out of them, to whose option he entirely left it.

This declaration had a great effect upon the most generous part of the nation, who said, it would be a shame to use any further violent proceedings against a prince, who made so noble a proposal ; and the principal part of the French nobility, who are very nice and delicate in punctilios of honour, said publicly, " That the " duke ought to accept the challenge, and think him- " self highly honoured, in having an opportunity of " drawing his sword against so brave and illustrious a " personage." It was not for want of courage that the duke declined the challenge, but he considered that to draw the sword against a prince of the blood, was looked upon as a sort of parricide in France, and that it would moreover reduce the cause of religion, and the public, to a private quarrel ; and that though he should accept it, he was not sure the league, who considered themselves as a body, in which one member was not superior to another, would consent to it : He therefore prudently answered, " That he had a very " great personal esteem for him ; that he honoured him " extremely as a prince of the blood, and K. of Navarre, " and had no particular quarrel of any kind with " him ; that the only motives that had prevailed upon " him to take up arms, were the imminent danger " the catholic faith was in, and the regard he had for " the peace of his country, which entirely depended " upon a religious preservation of it."

The second step that the K. of Navarre took was to complain of the Pope's violent proceedings to the K. of France, and to remonstrate, " That he was much
" more

" more nearly concerned to oppofe them than himfelf,
" for that if the Pope took upon him to limit the fuc-
" ceffion of his crown, and to declare a prince of the
" blood incapable of fucceeding to it, he might very
" likely in the end, lay claim to his dominions, and
" difpoffefs him of his throne, as Pope Zachary had
" formerly done by his predeceffor Childeric III.

This made fo ftrong an impreffion upon the king of
France, that he would not fuffer the excommunication
to be publifhed in his kingdom, tho' the nuncio, and
chiefs of the league, preffed him moft vehemently to
it, and even proceeded to threaten him with his holinefs's difpleafure, if he refufed.

The K. of Navarre was not content with this; he
found fome friends, amongft the great number he had
at Rome, bold enough to ftick up his proteft, with that
of the P. of Conde, in every ftreet, upon all the cardinals doors, and even upon the gates of the Vatican, in
which they appealed from the fentence of excommunication pronounced " by one Sixtus (who ftiled himfelf
" the Roman Pontiff) to the high court of peers in
" France, calling him an infamous and abandoned liar,
" for accufing them of herefy, which was a falfe and
" malicious charge, aud more properly belonged to
" himfelf than them, as they would fully prove before
" a free and general council, lawfully called, not by
" the pretended Pope who had no right to convoke it,
" but by fuch as had due power and authority : They
" declared him Antichrift, if he did not appear before
" fuch an affembly, and fubmit to its decrees; and
" upon that account faid, they would wage eternal and
" irreconcileable war againft him, and never lay down
" their arms, till they had feverely revenged the outra-
" gious affront he had offered to their fovereign, his
" royal houfe, and all the nobility of the kingdom."

As this was the common caufe of crowned heads,
and every monarch was concerned in the confequences, " they implored the affiftance of all Chriftian
　　　　　　　　　　　　　　　　　　" princes,

" Princes, efpecially the friends and allies of France,
" to enable them, before it was too late, to refift the
" tyranny of the Pope, and to fhake off the yoke he
" was preparing to fix upon their necks, in order to ferve
" his own private interefts, to gratify the ambition of
" the league, and to fubvert the kingdom of France."
They concluded with declaring, " that they looked upon
" the Pope, and the league which was abetted by him,
" as reprobates of God, rebels to the king, and trai-
" tors to their country.

The Pope was already above meafure exafperated
at the anfwer drawn up by du Pleffis, of which many
copies were handed about, both in manufcript and in
print; the fubftance of which was, " That kings were
" the immediate vice-gerents of God upon earth, and
" as fuch, invefted with an authority, not fubject or
" accountable to any other perfon: That the power of
" excommunication was not lodged in the hands of
" one man only, liable to paffion and caprice, but of
" the whole church.   To prove which, he alledged
" the example of Mofes, who tho' appointed by God,
" a leader and conductor of his people, was obliged
" to affemble a councel of the elders, without whofe
" advice and concurrence, he never undertook any
" thing of importance: Of David, who, upon all e-
" mergencies, confulted with the princes of the peo-
" ple: And to Jefus Chrift himfelf, who would not
" pafs fentence alone, upon the woman that was caught
" adultery.   But fuppofing, though not granting,
" that the Pope had fuch jurifdiction over princes;
" what honour would redound to the church of Rome
" by excommunicating thofe that had already feparat-
" ed themfelves from it, and held it in contempt and ab-
" horrence? What elfe could be expected, but inftead
" of bringing them back by mild and gentle methods,
" to widen the breach and drive them away for ever,
" only to oblige the league? This was to apply a fword,
" and not a falve to the wound, and to heap weight up-
" on thofe that were already finking; a conduct quite

X   " oppofite

" opposite to the mercies of God, and the spirit of the
" gospel, which commands us not only to receive a
" repenting son with open arms, but even to go and
" search for sheep that are lost, and that zeal and af-
" fection of St. John, who enjoins us *to pray for a bro-*
" *ther if we see him commit sin.*

" Now as the proceedings of the Pope are directly
" contrary to these righteous precepts, they must of
" course be deemed wicked and unjust ; and as they had
" already occasioned a fatal division in the church, in or-
" der to avoid a greater scandal, it was necessary to hold
" them in abhorrence, and endeavour to extinguish
" the remembrance of them amongst mankind."

As the reader has already been acquainted with the
choleric and furious disposition of Sixtus, it is easy to
conceive the rage he was in, at the appeal of these two
princes from his authority ; which was not a little en-
flamed by several pasquinades, and biting satyrs that appeared immediately after ; one of the bitterest of them
was entitled, Brutum Fulmen, and said to be penned by
Francis Hottman, a lawyer.

He called a consistory to deliberate upon means of revenging so flagrant an indignity ; he sent for all his spies,
and examined them strictly, and separately, concerning
the sticking up of the papers, but they could not give
the least account of them.

It was remarkable, and very uncommon in him,
that after the first transports of his fury were a little
subsided, he spoke of the K. of Navarre, in terms of
the highest respect, and said, " He could not sufficient-
" ly admire his courage, and greatness of mind, who,
" at that distance, had taken so proper and bold a me-
" thod to shew his resentment." From that time he
conceived so high an opinion of him, that he said,
" Of all the crowned heads in Europe, there is not one
" that is fit to be trusted with a secret but this Prince,
" and the Queen of England." And tho' he was daily importuned by the league, to contribute towards the
expence

expence of the war, he never advanced them one shilling. He had so great an opinion of him and Q. Elizabeth, that he often said, " Three such princes as Henry " of Navarre, Elizabeth of England, and Sixtus of " Rome, were sufficient to govern the world." That Queen had no less an esteem for him ; and when any body spoke to her of matrimony, used to say in a jocose manner, " I will have nobody but Pope Sixtus." Which being told to him again, he laughed and said, " If we " were to lie together one night, we should get ano- " ther Alexander."

Queen Elizabeth received news of his exaltation, about a fortnight after it happened; but the courier coming away in haste, only brought word in general, " That he had taken the name of Sixtus V. and " already given proofs of being a very different sort of " a man from what was expected." Soon after, she had a more particular account of his proceedings, with a mezzotinto picture of him, which she looked attentively at, some time, and said, " She believed what " was reported of him, but did not think he would be " any great friend to the Spaniards." Early the next day she held a council to consider of means to secure his friendship; as a Pope of his enterprizing genius might possibly engage the other R. Catholic powers to join in a league with Spain against England.

For this purpose the Earl of Essex sent for Mr. Carr [3] a Roman Catholic gentleman, that stood obliged to him for his life and fortune. The Earl had obtained leave for him to return from Rome, where he had resided six years (the two last by the Queen's express com-

---

[3] I can find no account of any such person in the English history of those times. There is mention made of one Sir Robert Carey, who seems to have been in favour with Q. Elizabeth, and was employed by her to carry the news of the Q. of Scots death to her son James VII; perhaps he was the person. It is not very material, and a pardonable mistake, in an author that writes of foreign affairs. I wish it had been the only one that I met with in Leti.

mand)

mand) after the publication of the edict againft Papifts.
When he came before the council, he confirmed what
he had before told the Earl in private, viz. " That he
" had been particularly acquainted with the prefent
" Pope, whilft he was Cardinal Montalto; that he was
" his confeffor, and had often formerly had many free
" converfations with him about the affairs of England;
" that he was but a weak, fimple fort of a man, and
" lived in a very private and obfcure manner, and there-
" fore could not believe what was now reported of him."
He further added, " That he knew his nephew Alex-
" ander Peretti very well, and had frequently enter-
" tained him at his houfe."

The council was very well pleafed with this account,
and thought him a proper perfon to obferve the Pope's
actions, as they might confide in him, upon the account of the obligations he lay under to the Earl of
Effex; fo that he was immediately furnifhed with bills
of exchange, and the Queen's picture, fet with diamonds, to make a prefent of to the Pope's nephew
(if he would accept of it) as he was fure to be a cardinal, with inftructions to draw for what fums he
pleafed, and fpare no expence to renew his acquaintance with Peretti, to find out (if poffible) the defigns
of Sixtus, and how he ftood affected to Spain. Carr
would have gone thro' fire and water to ferve the Earl,
and was not a little glad of an opportunity of ingratiating himfelf with the Queen, as moft of his relations
were R. Catholics.

When therefore, he had received his laft orders, he
gave out amongft his friends, " That he had taken fo
" great a liking to Rome, that he was defirous of fpend-
" ing a few years more there, if her majefty would be
" fo good to give him leave." This being obtained
(to be fure without much difficulty) he fet out for Rome,
and arrived there juft as Peretti was made cardinal : Glad
of fo favourable an opportunity, he went immediately
to pay his compliments to his eminence, who received
him very affectionately, and offered to introduce him

to

to the honour of kissing his Holiness's feet. This was what Carr wished for, tho' he was under some apprehension, that if Sixtus was so much changed, as had been reported, he would not know him again; however, he accepted the offer, and desired him to appoint a day.

In the mean time he happened to be a witness of the Pope's behaviour to the Spanish ambassador, upon his paying tribute for the kingdom of Naples, which he looked upon as a sure indication of his not being very favourably inclined to the court of Spain, and immediately wrote an account of it to England. Soon after Peretti introduced him to his Holiness, whom he beheld with a sort of astonishment, when he saw how great an alteration there was both in his person and behaviour. The Pope received him in a very affable manner; and calling to mind several occurrences that had happened in the course of their former acquaintance, amongst other things, said, " Sir, you often used to in-
" vite our nephew to dine at your house, for which
" reason, he ought now to invite you;" and turning to the cardinal, said, " Pray see that you make this Eng-
" lish gentleman welcome." The cardinal asked him several questions at dinner concerning the state of affairs in England, and seemed to be much pleased, when he found he was so well acquainted with the Queen's great favourite the Earl of Essex; and hinted to him, at his taking leave, " That he might expect the honour
" of frequently seeing his Holiness." From this conversation of his nephew, and his sudden return to Rome, the Pope began to suspect he was sent by the Queen to observe his proceeding, and find out how he stood affected to the Spaniards. This suspicion, however, he carefully concealed; and instead of treating him like a spy, endeavoured, by a shew of openness and affability, to draw out of him such secrets as he wanted to know, relating to the English nation.

In a few days he sent for him again, and enquired particularly (as out of curiosity) concerning the temper

per and difpofition of the Queen, her garb, perfon,
manner of fpeaking, &c. When Carr had given a
fatisfactory anfwer to all thefe queftions, he fhewn him
her picture, which he had in his pocket: The Pope
having looked at it fome time, with a great deal of
feeming pleafure, faid, " This Princefs reigns with wif-
" dom, and will be fortunate: We muft make a match
" of it, and get an Alexander." Carr was highly pleafed
with the Pope's humour, and judged from thence,
that he had no particular averfion to his miftrefs. Sixtus then afked him, " How the Englifh and Spaniards
" agreed now, as the latter were *volucres cæli*, pretend-
" ing to fly over every body's head;" and without
ftaying for an anfwer, added, " We fancy your Queen
" is a good deal embarraffed at prefent, as the maxims
" of her government muft naturally incline her to
" fend a fpeedy and effectual fuccour to the Hollanders;
" and on the other hand, we imagine fhe is afraid to
" do it, left it fhould provoke K Philip to fall upon
" her with all his forces: But, if fhe ftands in awe of
" him now, fhe will have greater reafon to do fo, when
" he has conquered them, and acquired fo much more
" ftrength. It is impoffible thofe provinces fhould hold
" out long, as no body is capable of affifting them
" but the Q. of England, and fhe dares not, tho' it
" is her intereft: But, pray tell us, what will become
" of England, when he is mafter of the Low Coun-
" tries? We fhall then order a requiem [4] to be fung
" for it " From this difcourfe Carr gueffed that the
Pope, either knowing, or fufpecting that he was employed to fend intelligence to England, took this method of hinting to him, that it was his opinion, fhe
fhould take the ftates of Holland into her protection;
and as he was ordered to acquaint her with every thing,
he fent immediate advice of it, with a minute detail of

---

[4] A folemn fervice in the Romifh church, that is performed
for the repofe of departed fouls; fo called from the beginning of
it, *Requiem æternam dona eis, Domine, &c.*

whatever

whatever elfe had paffed fince his arrival at Rome, in a cypher to the Earl of Effex. At the receipt of thefe letters, the Queen was freed from the apprehenfion fhe had entertained of the Pope, and laid them before her privy council, who unanimoufly advifed her to fend fpeedy relief to the Low Countries.

The next day Peretti introduced a converfation pretty much to the fame purpofe, (probably by his uncle's order) pointing out the particular ways and means, by which it would be moft proper to affift the Hollanders, and faid, " His Holinefs had conceived an " uncommon efteem for her majefty of England, from " the account he had given him of her, and was much " pleafed with the picture he had fhewn him, which " he likewife fhould be very glad to fee himfelf, if he " had no objection to it." Carr immediately took it out of his pocket, and defired, " He would do him the " honour to accept of it." The cardinal, at firft, civilly refufed, but at laft agreed to take it, upon con- dition that he would give him leave, in return, to pre- fent him with one of his uncle; and ftepping to his cabinet, brought him the Pope's picture, in a gold frame, fet with diamonds, inclofed in an ivory cafe of curious workmanfhip, worth 2000 crowns (though the Queen's was of much greater value) and faid, " Take " it and difpofe of it as you pleafe; perhaps your " miftrefs may have a curiofity to fee it;" which was a hint that he expected he fhould make her a prefent of it. As Carr knew it would be very acceptable to the Queen, he fent it by the fame perfon that took his cypher, with an account how he came by it, and of the converfation that paffed between him and Peretti : He alfo fent 12 gold medals of the Pope, and wrote upon the paper they were wrapped up in. " This is the " man that hates England."

The prefent was delivered into the Queen's own hand, by the Earl of Effex : when fhe had caft her eye upon it, fhe faid, " I like to fee the Pope drawn after " this manner, without that ftrange, foolifh crown up-
" on

" on his head." After she had viewed it some time, with a good deal of satisfaction, and talked to the Earl about the features and lineaments, she said, " If he " would cut off his beard, I would consent to marry " him, if it was only to gratify his humour of having " an Alexander." Upon which the Earl told her, " That " the habit did not make the monk, nor a beard the " hermit." " True, said she, but as it would be a " double sin to marry a priest and a great beard at the " same time, I would willingly commit but a single " one." " If that be the case answered he, you are " half married already." After some other conversa- tion upon the same subject, she said, " I own I like the " picture, but much more the character I hear of his " government, and his civility in expressing so much " respect for me, tho' he is a Pope; and, upon my " royal word, I would marry him with all my heart, " and no other person, if he was a temporal prince; " and think it would be for the good of all Europe." " Without doubt said the Earl, but princes generally " marry for the sake of having children; and you both " are rather too far advanced in years to expect that " blessing." To which the Queen smartly replied, " My lord, the flesh is not always weak, when the " spirit is willing."

She was so delighted with this picture, that she wrote to Carr to procure her one of Cardinal Peretti; telling him she liked the name of Alexander, and the account he had given her of his respectful behaviour, so much, that she was desirous of seeing whether his countenance corresponded with his actions; ordering him at the same time to neglect nothing that might tend to im- prove the favourable disposition he found in the Pope and his nephew; and if possible, to stir him up against the court of Spain, but with great caution and secrecy, lest it should come to the Spaniards knowledge; and, to cover his designs the better, gave him instructions to pretend to be now out of favour at home: For this purpose there was a printed order sent to Rome, com-

manding

manding him to return in three months, on pain of being declared a rebel, and having his goods confiscated, which was actually put in execution, as he wrote back, " That he had rather ftay in exile; than " return to a kingdom, where he fhould have the mor- " tification of feeing the R. Catholics treated with fo " much feverity."

All this was reported by the cardinal to his uncle (who prefently faw thro' it) tho' he did not think proper to let him know that, but fent for him at leaft once a week, excufing himfelf to the Spanifh ambaffador, by faying, " That he could not help compaf- " fionating poor Carr's misfortunes, as he was fo great " a fufferer for his religion."

There was at this time a prelate, whofe name was William Allen, an Englifhman, and much hated by Q. Elizabeth, for his zeal and affection for the Spaniards. The K. of Spain often confulted with him about the Englifh affairs, and had given him a bifhoprick in Flanders, that he might be near England, to receive the intelligence that was continually fent him by his R. Catholic friends in that kingdom, whom he was continually inciting to a rebellion againft their fovereign, as they put great truft and confidence in him : When he had feen the proclamation that was iffued out againft Carr, and knew him to be a Roman Catholic, not fufpecting there was any fineffe in it, he wrote him a letter to Rome, in which he earneftly exhorted him to perfeverance, recommending him warmly in other letters, to his Holinefs's protection (who probably, laughed at his fimplicity.)   As he had a great opinion of Carr's fincerity and integrity, he often wrote to congratulate him upon the profpect there was of things foon taking another turn, and his country being delivered from the tyranny it then groaned under, with whatever elfe he knew of England; all which advices were fent directly to the queen by Carr, who now defired leave to return home, being fully convinced of the Pope's hatred and averfion to the Spaniards, and

that

that it was not only his opinion, but desire, that their over-grown power should be curbed and restrained, which indeed he did not take much pains to conceal; for when Carr acquainted him with the treaty, which her majesty had lately concluded with the United States, and her resolution of sending over the earl of Leicester, as general, with a large body of troops to their assistance, he could not help smiling, which shewed he was pleased with it; and soon after the cardinal his nephew, asked him, "Whether the earl of Lei-" "cester was embarked?" Whence it was easy to guess, that the Pope was impatient to hear of it. As to the cardinals picture, which she desired, he mentioned it one day to the Pope himself, and said, "That his " great friend and patron, the earl of Essex, had made " his peace at home, and that the queen, having had " the good fortune to procure a picture of his Holiness, " had given it a place in her cabinet, amongst her " most valuable jewels; desiring the earl to get her " one at any rate, of his nephew, the cardinal Montal-" "to." The Pope said, " He wished to God the sight " of his picture might make a convert of her, and " then he would send his nephew himself, as Legate " a latere." A few days after, the cardinal gave him one by the Pope's order, of great value, with his name, ALEXANDER PERETTI, wrote round it; for which the queen presented him with a large crucifix of gold, set with jewels.

As Sixtus loved to be meddling in other people's affairs, he was continually expressing his surprize at the duke of Ossuna's lethargy, as he called it; but there was little reason to find fault with his conduct, for he was a very wise man, and a good politician: What he blamed him for was his neglect, or delay, in punishing the ring-leaders of the sedition at Naples, as he pretended it would be a reflection upon the kingdom in general to let them escape with impunity.

Whenever the Spanish ambassador was admitted to an audience, the Pope used to turn the conversation
upon

upon this fubject, and fay, " We always had a very
" high idea of the duke of Offuna, and thought him
" one of the moft able minifters the king your Maf-
" ter. had, but we find we are miftaken, fince he has
" not courage enough to punifh the authors of Starace's
" death."

One day the ambaffador, endeavouring to defend
the duke's proceedings, faid, " That what was deferred
" was not forgot; that he had taken proper meafures
" at Naples, and planted guards in every quarter of the
" city, to keep the people in their duty."   But Sixtus,
who was of opinion that fuch crimes fhould be punifhed
without mercy, anfwered, " The people want but two
" things, bread and cold iron, bread and cold iron;"
repeating the words feveral times.

Thefe upbraidings fo worked upon the duke at laft,
that he began to think in earneft of punifhing the
fomenters of that infurrection, in an exemplary manner ; and for that purpofe ordered the principal of them
to be taken up, one by one, and condemned for other
crimes; but at laft he threw off the mafk, and proceeded againft them in a more open manner, to which he
was encouraged by feveral of the moft powerful inhabitants, who being defirous of ingratiating themfelves
with the viceroy, at the expence of their fellow citizens, went, as they pretended, in the name of the people (though they had not any commiffion of that kind
from them) to defire they would bring thofe delinquents
to juftice; and faid, " It would be highly agreeable to
" them, as it would let the world fee, it was the crime
" only of a few, and not of the whole city."   Upon
this he immediately appointed two officers of juftice,
Ferrante Fornaro, and Jeremy Olgignano, the firft as
judge, the other, who was his great favourite, as attor-
ney general, men that were but little inclined to mercy.
The prifons were foon filled with thefe wretches; 37
of them were hanged, and their quarters ftuck upon
the gates of the city, 200 fent to the gallies, above
1000 banifhed, befides a vaft number that fled out of
the

the kingdom : As they went to their execution, they
could not help upbraiding their fellow citizens with
cowardice and ingratitude, in fuffering them to be
brought to that ignominious death, for exerting themfelves in the caufe of liberty and the public, by their
advice and inftigation.

The viceroy did not think this fufficient, but (being
defirous to let the Pope fee he knew how to exercife
wholefome feverity, as well as he did, when it was neceffary) caufed the houfe of John Pifoni, an apothecary, to
be pulled down, as he was faid to be the chief of the
rioters. Happily for him, he himfelf had made his efcape ; the materials of the houfe were burnt upon the
fpot, and the place where it ftood ploughed up, and
fowed with falt [5] ; and to add to the difgrace, a marble
pillar was erected there, with an infcription, to render
the memory of Pifoni infamous ; though fome thought
it was rather an honour to him than otherwife.

The duke further ordered feveral niches to be made
in the pillar, in which he fixed 20 heads, and other
parts of thofe that were executed, upon fpikes, with

[5] This was a cuftom with many nations, in former times,
Vid. Ifidor. lib. xv. cap. 11. Cel. Rhod. lib. xxvi. cap. 5. Alex. ab
Alex. lib. vi. cap. 14. who fay, that the plough was made ufe of
in deftroying the foundation of cities, as well as in the firft laying them out, according to that of Horace :

> Iræ Thyeften exitio gravi
> Stravare, et altis urbibus ultima
> Stetêre caufæ, cur perirent
> Funditùs, imprimeretque muris
> Hoftile aratrum exercitus infolens.

Sometimes the conquerors fowed corn in the place where the city
had ftood ; but if the citizens had been either rebels, or behaved
in an obftinate or ungenerous manner, they fowed it with falt, and
gave it up to perpetual barrennefs and fterility. This feems to be
of very ancient date, as we meet with it in the book of judges,
ix. 45. where Abimelech, being provoked at the infolent behaviour
of the *Shechemites*, *took their city, and flew the people that were
in it, and beat it down, and fowed it with falt.*

grates

grates before them, enclofing the whole with iron rails: This fpectacle was beheld with horror by the people, who feemed much affected at it, but durft not open their mouths, as the duke kept a great number of fpies, who gave him a punctual account of whatever was done in the city every day: It was commonly faid, that the Pope and he expended more in fpies, than it coft all the other princes of Italy to maintain their foldiery; and that Sixtus envied the duke, as he thought he was better ferved than him, in this refpect.

The news of thefe feverities made him change his note; inftead of fpeaking with contempt, as he ufed to do, he was extravagant in his praifes of the duke.

Politicians reafoned differently upon his conduct in this affair, but the Spaniards thought he had made ufe of their ambaffador, as a tool to ftir up the duke to thefe violent proceedings, in order to occafion ill blood and difaffection in the kingdom, the better to promote his defigns upon it: Certain it is, that if this infurrection had happened but a year or two after his exaltation (whereas it fell out in the firft month of his pontificate, before he was well fixed in the throne) it would have been attended with other confequences; for, as he had fet his heart upon the acquifition of that kingdom, he would have found fome means to raife a rebellion there, as we may judge, by his faying one day to Rufticucci, upon the news of Starace's death, "It " would have been of great fervice to us, if this man " had lived but a year longer.

Cardinal Sirletti, dying about this time, Sixtus fpoke of it with much regret, and faid, " He did not know " where to find a man worthy to fill his place." He left a large collection of curious books, which was offered to cardinal Montalto, for 6000 piftoles; but the Pope would not let him buy them, and faid, "His in- " ftructions would ferve him inftead of books whilft he " was alive, and, after his death, he would have fome- " thing elfe to do than read." He put great confidence

dence in his nephew, and employed him in the management of the moſt important affairs, as he had very
good parts, and a maturity of judgement far above his
years, ordering him to receive the reports of his ſpies,
and give him a faithful account of them; but ſtrictly
forbid him, as he had done his ſiſter Camilla, to aſk any
favour: This was not for want of natural affection, for
he loved them tenderly, but becauſe he had a mind to
take the care of providing for them, and making their
fortune, entirely upon himſelf, and often uſed to ſay,
" Have patience, don't be uneaſy, leave yourſelves to
" me, I'll take care of you; perhaps you may make
" uſe of unjuſt means to enrich yourſelves; what I
" give you ſhall be honeſtly got, and will bring a bleſ-
" ſing with it."

His ſpies informing him that his name was become
ſo terrible in Rome, that people trembled whenever he
was mentioned, he had a mind to let the world ſee, that
the reaſon why he adminiſtered juſtice in ſo rigid a
manner, was becauſe he thought it, at that time, abſolutely neceſſary for the good of his ſubjects, and that
he was not deſtitute, as perhaps they imagined, of humanity or compaſſion; that he knew how to reward
merit, and remembered the kindneſſes he had received
from his friends, when he was in a low eſtate. He
therefore, to qualify, in ſome meaſure, the great dread
and apprehenſion people had of him, began to open
his bowels, and yield to the dictates of gratitude and
generoſity.

Whilſt he was a monk, he compoſed a diary, in
which he daily ſet down the tranſactions that fell under
his obſervation, what he himſelf did, and what good
or evil befel him, with the names of his enemies and
benefactors: This he called his memento vivorum, and
had made three of them whilſt he was a monk, and
another after he came to be cardinal, with which he
uſed to entertain himſelf often at his leiſure intervals,
calling to remembrance the occurrences of times paſt,
eſpecially after his exaltation; and though he then
                                            cauſed

caufed moft of his letters and manufcripts to be burnt,
he carefully preferved thefe in a private drawer of his
cabinet.   In turning over thefe memorandums, he met
with the names of feveral perfons that he had been formerly obliged to, which afforded him proper opportunities of fhewing his gratitude.

Whilft he was regent in the convent of St Lawrence, at Naples, he had cultivated a particular friendfhip with Signior John Caponelli, a lawyer, who did
him many fervices: His wife, Prudentia Fava, had fo
great an opinion of him, that fhe left her confeffor, a
Carmelite Friar, and made choice of him for her fpiritual director.   They frequently invited him to dine and
fup with them, and made him feveral little prefents of
linen, and other wearables.   As he ufed to entruft them
with his neareft concerns, and acquainted them with
all the quarrels and broils he was from time to time engaged in with his brethren; they were his conftant ad-
vocates, defending him with great warmth in all companies, and were fo loth to part with him, when he
left Naples, that they came a day's journey with him
in their coach.   He kept up a correfpondence with
them about a year; but, Caponelli dying, he heard no
more from Fava.

As he was looking one day into his memento, he
happened to meet with an account of the friendfhip,
and many favours he had received from thefe two perfons; upon which he ordered a meffenger to go on purpofe to Naples, and bring him a particular account of
the circumftances of Caponelli's family; when he heard
that both he and Fava, who had married a fecond hufband, died without children, he expreffed a good deal
of concern, as it deprived him of an opportunity of
making them any recompence: This induced him to
make a frefh enquiry, whether Caponelli, or Fava, had
any relations, tho' never fo diftant, and of what occupation they were: At laft he found out a notary, that
called himfelf coufin to Caponelli, who was very poor,
and had a large family.   He heard likewife of a nephew to

Fava,

Fava, who was a foldier, and ferjeant under Alexander Farnefe, then in Flanders. For the notary, he immediately bought a very good houfe in Naples, and gave him 3000 crowns, the intereft of which he was to receive for his own ufes, and the principal to provide his three daughters with fortunes, when they married, or put on the veil: Befides this, he made him a prefent of 500 more, in ready money, and recommended him to the notice of feveral public officers and magiftrates, who employed him in all their affairs, out of regard to Sixtus, and promoted him to a very profitable poft in the law.

He likewife fent for his two fons to Rome, the eldeft about ten, the other eight years old, furnifhed them with clothes and neceffaries, and fent them to fchool at Bologna, where one of them died foon after: The other came to be nuncio at Malta, in the time of Paul V. The nephew of Fava was made colonel of the infantry at Rome, and married, by the particular requeft of Sixtus, who was defirous the name of Fava fhould be kept up, and gave him another honourable employment at Naples, whither he retired, after his benefactor's death, his commiffion being taken from him, by the next Pope, for behaving difhonourably in a duel that he was engaged in.

Whilft he was bachelor in divinity, and refided at Macereta, he went, one day, to a fhoe-maker's fhop, to buy a pair of fhoes; after they had difputed a good while about the price, the fhoe-maker told him, "He " would take no lefs than feven Julios [6]." Montalto could not afford then to give more than fix; and faid, " Perhaps, I fhall be able to give you the feventh fome " time or other." "Some time or other, replied the " fhoe-maker, but when will that be ? When you come " to be Pope ?" Yes, faid Montalto, that I will, with " all my heart, and pay you intereft for your money " too" " Well then, anfwered the fhoemaker, fince

[6] A Julio, is an Italian coin, worth about Sixpence.

" I fee

" I fee you are not without hopes of being Pope, you
" fhall e'en have them upon thofe terms." Montalto
afked him his name, and faid, " He would be fure to
" remember the bargain," which fet the fhoemaker a
laughing. This he put down in his diary, amongft
other occurrences of the day, at his return to the
convent.

When he met with it, in turning over his journal,
after he was Pope, he fent to Macerata, to know if the
fhoemaker was yet alive ; and being informed that he
was, he ordered the governor of that place to fend him
up directly to Rome, guarded by one of his officers,
without letting him know the reafon of it.

As it was above 40 years fince this affair happened,
the fhoemaker had entirely forgot it, and could not
conceive the meaning of being fent for by his Holinefs.
As foon as he arrived at Rome, he was introduced into
the Pope's prefence, who afked him, " If he had ever
" feen him at Macerata." The poor fhoemaker almoft
frighted out of his wits, faid, " Never, that he re-
" collected." " No, fays Sixtus, don't you remember
" that I once bought a pair of fhoes of you there ?"
The fhoemaker, more confounded than ever, faid,
" He knew nothing at all of the matter." " Well then,
" fays the Pope, I muft remember for you ; I am in
" your debt, and fent for you hither to be paid." The
fhoemaker, who could not comprehend the meaning
of this, ftood fpeechlefs, till the Pope explained the
myftery, by faying, " You formerly fold me a pair
" of fhoes, in the price of which you gave me credit
" for a julio ; that I promifed to pay you with intereft
when I was Pope ; now that is come to pafs, I have
" a mind to fhew myfelf an honeft man, by being as
" good as my word ;" and immediately ordered his
majordomo to fee how much the intereft of a julio, at
5 *per cent.* came to in 40 years, and then to pay him
both principal and intereft, difmiffing him with, *An-
date in pace, Go in peace.* The fhoemaker went away
very well pleafed, and had already fwallowed a large

fum;

fum; but when the majordomo came to him again, with three julios in his hand, and faid, " There's your " money, write a receipt for it," he began to mutter; and meeting fome of his countrymen, who waited, with impatience, at the gates, to know on what account he was fent for, he told them, " His Holinefs had made " him come to Rome only to pay him three julios; " complaining, that his journey had already coft him " above 20 crowns, without reckoning the expence of " his return."

Sixtus could not help laughing very heartily, when his fpies gave him an account of the fhoemaker's behaviour; and that he was fetting out again directly for Macerata in a very peevifh humour. But he had fcarcely got out of Rome, before he was overtaken by a meffenger, with orders to return; " for his Holinefs " had forgot fomething that he defigned to fay to him." When he came before the Pope a fecond time, he was afked by him, " Whether he had any fon; and an- fwering, " That he had one, who was in orders, and " a fervite," the Pope bid him fend for him to Rome, and ftay himfelf till he came. In the mean time, he made a ftrict enquiry into his life and converfation; and finding him a man of good character, he gave him a bifhopric in the kingdom of Naples. The fhoemaker coming foon after to return thanks, Sixtus faid to him, " We hope you are now fatisfied for the ufe of your julio."

Not lefs grateful and humorous was his behaviour to father Salviati, of the Auguftine order. We have already taken notice of the manner in which he left Florence, in the year 1564, upon the account of fome difputes with his general, who fent to all the convents of the Francifcans, between that place and Rome, to apprehend and confine him as a deferter; that Montalto fufpecting it, took another rout, and avoided all the houfes of that order. In this expedition he arrived one evening, at a convent of Auguftines, of which father Salviati, a young man, very civil and obliging in

his

his behaviour, was the prior. Tho' Montalto thought fit to conceal the rank he held in his order from him, he, neverthelefs, received him very hofpitably; and, as the chamber where ftrangers ufually lodged at that time, happened to be out of repair, he gave him part of his own bed. When Montalto took his leave, in the morning, either becaufe he really wanted money, or to make a trial of his friendfhip, he afked him to lend him four crowns, which he promifed to pay again in a fhort time. Salviati readily complied with the requeft, and took his note, which he had wrote in a different hand from what he commonly ufed, and figned with a fham name. The Auguftine having waited a long time without hearing any thing from his debtor, afked fome of the Francifcans if they knew fuch a one of their order, calling him by the name which he had fubfcribed to the note, but could not get any intelligence of him, there being no religious of that name, that he could find, amongft the Francifcans. Sixtus, meeting with an account of this adventure in his journal, ordered the general of the Auguftines to fend for father Salviati, if he was yet alive, for he wanted to fee and fpeak to him. This religious being engaged, at that time, in a quarrel with his bifhop, about fome trifling matter (as is often the cafe betwixt bifhops and regulars) the bifhop complained of him to the congregation of cardinals, that is appointed to adjuft fuch difputes; and the general imagined his Holinefs had fent for Salviati, to reprimand, or, perhaps, to punifh him for his contumacy: He was confirmed in his opinion, by the grave, or rather angry manner, in which he had given him that order; and, thinking it would pleafe the Pope, delivered him into the hands of four monks, to be guarded by them all the way, who were as lordly, and kept as ftrict a watch over him, as if they had been fo many archers.

The bifhop, hearing of the manner in which Salviati was conducted to Rome, began to triumph exceedingly, as he thought it was in confequence of the com-

complaint he had made againſt him by the cardinals
to the Pope, who, he did not queſtion, would handle
him with his uſual ſeverity ; and could not help ſaying
to his chapter, in the gaiety of his heart, " I'm mighty
" glad I have found a way to curb the inſolence of this
" Auguſtine; we muſt do theſe things ſometimes,
" to humble ſuch people, and teach them to behave
" with proper reſpect to their biſhop."

Salviati thought himſelf ruined; all his friends ad-
viſed him to wait upon the biſhop, and make a ſub-
miſſion to him, to ſee if it was poſſible to ſoften him
that way, but the monks that were ſent to attend
him, were ſo officious, they would not give him time
to do this. When he arrived at Rome, he was carried
directly to the Pope, by his general, who, being ordered to withdraw, left him alone with his holineſs:
poor Salviati trembled ſo, that he could hardly ſpeak;
and began to make apologies and excuſes for his behaviour to the biſhop, as he could not poſſibly think of
any other reaſon why he was ſent for: Sixtus, who
knew nothing at all of this difference, pretended to be
acquainted with it, and ſaid, " You are highly to be
" blamed for behaving in that diſreſpectful manner to
" your biſhop, who is a prelate of great worth : but
" that is not the occaſion of our ſending for you at pre-
" ſent : you are accuſed of embezzling the goods and
" revenue of your convent, which we ſhall call you
" to an account for ; but firſt we are willing to hear
" what you have to ſay for yourſelf." Salviati took a
little courage, when he found he was ſent for upon an
affair that would prove much to his honour, if it came to
be examined into, as he had conſiderably augmented the
eſtate of the convent, by his good management and
œconomy; and ſaid, in a very humble manner, " He
" ſhould willingly ſubmit to any puniſhment his Holi-
" neſs thought proper to inflict upon him, if he was
" found guilty of what he charged him with." Sixtus
replied, in a ſtern manner, " Take care what you ſay,
" we have proof ſufficient to convict you. Is it not true,
" that

" that when you were Prior of an Auguftine convent,
" in the year 1564, a religious of the Francifcan order
" lodged with you one night, and borrowed four crowns
" when he went away the next morning, which he ne-
" ver paid you again? Now we defire to know, what
" right you had to difpofe of your convent's money
" in that manner." Salviati recollected the thing, but
did not in the leaft dream, that Sixtus was the perfon
he had formerly lent the money to; and ventured to
fay, " It is very true, moft holy father; and I fhould
" have lent him more if he had afked me, for he feemed
" to be an honeft man, but he proved a knave, and
" a rafcal, and gave me a note with a fham name to
" it; and notwithftanding I have made all poffible
" enquiries, I have never been able to hear any thing
" of him." The Pope could not forbear fmiling, and
faid, " You need not be at any farther trouble in
" in your enquiries; for, take my word for it, you will
" never find him: But he has ordered us to pay that
" debt, and to return you his thanks. Are you content,
" to take us for your debtor?" Salviati, upon this,
began to think he remembered fomething of his face,
and to fufpect he was the very man; fo that the pleafure he received from what the Pope faid laft, was much
abated by the fear he was in, of having provoked him
by the harfh names of knave and rafcal. Sixtus,
who eafily perceived from outward appearances, how
violently he was agitated within, and was impatient to
acknowledge the favours he had received from him,
put an end to his pain, by faying, " It is high time to
" fhew our gratitude; we are the perfon you were fo
" kind to; and you received us hofpitably in your
" convent, it is but juft we fhould entertain you in the
" fame manner: And calling for cardinal Montalto, he
ordered him to appoint Salviati an apartment in his palace, and to entertain him at his table, till he found
fome way of providing for him.

The general of the Auguftines, who waited to fee
the iffue of this interview, was very well pleafed to find

it

it fo different from what he expected; and went with Salviati to wait upon Cardinal Montalto, who treated them with much courtefy and complaifance : But it is fcarce poffible to exprefs the aftonifhment of the bifhop, when he was informed by a friend (whom he had defired to fend him an exact account of the proceedings againft Salviati), " That inftead of being fent " for to be punifhed for his infolence, as he expected, " he had an apartment affigned him in the vatican, and " was entertained by his Holinefs like one of his re-" lations."

During the fpace of a month or more, that he ftaid at Rome, the Pope fent for him feveral times, to examine his capacity, and find out what fort of preferment would pleafe him beft : He at firft defigned to have made him general of his order, and the general a bifhop ; but as he perceived he was defirous of leaving the regulars he gave him a confiderable bifhopric, that happened to be vacant at that time. This promotion, which was a fufficient recompence, and much greater than he could expect, was highly agreeable to Salviati, an honour to his order, a heart-breaking to his adverfary, to fee him upon an equal footing with himfelf, a furprize to all the world; and gave Pafquin occafion to fay, *that bifhoprics were now fold for four crowns a-piece.*

Several other things of this kind he did, to the great aftonifhment of every body, as it was inconceivable how he could recollect the moft trifling and minute circumftances of tranfactions that happened fo long ago. If we confider the great care and exactnefs with which he regiftered every accident that had befallen him thro' the whole courfe of his life, one would think he muft have had fome prefentiment, or foreknowledge of what he was to be : But nothing gave him fo much pleafure, as looking over the occurrences that happened whilft he lived in a cloyfter.

When he heard of any one's death, that had ever done him a fervice, he feemed much concerned that he

had

had loft an opportunity of making them a recompence, which he ufed to do commonly to the nearest relations: As for thofe that had at any time done him a prejudice, if he did them no good, he at leaft did them no harm, but feemed to defpife the injuries his enemeies had endeavoured to do him.   Whenever he exhorted any body to forgive affronts, or ill ufage, he ufed to propofe himfelf as an examle to them, and faid, " If we were " to revenge all the perfecutions that have been raifed " againft us, we muft deftroy no inconfiderable part " of the Francifcan order."

Toward the latter end of the year he ordered a feftival to be celebrated, in honour of St. Bonaventure, as a doctor of the church [7]: He had fo great an efteem for the works of this father, that he began a commentary upon them whilft he was a monk, from the finifhing of which he was prevented, as he faid, by the

[7] Doctor of the Church, is a title given to fome of the fathers, whofe doctrines and opinions have been the moft generally followed and allowed.   In the Greek church are, Athanafius, Bafil, Gregory Nazianzen, and Chryfoftom : In the Latin, Jerome, Auguftine, Gregory the Great, Ambrofe, and Bonaventure. In the Roman breviary, there is a particular office for thofe that are doctorated.   Doctor, is alfo an appellation, joined to feveral fpecific epithets, wherein the merit of fuch as the fchools acknowledged for their mafters confifted.   Thus Alexander Hales is called the irrefragable doctor, and the fountain of life, as Poffevinus fays ; Thomas Aquinas, the angelical doctor ; Bonaventure, the feraphic doctor ; Duns Scotus the fubtile ; Raymond Lully, the illuminated ; Roger Bacon, the admirable ; William Ocham, the fingular ; John Gerfon and Cardinal Cufa, the moft Chriftian ; Dionyfius, the Carthufian, the extatic doctor ; and an infinity of others to be met with in ecclefiaftical writers.—Eodem anno Sixtus S. Bonaventuram ex Francifcano ordine, Balneo Regio in Etruriâ natum, qui anno Chrifti 1274 Lugduni deceffit, et fepultus eft, jampridem inter fanctos Sixto quarto itidem Francifcano olim relatum, ordini fuo ac profeffioni majorem ex eo auctoritatem conciliare cupiens, Ecclefiæ Doctorem pronunciavit, et Beatis Hieronymo, Auguftino, Ambrofio, Gregorio P. P. quintum adjenxit, ac omnia ejus fcripta undique conquifitia, et adprobatà Conftantii Samiani, ex eodem ordine Cardinalis ftudio ac curâ edi, et tanquam canonica fine cenfurâ admitti voluit.   Thuan. lib. 100.

continual

continual fquabbles he was engaged in with his brethren; a circumftance that he often mentioned with regret; and declared, "It would give him great fatisfac-
"tion, if any one elfe would go thro' with it."

The popes, according to antient cuftom, had always
held the chapels [8] in St. Peter's; but Sixtus ordered
them to be held in all the principal churches, as he
thought it unreafonable that only one church fhould enjoy this honour.

The Jefuits, who had been favoured with a large
fhare of power under the late Pope, ufed their utmoft
endeavours to infinuate themfelves into the good graces
of Sixtus, and with that view paid great court to his
nephew, whom they ufed frequently to invite to entertainments, made on purpofe for him at their convent. They got him to propofe one of their order to
his Holinefs for a confeffor; but he faid, pretty fmartly, "It would be better for the church, if the Jefuits
"confeffed to the Pope, inftead of the Pope confef-
"fing to them." One day, at the requeft of thefe fathers, he went to hear mafs in their church; after it was
over, their pupils repeated feveral declamations, and
copies of verfes, in praife of his predeceffor, who was
the founder of their college, and had beftowed many
other confiderable favours upon them, to which he
liftened with great attention; and when they had done,
faid, "To be fure, you thought you were fpeaking to
"Gregory, but our name is Sixtus." Another time,
being invited to honour one of the feftivals with his
prefence, and they defiring him to walk thro' their
convent, and take notice of the neatnefs of their
kitchen, the convenience of their refectory, and lodg-
ing-rooms, "We had much rather fee your trea-
"fury," faid he; but the rector modeftly excufed it,
by faying, "They were never fo poor as at prefent."
"So much the better," anfwered Sixtus, "for riches

[8] The ceremony of canonization, or creating doctors of the
church, is called, *holding a chapel.*

" spoil ecclesiastics." The saying was a little severe, tho' he had an esteem for the order, and employed them upon many occasions, especially as spies; and often used to say, " They were the most useful society belonging to the church; and that he had the greater " value for them, as they seldom asked him for any " thing."

Before his time there were only 13 wards, or divisions, in the city, but he added another, viz. Del Borgo; and appointed a commissary over each of them, whom he ordered to give him a weekly account of every thing that happened in his respective district; especially of all strangers that either resided in Rome, or passed thro' it. One of these commissaries, a person of good esteem and reputation, being guilty of some little omission in the discharge of his duty, Sixtus ordered him to be stripped in the most public place of his division, by a fellow with a cat of nine tails in his hand, as if he was to be whipped; but after all, excused him for that time, with threats of punishing him severely the next.

He sent officers through the whole ecclesiastical state, to prevent the exportation of grain, commanding his subjects, on the heaviest penalties, not to sell any to foreigners; and fined several merchants who had disobeyed his order. This foresight caused such plenty, and filled the public magazines at so cheap a rate, that besides good interest for the money, the apostolic chamber reaped no small advantage from it.

It was his design to have made all the courtezans live by themselves in one division, like the Jews; but the governor having represented the impossibility of it, from the vast number there was of them, he expressed a concern that they should be suffered to live promiscuously amongst modest women. The most notorious of them he banished, thinking, when he had reduced the number, he could easily accomplish his first design; but he met with so many difficulties in his project, that he was forced to give it up.

This

This banifhment was the caufe of two evils, in particular; firft, that they who were whores in private, now become profeffed ones: In the fecond place, it occafioned another execrable vice to encreafe to fuch a degree, that many of the confeffors went on purpofe to inform the Pope of it, fo that he was obliged to recall his edict, and fuffer them to return [9].

At this time flourifhed father Chriftopher Clavious, a Jefuit, of the German nation, and the ableft mathematician Europe had feen of many ages; he was in fo much efteem with Sixtus, that he ufed to fay, "The "having educated fuch a man was fufficient honour to "the Jefuits, even tho' they had no other merit to "plead." He had, likewife, a very great refpect for father Philip Diaz, an Obfervantine [10], Thomas Tragillo, a Dominican, Henry Henriquez, Francis Le Defme and Lewis Molina, Jefuits, all celebrated divines, often declaring, it would be a fincere pleafure to him to reward their labours, if they would apply themfelves to the advancement of Chriftianity, and the converfion of heretics.

He was not only an encourager of learning and arts, but of arms, and military fcience, and as he had vaft defigns to carry on, very foon after he came to the pon-

[9] In meretrices etiam, quarum Romæ a multo tempore frequens et publicum mercimonium erat, multa fevera decrevit; quas aut urbe quam primum excedere, aut nubere, et, fi non obtemperarent, publice flagellis cædi, juffit. Cum vero moneretur inter tot cælibes, fublatis fœminis, majoris vitii, quod Romanis jam olim B. Paulus exprobravit, periculum fubeffe; ita eas tulit, et lupinari includerentur, nec, ut prius, libere per totam urbem interdiu noctuve vagarentur; ratus, pudore utrinque incuffo, et illas priori vitæ renuntiaturas, et viros infamiam veritos, ad ea loca non ituros: Eas vero que in meretriciâ profeffione morerentur in fterquilinio defodi mandavit. Interceffit initio Senatus, a Sacro ordine, qui palam non audebat, clam inftigatus, hoc decreto, hofpitiorum pretia vilefcere, et ad nihilum redigi, et libertatem antiquam tolli, idemque, quod dixi, periculum imminere, dictitans, nec matronarum pudicitiam inter tot cælibes integram et inconcuffam, aliter fervari, nifi priftina libertas reftituatur, Thuan.

[10] A branch of the Francifcan order.

tificate,

tificate, he laboured, with much diligence, to eftablish funds, to raife forces, to build gallies, to erect fortifications; and for this purpofe fent for Clavius to affift him, as engineer.   The world was furprized to fee that a perfon, educated in acloyfter, whofe fole ftudy had been divinity, without any military knowledge, or inftruction, fhould on a fudden commence foldier, and make fuch preparations for warlike undertakings.

He put an end to this year by creating eight cardinals (tho' there were ten hats vacant) all men of extraordinary merit, and moft of them perfons of high birth; one of them was Hippolitus Aldobrandino, afterwards Clement VIII. His promotion was fo agreeable to the people, that the whole city rung with acclamations of long live Cardinal St. Pancras, which was the title he had taken.   It gave him great fatisfaction that his choice was fo well approved of, as he had publifhed a bull not long before, in which he declared, "He would " call none to any function in the church whatfoever, " but thofe that he knew worthy of it; that it fhould " be his particular care to fearch for fuch perfons, " wherever they were to be found, without any appli- " cation, or importunity, or intereft making, which he " abhorred, and would always difcourage to the utmoft " of his power; that fuch as had really any merit " would fully it, in his opinion, by making ufe of thofe " methods to advance themfelves; and fuch as had " none, might be affured, that no recommendation " fhould ever procure them any."   Never any Pope was lefs teazed, or importuned, than he, in fuch affairs; as every body was afraid to folicit any favour, after fo public a declaration.

End of the Sixth Book.

B O O K

BOOK THE SEVENTH.

THE firſt interval of leiſure that Sixtus had after his coronation, he undertook, with infinite labour and expence, to tranſport the obeliſk that now ſtands in the piazza of the vatican. It lay buried in dirt and obſcurity behind the ſacriſty of St. Peter's where he uſed to go ſometimes, whilſt he was a monk, to admire this monument of the grandeur of ancient Rome, often expreſſing his concern, to ſee it neglected in that ſhameful manner; and ſaid, " He could wiſh " tó be Pope, if it was only to reſtore it to its former " glory." And, indeed, next to juſtice, he beſtowed his firſt cares upon it, labouring a whole year without intermiſſion, only to remove it to that piazza: For this purpoſe he cauſed a wonderful engine, of new invention to be conſtructed, which drew great numbers of people from all parts of Italy, and elſewhere, to ſee it. This obeliſk is made of a kind of marble, called Pyropecide, from its being variegated with marks that look as if they were occaſioned by fire: It is termed by ſome, Oriental Granite, by others, Syeneſe ſtone, from its being got at Syena, a town of that name near Thebes, where the kings of Egypt, who were very fond of erecting obeliſks, pyramids, and ſuch like fabrics, uſed to dig up their ſtone: It was hewn out of the quarry about the time of Numa Pompilius, by Nocoreus, or Nuncoreus, king of Egypt. Some authors ſay, that it is not now entire, but fell as they were endeavouring to erect it, and broke into two pieces; Nocoreus took the larger, which was about 100 cubits long [1], and

con-

[1] In the ſcripture we find two different cubits, one of them equal (as Dr. Arbuthnot ſays) to an Engliſh foot, nine inches, and $\frac{888}{1000}$ of an inch; being a fourth part of the fathom, double the ſpan, and ſix times the palm. The other equal to one foot, and $\frac{9.6}{1000}$ of a foot, or the 400th part of a ſtadium. The Romans too

had

confecrated it to Apollo,- by the direction of an oracle,
which he had confulted, to know what he muft offer
to that deity, upon the recovery of his fight, after he
had been many years blind : The other piece, about
72 feet long, is the obelifk we are fpeaking of, and
was brought to Rome, with 42 others of various fizes,
which were fet up in different parts of the city : It was
dedicated to the emperor Auguftus, and Tiberius, his
adopted fon, with this infcription, which is yet legible:

DIVO. CAESARI. DIVI. IVLII. F. AVG.
TIBERIO. CAESARI. DIVI. AVG. F.
AVGVSTO. SACRVM.

It was imagined by many, for a long time, that the
afhes of the emperor Auguftus were enclofed in a great
ball of bronze, which was placed on the top of this
obelifk ; but Dominick Fontana, a celebrated architect,
whom the Pope fent for to tranfport this enormous
weight, after a careful examination found, that it was
folid, and caft in a mould, without any appearance that
there had ever been the leaft aperture, through which
they could put any thing into it ; that the holes now
feen in it were made by mufket, or harquebufs fhot,
when Rome was laft taken ; and what was imagined to
be the afhes of Auguftus, nothing but common duft,
that had got into them.   The abfurdity of this opinion
is further evinced by the fuperb Maufoleum, which that
emperor built for himfelf and his family, of which the
magnificent ruins are yet to be feen, near the gate of
Madonna del Popolo, in the quarter of St. Roche.
    Many of Sixtus's predeceffors had the fame defign
in the beginning of their reign, among others, Julius II,

had a cubit equal to one Englifh foot, five inches, and $\frac{406}{1000}$ of
an inch. Father Mercenne makes the Hebrew cubit, one foot,
four digits, and five lines, with regard to the foot of the capitol.
According to Hero, the geometrical cubit is 24 digits ; and according to Vitruvius, the foot is $\frac{2}{3}$ of the Roman cubit, i. e. fixteen
digits, or finger breadths.

lius II, Paul III, Paul IV, used their utmost efforts to accomplish it, and consulted with the most skilful architects of their times; but the difficulty, as well as the expence of such an undertaking, or perhaps their attention to some other affair of greater importance, occasioned them to lay it aside; and Sixtus, who made it a point of honour to surmount every obstacle that impeded his designs, not only undertook, but accomplished that arduous and noble enterprize, contrary to the opinion and expectation of all the world.

He appointed a congregation of cardinals, and other persons of experience in such affairs, to concert proper measures for the execution of this design, frequently assisting at their meetings, and at last fixed upon a method that succeeded; several medals of bronze were laid under the foundation of the pedestal, to perpetuate the remembrance of the fact, with two coffers, or chests of stone, in which they enclosed 12 coins, with the head of Sixtus on one side, and different devices on the other; on some of them, was represented a man sleeping under a tree, in an open field, with this motto, PERFECTA SECVRITAS, perfect security: On others were three mountains, upon one of which was a Cornucopia; upon another, a branch of laurel; and upon the third, a sword, with the point upwards, which served for a prop, or fulcrum, to a ballance, with the motto, FECIT IN MONTE CONVIVIVM PINGVIVM, alluding to his coat of arms, and to the peace, plenty, and justice, that he had established in the ecclesiastical state [2]. There were some with St. Francis, kneeling before a -crucifix, near a church, that seemed falling, with these words, VADE FRANCISCE, ET REPARA DOMVM MEAM QVAE LABITVR: " Go Francis and repair my " falling house." Some with Pius V. on one side, and religion, and justice, holding a ballance on the other. Two of them were of gold, in honour of that pontiff.

[2] *In this mountain shall the Lord of Hosts make, unto all people, a feast of fat things, full of marrow,* Isaiah xxv. 6.

They

They laid others upon a piece of Travertine ftone (fo caueu, from the name of the quarry where it was got) in the foundation, with a flab of white marble over them, on which was engraven, in Latin, the name of the Pope, and that of the architect, his country, and family; with an infcription relating the means that were ufed, 'and the time it took to erect the obelifk. Upon this were placed feveral medals of Sixtus, with another fmooth piece of marble over them: after which, they laid the' firft ftones of the pedeftal, and finifhed it in a beautiful manner, with a cornice, and entablature of bronze, that fupported the whole.

Many of the cardinals, and nobility, efpecially the Medicis, Colonne, and Urfini, defired the Pope would give them leave to bury fome medals, with their name and effigies upon them; which he confented to, on condition that his own head fhould be on the other fide. Several of the ambaffadors, and minifters of foreign powers, refiding there at that time, threw in others, on which their mafters were reprefented upon their knees at his Holinefs's feet: but count Olivarez, ambaffador from the king of Spain, having ftamped fome with his mafter on one fide, and himfelf on the other, the Pope defired "He would be pleafed to keep them "till they built fome palace at Madrid."

To erect this obelifk, Fontana, who was the architect, fpent above a year in making the wooden machine, or caftle (as it was called) before mentioned; there were 40 capftans made ufe of, each of which was worked by four of the beft horfes, and 20 of the ftrongeft men they could get fo that thefe alone employed 160 horfes, and 800 men, befides 400 more that were engaged in other fervices, and this for the fpace of a whole month.

Upon the top of the machine there was a bell, and a trumpet; when Fontana made a fignal to the trumpeter, he founded the trumpet, upon which all hands heaved together, till the bell rung, which was a fignal

to

to leave off. By this method, the confufion was-pre-
vented, which would otherwife have happened from
the variety of noife, that muft neceffarily have been
occafioned by fuch a number of men, and every thing
carried on with the greateft order and regularity. It
was finally erected upon Wednefday the 10th of September 1586, and confecrated the Friday following to the
Holy Crofs. On the top of which was placed a crucifix,
wherein was inlaid a piece (as it is faid) of the real
crofs on which our Saviour fuffered.

Sixtus granted great indulgences to thofe that
kneeled down to it, and faid three pater nofters and
as many Ave Marias, with a prayer for the exaltation
of the Holy Church, and the profperity of the Pope. So
that whilft he lived, either out of devotion or complaifance, there were daily thoufands of people upon their
knees before it, which gave great pleafure to Sixtus,
who ufed to look at them out of his window.

On the top of it was written in gold letters, fo
large that they were legible to thofe that ftood on the
ground:

SANCTISSIMAE CRVCI SACRAVIT
SIXTUS V. PONTIFEX MAXIMUS,
A PRIORE SEDE AVVLSVM
ET CAESARIBVS AVGVSTO ET TIBERIO
I. L. ABLATVM. *

The pedeftal is of marble, and 36 feet high; the
obelifk itfelf 72, and the crofs 5; fo that the whole
height is 113 feet. Upon each angle of the bafe, is
a lion of folid bronze, in a couchant pofture, which
fupport the obelifk upon their backs. The expence
of tranfporting and erecting it, with the ornaments
and gilding, amounted to 38,000 crowns, befides the
metal for the crofs and lions, which was paid for out

* Schroderus fays OBLATVM, and leaves out I. L.

of

of the Apoftolic Chamber. Upon the four fides of the bafe are the following infcriptions:

On that towards the Eaft,
ECCE CRVX DOMINI,
FVGITE PARTES ADVERSAE,
VICIT LEO DE TRIBV IVDA.

To the Weft,
CHRISTVS VINCIT, CHRISTVS REGNAT,
CHRISTVS IMPERAT,
CHRISTVS AB OMNI MALO PLEBEM [3] SVAM
DEFENDAT.

To the North,
SIXTVS V. PONTIFEX MAXIMUS,
CRVCI INVICTÆ,
OBELISCUM VATICANUM,
AB IMPVRA SUPERSTITIONE EXPIATUM,
IVSTVS AC FELICIVS CONSECRAVIT,
ANNO MDLXXXVI. PONT. II.

To the South,
SIXTVS V. PONT. MAX. OBELISCUM VATICA-
NUM,
DIIS GENTIVM IMPIO CVLTV DICATVM,
AD APOSTOLORVM LIMINA OPEROSO LABORE
TRANSTVLIT,
ANNO MDLXXXVI. PONT. II.

A little below the infcription on the third fide Six-tus permitted the following to be engraven, to immor-talize the memory of the architect.
DOMINICVS FONTANA,
EX AGRO MILIAGRI, NOVOCOMENSIS,
TRANSTVLIT ET EREXIT.

[3] I fhould think *Plebem* a very indifferent word to be made ufe of upon this occafion; but it muft be placed to the account of Sixtus. I doubt the reader will meet with feveral expreffions in his Latin, that are juftly liable to exception.

Z

Many

Many of the poets and wits of thofe times offered
their fervice to write infcriptions for it ; but Sixtus civilly refufed them ; and, avoiding all pomp of expreffion,
compofed them himfelf, in that plainnefs and fimplicity
of ftyle, which he thought would be the longeft intelligible.

In the month of March, the fame year, the duke of
Offuna, viceroy of Naples, arrived at Rome, with a ve.
fplended and numerous train, to kifs the Pope's feet, in
his mafter's name. The great reputation he had acquired of an able minifter and politician, made his Holinefs very defirous of feeing him, fo that he was received with extraordinary marks of honour and favour,
as his public entry was the moft magnificent of any
ambaffador's, fince his acceffion to the pontificate.
Sixtus admitted him to four or five audiences ; feeming to take much pleafure in hearing him difcourfe upon affairs in general, and fuch as did not immediately
concern or relate to the Spanifh intereft, tho' he wanted
(according to his mafter's inftructions) to have entered
into a private negociation with him ; but the Pope always declined it, and turned the converfation upon
fome other topic,, which occafioned the duke to tell
the ambaffador in ordinary, who afked him one day as
he came from the Pope, "How his negotiation fucceed-
" ed ?" " That he gave him many fine words, but per-
"formed nothing." To which the other replied,
" Then your excellency is a favourite with him ; for
" he not only avoids coming to the point with us,
" but abufes us into the bargain."

The viceroy, after having met with much outward
refpect and ceremony, left Rome a good deal diffatif-
fied, that he had not been able to draw the Pope into
any negociation, or to obtain the leaft favour he afked
of him. Don Pedro de Toledo, who commanded the
gallies of Spain, was juft arrived at Gaieta, with a defign to make a defcent upon the coaft of Barbary, and
fent to compliment the viceroy with an offer of con-
voying him back to Naples : But this civility occafioned
a fort

a fort of difpute betwixt them about the titles they gave each other in their letters, which ended in a quarrel: Such are the confequences that attend the foolifh cuftom of affuming pompous and magnificent titles, now happily almoft laid afide in Italy.

The difference betwixt thefe two great noblemen being much talked of by every body, the Pope called a confiftory, and ordered the cardinals to receive no letters from any prince whatfoever, that were not fuperfcribed with the titles that were due to them, which occafioned people to fay, " That his Holinefs gave the " fpit to others, but kept the meat himfelf."

The duke was glad to get away from Rome, not only upon account of the vaft expence he was at to keep up the fplendour of his embaffy, but becaufe his prefence was neceffary at Naples, to give orders about the public rejoicings that were foon to be celebrated there upon the birth of the duke of Savoy's firft fon, by Donna Catherino, daughter of the K. of Spain. Sixtus, upon this occafion, fent a nuncio extraordinary to congratulate the duke at Turin, for whom he profeffed a very high efteem, and ufed to call him the fourth evangelift; meaning by the other three, the K. of Navarre, Queen Elizabeth, and himfelf.

About this time news came to Rome, that the Proteftants had over-run all the country about Cologne, burnt above 50 villages, taken a fort at Bonne, and been tampering with the garrifon of that city to revolt, which put the elector into fuch a confternation, that he determined to retire into Bavaria, and leave the whole province to their mercy.

When the Pope was informed of this, he immediately wrote to the bifhop of Vercelli, his legate in that country, to diffuade the elector from a defign fo prejudicial to his honour, and the caufe of religion; to encourage him by his affurances of certain and fpeedy affiftance from the catholic powers, to whom he himfelf fent very preffing letters for that purpofe; earneftly exhorting Alexander Farnefe, who then commanded the

Z 2   K. of

K. of Spain's armies in Flanders, with great renown, to exert himself vigorously in the Elector's defence: Which had so great an effect upon him, that he marched immediately to his relief; and having taken Grave and Venlo, he came in person before Nuis, a place about ten leagues from Cologne, and subject to the Elector, where the Protestants were so well fortified, that they thought it impregnable, both with respect to their number, plenty of provisions and ammunition, and its advantageous situation. But Farnese trusting to his valour, or rather, as he said, to the assistance of the Lord of Hosts, sat down before it, and carried on the siege with so much resolution, that, notwithstanding their bravadoes, and giving out, " That they would " defend themselves to the very last drop of their " blood," the courage of the besieged began to fail.

To animate this general to carry on the war with vigour, his Holiness sent the Abbé Grimani (one of his chamberlains, and afterwards Patriarch of Venice) with a hat and sword, which he had solemnly confecrated at Rome. When Farnese heard of the Abbé's arrival at a place near Nuis, the 22d of July, he sent an Aid du Camp to desire, " He would be pleased " to suspend the ceremony, and stay at Ruremond, for " fear of causing any delay or interruption in an en- " terprize he had undertaken for the glory of God, " and defence of the Catholic religion, and to which " he had at present devoted his whole time and appli- " cation;" and said, " That if, by God's blessing, he " succeeded in it, he should have a better title to the " honour which his Holiness was pleased to confer upon " him, in sending him so inestimable a present, and " should be at leisure to receive it in a proper manner, " and with a ceremony suitable to the occasion."

The town was taken in four days, and not only plundered, but burnt to the ground; the officers not being able to restrain the fury and rage which the soldiers expressed against the Protestants. The shortness of the time in which the place was taken, was a great addition to Farnefe's glory, as it had formerly been, in vain, attempted by Charles of Burgundy, with a numerous army, who was forced to abandon it, after a fiege of eleven months.

Amongft the compliments and congratulations, that were fent him by all the neighbouring Princes upon this fuccefs, the duke imagined it would be a proper time to receive Grimani with the prefents from his Holinefs; and the Elector preffed him very earneftly to celebrate the feftival in his capital; but he thought it would be more honourable, as well as foldier-like, to do it in the camp, and in his own tent, which was pitched over-againft Guadenthel, one of the principal forts, in the taking of which he had behaved with uncommon bravery. It was extremely grateful to the foldiers, to fee themfelves admitted by their general to a fhare in the rejoicings that were to be made upon this occafion; and they omitted no pains to prepare every thing that could conduce to the fplendor of the ceremony.

On the firft of Auguft, the whole army being under arms, and divided into three battalions, were drawn up round the duke's tent, which was converted into a chapel, richly decorated, for the reception of the general officers, the ambaffadors of the Pope and Emperor, and fome other princes and towns in Flanders, and the Low Countries.

The duke of Parma, having the Elector of Cologne on his right hand, and the duke of Cleves on the left, received the facrament from the bifhop of Vercelli, who reprefented his Holinefs, and the confecrated fword and hat, as an acknowledgement of the fervices he had done the church, from the hands of Grimani, who was introduced by fome officers of the higheft diftinction in the army: The hilt and fcabbard of the fword were fet with jewels of great value: There were many alfo upon the hat, which was made of black velvet, fringed with gold. His Holinefs, fparing no expence to reward a general that had fo valiently defended the

catholic

Catholic faith, and at the fame time to fhew his efteem for cardinal Farnefe, his uncle, who feemed to
apprehend that he had loft the Pope's favour.

To add to the folemnity, the bifhop of Vercelli harangued them in an eloquent oration, in which he acquainted them with the nature, origin, reafon, and antiquity of the Popes confecrating armour, upon the
evening of Chriftmas-day, to make prefents of to fuch
princes and generals as worthily exerted themfelves in
the defence of the Chriftian Religion; concluding with
a prayer to God, "That the hat might be an helmet
" of falvation to the duke, and his whole army; and
" the fword prove, like the fword of Gideon, always
" victorious in his hands, againft the enemies of Jefus
" Chrift."

This was fucceeded by the fhouts and acclamations
of the whole camp, the firing of the artillery, tilts,
and tournaments, with every fort of mirth and rejoicing.

The duke then gave a magnificent entertainment to
all the perfons of diftinction, that had affifted at this
ceremony, and made the bifhop of Vercelli fit on his
right, and Grimani on the left hand; amongft many
other healths at dinner, that of the Pope was drunk
upon the knee, with drums beating, trumpets founding,
and a difcharge of all the artillery.

About this time, the Pope judging it neceffary to
fend a nuncio into Poland, fixed upon Hannibal de Ca-
pua, archbifhop of Naples, with whom he had cultivated a friendfhip, when he formerly read divinity
lectures in that city, that had continued ever fince:
It was not, however, the friendfhip he had for this prelate, but his great merit that had induced him to make
choice of him; he being likewife of a very noble family, and long experience in the management of ftate
affairs.

He fet out in October, with an equipage fuitable to
his dignity; but whilft he was upon his journey, the
news of the king of Poland's death arrived at Rome.
As this prince died without children, there was great
reafon

reafon to apprehend the fatal diftractions, that ufually attend the election of a king in that country; upon which account, the Pope immediately called a confifto-ry, to deliberate upon proper meafures to avert thofe evils; in which fome of the cardinals, entreated him to fend one of their brethren, of the greateft prudence, and diftinction, who, by his weight and influence, might prevail upon the Poles to chufe a perfon worthy of the crown, not only for his princely qualifications, but his zeal and attachment to the H. See.

Sixtus, however, who plainly perceived their defign in this was only to have the archbifhop recalled, took little notice of their requeft, either becaufe he faw it proceeded from envy, or thought him fufficiently qua-lified for that embaffy, and faid, " He did not fee why " there might not be as many brains under a green " hat [4], as a red one." And fent orders to the nun-cio to proceed on his journey.

This winter the duke of Offuna left Naples, having governed that kingdom as viceroy four years, and dif-patched a gentleman to acquaint the Pope with his de-parture, defiring his benediction. Sixtus feemed pleafed with the compliment, and fent back the perfon that brought it, loaded with medals and relics. Don John de Zunica, count de Miranda, fucceeded him, who had the reputation of being a very juft and incorrupt ma-giftrate; but was of fo mild and gentle a difpofition, that many looked upon him as a weak man, and not fit for that high poft.

The Pope feemed glad of Offuna's departure; he was too vigilant and clear-fighted to be furprized, or de-ceived; his care and prudence, had hitherto traverfed all defigns upon that kingdom, and his inviolable fide-lity to the interefts of his mafter, made Sixtus look up-on him with a degree of impatience, as he found him an obftacle to his defigns upon feveral parts of Italy: Whereas the fupinenefs and indolence of Zunica, gave

[4] The Roman Catholic archbifhops, and bifhops, wear green hats, and the cardinals red ones.

him

him reafon to hope, that he might now eafily bring his fchemes to bear.

Margaret of Auftria, a natural daughter of Charles V whom he had four years before his marriage, by Margaret Van Geft, a Flemifh lady, died the beginning of this year, at Aquala, a city in Naples. She firft married the duke of Florence, and then the duke of Parma and Placentia, and was one of the moft illuftrious perfonages of her time, having been ufed to government and command from her youth, and had conducted feveral of the moft arduous and important affairs of Europe, with a fpirit and addrefs, that will make her memory immortal. Her brother, cardinal Farnefe, caufed her funeral obfequies to be performed at Rome, in a very magnificent and folemn manner; the Pope himfelf affifted at them, and not only fent a compliment of condolence to the duke of Parma, her fon, but fpoke with the higheft commendation of this princefs, upon all occafions; and faid in public, "That " fhe had fupported the interefts of religion, with as " much zeal and conftancy as the braveft captains " could have done."

In the mean time, Sixtus did not forget his defign to beautify and embellifh the city: After he had erected the grand obelifk, he gave orders for another to be dug up near St. Roche's church, which formerly, in all appearance, had belonged to the Maufoleum of Auguftus: It was broke in three pieces, but the architect had fo fkilfully joined them together, that it was very difficult to perceive the fracture.

This was alfo erected by Fontana, over againft St. Maria Maggiore, and many medals thrown into the foundation: It is 42 feet high, with a pedeftal of common marble, upon the four fides of which are the following infcriptions, compofed by Sixtus:

On the Firft,

CHRISTI DEI IN AETERNVM VIVENTIS CVNA-
BVLA LAETISSIME COLO,
QVI MORTVI SEPVLCHRO AVGVSTI
TRISTIS SERVIEBAM.

On

On the Second,

CHRISTVS PER INVICTAM CRVCEM POPVLO
FACEM PRAEBEBAT,
QVI AVGVSTI PACE [5],
IN PRAESEPE NASCI VOLVIT.

On the Third,

CHRISTVM DOMINVM,
QVEM AVGVSTVS DE VIRGINE NASCITVRVM
VIVENS ADORAVIT,
SEQVE DEINCEPS DOMINVM DICI VETVIT,
ADORO.

On the Fourth,

SIXTVS V. PONT. MAX.
OBELISCVM AEGYPTO ADVECTVM
AVGVSTO IN EIVS MAVSOLEO DICATVM,
EVERSVM DEINDE, ET IN PLVRES CONFRAC-
TVM PARTES
IN VIA AD SANCTVM ROCHVM IACENTEM,
IN PRISTINAM FORMAM RESTITVTVM,
SALVTIFERAE CRVCI, FELICIVS HIC ERIGI
IVSSIT
A. D. MDLXXXVII.

Since we are speaking of these ornaments and alterations which Sixtus made in Rome, it will be better, for the sake of perspicuity, to give an account of them all in this place; tho' according to the strict rules of history, every particular of this kind ought to be mentioned in the year it was undertaken, or finished; but that will be known from the date of the inscriptions.

[5] I don't know what his Holiness meant by the word pace, except the peaceable interval of Auguftus's reign, which is badly expreffed.

He

He dug up two other obelilks, that had lain buried a great number of years in the Circus Maximus, with an intention to have placed one of them (which, it is faid, was the largeft that ever was brought to Rome) in the piazza of the Holy Apoftles; but finding the place too narrow, he laid that defign afide, and carried it to the piazza of St. John de Lateran. This, likewife, was broke into three pieces; but neatly put together again, and erected by the fame Fontana. It was dedicated to the Holy Crofs, and coins laid in the foundation. There are many hieroglyphics, and Egyptian figures, in bas relief, on every fide of it, being tranfported from Egypt to Rome, by the emperor Conftantius, fon to Conftantine the Great. The higheft is 112 feet, without the bafe, and the dimenfions, at the bottom, nine feet and a half by eight. Ammianus Marcellinus fays, it was formerly dedicated to king Ramifius [6], and that the letters and figures round it are panegyrics upon him. The veffel, on board which it was brought over, was the largeft then in the world. On the four fides of the pedeftal are the following infcriptions:

On the Firft,

FL.CONSTANTIVS AVG.CONSTANTINI AVG.F.

OBELISCVM A PATRE, LOCO SVO MOTVM,

DIVQVE ALEXANDRIAE IACENTEM,

TRECENTORVM REMIGVM IMPOSITVM NAVI

MIRANDAE VASTITATIS,

PER MARE TIBERIMQVE

MAGNIS MOLIBVS, ROMAM CONVECTVM

IN CIRCO MAX. PONENDVM S. P. Q. R. D. D.

[6] Ramifius, or Ramefes, was K. of Egypt 1292 years before Chrift.

On

On the Second,

FLAVIVS CONSTANTINVSMAX. AVG.
CHRISTIANAE FIDEI VINDEX ET ASSERTOR,
OBELISCVM
AB AEGYPTI REGE IMPVRO VOTO SOLI DEDI-
CATVM,
SEDIBVS AVVLSVM SVIS,
PER NILVM TRANSFERRI ALEXANDRIAM
IVSSIT,
VT NOVAM * ROMAM A SE TVNC CONDITAM
EO DECORARET MONVMENTO.

On the Third,

SIXTVS V. PONT. MAX.
OBELISCVM HVNC SPECIE EXIMIA
TEMPORVM CALAMITATE FRACTVM,
CIRCI MAXIMI RVINIS, HVMO LIMOQVE ALTE
DEMERSVM,
MVLTA IMPENSA EXTRAXIT,
HVNC IN LOCVM MAGNO LABORE TRANSTV-
LIT,
FORMAEQVE PRISTINAE ACCVRATE RESTI-
TVTVM
CRVCI INVICTISSIMAE DEDICAVIT
ANNO MDLXXXVIII. PONT. IV.

On the Fourth,

CONSTANTINVS PER CRVCEM VICTOR,
A S. SYLVESTRO HIC BAPTIZATVS
CRVCIS GLORIAM PROPAGAVIT.

The other obelisk is less than this, and is also full
of hieroglyphics; they dug it up by pieces, which
are now joined together: It was transported into the

* Conftantinople.

piazza

piazza of St. Maria del populo, and there erected and
confecrated as the others.   This was brought to Rome
by Auguſtus Cæſar, and dedicated to the ſun, as one
may ſee by the following ancient inſcription, ſtill remaining,   •

IMPER. CAESAR. DIVI. F. AVGVSTVS.
PONT. MAX. IMPER. XII. COS. XI. TRIB. POT.
XII.
AEGYPTO. IN. POTESTATEM. POPVLI. ROMA-
NI. REDACTA.
SOLI. DONVM. [7] DEDIT

It is 88 feet high, and was erected the laſt of all
the four: Fontana invented a new machine for this,
and raiſed it with much more eaſe, and leſs expence,
than he had done any of the others.   The baſe is finely carved, and on two of the ſides are theſe inſcriptions :

On the Firſt,
SIXTVS V. PONT. MAX.
OBELISCVM HVNC A CAES. AVG. SOLI IN
CIRCO
MAXIMO RITV DICATVM IMPIO,
MISERANDA RVINA FRACTVM, OBRVTVM-
QVE
ERVI, TRANSFERRI, FORMAE SVAE REDDI,
CIRCIQVE INVICTISSIMAE DEDICARI IVSSIT
ANNO MDLXXXIX.

On the Second,
ANTE SACRAM ILLIVS AEDEM
AVGVSTIOR LAETIORQVE SVRGO,
CVIVIS EX VTERO VIRGINALI AVG. IMPE-
RANTE,
SOL JVSTITIAE EXORTVS EST.

The

[7] Leti ſays bonum : Roma antiqua figurata, Domum, both
which are nonſenſe.

The expence of digging up and erecting thefe obelifks was very great, but they were fo prodigious an
ornament to the city, that the people, far from mur-
.muring, paid it with chearfulnefs. Tho' Sixtus was
naturally inclined to parfimony, and defirous of filling
the treafury, yet he was never deterred from the profecution of any defign that he had fet his heart on, by
the expenfivenefs of it.   He founded a very fine chapel, in honour of the manger, that our Saviour was
laid in at his birth, in the church of St. Maria Maggiore, which he had begun three months before he
was Pope, out of veneration for this facred cradle,
which had been preferved a long time in a place near
this new building. Many of the cardinals, and the
architect himfelf, advifed him, immediately after his
election, to enlarge it and make it more magnificent;
but he would not alter his firft plan, and only confented that the infide fhould be of fine marble, inftead
of ftucco, ornamented with feftoons, and fome figures
in relief, which were fo well executed, that, when
Sixtus came to fee it, he made the architect and work-
men a handfome.prefent.

In the old chapel that was dedicated to the holy
manger (yet entire) which he had a mind to have preferved, upon the account of its antiquity, and the great
refpect people had for it, he built a noble monument to
the memory of Pius V, [8] to fhew his gratitude for
the many favours he had received from him, whither
he ordered his bones to be removed as foon as it was
finifhed.   Another tomb he built there for himfelf, upon which he is reprefented on his knees before the
manger.   To this chapel he granted feveral privileges,
endowed it with a handfome revenue; and, by a Bull

---

[8] There is the following infcription upon it.

PIO V. PONT. MAX. EX ORDINE PRAEDICATORVM,
SIXTVS V. PONT. MAX. EX ORDINE MINORVM,
GRATI ANIMI MONVNENTVM POSVIT.

which

which he publifhed, beginning after this manner, *Glo-riofæ et femper Virgini Genetrici Mariæ*, &c. invefted the right of prefenting to it, in his own family.

The firft year of his pontificate was not quite finifhed, when he formed a defign of bringing water to the pa-lace at Monte Cavallo, (anciently Mons Quirinalis), which was much wanted ; as the Popes generally refide there two or three months in the heat of the fummer, for the fake of coolnefs and frefh air. He carried his fearches for water as far as a place called Colonne, where they found a very wholefome and copious fpring. So many difficulties attended this undertaking, that it was generally thought impoffible ; yet he happily conquered them all, to the great furprize of every body, after eight months labour, during which time there were two or three, and fometimes four thoufand men employed every day, according to the impediments they met with, in undermining and clearing away the earth. This Aqueduct coft 10,000 piftoles, including 25,000 crowns paid to Martini Colonna, lord of the foil. To receive this water he erected a beautiful fountain and bafon in the piazza of St. Sufanna near Dioclefian's baths, which he would have called after his own name, Fonte Felice, with this infcription upon it :

SIXTVS V. PONT. MAX. PICENVS,
AQVAM EX AGRO COLVMNAE,
VIA PRAENESTINA, SINISTRORSVM,
MVLTARVM COLLECTIONE ENARVM DVCTV
SINVOSO,
A RECEPTACVLO MILL. XX. A CAPITE XXII.
ADDVXIT,
FELICEMQVE DE NOMINE ANTE PONT. DIXIT.
COEPIT PONT. ANNO PRIMO,
ABSOLVIT III. MDLXXXVIII.

He likewife built the gallery which is over the por-tal of St. John de Lateran, from whence the Popes give their benediction to the people, and embellifhed it with
paintings,

paintings, which reprefent the nine hierarchies or
orders of angels, the apoftles, prophets, martyrs,
virgins, pontiffs, confeffors, the emperor Conftantine,
and many others, worthy the notice of ftrangers. Clofe
to this he built a palace for the reception of the Popes,
when they fhould come to vifit this church. There is
not in the whole city, a fabric of that grandeur, begun and finifhed by the fame perfon. In it are many
noble and magnificent apartments, and two large halls,
in which there are many hiftory-pieces of the Popes
and emperors. The front of it, facing the obelifk,
is 340 feet long; and that which looks towards St.
Maria Maggiore 335, and 137 high. There is room
in it to entertain feveral princes at once, and all the
cardinals, if ever a canonization or confiftory fhould
be held there: But his principal view was to lodge the
emperor in it, if at any time he fhould come to Rome:
And, to keep it in good order, he publifhed a decree,
enjoining his fucceffors to refide there two months in
the year; who have fhewn fo little regard to it, that
this noble edifice, which would be one of the greateft
ornaments of Rome, is now, miferably out of repair,
and almoft a ruin for want of being inhabited.

This year he likewife caufed the holy ftair-cafe,
which was buried under the ruins of old houfes, to be
tranfported to the Sanctum Sanctorum, and beautified
that place with many fine paintings, to increafe the devotions of pilgrims, who came for the fake of the indulgencies, which he granted to all thofe that went up
this ftair-cafe upon their knees. It confifts of 28 fteps,
and is faid to be the fame that was in Pilate's palace
in Jerufalem, which (according to tradition) our Saviour afcended and defcended twice.

His next undertaking was a very large and convenient hofpital, for the fick, wounded, maimed, and
fuch as were not able to maintain themfelves by labour,
capable of containing 2000 people, without incom-
moding each other: This was fituated near a bridge,
which he had built over the Tyber, called by his own
name

name [9], at the top of the Julian ftreet, and endowed with a yearly revenue of 5000 piftoles, with apartments for the governors and other officers belonging to it. The arms of Sixtus are fixed over the gate, with this infcription:

SIXTVS V. PONT. MAX. PICENVS,
PAVPERIBVS PIE ALENDI-,
NE PANE VESTITVQVE CAREANT,
MVLTO SVO COEPTANS AERE, HAS EADES EX-
TRVXIT,
APTAVIT, AMPLIAVIT, PERPETVO CENSV
DOTAVIT.
ANNO MDLXXXVI.

He placed a gilded bronze ftatue of St. Peter, 14 feet high, upon the top of Trajan's pillar, which he confecrated to him. It was firft dedicated by the Romans to that emperor, to perpetuate the memory of his victories over the Parthians and Dacians (now called Tran-

[9] *Il Ponte Sifto tras Tevere.* This bridge was built by Sixtus IV, and only repaired by Sixtus V, as appears from the following infcription upon it, to be found in Schraderus:

SIXTVS IV. PONT. MAX.
AD VTILITATEM POPVLI ROMANI,
PEREGRINAEQVE MVLTITVDINIS AD JVBI-
LAEVM VENTVARAE,
PONTEM HVNC QVEM MERITO RVPTVM VO-
CABANT
A FVNDAMENTIS MAGNA CVRA ET IMPENSA
RESTITVIT,
SIXTVMQVE SVO DE NOMINE APPELLARE VO-
LVIT.
ANNO MCCCCLXXV.
QVI TRANSIS SIXTI IV. BENEFICIO
DEVM ROGA VT PONTIFF. O. M. DIV NOS SAL-
VET AC SOSPITET.
BENE VALE, QVISQVIS ES, VBI HAEC PRECATVS
FVERIS.

Tranfylvanians and Wallachians), which are recorded upon it in Alto Relievo.

After this, he confecrated Antoninus's pillar to St. Paul, whofe ftatue he erected upon it, of equal dimenfions and value with that of St. Peter. This pillar was firft dedicated to the emperor Antoninus, furnamed, The Pious, by Marcus Aurelius, his fon-in-law, who embellifhed it with Baffo Relievos, reprefenting the exploits he had performed in Germany, againft the Marcomanni, now called Bohemians and Moravians. It was much defaced by time, but he reftored it to its former beauty.

Trajan's pillar is of the fpiral kind, and ftands in the piazza of St. Mary of Loretto : You afcend to the top of it by an hundred and eighty two fteps [10] in the infide. There are 44 windows to give light to the ftair-cafe. Round the capital is the following infcription, in large letters :

SIXTVS V. PONT. MAX.
B. PETRO APOSTOLORVM PONTIFICI,]
ANNO PONT. IV.

The other is in the piazza delle Colone, all of marble, with a winding ftair-cafe, and 190 fteps (which is eight more than there are in Trajan's) and 41 windows; the ftairs are likewife much higher. The figures upon it are fo well executed, and in fo juft a proportion, that the higheft don't appear lefs than the loweft. The ftatue of St. Paul on the top, has this infcription under it, in capitals :

SIXTVS V. S. PAVLO APOST.
PONT. A. IV.

[10] Roma antiqua figurata, fays 123 fteps and 15 windows; that it is 128 feet high, and the work of Apollodorus. It is reckoned the fineft piece of fculpture and architecture in the world, fays Relation de la Cour de Rome ; and that it is 140 feet high, with 192 fteps and 44 windows.

A a

And

And upon the fides of the pedeftal the following:

On the firft,

SIXTVS V. PONT. MAX.
COLVMNAM HANC AB OMNI IMPIETATE EX-
PVRGATAM,
S. PAVLO. APOSTOLO,
AENEA EIVS STATVA INAVRATA,
IN SVMMO VERTICE, POSITA
D. D. ANNO MDLXXXIX. PONT. IV.

On the Second,

SIXTVS V. PONT. MAX.
COLVMNAM HANC COCHLIDEM
IMP. ANTONINO DICATAM
MISERE LACERAM, RVINOSAMQVE,
PRIMAE FORMAE RESTITVIT
ANNO MDLXXXIX. PONT. IV.

On the Third,

MARCVS AVRELIVS IMP.
ARMENIS, PARTHIS, GERMANISQVE BELLO
MAXIMO DEVICTIS,
TRIVMPHALEM HANC COLVMNAM,
REBVS GESTIS INSIGNEM,
IMP. ANTONINO PIO PATRI DEDICAVIT,

On the Fourth,

TRIVMPHALIS ET SACRA NVNC SVM,
CHRISTI VERE PIVM DISCIPVLVM FERENS;
QVI PER CRVCIS PRAEDICATIONEM
DE ROMANIS BARBARISQVE TRIVMPHAVIT.

He repaired, at a great expence, the ftatues of the
two horfes at Monte Cavallo, which, tho' of marble,
had not been able to refift the force of time. Each
ftatue reprefents Alexander the Great naked, breaking
his

his horfe Bucephalus, who was fo fierce that he would let no body mount him but that prince and his father Philip. They were brought by Tiridates, king of the Armenians, to Rome, as a prefent to Nero, and after-wards placed in the baths of Conftantine, from whence Sixtus removed them to the Mons Quirinalis, which from them was called Monte Cavallo. They are ad-mirably executed, and the work of Phidias and Praxi-teles, the moft famous ftatuaries of their times. Praxi-teles lived long after Phidias, and is faid to have vied with him in this performance [11].

Under the horfe of Phidias is infcribed:

PHIDIAS NOBILIS SCVLPTOR,
AD ARTIFICII PRAESTANTIAM DECLARANDAM,
ALEXANDRI BVCEPHALVM DOMANTIS EFFI-
GIEM,
E MARMORE EXPRESSIT.

Under that of Praxiteles.

PRAXITELES SCVLPTOR
AD PHIDAE AEMULATIONEM SVI
MONVMENTA INGENII POSTERIS RELINQVERE
CVPIENS,
EIVSDEM ALEXANDRI BVCEPHALIQVE SIGNA,
FELICI CONTENTIONE PERFECIT.

A a 2   Upon

[11] Leti has fallen into an error here in common with many hiftorians. For Donatus and other chronologifts plainly fhew, that Phidias lived about the 83d olympiad, and Praxiteles about the 104th, above 80 years after; and Alexander about the 114th, 40 years after Praxiteles. Thefe ftatues were not prefented, as Fulvius, Leti, and others pretend, by Tiridates to Nero, but brought by Conftantine out of Greece; and are more likely the ftatues of Caftor and Pollux, and their favourite horfes. Urban VIII erafed the modern infcription, and only left the ancient one, viz.

OPVS PHIDIAE, upon the one, and
OPVS PRAXITELIS, on the other.

Duos

Upon the Bafe,

SIXTVS V. PONT. MAX.
SIGNA ALEXANDRI MAGNI CELEBRISQVE EIVS
BVCEPHALI,
EX ANTIQVATATIS TESTIMONIO,
PHIDIAE ET PRAXITELES AEMVLATIONE,
HOC MARMORE AD VIVAM EFFIGIEM EXPRESSA
CONSTANTINO MAX. E GRAECIA ADVECTA,
SVISQVE IN THERMIS IN HOC QVIRINALI MON-
· TE COLLOCATA,
TEMPORIS VI DEFORMATA LACERAQVE
AD EIVSDEM IMPERATORIS MEMORIAM VRBIS-
QVE DECORVM,
IN PRISTINAM FORMAM RESTITVTA,
HIC REPONI IVSSIT,
ANNO MDLXXXIX. PONT .IV.

Every body was amazed to fee fo many vaft undertakings executed with fuch refolution and celerity, by
a perfon who was at the fame time fo attentive to the
concerns both of church and ftate: It is faid, what
he did in the few years that he was Pope, toward
beautifying and adorning the city, exceeded all that
had been done by the Roman emperors.

Having been informed that the palace at Monte Cavallo, to which he had made confiderable additions,
was not yet large enough to contain his houfhold, when
he fhould pleafe to refide there, he built another adjoining to it, with a barrack to lodge his Swifs guards
in, confifting of 200 men, who before had no convenience of this kind.

Thefe occupations, in which he feemed wholly employed, did not hinder him from thinking of his own
family: After he had given them his palace, near St.

Duos item equos infignes e Pario marmore, fed injuria temporis
ac cœli admodum mutilitas, qui falfis infcriptionibus Phidiæ ac
Praxiteles nomina pre fe ferunt, in Monte Quirinali rarâ artificum
induftriâ refici juffit. Thuan. lib. 100.

Maria

Maria Maggiore, he added feveral royal apartments to it, with all manner of conveniencies, and a garden, that for beauty and elegance, vied with that of the Vatican, which, they fay, far exceeds any in Europe.

He drew a plan for building feveral new ftreets, which he began the fame year; the moft confiderable of them runs from the church, *di Santa Croce in Jeru-falem*, and reaches *Trinita di Monti*, from whence he defigned to have continued it to *Porto del Populo*; but died before it was finifhed. It was carried on, however two miles (above one in a right line) fo wide that five coaches might eafily go abreaft, and called it after his baptifmal name, *Strada Felice*.

He likewife built two others, which begin at St. Laurence's without the walls; one of them reaches to St. Maria Maggiore, and the other to the place where Dioclefian's baths ftood, on the back fide of this palace. Another he built, which goes from St. Maria Maggiore to the palace of St. Mark, belonging to the Venetians. Another, which begins at St. John de Lateran, and reaches to the ancient Colifeum [12]: And another from Porta Salaria, to Porta Pia. Though thefe new ftreets were of very great convenience to the public, fome people could not help murmuring, and faid, "That he built them for the fake of his palace there."

He ordered his architect, Fontana, to take a furvey of the Vatican, and let him know what number of perfons it would lodge; and being informed that it was not large enough to contain fuch a houfhold as the dignity of the pontiff required, he added another palace

[12] Coloffeum, corruptly called Colifeum, and Culifeum, an immenfe amphitheatre, built by the emperors Vefpafian, Titus, and Domitian; fo called from being fituated near the Coloffus erected by Nero. It was reckoned the largeft and moft magnificent piece of architecture in Rome, capable of containing 87,000 fpectators, without inconvenience, or crowding each other. Martial fays of it,

Omnis Cæfario cedat labor amphitheatro;
Unum pro cunctis fama loquator opus.

to it, joining to the gallery which the Popes Leo, Pius, and Gregory, had adorned with the fineſt paintings in the world; ſo that now the Vatican is by much the largeſt and moſt ſuperb palace in Europe.

He ſpared Gregory's chapel, and made a paſſage thro' it, tho' he pulled down ſeveral other buildings, that were in his way, when he made the grand ſtair-caſe that goes out of the Vatican to St. Peter's. This ſtair-caſe is of great convenience, and there is a ſort of dignity in it; for as the Popes were before obliged to go out of doors, and over the piazza, every time they went to church, they can now paſs thither ſecretly, without being expoſed to the weather, or the importunities of the people.

He repaired the tower in the Belvidere, which time had almoſt deſtroyed; thinking it a pity, that a work ſo beautiful, as well as neceſſary, ſhould fall to ruin. He likewiſe took compaſſion on the very ancient church of St. Sabine, of which there were hardly any remains left, and rebuilt it in ſuch a manner, that it now exceeds any in Rome, of the ſame ſize and extent. He repaired the beautiful church of St. Jerome a Rapietta, from which he took his title, when he was cardinal, and granted ſeveral indulgences to it.

The prodigious number of edifices we have already mentioned, are ſufficient, one would think, to make his name immortal; but all theſe are nothing in compariſon of what he did to St. Peter's, as the undertaking ſeemed impoſſible to the very architects themſelves: To finiſh this noble ſtructure, there wanted a dome, or cupola, proportionable to its vaſt height and extent: His predeceſſors durſt not ſo much as attempt it; Sixtus, however, whoſe courage and reſolution nothing could daunt, being determined to conquer this difficulty, ordered an architect to draw the plan in his preſence, commanding him, without any regard to expence, to exert his utmoſt art and endeavours to accompliſh it; which he did, in that grand and wonderful manner we now ſee it.

It

It is faid to be the higheft edifice in Chriftendom. He was fo impatient to fee it finifhed, that he daily employed above 600 men about it, and would have doubled the number, if the architects had not affured him, that fuch a multitude of people would create confufion, and rather retard than expedite the work. The infide is of Mofaic, in which there are the four evangelifts, of an immenfe fize.

One may form a judgment of the height of this dome, by the appearance of the ball on the top of it, which, tho' large enough to contain 15 or 20 perfons in the infide, feems no bigger than a foot ball to thofe who ftand on the ground. It may alfo be gueffed at, from a window which is about half way from the bottom to the top, where men appear no bigger than pigmies, and the beft eyes in the world cannot diftinguifh any particular perfon from another.

He pulled down an old tower, built of very fine marble, by the emperor Severus, called the Septizonium [13], and made ufe of the materials in the dome of St. Peter. The city was not pleafed at the demolition of this monument of the ancient Roman grandeur; but Sixtus intent upon new ornaments, did not give himfelf much concern about the glory of the ancients.

He gave many proofs of the affection and refpect he had for his order, in granting them feveral privileges, and taking care to defend them againft the incroachments of the Reformed Conventuals, or Zoccolant friars, who had made many attacks upon them, and under pretence of reformation, had difpoffeffed them of feveral convents, with the confent of his prodeceffors. This branch of the Francifcan order he fuppreffed, as ufelefs, or rather prejudicial to the ancient and true difcipline of the Conventuals, and ordered them, on

[13] The Septizonium, was a fort of a tower, or buryingplace, built by the emperor Severus; fo called from feven colonades, or zones of pillars (with which it was furrounded) one above another, growing lefs and lefs to the top.

the

the fevereft penalties, to re-unite with them, to apply their revenues to the fame ufes, and to admit no more to the noviciate; fo that in a fhort time they had only one convent left, viz. St. Lucia del Monte, at Naples, which now belongs to the old Conventuals, who owe the re-eftablifhment and prefervation of their order entirely to Sixtus.

He founded a college in the convent of the H. Apoftles, and endowed it with the revenue of a rich abbey in Calabria, for the maintenance of 25 ftudents. This foundation, which was very advantageous to the religious of his order, as it gave them an opportunity, and infpired them with an emulation to ftudy, that they might qualify themfelves to be admitted into this college, where, after they had refided three years, they proceeded regents, or lecturers of divinity. It is true, the rules and orders obferved in this houfe were very ftrict and fevere; but Sixtus, who was well acquainted with the manners and behaviour of monks, thought this the beft, and moft likely method, to make it truly ferviceable. This difcipline was kept up a long time and to fay a perfon was a fcholar of St. Bona-venture (to whom he had dedicated this college, and called it by his name) was the fame as to call him a very good fcholar, and a learned divine; but when it began to relax, diforder and riot crept into the college, and it was foon filled with ignorant and diffolute people, to the utter ruin and fubverfion of it; tho' Sixtus had taken all imaginable precautions for its continuance, by making it not fubject to the common protector of the order, but a particular protector, to be chofen by the rector, and other members of it; and ordered, that whenever there fhould be a cardinal of the houfe of Peretti, he fhould be the patron of it.

His munificence was not confined to Rome alone; he extended it to the country round about, as far as the frontiers of the ecclefiaftical ftate, not only in the care he took for the peace and fafety of his fubjects, but in building colleges, aqueducts, bridges, and an

infinity

infinity of other works, merely for the public fervice: He began with the province of La Marca, his own country, which he excufed from paying taxes equal to the reft, tho' he did not entirely exempt it; and having obferved, before he was Pope, that there was a great fcarcity of learned men in that country, in order to encreafe the number, and to encourage virtue and merit, he built a college in Bologna, which he endowed with a revenue fufficient to maintain four ftudents, befides a principal, lecturer and other officers.   He once intended to have built it in Rome, but two reafons determined him againft it : In the firft place he thought it would be looked on with an envious eye by his fuccefors, who would therefore be tempted to deftroy it, or at leaft pervert the rules and defigns of its inftitution.   As he intended it only for the natives of La Marca, he was apprehenfive they might hereafter chufe the ftudents indifferently out of any other parts of the Ecclefiaftical ftate, which he imagined would be prevented by placing it at a diftance from Rome, and out of the immediate notice of his fuccefors.

The fecond reafon was, to make Bologna more refpectable; as he likewife thought it a very plentiful place, and much cheaper than Rome.

He enriched that province with two other ornaments, which brought it into greater renown; the firft was the effect of his particular devotion; the fecond of his love for the place of his nativity : As he always profeffed himfelf highly obliged, upon many accounts, to the virgin of Loretto, whofe church is fituated in the middle of it, he determined to enlarge and beautify that town; and faid, " It was but juft, that a man " born in La Marca, fhould fhew himfelf grateful to " the mother of God, for making choice of that pro- " vince for her refidence, and tranfporting the houfe " fhe formerly inhabited in Judæa to the village of " Loretto *." He therefore gave immediate orders for

* Her church at Loretto was faid to be miraculoufly removed thither from Judæa, in a night's time.

laying

laying the foundations of a new city, and granted many privileges and exemptions to fuch as would come to live in it: But as it would not properly be a city without an epifcopal fee, he erected one there, and curtailed the revenue of the bifhopric of Recanati, upon which Loretto was before dependent. This was a great mortification to the bifhop of Recanati; but as there was no remedy he was forced to fit down content.

He once thought to have ordained, by a decree, that nobody fhould ever fucceed to that bifhopric, that was not born in the province of La Marca; but as he apprehended that would not be long obferved, he dropt it. The officers of that church, erected his ftatue, as big as the life, over againft the main gate, out of gratitude for the many favours he had beftowed on them.

His next undertaking was to build a city at Le Grotte di Montalto, round the houfe where he was born; for the peopling of which he had already concerted meafures, but was obliged to lay it afide, as impracticable; and it was the only project he undertook, and did not execute, during his pontificate.

Not being able to accomplifh this, he fixed upon Borgo di Montalto, the largeft of thofe villages that were near the place of his birth. After he had granted it feveral franchifes, and immunities, he caufed a new plan to be drawn by an able architect, and having examined it, corrected thofe parts that he did not approve of, with his own hand: He then appointed a commiffary, and an engineer, to execute it, with orders to fend him an account every week of the progrefs and expence of the work, daily employing there 500 labourers, befides the inhabitants; and as it could not otherwife well be called a city, he enclofed it on every fide with a ftrong wall, and other fortifications.

This enterprize he found attended with very great difficulties, as it was neceffary to cut above 700 fathoms thro' a hill, where there was a rock as hard as
flint,

flint, which the engineer was not aware of. Many of the cardinals murmured in secret at it, though they durst not speak out, for fear of the spies that continually beset them, as they knew what methods he generally took to stop people's mouths. They could not, however, forbear privately condemning this sort of ambition, which was no service either to the church or state.

Sixtus, who was informed of every thing they said, pressed forward the work with so much the more vigour and earnestness, and sometimes said to them, in a taunting manner, " What we are doing at Montalto, " is only by way of recreation, and amusement, to un- " bend ourselves a little, after the great labour and " fatigue we have undergone in beautifying Rome." Here, likewise, he erected a bishopric, with a handsome revenue, and great privileges; and built at the same time a bridge over the Tiber, betwixt Borghetto and Utricoli, for the convenience of trade and passengers, who were often stopped there by the floods.

Tho' the Ecclesiastical state is finely watered with several rivers and lakes, which make it extremely fertile and pleasant, Sixtus, who had always some great design in view, intended to bring the river Teveron to Rome: This, besides the advantage which the adjacent lands were sure to receive from it, would have been very serviceable to commerce, and the transportation of provisions and fruit, out of the country to the city: But what he considered most, was the refreshing and purifying the atmosphere, to which, streams of running water very much contribute, by the constant undulation which the vapours that arise from them occasion in the air, nothing being more dangerous than a long calm, as it produces a stagnation, and consequently a putrefaction of it, very often fatal to the inhabitants of the country round about Rome.

Many people, it is probable, would likewise have been tempted to build country-houses, mills, magazines,

zines, and other edifices; to make gardens, orchards, walks, and groves, upon the banks of this new canal; which would have furnished a beautiful landscape, and very much embellished the neighbouring campaign.

It was further said, that the inundations of the Tiber, which have often done so much mischief, would have been considerably diminished, and that the quality of its water would not have been altered for the worse, by diverting the course of the Teveron, that falls into it some miles above Rome: Tho' it is supposed to be strongly impregnated with sulphur, by passing thro' Tivoli, that abounds with strata of that mineral, which is looked upon as a circumstance that makes it more wholesome. But admitting the water of the Tiber had not been quite so good, the detriment would have been over-balanced, by many advantages that might have resulted from the execution of this design. In cases of medicine, it often happens, that the physician can't relieve one member that is indisposed, without, perhaps, some prejudice to another; so in civil affairs, whilst we endeavour to remedy one inconvenience, it is often impossible to avoid occasioning another; it must therefore suffice to chuse the less of two evils; and Sixtus would have actually undertaken it, if the engineers had not represented it to him as utterly impossible.

After he had laboured with so much application, and reduced both the spiritual and temporal affairs of the ecclesiastical state into good order, he began to think of regulating his militia: For which purpose he gave orders to have muster-rolls made of all the soldiers in his service, and to form them into battalions, ready to take the field upon any emergency. All his subjects who were able to bear arms, he had enrolled, and appointed officers in every city, to discpline and exercise them, granting them several immunities. To this regulation was owing the success of Clement VIII, at Ferrara, in the year 1599. All the world was surprized to see 20,000 foot, and 2000 horse, all subjects

of

of the Holy See, affembled in lefs than a month A
thing few princes in Europe were able to do, and which
he himfelf could not have brought to pafs, if it had
not been for the forefight and prudent difpofitions made
by Sixtus.

He fent for three of the beft engineers that could
be any where procured, to give him their opinion what
places it was moft neceffary to fortify in the Ecclefiaftical ftate. After a long confultation about it in his
prefence, one of them faid, " It was very neceffary to
" purfue the plan of fortification at Caftello Franco, be-
" gun by Pius V, which he was obliged to abandon by
" the war of Cyprus." This place is fituated in the
middle of a plain, eafy to fortify, not commanded by
any eminence, in a plentiful country, near Bologna,
which would be obliged to fuccour it, for its own fafety, and that of its dependencies, and might eafily be
defended againft a very great army.

It is true Sixtus, out of regard to the memory of
Pius, had fome thoughts of finifhing the works begun
there by that pontiff: But as the conqueft of Naples
was his principal view (tho' he did not then think fit
to communicate that fecret to any one) he was chiefly
concerned to fortify his frontier on that fide, and take
every preparatory ftep that might conduce to bring that
enterprize to a fuccefsful iffue.

The engineers, by his order, went to fee what
towns it would be propereft to garrifon. They reported, " That the length of the frontier required feveral;
" that the moft convenient would be Ripa, Tranfona,
" Offida, and Afcoli, particularly the laft, which ought
" to be very well fortified, as it immediately bordered
" upon Naples, and was the beft qualified to annoy the
" enemy, by the advantage of its fituation, and the
" bravery of its inhabitants." On the fide of Terra
Sabina [14], they advifed him to fortify Rieta, a fine
town furrounded by a very fertile country, which it was

[14] The country of the antient Sabines.

highly

highly neceffary to fecure from the inroads of an invader. They were of opinion that Terracina, Frufinone, Firentino, Segna, and Anagni, but particularly Frufinone and Anagni ought to be well fecured; and that all the little fortreffes near Rome fhould be demolifhed, that they might not be of any ufe to an enemy, if they fell into his power.

They further reprefented to him, that as Civita Vecchia, which muft be his fea-port, was very ill fupplied with frefh water, it was abfolutely neceffary to furnifh it with a fupply, to prevent the fatal confequences that might fome time or other proceed from fuch a fcarcity. Upon this he gave immediate orders to begin upon an aqueduct, which was fpeedily finifhed, to the great advantage of the town, as a fortified place, and the joy of the inhabitants.

He had a huge cheft or coffer of bronze made, 16 feet long, 12 wide, and as many in height, which he called the Ærarium Romanæ Ecclefiæ, the treafury of the Romifh Church, with three very ftrong locks to it. In this there were two chinks or nicks, to prevent the trouble of often opening it; one for gold, the other for filver to be dropt thro'. For the greater fecurity, it was placed in the tower of St. Angelo, as he propofed to lay up a million of crowns in it every year (for ufes that will be mentioned hereafter), of the beft money, that was then current, which he would fometimes be at the trouble of feeing picked out himfelf.

All manner of people were welcome to him that could point out any way of raifing money; for which purpofe he eftablifhed a committee, confifting of 12 perfons, who were to meet in his apartment once a week. They were all men well fkilled in accounts, and fuch as were thoroughly verfed in money-matters, in trade and the management of the finances. Every one of them was to bring fuch a fcheme in writing, as he thought beft to enrich the treafury, without opprefsing the people. Each took an abftract of the other's fcheme; and at the next meeting put down in writing
what

what he thought good or bad in it, or if he had any thing elfe to propofe that he thought would turn to better account. The whole was examined and debated before the Pope, who referved the decifion to himfelf, after he had left it to be reconfidered by a congregation appointed for this purpofe. Indeed, he did every thing with the matureft deliberation, as he was very unwilling to give up any defign that he had once undertaken.

Thefe preparations gave great fufpicion and jealoufy to the neighbouring princes, efpecially the Spaniards, who faw him fo intent upon fortifying his frontiers, and putting his militia in fuch order as to be able to attack them on a fudden.

This was not a little increafed, when they perceived he likewife intended to have a force at fea, having given orders for the building of ten ftout galleys, and fent to Venice for fome of the beft fhipwrights that could be got. " This he gave out, was to do honour " to the Holy See, and for the common fervice of the " ftate."

Before he began to build the galleys, he held a congregation, to fettle a fund for their fupport. As this expence was to be defrayed by the fubjects of the Ecclefiaftical ftate alone, he gave orders that no cardinals, but thofe that were born fubjects of the Holy See, fhould affift at it, that they might advife fuch ways and means of raifing the money, as would be the leaft grievous to their relations, and the reft of the ftate.

The other cardinals refented this exclufion, and faid, " That as they had an equal title with the others " to be fummoned, it feemed as if his Holinefs defigned " to deprive them of the fhare they ought to have in " thofe confultations, and to admit none but fuch as " were born in the dominions of the church." They defired Cardinal D'Efte*, to make remonftrances of this kind to the Pope, which he did in a long confe-

* The French fays Medicis.

rence that he had with him upon this occafion; and
faid, " that the common character and dignity of
" cardinals, made them all equal, and that they were
" princes of the church as well as others." Sixtus
who had his anfwer ready, heard him contrary to his
cuftom, with a great deal of patience, and then faid,
" We are very willing that your eminence and your
" brethren fhould be entitled princes of the church,
" but not of our ftate." The fharpnefs of the reply
ftung D'Efte to the quick ; and tho' he knew how dangerous it was to provoke Sixtus, the courage and magnanimity hereditary in that noble family, and the intereft he had in the fuccefs of an affair that was left
to his conduct, prompted him to fay, " if this be the
" cafe, Holy father, we might as well ftay quietly at
" home." " I fhall commend you for fo doing, re-
" plied Sixtus, and God be with you." D'Efte was
determined to retire that night, but all the other cardinals being affembled upon this occafion, reprefented
to him, " that if he did, they muft be obliged to do
fo too, which would ftill more incenfe the Pope, by
" whom they would be fure to be roughly treated for
" fuch fort of behaviour." This made him alter his
refolution, and the affair dropped, Sixtus and the other
cardinals laughing in their fleeves.

It was agreed in this congregation, where the Pope
managed every thing himfelf, that thefe gallies fhould
be built at the expence of the provinces and moft confiderable towns in the Ecclefiaftical ftate ; and there
was a bull immediately iffued out, which obliged them
to pay their yearly quota: Upon a calculation which
his Holinefs ordered to be made, it was found that it
would amount to the fum of 100,000 crowns per annum.

For the greater exactnefs he had an account taken
and brought of the number of families in every province, that they might contribute in proportion to their
abilities. He taxed the fenate and people of Rome at
12,000 crowns; the city and territory of Bologna,

the

the province of Umbria and that of Romagna the fame. The province of La Marca he would willingly have excufed, but thinking it would be a manifeft injuftice to the others, and that his fucceffors, looking upon it as an act of partiality, might fome time or other take an opportunity of making it pay double taxes; as it was the richeft and moft populous province in the Pope's dominions, he charged it with 12,000, like the reft. The patrimony of St. Peter, which is the leaft of any, was taxed only 5874; that of Campania, which is fomething richer, 6126; the city of Ancona, with its dependencies, at 1810; Fano the fame, though it is lefs than Afcoli, which was included in the dependencies of Ancona. The clergy were taxed 12,000 (a very fmall proportion) every ecclefiaftic according to his benefice. They levied yet 5000 more upon the city and diftrict of Benevento, and 8000 upon two eftates belonging to the public, in all 100,600 crowns.

The firft year's tax was immediately collected, in order to build two galleys directly, which he was impatient to fee finifhed, to receive fome of the criminals, as every prifon was full of them. This pontificate having been, out of the neceffity there was for ftrict juftice, the fevereft and moft rigorous that ever was remembered, infomuch that it was ufual to fee wretches dragged to prifon or execution every hour of the day, with heads and quarters ftuck upon poles in all the public places of the city.

The Catholic Swifs cantons fent ambaffadors this year to Rome, not only to pay their obeifance to the new Pope, and kifs his feet, but likewife to inform him of the dangerous and pitiable fituation they were in, with refpect to the neighbourhood of the Proteftants, whofe force and numbers increafed every day.

Sixtus received them with a great deal of humanity, and having been informed by them of the ftate of affairs in their country, thought proper to fend a Nuncio, to encourage them to fteadinefs and perfeverance in the Catholic religion. After he had maturely confidered of a perfon fit for an employ of this importance, he appointed John Baptift Santorio, bifhop of Tricario, a man of great merit and long experience in negocia-tions; and in a full confiftory declared him Nuncio to the Catholic cantons, their confederates and al-lies.

This prelate was not a little pleafed with an oppor-tunity of fhewing his zeal in the fervice of the church: he left Rome in the hotteft feafon of the year, with a very flender attendance; and, at his arrival in Switzer-land, found things in the utmoft confufion, occafioned by not having had any Nuncio there for feveral years. They feemed to have been abandoned by the Holy See, as if they had not been members of the Romifh com-munion: whereas, if a Nuncio of prudence and ad-drefs had been there, when thefe Proteftant preachers every where propagated their new doctrines, it might have prevented them from embracing the Lutheran religion, and kept them fteady in the purity of the Catholic faith, to which they were now become fo indifferent, that it was believed all the cantons would have foon turned Proteftants, if they had not been pre-vented by the arrival and indefatigable labours of this Nuncio.

As foon as he came there, he acquainted them that he fhould be glad to meet them affembled in a general diet, and defired they would fend a greater number of deputies thither than ufual. Upon which intimation there was one called immediately, and affembled the 5th of October.

In this meeting there were two points carried of great importance to the Holy See, for which the Pope wrote a particular letter of thanks to the Nuncio. The firft was, that after he had himfelf given the facrament to all the deputies, he concluded a perpetual alliance be-twixt them and the See of Rome, to the fervice of which they devoted themfelves, their children, their lives and fortunes, by an oath taken on their knees before the altar, with their hands upon the Miffal,
which

which he held open. This was paffed into a folemn
act, figned and fealed by them all.

The fecond was, the confent which Santorio obtained
from the deputies, to have a particular place a figned
for the eftablifhment of a free and independent eccl-
fiaftical jurifdiction, which fhould take cognizance of
all caufes, as well criminal as civil, belonging to ecclefiaftics, with liberty to imprifon and punifh them according to the nature of their offences. They likewife
allotted him a piece of ground to build a prifon upon
for this purpofe, to fhew the authority of his jurifdiction; and refufed him nothing elfe that he thought proper to afk, in order to affert and maintain the intereft
of the Holy See.

It is true, the Nuncios formerly enjoyed all thefe
privileges amongft the Swifs; but the magiftrates refenting the contempt, as they thought it, of none
being lately fent to them, as there were to crowned
heads, following the example of the Venetians, abolifhed the ecclefiaftical jurifdiction, imprifoned and
punifhed the ecclefiaftics themfelves : but Santorio, at
his arrival, recovered this power, and re-eftablifhed the
antient rights and privileges of the court of Rome, at
the expence of their fovereign authority; a lofs which
they have fo much regretted fince, that if it was to be
done again, without doubt they would be more tenacious of their liberties.

The Nuncio applied himfelf with great diligence to
exercife them almoft continually in the duties of religion, and reformed feveral abufes that had crept in a-
mongft them. To overcome the difficulties which the
Proteftants threw in his way, he caufed feveral monafteries of the capuchins to be built, and particularly in
Apenzel, which is a neutral canton; and wrote to the
general of the order, to fend him fome fathers, capable of edifying and confirming the Catholics by
their good example, and to make head againft the Proteftant preachers, who came from Geneva, and other
infected places, to fpread their falfe doctrine amongft

B b 2   the

the people, and to support those that were already tainted with their principles.

There happened some disputes betwixt the Protestants and Catholics about their limits and boundaries, which not a little embarrassed the Nuncio, and had like to have set the whole country in a flame, and lost him the Pope's favour. To execute the power given him of imprisoning the ecclesiastics with greater authority, he had a marshal and a party of archers, which without doubt, was a most violent attack upon the sovereignty of the cantons : they winked at it, however, either out of respect to the See of Rome, or the esteem and affection they had for the Nuncio.

The marshal having received orders to apprehend a preacher, pursued and took him in a house, which was in the Protestant confines, and conveyed him to prison, though the priest protested strongly against it, and insisted that he had no power to apprehend him in a place that was not in the Nuncio's jurisdiction. Some Protestants, that had been witnesses of this proceeding, gave immediate information of it to their magistrate, who sent to demand the prisoner back, and to complain that he had been seized in their territory ; but received for answer from the canton, " That it was no " affair of theirs, that it was the Nuncio's doing ; that " the preacher was in his prison, and that he must apply " to him for redress."

The Protestants, upon this, reproached them with the authority they had given the Nuncio, to the prejudice of their own, of which they would one time or other feel the consequence, when perhaps it was too late to remedy it ; declaring, they acknowledged no such power as the Nuncio pretended to, and threatened reprizals, if their preacher was not immediately set at liberty.

As these remonstrances had no effect, they took an opportunity of seizing a priest, that did not live far from their confines, in his own house, and carried him to their prison, with a resolution not to release him till

they

they fent their preacher back again. This action fet
all the cantons in an uproar ; both the Proteftants and
Catholics held councils to deliberate what was proper
to be done in fo nice a conjuncture. The Nuncio fent
an account of it to the Pope, from whom he received
this anfwer ; " We fent you into Switzerland, not to
" create confufion, but to reftore peace and unanimity
" amongft the Catholics ; not to force the Proteftants
" to take up arms againft them, but to labour for the
" converfion of the one, and the prefervation of the
" other: You need to be informed, that nothing is
" of fo delicate a nature as the point of jurifdictions,
" and that affairs of this kind ought to be managed
" with the greateft prudence : popular tumults and fe-
" ditions are as prejudicial to the Catholics, as they
" are ferviceable to the Proteftants ; for which reafon
" you ought to take all imaginable care to prevent, at
" leaft not to occafion them. It would be a wrong
" meafure, indeed, to give them any advantage, but
" imprudent to take any thing from them, for fear of
" the confequences ; we therefore charge you, for the
" future, to proceed with the utmoft caution, both for
" the fake of our repofe and your own."

This anfwer, wrote with the Pope's own hand, whofe
temper the Nuncio was fo well acquainted with, obliged
him to ufe all his dexterity and addrefs to accomo-
date the matter ; which, after a long negociation, was
at laft thus compromifed : the Proteftants confented,
that their preacher fhould come out of prifon as if he
had made his efcape, and the Catholics agreed that
theirs fhould be releafed after the fame manner.

About this time above 50,000 Germans, Swifs, and
other Proteftants, declared in favour of the king of Navarre, and took up arms in his quarrel. The Catholic
cantons were apprehenfive this great body of men
intended to invade them, and held a council upon it
at the Nuncio's houfe, at which the ambaffadors of
all the Roman Catholic powers then refiding there were
prefent, whom they humbly befought to fuccour them

if

if they should be attacked. The Nuncio promised them every thing that could be expected or hoped for from the Pope, and sent an express to inform his Holiness of it. Sixtus wrote immediately to all the Catholic cantons, and assured them, he would send both men and money to their assistance, if there should be occasion, exhorting them to continue steady in the Catholic faith, and promised, upon the word of a Pope, that he would never abandon them.

Some days afterwards, 14,000 of the Swiss Catholics engaged in the service of the league, at the request of the king of France; the Nuncio who endeavoured to make himself a party in all public transactions, caused these troops to be drawn up before their departure, and gave them the sacrament with his own hand; he also made them swear upon the Holy Evangelists, which he tendered to them, that they would never fight but for the interest of the Catholic religion, and that if the king should at any time join with the Protestants, they would immediately lay down their arms, and return home.

These proceedings of the Nuncio, which were extremely agreeable to the court of Rome, were followed by another attempt, equally remarkable, to extend his authority. The canton of Lucerne, after the time of harvest, claimed a large quantity of grain from the canons of Brone, contrary to the especial edicts and decrees of the Pope, which forbid the laity to make any demand of that kind from the clergy, as it would be usurping a power over them, that he had expressly commanded them not to acknowledge: the Nuncio, piqued at this demand, enjoined the canons not to comply with the summons of the secular magistrate, or own their authority, and threatned, in case of disobedience, not only to write to Rome, but immediately excommunicate them.

Upon this occasion, the Protestants did not fail to represent to them, " How much their honour was con- " cerned, nay, that their very independence and liber-

" ties

"berties were at stake; and that if they acknowledged
"the nuncio's jurisdiction, instead of being sovereigns,
"they would soon become slaves."

The nuncio, who was acquainted with these endeavours of the Protestants to embroil the canton of Lucerne with the court of Rome, used every artifice to
make their instigations of no effect. For this purpose,
he called together all the principal inhabitants of the
canton in the great church, without letting them know
the occasion of it, and as soon as they were assembled
exposed the holy sacrament, amidst a great number
of lighted candles, upon the high altar, on the left
hand of which he stood, accompanied by three Jesuits,
and made a discourse, in which he represented to them,
with much vehemence, the reasons he had to complain
of them, omitting no argument that he thought could
move them to repent, and acknowledge their fault.

This harangue delivered in so pathetic a manner,
had such an effect upon them, that they expressed a
great deal of concern for what they had done, and
swore solemnly never more to make any demnd upon
the canons of Brone. Before they went out of the
church, the nuncio prevailed upon them to sign an
instrument drawn up to the same purpose, which he immediately sent to Rome. Many of them publicly asked
his pardon, and said, "They had been put upon it
"by the Protestants."

After the difference occasioned by the change of
nuncio's, betwixt the Pope and K. of France was
composed, as we have related, the K. wrote to the
Pope to desire his leave to levy 100,000 crowns upon
his clergy, assuring him he would employ it to the extirpation of Hugonots, who daily encreased in his kingdom. He likewise entreated the nuncio, who saw the
distress he was in, to represent it to his Holiness; and
Pisani delivered memorials every day at Rome to the
same effect, urging him, in the most pressing manner,
not to refuse his master this favour, as there were so
many strong and just reasons for granting it.

The

The Pope was not willing either to grant or deny this request, but answered according to the custom of that court, when they have not a mind to give their consent to any thing that is asked of them, " We shall " see; we shall consider of it [15];" which in effect, is the same as an absolute denial. Pisani understood this sort of language pretty well, and sent word of it to the court of France; from whence the King and his ministers perceived that the Duke of Guise and the league had been persuading the Pope not to comply with it; and seeing himself without money, ready to be crushed betwixt the two factions of the league and the Hugonots, thought it would be no bad expedient to enter into a treaty with the latter, the management of which he left to the Queen mother, who concluded it with them, upon the following conditions, viz. " That " the town of Marans should remain neutral for the " benefit of both parties; that the K. of Navarre " should appoint a governor of his own religion; " that the garrison, should be one half Catholics, and " the other Proteftants; and that the King should re- " tire with his troops to the further side of the " Charante:" With some other articles, very advantageous to the Hugonots.

The league and the Parisians were terribly alarmed at this treaty, but above all the Duke of Guise, who sent an express to Rome, wrote with his own hand, in which he said, " That the interests of religion were " betrayed in France; that the Hugonots were openly " favoured, as appeared by stopping the course of the " war, which must of necessity have been very soon " ended, to the honour of the holy league; that the " King was plainly estranged and alienated from the " Catholic cause, and used all means to cherish and " support heresy in the kingdom."

Tho' the king so carefully concealed his designs, that nobody was able to penetrate into them, this treaty

[15] *Vederemo, diremo, faremo sopra cio refleffione.*

with

with the Hugonots gave people occafion to harbour fentiments, not at all to his advantage, and fo encreafed
the Duke of Guife's fufpicions, who was very difcerning and quick-fighted, that he thought himfelf obliged
to fend an account of it to Sixtus.

As foon as it was known at Rome, the Pope fent for
the French ambaffador, and made heavy complaints of
his mafter's behaviour, with many reproaches, and
treated him as a Heretic. After this he called a confiftory, in which he fpoke of that prince with the
higheft refentment, and declaimed in a moft furious
manner, againft the treaty which he had made with
the K. of Navarre, whom he had fo lately excommunicated. He fent orders at the fame time to his nuncio in France, to go in his name to the King, and tell
him, " That he would never forget the grievous affront
" he had offered to him and the H. See, and that he
" found it impoffible not to refent it."

The nuncio, who, at the Duke of Guife's folicitation, had already made his complaints to the King,
before he received the Pope's orders, had nothing further to add upon that head ; however, he thought proper to renew his inftances; and to give them the greater weight, went with the Pope's letter to his majefty.

The King anfwered the nuncio's reproaches with
fome fharpnefs, tho' he was naturally of a very mild
and gentle difpofition, and faid, " That having per-
" ceived the obftinacy and unwillingnefs of the clergy
" in his kingdom, to contribute like faithful and loy-
" al fubjects, to the immenfe expences of the war,
" and the difficulty which the court of Rome made of
" granting him a power to levy the infignificant fum
" of 100,000 crowns upon them, he thought he
" might liften to the propofals of peace that were made
" to him, without doing violence to his confcience, or
" acting in a manner unworthy of a Chriftian prince,
" in procuring the peace of his people, after they had
" been fo long and fo cruelly harraffed by the mi-
" feries of a civil war : That it was a very fine thing
                                                " indeed

" indeed for his Holinefs to fit down at a diftance,
" and regulate the affairs of his kingdom by letters
" and meffages; and that it was the duty of a good
" fhepherd to watch over his flock himfelf, to be al-
" ways prefent with them, to be anxious for their
" fafety, and to relieve their wants, and not to abandon
" them to the careleffnefs and negligence of ftrangers
" and hirelings."

The nuncio replied, " That the only way to efta-
" blifh a firm and lafting peace in his kingdom, was
" to pluck up herefy by the roots, to prevent it ever
" fprouting again; that the falvation of his foul was
" to be confidered before all the advantages of this
" world; that the only intention of the war, under-
" taken by the league, was to give repofe to the
" kingdom; that the king of Navarre, and the prince
" of Conde, being both excommunicated, would not
" be able to hold out long." To mollify the King a
little, and to diffuade him from putting the laft hand
to this treaty, he added, " That fome of the prelates
" of his kingdom, had never refufed to contribute to-
" wards the expences of the war, and that others
" would be more fubmiffive for the future." And concluded with faying, " That he durft take upon him
" to affirm, he might depend upon his requeft being
" granted by the court of Rome; that his Holinefs
" feemed well difpofed to it, and that nothing was
" wanting to accomplifh it, but a proper behaviour
" and complaifance."

When the King found the nuncio began to talk in
terms of more refpect, he likewife, on his fide, feemed
to moderate his refentment, and told him, in a very
civil manner, " That to free himfelf from that inun-
" dation of foreigners, with which his kingdom was
" then overwhelmed, it was abfolutely neceffary to
" temporize a little, and accommodate himfelf to the
" prefent circumftances of affairs:" Conjuring him to
affure his Holinefs, " That he would never do any
" thing prejudicial to the interefts of the Catholic
                                        " religion

" religion, the honour of the Holy See, or the peace
" of his own confcience." With which declaration
the nuncio was highly pleafed, and fent an immediate
account of it to the Pope.

The ambaffadors of the Proteftant German princes
arrived at Paris at this juncture, to treat in favour of
the Hugonots, with orders to make remonftrances upon
feveral heads, which all centered in complaining, " Of
" the King's not keeping his word ; the infraction of
" feveral declarations, in which he had promifed and
" fworn to grant liberty of confcience to his Proteftant
" fubjects, and faying they were perfuaded he had
" done it out of complaifance to the Pope, whofe in-
" fatiable ambition and thirft of Chriftian blood made
" him unworthy of his name and office, or to have any
" refpect fhewn him by other princes.

They concluded their difcourfe in a menacing fort
of a manner, and gave him to underftand, " That if
" he continued to follow the counfels of Rome, their
" mafters, united with the Proteftants by the ties of
" birth, intereft, and religion, would certainly declare
" in favour of thofe in France.'

The King, jealous of his authority, to the laft degree, was extremely provoked at their infolence ; and
anfwered, " That he held his crown from God alone ;
" that he had power to make laws or publifh ordi-
" nances, and grant fuch favours and privileges, as
" he thought neceffary for the welfare of his fubjects ;
" that he was entirely at liberty to alter or abrogate
" them, whenever he judged proper, according to the
" infpirations of the Almighty." And, to their great
furprize, faid many things in juftification of the Pope,
againft the complaints they had made of him.

They defired he would give them his anfwer in
writing ; but he refufed it, and faid, " He could not
" fufficiently wonder at their pretending to bufy them-
" felves in the affairs of his kingdom." And without
granting them any other audience, difmiffed them the
next day, very much diffatisfied and difcontented.

The

The same day the nuncio had an audience of his majesty, who acquainted him with every thing that had passed betwixt him and the German ambassadors, of which he sent immediate advice to Rome. His Holiness was extremely pleased with a behaviour so obliging and full of respect to himself and the H. See ; and instantly ordered a brief to be drawn up, giving him power to raise the 100,000 crowns, to which he added 20,000 more than the King had asked, to shew how much he approved of his conduct ; and commanded the nuncio to oblige the clergy to pay it immediately, without delay or remonstrance.

It is not to be imagined what indefatigable pains Sixtus took to aggrandize the H. See, and to encrease the splendour and majesty of it in the eyes of the world. He thought. it below the character and dignity of the Apostolic nuncios, when they were sent to other courts, to live in hired houses, and liable to be turned out at the caprice or disgust of the owner. To avoid this, he designed to purchase a palace, suitable to their rank, in every place where they resided, which should be their constant habitation for the future. With this view he gave them orders at their respective courts, to fix upon places proper for that purpose, and said he would pay for them : desiring all the ambassadors at Rome to write to their masters, and entreat them to assist his nuncios in this affair.

Even the senate of Venice, who are more watchful over the Pope's proceedings than any other state, as soon as they heard of his intention, sent instructions to their ambassador at Rome, to assure his Holiness, the republic was so well disposed to second his endeavours, that they would make a present to the Holy See of a palace, for the constant residence of his nuncio at Venice, and appointed a very magnificent one in the Piazza delle Vigne, for Jerome Mattenci, who was nuncio there at that time, causing an instrument to be drawn up, which they signed and sealed, acknowledging that palace for the future belonged to the See

of

of Rome, and sent a counter-part of it to his Holiness, after which the nuncio was put in possession of it with the usual ceremonies.

When Sixtus received an account of this piece of generosity in the Venetians, he returned his thanks, in person, to their ambassador, and ordered his nuncio to do the same to the senate; and not being willing to be out-done by them, in point of munificence, presented the senate with a noble palace at Rome, which is now called St. Mark's, for the perpetual residence of their ambassadors, an edifice large enough for the reception of an emperor.

This design did not succeed so well in other courts; and was either opposed for reasons of state, or prevented by contingencies, which hindered most of his nuncios from appropriating such houses to themselves. Some say, that the vast expence attending such a number of purchases, occasioned Sixtus to give it up. But it is not likely that he, who never abandoned any scheme, but what was absolutely impossible, let the expence be never so great, and whose ambition had filled Rome and the Ecclesiastical state with obelisks, palaces, aqueducts, bridges, hospitals, and innumerable other most sumptuous fabrics and ornaments, would neglect so fair an opportunity of rendering the grandeur of the H. See, and the glory of his name, immortal, in all the considerable cities of Europe.

It is said by some, that, when other princes heard of the exchange betwixt him and the republic of Venice, they offered to do the same, but that Sixtus thought there were not palaces enough vacant, or to be procured for that purpose. Perhaps he was apprehensive, too, that it might occasion envy and jealousy amongst them, as it was likely every one would endeavour to procure a palace in the best and most commodious part of the city, which would give rise to frequent disputes about rank and precedence; and instead of contributing, as his intention was, to establish unity and concord amongst the powers of Christendom, would

involve

involve them in everlafting ftrife and contention.
What determined Sixtus, moft likely, was the fear of
leffening his own authority in Rome, by fubjecting fo
many noble palaces to the jurifdiction of foreign
princes, who feeing themfelves eftablifhed, by long
poffeffion, in the enjoyment of them, might probably
fortify, or make them places of arms, to the great
difturbance of the public peace, and perhaps danger
of the city. However, before he died, he bought
palaces in many cities for the refidence of the nuncios.

Philip II. of Spain was, at this time, fetting all engines at work, to prevail upon the Pope to unite the
Catholic powers in a fort of crufade, or league, a-
gainft Q. Elizabeth of England, whofe view was, as he
faid, totally to extirpate the true religion. Sixtus, who
defired nothing more than to engage the K. of Spain
in a tedious and expenfive war, in order to weaken or
divert him in fuch a manner, as might prevent him
fending any fuccour to the relief of Naples, which he
intended to invade, whenever a convenient opportunity
offered, was, however, a little at a lofs what to refolve
upon, as he was defirous Philip fhould ftill keep up his
inveterate hatred againft England; and, on the other
hand, did not care to fee him become too powerful, by
the affiftance of many allies, left it fhould terrify the
Q. of England, and put her upon feeking a reconciliation, at any rate, with fo formidable an adverfary.

He intended, at firft, to make heavy complaints
againft K. Philip at all the courts in Europe, for having
concluded a treaty with the Turk, in which it was mu-
tually ftipulated betwixt the Porte and the houfe of
Auftria, not to offend or annoy each other at any time,
or upon any pretence whatfoever: An action unworthy
of a king, who bore the title of Catholic, and defender of the H. See. But he altered his refolution:
and, contrary to his ufual practice, (which was to take
all opportunities of raifing a clamour) pretended not
to know any thing of it, or at leaft to connive at it,
whilft

whilft he fecretly fpirited up Elizabeth, by the means of Carr (with whom he ordered his nephew to corref-pond) to fpare no expence to fet the Turk upon the houfe of Auftria, either in Hungary or Sicily, whilft fhe attacked them in the low countries.

If Elizabeth had the character of a fubtle and in-triguing princefs, Sixtus deferved it no lefs, confidering the many ftratagems and fineffes he made ufe of to draw both Elizabeth and Philip into his fnare. He thought, by ftirring up the former againft the latter, he fhould plunge her into an expence that would gall her fubjects to fuch a degree, as perhaps would occa-fion a rebellion, or at leaft oblige her to defift from perfecuting the Catholics; and, on the other hand, by whetting up Philip againft Elizabeth, he fhould make him fpend all his force in Flanders and England, and fo thoroughly entangle him in a hot war with thofe two powers, that being drained both of men and mo-ney, it would be impoffible for him to oppofe the de-figns he meditated againft him: For that purpofe, he extolled Philip's piety and zeal for religion to the fkies, admiring his greatnefs of mind; and told him, what a ftain it would be upon his glory, if he fuffered a wo-man, a weak as well as impudent and wicked woman, to fupport or protect his rebellious fubjects; a woman that was not content with withdrawing her allegiance from the H. See, but took upon her to incite others to rebel againft a monarch, whom no other potentate up-on earth durft prefume to treat after that manner. In fhort, there was no offer, no promife, nor perfuafion, nor argument, nor adulation of any kind, which he did not make ufe of to induce him to exert his utmoft ftrength to diftrefs Elizabeth, at the fame time that he acquainted her with the defigns of Philip, informing her of the ftrength and number of his forces, what places were to be attacked; reprefenting to her, "That " it was abfolutely neceffary, nay, her indifpenfable " duty and intereft, to pull down that Coloffus, to " humble

" humble that haughty and overgrown tyrant that
" kept the world in terror; that only to enter the lifts
" with him would make her name glorious, but im-
" mortal if fhe got the better of him, as fhe certainly
" would, provided fhe drew het fword in earneft; that
" fhe was the only power in Europe that was capable
" of undertaking it; and that the antient and well-
" known valour of the Englifh nation, conducted by
" a princefs of her confummate wifdom and prudence,
" could not fail of fuccefs."

Elizabeth, who had always been afraid the Pope was
contriving fome mifchief againft her, being now convinced that there was no danger to be apprehended
from that quarter, began to behave very haughtily
to Philip, and think in earneft of making war upon
him.

On the other hand, Philip being thus encouraged by
the Pope, and fpurred on by revenge, and other political motives, fent orders to all his fea-ports to fill
their magazines with arms, ammunition, and provifions, and to labour day and night to get a powerful
fleet ready with all expedition, to lift and difcipline
foldiers, and to make all manner of warlike preparations throughout the whole kingdom, writing a letter
to the emperor, to defire he would affift him with fome
forces; and another very refpectable one to his Holinefs,
to entreat his blefling upon the expedition.

When the Pope received this letter, wrote with the
king's own hand, from the ambaffador, he read it in
his prefence, and feemed wonderfully pleafed with the
zeal and pious refolution of his mafter; but immediately fent a copy of it to Carr, who was to communicate it to the Queen, with advice, " Not to let her
" courage fail, but put the kingdom in a proper ftate
" of defence, and be ready to receive him: that it
" was more than probable this expedition would at
" leaft prove fruitlefs, if not prejudicial to the K. of
" Spain."

The

The Queen thought this advice too good to be neglected; and, it is certain, if she had not received it in time (tho' no kingdom in the world is so powerful in shipping as England) she could not have fitted out a fleet that would have been able to keep the seas against him.

Whilst Philip was making these open preparations for an invasion, he likewise endeavoured to promote his designs, by fomenting plots and conspiracies in England. Several of that nation, of whom Anthony Babington was the chief, engaged in a conspiracy to assassinate the Queen, whom they were to pistol, the first time they met her, either on horseback, or in her coach, and immediately shout, *long live our Queen,* Mary of Scotland; who was to have been taken out of the prison where she was, and set upon the throne. It is said, this conspiracy was hatched at Paris, in the duke of Guise's lodgings, with the assistance of his brother the cardinal, and the two ambassadors of Spain, who, in their master's name, promised great rewards to all the conspirators, particularly to Babington. It would not have been difficult to put it in execution, as there were several persons of distinction concerned in it, and numbers of Catholics ready to take arms: But, providentially for Elizabeth, their hearts failed them when they came to the point, and the whole was discovered. Babington, and three others, had desired the cardinal to procure them an absolution from the Pope in articulo mortis, in case they did not succeed in their undertaking, which the Pope granted; and as they say, sent an immediate account of it to Carr, with advice to the Queen, to take proper care of herself.

The Protestants, who think the Jesuits have a hand in every thing, did not scruple to charge them with being the authors of the plot; which suspicion, perhaps, might arise, from most of the conspirators having been educated under these fathers. It is certain, the education of youth, which is almost wholly engrossed by that order, has given them great power and

credit

credit in the world For, as many of their pupils come afterwards to be prelates, and nobles, and princes, and fill all the dignities and offices about courts, it is eafy, by their means, to become refpectable, and infinuate themfelves into the fecrets and management of affairs; and indeed there has hardly been any Pope or cardinal in our times, who was not their difciple.

There happened a ftrange adventure at Rome towards the end of this year [1586]. As the Pope was going one day to his devotions, there was, according to cuftom, fo great a crowd to fee him, that no body could pafs, which obliged the Swifs guards, that always attend upon his holinefs when he ftirs out, to make way with their halberds. There was, unluckily, amongft the crowd, a Spanifh gentleman, lately arrived at Rome, with his uncle, who was a learned and eminent divine. This unfortunate perfon being one of the foremoft, was pufhed back a little roughly by one of the guards, with the ftaff of his halberd, which he thought fo great an affront, that he vowed revenge. The poor Swifs going one day foon after to mafs at St. Peter's, had quite forgot the affair, when the Spaniard, who juft came in, perceiving him upon his knees before the altar, thought it a proper opportunity to gratify his refentment ; and taking up a pilgrim's ftaff, that was reared againft one of the pillars, gave him fo violent a ftroke upon the head, that he immediately dropped down dead, without fpeaking a word. The murderer endeavoured to make his efcape, by flying to the Spanifh ambaffador's houfe, who had a friendfhip for him upon his uncle's account, but was ftopped by two other Swifs, that were witneffes of the fact.

When Sixtus heard of it, he was extremely enraged, and faid, " We thought our character had been too " well known for any one to prefume to commit fo " flagrant an action ; but, if it is not, we will foon " make it :" And immediately fent for the governor of the city, who having been informed of the tranfaction, was already come on foot to enquire into it,

to

to shew his zeal and diligence in the execution of his office.　As soon as he appeared, the Pope accosted him in this manner: " Well, Sir, What do you think of " a murder committed in the house of God, and al- " most before our face ? It is your business to see that " strict justice be done directly, and a proper punish- " ment inflicted upon the offender, for so daring an " insult upon our authority." The governor answered, " He had given orders, as he came into the palace, to " have informations taken, and a process to be com- " menced against him speedily." A process !" said Sixtus, "What occasion is there for a process in such " a case as this?" The governor happening to say, " That he thought it had been necessary to observe the " usual forms of the law, as the criminal was nephew " to a person of consideration, and under the protec- " tion of his Catholic majesty's ambassador :" The Pope answered, in a very furious manner, " Don't talk " to us of forms and ceremonies ; It is our pleasure " that he shall be hanged before we sit down to dinner, " and we intend to dine early to day, being somewhat " hungry."

As soon as the governor knew his Holiness's plea- sure, he immediately gave directions to hasten the exe- cution ; and, as he went out, the Pope ordered him to have the gallows erected in some place where he him- self could see him hanged out of his window. The governor took this as an order for instant execution, and directed the gallows to be set up in the piazza of St. Peter's, over-against his apartment, whilst he was trying him. His trial, indeed, was not a very long one, as there were not above four hours and a half be- twixt the fact and the execution ; during which time, the Pope did nothing but fume and stamp about the room, looking out every minute, to see whether they were bringing him to be hanged.

The ambassador of Spain, and four cardinals of that nation, waited upon his Holiness, not to ask his life, for they knew that it was to no purpose, but to

　　　　　desire

defire "his punifhment might be changed into behead-
" ing, as he was a gentleman, out of regard to the
" honour of his family, and that of the whole nation."

But the Pope faid fternly to the ambaffador, who
was moft earneft in it, "A crime of fuch a nature muft
" be punifhed by a halter; and we fhould difhonour
" ourfelves, and you too, if we granted what you afk;
" neverthelefs, we fhall fhew you fome favour, and
" take care that the reputation of hi*family does not
" fuffer, by the honour we fhall do him in being a
" witnefs of his execution." And, indeed, he never
ftirred from the window, till he faw him quite dead;
and then, turning round to thofe that were in the room
with him, faid, "Let them ferve up dinner, we fhall
" eat heartily now; this piece of juftice has ferved
" for a whet to our appetite."

Whilft dinner was coming up, he entertained the
company with a difcourfe concerning the neceffity of
prompt juftice in fuch cafes, and feemed much pleafed
at his morning's work; repeating, with marks of great
fatisfaction, that paffage in the Pfalms, *I fhall foon deftroy all the ungodly that are in the land, that I may root
out all the wicked doers from the city of the Lord.* After
dinner was over, he faid grace himfelf; and rifing
from the table, added, "Thanks be to God, we have
" eat very heartily to day."

Early next morning Pafquin appeared, with a large
difh full of gibbets, wheels, axes, chains, and other
inftruments of death and torture in his hand; and being afked by Marfario, *Whither he was carrying them?*
Anfwered, *To the Pope, for a whet, to get his Holinefs an
appetite to his dinner.*

I believe we may venture to fay, this was the firft
inftance of a murder committed, the criminal apprehended, the witneffes examined, a procefs finifhed,
fentence of death pronounced, and executed in lefs
than five hours. He feemed to pride himfelf much upon the terror fuch an example had ftruck into the people, and the firmnefs he had fhewn in refufing to
change

change the punifhment, though the Spanifh ambaffador
had afked it in his mafter's name.   It occafioned all the
other foreign minifters to charge their followers and
dependents, to take particular care of their conduct,
for fear " of falling in the Pope's hands, from whom
" they muft expect no quarter;" which had fo good
an effect upon them, that the domeftics of ambaffadors never behaved themfelves fo well as in the time
of Sixtus.   It was his intention, that all due reverence
and refpect fhould be paid to their mafters, but he declared, " He would not fuffer the infolent and licentious
" manner they behaved in during the reign of his pre-
" deceffor:"   nay, he went further, and commanded
the Provoft Marfhal, " if any criminal took refuge in
" the palace of a cardinal, to go and apprehend him,
" without any confideration, or refpect of perfons, and
" let them oppofe him that durft.

This year died Philip Buon Compagnon, nephew to
the late Pope, of a malignant fever, after a few days
illnefs.   Neither his youth (being but 38 years old)
nor the ftrength of his conftitution, confirmed by the
moft temperate courfe of life, could refift the fury of
the difeafe.   The Pope went to fee him twice whilft
he lay ill.   It was commonly believed, that he paid him
the firft vifit out of the great friendfhip and efteem he
had for him;   but others, who pretended to know the
Pope better, faid it was to draw out of him the fecret
of fome important affairs, that had been tranfacted in
the pontificate of his uncle;   thinking this a proper
opportunity of extorting from him, what he had often
in vain attempted to come at the knowledge of, whilft
he was in health, and for this purpofe ftaid with him
above half an hour: the fecond vifit he paid him
when he lay in his laft agonies, to give him his benediction (according to cuftom) in the article of death.

This cardinal left an an immenfe fum of money to his
relations, and the richeft furniture in Rome, with feveral legacies to the Pope, his nephew, and other
cardinals ;

cardinals; but little or nothing to his fervants and domeftics.

The office of Grand Penitentiary [6], conferred upon
him by Gregory, was vacant by his death : as it is a
poft of the higheft truft and confideration, it was the
general opinion the Pope would give it to his nephew,
and appoint a vice-penitentiary to exercife the functions of it, till he fhould be of years and experience
enough to fill it himfelf : but Sixtus had a mind to let
the world fee, that in the difpofal of places of fuch
importance, he had no regard to kindred or relation,
but to merit alone; and beftowed it upon cardinal
Aldobrandino, a perfon of the higheft virtue and wifdom, as a reward for the many fignal fervices he had
done the church, in the feveral employments he had
worthily difcharged. The whole court rejoiced at it,
and expreffed their approbation of fo juft a choice.
The cardinal dean faid, in a full confiftory, " That
" he fincerely wifhed, and prayed to God, that all the
" fucceffors of his holinefs would fhew the fame re-
" gard to merit as he had done, in the choice of per-
" fons to fill places of that confequence.

On Chriftmas eve, there happened an event which
made the name of Sixtus ftill more terrible : he had
a mind to celebrate mafs himfelf (as is ufual) at mid-
night, in St. Peter's, and was carried to the gates of
the church incog. in a fedan chair, where he was received
by the canons, with the cuftomary form and folemnity.
Immediately upon his arrival there, a woman ftepped

[16] The Chief, or Grand Penitentiary, is always a cardinal,
and has the power of regulating all affairs relating to confeffors
and confeffions. He fits, with great folemnity, fometimes in one,
and fometimes in another of the three cathedral churches, viz.
St. John de Lateran, St. Peter, and St. Maria Maggiore, upon a
feat, to which he afcends by three or four fteps, in the form of a
tribunal, with a ftaff of office in his hand, to hear confeffions,
and grant abfolutions in referved cafes. His congregation confifts
of the prelate that keeps the feal, and two or three other divines,
who are commonly Jefuits, and one canonift. He has feveral offices under him that are vendible, and the profit arifing from the
fale belongs to him.

forwards

forwards out of the crowd, and threw herſelf at his feet, crying, " Juſtice, holy father, juſtice. Let me " beſeech you, who are a righteous judge, to cauſe " my poor daughter, the comfort of my old age, that " has been carried off by violence about two hours " ago, to be reſtored to me." The agony ſhe ſeemed to be in, and the tears which ran down her cheeks, ſo moved his holineſs, that he did not ſtay to hear the particulars of her ſtory, but ſending directly for the governor, ſaid to him, " We are going to pay our de- " voirs to God, go you, and pay yours to juſtice: " enquire into this affair, and let me have an account " of it before day-light."

The governor learned, from her examination, that the woman was the widow of a captain, that former-ly belonged to the garriſon of St. Angelo, by whom ſhe had a very beautiful daughter; that one Pignoni, a baſ-tard of a Neapolitan gentleman, of that noble family, falling deſperately in love with her, had with the aſ-ſiſtance of another perſon, forcibly carried her off, af-ter he had obtained admiſſion into the houſe by knock-ing at the door, and deſiring to light a candle.

Early in the morning, there was publiſhed a moſt ri-gorous edict, commanding every body to uſe their endeavours to bring two ſuch notorious offenders to juſ-tice, promiſing a reward to any one that would diſco-ver them, and threatning thoſe with the ſevereſt puniſh-ment, that ſhould dare to harbour or conceal them. In ſhort, they were both apprehended before night, and the governor himſelf went to acquaint Sixtus with it, who expected him with the utmoſt impatience: when he had heard the particulars of his report, he walked briſkly about his apartment, and ſaid, " If it " was not too late, they ſhould be hanged to day." " It is not poſſible, holy father," anſwered the gover-nor, " that they ſhould be either executed or tried this " week, as it is the time of Chriſtmas holidays." " Chriſtmas holidays!" replied the Pope, in a contemp-tuous tone, " It is a ſhame, ſir, that a governor of
                                                    Rome

" Rome fhould not underſtand his duty better : what!
" fhall two wretches dare to profane ſo holy a night
" with the rape of a virgin, in contempt of our au-
" thority, and the judges make a ſcruple of putting
" them to death, becauſe, forſooth, it is Chriſtmas ho-
" lidays?" With this compliment he diſmiſſed the
governor ; but perceiving him a good deal perplexed,
and confuſed, he called him back again, and ſaid,
" Pray, good ſir, be pleaſed to lay aſide your ridicu-
" lous, nonfenſical qualms, and believe us upon our
" authority, when we tell you, that the puniſhment
" of the wicked, is an acceptable ſacrifice to God."

There was no occaſion to ſay any thing farther ; ſentence was paſſed the next morning, " That the houſe
" where the rape was committed, fhould be demoliſhed,
" and the owner of it ſatisfied out of the city cham-
" ber ; that a gallows fhould be erected upon the ruins,
" on which the two criminals fhould be hanged, and
" their goods appropriated to the uſe of the young
" woman." They were accordingly executed the ſame
day, which was St. Stephen's, to the great horror and
conſternation of the whole city.

The ſame night Andrew Marra, a prieſt, had his
houſe robbed whilſt he was ſaying maſs in the church
of St. Maria Maggiore ; and as the laws were ſo ſevere
againſt thoſe that knew of any offences, and did not
diſcover them, he went directly, and reported it to the
lieutenant criminal, and ſaid, " He had ſome ſuſpi-
" cion of a woman that uſed to come and affiſt an
" old ſervant of his, when ſhe had any extraordinary
" buſineſs to do." The Pope, hearing this, was not
a little mortified, as he had taken ſuch pains to make
people honeſt, and been remarkably ſevere upon
thieves of all ſorts ; for which reaſon he ordered the
governor to uſe all poſſible means to find out the perſons that had committed the robbery ; which he did in
a few days, and apprehended the woman at Orvieto,
whither ſhe had fled, with a corporal of the archers,

who

who was an accomplice in the theft, and promifed to marry her.

In the mean time, the prieft (confcious of his guilt) hearing the woman was taken, and afraid his crime would be made public, began to fell off his goods, with a defign to abfcond ; which the magiftrates being aware of, took him up, and fent him and the old woman, his fervant, to prifon ; when the archer, and the other woman came to Rome, they, together with the prieft and his fervant, were brought to an examination ; from whence it appeared, that fhe had been the prieft's concubine above a year ; that the old woman, who was her relation, had acted as a bawd, and brought her, from time to time, fecretly into the houfe. Not long before, fhe had an opportunity of being married to this archer, and afked the prieft's confent ; but he, it feems, could not fpare her ; which put her upon making an efcape from him.   She confeffed, with tears in her eyes, that fhe was determined to marry, for two reafons ; the firft was, to deliver herfelf out of that finful courfe of life which fhe led with the prieft, as it often gave her a great deal of uneafinefs and remorfe.   The other was, that being informed of the fevere laws, which the pope had made againft priefts keeping concubinnes, fhe trembled every moment at the thoughts of being detected, and becoming liable to the penalties therein fpecified ; and thought herfelf obliged to make it known, efpecially, as fhe had often, in vain, entreated the prieft to difmifs her, that they might both exonerate their confciences, and avoid falling into the hands of a pope, that fpared nobody.

She further frankly confeffed, fhe had often defired the old woman to intercede with him, and procure her that liberty, which fhe refufed, upon many confiderations ; but chiefly, as fhe fuppofed, becaufe fhe found her account in it: So that the prieft having 100 crowns of her's in his hands, and keeping her clothes locked up, fhe was perfuaded by the corporal to take this method of paying herfelf, without any defign to

rob

rob or defraud him of the leaft thing that was his, or take more than was due to her, tho' fhe had never received any thing for her fervices to the prieft, more than bare promifes.

After the Pope had heard the whole, he fent to tell the governor, "That if he was judge, he knew what "fentence he fhould pronounce upon fuch crimes;" which he took as a hint not to pafs a very mild one, and condemned the prieft to be deprived of his benefice, and imprifoned for life ; the old woman to be whipped; the archer and the concubine to be hanged for the robbery : But Sixtus was not pleafed with this, and complained of the governor for loading the city chamber with the expence of maintaining thofe two perfons in prifon. The governor anfwered, "He was "not willing to inflict a more ignominious punifhment "upon the prieft, as it would be matter of concern "to the Catholics, and derifion to the Heretics." Sixtus replied, "That, on the contrary, it was the "true way to edify both the one and the other." The fentence, however, was changed, and the prieft fent to the gallies for keeping a concubine, and not fuffering her, *To turn away from her wickednefs, and fave her foul alive*. The concubine was condemned to be whipped once a month, for three months, thro' the city, and then banifhed for ever. The corporal and the bawd, who had been the contriver of this iniquitous fcene, were hanged, tho' fhe was 56 years old; all the archers marched two by two before their brother. The gardener, and a niece of the old woman, who were often in the houfe, and knew of the affair, were feverely whipped for not difcovering it.

It was not long before he renewed the fears of the people by a frefh inftance of his feverity. Pafquin was dreffed one morning in a very nafty fhirt; and being afked by Marforio. *Why he wore fuch dirty linen?* anfwered, *He could get no other, for the Pope had made his wafher-woman a princefs.* Meaning Donna Camilla, the Pope's fifter, who had formerly been a laundrefs.

This

This ftinging piece of raillery was carried directly to his Holinefs, who ordered a ftrict fearch to be made for the author, but to no purpofe. Upon which he ftuck up printed papers in all the public places of the city, promifing upon the word of a Pope, to give the author of the pafquinade 1000 piftoles and his life, provided he would difcover himfelf, but threatened to hang him, if he was found out by any one elfe, and offered the 1000 piftoles to the informer.

The author of it, tho' he had trufted no other perfon with the fecret, was fo tempted with the promife of a thoufand piftoles, that he was fimple enough to go and make a full confeffion of it to the Pope, demanding the money, and to have his life fpared. Sixtus was fo aftonifhed at his folly and impudence, that he could not fpeak for fome time, and at laft faid, " It " is true, we did make fuch a promife, and we fhall " not be worfe than our word : We give you your " life, and you fhall have the money immediately ;" ordering the 1000 piftoles to be inftantly paid him down.

When he had received the money, Sixtus afked him " If he he was fatisfied," and he anfwering, " that he " was," Sixtus faid, " We promifed you your life and " 1000 piftoles; you have received both, and fay you " are fatisfied : But we referved to ourfelves the power " of cutting off your hands, and boring your tongue " thro', to prevent your being fo witty for the future ;" which was directly executed. Sixtus declaring, " that " he did not deferve the punifhment fo much for the " pafquinade, as for being fo audacious to avow it." The novelty of the fentence filled every one with terror and amazement, efpecially as it was foon followed by another equally remarkable.

Charles Matera, a Neapolitan poet, who lived at that time in Rome, had publifhed a fmall book of poems, in compliment to fome ladies; amongft whom there was one whofe name was Ifabella, a woman of unfpotted character, and the wife of an advocate, with whom

he

he had lately had a quarrel. After he had faid a great many fine things of her in the firft lines of every ftanza, he always concluded after this manner :

But Ifabella *is a whore:*

Thefe being handed about the town, a copy of them fell into the hands of the advocate, and he carried it ftraight to the Pope, who gave immediate orders to the provoft marfhal to apprehend and bring Matera before him ; as he had a mind to interrogate him himfelf, and know the truth of the accufation from his own mouth. The advocate, who was afraid Matera would runaway, and he fhould lofe his revenge, made fo diligent a fearch after him, that he was arrefted that day. When he faw himfelf furrounded by the archers, and hurried away to the vatican, he was ftrangely furprized, being quite ignorant of the caufe, tho' he began to fufpect it, upon fight of the advocate amongft the archers. When he came before the Pope, who had the verfes in his hand, being afked by him, whether he was the author of them, he ingenuoufly confeffed he was ; either expecting to meet with fome favour, for fpeaking the truth, or becaufe he knew it was in vain to deny it, as there was fufficient proof againft him. Sixtus then ordered him to read the verfes himfelf : and when he came to the line that reflected upon Ifabella, he made him repeat it twice, afking, " What had provoked him to take fuch liberties " with the reputation of a modeft woman ?" To which he anfwered, " I folemnly proteft and fwear to " you moft holy father, that I had not the leaft in- " tention to wound the fame of this lady ; and if " there is any thing that feems abufive or reflecting " upon her, in my verfes, it is merely poetical li- " cence. Your holinefs, 1 am fure, very well knows, " that there is nothing fo firmly eftablifhed, and fo ge- " nerally allowed in the world, as the liberty that has " ever been taken by painters and poets : And " you will pleafe to take notice, moft holy father,
" that

" that the word FONTANA, which ends the laſt verſe
" but one of every ſtanza, puts me under a neceſſity,
" for rhyme's ſake, of uſing the word * PUTTANA,
" without any deſign to make the world believe that
" ſhe is really ſo, but to give more grace and beauty
" to the lines, by the richneſs and harmony of the
" rhyme." The ſtanders-by could not help ſmiling
at ſo poor an excuſe, and the gavity with which the
Pope heard him ; who looking ſternly at him, ſaid,
" If poetaſters like you, are allowed ſuch licence,
" ſurely the Pope may expect the ſame indulgence.
" Let us ſee, then, if we can't compoſe a couplet,
" with the aſſiſtance of a little poetical licence :" And
having pauſed a moment or two, he brought forth the
two following lines:

Good Maſter Sing-ſong, for being ſo arch,
Thou ſurely, this day, to the gallies ſhalt march [17].

" Pray, Sir, ſays he, what do you think of our extem-
" pore performance ? How does it ſound in your ear ?
" Are the rhymes rich and full ?" But the poor poet,
half dead, and ready to ſink into the earth with fear,
not being able to make any anſwer, Sixtus ordered him
to be carried away to priſon. The judge criminal,
who was preſent, aſking him, " If he was in earneſt,
" and really deſigned he ſhould be condemned to the
" gallies ;" he anſwered in a great rage, " How dare
" you preſume to aſk ſuch a queſtion ? Can you make
" any ſcruple of paſſing this ſentence upon him ? If
" we leave ſuch an inſolent outrage unpuniſhed, for
" the ridiculous excuſe of poetical licence, ſome im-
" pertiment ſcribbler will, ſhortly take the liberty of

* A whore.

[17] Ital.	*Merita ben queſto Signor Matera*
	D' haver per Stanza propria un' Galera.

Fr.	*Vous meritez Seigneur Matere,*
	De ramer dans une Galere.

" calling

" calling us ourfelves ignominious names, on a pre-
" tence of its being neceffary, for the rhyme and ca-
" dence of the verfe. Is it not right then to prevent
" fuch confequences, by making an example of this
" fellow ?"

The governor finifhed his procefs that day, and condemned him for five years to the gallies, notwithftanding the follicitations of the Urfini family, under whofe
protection he was, and the interceffion of Cardinal
Montalto, to whom he had dedicated a poem upon
the Pope's coronation, which had met with the appre-
bation of many people of tafte, and was faid to have
fome merit.

Notwithftanding the fevere punifhment that the author of the laft pafquinade met with, there foon appeared another. On the Sunday after, Pafquin was reprefented holding a wet fhirt to dry in the fun; and
Marforio afking him, *Why be could not ftay till Monday,
before be dried it ?* He anfwered, *there's no time to lofe;
if I ftay till to-morrow, perbaps I muft pay for the fun-
fhine*; hinting at the taxes that Sixtus had laid upon
all the neceffaries of life, and from which there was
hardly any thing exempt but the light and heat of the
fun. When Sixtus heard of it, he faid, " if we could
" catch the author, we would dry fomething elfe for
" him, befides his fhirt." But, whether he thought
he fhould increafe the number, by punifhing the authors, or that it was better to defpife them, and did
not care to be at the trouble of refenting affronts,
that it was in every body's power to offer him, he gave
no orders to fearch for the author, nor took any farther notice of it: An unufual piece of moderation,
and contrary to the expectation of every body, who
thought to have feen him in great wrath upon this occafion.

Tho' he would not fuffer fuch grofs abufes, and feverely punifhed all manner of calumny, detraction, and
defamatory libels, he was no enemy to delicate raillery, or fatire, that was confined within the bounds of
decency;

decency; and often faid, when he heard of any fmart faying or pafquinade, that was not too fevere, " If the " authors of thefe would make better ufe of their wit, " we would be their friend."

The little notice that was taken of the laft, gave encouragement to feveral others, that made their appearance about this time, which, as we are upon the fubject of pafquinades, it may not be amifs to mention here.

The firft was a pear-tree [18] full of pears, from one of which there was a label hung, with thefe words, *I fhall be four till I drop*; alluding to the harfhnefs and afperity of the Pope's government, and fignifying that he would never grow mellow; that is milder or more gentle, whilft he lived. Marforio attempting to eat one of the pears, Pafquin fays to him, *Take care it does not choak you friend*; to which Marforio anfwered, *So much are we obliged to the cardinals for giving us this choak pear.*

In the fecond, Pafquin was drawn with a belly as big as a tun, and this motto, *I am ready to burft for want of fpeaking*; hinting at the great awe in which Sixtus kept the city, and the feverities he had inflicted upon the authors of pafquinades.

Another very fevere one was ftuck up in feveral parts of the city, on the fame day, taken out of Æfop's fables. It was a picture reprefenting the ftump of a tree, with a papal crown upon it, and a ftork ftanding near it, in pontifical robes, preying upon the Romans, who were fwimming about, like frogs in a pool with this motto coming out of their mouths, *Merito hæc partimur*; *We deferve all this.* The moral of it, I fuppofe, was, that the Romans having looked upon, and treated Gregory as a log of wood, Heaven, in its anger, had fent a ftork to devour them, which was Sixtus. Without queftion his

[18] Pera, in its diminutive Peretta, fignify a pear, in the Italian. Pero and Peretta, a pear-tree.

.government

government was very rigorous, not to call it cruel; but it muſt be conſidered, in his defence, that it did not proceed from paſſion, or revenge, or blood-thirſtineſs, as ſome have ſaid, but from his being forced to it, by the neceſſity of the times; that his deſign (which was a very laudable one) was to reform that general diſorder and licentiouſneſs, which had been introduced by the too great lenity of his predeceſſor. It may be looked upon as a remarkable interpoſition of Providence, that a perſon of his temper and ſpirit ſucceeded Gregory; for if he had not, in all likelihood the Eccleſiaſtical ſtate had been ruined. Wiſe men were ſenſible of this, as was evident from ſeveral pictures and devices that were fixed up in the public places. In one of them, the Eccleſiaſtical ſtate was repreſented by the figure of a man, in a dying condition, full of ulcers and ſores; near him ſtood Sixtus in the habit of a phyſician, with a great number of judges, and governors of provinces and cities, dreſſed in the ſame manner, conſulting what kind of remedies it was moſt proper to adminiſter in this deſperate condition. Sixtus gives his opinion in theſe words: *We muſt open every vein, or he is a dead man.* The patient ſays, Gregory *has brought me to death's door by palliatives*; Sixtus *cures me by inciſion.*

In another, Gregory is pictured in woman's cloaths, with a diſtaff and ſpole in his hand, ſpinning hemp: Near him ſtands Sixtus, with a great number of hangmen and executioners, knotting halters and grinding axes, with this motto, Gregory *ſpun the halters, and* Sixtus *makes uſe of them.*

On a third was figured, gallowſes, axes, wheels, chains, fetters, and other engines of torture; and the ſtatue of Paſquin, with a label coming out of his mouth, with theſe words upon it; *It's well for me that I am made of marble.* The application is eaſy.

With things of this kind, Sixtus was not at all offended; on the contrary, he ſeemed much pleaſed when he heard any thing ſaid of the ſeverity of his
juſtice.

juftice. His nephew, talking with him one day, a-
bout the two laft mentioned pictures, faid, "He thought
" they were a great reflection upon his holinefs, and
" not to be fuffered:" but he anfwered, "You entirely
" miftake the matter, my dear nephew; the character
" of feverity, inftead of diminifhing, increafes our
" glory: don't you fee what a joke every body makes
" of Gregory's clemency and forbearance; they laugh
" at it as downright folly, and in truth it was no bet-
" ter: on the other hand, our rigour will get us the
" name of a juft and honourable judge, and of
" one that is refolved to do juftice with his eyes fhut.
" The punifhment of the evil, is the prefervation of
" the good. In fhort, what can we do more benefi-
" cial to the ftate, or more glorious to our pontificate,
" than to employ the authority of the one, for the fe-
" curity of the other: this can never be effected, till
" we have taught the people to ftand in awe of our
" juftice, and revere our power."
    We fhall relate fomefarther inftances of the pecu-
liarity of his juftice, from which one would be tempted to imagine, he proceded with that uncommon
degree of rigour, not only to purge the ftate, as he
ufed to call it, but merely for the fake of being talked
of.
    It was currently reported in Rome, that Drake, had
taken and plundered St. Domingo, in Hifpaniola, and
carried off an immenfe booty: this account came in
a private letter to Paul Secchi, a very confiderable
merchant in the city, who had large concerns in thofe
parts, which he had infured. Upon receiving this
news, he fent for the infurer, Sampfon Ceneda, a Jew,
and acquainted him with it. The Jew, whofe intereft
it was to have fuch a report thought falfe, gave many
reafons why it could not poffibly be true; and, at laft,
worked himfelf up into fuch a paffion, that he faid,
" I'll lay a pound of my flefh it is a lye." Such
fort of wagers, it is well known, are often propofed
by people of ftrong paffions, to convince others that

D d

are

are incredulous or obftinate. Nothing is more common than to fay, " I'll lay my life on it; " I'll forfeit " my right hand, if it is not true, &c.

Secchi, who was of a fiery hot temper, replied, " If " you like it, I'll lay you 1000 crowns againft a " pound of your flefh, that it is true." The Jew accepted the wager, and articles were immediately executed betwixt them, the fubftance of which was, " That if Secchi won, he fhould himfelf cut the flefh, " with a fharp knife, from whatever part of the Jew's " body he pleafed [19]." Unfortunately for the Jew, the truth of the account was foon after confirmed, by other advices, from the Weft-Indies, which threw him almoft into diftraction; efpecially, when he was informed that Secchi had folemnly fworn, he would compel him to the exact literal performance of his contract, and was determined to cut a pound of flefh from that part of his body which it is not neceffary to mention. Upon this, he went to the governor of Rome, and begged he would interpofe in the affair, and ufe his authority to prevail with Secchi to accept of 1000 piftoles, as an equivalent for the pound of flefh : but the governor, not daring to take upon him to determine a cafe of fo uncommon a nature, made a report of it to the Pope, who fent for them both, and having heard the articles read, and informed himfelf perfectly of the whole affair, from their own mouths, faid, " When " contracts are made, it is juft they fhould be fulfilled, " as we intend this fhall: take a knife therefore " Secchi, and cut a pound of flefh from any part you " pleafe, of the Jew's body. We would advife you, " however, to be very careful; for if you cut but a " fcruple, or a grain, more or lefs than your due, you " fhall certainly be hanged: go, and bring hither a

[19] The fcene betwixt Shylock and Antonio, in Shakefpear's Merchant of Venice, feems to be borrowed from this ftory : though the poet has inverted the perfons, and, decently enough, altered fome of the circumftances.

" knife,

" knife, and a pair of fcales, and let it be done in our
" prefence."

The merchant, at thefe words, began to tremble
like an afpin leaf, and throwing himfelf at his holinefs's feet, with tears in his eyes, protefted, ·" It was
" far from his thoughts to infift upon the performance
" of the contract." And being afked by the pope,
what he demanded; anfwered, " Nothing, holy fa-
" ther, but your benediction, and that the articles
" may be torn in pieces." Then, turning to the Jew,
he afked him, " What he had to fay, and whether he
" was content?" The Jew anfwered, " He thought
" himfelf extremely happy to come off at fo eafy a
" rate, and that he was perfectly content." " But
" we are not content," replied Sixtus, " nor is there
" .fufficient fatisfaction made to our laws: we defire
" to know, what authority you have to lay fuch wa-
" gers? the fubjects of princes, are the property of
" the ftate, and have no right to difpofe of their bo-
" dies, nor any part of them, without the exprefs
" confent of their fovereigns."

They were both immediately fent to prifon, and the
governor ordered to proceed againft them with the utmoft feverity of the law, that others might be deterred,
by their example, from laying any more fuch wagers.
The governor, thinking to pleafe Sixtus, and willing to
know what fort of punifhment he had a mind fhould be
inflicted upon them, faid, " Without doubt, they had
" been guilty of a very great crime, and he thought
" they deferved each of them to be fined 1000 crowns."
·" To be fined, each of them 1000 crowns!" anfwered
Sixtus, " Do you think that fufficient? What! fhall
" any of our fubjects prefume to difpofe of his life
" without our permiffion? Is it not evident that the
" jew has actually fold his life, by confenting to have
" a pound of flefh cut from his body? Is not this a
" direct fuicide? And is it not likewife true, that the
" merchant is guilty of downright premeditated mur-

" der

" der, in making a contract with the other, that he
" knew muſt be the occaſion of his death, if he in-
" ſiſted upon its being performed, as it is ſaid he did?
" Shall two ſuch villains be excuſed for a ſimple fine?"
The governor alledging, " That Secchi proteſted he
" had not the leaſt deſign of inſiſting upon the per-
" formance of the contract; and that the Jew did
" not at all imagine he would, when he laid the wa-
" ger :" Sixtus replied, " Theſe proteſtations were on-
" ly made out of fear of puniſhment, and becauſe
" they were in our preſence, and therefore no regard
" ought to be had to them : let them both be hanged;
" do you paſs that ſentence upon them, and we ſhall
" take care of the reſt." In a word, they were both
condemned to ſuffer death, to the great terror and
amazement of every body, though no one durſt open
his mouth, or call it an unjuſt ſentence.

As Secchi was of a very good family, having many
great friends and relations, and the Jew one of the
moſt leading men of the ſynagogue, they both had
recourſe to petitions; ſtrong application was made to
cardinal Montalto, to intercede with his holineſs, at
leaſt to ſpare their lives. Sixtus, who did not really
deſign to put them to death, but to deter others from
ſuch practices, at laſt conſented to change the ſentence
into that of the gallies, with liberty to buy off that
too, by paying each of them 2000 crowns, to be applied to the uſe of the hoſpital (which he had lately
founded) before they were releaſed.

Two other perſons of ſome diſtinction, were alſo
fined, for laying wagers, together with the people to
whom it was left to decide them, and their fines appropriated to the ſame uſe ; which gave occaſion to a
Paſquinade, importing, *That he robbed the rich to feed
the poor.*

It is not much to be wondered at, that Sixtus undertook and accompliſhed ſuch prodigious things, without
prejudice to his revenues, when we conſider how fertile

tile he was in expedients to raife money, and with what eagernefs and avidity he put them in execution. He publifhed two bulls in the beginning of his pontificate; in the firft of which, he confined the power of the inquifition, to things only relating to religion and the doctrines of the church, and that too, chiefly where ecclefiaftics were concerned; referring blafphemies, oaths, perjuries, fcandal, profanations, and offences committed by the laity againft the clergy, to the cognizance of the fecular magiftrate: this he did, becaufe the tribunal of the inquifition does not ufually punifh by fines, but corporal pains; whereas, the other power fentences the criminal to whipping, or imprifonment, or the gallies, or death, with leave to commute for a handfome fum of money, of which we fhall give the reader two more inftances.

A French taylor, who had lived fome time in Rome, and heaped together a good deal of money, meeting another of the fame occupation in the ftreet, with whom he had a quarrel, flew into fuch a paffion with him, that, forgetting all decency and referve, he rapped out, *Rinigo Iddio, God I renounce thee.* The magiftracy, who have fpies to inform them of people's words and actions, being acquainted with it, having fummoned the taylor before them, tried and condemned him to be publicly whipped; with a power, however, to buy it off for 500 crowns. The fum would have been much larger, if the French ambaffador had not interfered.

Another perfon, who was a native of Rome, and of a noble family, after a long run of ill luck at play, one night, was fo out of patience and humour with the Virgin Mary, that he cried out, *Puttana d' Iddio* (an expreffion too horrid to be tranflated). It was immediately carried to the Pope, who inftructed the judge to fentence him to be publicly expofed upon a ftage with a bridle in his mouth, and then to be fent to the gallies for five years; but, out of refpect to

his

his family, he was excufed, upon paying 1000 crowns
to the ufe of the hofpital.

It had been a cuftom in Rome, and the ecclefiaftical
ftate, to excufe crimes of the moft flagitious nature,
for a pecuniary confideration, which went to the judge
or governor of the place where they were committed.
As the number of them was confiderable, the magiftrates always came very rich out of their offices:
But Sixtus having occafion for large fums, to carry on
his vaft defigns, publifhed a bull, in which he ordered,
" That all manner of fines and mulcts, of what kind
" foever, fhould be returned into the Apoftolic cham-
" ber; and that no judge, governor, or magiftrate,
" fhould accept any reward or confideration more than
" their falary;" an ordinance of as great prejudice
to them, as emolument to the Pope; which was the
occafion that very few cared to accept of any office of
judicature in this pontificate : but Sixtus foon found a
remedy for this, by iffuing out another bull, declaring
that he would feverely punifh thofe that prefumed to refufe any office, to which they fhould be nominated ; fo
that nobody durft fhew the leaft repugnance, pretty well
knowing his temper and appetite for money, though the
magiftrates were little better than galley flaves, as they
lived in continual fear of making fome falfe ftep, and
received a very fmall reward for their labours. It is
computed that, in the five years of his pontificate, he
raifed two millions and 300,000 crowns, by the fines
and commutations of delinquents.

Notwithftanding his immoderate hunger and thirft
after money, he never would allow any to be taken in
capital cafes; as theft, robbery, affaffination, rape, murder, and fuch like crimes. It is true, he would often
magnify the nature of an offence, that he might impofe a large fine with a better face ; though it was not
ufual with him to lay a fine immediately upon any
one, but firft to fentence him to a whipping, or imprifonment, or the gallies, and then give him leave

to

to buy off his punifhment, upon much folicitation, which they were glàd to do when fentence of death, or the gallies, hung over them, and they confidered the inexorable temper he was of: This occafioned Pafquin to fay, He has found a way to rob us, under a pretence of doing us a favour.

End of the SEVENTH BOOK.

BOOK THE EIGHTH.

WHILST Sixtus thus made himfelf terrible, by fines and impofitions, to the rich, he was fo beloved and adored by the generality, for the great care and affection he had fhewn to the city, by beautifying it with fo many fumptuous ornaments, and the abundance of all things which he had eftablifhed in the ecclefiaftical ftate, at a time when all the other parts of Italy laboured under a fevere famine, that they erected a ftatue to him, with the following infcription upon the pedeftal :

SIXTO. V. PONT. MAX.
OB. QVIETEM. PVBLICAM.
COMPRESSA. SICARIORVM. EXVLVMQVE. LI-
CENTIA. RESTITVTAM.
ANNONAE. INOPIAM. SVBLEVATAM.
VRBEM. AEDIFICIIS. VIIS. AQVAEDVCTIS. ILLVS-
TRATAM.
S. P. Q. R. D. D.

There happened two adventures this year, with which he was much diverted. Going very early one morning to vifit the convent of the Holy Apoftles (as he often did) without giving the guardian any notice of it, he knocked, pretty brifkly, at the cell door
of

of a monk, that had but lately arrived from Naples, and was not acquainted with the Pope's custom of visiting the convent after that manner, without any train or attendance. Hearing this noise at the door, the monk asked, Who was there? and Sixtus answering, The Pope; he, not thoroughly awake, replied, in very coarse terms, *E uno stronzo* [1], and bid him, Go about his business. The warden, who attended his holiness, was so angry and ashamed of his beastly answer, that he would have broken open the door to chastise the monk for his ill-manners; but the Pope would not suffer him, as he knew it was done without any design to affront him; and as he went away, said, *De stercore erigit pauperem, He lifteth the beggar from the dunghill.* 1 Sam. ii. 8. When this came to be known at court, it occasioned a good deal of mirth amongst the cardinals and ambassadors: Sixtus himself could not forbear laughing, whenever he told this story, or heard it mentioned by any body else.

Another time, as he passed through the city, seeing the gates of that convent open, he suddenly got out of his chariot, and went into the porter's lodge, where he found the porter, who was a lay-brother, eating a platter of beans, with oil poured over them. As the meanness of the repast put him in mind of his former condition, he took a wooden spoon, and sitting down close to the porter, on a stair case, first eat one platter full with him, and then another, to the great surprise of those that were with him: after he had thanked the lay-brother for his entertainment, he turned to his attendants, and said, " We shall live two " years longer for this; for this we eat with an ap- " petite, and without fear or suspicion." And then,

[1] I could wish to be excused from translating this passage, if the reader pleases; but if he insists upon having the meaning of it in plain downright English, I must e'en tell him, it is neither better nor worse, than a Sirreverence.

lifting

lifting up his eyes to heaven, faid, " The Lord be
" praifed, for permitting a Pope, once in this life, to
" make a meal in peace and quietnefs."

He did not fay this without reafon, as many of his
predeceffors died by poifon, and it was ftrongly fufpected that he did himfelf, at laft, though he took all
poffible care to prevent it, and placed a continual guard
upon his cook, to hinder him from going out of the
kitchen, or having any private converfation with other
people. The next day, he ordered the fuperiors of
the convent to admit the porter as a profeffed, and
faid to him, when he gave him his benediction, " W
" have formerly been what you are, let it be your
" endeavour to be what we are."

It was his pleafure there fhould be a general Chapter of the Francifcan order held this year, and that
all the members, as well as thofe that had votes, as
thofe that had not, fhould affift there, and furnifhed
the whole expence of it himfelf. He condefcended to
honour one of their meetings with his prefence, dining
with them in the refectory (attended by two cardinals) where a moft fumptuous entertainment was prepared, and drank profperity to the order; defiring the
filence and reftraint that are ufually obferved upon
fuch occafions, might be laid afide at that time.

Many of them petitioned him for the generalfhip;
but he left it entirely to the body to chufe one for
themfelves, left it fhould be faid, he affembled them
only to recommend a general; notwithftanding he
had a power to appoint one himfelf, if he pleafed,
without their confent or approbation. It was faid,
he was not pleafed they had not the civility to afk,
what perfon would be moft agreeable to him; but he
took no further notice of it. His nephew, however,
who did not want penetration, could not forbear faying, " Thefe people have neither gratitude nor good
" manners." Sixtus anfwered with a fmile, " We know
" them

" them pretty well: we are no stranger to the temper
" and behaviour of monks."

He strictly forbad them to make any panegyrics
upon him in the exordiums, or conclusions of their
Theses, during this chapter: two of which were
afterwards printed, and dedicated to him. Some of
these exercises he would have performed before him,
in the pontifical chapel, by the most learned and
able divines. One of them, a Dominican friar, was
so heated and transported with passion, in the course
of his disputation, that some of the cardinals were
very much offended at his indecent language and
behaviour; and said, " He ought to be silenced."
But either the respect he always had for that order,
for the sake of his old benefactor, Pius V, or because
it was some sort of diversion to him, he would not
suffer it, letting him run his full career; and said to
the cardinals, who seemed extremely disgusted at it,
" Very probably we might have behaved so our-
" selves, if we had been in his place; for it is hardly
" possible to contain one's self always, in such cir-
" cumstances."

After the chapter broke up, the whole order,
with the new general at their head, came to the
Vatican, in procession, to kiss his holiness's feet, in
expectation of receiving some mark of his kindness,
as he had ordered the cardinal protector to acquaint
them the day before, " That he would grant every
" one of them (without exception) some favour;
" that he would have them consider what would be
" most agreeable to them, and that it was but just
" he should take some method of convincing the
" world, how great an esteem and affection he re-
" tained, for people that had formerly been his bre-
" thren."

When the protector informed them of his holiness's
intentions, it is not possible to express the joy that
appeared through the whole body, or the envy and
difcontent

discontent it occasioned in the other orders, particularly the Dominicans; they began to murmur and complain of Pius V, who had never done the least thing for them, or granted them any favour; especially when they remembered how ill used Sixtus had been by his brethren, whilst they had always shewn the highest regard and veneration for Pius.

On the other hand, the cardinals were not a little piqued at this sudden change of temper, and called it a prostitution, nay, a profanation of his favour, as they were disgusted to see such a profusion of liberality squandered away upon a parcel of dirty monks, by a pontiff that had behaved with so much reserve, and been remarkably close-fisted and niggardly to the H. College.

The Pope had acquainted them with this resolution the day before, to give them time to consider what to ask: As the news of it soon came to be spread about the city, Pasquin appeared, putting on a monk's habit, with this label, *It is better to be a Cordelier than a Cardinal, in these times.* But Rusticucci, who knew the Pope as well, or better than most people, said to a person who was speaking to him of this affair, " Time will discover something that we are not " aware of at present."

Sixtus received them all in the great hall, where the consistories are held, seated upon his pontifical throne, with a secretary upon his left hand, to take down the name and request of every monk, as he came in his turn to kiss his feet. The general was the first that advanced, and after prostrating himself before the Pope, he returned his most humble thanks for the great favour he had received in being appointed general of the order, and said, " The only request he " had to make was, that his Holiness would vouch- " safe to honour him with his patronage and protec- " tion, and be pleased to support him in the execution ' of an office, that was conferred upon him in a chap-

" ter

" ter fummoned by his command, maintained by his
" bounty, and honoured with his prefence."

Others that followed, according to their rank and
feniority, had their petitions regiftered. Some were
of fo whimfical and extravagant a turn, that Sixtus
feemed much diverted with them : One of them defired a brief, forbidding all the other religious to give
him any trouble or moleftation, or to fay any thing
abufive, or reflecting upon him. It feems he had fome
reafon to afk fuch a favour, as he was a moft infolent
and incorrigible fellow, continually plaguing and provoking his brethren, to that degree, that he was
hated and avoided by the whole community. Another afked for two rooms in the convent, in which he
might do whatever he pleafed, without being accountable to his fuperior, or even the Pope himfelf; and
faid, " He would willingly fubmit to the difcipline of
" the order, when he was in any other part of the
" convent;" but infifted upon a total independence,
and exemption in thofe apartments, where he fhould
not be prevented from fhutting himfelf up, whenever
he had a mind, by any perfon, or upon any pretence
whatfoever; and that if he hereafter happened to deferve punifhment, he fhould be permitted to retire into one of thefe rooms, and confider whether he liked
the kind of punifhment, or not; and if he did not,
he fhould have the liberty of changing it to fuch a one
as he did like.

A Neapolitan lay-brother, after he had kiffed the
Pope's feet, begged leave to make his wants known to
him in private; upon which, the Pope gracioufly in-
clining his ear to him, he defired " his Holinefs would
" be pleafed to give him leave to quit his habit and
" marry, or at leaft keep a whore, without the war-
" den's having it in his power to hinder it."

A bachelor of Bologna defired " A brief, with per-
" miffion to preach in any church, either regular or
" fecular, and at what hour he pleafed, without li-
" cence

" cence from the ordinary, or superior, and to have
" for his own use, all the money that was collected at
" his sermons."

Father Poppa, the provincial of Puglia, requested,
" That his family might be called relations of his Ho-
" liness, which, he said, would be the highest honour
" he could ever receive in this world. The Pope
said, " He would give his consent, if there was the
" least colour of foundation for it:" And asked him
what family he was of; to which the provincial answered, " That he was of one of the most ancient and
" richest families in Italy." " I don't see then," replied Sixtus, " how we can possibly make out any
" relationship, since we were only poor hog-keepers,
" and you people of great fortune and estate; yet we
" think we have hit upon an expedient to gratify you,
" which is, that you give up your riches to the use
" of an hospital we have lately founded, and be-
" coming poor, turn hog-keepers, as we were : As for
" you yourself, we will give orders, after you have
" been stripped of your habit, that you shall be sta-
" tioned under our eye, somewhere near the city, that
" we may see if you behave well in your new occu-
" pation, and then we will acknowledge you for our
" kinsman." The poor provincial was strangely surprized at this answer, which was moderate enough,
considering the impertinence of the request. It was
expected by some, who knew the disposition of Sixtus,
that he would actually have put his expedient in execution, i. e. that he would have degraded him, and
turned him out of his convent.

No less ridiculous and mal a propos was the demand
of father Sarco, of Umbria, who desired the Pope,
" To grant him a bull, that the convent to which he
" belonged, and had been so much enriched by the
" alms that were collected at the sermons which he
" had preached, might be converted into an abbey;
" that the jus patronatus, or right of presenting to it,
" might

" might be invefted in his family; that no monk
" fhould be admitted into it, that had not firft been
" three years a fervant in his family, or at leaft to
" fome of his relations; and that he would be pleafed
" to grant to the faid abbey, one half of the tythes
" that belonged to the bifhop." The Pope could not
help drawing up his mufcles, and faid, *Paſſate, Paſſate,
Go along, go along ; we can't give abbeys to every fool.*

He was not a little pleafed at the fimplicity of a good
old man of 77 years of age, who was a religious of
the province of Rome, and having affifted at feven general chapters, was carried to Rome, in order to have
the confolation of feeing this before he died, as he
heard it would be a very fplended one. After he had
kiffed his Holinefs's feet, he addreffed him in this manner: "I fhould be very glad, holy father, if you
" could add ten years to my life ; but as that is in the
" power of Heaven alone, I only defire an indulgence
" in the hour of death, which now cannot be far off."
He pronounced thefe laft words with fo good a grace,
that the Pope faid, " He wifhed, with all his heart, he
" was able to work a miracle, for his fake ; but that
" he thought, as he had lived fo long, he might now
" be very well content to die."

It is hardly poffible to conceive the folly and abfurdity of fome other of their requefts, with which the
Pope was grievoufly offended. Some afked for cardinals hats, archbifhoprics, abbeys, and other dignities in the church: Some for offices that were appropriated to particular orders. A young bachelor
afked for the place of mafter of the palace, which is
always poffeffed by a Dominican ; others defired bifhoprics that were not yet vacant. If he had been inclinable to gratify even thofe that afked for preferments
in their own order, he muft have turned every thing
topfey turvey ; as fome wanted to be perpetual provincials ; others, to have the power of vifiting whatever
provinces they pleafed, during life: Others, again, to
chufe

chufe what convents they liked beft to refide in, or not
to be fent far from the place of their birth. Many
afked for money to build houfes of pleafure, with confiderable penfions; and not a few petitioned his Holinefs
to give them leave to lay afide the cowl, as they were
thoroughly tired of a monaftic life.

Laft of all came a lay brother about 60 years old,
30 of which he had fpent as a fervant to the cook
and butler of the convent of the H. Apoftles. The
old man, bowing down to kifs the Pope's feet, who
remembered him very well, faid, "Holy Father, I
" am a poor lay brother, in one of the loweft offices
" that belong to the convent, and not worthy to ex-
" pect the leaft of your Holinefs's favours. The ho-
" nour I have had of feeing you become head of the
" church, after having remembered you a private
" religious, will not give me leave to hope for any
" thing further. A miferable lay brother, like me,
" ought not to prefume to afk favours from a fove-
" reign as you are: Neverthelefs, as your Holinefs
" has been pleafed to include even me in the number
" of thofe that you have thought fit to diftinguifh by
" your princely munificence, with the moft profound
" reverence, I humbly befeech your charity to make
" a fountain in our convent, which is in great
" want of water, as your Holinefs may pleafe to re-
" member, from the inconvenience which you your-
" felf have often fuffered by it."

It is faid, that the Pope was fo affected with the old
man's fpeech, that he could hardly refrain from tears.

When they had all kiffed his feet, and prefented
their feveral petitions, they were called back into the
fame hall, from whence they had gone out, to avoid
confufion; and the Pope fpoke to them in the following manner: "If your defires had been conformable
" to my good intentions, I fhould willingly have com-
" plied with them; but as they are of fo extraordi-
" nary a nature, that there is no poffibility of grant-
" ing

" ing them, I find myfelf under a neceffity of giving
" you an abfolute refufal. I did not expeﬄ that any
" of you could have been fo mean to think of your
" own private intereﬅ, without any regard to that of
" the order in general. Your folemn vows and pro-
" feﬂions at your entrance into a religious life,
" ought to have made you forget the one, and the
" concern which every good member ſhould have for
" the welfare and prefervation of the body, ſhould
" have put you in mind of the other. Your avarice,
" your ambition, and fenfuality, have prevented my
" good defigns; and I ſhould think it a great fin to
" feed and encourage them by my generofity. It is
" with ſhame and horror that I fee but one, out of fo
" great a number of you, that has ſhewn any regard
" for the good of the public."

After this manner he difmiﬀed them from his prefence, in the higheﬅ confufion and mortification; and
turning to the poor lay brother, promifed that what
he had aſked ſhould be performed; and, with high com-
mendations of his public fpirit, recommended him to
the notice and proteﬄion of the general.

When this came to be publicly talked of in the
city, they who had been the forwardeﬅ to find fault
with the pope's extravagant generofity, now highly applauded his contrivance, when they found it was only
to expofe and difcountenance the folly, felfiſhnefs, and
ambition of the Cordeliers.

The next day Pafquin was ſhuffling off his monk's
habit, and putting on the cardinal's again, with this
label, *If one muﬅ be made a fool of, it is better to be
fooled in the college, than in the cloyﬅer.* Ruﬅicucci,
who had always fufpeﬄed it was fome trick of the
Pope's, feeing what had happened, faid to fome of the
cardinals; "He that does not know the Pope, is fure
" to be deceived by him; and let him that knows him,
" take care how he truﬅs him; we had the honour of
" being the firﬅ fools he made."

The

The very next day he gave orders to have the lay-brother's requeft executed; and was fo well pleafed with it, that he faid, "It was a thing very much " wanted in that convent, which fuffered extremely " from the fcarcity of water ; that he had often been " fo fatigued himfelf, with drawing it out of a very " deep well, for his own ufe, that it made him almoft " tired of his life ; that the weight and multiplicity of " his cares, fince his affumption to the pontificate, " had caufed him to forget a defign he once had of " making a fountain there ; and that he was highly " obliged to the lay brother for recalling it to his " memory."

Soon after, Sixtus went himfelf with an architect and engineer, and fixed upon a proper place for the fountain, which was to be fupplied by the fame ftream that he had brought to Monte Cavallo. It ftands in a great bafon in the middle of the court, beautified with the arms of Sixtus, from whence the water is conveyed through pipes all over the houfe, and in great plenty to the door of the refectory, for the covenience of wafhing before and after meals. Other pipes carry it not only into the kitchen, but into the very kettles and coppers. The convent, which in general is now the beft watered of any in Rome, owes this convenience to the public fpirit and difinte-reftednefs of the lay brother.

He eftablifhed fifteen congregations of cardinals there were fome already inftituted by other popes, but they were fo altered and new modelled by him, that he may properly be called the author. His fucceffors have abolifhed fome, and fubftituted others in their room, fo that the number is ftill the fame : we fhall here give the reader a detail of them.

The firft is the congregation of the H. Office, efta-blifhed by Pius IV, reformed by Pius V, and reduced into a ftill better form by Sixtus. It meets twice a week, viz. on Wednefday at the convent Sopra la Minerva, belonging to the Dominicans, where the

office

office is held; and on Thurfday in the pope's prefence,
to take cognizance of matters of herefy. This affembly confifts of at leaft 12 cardinals, deputed by
the pope, with feveral other prelates and divines of
different orders, who are called confultors of the H.
Office, with a commiffary (always a Dominican) and
an affeffor to make a report to his holinefs of what
paffes in the congregation, if he is abfent.

The fecond takes cognizance of all differences that
happen betwixt bifhops and their fubjects, whether
regulars or feculars: this he eftablifhed to rid himfelf
of the trouble of hearing the frequent difputes that
arife amongft them; referring them to this tribunal,
which is held every Friday in the palace of the cardinal prefident, where there are fometimes fo many
memorials and complaints, that it is not poffible to hear
them all.

The 3d, is to take care that the canons, made at
the council of Trent, are duly executed, as there at
firft, occurred many difficulties in them, with which
he was not a little embarraffed. This congregation
was charged with the care of interpreting and ex-
pounding them. If there fhould arife any difpute
concerning the doctrine or difcipline of the church,
in whatfoever part of Chriftendom it happens, the parties concerned in it muft have recourfe to this court
for a decifion. They commonly affemble on Thurfday
and Saturday every week, at the palace of the oldeft
cardinal that is member of it, though he is not the prefident, who alone has the power of convoking them.

The fourth is the congregation of ftate, to provide
for the well government of the pope's dominions; and
confifts of all the cardinals that have ever been nuncios,
and a fecretary of ftate. It is moftly held in the pope's
prefence, and when he cannot affift, at the cardinal
nephew's.

The 5th, is that of rites; to determine all difputes
concerning cuftoms, ceremonies, precedence, canonizations of faints, &c. The oldeft cardinal is prefident

dent of it : he calls them together once a month, and oftner, if neceffary. This is a power that belongs to the prefidents of all congregations.

The 6th, is the congregation of waters, whofe province is to take care of all rivers, brooks, water-courfes, and bridges : the pope eftablifhed this to affift him in conducting the water to Monte Cavallo. The oldeft cardinal is always prefident.

The 7th, is the congregation of ftreets and fountains, of which the cardinal chamberlain is prefident, and fummons it at the houfe of the oldeft commiffary, as often as there is occafion. Their bufinefs is to take care of the aquæducts and pipes, which bring the water to Rome, to fee that it is diftributed in a convenient manner, and to make the ftreets large and commodious. He firft inftituted this to fuperintend the new ftreets he was then building ; and feeing the fervice it was of, eftablifhed it by a bull for ever.

The 8th, is the congregation dell indice, to correct and cenfure fuch books as they think proper. He erected this upon the account of a printing-office, which he defigned to eftablifh at Rome. The Prefident is always a cardinal, who calls them together at his houfe, when there is occafion.

The 9th is the congregation della confulta, for the government of the church ; the cardinal nephew prefides at it pro tempore. Montalto, the pope's nephew, acquired great reputation in this office, and went out of it with the higheft applaufe. It confifts of fix cardinals, fix prelates, and a fecretary, who is generally a bofom friend of the prefident, at whofe houfe it is affembled every Friday : whatever concerns or relates to the government of the church, falls under its jurifdiction. To this court all the vice-legates, governors, and other officers of ftate have recourfe, when they meet with any thing difficult or extraordinary in the exercife of their functions : upon this they deliberate ; and when they come to a conclufion, the fecretary draws it up in writing, which

is figned by the prefident, and all the prelates that
are prefent. They have every one of them a feparate province in the ecclefiaftical ftate, and report
whatever they think worthy of notice, in that province, to the congregation. The legation of Avignon, the government of Benevento, in the kingdom of
Naples, and the city of Ceneda, in the ftate of Venice,
don't acnkowledge the jurifdiction of the confulta.
Fermo and Spoletto claim the like exemption. Every
prelate of this congregation has a yearly falary of
1000 crowns, and the fecretary of 2000.

The 10th congregation degli Sgravi, or, de bono
regimine, likewife owes its inftitution to Sixtus. The
cardinal·nephew is prefident. This court hears and
redreffes all grievances, oppreffions, and vexations of
the fubject. It meets every Saturday in the place
where the confulta is held. The members are likewife the fame, and have the fame falary for affifting
in this congregation, with the further privilege of
wearing a purple or violet-coloured habit, and being
called the pope's familiars.

The 11th, is the congregation of the mint, to
which belongs the care of coining money, regulating
the ftandard of foreign gold, and fettling its currency
in the ecclefiaftical ftate. It is generally compofed
of four cardinals, and two chamberlains, of the
pope's appointing, with a prefident who calls them
together upon any emergency.

The 12th, is the congregation of confiftorial affairs,
which is of great relief to the pope, and was projected
by Sixtus long before his exaltation. The dean of
the H. College is the prefident. There is no certain
day fixed for its meeting, fo that it only affembles at
the prefident's houfe, when the pope refers any affair
to its confideration. It generally takes cognizance of
the refignation of bifhoprics, taxes, impofitions upon ecclefiaftics, and fuch things. As the cardinal
nephews, at prefent, take the whole of affairs into
their

their own hands, there is but little bufinefs now done in this court.

Thefe are 12 of the 15 congregations eftablifhed by Sixtus; his fucceffors have abolifhed three, and inftituted three others in their room; fo that the number of them is the fame as it was under his pontificate. The firft was eftablifhed by Clement VIII, for the examination of perfons nominated to bifhoprics. That pope ufed to examine all fuch as had ftudied the civil law himfelf, and thofe that had proceeded in divinity he referred to cardinal Bellarmine. This congregation is always held in the pope's prefence. It confifts of eight or ten cardinals, as many bifhops, and fome doctors of different faculties and orders: By them are examined fuch perfons as his holinefs intends to promote to bifhoprics that lie in Italy; for thofe that do not are excufed from this formality.

He that is examined, kneels down upon a cufhion before the pope, and is liable to be interrogated by any member of the congregation; when he has undergone this examination, which is fufficient, if he is tranflated to any other fee, the fecretary enters his name in a regifter: But if a bifhop, who has been any time in poffeffion of a foreign fee, is tranflated to one in Italy, he muft go thro' this examination, except he be a cardinal, as the H. College claim an exemption from it. But the approbation of the examiners does not put him in immediate poffeffion of his bifhopric; he is to pafs thro' the following ceremonies before it can be done. In the firft place, he muft make a profeffion of his faith before a cardinal, called, *Il cardinal potente*, *The cardinal propofer*, who is fo named from being appointed by the Pope to propofe him to the other cardinals. In the next place they examine witneffes, who give information upon oath, concerning the ftate of the fee to which he is to be promoted, the birth, quality, and morals of the candidate. After this, the cardinal orders his au -

ditor

ditor to draw up an inftrument, which is figned by the
notary of the cardinal vicar, or auditor of the apoftolic chamber. The candidate muft then exhibit
a certificate of his doctor's degree, and other titles
and privileges, if he has any, with his teftimonials
and letters of orders: Other witneffes are then examined to prove that he was born in lawful matrimony; that his father and mother were never fufpected
of herefy; and that he is above 30 years of age, as
the canons of the council of Trent require; after
which, enquiry is made into the quality, circumftances, and revenue of the bifhopric, in what province
it is fituated, whether immediately dependent upon
his holinefs, or fuffragan to any archbifhop; what
extent of land, what towns, what number of fouls
there are in the diocefe, what religious houfes,
what relics are there held in veneration, what
is the annual income of the church, the number
of canons, the different dignities: If there be
any feminaries, how many nunneries, parifhes,
churches, and feveral other particulars of the like
nature. The cardinal propofer figns an account of
thefe proceedings, and fends it to be revifed by three
other cardinals, protectors of their orders, who fign
and fend it back to the fame cardinal, and he keeps
it ever afterwards. The candidate is then proclaimed
in the firft private confiftory that is held; and in the
next he is prefented in a Latin fpeech, which is generally a panegyric upon his life and character. But
before the cardinal propofer fpecifies the fee, the candidate gives the receiver of the revenues of the H.
College two notes of hand, figned by himfelf, in
which he promifes to pay whatfoever is due to the
cardinal, the apoftolic chamber, the H. College,
and the officers of the chancery for his difpatches.
The day before he is propofed, the cardinal ponente
fends an abftract of the proceedings to all his brethren,
to fee if they have any objection to the candidate,
and as foon as he is propofed, turns to the pope, and
then

then to the cardinal dean, and afks them " If they
" know of any reafon why he fhould not be en-
" throned?" If they do they immediately declare it; if
not, they rife from their feats and fignify their approbation. The pope then, by a decree, orders him to be put
in poffeffion of his bifhopric, of which the cardinal vice-
chancellor keeps a copy; and the proper inftruments
for that purpofe are immediately made out. The cardinal ponente claims a right to 15 per cent. out of the
firft year's revenue, and when the Pope propofes him
himfelf, this perquifite belongs to his fecretaries. If a
cardinal is propofed, who has never been at Rome, he
pays the fame fees; but if he is prefent, or has been
there, he is excufed from it.

The new prelate keeps the houfe all the morning
of the day he is propofed, and takes care to provide a
mitre: After dinner he dreffes himfelf in his epifcopal robes, puts on a hat, with a green border and hat-
band, and then goes to the vatican, when he is prefented by the maeftro della camera, to kifs the pope's
feet. He takes with him a rochett, which the pope
puts upon him with his own hands, and then goes to vifit the whole college of cardinals, beginning with the
dean.

I have been more particular in the account of the
laft congregation, as the greateft part of thefe ceremonies were inftituted by Sixtus. It is true, Clement
made feveral additions to them, and put thofe that
were already eftablifhed into a better method; fo
that Sixtus may very well be called the author of it; at
leaft, be faid to have laid the foundation, which Clement
afterwards built upon.

The next congregation is, for the propagation of
the Chriftian faith, founded by Gregory XV, to confider of ways and means to eftablifh the Chriftian religion in all parts of the world, and meets
the firft Monday in every month in the pope's prefence; tho' it is held fometimes in a palace, which
they have built for that purpofe. It confifts of many
cardinals,

cardinals a prothonotary a secretary of state, a judge, who is commonly a referendary [2] of both signatures, an assessor of the H. office, and a secretary of the congregation. All those that come to Rome out of devotion, after they are converted, are lodged in this palace which is very large and magnificent. Bishops also, whose revenues are small, are received and entertained there with all manner of necessary accommodations. They have set up a press to print breviaries, missals, and other books that are used by the Romish church in all manner of languages.

The congregation of ecclesiastical immunities, which is the last we shall mention, was instituted by Urban VIII. He found the want of it when he was nuncio, in several disputes and controversies, concerning such exemptions and privileges, upon which it was necessary to have the pope's opinion, and he usually referring these matters to commissaries, occasioned them to be spun out to an immoderate length. This made him resolve to establish a congregation, which might determine what immunities ecclesiastics ought, and what they ought not to enjoy. It is held every Tuesday, in the house of the oldest cardinal that is member of it, with an auditor of the Rota [3], a clerk of the chamber,

[2] Referendaries are prelates that propose suits, commissions, supplications, &c. in the signatures of Justice and Grace, and take cognizance of causes not exceeding the sum of 500 crowns: for if they exceed that, they are referred to the Ruota or Rota.

[3] The Ruota or Rota, is a particular court of jurisdiction, and takes cognizance of beneficiary matters, &c. It consists of 12 doctors taken out of the four nations of Italy, France, Spain, and Germany; three of them being Romans, one a Florentine, one a Milanese, one of Bologna, one of Ferrara, one a Venetian, one a Frenchman, two Spaniards, and a German, each having four clerks or notaries under him. Their office is to judge of all beneficiary causes, both within Rome, and thro' the whole Ecclesiastical dominions (in case of appeal) and of all civil processes, for above 500 crowns. Du Cange says, this court is so called from the
Rota

chamber, an advocate of the fignature, and a referendary. The prefident is keeper of the feals, and has
a penfion of 700 crowns per annum.

Whilft Sixtus was thus employed at home in making
provifion for the well government of the church and
ftate, Q. Elizabeth was no lefs active in her endeavours
to extirpate the R. Catholic religion out of England.
Tho' it was with great regret the Pope faw his authority entirely loft in fo flourifhing a kingdom; and tho'
he often lamented it in the confiftory, and prefence
of foreign ambaffadors, he, upon all other occafions,
teftified the moft profound regard for the Queen;
and faid, " He fhould have efteemed it the higheft
" honour to have had fuch a princefs in the fame com-
" munion with him." Which being told her, fhe was
fo pleafed with it, that fhe faid, " If he continued Pope
" long, fhe would find fome means to reconcile her
" kingdom to the See of Rome;" which was looked
upon by every body as a mere compliment.

She had detained Mary Q. of Scotland, daughter to
James VI, a long time prifoner in England, for reafons
of ftate, and endeavouring, as it is faid, to foment a
rebellion in her kingdoms. Moft of the crowned heads
in Europe had ufed their interceffion for her releafe,
which fo increafed the jealoufy of Elizabeth, that fhe
at laft determined to put her to death.

To give fome fort of varnifh to fo foul a deed, fhe
fent an ambaffador to acquaint the king and queen
of France with it, and to let them know, " She was
" obliged to proceed in that manner, not out of jea-
" loufy, to gratify any private refentment, but by the
" efpecial advice of her parliament; that fhe fubmit-
" ted to it with the utmoft reluctance; but that juf-
" tice the majefty of crowned heads, and the pefer-
" vation of herfelf and her kingdoms, abfolutely re-
" quired it." She at the fame time fignified the refo-

Rota Porphyretica, becaufe the pavement of the chamber, where
they formerly fat, was of Porphyry, and fafhioned like a
wheel.

lution

lution of the parliament to the Q. of Scotland, and
that sentence of death was passed upon her. Which it
is said, the queen received with a great deal of courage and firmness.

The king of France, that he might not seem wanting in his endeavours to save a princess so nearly related to him, sent Bellievre into England, with a full answer to every article of the accusation upon which she
had been condemned to die. This ambassador had
instructions to give out in public, " That he came
" only to demand her life, in the name of the king
" his master, and the whole French nation."

When the pope was informed of this, he said,
" That when sovereign princes were once embarked
" in such designs it was not usual for them to desist
" at the simple request of an ambassador." And
talking one night at supper, with his nephew, about
Bellievre's success in England, he said, " We don't
" know what Elizabeth designs to do with the queen
" of Scotland ; but we know what we should do, if
" we had a crowned head in prison." The cardinals
in the French interest entreated the pope, that there
might be prayers and supplications, and the Host exposed for forty hours (as is usual upon such occasions)
at every church in Rome, to implore the blessing of
God upon Bellievre, in an undertaking of such importance to all Christendom. To which Sixtus gave his consent,
tho' he judged that the release of the Q. of Scotland
was only a feint, and that the real design of sending
Bellievre into England, was to negociate some affairs
of far greater importance and advantage to his master, and said to cardinal Farnese, " He was thorough-
" ly persuaded it was all a pretence, and that he
" would find things quite contrary to what they ap-
" peared." It was known soon after, that the ambassador's application, in behalf of the Q. of Scotland, met
with little success. Some said he was very cool and indifferent in this matter, and others did not scruple to
affirm,

affirm, that he actually promoted and advised her death.

Bellievre was secretly instructed by his master, to press Q. Elizabeth to make use of the influence and authority she had with the K. of Navarre and the P. of Conde, to persuade them to listen to a peace with him. He was further ordered to discover, if possible, the sentiments of this Queen, concerning a treaty he heard she had entered into with some of the German princes, and to encourage her to conclude it. Upon which Sixtus said, by way of excuse for him, " That the " civil wars which at that time miserably distracted " the kingdom of France, would not permit Hen- " ry to quarrel with England, and that his own " crown ought to be dearer to him than that of " any relation."

The arrival of Bellievre, having for some time put a stop to the execution of the sentence that had been passed upon the Q. of Scotland, it was apprehended by some, that the K. of France's remonstrances had shaken the resolution of Elizabeth. This delay alarmed some of the queen's ministers, especially Leicester, Cecil, and Walsingham, who had been the principal advisers of her death, when they considered, that, in case their mistress should die, the crown would of course, by indisputable right descend to Q. Mary, who (when she was established in the possession of it) would infallibly work their destruction; not only upon the mortal and irreconcilable aversion she had to all Protestants, but out of resentment for the long and ignominious imprisonment she had suffered, and the cruel sentence they had occasioned to be passed upon her.

At a proper opportunity therefore, they represented to the Queen, in a complaining manner, " That " her lenity and forbearance to put the sentence in " execution was a contempt shewn to the advice of " her parliament and council, and that the whole ' kingdom expected it with the utmost impatience."

She

She affected by this delay to shew a regret and unwillingness to consent to it, and at last pretended, " That " the fear of disobliging her subjects (a consideration " that, she said, had a greater weight with her than " any other) prevailed upon her, tho' with the highest " reluctance, to give orders for the execution."

When this was reported to the queen of Scotland, at Fotheringay castle, she did not shew the least sign of fear or concern; but thanked God " She was thought " a person of such consequence, as to be able to re- " establish the R. Catholic religion in England, for " which cause she supposed she was condemned to " die." After this having obtained leave to write three letters, she addressed one of them to the Q. of England, another to the K. of France, and a third to the Pope; and said in the last, " That she esteemed it " a great happiness to lay down her life for the sake " of a religion, in which so many kings, her illustri- " ous ancestors had lived and died." She was soon after beheaded at Fotheringay castle.

In this manner, Mary Stuart, Q. of Scotland, finished a life, abounding with examples, both of good and bad fortune; after a confinement of about 20 years, during which time she had been in six different prisons, rigorously treated by her keepers, abandoned by her nearest relations, and destitute of all worldly comfort, except some letters from Gregory XIII, and Sixtus V, who had found means to have two secretly conveyed to her; one of which came to the hands of Q. Elizabeth, who read it over several times with much pleasure, tho' it was filled with instructions and exhortations, proper to confirm her in the Catholic religion, which Elizabeth held in abomination; but had so particular a regard for him, that she said to the person that gave her the letter, " The Q. of Scotland had no reason to complain of " her prison, when she received an honour there, " that we have long wished for above all others." And, without doubt, she would have been very glad to

have

have entered into a stricter correspondence with him, if she had not thought it would be disgustful to her subjects.

The news of this mournful catastrophe was soon spread all over Europe. The nuncio, that resided at Paris, sent an express, with an account of it, to Rome. Sixtus was just got up from supper, and stood leaning against a window, when cardinal Montalto gave him the nuncio's paquet, which he desired his nephew to read to him. All the while he was reading the letters, he looked stedfastly at him, and, when they were finished, struck his hand with great vehemence upon the window shutter, and fetched a deep sigh, turned his face towards England, as if he had a mind to speak to Q. Elizabeth, and said, aloud, *O glorious Queen!* From whence it was conjectured, that he envied her the happiness of cutting off a crowned head; tho' as there could be no certainty of that, such a conclusion seems unwarrantable.

The Q. of England, to skreen herself from the infamy of having shed royal blood, seemed to be under the deepest concern, and stormed at her secretary, who, as she pretended, hastened the execution, contrary to her orders; for which reason she threw him into prison, and laid a heavy fine upon him. But all the world laughed at this grimace, when they saw bonfires, illuminations, ringing of bells, and every sort of rejoicing, quite thro' the nation, at the same time.

The secretary wrote a justification of himself, and sent it to every court in Europe; wherein he asserted, that he had done nothing without the express commands of his mistress; which was generally believed. It is certain she drew upon herself the odium of all the princes in Christendom, by so flagrant and cruel an attack upon royal majesty.

As there is no place in the world where the conduct of princes is more freely examined and discussed than at Rome, they talked of Elizabeth there in terms of
the

the greatest abuse and indignation; thousands of satyrs and libels were daily published, in which she was
branded with the approbrious names of murdress, cro-
codile, barbarian, sacrilegious heretic, and all manner of the bitterest invectives. The authors of these
works were particularly severe upon her dissimulation
and hypocrisy, in pretending to shed tears at a tragedy
in which she had acted the principal part.

Upon this, Sixtus issued out an edict, forbidding
his subjects, on pain of the gallies, to write or say
any thing derogatory to the honour of that princess.
She was so pleased, when she was told that he said,
" Though she was a Heretic, she ought to be treated
" with respect, upon the account of her high rank
" and merit," That she redoubled the esteem she had
for him; and said, " He was a great prince, tho' he
" was a pope, which obliged him to be her enemy,
" contrary to his inclination."

From this mutual respect, which each expressed for
the other, the people of Rome suspected there was an
actual correspondence betwixt them; and tho' the
great number of spies deterred them from speaking
their opinion of it, they were impudent enough to
dress Pasquin like a courier, answering to Marforio,
who asked him, Whither so fast? I am going to England to carry the pope's letters to Q. Elizabeth.

It is said, tho' I think it scarce appears credible,
that the resolution which Q. Elizabeth had shewn in
bringing the Q. of Scotland to the block, inspired Sixtus with an ambition of putting some prince to death;
that he thought it an heroick action, and envied the
good fortune of Elizabeth, that he had thrown such an
opportunity in her way; that he often caused the
whole story of her life and death to be read to him;
and when they came to the circumstance of the Q.
of England's sending her word she must prepare for
death, he would stamp his foot, and say, " My God,
" what a glorious princess! What would I give to
                                                    " have

" have it in my power to fignalize myfelf in the fame
" manner."

Whilft he was feeking for an opportunity of gra-
tifying this inhuman appetite of fhedding royal blood,
it happened that Ranucius Farnefe, prince of Parma,
eldeft fon to the great Alexander Farnefe, duke of
Parma, general of the K. of Spain's armies in the
Low Countries, whom we have had occafion to mention before, came to Rome. This young prince happened, unluckily, to carry fome fort of arms, which
the Pope had forbid, by a very fevere edict, not
thinking himfelf liable to the penalties therein fpecified, as he was an independant prince: But when
Sixtus was informed of it, he gave orders for him to
be arrefted, and carried to the caftle of St. Angelo;
which were fo well obeyed that he was feized the very
next morning, armed, in the pope's anti-chamber
(which was looked upon as a very great aggravation
of his crime,) where he waited to be introduced to his
Holinefs, and directly hurried away to prifon.

The fuddennefs, and other extraordinary circumftances, of his arreft, made a great commotion in the
city, and exceedingly fhocked all the friends and par-
tifans of the Farnefe family, efpecially the cardinal,
who went with them immediately to the pope, to
defire he would forgive the prince, upon the account
of the great merit and fervices of the father, to whom
this would be offering a moft outragious indignity in
the perfon of his fon; and faid, " It would be a mat-
" ter of everlafting infamy and reproach to the H.
" See, that whilft the father, who was a fovereign
" prince, was bravely afferting the rights and inte-
" refts of the church, his fon and heir fhould be
" fhut up in prifon by his holinefs's order, for a tri-
" fle hardly worth taking notice of." They farther
reprefented to him, " That foreign princes were not
" obliged to pay obedience to edicts, or even laws,
" that were enacted to preferve order and decorum
" amongft the common people: That his crime (if
" it

" it was one) was rather the effect of youth and inad-
" vertence, than a premeditated defign to offend his
" holinefs, by infringing his laws : That if his of-
" fence had been of a more heinous nature, he de-
" ferved indulgence, upon the account of his youth,
" and the almoft unexampled fervices of his father."

Sixtus anfwered, " That he had too great a regard
" for merit, not to entertain the higeft refpect for
" the D. of Parma; but that, at the fame time, no
" confideration fhould ever prevail upon him to de-
" viate from juftice, if any one (let their quality be
" never fo confiderable) fhould be prefumptuous e-
" nough to tranfgrefs his laws; that he fhould have
" treated his neareft relation in the fame manner, if
" he had been guilty of fuch a crime; that he had
" much rather refign his crown, and return to a
" cloyfter, than fee the ordinances he had made,
" openly defpifed and trampled upon before his face;
" that he expected them to be obferved by every bo-
" dy, without exception; that a fovereign was no
" longer fo, when he was out of his own dominions,
" but bound to obey the laws of the ftate he refided
" in; that his youth was no manner of excufe; al-
" ledging, that the D. of Parma was a vaffal or feo-
" datary of the H. See; and that if he was not, there
" could be no defence made for fuch behaviour.'

At laft, he worked himfelf up into fuch a heat, and
treated them with fo much roughnefs, that they
thought proper to retire, and leave him to vent the
firft fallies of his paffion, waiting till his fury fhould
begin to fubfide : But the cardinal, who was acquainted with the obftinate and inflexible temper of Sixtus,
fearing left he fhould perfevere in his refolution, was
fo uneafy, and in fuch agitation of mind, when he got
home, that he returned to the vatican to renew his application, and fully determined not to leave it till he
had fucceeded. The Pope, who expected to be much
teazed and importuned upon this occafion, had already
given a ftrict charge to the gaoler, to put the prince
                                                    to

to death at fuch an hour. When the cardinal came again to folicit for his nephew, Sixtus pretended to fuffer himfelf to be prevailed upon, and gave him a written order to the keeper of the prifon, commanding him to deliver the prince up to him at the fecond hour of the night, meaning his body; for he had given him pofitive inftructions to cut off his head an hour before that time; which coming to the cardinal's knowledge, he found means to defer the execution till the fecond hour; a little before which he went himfelf, with the Pope's order, to the prifon; at the fight of which, the keeper, without any fcruple, gave the prince up into his hands.

The moment he was at liberty, he mounted a fwift horfe, which, by the cardinal's directions, was kept in readinefs for him; and made fo good hafte, that in 30 hours he was in his father's dominions in Lombardy. When the pope came to know how he had been over-reached, he was in fo great a rage, that it was apprehended he would have taken fome violent meafures to revenge himfelf upon the cardinal; but after he came to be cool, he could not help applauding his affection and addrefs, in outwitting both himfelf and the keeper.

For my own part, I cannot give any fort of credit to this ftory: It feems hard to believe, that the pope fhould dare to put a perfon of his quality to death for fuch a trifle, and in fo fhort a time, as it would certainly have been feverely revenged by the K. of Spain, with whom he was a great favourite; which might poffibily have turned Rome upfide down, and entirely ruined the Catholic intereft in the Low Countries: It rather looks like a malicious invention of his enemies, or fome perfon that miftook the extreme rigour with which he was neceffitated to adminifter juftice, for a cruel difpofition and blood-thirftinefs of nature. However, as it was a common report in thofe times, and is taken notice of by other authors, I thought it my

F f   duty,

duty, as an hiftorian, not entirely to omit the mention of it.

During the exceffive heats of the fummer feafon this year, the pope had a fever, without intermiffion, for feven days, of fo malignant a kind, that the phyficians defpaired of his life: The cardinals were fo far from being afflicted at it, that they rather wifhed for his death than recovery, as it would reftore the authority he had fo violently wrefted out of their hands, by taking the fole management of affairs to himfelf, and treating them like valets and flaves. The fury of his difeafe did not hinder him from attending to bufinefs and the government of the ftate, tha' his phyficians advifed him not to fatigue himfelf with it. He ftill continued publifhing edicts as ufual, and fent for the governor of the city, and the other magiftrates, every day, to give an account of their office, and to receive frefh inftructions.

His nephew was very urgent with him to fpare himfelf a few days, as too much application would certainly increafe his diforder; but he anfwered, " that a " prince ought never to quit his poft but with his " life;" charging him to double the number of fpies in Rome, as he thought the time of his illnefs would give him a proper opportunity of knowing in what degree of favour and efteem he ftood with the people. His nephew did as he was commanded; but nobody durft open their lips concerning him, for fear it fhould be a feigned ficknefs. They that hated him moft, were the forwardeft to frequent the prayers that were made for his recovery in all the churches of Rome, where the hoft was expofed for a whole day. When the pope heard of this, he ordered them to be fufpended; and faid to his nephew, " So much praying will " make the people think we are in effect, a dead " man; but we intend to let them know that we " are yet alive."

He lay one whole day as if he had been dead, and his phyfician feeing him motionlefs, gently touched his
nofe,

nofe, to fee if there remained any natural heat in him : Sixtus perceiving it, ftarted as if he had been frighted by fome terrible dream, and looking the phyfician full in the face, faid in an angry manner, " Pray, fir, who " are you, that have the impudence to take the pope " by the nofe ?" In a few days however he entirely recovered, and appeared again in public.

This illnefs did not at all abate the rigour of his juftice, nor infpire him with a more merciful difpofition. He was hardly got well, when he ordered two poor gentlemen to be hanged, for having kept fome fort of correfpondence with Mangone D'Evoli, one of the banditi. This man, who was of a very mean extraction, commonly took fhelter in the neighbourhood of Naples, from whence he ufed to fally, like a lion out of his den, and commit many murders and robberies in the ecclefiaftical ftate : but being taken at laft, he was broke upon the wheel at Naples. At his execution, he confeffed that he had been guilty of numberlefs crimes, impeaching feveral of his accomplices, and faid, " Thefe two gentlemen had often affifted him in his " efcape from the hands of juftice." The governor, who had fent them to prifon, found fufficient reafon to condemn them ; but out of compaffion to their families, put off their execution; either in expectation that Sixtus would die, or if he lived, to give their relations time to make intereft for a pardon. When he was informed of this delay, he was exceedingly enraged at the governor, threatning to turn him out of his office, for his dilatory proceedings, and ordered them to be immediately executed, though many ambaffadors feconded the petitions and entreaties of their friends to fpare their lives.

The court was no lefs alarmed at the feverity with which he punifhed Signior Bellochio, his chief cupbearer, and Guilterucci, fecretary to the H. College, a prelate of great character, and who, by his long fervices, had acquired the favour and confidence of his holinefs ; they were both fentenced to the gallies,

with

with another fecretary. Bellochio died of grief, not
being able to procure a pardon, though the whole court
interceded for him. He was condemned for having,
in a clandeftine manner, taken the Annulus Pifcatoris,
the fifherman's ring, which is the Pope's feal, and
fet it to a brief, which he had long importuned Sixtus
for in vain, as he thought it an unjuft and unreafonable requeft. The affair was this; Bellochio defigning to build a magnificent palace in his own
country, had occafion for a houfe which the propri-
etor would not part with. When he faw himfelf difappointed in his fchemes, he counterfeited a brief,
commanding the perfon to fell his houfe, which he
immediately obeyed, for fear of incurring the pope's
difpleafure, and fold it for much lefs than it was
worth.

Gualterucci, and the other, were likewife condemned for being privy to, and affifting in this knave-
ry. Every body was fenfibly touched with Gualterucci's fentence, as he was endowed with many excellent qualities, and his fhare of guilt fo inconfiderable, that it would have been taken no notice of in
any other pontificate. The whole college of cardinals, the ambaffadors of Spain and Venice, and many
other perfons of the firft rank, fued for his pardon:
but the pope would not fo much as hear them, and
faid, "He was called to the pontificate by God, to
" execute juftice, and not to grant pardons, which
" were only encouragements to commit frefh crimes.
" That he was a friend to his fervants, whilft they
" ferved him with fidelity; but would be the firft to
" punifh thofe that betrayed their mafters. That he
" could eafily forgive injuries done to his own per-
" fon, but would give no quarter to fuch as were
" offered to the H. See; that he fincerely wifhed no
" body was concerned in the prefent affair but him-
" felf, for then he would willingly have pardoned the
" offenders."

Gualterucci

Gualterucci remained in the gallies till the death of Sixtus, when he was fet at liberty to the great joy of all his acquaintance, who had heartily fympathized with him in his misfortune.

Francis di Medicis grand duke of Tufcany, dying this year, 1587, without heirs, his title and dominions devolved to his brother Ferdinand, the cardinal ; upon which account he fent ambaffadors to Rome on purpofe to refign his hat, with the ufual ceremonies, into the pope's hands, who obliged him to make rich prefents, for that indulgence, to the church of St. John de Lateran. This prince, fome time after, took to wife Chriftiana, daughter to the duke of Lorrain. Sixtus was not much concerned at his refignation, as it occafioned a vacancy in the College, and freed him from the infpection of a very quick-fighted perfon, and one, who, by the great authority refulting from his birth, was rather troublefome to him than otherwife [4].

Stephen Battori, prince of Tranfylvania, and K. of Poland, died alfo about this time, after he had

[4] Eodem tempore Ferdinandis Medicis cardinalis magnus etruriæ dux de uxore ducendâ ; et liberis ad firmandum imperium tollendis cogitans, cum in galliâ jam cum rege et reginâ parente, de accipiendâ Chriftiernâ Caroli Lotaringiæ Ducis et Claudiæ regis fororis filiâ conveniffet ut fe, cardinalis dignitate cum bonâ pontificis gratiâ, honorifice abdicaret, Nicolaum Tornobonum, Sancti Sepulchri epifcopum, Romam miffit cum literis ad pontificem et collegium cardinalium, quibus caufas petitionis fuæ exponebat. Huic et Johanni Nicolmo oratori apud pontificem fuo fenatus datus iv. calend. Octob. porrectifque literis, Cæfar Marfilius advocatus confiftorialis, pro oratoribus verba fecit. Tum recitatis publice literis, pontifex cum cardinalibus in fecretius cubiculum confeffit, ubi, exquifitis eorum fententiis, juftam Ferdinandi petitionem effe pronuntiavit, et quando facris nondum ullis ordinibus initiatus effet, ut uxòrem ducere poffet, gratiem fecit. Actæ ab oratoribus gratiæ, et pro gratâ tanti beneficii memoriâ duæ pulchri artificii ftatuæ argentæ. fingulæ 60 pondo ad S. Johannis in Laterano Bafilicam, cujus effigiem referebant, Ferdinandi nomine appenfæ funt. Mox Horatius Oricelarius, qui Paulo ante in patriam, invidiofis, ex Salinario vectigali, comparatis opibus relictâ Galliâ conceflerat, cum mandatis miffus, ut nuptias conventas fiduciariâ poteftate contraheret. Thuan. lib. xcii.

reigned

reigned nine years, lamented by all Chriftendom. This prince was very zealous for the R. Catholic religion, a great foldier and politician, had always kept the Proteftants in awe, happily put an end to many civil wars, and bravely recovered the duchies of Sueve and Smolenfko, which the Mufcovites had formerly taken from the Poles, more by ftratagem than valour. He fhewed no lefs courage in the year 1584, when the Turk, according to ancient cuftom, demanding a certain number of troops to make war upon the Perfian, he fent him word, " That the Polifh " eagle *, which had been fo long difplumed, began " to recover its former vigour, and had whetted its " 'beak   ' talons." Which bold anfwer prevented the infid. making any attempts upon his dominions (as they ui d to do) during his reign.

The great good qualities of Stephen, put the Poles to a difficulty in the election of another king, as they were defirous of fetting a perfon upon the throne that fhould fill it with equal dignity, and fupport the kingdom in the ftate he left it. Many thought the emperor Rodolphus would have been chofen; as it was agreed when his father Maximilian was elected by the favour of the houfe of Auftria, that his fon Rodolphus fhould immediately fucceed him, without any interregnum, when he died, which happened foon after, as they had forefeen from his weak conftitution and infirm ftate of health.

Some thought the D. of Parma ftood no bad chance for that crown, as he was one of the wifeft men, and greateft generals of the age; and his uncle, the cardinal, had acquired fo much efteem and reputation amongft the Poles, by the many fignal fervices he did them when he was the cardinal protector of that nation. But others were of a quite different opinion, founding their arguments upon the contrariety of humour betwixt the Poles and Italians.

* The arms of Poland.

It

It was likewife fufpected, that the duke's great valour was attended by a proportionable fhare of pride
and feverity, and that the Turks would be difgufted
at their having chofen a perfon to be their neighbour,
that was fuch a favourite, and fo much in the interefts of Spain, which nation they mortally hated.

The Vaivode [5] of Tranfylvania, and his coufin
the Cardinal Battori, likewife afpired to the crown.
The firft, who was a young man, full of courage
and ambition, depended upon the fuccour of the
grand fignior, and the immenfe riches and influence
of his family; on the other hand, it was a difadvantage to him, that he was nephew to the late
king, who, notwithftanding his great valour, and
the many fervices he had done the nation, was much
more feared than beloved by the nobility. They
complained that he had not obferved the ancient
cuftoms of that kingdom in the difpofal of places
and honours, that he had given them away, contrary
to the advice of the principal grandees; that as their
ftate was a fort of commonwealth, of which the
king was only the head, he could not, without the
concurrence and approbation of the diet, either make
war or peace, nor condemn any perfon to death,
that was accufed of capital crimes, as he had done,
which they looked upon as an infringement of their
liberties, and a downright ufurpation of the whole
fovereign authority.

The fame reafons were in force againft the cardinal, who was likewife a nephew to the late king.
He was otherwife poffeffed of fo many royal virtues,
and fo well qualified to reign, that many were perfuaded his merit alone would give him the preference
to all other competitors.

[5] Vaivode, or Woiewoda, fignifies a prince, duke, governor,
or chief magiftrate, and in the northern parts is generally a feu-
dal dignity : There is in Selden's Titles of Honour, an inveftiture,
folemn livery, or infeodation of Moldavia, to Stephen as Vaivode
thereof, in the year 1485.

The

The duke of Ferrara was alſo talked of: He was a great prince; had done ſeveral good offices to the kingdom; but was an Italian, and had been propoſed at a former election, and rejected, which diſcouraged many from giving him their ſuffrage, who had voted for him before.

Several of the Poliſh nobility likewiſe flattered themſelves with the hope of being elected; but their ambition was ill-grounded; they ſeemed to have forgot, that the Poles dread nothing ſo much as a king of their own nation; that there had not been one for above 600 years; and that if their anceſtors did not chuſe foreigners before that, it was becauſe the government was not then thoroughly ſettled, and at a time when the laws had but little authority, and that they were not ſo good politicians in thoſe ages as they have been ſince. Beſides, if the Poles had been inclined to chuſe one of their own nation, they would not have fixed upon a Piaſte (that is, a gentleman of a family that pretends to be deſcended from their ancient kings) but upon the chancellor Zamotſki, who had been truſted with the entire adminiſtration of affairs under Stephen. That Prince uſed to conſult him in the minuteſt affairs, and was wholly governed by his advice: his levee was as numerous and ſplendid as the king's; the quality of general of the crown army, ſerving as a pretext for the royal ſtate and magnificence in which he lived. His experience and readineſs in buſineſs, joined to his bravery, and the prodigious love the ſoldiery had for him, would infallibly have facilitated his deſigns upon the crown.

The lot however did not fall upon any of the candidates that we have mentioned. The nation was divided into two powerful factions, which, in the end ſwallowed up the ſmaller; one of them declaring for the prince of Sweden, the other for Maximilian, arch-duke of Auſtria, brother to the emperor Rodolphus, whoſe generoſity, mildneſs, and love of juſtice, had gained him a conſiderable party in the diet; which

which being fupported by the Auftrians, he was proclaimed king by one of the factions.

The other, which was compofed of fuch as had an irreconcileable hatred to the Germans (with whom the court would have been immediately filled, and who would have had the preference to natural born fubjects in the difpofal of all places of honour and profit) was further apprehenfive, that if the arch-duke fhould ever fucceed his brother the emperor, he might join Poland to the empire, as an hereditary ftate, like Hungary and Bohemia, which were formerly elective kingdoms, but annexed to the imperial crown by his anceftors.   It was likewife feared they might difoblige the Grand Signior, whofe power was always formidable to them, by chufing a prince of the houfe of Auftria, which he could not endure, as has been remarked.

These reafons prevailed upon that faction to chufe the prince of Sweden, about 20 years old, of the houfe of the Jagellons, whofe name was held in great veneration for the many noble atchievements they had performed, befides the joining the great duchy of Lithuania to the crown of Poland.   The ready money of Sweden might likewife have fome influence upon them, and many were of opinion, that the king of Sweden had a defign of uniting the two kingdoms in favour of this his only fon, whom he loved tenderly.

But the moft penetrating thought otherwife: That monarch might yet have more children, and had at prefent other heirs of his own name; but, admitting he had not, what reafon could there be for giving his crown, which was hereditary in his family, to the kings of Poland who are ftrangers, often fet upon the throne by brigue, or fortune?

What determined them, moft probably, in this election, was, that the Poles had a mind to make fure of Lithuania, upon which the K. of Sweden might make fome attempt by fea; whereas by chufing his fon, they fhould deliver themfelves from a long and
cruel

cruel war. They likewife confidered that their chief ftrength confifted in their cavalry, and the utter inability they lay under·to raife any confiderable force, except by land; that the K. of Sweden could at any time fend out a powerful fleet, by which means they fhould make themfelves formidable, both by fea and land, to the Mufcovite, who had long been called, *The Dragon of the North,* and to whom they had always entertained an implacable hatred. Thefe reafons, having engaged one of the factions to chufe the P. of Sweden; there was a double election; and the two princes, being informed of all that had been tranfacted in their favour, affembled fome troops, and marched at the head of them, to take poffeffion of the crown.

Whilft the diet was fitting, Sixtus fent two couriers to the archbifhop of Naples, his nuncio in Poland, with orders to attend it, and ufe his utmoft endeavours to promote the election of Maximilian; enjoining him, however, to conduct himfelf with prudence and difcretion, and not to make too open profeffions of his attachment to him, for fear of irritating the Swedes, as it might be inconfiftent with the honour of the H. See to engage too far in an undertaking, the event of which was yet uncertain.

He ftrictly charged him to pay clofe attention to the deliberations of the affembly, with inftructions, " If he faw Maximilian's party not likely to prevail, " then to declare for him that was the ftrongeft." Which was, in effect, to name the prince of Sweden. Great was his joy when the nuncio fent him word that Maximilian was chofen; but being informed, foon after, that his election was likely to be attended with much oppofition, he was highly difpleafed at the archbifhop, and wrote an angry letter, to upbraid him with fending falfe intelligence; but at the fame time remitted 22,000 ducats to the bifhop of Nais in Silefia, for the affiftance of Maximilian, with a promife of more confiderable fuccours.

It

It is thought, if Maximilian had marched with a larger force, directly to the gates of Cracow (the capital of Poland, and residence of the kings, where the Regalia are kept) he would infallibly have made himself master of it, and that the rest of the kingdom would of course have been obliged to acknowledge him: But he arrived too late, and came to a plain that lies near the city, with only 16,000 men, about the middle of October, 1587.

When he had marked out a camp, he sent to notify his election to the inhabitants, requiring them to admit him into the city: But they shut their gates, and immediately sent an express to the P. of Sweden, conjuring him to hasten his arrival; representing to him the peril and hazard of any delay; and that they had fixed the ceremony of his coronation upon St. Luke's day. In the mean time they fortified themselves in the best manner they could, and burnt some part of the suburbs, and neighbouring villages, casting up trenches and breast-works, to defend themselves, if they should be attacked by Maximilian, as there were every day some skirmishes betwixt his army and the Poles, generally to the advantage of the latter.

Whilst things were in this situation, ambassadors arrived from the prince of Sweden, with advice, " That their master was at Dantzick; that he had " been prevented from arriving there sooner, by the " bad weather they met with at sea ; that he was o- " bliged to make a short stay there to refresh his troops " and attendants; so that it was not possible for him to " be at Cracow on the day appointed for the corona- " tion, and desired it might be deferred till St. Mar- " tin's day, the 11th of November." To which the Cracovians sent for answer, " That it had always " been the custom to crown their kings upon a Sun- " day, which was the reason they had fixed upon St. " Luke's day, as it fell on a Sunday that year; and " that if he could not be with them by that time,
" they

" they muſt put it off till the Sunday after St. Mar-
" tin's day."

In the mean time Maximilian's army, encamped
upon the plain before Cracow, grew weaker and weaker every day; his ſoldiers being ill-cloathed, could
not ſtand the inclemency of the ſeaſon, which was at
that time more than commonly rigorous: The want
of wine obliged them to drink water, or very bad
beer, which gave them fluxes and dyſenteries, with
a malignant fever, that at laſt became contagious,
and daily carried off great numbers; tho' the general did every thing that man could do to remedy this
evil, but to no purpoſe, as he had neither wholeſome
food, nor warm and convenient lodgings, without
which it is not poſſible to ſtop the progreſs of theſe
diſtempers.

There was no leſs a mortality in Petrocovia, where
the P. of Sweden being now arrived, a young Pole,
whoſe name was Corfinſki, a follower of Maximilian,
took upon him to deliver a letter into his hand, which
he effected in the following manner: He had an uncle in the P. of Sweden's camp, that was his chief favourite and confidant, to whom he addreſſed himſelf,
begging him to intercede with the prince in his behalf, to acquaint him how ſorry he was that he had
taken up arms in Maximilian's cauſe, and how deſirous to atone for that fault, by now entering zealouſly
into his highneſs's ſervice,

His uncle, who expreſſed much ſatisfaction at his
reſolution, eaſily obtained his pardon, and permiſſion
to kiſs the prince's hand: But as ſoon as he was introduced, inſtead of paying him that mark of reſpect,
he had the aſſurance to deliver him a letter from
Maximilian, telling him, "He muſt not be ſurprized
" if that prince was now obliged to make uſe of a
" ſtratagem to convey a letter into his own hand,
" after he had wrote five or ſix, which, he had rea-
" ſon to believe, were never delivered." The prince
enraged at the inſolence of ſuch a proceeding, ordered
him

be thrown into a dungeon, after he had firſt
t Maximilian's letter before his face. Some ſay
id not burn it, but gave it, unopened, to one of
ecretaries, to ſhew the contempt he held him in.
ever, when he came ſoon after to reflect upon
e was ſo ſtruck with the intrepidity of the action,
the Pole's fidelity to his maſter, that he ſet him
erty.

aximilian being obliged to decamp from before
ow, took the rout of Petrocovia, with the remains
is army, fully reſolved to give the Swedes battle,
ever he met them, not imagining they were ſo
g, as he was afterwards informed, tho' they were
e 30,000, and his army reduced to about a third
of that number: But whether he was deterred
he ill fortune he had in a ſkirmiſh with them, or
ced by ſome other ſecret motive, he quitted his
deſign, and returned to make another attack up-
racow, in which he loſt a great many men, and
with no better ſuccefs than he had done in the
At laſt, being obliged, for his own ſafety, to
e to Bellon, the chancellor determined to purſue
with 12,000 men.
Then Maximilian heard this, he was forced to leave
n, and retiring out of Poland, came to Pilſen, a
: ſituated upon the frontiers of Sileſia, belonging
he duke of Brigen, where the chancellor, hav-
had the advantage of him in ſeveral ſkirmiſhes,
him up, and he being in want of all ſorts of am-
ition and proviſions, was compelled to ſurrender
elf priſoner the beginning of January, 1588.
he chancellor, overjoyed at the victory he had
ined, cauſed an inventory to be taken of all the
gage that was in Maximilian's camp, and ſent him
ner, under a ſtrong guard, to a place at ſome
nce; leaving him, for the uſe of his table, only
ſilver diſhes, eight plates, two ſpoons, and two
s. It was a cruel mortification to the unfortu-
prince to ſee himſelf treated in that manner.
All

All that knew him were fenfibly affected with his difgrace. The town of Pilfen was given up to the infolence and avarice of the foldiers, who plundered it with a barbarity hardly to be paralleled. Every court in Chriftendom was concerned at Maximilian's defeat, and none more deeply than Poland itfelf; the ftates of which, having agreed to take part with neither fide, faw, with afflicton and regret, the indignity that Maximilian had received; and the pillaging of a town in Silefia, which was part of the kingdom of Bohemia, by an army of Poles, commanded by a chancellor of their own nation. But of all the fovereigns that bewailed Maximilian's misfortune, there was not one of them that was fo ready to fuccour, or fent him earlier afliftance, than Sixtus, as we fhall relate in the next book, being obliged, for a little while, to refume the affairs of France.

The pope began now in good earneft to be very attentive to what paffed in that kingdom. He made a prefent of a fword to the duke of Guife, who was head of the league, like that which he had formerly fent by the abbé Grimani to the D. of Parma, in the Low Countries; and ordered the prelate, that was charged with this commiffion, to affure him of " his " fincere affection; and that he filled the firft place " in his heart."

When the duke received this prefent at Paris, there were fuch rejoicings and acclamations amongft the citizens, that it excited the jealoufy of Henry III; tho' the duke feemed to receive thefe honours with a great deal of modefty, and rather to decline than affect popularity.

It was with the higheft concern that the king faw the deplorable condition to which France was reduced, by the miferies of civil war, and the daily diminution of his own authority. The pope, who could never bear to hear with patience of any incroachment upon the rights of fovereigns, wrote a letter to him with his own hand, in which he exhorted him, " To fhew
himfelf

" himſelf couragious in the defence of his crown;
" to chaſtiſe the inſolence of his rebellious ſubjects;
" to have recourſe to amputation and cauſtics, now
" the diſtemper was grown inveterate; adviſing him
" to make frequent uſe of phlebotomy, as they
" ſeemed wanton and full of blood."

This letter, which occaſioned many ſtrange reflec-
tions and reſolutions in the king's heart, was very
carefully preſerved by him, and more than once
ſhewn to the D. of Guiſe. He read it one day to his
council, whom he had aſſembled to conſult upon proper means to heal the wounds and diviſions, that were
made in the kingdom, to ſhew his miniſters the Pope
was in his intereſt, and that he was not inclined to
follow the violent councils he gave him, but to be
tender of his people's lives. All that were preſent,
even the very Proteſtants, were above meaſure ſurprized to ſee his holineſs ſo forward to ſhed the blood
of a flock, over which he pretended to be the true
ſhepherd. One of them (a Proteſtant) was ſo tranſ-
ported he could not forbear ſaying, " That the pope
" had made a downright ſhambles of human fleſh at
" Rome, and wanted to do the ſame at Paris; that
" it was not at all to be wondered at, that he ſhould
" adviſe other princes to exerciſe ſuch cruelties to
" their ſubjects, when he treated his own after the
" ſame manner, nor that his counſels ſhould be as
" bloody as his conduct."

The Proteſtants took occaſion from this to publiſh
many ſatyrs and libels againſt the pope, who, when
he found it had been read in full council, ordered his
nuncio to complain of it to the king, and to ſignify
to him, " That as he had written to his majeſty out
" of the fulneſs of his paternal affection, and opened
" his ſentiments in a very ſincere and explicit man-
" ner, he did not expect he would have ſhewn ſo
" little regard for him, as to expoſe his letter, or
" make uſe of his name, without permiſſion." The
king made the beſt excuſe he could for it; but Sixtus

tus would never write to him again; always ordering his nuncio, upon any matter of confequence, to communicate what he had to fay by word of mouth. This did not give the king much concern, as he often difapproved of the pope's advice, whofe temper was very different and difagreeable to his own.

The K. of Navarre's agents in Switzerland, were very active at this time preffing the Proteftant cantons to affemble their forces, and join them with thofe of the K. of Denmark, the duke of Saxony, the marquis of Brandenbourg, and prince Cafimir, who, by the affiftance of 60,000 ducats, which the Q. of England had already fent them, were refolved to oppofe the progrefs of the league againft the Proteftant preacher, was then amongft the Swifs, who held him in very great reverence, for his zeal in their religion; the K. of Navarre's agents, to give a fanction to their negociations, applied to him, and prefented him with letters from their mafter conceived in terms of the higheft refpect. Upon which Beza, who was indeed very zealous for the advancement of the Proteftant religion, and ambitious of fhewing his influence over thefe people, began to go about from canton to canton, preaching, exhorting, and fpiriting them up in fuch a manner, that they not only gave orders for raifing the forces which the K. of Navarre folicited; but collected a very large fum of money to fupport them, and lodged it in the hands of prince Cafimir.

The Catholic cantons, who were grievoufly offended at his proceedings, wrote to feveral prelates and cardinals in Rome, defiring them to inform the pope "of the horrible mifchief he was doing by his " oftentatious fhew of zeal, and continual endeavours " to confirm the Proteftants in their infatuation, to " the great prejudice of the Catholic intereft; upon " which confideration it would be highly proper to " think of fome expedient to ftop his progrefs, and
" concert

concert means to remove or take him off, as they rendered the safety and preservation of the true religion in those parts."

There were two consultations held upon this subject which the pope was present, when some of cardinals said, "That without doubt a method might be found to draw him out of Geneva, either by stratagem, or promises, or allurement of some kind or other, and then there would be no obstacle to prevent the entire conversion of that city; that though his holiness had signalized his pontificate by many illustrious actions, this would outshine them all in the annals of his reign; that was therefore absolutely necessary, nay, his duty, to use his utmost endeavours and authority, to banish this pest from Geneva, which would infallibly restore the true Catholic religion, to the eternal confusion of the Protestants and their new doctrines."

They added, "That the conversion of this city was a point of the highest importance; and that the preservation, not only of Switzerland, but of France, was likewise concerned at it, as it was the key of the Protestant cantons, and an asylum to such as fled thither out of France, upon any persecution; that there was no doubt, but, if Geneva was reduced to its duty, the whole kingdom of France, would of course follow its example, and the hope of the one, and the support of the other, being entirely taken away, the Catholic religion might easily be re-established in both."

Sales, the titular bishop of Geneva, being at that time in Rome, was sent for by the Pope, to consult what would be the likeliest method to remove Beza out of Geneva. He said, "He thought the best way would be, to furnish the duke of Savoy with a force sufficient to besiege the city; for that there was but little probability of enticing him out of it, as he was very subtle, and not a little proud

G g

" of

" of the authority and power he faw he had obtained a-
" mongft them, and fo well acquainted with the
" nature of his fituation, that he was aware the
" Catholics had all engines at work to get his per-
" fon into their hands; that he therefore took no
" ftep without great care and circumfpection; was
" very fhy of entering into an acquaintance with
" any body he did not know, and would not admit
" even a fervant into his houfe, whofe fidelity he
" was not well affured of; that he was conftantly
" attended by five or fix Proteftants by way of
" guard, when he ftirred abroad, and very feldom,
" upon any occafion, went out of the city, which
" precautions had entirely defeated the duke of
" Savoy's defigns, who had taken great pains to
" get him poifoned or affaffinated."

Sforza, who was at the confultation, advifed,
" That cardinal Montalto fhould fend him a letter
" by fome perfon, in the character of a young
" nobleman upon his travels, and make him an
" offer of a cardinal's hat, if he would abandon the
" Proteftants, and return into the bofom of the
" church, in which fo many of his family had glo-
" rioufly lived and died." The congregation was
much divided in their opinions upon this propofal;
fome applauded it, and faid, "That as Beza was
" reported to be a vain-glorious and ambitious man,
" it was not to be doubted that he would fwallow
" the bait, and be glad to embrace an opportunity
" that would put him upon a level with princes."
" Others faid, "It would be making the purple too
" cheap to offer it to a heretic, who, they might
" be affured would infallibly refufe it, tho' it might
" be reafonably fuppofed he would be very defirous
" of fo great an honour, but was too cunning to be
" caught in a trap, and would not truft their pro-
" mifes; that fuch a meafure would encreafe his au-
" thority, and add to his reputation, amongft his
" followers, and might poffibly ferve to confirm them
                                          " in

" in their errors, as it would give them caufe to be-
" lieve their religion was the true one, when they
" faw a man of his diftinction and learning refufe
" the dignity of a cardinal, and refolutely perfevere
" in his principles."

Sixtus heard their feveral opinions, as ufual, and
then faid, " He had little or no occafion for advifers
" in fuch matters; that the right of difpofing of car-
" dinals hats entirely belonged to him, and was one
" of his prerogatives; that he thought it impertinent
" in any one to direct him to whom, or upon what oc-
" cafion he fhould beftow them; that he had rather
" drive three cities from their obedience to the H.
" See, than call one heretic to Rome, and clothe him
" in purple; that when it came to be known, that
" he gave away cardinals hats to reclaim Hugonots
" and bring them back to the Catholic faith,
" many would turn heretics to obtain that honour;
" that he thought it was the beft way not to make
" them confiderable by taking too much notice of
" them, and then they would probably make ad-
" vances of themfelves or dwindle away by degrees
" in courfe of time."

He was much more alarmed at the murmurs and
complaints that were raifed all over Europe upon Q.
Elizabeth's putting the Q. of Scotland to death in fo
cruel a manner, without any regard to nearnefs of
blood, or the majefty of crowned heads, to gratify
her own mean jealoufy; or, as fhe pretended, for
reafons of ftate. It was objected, that if there were
in reality any fuch exifting, it was acting according
to the maxim of the Jews, who held it lawful to
put one perfon to death, tho' innocent, for the prefervation of the whole.

All Chriftendom rung with execrations and curfes
at this inhuman manner of proceeding. The very
Proteftants themfelves looked upon it with horror and
deteftation. As Sixtus had thefe reproaches daily
echoed in his ears, from all quarters, by his fpies

and nuncios abroad, and was informed, "That it
"was much wondered at by all the world, that a
"Pope, who was so strenuous an asserter and main-
"tainer of the Catholic faith, should not take
"particular notice of such an unprecedented attack
"upon it, and give some consolation to the faithful,
"by publicly shewing his resentment and abhor-
"rence of a murder barbarously perpetrated upon a
"princess whose only crime was her zealous attach-
"ment to the religion of her ancestors."

But the Spaniards raised the loudest clamour, and
were perpetually teazing the Pope to furnish them
with assistance to make war upon Elizabeth; so that
he (to whom nothing could be more agreeable than
to engage the K. of Spain in such a war, more with
a view to serve his own particular interest than out
of any zeal to religion) thought it would be no ill
policy, in some measure to comply with their re-
quests, and make a shew of being vehemently in-
censed at the conduct of Elizabeth: But to do this
in a manner that would be the least expensive to
him, he judged it would be the properest to make use
of ecclesiastical censures. For this purpose, having
called a consistory, he furiously declaimed against the
wickedness of Elizabeth, and highly commended the
zeal and piety of the K. of Spain, and his intended
invasion; acquainted them, at the same time, with
his intention to anathematise her. And they all applauding his resolution, he accordingly proceeded to
excommunication; first in the consistory, and then
publicly; a bishop in black robes reading the sentence, with a lighted candle in his hand, and all the
other ceremonies used upon such occasions [6].

The contents of the bull published for that purpose,
are as follow:

[6] As I met with the contents of the bull in Thuanus, l. lxxxix.
I thought it would not be disagreeable to the Latin reader, if I
here inserted it.

. Diplomate

Diplomate autem illo, pontifex pro poteſtate
a deo ſibi, legitimâ Ecclesiæ Catholicæ ſuc-
ceſſione, delatâ, ob defectionem Henrici octavi,
qui ſe ſuoſque a communione Chriſtianorum vi ſe-
queſtravit, ab Edvardo longinuś promotam, et ab
Elizabethâ, quæ in eâdem rebellione, et uſurpati-
one, pertinacem et mimine pænitentem ſe pre-
bens, magna vicinorum principum ac populorum
offenſione ac periculo perſeverat, continuatam,
aſſiduis plurimorum hortatibus, et anglorum ipſo-
rum ſupplicibus precibus incitatus, apud diverſos
principes, ac præcique præpotentem Hiſpanorum
regem, diligenter egiſſe dicit, auxiliumque implo-
ràſſe ut vires omnes a deo O. M. datas in id con-
ferret, quo fœmina illa de gradu dejiceretur, eique in regno faventes, homines pernicioſi, pro
ſcelerum gravitate punirentur, et regnum, cujus
ſalus ad univerſam rem Chriſtianam pertinet, in-
ſtauratâ religione, priſtinæ quieti reſtitueretur.
Tum cauſæ additæ, ob quas denuo cum fœminâ
hâc tam ſevere actum eſſet, quod, videlicet, ſciſ-
ſuræ cauſam ſectariâ pravitate dederit, ob id a
* deceſſoribus P. P. ecclesiæ communione ſum-
mota, contra omnia jura divina et humana, auctoritatem et juriſdictionem in rebus ſacris ſibi ſump-
ſerit, quod regnum contra jus omne uſurpet, abo-
litâ veteris contractûs inter S. S. et regnum Angliæ
initi, temporibus Henrici Secundi, ob cædem S.
Thomæ Cantuarienſis, religione, item ob crebras
injurias, vexationes violentas, ab ipſa et aliis ejus
permiſſu in homines innocentes perpetratas, ob
ſeditiones ac rebelliones inter vicinarum provinci-
arum populos, contra legitimum magiſtratum ac
principem excitatas, ob hoſpitium datum tranſ fu-
gis, rebellibus facinoroſis, aliiſque publicis male-
ficis, eorumque patrocinium magno Chriſtianorum
opprobio ac detrimento ſuſceptum, ob accerſitum
et concitatum præpotentem Chriſtiani nominis
hoſtem Tuream, ob indeſinentem contra ſanctos

* Predeceſſors.

" dei

" dei epifcopos crudelitatem, et male habitos, fpo-
" liatos, carceri mancipatos, variifque tormentis
" fubjectos facerdotes, ob inhumanam et iniquam
" captivitatem, et infolenti more captum de Mariâ
" Scotorum reginâ, quæ fupplex acceptâ fide in
" Angliam confugerat, fupplicium, ob exturbatam
" antiquam religionem : Et ut etiam, quantum ad
" civilem adminiftrationem, in regna ac ditiones
" alienas jus coercitionis fanctæ fedi competere
" oftenderetur, crimini ulterius Elizabethæ datum
" fuit, quod rejectâ antiquâ nobilitate, homines
" novos, obfcuros, et indignos, ad dignitates tam
" facras quam civiles provexiffet, et confufo omni
" humano ac divino jure, fœdiffimam munerum
" publicorum nundinationem hâc ratione conftituif-
" fet : Ob quas et alias caufas, plenius in Pii V, et
" Gregorii XIII diplomatibus expreffas, Sixtus eam
" denuo profcribebat, omnemque regiam dignitatem
" titulos ac jura ad Angliæ et Hiberniæ regna com-
" petentia profcriptæ adimebat, illegitimam ipfam,
" et horum regnorum verè ufupatricem declarans,
" fubditis ejus a fidei et obfequii jurejurando abfolu-
" tis. Tum omnes, cujufcunque conditionis effent, i-
" ram omnipotentis Dei, ni parerent, incurfuros inter-
" minatus, obteftabatur, ne, ubi mandati hujus notiti-
" am habuerint, ullâ ope, favore, auxilio, gratiâ pro-
" fcriptam reginam juvent : Sed omnes vires fuas
" ultro conferant ut dignum fupplicium de illâ fumi
" poffit. Mandabat infuper omnibus horum regno-
" rum incolis, ut mandata hæc diligenter exequeren-
" tur, et fimul ac de claffis adventu certiores fierent,
" Hifpanorum exercitui vires fuas jungant, et duci
" parmenfi, qui fummo cum imperio a Philippo,
" cujus aufpiciis expeditio fufciperetur, ei præpofitus
" fuit, ad omnia obediant, fide datâ ut nihil de reg-
" norum antiquis legibus, confuetudinibus privilegiis,
" immunitatibus, libertatibus, nifi ex S. M. et ordi-
" num concordi decreto immutetur aut detrahatur:
" Sed quæ ad inftaurationem antiquæ religionis, et

fœminæ

" fœminæ hujus abdicationem, controverſiaſque ex
" eâ orituras pertinent, amicè componantur, et jux-
" ta leges ac Chriſtianam æquitatem, ſine ullius dam-
" no vel in juriâ decidantur, Catholicis ab omni inju-
" riâ ac direptione tutis, et aliis præteria qui pœni-
" tentiâ factâ ad parmenſis partes ultro ſe applica-
" bunt: Propoſita interea præmia luculenta iis qui in
" fœminam proſcriptam manum injicerent, eam ca-
" perent, et Catholicæ parti ad ſumendum de eâ ſup-
" plicium traderent. Pro clauſulâ ſolenni, pontifex
" ex ecclesiæ promptuario fidei ſuæ credito, opes de-
" promit, et plenam delictorum omnium, iis qui
" huic expeditioni nomen darent gratiam facit,—
" Conventum eſt in arcano ut Philippus regnum ad
" ecclesiæ obedientiam redactum, tanquam S. S. be-
" neficiarium, juxta contractus ab Ina, Henrico Se-
" cundo, et Johanne initos, et renovatos, legeſque
" a pontifice cum titulo defenſoris fidei acciperet."

This was followed by orders to his nuncios reſi-
ding at foreign courts, to ſee that all the biſhops in
Chriſtendom publiſhed the excommunication in their
reſpective dioceſes, for three Sundays ſucceſſively;
which was punctually executed in the eccleſiaſtical
ſtate, and throughout all the K. of Spain's dominions, to excite his ſubjects to contribute willingly to
the expence of the war he was now reſolved to engage in with Q. Elizabeth. To make the greater
impreſſion upon the people, he ordered his royal
chapel to be hung in black, when the nuncio publiſhed the excommunication before the king, and
moſt of the grandees and nobility of Spain.

But the Venetians, who are always very circum-
ſpect in their proceedings, eſpecially where the court
of Rome is concerned, would not conſent to have it
publiſhed in their dominions; making excuſes from
time to time, to the nuncio, for putting it off. The
nuncio at laſt, by the inſtigation of the Spaniſh ambaſſador, complained to the ſenate; and, finding after

ter all, he could get no pofitive anfwer, he wrote
an account of it to the Pope, who fent him word,
" That he approved of his prudent conduct, and
" fhould be ftill more pleafed with it, if he could by
" any means bring the Venetians to acknowledge that
" they did not do this out of any contempt or difre-
" gard to the H. See, but for political reafons, and
" for fear of affronting thofe that had it in their
" power to be either good friends or dangerous ene-
" mies."

The nuncio perceived by this anfwer, the Pope
was not exceedingly folicitous that he fhould prefs
the Venetians much about it. Queen Elizabeth was
fo pleafed with this demonftration of their efteem and
refpect for her, that fhe fent to return her particular
thanks to the fenate for it.

When fhe was informed that Sixtus had excommunicated her, tho' fhe was fully convinced he did it
only to flatter and amufe the Spaniards, and not out
of any real hatred to her : However, to let the world
fee that fhe did not fear the forces of Rome and Spain,
tho' united, and that fhe had as much fpiritual authority in her dominions as the Pope had in his, fhe fummoned all the nobility and principal perfons of the
kingdom, with the magiftracy of London, to attend
her at St. Paul's church ; and there caufed the bifhop of the diocefe (to the great mortification and
offence of the Catholics) to pronounce fentence of
excommunication againft the Pope, and all perfors
that had any hand in excommunicating her ; and entertained them the fame day at a fumptuous banquet,
where they all folemnly promifed and fwore, " To
" ftand by her with their lives and fortunes, and
" fpend the laft drop of their blood in the defence
" of her perfon and crown, againft all open and fe-
" cret enemies." When Sixtus was acquainted with
this, he faid to the perfon that informed him of it,
" We perceive our excommunication has not much
                                        " frighted

" frighted the Q of England ; and this is all we fhall
" do for the Spaniards."

Francifco Maria dello Rovere, duke of Urbino, was
about this time engaged in a broil with his holinefs,
who, tho' he had a very great refpect for the memory of Sixtus IV, the founder, as it were, of that
family, could not help thinking it unjuft that fo fine
a duchy, containing fuch a number of cities, caftles, villages, territories, and dependencies, fhould
be difmembered from the pope's dominions, though
the dukes held it as a fief of the church. It galled
him fo much the more, as it lay almoft in the midft
of the ecclefiaftical ftate ; fo that from the beginning of his pontificate he had formed a defign of re-
uniting it to the Holy See.

Indeed the fchemes of Sixtus were very great, if
credit may be given to what cardinal Montalto told
fome of his friends, after the pope's death. He faid
that his uncle, confidering the ftrength of his conftitution, expected to have lived ten years longer, which
would be time fufficient to lay up an immenfe fum of
money, and make all neceffary preparations for the
invafion and conqueft of Naples, which expedition
he intended to honour with his prefence. This he
thought would be eafy to accomplifh, and give him
an opportunity of afterwards wrefting the duchies of
Urbino and Ferrara from the families Della Rovere,
and D'Efte.

For my own part, I can't help thinking he would
have met with many difficulties in his firft undertaking; not only upon the confideration of Philip II.
being a prince of great wifdom and forefight, as well
as ftrength and power, but becaufe the Neapolitans,
tho' they hate the Spanifh government, have a much
greater averfion to ecclefiaftical tyranny ; and would
therefore, of two evils, naturally chufe the lefs. If
he had fucceeded, he would certainly then have made
an attempt upon Tufcany and Lombardy.

But

But as his defign upon Naples was not yet ripe for execution, and great treafure and much time were neceffary to bring it to maturity, he altered his fcheme, and determined to begin with Urbino, not by violence, or force of arms, but under a pretence of juftice, and a legal title to it. For this purpofe, he fent a nuncio to the duke of Urbino, whofe name was Pignoni, an arrogant and fupercilious man; and fo rigid an afferter of the ecclefiaftical privileges, that he often ufed to fay, " He would fooner fuffer " himfelf to be cut to pieces, than give up the leaft " atom or particle of the church's rights."

Immediately after his arrival there, he fet up a jurifdiction, in direct contempt of the fovereignty of that prince, eftablifhing a tribunal in his palace, under the colour of examining into the validity of marriages, that had been celebrated above ten years before; in many of which it was pretended there had been great abufes and clandeftine practifes; taking upon him to cite feveral of the principal perfons of the court to appear before him, and to fend fome of them to Rome, after having feveral times examined them. The duke had private intelligence, that his Holinefs fent this nuncio on purpofe to provoke him to fome act of refentment, that fo he might have a plaufible excufe for proceeding againft him, as a contumacious rebel to the Holy See.

After he had with incredible patience fubmitted to his infolent behaviour, for the fpace of fome months, not being able to bear with him any longer, he publifhed an edict, forbidding his lay fubjects, on fevere penalties, to appear at the nuncio's court; and fent him word, " That when he had occafion to examine " any perfon, he muft apply to his chief juftice, " who fhould take his examination, and fend it to " him." This fet fire to the train; and the nuncio, after much perfonal abufe, proceeded fo far as to threaten, " that he would make the duke feel the
" weight

' weight of his authority;" and sent an account of
he whole affair to Rome.

Tho' it is probable the pope hourly expected to
hear something of this kind, he could not help fall-
ng into so extravagant a passion, that, without ever
advising with the consistory, as he ought to have
done, he sent a monitory by the same courier to the
duke, in which he commanded him, on pain of excommunication, " Not only not to molest the nuncio
" in the execution of his office, and to admit of his
" tribunal, but to come himself directly to Rome,
" and give an account of his behaviour, or he would
" treat him as a rebel." The duke was supported
by the grand duke of Tuscany, the Venetians, France
and Spain, who all exerted themselves strenuously
in his favour, but none of them so much as cardinal
Aldobrandino, who was under obligations to the duke,
and in great favour with Sixtus: By his good offices
the matter was compromised, and the duke obliged
to send a formal embassy to ask the pope's pardon;
upon which the nuncio was recalled, and not taken
any notice of afterwards; the duke being very glad to
come off so well.

Not long after, Sixtus had a quarrel with Rodolphus
II, tho' he always professed the highest veneration
for the house of Austria. The emperor had sent instructions to the duke Savelli, his ambassador at
Rome, to treat with the pope about some ecclesiastical affairs in Germany, as he pretended to have a sovereign jurisdiction over his own clergy; and as many prelates, perhaps encouraged by the court of
Rome, claimed certain immunities and exemptions,
which the emperor thought derogatory to his imperial power, he made heavy complaints of it to his holiness, protesting " He would never part with the
" right he had to take cognizance of those affairs,
" and especially the nomination to several dignities
" in the church;" ordering his ambassador to acquaint the pope with this his resolution.

Tho'

460 THE LIFE OF BOOK VIII.

Tho' the ambaſſador was no ſtranger to the pope's temper, and knew how obſtinately tenacious he was of what he thought his right; having often heard him declare, " He would ſooner die the crueleſt " death, than give up a hair's breadth of it;" and was convinced that ſuch a negociation would be very diſagreeable to him, and conſequently of diſſervice to his maſter; he neverthelefs, in obedience to his inſtructions demanded an audience of the pope; and, with a great deal of modeſty, ſet forth the emperor's claim : To which the pope anſwered, with ſome ſharpneſs, " That the ſword had been given to the " emperors by the good-will and generoſity of the " popes, to defend the faith with it, not to rob the " H. See of its privileges and immunities ; that the " pontiffs were the vicars of God, from whom they " received the authority which they had over the " church, and were accountable to none but him; " and as they had never attempted to interfere in " the emperor's temporal concerns, ſo he conceived, " the emperor had no right to buſy himſelf in things " that belonged to the church; and that he would " never ſuffer him upon any account, to exercife " the leaſt authority over the rights or perſons of the " clergy."

The ambaſſador had likewiſe another knotty point to ſettle, concerning the right of the prefectſhip of Rome [7]. This is an office of great dignity, former-ly

[7] The following account of this office is given in the Relati-on de la Cour de Rome, and Gutherius de Offic. Dom. Auguſt.

The prefectſhip or prefecture of Rome, is a very noble and antient dignity, firſt inſtituted by the Roman emperors, and conti-nued by the Popes: It was a long time in the noble families of the Urſini and Della Rovere. After the death of Franciſco Maria, the laſt duke of Urbino, it was granted by Urban VIII. to Taddeo Barberini, and his heirs, to the third generation. It was veſted with great authority, and many prerogatives; one of which was, to carry the ſword of ſtate immediately before the emperors in their cavalcades; and it is remarkable, that in delivering the

ſword

y eſtabliſhed by the emperors, when the empire was
ransferred into Germany, to ſupport and repreſent
heir perſons and authority in Rome, by way of lieu-
enancy. Rodolphus, perceiving the popes had ſeized
ipon it, and uſed commonly to give it to their own
elations, was deſirous of recovering it, as it was
iis unqueſtionable right, and for that purpoſe ordered his ambaſſador to complain of this uſurpation
o the pope, and deſire, " he would give the pre-
‘ fectſhip up, as the electoral college was exceed-
‘ ingly offended at ſuch an incroachment upon the
‘ rights of the empire, and very urgent with him
‘ to demand a reſtitution from the court of Rome."
Which indeed had been done in the time of Gregory
XIII, and it is thought would have been obtained,
f that pontiff had lived a little longer.

Savelli had mentioned it to the pope ſeveral times,
amongſt other things, in common converſation; but
having now received more particular orders from his
court to preſs the matter home, and to inſiſt upon
in explicit anſwer to ſatisfy the electors, he was ve-
·y urgent with the pope, and made uſe of all his
·hetoric to prevail upon his holineſs to comply with
he emperor's demand, repreſenting to him the in-
convenciencies and dangers that might attend any de-
iial or evaſion.

Sixtus was not a little nettled at his importunity,
ind to get clear of him, told him in an angry man-
ier, " That he could not conceive how a perſon of
‘ the emperor's wiſdom and underſtanding, could
‘ fall into ſuch a grievous error; that it was true he
‘ was titular king of the Romans in Germany, but
‘ had no manner of authority at Rome; that in o-
‘ ther times there were other maxims of govern-
‘ ment; and the emperors formerly reſided at Rome,
‘ at leaſt by force, if not by any right they had to

word to the prefect, Trajan ſaid to him, " Take this ſword
‘ and defend me with it, if I purſue the intereſt of my country ;
‘ but uſe it againſt me if I reign tyrannically."

"it,

" it; but now, the popes were emperors of Rome,
" the prefectſhip of courſe belonged to them; and as
" he was fully ſatisfied his authority was lawful,
" and ſupported by a good title, he would exerciſe
" it upon any perſon that ſhould preſume to call it
" in queſtion, or diſturb him in the execution of it;
" that the law of God, as promulged in the h. ſcrip-
" ture, commanded us to *give to Cæſar the things*
" *that are Cæſar's, and to God the things that are*
" *God's*; but in the preſent caſe, that heavenly pre-
" cept was inverted, and Cæſar was deſirous of ta-
" king to himſelf the things that belonged to God;
" which he, as God's vicegerent, thought himſelf
" obliged to oppoſe, to the utmoſt of his power,
" both out of regard to his imperial majeſty's cha-
" racter, as defender of the church; and his own, as
" the vicar of Jeſus Chriſt."

After a warm conteſt, the emperor was at laſt
forced to give the matter up; either becauſe he did
not think it of conſequence enough to occaſion an
open rupture, as it muſt have done if they had proceeded any further, or out of the great regard he
had always profeſſed for the H. See, and his title of
defender of the church. Such was this pope's method
of treating princes and emperors, of whom he was
no great reſpecter, when the rights and immunities
of the church, as he termed them, were called in diſpute; and in this manner he publicly defrauded
Cæſar of the things were Cæſar's.

He carried the affair of eccleſiaſtical immunities
to a great height likewiſe in Spain, and, after Pius
V, may be ſaid to be the founder of an *imperium in
imperio*, in that kingdom, that is, a ſeparate, diſ-
tinct, power, entirely independent upon the original
ſovereignty, which evidently exiſts to this day.

End of the EIGHTH BOOK.

THE
L I F E
OF
Pope SIXTUS the Fifth.

BOOK THE NINTH.

IT has been commonly reported that Sixtus kept a miftrefs in Rome, whom he was exceffively fond of, and trufted with all the fecrets of his government; and that by her means Q. Elizabeth of England knew every thing that was tranfacted at that court, and the defigns of the pope, much better than either the French or Spaniards; that he was not averfe to fuch a correfpondence, either becaufe he had a great efteem for that queen, and was defirous of fupporting her fecretly againft K. Philip; or, being covetous, and fet upon heaping up riches, he was not difpleafed that his favourite fhould be enriched at another perfon's expence; as it was faid Elizabeth made her very great prefents.

But I think it feems to the laft degree improbable, that a man who had lived 15 years in the manner he did when he was cardinal, and deceived his very friends, and relations, and domeftics, by a conftant courfe of penance and mortification, and a pretence of ficknefs and infirmity, without feeming to take pleafure in any worldly thing, fhould think of keeping a miftrefs, after he was 64 years old, and came to be pope; that a man, who was ambitious of immortalizing his name, and fo rigoroufly punifhed

concubinage

concubinage in others; that a man of his fevere and inflexible nature, who fhewed no refpect to the greateft princes, and would not admit his own fifter, whom he loved dearly, to any fhare in his government, fhould be fo fafcinated by a woman of that character, as to fuffer her to correfpond with an heretical princefs. For my own part, I am fo far from believing this ftory, that I am firmly of opinion, he would have ftrangled her with his own hands, if he had but barely fufpected her of fuch practices.

This report perhaps may be accounted for in the following manner. Mrs. Anne Afton, a young Eng-lifh widow lady, of great beauty and very genteel behaviour, came to Rome about this time. As fhe was a zealous Catholic, fhe could not bear to live in England, under the fevere government of Q. Elizabeth, and for that reafon, left the kingdom, with an only fon, about eight years old. As foon as Sixtus was acquainted with their arrival, and that they both fpoke Italian pretty well, he was defirous of being informed, from her own mouth, of her condition, and the motives that had induced her to leave her native country; and was fo pleafed with her zeal, her addrefs, and the politenefs of her behaviour, that he thought fhe might be of fervice to him, in procuring information concerning the ftate of affairs in England, by a correfpondence with her friends in that kingdom. As fhe had relinquifhed a confiderable fortune for the fake of religion, the pope took care to provide for her, and recommended her to the care and acquaintance of his fifter Donna Camilla, in whofe palace fhe had a table, and an apartment, with a yearly penfion of 500 crowns. She brought about 1500l. with her, which was put out to intereft for her ufe, and the education of her fon. The pope took the more notice of her, as fhe was in fome degree related to Carr, and was recommended by him to his Holinefs. By her agreeable and infinuating manner

ner, she in a short time, made herself absolute
ress of Camilla's confidence and affection.

asquin who spares nobody, had the impudence
y one day, *his Holiness has banished all the bawds
of the city, except his sister.* It was much more
y that cardinal Montalto deserved this slander,
:r than his uncle, as he was a young handsome
, and used frequently to go incog. and stay ma-
ours together with this lady.

mongst the many great designs which Sixtus ined to execute, we may reckon that of abolishing
quarters [1] none of the least: For this purpose,
ent for all the ambassadors then at Rome, and
them, " it was his pleasure they should write to
eir respective courts, and to acquaint their mas-
rs, that he was determined no body should reign
Rome but himself; that there should be no pri-
lege or immunity of any kind there, but what
:longed to the pope, nor any sanctuary or asy-
m, but the churches, and that only at such
nes, and upon such occasions, as he should
ink proper; that his intention was to have jus-
ce strictly observed, and rigorously executed, in
l places, as well in the palaces of princes, car-
nals, and ambassadors, as the houses of private
:rsons, desiring them to take that for sufficient
otice."

few days after it happened, that as the archers
pursuing Cola di Lucca, one of the banditi, he
for refuge to the palace of the Imperial ambas-
:; upon which the archers turned back, as they

I quartieri, quarters or franchises, is a privilege that
n ambassadors claim at Rome, of giving sanctuary to crimi-
nd outlawed persons, in their palaces, and a certain distance
them, which is called the verge. The reader may find a
account of this transaction, in a book called Modern History,
monthly account of all the considerable occurrences, civil,
stical, and military, in Europe; in the month of Novem-
nd the subsequent months of the years 1687 and 1688.

either were not acquainted with what the pope had faid to the ambaffadors, or were afraid to proceed to any extremity in that place.

When the pope heard of this, he fent for the governor of Rome, and demanding an account of the criminal, afked him, " How it happened that he was " not in prifon before that time; to which he an- fwered, " that having been informed he was in a " certain public houfe, he had fent fome archers " to apprehend him; but that he had made his ef- " cape thro' a window, and fled to the palace of the " Imperial ambaffador; and that they durft not pro- " ceed any further, for fear of breaking the privile- ". ges of that minifter." Sixtus replied, in a great rage, " What fear? What privileges are you pra- " ting of; we fuppofe you think you are talking to " Gregory; but we fhall let you know that our name " is Sixtus." And the governor faying, " He was " informed the criminal was protected by fome of " the ambaffador's domeftics, and fhut up in his " chapel:" Sixtus was fo enraged, that lofing all pati- ence and forgetting the decency and gravity due to his character, he faid, " He would have him before " night, tho' he was in the belly of Jefus Chrift."

Indeed this was his great foible; he would fome- times fuffer himfelf to be fo tranfported with paffion, efpecially when he met with any obftruction or im- pediment, in the execution of juftice, that he totally laid afide all decorum, and would break out into fuch expreflions as are hardly fit to be related, tho' very feldom or never upon any other occafion.

The governor coming one day to acquaint him, " that a nephew of cardinal Rufticucci was in pri- " fon, and that if his holinefs was not willing to fhew " fome regard to the cardinal, his crime was of fuch " a nature, that he could not help fentencing him to " the gallies;" Sixtus anfwered in his ufual fury, " if he deferves it, he fhall go to the gallies, tho' " he was nephew to our Saviour."

Another

Another time, having fent a lady to prifon, upon
)icion of fheltering fome banditi in her houfe, and
ng told fhe was a relation to the houfe of Conti ;
anfwered, " He did not care if fhe was full fifter
:o the lady of Loretto ;" that is, the Virgin Mary.
After they had taken the criminal we were fpeak-
; of, out of the ambaffador's houfe, who delivered
i up for fear of quarreling with the pope, he was
nediately tried and hanged, notwithftanding the
ft earneft entreaties of the ambaffador to the
trary.

A few days after Sixtus iffued out a bull, in which
:onfirmed two others of Pius IV, and Gregory XIII,
cerning the abolition of quarters, and other im-
nities, in the houfes of " Ambaffadors, cardinals,
1obles, or prelates, with this addition, that who-
ver fhould dare to fkreen, protect, entertain, or
iny way affift, encourage, or abet the banditi, or
)ther malefactors, in their houfes, or in any degree impede or obftruct the courfe of juftice, by
nolefting the archers, or other officers, in the
:xecution of their office, by fecreting the per-
ons of fuch criminals, either directly or indirectly,
)r excite and inftigate others to it, fhould be
leemed ufurpers of the fovereign authority, which
)nly belonged to the pope, guilty of *læfæ majefta-
is*, *ipfo facto* excommunicated, and not to be ab-
olved by any but the pope himfelf, except in the
article of death."

Julius II. was always a profeffed enemy to thefe
rileges: He was indeed of a martial difpofition,
l fitter for the fword than the crofier; whence he
d to fay himfelf, " That the cardinals and elec-
ors were guilty of an egregious blunder, in not
naking him emperor, and Maximilian pope." As
was fully determined to abolifh them, he publifhed
ull, in which there is the following claufe: " Nos
ibominabile et deteftandum franchigiarum hujufmodi nomen penitus abolemus, et perpetuo aboli-

" tum fore decernimus." But the proceedings of
Julius were mild and gentle, when compared with
thofe of Sixtus. It muft be owned that pontiff fhewed
courage and fpirit in publifhing fuch a bull; but wanted refolution to enforce the obfervance of it; and
was obliged to fuffer many irregularities and enormities for want of putting it in execution. Sixtus, on
the contrary, would not ,fuffer the leaft violation or
infringement of his edicts, after they were once publifhed, all the while he was pope; and punifhed any
perfon that prefumed to difobey them, in the moft
fevere and exemplary manner.

Count Olivarez, the K. of Spain's ambaffador,
went poft from Rome incog. to the confines of the
kingdom of Naples, to have a conference with the
viceroy, who was to meet him: Whilft they were
there, the archers purfued a criminal that had been
guilty of murder, and fled to his palace, where he
hoped to find an afylum, as he had an uncle in the
count's fervice, by whofe intereft he thought he
fhould be protected. The domeftics, not knowing
how to act in this cafe, as the ambaffador was abfent,
fhut the gates upon the archers, who pofted themfelves on the outfide, and befet the houfe; which the
governor hearing of, fent one of the judges of his
tribunal to demand the criminal of the domeftics,
and to let them know they had no right to protect
him. But when he came there, they refufed to open
the doors; and anfwered him thro' a window, "That
" they were only fervants, and could not tell what
" to do in a matter of fo great importance, as the
" count was not at home; that they expected him
" every moment, and then he, who underftood the
" laws and cuftoms of Rome, might act as he thought
" proper." Tho' the governor feemed fatisfied with
this anfwer, he ordered the archers to continue there,
till the ambaffador returned. Sixtus, however, was
not content; he inftantly fent for the governor, and
having rated him foundly, faid, "He had not taken
" away

away privileges from ambaſſadors to give them to
their domeſtics." And then turning to his ma-
domo, who ſtood by, aſked him, " What o'clock
was ?" and being told the hour, he ordered the
vernor to go and demand the criminal; and if he
s not delivered up in two hours to take his own
ards and affiſt the archers in breaking down the
ɔrs of the palace, and carrying, not only him,
t every one of the ambaſſadors domeſtics to pri-
ɪ.

We muſt beg the reader's pardon, if we make a
ɪrt digreſſion here, to draw a parallel betwixt the
ɪaviour of Sixtus, and that of Odeſchalchi (Innocent
.) upon a ſimilar occaſion. They that remember
conduct of the marquis of Lavardine (ambaſſa-
· from Lewis XIV.) and with what inſolence he
ɪported the privilege of quarters, in contempt of
pontiff, and his excommunications, will not know
ᴠ to condemn Sixtus for ſo ſtrenuouſly aſſerting the
ɪts and juriſdictions of the Apoſtolic See. I am
ſible it may be objected, that the complexion of
times was very different; in the reign of Sixtus,
.nce was plunged in an abyſs of miſery and diſtrac-
ɪ; whereas in the pontificate of Innocent, the K.
France was the moſt formidable power in Europe:
is is very true we confeſs; but then it muſt be
ɪembered that Philip II. of Spain, whoſe ambaſſa-
Olivarez was, might at leaſt be looked upon as
ally reſpectable in this day, and that the power of
houſe of Auſtria was then arrived at a pitch of
ɪdeur, that aſtoniſhed and terrified all the Chriſ-
ɪ world,
ɪxtus kept France in awe with excommunications,
treated both the Spaniſh and Imperial ambaſſa-
ɪ after ſuch a manner as no petty prince or ſtate
ɪld have borne from any other pontiff. He per-
ned miracles, becauſe he generally acted with pru-
ce and reſolution. He was ſlow in projecting,
ſwift and intrepid in executing his ſchemes;
which

which, we may juftly fay, was the reafon that they
were for the moft part crowned with fuccefs. It was
faid of him, " That he had a head of fteel, a heart
" of adamant, hands of iron, and feet of mercury."
And tho' he had not all the innocence and fimplicity
of the dove, he certainly did not want the wifdom of
the ferpent, which he refembled alfo in fhewing his
refentment as foon as he was provoked.

On the contrary, one might truly fay of Innocent,
that he had the head of a mule, the heart of a deer,
hands of ice, and feet of lead. The Hugonots, indeed, that were banifhed out of France, cried him up
for one of the greateft and beft popes that ever
reigned, only becaufe they knew he hated Lewis XIV,
and was willing to throw in his mite with others to
lower his greatnefs; and there is no doubt but he
would have been glad to have feen it effected; as he
had actually formed fome fchemes for that purpofe,
which yet he had not fpirit to go thro' with. He
could protect, but not act; and ftir up others, tho'
he kept himfelf out of danger, fketching out magnificent plans, whilft he moved with leaden feet to execute them. In matters of great weight and importance to the public, he was variable and capricious,
whimfical, and irrefolute; ever fluctuating and undetermined; but in things of indifference or little
moment, inexorable, pofitive, and obftinate to the
laft degree. Certainly, never any pope was fonder
of his own conceits, or lefs confidered the good or
harm which the public would receive from the
execution of them.

What could be more mean and pufillanimous than
his proceeding with the clergy of France? He quarrelled with them, without any fort of reafon or occafion, merely to fhew himfelf a zealous affertor and defender of the Apoftolic privileges againft the incroachments of the Gallican church; and when they
rofe up in their own defence, and both wrote and acted in a very vigorous manner againft his authority,
he

he did not shew the least resentment; nor when, at last, he was made sensible of the affront that was offered him, tho' spurred and goaded up to it by others, with the most stinging reproaches, did he take any means to obtain satisfaction.

He published a severe bull to abolish the quarters in Rome, and confirmed those of Pius IV, Gregory XIII, and Sixtus V, with terrible denunciations of his wrath against any that should presume to disobey them, thundering out the greater excommunication against Lavardine, the French ambassador, and was deaf to the arguments of those that endeavoured to convince him of the unreasonableness and absurdity of such a proceeding. But as soon as he heard the K. of France was resolved to support his pretensions, he lowered his topsails; his courage failed him; he began to droop and grow irresolute, to the advantage of France, the great prejudice of the H. See, and the laughter and derision of all the world.

It was pleasant enough, whenever cardinal D'Estrees went to expostulate with him upon the impropriety of such a behaviour, to see him swagger and knit his brows, and bellow out, " As to the abolition of quarters we " are thoroughly resolved upon it, and shall shew our- " selves another Sixtus in that matter." One day, when some of the cardinals in the consistory were proposing expedients to accommodate the disputes with France, and prevent coming to an open rupture with that power, to the great scandal of Christendom, and detriment of the R. Catholic religion, he said in a haughty manner, " We are so fully convinced that the proceedings " of Sixtus, in regard to abolishing the quarters, was " a very just and wise measure; that we are deter- " mined to follow his example thro' the whole, and " shall not suffer ourselves to be prevailed upon to " deviate from it, by any motive or consideration " whatsoever." But I am ashamed, and if the impartiality of an historian did not oblige me to it,

could

could heartily wifh to be excufed from relating the fubfequent behaviour of this great imitator of Sixtus, to
France, and that of France to him. For, upon the
death of the duke D'Eftrees, ambaffador from the
French king to the court of Rome, Innocent gave orders to his nuncio at Paris, to acquaint his majefty,
" That he would upon no account whatever, receive
" another ambaffador from him, except he would firft
" promife and fwear, in his name, for ever to renounce
" the privilege of quarters ; as he was refolved in that
" particular, to copy after his predeceffor Sixtus V, of
" glorious memory ; and, for that reafon, defired the
" K. of France would, on his part, take his meafures
" accordingly."

That monarch, with great coolnefs, and his ufual
magnanimity, told the nuncio, " He did not under-
" ftand what his Holinefs meant by imitating the ex-
" ample of Sixtus; that the times and circumftances
" of affairs were in many refpects altered from what
" they were then ; that he did not pretend to know
" particularly what proceedings there had been upon
" that occafion, betwixt his anceftors, and the prede-
" ceffors of his Holinefs ; but that he knew he was
" thoroughly determined, at all events, to maintain
" the rights of his crown, and, for that purpofe, fhould
" very foon fend an ambaffador to Rome."

How did poor Innocent behave upon thefe threats?
When he received the anfwer, he fell upon his knees
before a crucifix that was in his apartment, and
prayed to God, " Who had given his holy fpirit
" and refolution, to his vicar, Sixtus V, to exert
" himfelf to the utter abolition of the quarters, fo
" prejudicial to his glory and the intereft of religion ;
" that he would be pleafed of his infinite mercy, to
" infpire him with the fame courage and ftrength, to
" carry him thro' all difficulties, as he had deter-
" mined to act in the fame manner as foon as he was
" able, refigning the direction of his conduct entire-
" ly

ly into his hands, whofe almighty power was able
to bring all things to a profperous conclufion.
What would Sixtus have done? How would he
ve acted upon this occafion? It is paft doubt, that
ftead of going to his pater nofters, he would have
ımediately fent for his officers of juftice, and im-
ifoned a perfon, if not put him to death, that
d the infolence to obtrude himfelf upon him in
e character of an ambaffador, without his per-
iffion, or acknowledging him as fuch; this much
certain, that the king of France would never have
nt one upon that errand.

His majefty was as good as his word; for the
ıncio was hardly got out of his prefence, when he
mmoned a council, and notified his intention of
nding the marquis of Lavardine ambaffador to
ome; and immediately gave him orders to prepare
ʳ his journey. He accordingly fet out from Paris a
w days after; and when he arrived at Bologna, was
ıet by one of the pope's mafters of the ceremonies,
ho acquainted him, " That if he did not confent
to give up the privileges of quarters, by an inftrument under his hand, before a public notary,
his Holinefs would not acknowledge him an am-
affador of France." The marquis anfwered calmly,
That he fhould make known the intention of his
mafter, upon that head, to his holinefs, when he
arrived at Rome, and to no other." After which,
=parting from Bologna, he continued his rout thro'
lorence, and the confines of Tufcany, where he was
ined by his train, and fome military officers, that
ıd embarked at Marfeilles, and landed at Leghorn,
l good ftaunch Catholics, that they might not be
ıble to cenfure or reproach, upon the account of
ıeir religion.

Innocent, tho' he had advice that Lavardine was
ıarching towards Rome, with 700 armed men, made
ɔ other preparation to receive him, than ordering
ıazza, affeffor of the H, office, to go to the houfes of
all

all the cardinals and prelates, and commanded them not to fpeak to, or have any correfpondence with Lavardine, on pain of excommunication. People could not forbear wondering at this daring and fool-hardy beha-ᐧ viour in Lewis, who was efteemeed one of the-wifeft princes in Europe. They faid to themfelves, " Surely " the king is not acquainted with the character of this " pope; he has made choice of a wrong man to play " tricks upon; he'll find he has another Sixtus to deal " with."

Lavardine, upon his arrival at Rome, chofe to make his public entry upon a holiday, that it might be the more remarkable, and taken notice of by the pope. His train confifted of 200 military officers, 300 private men, as guards; 100 gentlemen, and 100 fervants. The cardinals D'Eftrees and Maldachino went out to meet him, each with three chariots and fix, a mile out of the city, which he entered at the Porto del Popolo (as all ambaffadors do) in a moft fuperb coach, in which the two cardinals accompanied him. When he arrived at the gate, the Cuftom-houfe officers came to examine his baggage, which was carried by forty fumpter mules, in rich caparifons, curioufly adorned with filver fleurs de lis. The ambaffador's attendants anfwered, " They had orders to cut of the nofe and " ears of any one that durft prefume to ranfack his " excellency's baggage." When the officers heard this, they made them a very low bow, and left them to themfelves. The mafter of his houfhold rode before them, fcattering money and medals by handfuls, with the arms and effigies of Lewis upon them, which the populace was ready enough to gather up, attending the cavalcade with acclamations and fhouts of, " The king " of France for ever."

In this manner, with royal pomp, Lavardine entered Rome, traverfing above one half of the city; and took up his refidence in the palace of the Farnefe, which is by much the fineft in Rome. The

foldiers

ldiers were drawn up in good order, lining the
iazza before it, with their fwords drawn (which
1ade a very handfome appearance) and ftayed there
ι that manner till the whole train came up, and
ιe baggage was unloaded, which was all done in a
1ort time, without any hindrance or moleftation,
otwithftanding the infinite concourfe of people that
'ere affembled, not only out of curiofity, but afto-
iſhment, to fee an ambaſſador enter Rome in a
oftile manner, and with an armed force, in contempt
f the pope, and to the eternal difgrace of the holy
ity. Some of the moft zealous could not forbear
rying out aloud, ".Would to God old Sixtus was
' in the Vatican, monfieur Lavardine durft as well
' have been hanged as come to Rome."

The dread of the marquis was fo great in the
ity, that the governor, with his archers and imps
f juſtice, durſt not appear in the ſtreets; it be-
1g given out, "That the ambaſſador had ordered
' his guards to patrole night and day round his pa-
' lace (as they actually did) and cut off the ears of
' any one that offered to difturb or oppofe them."

The ambaſſador further declared, in the prefence
f many people, that fo it might be fpread all over
he city, "That if either he or his lady, the
' ambaſſadreſs, met with any of the cardinals, or
' other perfons who did not pay them the.honours
' that were due to the ambaſſador of the K. of
' France, he would ufe proper means to oblige them
' to it upon the fpot." So that no-body durft ftir
.broad, except fuch as had a mind to ſhew their
eſpect to his excellency, who affected to parade it
hro' the city, every day, with his lady, in two
lifferent chariots, attended by 200 of his horfe-
guards.

The pope, more frighted than any body elfe,
hut himfelf up in the Vatican, with cardinal Cibo,
lean of the H. College, his favourite minifter, enter-
aining himfelf every day at his window with the fight
of

of this cavalcade, which lafted nine months. No pontiff ever received fo grofs an affront, nor the city, at any time, fuch an infult as this. It hardly feems credible, that a fovereign prince of fuch a powerful ftate, with plenty of foldiers, both horfe and foot, and a ftrong garrifon in the city and caftle, which were very well fortified, befides many thoufands of other people able to bear arms, exclufive of 8000 ecclefiaftics, who would have been more than fufficient to knock them on the head with fticks and ftones, fhould not be able to prevent Lavardine making his entrance with about 700 men. If they had only fhut the gates, the K. of France was fo much embarraffed with other powers at that time, that he could not have fent any forces to befiege the city.

What made it ftill more galling, was, that the affront was not only offered to him as a temporal prince, but to his fpiritual power ; for tho' he declared Lavardine excommunicated, and put the church of St. Lewis, which he frequented, under an interdict, he laughed at it, and made a joke of the pope's authority in the midft of Rome, and under his very nofe ; for he commanded fervice to be performed as ufual, in that church, and in his own chapel, in fpite of his holinefs ; going fometimes to one church, and fometimes to another, and very often to St. Peter's. But the moft fhameful circumftance of all was, that in paffing thither, he was obliged to go under the very walls of St. Angelo, in the face of the pope's guards, and in fight of the Vatican, tho' there were four pieces of cannon planted before the gates, always ready loaded and primed.

In the mean time, the good pontiff ordered his guards to retire into the palace, and fecured the gates with bolts and chains, leaving the cannon out of doors for the ufe of the French, if they fhould have occafion for them. On the other hand, the ambaffador's guards, mounted on horfeback, to the number of 200, half of them with their fwords drawn, ·
and

and the other half with their muskets prefented and
matches lighted, took poffeffion of the piazza, pofting
themfelves in the very place where the pope's guards
ufed to be ftationed, directly oppofite to, and within
mufket fhot of the cannon of St. Angelo, where they
ftayed all the while the ambaffador was performing
his devotions in St. Peter's, and then efcorted him
back again in the fame infolent manner.

I dare venture to fay, pofterity will hardly believe
this; for who can imagine that there ever exifted
a man fo fimple, fo totally forfaken by all the fuccours of reafon, as to fuffer his enemy to come into
his houfe, and cudgel him foundly, when it was in
his power to have kept him out, only by fhutting
his doors? And yet the partizans of this pope highly
extol his prudence and long-fufferance, in fwallow-
ing this indignity to prevent a worfe.

We hope the reader will excufe this digreffion,
which we thought in fome meafure neceffary to juftify the memory of Sixtus, and fhew the weaknefs
of thofe who have fondly pretended to compare Innocent with him for fteadinefs, refolution and intrepidity
in defending the rights of the papacy, and in the abolition of quarters at Rome; a parallel indeed very in-
jurious to the memory of Sixtus, who never began an
undertaking which he did not finifh; whereas Innocent
hardly fucceeded in any thing: The refpect due to
the perfon and government of the popes, never being at a lower ebb than in his pontificate, tho' we
fhall do him the juftice to own, he had many qualities that conftitute the pious, good Chriftian, but not
the great prince.

No other pope ought to be mentioned in the fame
page with Sixtus, except thofe that are diftinguifhed
in the calendar by a red letter, which is an honour
that he did not much afpire to; taking a quite different road to fame, from thofe who are ambitious of
having their names recorded in breviaries and mar-
tyrologies.

He

He had no contemptible idea of military affairs, as appeared from the regulations, the order and difcipline which he introduced into his foldiery : And to this martial difpofition, perhaps, might be owing the inflexible rigour of his juftice.

If fuch an event as we have been relating had happened in his time, it is not improbable, if he acted confiftently with his character, that he would have gone out to meet Lavardine, and his train, with his guards, and the garrifon of St. Angelo, and put them all to the fword, except the ambaffador, whom perhaps he would have referved for a feverer punifhment; inftead of fuffering them to befiege him in his palace, to brave his authority, and to parade thro' the city, in fo triumphant a manner, with an armed force.

What example can the hiftory of former times produce of a prince more auguft, more magnificent, more truly great and refpectable than Sixtus ? What pontiff ever governed the church with more order and regularity, or better difcipline ? What ftatefman more provident and fagacious, more fubtle and refined in his politics, or that better knew how to command fortune, and fecure fuccefs in his great undertakings ? His nod was fufficient to make him obeyed ; his voice made the world tremble.

It is computed there were above 4000 banditti in Rome, at his exaltation, that had reforted thither whilft the fee was vacant, by the invitation and encouragement of more than 500 noblemen, who protected and fupported them : A body fufficient to have plundered the city, as it was commonly believed they intended. But the found of his juftice was no fooner gone forth into the world, but the city was prefently clear, both of them and their protectors.

Such a pope deferves to live eternally in the annals of fame, his memory ought to be for ever glorious, and dear to mankind.

Schah

Schah Abbas, the king of Perfia, was engaged at this time in a hot, but unfuccefsful war with the Turk, which obliged him to fend an ambaffador to Sixtus, whofe renown, as a great prince, had already reached thofe diftant regions, hoping to prevail upon him to unite the Chriftian princes in a league againft his enemy, whilft he attacked him with all his forces on the fide of Perfia.

His divan, it feems, had been divided in their opinions concerning this affair, fome thinking it would not fucceed; as without doubt the pope would require conditions in return, which perhaps their religion would not allow them to comply with. It was at laft, however, concluded to fend Babacchon Gord, one of the greateft and moft confiderable noblemen in his dominions, but with a very fmall train; it confifting only of 12 perfons, two of whom were monks, very learned in the rites of the Eaftern church, and fpoke Latin fluently, which was of great convenience to them, though they had an interpreter that underftood Italian tolerably well. The ambaffador was four months upon his voyage, and when he arrived at Rome, Sixtus, who loved pomp and pageantry, gave orders that he fhould be received in a royal manner, and appointed a magnificent cavalcade to attend him at his public entry.

He was a man of a grave deportment, with a venerable beard, and his domeftics, genteel well looking men, except the fecretary, that was to fucceed him if he died, who made but an indifferent figure; though he was a man of much knowledge and underftanding.

His firft audience (like that of all other ambaffadors of crowned heads) was in the royal chapel, with this additional circumftance, that the pope infifted upon all the cardinals and principal prelates of the court being prefent at it, to give a higher idea of the grandeur and magnificence of the pontifical court to thefe foreigners. There were fome little difficulties in the

the ceremonial, and particularly in prevailing upon
the ambaſſador to kiſs the pope's feet; but as he
came to aſk a favour, he at laſt complied. As ſoon
as he entered the royal hall, he fell down upon his
knees, and made his obeiſance to the pope, who ſat
upon his throne, repeating the ſame in the middle
of it, and when he came near enough to him, he
ſtooped and kiſſed his feet: After which he ſat down,
and made his ſpeech, with his head uncovered all the
while. As he ſpoke in his own tongue, one of the
monks, kneeling down, repeated what he ſaid, in
Latin, which was given to him before by the ambaſſador.

The ſubſtance of what he ſaid, was, "That his
"maſter Schah Abbas, K. of Perſia, having lately
"aſcended the throne of that kingdom, had been
"informed that the Almighty Governor of heaven
"and earth had been pleaſed to call his Holineſs
"likewiſe to reign over Chriſtendom, and thought
"proper to ſend him as his ambaſſador, to let him
"know what pleaſure it would give him to be ſerved
"by ſo auguſt and glorious a monarch, whoſe tran-
"ſcendent merit had exalted him far above the le-
"vel of all other Chriſtian princes, provided the pro-
"poſals, which he was ordered to make, were a-
"greeable to him, and deſired he would be pleaſed
"to grant him a private audience to acquaint him
"what they were."

This ſpeech was not reckoned very polite, but rather haughty than otherwiſe: It is true the letter written to the pope by the king, afterwards printed at
Rome, was much praiſed and admired; and very well
it might, as the greater part of it was compoſed at
Rome, promiſing many conſiderable advantages to the
Latin church. It is certain, that he did offer the
Roman Catholics liberty to enjoy their religion, to
build churches and convents, and ſome other privileges in Perſia.

When

When the ambaffador had finifhed his fpeech, his
)wers were admitted to the honour of kiffing his
inefs's feet, and after this ceremony was over,
linal Montalto invited the ambaffador to his pa-
, and made a noble banquet for him, at which,
the pope's exprefs command, he was treated with
utmoft deference and refpect. The Perfians ex-
fed their aftonifhment at the number, variety,
elegance of the difhes; the fplendor and richnefs
the plate, and the magnificence of the whole;
at that which they faw afterwards at the palaces
he other cardinals, who entertained them in their
is.

The pope appointed Gambacorta to confer with the
)affador, who was to report his propofals to car-
d Montalto, and the fubftance of them to himfelf:
ich was, in fhort, a reprefentation of the neceffi-
of entering into a vigorous war with the Turk;
That the pope, who was the chief of the Euro-
ean powers, ought to unite them in a league for
hat purpofe; that if it was neglected, he would
ery likely fee the Ottoman power make the
ime devaftations in Europe, that it had done in
Afia: On the contrary, if he made ufe of the pre-
ent opportunity, he might expect prodigious ad-
antages from the fpoil of fo rich and formidable
n enemy; that if the K. of Perfia made peace
vith the Turk, which he muft do of neceffity, if he
vas not fupported by other powers, the latter
vould infallibly turn his arms upon fome part of
.urope." He propofed likewife, "That thofe that
iy neareft to his confines, that were moft intereft-
d, fhould attack him firft:" And faid, "That
is mafter would never fheath the fword, except
vith the confent, and to the advantage of all the
.hriftian princes."

iut there was not much credit to be given to thefe
nifes: Without doubt fuch an opportunity would
e been much to be wifhed for at another time; but

　　　　　　the

the fituation of affairs would not then allow of it.
For, in the firft place, Sixtus was wholly taken up
with his defign upon Naples, and for that purpofe
was exceedingly attentive to the accumulation of
treafure, and to embroil Spain in a war with England;
fo that he did not care to empty his coffers in a ro-
mantic crufade againft the Turks. In the next, K.
Phillip was fully employed in the low countries, the
affairs of the league, and his intended invafion of
England, againft which he was determined to bend his
whole force. The emperor had bufinefs enough at
home; and the Venetians, who fufpected the pope
had fome great fcheme in view, did not care to engage in a foreign war, that they might attend to the
confufions which they daily expected would happen
nearer home.

After the ambaffador had ftaid about a month at
Rome, to the no fmall expence of the apoftolic
chamber, the Pope admitted him to his laft audience; in which he told him, " That he was extreme-
" ly concerned to find the princes of Europe, neither
" difpofed, nor in circumftances to embark in fuch
" an undertaking; that he prayed God, in his infi-
" nite mercy, to fend his mafter fuch fuccefs in his
" warfare as might tend to the good of his foul, and
" the peace of his kingdom." Difmiffing him with
many other compliments and fome few prefents.

Before their departure, he was defirous of fhewing
them an example of his juftice upon one Mozzi, a
furgeon by profeffion, and native of Syracufe, who
had married a woman with a tolerable fortune; but,
for fome reafon or other, left her at the end of three
years, and went to Naples, where he married a
courtezan, tho' his firft wife was alive; and having
ftaid with her till he had fpent all her money, which
was about 10,000 crowns, without being difcovered,
he ran away to Venice, and there married the widow
of a taylor, lately dead, that had left her 4000
crowns; but as fhe was not very handfome, he got,

the

the money into his hands and made off with it, leaving her to shift for herself. From Venice he came to Rome, and married a fourth wife, under a feigned name, as he had done the others (they being all three alive for any thing he knew to the contrary) with an intention, as he afterwards confessed, to leave her too, as soon as he had got possession of her fortune, which was above 6000 crowns, and return to his own country. But it happened unluckily, that whilst the priest was performing the ceremony, in the church of St. Pancras, the brother of the wife whom he last married, came by chance into the church, and knowing him again, dogged him to his lodgings, and then informed the governor of the whole matter; who immediately sent some archers, and took him just as he was going to bed, and carried him to prison.

As soon as Sixtus heard of it, he sent for him to be examined by himself. When he owned, " That " his first wife being an imperious termagant vixen, " he left her, and went to Naples, and married a se- " cond, of whom he was jealous, as he knew she " had been a whore ; and for that reason, growing " tired of her, he ran away, and came to Venice, " where he married another, who proving to be of a " disposition much unlike his own, he gave her the " flip, and came to Rome, and married another ; " with whom, he believed he should not have staid " long, as far as he could then judge, from the little " acquaintance he had with her." After a short pause, the Pope said, " That if he was so difficult to " be pleased, he doubted this world could not fur- " nish him with a wife to his taste ; for which reason " he would send him into another, where there was " greater plenty of women, and then he might chuse " such a one as he liked best." And turning round to the governor, ordered him to take care that he was hanged the next day.

At

At the beginning of this year, Charles Emanuel, duke of Savoy, fent an ambaſſador extraordinary to Rome, under a pretext of paying his devoirs to the H. See; but the true intention of the embaſſy, was to aſk the pope's aſſiſtance in his defigns upon Geneva, as he was now fully determined to make himſelf maſ- ter of that city, relying upon the fuccour of K. Phi- lip, whoſe daughter he had lately married, and fee- ing France ſo involved in domeſtic troubles, that it was impoſſible for that crown to afford them any re- lief.

Sixtus received the ambaſſador with much civility and affection, and ſhewed him great reſpect, upon the account of the royal houfe of Savoy, for which he always profeſſed much regard, and uſed to call it, the bulwark of Italy. But as to the affair of Geneva, tho' he affected to appear very zealous in it, yet out of fear of engaging in too great an expence, as the Swifs were much intereſted in the preſervation of that city, or that he ſaw the undertaking was likely to be attended with many other difficulties, he ra- ther declined it, and anfwered in ambiguous terms, " That, without doubt, the duke had both religi- " on and juftice on his ſide; but that he would not " advife him to proceed with too much precipitation, " left he ſhould draw himſelf into difficulties that he " was not aware of." Francifco Fabri, a native of Geneva, fon of Peter Fabri, whoſe family had been in the higheft efteem there above 200 years, was then at Rome; with him the Pope had frequent confer- ences upon this enterprize, and was informed by him of the feveral particulars relating to that city, and eſpecially of the biſhop's pretenſions in oppoſition to the duke: Upon which he began to grow very cool in the matter; and, after a long negociation, told the ambaſſador, and count Olivarez, who was or- dered by his mafter to fecond his inftances, " That " if the war he was going to enter into with the ſtate " of Geneva had been for the fake of religion, he

                                        " ſhould

" fhould have thought himfelf obliged, as head of
" the church, to join in it, and give him all the affif-
" tance that was in his power ; but as he found it was
" only a difpute, concerning temporal rights, he
" could not in confcience fquander away the trea-
" fure of the church in quarrels of that nature, which
" ought only to be employed in defending itfelf, or
" enlarging its own territories; that he might with e-
" qual reafon defire the duke to lend him his affiftance,
" and then did not doubt but he could reduce it to the
" obedience of the H. See."

The duke was exceedingly enraged at this anfwer,
and faid, " That Sixtus took more pleafure in fhed-
" ding Catholic blood at Rome, than in the reduction
" of Heretics at Geneva; and that under fuch a
" pope, it was better to turn Proteftant than continue
" in the fame communion with him, as he feemed to
" countenance and protect, rather than endeavour to
" fupprefs them ;" and wrote to his ambaffador to
come away directly from Rome, as he faw it was infected with herefy ; and faid, " That if he could not
" accomplifh his defigns upon Geneva, by the help
" of the pope, he would try what he could do with
" his own fword, which he thought no prieft would
" dare to oppofe."

During the courfe of this negociation, count Olivarez had feveral conferences with the ambaffador
of Savoy; and faid to him, as they went to their laft
audience, " I would not have his highnefs your maf-
" ter deceive himfelf any longer, with expectations
" of affiftance from the pope, in the affair of Geneva ;
" churchmen are made of a different fort of clay
" from other men: I have had a long acquaintance
" with them, and know, by experience, the hu-
" mour of this pope in fuch affairs, from his beha-
" viour to my mafter, in regard to England. I am
" well affured he has fome defign upon Geneva him-
" felf ; and it will be better for the duke to let it
" continue in the hands of them that now poffefs it.
" The

" The Proteftants refpect him, and live amicably
" with the neighbouring ftates: but if it comes in-
" to the power of the ecclefiaftics, they will be trouble-
" fome to both the duke, and other contiguous ftates.
" In fhort, it is a bad thing to live in the neighbour-
" hood of priefts."

To underftand the reafonablenefs of the count's complaint againft the pope, in relation to the affairs of England, it is neceffary to inform the reader, that Sixtus
had been perpetually teizing the K. of Spain, ever fince
the beginning of the year 1587, to make a defcent upon that ifland, and had taken all the pains he could to
irritate him againft Q. Elizabeth. He wrote a letter to
him, with his own hand (which is reckoned a prodigious favour) and told him, " If he had any regard for
" his title of Catholic Majefty, or the leaft affection
" left for a people he once governed, he ought to fet
" himfelf in earneft to avenge the violence and indigni-
" ties that were daily offered there to the Roman Catho-
" lics and their religion ;" promifing to bear part of
the expence, and to advance a million of crowns, as
foon as he fhould be certainly informed his forces had
landed in England. The count took great pains to
prevail upon the pope to difburfe one half of
this money immediately ; and the duke of Parma fent
count Sefis to Rome for the fame purpofe ; but all their
arguments and perfuafions were thrown away upon
him, for he continued firm, and would not part with
a crown till the time propofed.

To make him amends for this refufal of the money, he made William Allen (whom we have formerly
mentioned) a cardinal at his recommendation ; a perfon that had deferved very well of the church, and
done great fervices to the Catholic religion ; and,
which is a very uncommon inftance of modefty, had
refufed a hat when it was offered him by Gregory
XIII : but Sixtus obliged him to take it, with a defign
to fend him (as the king defired) legate into England,
when he fhould have conquered it, as cardinal
                                                    Pole

Pole had been in the time of Q. Mary. The pope took occafion to tell his Majefty, " That as his de- " fign upon England muft now be penetrated by this " ftep, it behoved him to put to fea with all expedi- " tion, and come upon the Englifh before they were " prepared, and to prevent them exercifing further " feverities upon the Catholics, as they would undoubt- " edly double their rigour towards them upon this oc- " cafion."

This method of proceeding in Sixtus made fpecula- tive people fufpect, that his inftigation of the Spani- ards to invade England, did not proceed from his zeal for religion, but from motives of private intereft, and being defirous to embarrafs the king in a long and expenfive war, the event of which might be doubt- ful, that fo he might take a proper opportunity of ex- ecuting his defign upon Naples : as that kingdom, being drained of foldiers and money, would then eafily fall a prey to the firft invader ; fince the vaft armada that the Spaniard was fitting out, had already pretty well exhaufted his treafure, and fwept off the flower of his nobility.

Though Sixtus was firmly refolved not to affift him with any money in this enterprize, he left nothing unattempted that might excite him to it. He gave him the inveftiture of the kingdom of England ; and as he knew the Spaniards are dazzled with appearan- ces, he fent the king, for the ufe of the armada, feveral huge chefts of agnus dei's, medals, crucifix- es, relics, pardons, and indulgencies, with which the men, efpecially the officers, were fo loaded and in- cumbered, that they looked more like pilgrims than foldiers.

The Armada confifted of 150 very large fhips of the line, befides an infinite number of frigates and fmall veffels. It was furnifhed with 2000 pieces of cannon, great plenty of all forts of provifions and ammunition, and a land force confifting of 23,000 men.

When

When every thing was in readiness, the duke of
Medina Sidonia, who was appointed admiral of it,
put to sea, and steered right away for the English
coast; where meeting with the famous sir Francis
Drake, whom the Q. of England had preferred to be
an admiral in her navy (in the raising of which she
had been forced to pawn her very jewels) they had several skirmishes, but never came to a general engagement; either because the duke of Medina, who was
not a very expert seaman, endeavoured to decline it,
or had orders not to engage at sea, except he was sure
of success. Whatever was the reason, the two fleets
parted without coming to any considerable action; and
that of Spain being caught in a violent gale of wind,
the greatest part of it perished, and the other with much
difficulty, and terribly shattered, escaped into their
own ports.

In this interval the pope went in person to Civita
Vecchia, attended by the whole court, where he pronounced a solemn benediction upon the gallies which
he had lately built for the service of the church. All
the princes of Italy, who knew his ambition, the
Spaniards in particular, were alarmed at this. The
viceroy of Naples doubled his garrisons upon the frontiers, and sent several spies to Civita Vecchia, to watch
the pope's motions, who gave orders for the gallies
to be got in readiness with all possible expedition, and
furnished with ammunition and provisions, and every
thing else that was necessary to execute some important design: he visited the fortifications of the place,
and directed new ones to be built, where the old did
not appear sufficiently strong, to the great suspicion and
uneasiness of the Spaniards.

At his return to Rome, count Olivarez delivered
him a letter from the elector of Cologne, in which he
set forth, " That he had lost not only Bonne, a consi-
" derable town in his dominions, but was in great
" danger of seeing Cologne itself in the hands of his
" enemies; and that in order to put a stop to the
" progress

progrefs of their victorious arms, he was obliged to
have recourfe to his Holinefs." The duke of Ba-
ɪria, who was much efteemed by Sixtus, wrote at
e fame time, " Befeeching him to compaffionate the
diftrefs not only of his brother the elector of Cologne,
but that of the whole church, in thofe parts, which
was threatened with a total fubverfion by the fuccefs of the Proteftants, who had over-run almoft all
the country."   ˌ,
Sixtus promifed to affift the elector, but (according
ɪ his cuftom) upon feveral conditions to be fulfilled
y that prince, highly advantageous to the Holy See;
ɪd gave orders for 10,000 piftoles to be paid immedi-
ely into the count's hands, for the elector's fervice;
furing him, " That the army in the Low Countries,
commanded by the D. of Parma, fhould march in a
fhort time to his affiftance."

He had wrote a letter of confolation to the K. of
ɔain, upon the deftruction of his Armada, as foon as
ʋer he heard of it. Many were of opinion that he
as not fo much affected with that prince's lofs, as
ɛfirous to prevent him from afking any thing towards
ɪe repair of it: For in this letter he found fault with
ɪe conduct of all his officers and minifters, except Alex-
ɪder Farnefe, of whom he fpoke with the higheft com-
ɪendations, in the prefence of count Olivarez. As
ɪme did not fpare even that general, Sixtus was ex-
ːedingly enraged at the authors of fuch fcandalous cen-
ɪres, and extolled the duke's valour and military fkill
ɪ the moft extravagant terms, not only to Olivarez,
ut in a full confiftory; for which, cardinal Farnefe re-
ɪrned thanks to his Holinefs and wrote to acquaint his
ephew with it, which was of no fmall fervice to him,
ѕ the approbation of fo great a pope was fufficient to
lence all calumny and reproach.

He fent the letter which he wrote to the K. of
pain, to his nuncio at Madrid, with orders to make
handfome compliment himfelf upon this occafion,
when

when þe delivered it. The king read it with the fame indifference as if it had been a letter of congratulation, inftead of condolence; So little impreʃʃion did his lofs make upon him, and with fuch refignation and magnanimity did he bear the ʃhock of that melancholy difafter. He thanked the nuncio, and faid, " He would fend the pope an anfwer in a ʃhort " time ;" as he did two days afterwards, in which he defired his Holinefs " to join. with him in giving " God thanks for preferving fome part of his fleet; " and faid, that he could not exprefs the fenfe he had " of his mercy and favour, for leaving it in his power " fpeedily to repair the lofs, and to fit out an arma- " da, in no degree inferior to the other ; that there " was no danger of the ftream failing, whilft he was " in poffeffion of the fource; that he had fent his " fleet to fight with the enemies of the true faith, and " not to oppofe the decrees of Providence; that he had " no reafon to blame his officers, as they could not com- " mand the winds and waves, or infure it againft ftorms ". and hurricanes." He faw, by the tenour of the pope's letter, how little affiftance he muft expect from him; and as he was a prince of courage not to be daunted, intrepid, conftant and immoveable in danger or adverfity, he defpifed what he faw he was not likely to obtain, and reproached him with want of zeal, and the little concern he expreffed for the welfare of Catholic princes, who had always defended the caufe of religion with fo much ardour. and bravery.; and concluded with faying, " That the misfortunes of his fleet " ought to be efteemed a lofs common to them both, " as he had entered into this expedition merely at his " inftigation ; that if it was not an honour, it was " at leaft a confolation to him, when he reflected, " that his fleet perifhed in the fervice of God, and " endeavouring to advance the true religion; that " he thought fuch a general calamity ought to be " more afflicting to the common father of the faith-
" ful,

ful, and the head of the Chriſtian church, than
to himſelf; and for the future, however, ſince he
ſeemed ſo unconcerned about it, he ſhould leave
him to fight the battles of the church himſelf; or
if he ſhould be ſtill generous enough to enter into
them as an auxiliary, he ſhould expect to ſee his
Holineſs act as a principal; that his ambition
would let him ſit down very well contented with
the honour of the ſecond poſt, under ſo great a
leader."

He had a mind, without doubt, to let him ſee by this
ſwer, that he was acquainted with his deſigns upon
kingdom of Naples, and that it did not give him
leaſt uneaſineſs or apprehenſion, though he heard
was daily laying up money, and making other pre-
rations for it; and that, notwithſtanding the misfor-
ne of his fleet, he had ſtill ſtrength enough left to de-
nd his dominions againſt any perſon that ſhould dare
invade them.   Count Olivarez, who obſerved the
pe's proceedings very narrowly, ſaid to him, after he
d read the king's letter, "That his majeſty could
eaſily repair the loſs of his fleet, by taking away the
dominions of ſuch as ſhould be hardy enough to attack his."

The nuncio at Madrid having informed Sixtus, in one
his letters, with what ſpirit and firmneſs Philip bore
s misfortune, he ſaid to ſomebody that was preſent,
Of all this prince's great qualities, there is not any
that I envy him, except his equanimty and patience
in adverſity." His moderation in proſperity was no
ſs remarkable.   When a courier brought him an ac-
unt of the great victory gained over the Turks, in
e year 1571, by his brother Don John of Auſtria, who
mmanded the Chriſtian army; ſome of the grandees
his court, with whom he was the moſt familiar, ran
ith the news to his apartment, where he was reading the
fe of his father Charles V.   They thought to have ſeen
m in great tranſports of joy upon this occaſion,
                                        whereas

whereas he did not fhew the leaft emotion : But after he
had heard the particulars of that memorable battle, he
fhrugged up his fhoulders, and faid coolly, " Don John
". ran a great rifk, and might as well have loft the bat-
" tle as won it ;" and then returned to his book. Again,
when a courier arrived with the news of his armada being deftioyed, Chriftopher de Mourra and John In-
diafquez, both great favourites with him, were by chance
in his ante-chamber.   They judged by his countenance
that he brought no favourable account ; but when they
had heard the particulars of the ftorm, and great lofs
that was fuftained, they were in fuch confternation that
neither of them would venture to introduce the courier
to his majefty, who was at that time writing difpatches
to the duke of Medina.   At laft Mourra took upon
him that difagreeable office.   As foon as he entered
the apartment, the king perceiving him in a good
deal of confufion, afked him the reafon of it ; to
which he replied, prefenting the courier, " That there
" was bad news from the armada."   When the courier had given him a detail of the whole, he faid,
with his ufual calmnefs, " We fent our fleet to fight
" againft men, and not againft ftorms and tempefts ;"
and taking up his pen which he had laid down at the
beginning of the relation, he began to write again
with as much unconcern as if he had not heard of it.
Mourra, furprized at his phlegm, returned to Indiaf-
quez, who waited for him with impatience; and being afked, " In what manner the king received the
" account? anfwered, " He does not feem to give
" himfelf any fort of trouble about it ; and if he does
" not, I'm fure there's no reafon why I fhould."
Any other prince would have tore his beard at fuch a
difafter.   If it had happened to Sixtus, it is not unlike-
ly that it would either have killed him out-right, or driven him to diftraction.

    The K. of Spain had a long time folicited the pope
to canonize Diego, or Diacus, of Alcala, and offered
                                                    to

to be at the whole expence, out of the devotion he had for him. The pope, for his part, was not averfe to it, as he was of the order of St. Francis; and thought befides it would in fome meafure ferve to pacify the K. of Spain, and be of no expence to the Apoftolic chamber.

Although this affair had been pretty warmly preffed by the K. of Spain, the court of Rome which proceeds with much flownefs and deliberation in all things, did not feem to be very forward in it, and was mighty dilatory in examining witneffes, concerning the miracles which this holy man had wrought in his life-time. It was imagined the misfortune of the armada would have diverted the thoughts of this canonization; and that having great occafion for money to repair the lofs, he would not have any to throw away upon fuch ceremonies: The pope himfelf was of that opinion. But to the great furprize of every body, the king wrote to his ambaffador the fame week that he heard of that event, commanding him to apply to the pope in concert with the Spanifh cardinals, entreating him to expedite this canonization, and not to fpare any expence that might render it brilliant and magnificent. He alfo told one of the cardinals, to whom he wrote upon this occafion; " It was but reafonable, that he who had " facrificed fo much to the fea, fhould now offer up " fomething to God." The whole court of Rome was furprized at his magnanimity, and admired his policy, in endeavouring to obliterate the memory of his difgrace and make it forgot by the fplendor and eclat of this feftivity.

Don Carlos, the fon of K. Philip, who lived in the pontificate of Pius IV. had a particular devotion to this faint. It was at his defire that Philip was fo folicitous for his canonization; but this unfortunate prince, being ftrangled a while after on a fufpicion of a defign upon his father's life, St. Diego was no more thought of till the times of Pius V, and Gregory XIII, in whofe pontificates K. Philip renewed his inftances; but thofe

pontiffs

pontiffs were not very fond of the matter, either because they had not any great opinion of the faint, or
not sufficient proof of his miracles. But when Sixtus
was exalted to the chair of St. Peter, K. Philip made
fresh application to have him fainted for the honour of
the Spanish nation.

Sixtus was easily prevailed upon for the reasons a-
bove mentioned, and appointed a congregation to
examine witnesses and take depositions previous to
the canonization, which was at last celebrated, with
a magnificence that exceeded all others that had gone
before it. It is generally believed, that Sixtus composed the collect which was consecrated to St. Diego,
upon that occasion, as it is in some measure applicable
to himself, in regard to the meanness of his birth, and
wonderful exaltation to the pontificate. It is follows:

" OMNIPOTENS et sempiterne Deus, qui dispositi-
" one mirabili infirma mundi eligis, ut fortia quæque
" confundas, concede propitius humiliati nostræ, ut
" piis beati Didaci Confessoris tui precibus ad perennem
" in cœlis gloriam sublimari [2] mereamur."

Which being translated, runs thus:

" Almighty and eternal God, who in thy wonder-
" ful disposition of things in this world, makeft choice
" of the *foolish to confound the wife, and the weak to a-*
" *bafe the mighty*, we humbly beseech thee mercifully
" to grant, that, thro' the intercession of thy blessed
" faint and confessor Diego we may be thought worthy
" to inherit everlasting glory in the next."

This prayer he repeated in so strong a voice, that
the cardinals looking at one another said, " There is
" but little for us to hope, for the the pope grows young-
" er and younger every day."

[2] Sublimari seems to be a very bad word.

There

Γhere happened a quarrel, juſt before the canoniza-
ι, of ſuch conſequence, that it had like to have pre-
ιted it, and ſet the whole court in a flame.   It like-
ε gave the pope a good deal of uneaſineſs, as the ʴre-
ſt due to him was in ſome meaſure laid aſide, aſid the
ιce of the city for a while diſturbed, which he piqued
ιſelf upon having perfectly ſecured by his ordinances
ι regulations.

Count Olivarez, who never appeared at public cere-
ιnies (leſt he ſhould be obliged to give place to the
ιbaſſador of France, who conſtantly attended them)
ιlared his intention of aſſiſting at this, by a maſter of
ι ceremonies to the French ambaſſador ; and, " That
he expected to take place of all other ambaſſadors
that ſhould be there ; for as the canonization was obtained at the requeſt of his maſter, and concerned
nobody but the Spaniſh nation, that honour undoubtedly belonged to him." The French ambaſſador
ſwered, " That ſuch ceremonies as were publicly celebrated in St. Peter's, could not be deemed particular,
or appropriated to any one nation : All the world had
a right to be preſent at them ; and that at ſuch times
eſpecially, every one ought to maintain his proper
rank and ſtation." In anſwer to this, it was ſaid, " That
he might for once at leaſt abſent himſelf from the ceremony." But he did not care to conſent to that ; and
d, " his character would not admit of it; that he ſhould
incur his maſter's diſpleaſure by acting in that manner." And made ſome other excuſes and compliments
ιon the occaſion. The count remonſtrated, " That he
was obliged to perform certain particular functions
that day, and to make ſome preſents to his Holineſs ; with other ceremonies, which abſolutely
required him to be near the pope's perſon." The
ther replied, " that his preſence need not any ways
prevent him performing this ; and that as ſoon as
he had done, he might either go out of the chapel,
or retire to his proper place.   This conteſt made

a great

a great noife in Rome, and the pretentions of both
fides were difcuffed with much warmth and animofity; the French minifter obftinately refufing to give
up the leaft particle of his privileges.

Olivarez, who was embarraffed to the laft degree,
affembled the cardinals of his own nation, to deliberate upon an affair of fuch nicety and importance.
They were divided in their opinions; the major part
thought, as they could not prevail upon the French
ambaffador, by any other means, "it would be the
"beft way to afk, as a favour, to give up his
"right to precedence, for that time only." But
this went againft the grain: as he likewife thought it
would be prejudicial to the honour of his mafter, his
Spanifh pride and gravity (which he was remarkable
for) would not let him ftoop to it. The wifeft, however, and moft experienced of the Spanifh cardinuls advifing him to it, he at laft confented, tho' with reluctance; and fent two of them to defire the favour of
the French ambaffador, to give him place, only for
that day. The French ambaffador anfwered, in civil terms, "That he fhould be very glad to oblige
"him in this particular, and thought it might be
"done without prejudice to the right of precedence;
"which undoubtedly belonged to him, by cuftom
"immemorial, provided he would affift at the firft
"chapel the pope fhould hold (at which ceremonies
"he never attended) and there taking his place
"below him, fign a formal acknowledgement, that
"the right of precedence was due to him."

Olivarez, nettled at this anfwer, called all the Spanifh cardinals together a fecond time; and told them,
with fome fharpnefs, "How wrong a ftep it had
"been in them to perfuade him to afk a favour,
"which he very well knew, would not be granted
"without prejudice to the honour of his nation:"
Defiring to know, "What they thought was proper
"to be done further, in fo delicate and critical a
"conjuncture?" They were unanimoufly of opinion

"That he ought not, by any means, to comply
with fo ureafonable a demand." In confequence
of which he returned for anfwer to the French ambaffador, "That he fhould take great care how
he gave up in writing a privilege, which, he was
thoroughly convinced, lawfully belonged to him;
and would find a way to obtain that, as his right,
which he had denied him as a favour."
The difpute was carried to fuch a height, that it
s hourly expected they would have recourfe to
ıs, to fupport their pretenfions: All the Spaniards,
t were in Rome, reforted to the count's palace; and
French, to that of their minifter; fo that people
re apprehenfive, this difturbance would not only
vent the canonization, but fet the whole city in
uproar.

Sixtus, being informed of thefe tumultuary pro-
dings, was highly offended at the minifters, and
l them, with his ufual roughnefs, "That they
were both in fault and ought to have known their
duty better; that he would not fuffer either of
hem to difturb the public tranquillity, or brave
he fovereign authority of the H. See; that as he
did not allow his nuncios at Paris, or Madrid, to
ake up arms upon any pretence whatfoever, he
would not fuffer either the French or Spanifh, or any
other minifters, to do fo in Rome." He then called a
fiftory, compofed chiefly of the cardinals of both
ions, and reprimanded them feverely, for not hav-
put an end to this difpute before. Some of them an-
red with a good deal of fpirit; fo that the confifto-
had like to have been in confufion, as well as other
ces: But the cardinals fearing left they fhould pro-
e Sixtus to treat them with ftill more afperity than
ufed to do, thought proper, at laft to give way to
impetuofity of his temper; and it was agreed, at
breaking up of the affembly, that every one of
m fhould ufe their utmoft endeavours to extin-
ifh the flame; which was at laft effected; but in

a manner

a manner very much to the honour of the French
, and the inexpreſſible mortification of Olivarez: He
was obliged, however, to ſit down contented, for
fear of preventing the canonization, which his maſter had been ſoliciting ſo many years, and with ſuch
eagerneſs and application.

The expedient that was hit upon to put an end
to the affair, was, that the count ſhould ſtay away
from the feſtival, on pretence of indiſpoſition; and
that cardinal Deza, who had a right to take place of
the French ambaſſador, ſhould repreſent him, and
diſcharge all the functions of the Spaniſh ambaſſador
that day. He was ſo galled at being obliged to keep
the houſe, all the day of ſo ſplendid a ceremony, and
which he had laboured with ſuch earneſtneſs and aſſiduity to bring about, that it was a long time before
he could forgive the French, or even ſpeak of them
with any tolerable patience.

It is ſaid, that an event, not certainly known,
which happened at this canonization, inſpired Sixtus
with a deſign of founding ſome great and public
charity, that ſhould be beneficial, not only to Rome,
but the whole Chriſtian world: For this purpoſe he
appropriated 3000 crowns per ann, for the redemption
of Chriſtian ſlaves out of the hands of the Infidels;
and ordered, that ſuch as were moſt deſtitute and
miſerable of them, ſhould be yearly ranſomed; and
that the ſubjects of the H. See ſhould have the preference of all others.

He eſtabliſhed many other noble charities; and
tho' he was naturally parſimonious, and an enemy to
profuſion, he was never ſparing in expence, for the
relief of thoſe that were really neceſſitous, and ob-
jects of charity, eſpecially ſuch whoſe modeſty would
not let them make their wants known.

He frequently diſtributed large ſums, by the hands
of ſome good eccleſiaſtics, whom he pitched upon
for that purpoſe, to poor widows, that were left with
large familiɛs, or had daughters marriageable, and
no

no fortunes to give them. He was particularly careful of young women; and never fpared thofe that had been guilty of debauching any of them, either by force or artifice; and condemned above fifty to the gallies upon this account, without any procefs, tho' fome of them had not been actually guilty of the fact, but an attempt only to commit it.

Two young rakes having been apprehended one day, and carried to prifon by the archers, who caught them breaking open a window to get into a houfe, where a young woman lived, the governor thought they only deferved a few days imprifonment; but fearing on the other hand, he fhould incur the difpleafure of Sixtus, who he knew would never bear to hear of any outrage of this kind, he went to inform him of it, and faid, "That as no violence had "been actually committed, he thought it might be "looked upon only as frolic of youth, and could "not deferve fo fevere a punifhment as the gallies." As foon as he had finifhed, Sixtus knit his brows, and anfwered, "We did not make you a judge to plead "for the guilty, but to punifh them as the law di- "rects. However, fince you have taken upon you "to turn advocate, we fhall difpofe of your place "to fomebody elfe, and then you may plead as long "as you think proper." The governor was not a little terrified at thefe threats, as he knew Sixtus was generally as good as his word, and endeavoured to mollify him, if poffible, with excufes and fubmiffion. Upon which he began to abate a little of his paffion, and faid, in a tone fomething fofter, "If we do not "punifh the wicked attempts of fuch people, by "fending them to the gallies, they would certainly "come to be hanged in a while, for an actual com- "miffion of the crime, fo that we think we are very "much their friends, and do them a confiderable "piece of fervice."

It is not eafy to be imagined how exact Sixtus was in this point, and how carefully he watched over the

K k 2   honour

honour of the female sex, and provided for their security, especially in the streets and public places, of which we shall give some instances.

A servant-maid going very late one night, to fetch a midwife to her mistress, who was in labour, happened to meet a gentleman's lacquey in the street, who knocked out the light that was in her lanthorn, and then endeavoured to give her a kiss; but she crying out, he took to his heels: However, she knew him, and complained of it to her master, a linen draper; who, as it was a trifling affair, took no further notice of it; but Sixtus being soon informed of it by one of his spies, sent for the governor, reproaching him with negligence in his office; and said, "He "he did not attend to, or seem, to give himself any "trouble about the government of the city;" and ordered him to take up the footman, and have him severely whipped thro' the street where he had abused the woman. As the master had shewn no regard to his servant's complaint, he was sent to prison, and kept there a considerable time, on a pretence of having preferred his private interest to that of the public, and concealed from the eyes of Justice what he ought immediately to have made known.

But his severity was still greater to the son of a Perugian advocate, that was lately come to live at Rome. This young man falling desperately in love with the daughter of a widow lady, of remarkable beauty, asked her in marriage; but the mother who designed her for one of her own relations, would not consent. Driven to despair by this repulse, he took the following method to obtain her in marriage: As she was going one day to church, he stopped her in the street, and lifting up her veil gave her a kiss, tho' she did all that was in her power to prevent it. Upon this, her mother making a great outcry, the mob began to gather about them, and the lover made his escape. The old woman, thinking the honour of her daughter sullied by this affront, went

to

to demand justice of the Pope, who immediately ordered a procefs to be commenced againft the young man, for having offered fuch a violence to a woman of modefty and reputation: But as he was protected by the Colonna family, who interefted themfelves in the affair, the mother confented that fhe fhould marry him, which was immediately agreed to by them both. As the young woman's relations thought that a fufficient recompenfe for the indignity which had been offered to her; they fent to inform his Holinefs that the matter was compromifed, and all parties fatisfied, and that they were going immediately to folemnize the marriage: But juft as they were fat down to their wedding-dinner, with all their friends and relations, that were affembled upon this occafion, in came the Provoft-marfhal, with his archers, and laying hold of the bride-groom, carried him away to prifon, by the Pope's order.

The reader may eafily figure to himfelf the aftonifhment of the whole company, and, particularly, the vexation and difappointment of the bride. Dinner was put off; and the parents of the new married couple, going to the governor, defired to know the reafon of this proceeding; but he faying he could only refer them to the Pope for an anfwer, they went the next day to entreat his Holinefs to releafe their fon; acquainting him, "That he had made " full recompenfe for the affront he had offered to " the young woman, by marrying her; and that all " fides were very well contented." He told them, " He was very glad to hear they were all content; " but it was neceffary juftice likewife fhould be fa- " tisfied;" and then addreffing himfelf to the go- " vernor, faid, "Pray, Sir, what is your opinion " of this match? Are you likewife content?" The governor, who had been before hand inftructed what he was to anfwer, faid, "That a fufficient fa- " tisfaction was by no means made to juftice, which " had been grievoufly infulted, by the contempt
" that

" that the young man had fhewn to the fovereign
" authority, in daring to offer violence to a modeft
" woman, in the open ftreet ; and that he demanded
" fatisfaction." "If that be the cafe, faid Sixtus, as
" every body elfe is fatisfied, it is but reafonable
" you fhould be fo too ;" and, upon this, he difmiffed them, fending the bridegroom back to prifon,
with orders to the governor to proceed againft him
immediately, and condemn him to the gallies for
five years.

The family of the Colonna, who were inftrumental in making this match, were fenfibly touched with
the young man's hard fate ; and as they were in great
favour with Sixtus, endeavoured to obtain his pardon,
but to no purpofe : For the Pope, laying afide the
friendfhip and refpect he had for them, and of which
he had given feveral remarkable proofs, faid, "We
" don't reckon thofe in the number of our friends,
" that are continually teazing and importuning us
" to let fuch crimes go unpunifhed : Indeed, how
" can we? when we fee them taking the part of a
" knave or a villain, againft law and juftice ;
" whofe crimes are owing to the many bad exam-
" ples of impunity and injuftice they have lately
" feen. If we leave fuch unpunifhed, they will au-
" thorize more. A perfon ought to feek a woman
" in marriage, not by force and violence, but in a
" civil and honourable manner. If we did not put
" a ftop to fuch practices, we fhould fee no end of
" difproportioned and incongruous marriages ; pa-
" rents would no longer have any power over their
" children, if every fhabby fellow was fuffered to go
" and kifs a young woman by violence, in the
" ftreets, on purpofe to oblige her to marry him.
" If women are not fafe in the public ftreets, which
" are immediately under our protection, how can it
" be fuppofed they fhould be fo in their own houfes,
" where they have no body to defend them ? God
" forbid that fuch crimes fhould go unpunifhed,
" whilft

" whilft we have the honour of governing his " church." Cardinal Colonna not being able to make any impreffion upon him, the poor man was fent to the gallies and the chain faftened to him, in the place where the offence had been committed. It affected his wife in fuch a manner, that fhe died in a few days after.

It was owing to thefe feverities, that, in the time of Sixtus, a woman might pafs the ftreets at any hour of the night, without the leaft infult or affront; and indeed, to juftify his memory, it muft be owned there was very great occafion for them, to reftrain the exorbitant degree of libertinifm and debauchery, that reigned in the days of his predeceffor, whofe uncommon lenity had fo encouraged the Roman youth in all manner of lewdnefs, that the chafteft and moft virtuous women were not fecure from violence, either in public, or in their own houfes, which obliged many to fend their daughters into convents, to protect them from the attempts that were daily made upon their chaftity.

His attention was not however fo wholly taken up in eftablifhing good government, and making regulations in the police, but he found fome time to employ in works of piety and devotion, of which we have already given feveral inftances. He further inftituted the feftival of the prefentation of the virgin [3], and that of St. Francis de Paul, at the par-

[3] This feaft of the Romifh church is held in memory of the H. Virgin's being prefented by her parents in the temple, to be there educated. It is pretended, that there were young women brought up in the temple of Jerufalem, which fome endeavour to prove from that paffage in the fecond book of the Maccabees, iii. 19. *And the women, girt with fackcloth under their breafts, abounded in the ftreets; and the virgins, that were kept in, ran, fome to the gates, and fome to the walls, and others looked out of the windows: And all holding their hands towards Heaven, made fupplication*; which is the glofs of Eutochius upon this paffage. And Lyranus obferves, that young women were educated till marriage, either in the temple, or in the buildings contiguous to it.

ticular

ticular requeſt of the Minims, of which order this
Saint was the founder, and celebrated maſs himſelf
in their church, upon the day of that ſolemnity,
which is the ſecond of April. The Auguſtines alſo
entreated him to appoint a feſtival in honour of St.
Nicholas of Tolentino, which he granted the more
willingly, as this Saint was a native of his own province La Marca. He likewiſe canonized St. Anthony
of Padua, by whoſe interceſſion, he ſaid, he had received many remarkable favours from Heaven,
whilſt he lived a monaſtic life. After this, the
archbiſhop and city of Naples prevailed upon him
to make a ſaint of Januarius, the martyr and biſhop
of that city, with his companions and fellow-ſuffer-
ers; as he did (at the inſtance of the Dominicans) of
St. Peter the martyr, who had been a religious of
their order.

It was by his particular command, that a feſtival
was appointed for St. Placidus, and his brothers,
Eutychien and Victorinus, with their ſiſter Flavia,
whoſe names he inſerted in the calendar. Their
bodies were found this year, in the church of St.
John Baptiſt de Meſſina, as they were digging up the
foundations of a very old wall, in order to have it
rebuilt. It was known, by the hiſtory of their lives,
that they were buried in that church, but no body
could tell the exact place. Placidus was a religious
of the order of St. Benedict, and contemporary with
him. He lived with his brothers and ſiſter at Meſſina; from whence, as they were going out one day,
to viſit that ſaint they were taken by the Saracens,
commanded by Abdalla, a bitter enemy and perſecu-
tor of the Chriſtian name, who put them to death,
after he had tortured them in the moſt cruel manner, to make them renounce their faith. To this
church he granted many privileges and indulgences,
by a ſpecial bull; and ordered the day of their tran-
ſlation, that is, the removal of their bones, to be
kept

kept as a feftival; and a particular fervice to be
compofed for that purpofe [4].

Whilft he was thus bufied in canonizations, and
other acts of charity and devotion, he let no opportunity flip, that he thought might ferve to extend
the power and influence of the H. See: and in order to
do this, he was conftantly thrufting himfelf into all
the differences of Europe, endeavouring to have them
referred to him, and propofing himfelf as a mediator.
With this view, when he heard of Maximilian's imprifonment in Poland, he determined to fend a legate a latere, to procure his liberty, under a pretence of compofing the civil diffenfions that raged in
that kingdom, and preventing the evils that threatned
Chriftendom.

Cardinal Hippolitus Aldobrandino was fixed upon
for this employment, and left Rome the 23d of May,
in the year 1588, attended by a numerous train, and
furnifhed with ample powers. The Pope conjured
him to make ufe of his utmoft addrefs to accomplifh this end; for, as both the fpiritual and temporal welfare of Poland entirely depended upon it, it
would add great weight and influence to the authority
of the H. See.

As foon as he arrived in Poland, he began to nego-
tiate with all parties: firft he conferred with the
emperor Rodolphus, and then with Sigifmond, lately
chofen king of Poland, and laft of all with the nobility of the kingdom, that were deputed for that purpofe; and was prefent at the diets that were affembled in Bohemia. After having furmounted difficulties that were thought almoft infuperable, a peace
was concluded betwixt the Poles and the Houfe of
Auftria, to the fatisfaction of both parties; and an
agreement made betwixt Sigifmond and Maximilian,
who was fet at liberty, upon condition that he would
never more pretend to the crown of Poland, in right

[4] Thuanus mentions this tranfaction, but feems to think the
ftory of Placidus fabulous.

of

of his former election, even though Sigifmond fhould die, and acknowledge him for the true and lawful fovereign of that kingdom; all parties folemnly fwearing to obferve their engagements before the legate, in the cathedral church of Cracow.

When this ceremony was over, the legate difpatched his nephew, Cynthius Pafferino, with the news of it to his holinefs. This young man was the fon of a fifter whom he loved tenderly : he was equally fond of his nephew, whom he brought with him into Poland, upon the account of his uncommon learning and prudence, and other qualities, very rarely to be met with at his age. When he was afterwards exalted to the pontificate, and took the name of Clement VIII, he gave him a hat, with the title of St. George, and would have him called cardinal Aldobrandinino, as he had been himfelf. He left Poland, attended by only two fervants, and made fuch hafte, that he arrived in twelve days at Rome. The whole court expreffed the greateft fatisfaction at his arrival; and the Pope was highly pleafed at the news he brought from Poland.

The legate fet out foon after his nephew, leaving behind him a wonderful opinion of his virtue and abilities. He was conducted to the frontiers of that kingdom, by a large body of the nobility, who with many demonftrations of regret and concern, upon his departure, at the fame time loaded him with bleffings, for having re-eftablifhed peace and tranquillity in their country.

To honour him with ftill greater marks of his confidence and efteem, the Pope fent him power to fettle feveral other affairs of the utmoft confequence in the ftates and cities, through which he was to pafs in his return; the governors and magiftrates of which, fhewed him the higheft refpect; efpecially at

Bologna,

Bologna, where he ſtaid two days to repoſe himſelf; during which, he was royally entertained at the expence of that city.

When he came near Rome, the whole college of cardinals, attended by the prelates and nobility of Rome, went to meet him, with a train of coaches and chariots, that reached above a mile; at the head of which, cardinal Montalto came to wait upon him, by his uncle's expreſs command, and conducted him into the city in one of his own coaches, attended by a party of guards, an honour never ſhewn before to any legate.

The magnificent palace, near St. John de Lateran, being lately finiſhed, the Pope cauſed it to be fitted up a few days before he arrived, on purpoſe to admit him to his firſt audience in that noble edifice. He was received in the grand ſaloon, by his holineſs, and all the cardinals, who liſtened with extreme pleaſure, to the account he gave of his embaſſy; applauding his conſummate prudence and abilities, in bringing that arduous and perplexed negotiation to ſo happy a concluſion.

The whole court went to compliment him upon the reputation he had acquired in the diſcharge of this office; which was likewiſe the common topic of all converſations in Rome for ſeveral weeks, and the Pope being every day more and more convinced of his capacity, entruſted him with a larger ſhare of power; and ſpeaking of him in the conſiſtory, ſaid, " He had, at laſt, found a man after his own " heart."

This year Sixtus built the famous library in the Vatican: as he ſpared no pains or expence to make it the fineſt in the world, it may not be diſagreeable, perhaps, to give ſome account of it here, for the ſatisfaction of thoſe that have never been at Rome; and we are not without hope that it will furniſh ſome entertainment, even to the learned, and ſuch as are lovers of antiquity.

In

In a very large area, belonging to the Vatican, called the Belvidere, there was a vaft and magnificent theatre; round which, Pius V. had built feats, of the fineft marble, for the convenience of the people, when he entertained them with any public fpectacle. Sixtus, thinking this a proper place for the purpofe, pulled down the feats, and made ufe of the materials in erecting this grand fabric.

The library alone, is above 300 feet long, and 70 broad, with a beautiful range of pilafters, from one end of it to the other, which fupport the vaulted roof. It is finely lighted, by many large windows, on the North and South fides, and at the Weft e.id: adjoining to the main library, are two other large rooms, in which are depofited the moft curious books and manufcripts: Into thefe, no ftrangers are ever admitted, except they be prelates, or perfons of diftinction, and well recommended to the librarian. There are feveral others for the under library-keepers, and the convenience of the literati, who come to confult the books; with an elegant apartment for the cardinal-librarian, when he pleafes to refide there. The walls are painted, both on the outfide and infide, by the moft celebrated mafters of that age.

On the outfide are feveral emblems, or reprefentations of the fciences and virtues, in frefco, with other curious devices relating to the feveral parts of literature, admired by all connoiffeurs.

On the infide are painted the great actions and atchievements of Sixtus, till that time, in the moft exquifite manner. There is, likewife, a reprefentation of the fixteen general councils, with an infcription under every one of them, which we fhall here infert, as they contain a fhort fketch of church hiftory.

Under

Under the picture of the first council of Nice,

SAN. SYLVESTRO. PAPA. FL. CONSTANTINO.
MAGNO. IMP. CHRISTVS. DEI. FILIVS.
PATRI. CONSVBSTANTIALIS.
DECLARATVR. .
ARII. IMPIETAS. CONDEMNATVR.
EX. DECRETO. CONCILII. CONSTANTINVS.
IMP LIBROS. ARIANORVM. COMBVRI.
IVBET.

Under the first of Conftantinople.

S. DAMASO. PAPA. ET. THEODOSIO. SEN.
IMP.
SPIRITVS. SANCTI. DIVINITAS. PROPVG-
NATVR.
NEFARIA. MACEDONII. HAERESIS. EX-
TINGVITVR.

Under the council of Ephefus. .

S. CELESTINO. PAPA. ET. THEODOSIO. IVN.
IMP.
NESTORIVS. CHRISTVM. DIVIDENS.
DAMNATVR.
B. MARIA. DEI. GENETRIX. PRAEDICATVR.

Under the first of Calcedon,

SANCT. LEONE. PAPA ET. MARCIANO. IM-
PERATORE.
INFELIX. EVTYCHES. [5]
VNAM. TANTVM. IN. CHRISTO.
POST. INCARNATIONEM.
NATVRAM. ASSERENS. CONFVTATVR.

[5]. I fuppofe this was intended for a pun.

Under

Under the second of Conftantinople,

VIGILIO. PAPA. ET. IVSTINIA NO. IMP
CONTENTIONES. DE. TRIBVS. CAPITIBVS.
[6] SEDANTVR.
ORIGENIS. ERRORES. REFELLVNTVR.

Under the third of Conftantinople,

S.AGATHONE. PAPA. CONSTANTINO. [7]
POGONATO. IMP.
MONOTHELITAE. HAERETICI.
VNAM. TONTVM. IN. CHRISTO. VOLVNTA-
TEM. ESSE. DICENTES.
EXPLODVNTVR.

Under the second of Nice,

ADRIANO. PAPA. CONSTANTINO. IREN. F.
IMPER.
IMPII. ICONOMACHI. REIICIVNTVR.
SACRARVM. IMAGINVM. VENERATIO. CON-
FIRMATVR.

Under the fourth of Conftantinople,

ADRIANO. SECVNDO. PAPA. BASILIO. IMP.
IGNATIVS. PATRIARCHA. CONSTANTINOPO-
LITANVS.
IN. SEDEM. SVAM. EXPVLSO. PHOTIO. RESTI-
TVITVR.

Under the firft of the Lateran,

ALEXANDRO. TERTIO. PONT. FREDERICO.
PRIMO. IMP.

[6] See Bower's Life of Vigilius.
[7] Conftantine the younger, firnamed Pogonates, or Pogona-
tus, i. e. Barbatus ; being remarkable for his great beard.

VAL-

VALDENSES. ET. CATHARI. [8] HAERETICI.
DAMNANTVR.
LAICORVM. ET. CLERICORVM. MORES.
AD. VETEREM. DISCIPLINAM. RESTITVVN-
TVR.
TORNAMENTA. VETANTVR.

Under the fecond of the Lateran,

INNOCENTO. III. PONT. FREDERICO. SE-
CVNDO. IMP.
ABBATIS. IOACHIMI. [9] ERRORES. DAMNAN-
TVR.
BELLVM. SACRVM. DE. HIEROSOLYMA. RE-
CVPERANDA.
DECERNITVR.
CRVCE. * SIGNATI. INSTITVVNTVR.

On one fide of this picture, St. Francis is reprefented fupporting the church of St. John de Lateran,
according to the dream of Sixtus, with the following
infcription under it,

[8] Cathari, or Puritans, fo called from the Greek word καθαρος
purus, a fort of heretics, pretending to great purity of life.
They maintained, that it was not lawful to take an oath, upon
any occafion whatfoever; that perfection in this life was abfolutely
neceffary to falvation; that repentance after baptifm was of no
effect

[9] A Calabrian by birth, and a monk of the Ciftercian order,
afterwards abbot and founder of the congregation of Flora: he
lived in the eleventh century, and wrote commentaries upon Ifaiah,
Jeremiah, and the Revelations, in which he fhews, that the Anti-
Chrift was already born at Rome, and to be exalted there. As
alfo a concordance of the old and new teftament, and feveral
prophecies concerning the Popes. He died in 1202, and foretold
in his writings (as well as cardinal Cufanus, Johan, Lightenber-
gius, Hildegarda, and St. Bridget) a general change of religion.
In this council, one of his treatifes, concerning the Trinity, was
condemned as heretical; but George Laudo, an abbot of his own
order, wrote a defence of it: he was a pious man, and of fome
learning; but looked upon as a vifionary, and enthufiaft.

* Crufades.

IN.

INNOCENTIO. III. PONT.
PER. QVIETEM. SAN. FRANCISCVS. ECCLE-
SIAM. LATERAN.
SVSTINERF. VISVS. EST.

On the other fide of it is the picture of St. Do-
minic; who, in the time of Innocent III, fuppreffed
a dangerous herefy that had fprung up at Tholoufe:
under it,

S. DOMENICO. SVADENTE.
CONTRA. ALBIGENSES. HAERETICOS.
SIMON. COMES. MONTIFORTENSIS.
PVGNAM. SVSCEPIT. EGREGIEQVE. CONFE-
CIT.

Under the firft of Lyons,

INNOCENTO. IV. PONT. MAX.
FREDERICVS. SECVNDVS. HOSTIS ECCLE-
SIAE. DECLARATVR.
IMPERIOQVE. PRIVATVR.
DE. TERRAE. SANCTAE. RECVPERATIONE.
CONSTITVITVR.
HIROSOLYMITANAE. EXPEDITIONIS. DVX.
LVDOVICVS. FRANCORVM. REX. DESIGNA-
TVR.
GALERO. RVBRO. ET. PVRPVRA. CARDINA-
LES. DONANTUR.

Under the fecond of Lyons,

GREGORIO. X. PONT.
GRAECI. AD. S. R. E. VNIONEM. REDEVNT.
IN. HOC. CONCILIO.
S. BONAVENTVRA EGREGIA. VIRTVTVM.
OFFICIA.
ECCLESIAE. DEI. PRAESTITIT.
TARTARORVM. REX.

A.

, F. HIERONYMO. ORDIN. MINOR. AD.
CONCILIVM.
PERDVCITER.
ET. SOLEMNITER. BAPTIZATVR,

Under that of Vienna,

CLEMENTE. V. PONT.
LEMENTINORVM. DECRETALIVM. ET.
CONSTITVTIONVM.
CODEX PROMVLGATVR.
OCESSIO. SOLEMNITATIS. CORPORIS. DO-
MINI. INSTITVITVR.
BRAICAE. CHALDAICAE. ARABICAE. ET.
GRAECAE.
LINGVARVM. STVDIVM.
PROPAGANDAE. FIDEI. ERGO.
. NOBILISSIMIS. QVATVOR. EVROPAE. A-
CADEMIIS.
INSTITVITVR.

Under that of Florence,

EVGENIO. IV. PONT.
GRAECI. ARMENI. AETHIOPES.
AD. FIDEI. VNITATEM. REDEVNT.

Under the laſt of the Lateran,

IO. SECVNDO. ET. LEONE. X. PONT. MAX.
BELLVM. CONTRA. TVRCAM.
QVI. CYPRVM. ET. AEGYPTVM.
OXIME. SVLTANO. VICTO. OCCVPAVE-
RAT.
DECERNITVR.
XIMILIANVS. CAESAR. ET. FRANCISCVS.
REX. GALLIAE.
LLO. TVRCICO. DVCES. PRAEFICIVNTVR.

Under that of Trent.

PAVLO. III. IVLIO. III. PIO. IV. PONT.
LVTHERANI. ET. ALII. HAERETICI. DAM-
NANTVR.
CLERI. POPVLIQVE. DISCIPLINA. AD. PRIS-
TINOS. MORES.
RESTITVITVR.

After the councils, the moft celebrated libraries that
have ever been in the world, are painted, with infcriptions under them ; the firft is the library of the Hebrews;
under which is the following,

MOYSES. LIBRUM. LEGIS. LEVITIS.
IN. TABERNACVLO. REPONENDVM. TRA-
DIT.
ESDRAS. SACERDOS. ET. SCRIBA.
BIBLIOTHECAM. SACRAM. RESTITVIT.

Under that of the Chaldeans in Babylon,

DANIEL. ET. SOCII.
LINGVAM. SCIENTIAMQVE. CHALDAEO-
RVM. ADDISCVNT.
CYRI. DECRETVM. DE. TEMPLI. INSTAV-
RATIONE.
DARII. IVSSV. PERQVIRITVR.

Under that of the Grecians at Athens,

PISISTRATVS. PRIMVS. APVD. GRAECOS.
PVBLICAM. BIBLIOTHECAM. INSTITVIT.
SELEVCVS. BIBLIOTHECAM. A. XERXE. AS-
PORTATAM
REFERENDAM. CVRAT.

Under that of. the Egyptians at Alexandria,

PTOLEMAEVS. INGENTI. BIBLIOTHECA. IN-
STRVCTA.

STRVCTA.
IEBRAEORVM. LIBROS. CONCVPISCIT. [10].
SEPTVAGINTA. ET. DVO. INTERPRETES.
AB. ELEAZARO. MISSI.
SACROS. LIBROS. PTOLEMAEO. REDDVNT.

Under that of the Romans,

TARQVINIVS. SVPERBVS. LIBROS. SIBYLLI-
NOS.. TRES.
ᵃLIIS. A. MVLIERE. INCENSIS. TANDEM.
EMIT.
AVGVSTVS. CAESAR.
ᵖALATINA. BIBLIOTHECA. MAGNIFICE. OR-
NATA.
VIROS. LITERATOS. FOVET.

Under that of Jeruſalem,

ᵢ. ALEXANDER. EPISCOPVS. ET. MARTYR.
DECIO. IMP.
IN. MAGNA. TEMPORVM. ACERBITATE.
SACRARVM. SCRIPTVRARVM. LIBROS.
HIEROSOLYMIS. CONGREGAT.

Under that of Ceſarea,

SANCT. PAMPHILVS. PRESBYT. ET MAR-
TYR.
ADMIRANDAE. SANCTITATIS. ET. DOC-
TRINAE.
SACRAM. BIBLIOTHECAM. CAESAREAE.
CONFICIT.
MVLTOS. LIBROS. SVA. MANV. DESCRIBIT.

Under that of the Holy-Apoſtles.

ANCTVS. PETRVS. SACRORVM. LIBRORVM.
ₜ THESAVRVM.

[10] Concupiſcit is a very indifferent word, I think.

L l 2   IN.

IN. ROM. ECCLES. ASSERVARI. IVBET.

Under that of the Popes,

ROMANI. PONTIFICES. APOSTOLICAM. BIB-
LIOTHECAM.
MAGNO. STVDIO. AMPLIFICANT. ATQVE.
ILLVSTRANT.

Then follow the pictures of those that invented letters.

Under that of Adam is written,

ADAM. DIVINITVS. EDOCTVS.
PRIMVS. SCIENTIARVM. ET. LITERARVM.
INVENTOR.

Under the fons of Seth, who were the grandfons of
Adam.

FILII. SETH. COLVMNIS. DVABVS.
RERVM.   CAELESTIVM.   DISCIPLINAM. IN-
SCRIBVNT.

Under Abraham,

ABRAHAM. SYRAS. ET. CHALDAICAS. LI-
TERAS. INVENIT.

Under Mofes, the general and legiflator of the Jews.

MOYSES. ANTIQVAS. HEBRAICAS. LITERAS.
INVENIT.

Under Efdras, the fcribe and prieft.

ESDRAS. NOVAS. HEBRAEORVM. LITERAS.
INVENIT.

Under

Under Mercury the Egyptian,

MERCVRIVS. THOTH.
ᴣGYPTIIS. SACRAS. LITERAS. CONSCRIP-
SIT.

Under Hercules the Egyptian,

ᴣRCVLES. AEGYPTIVS. PHRYGIAS. LITE-
RAS. CONSCRIPSIT.

Under Memnon,

MEMNON. PHORONEO. [11] AEQVALIS.
LITERAS. IN. AEGYPTO. INVENIT.

Under Ifis queen of Egypt,

S. REGINA. AEGYPTIARVM. LITERARVM.
INVENTRIX.

Under Phœnix,

IOENIX. LITERAS. PHOENICIBVS. TRA-
DIDIT.

Under Cadmus,

CADMVS. PHOENICIS. FRATER.
LITERAS. SEXDECIM. IN. GRAECIAM.
INTVLIT.

ich are painted above him. It is faid, Palamedes
led four, and Simonides four more, which make
the 24. Ariftotle, as quoted by Pliny, fays the
ient Greek letters were but 18; and that Epicharmus

11] Phoroneus was the fecond king of Argos, and fucceeded
father Inachus, about the year of the world 2247, and reigned
years. He was fucceeded by his fon Spartus, who built Spar-
Eufeb.

mus added two, and not Palamedes, how it was, is not possible to determine, at this distance of time.

Under Linus the Theban,

LINVS. THEBANVS. GRAECARVM. LITERA-
RVM. INVENTOR.

Under Cecrops king of the Athenians,

CECROPS. DIPHYES. PRIMVS. ATHENIENSI-
VM. REX.
GRAECARVM. LITERARVM. AVCTOR.

Under Pythagoras,

PYTHAGORAS. LITERAM. Υ.
AD. HVMANAE. VITAE. EXEMPLVM. INVE-
NIT. [12].

Under Epicharmus the Sicilian,

EPICHARMVS. SICVLVS. DVAS. GRAECAS.
LITERAS. ADDIDIT.

Under Simonides,

SIMONIDES. MELICVS.
QVATVOR. GRAECARVM. LITERARVM. IN
VENTOR.

Under Palamedes,

PALAMEDES. BELLO. TROIANO.
GRAECIS. LITERIS. QVATVOR. ADIECIT.

[12] Pythagoras used the Υ as a symbol of human life. The foot representing infancy, and the forked top the two paths of virtue and vice; one or the other of which all people enter upon when they arrive at years of maturity. They that have a mind to see the different letters invented by the above-mentioned persons, may consult Schraderus, p. 196, 197.

Under

Under Nicrofta Carmenta, the mother of Evander.

NICOSTRATA. CARMENTA.
LATINARVM. LITERARVM. INVENTRIX.
VIZ.
A. B. C. D. E. G. I. L. M. N. O. R. S. T. V. *

Under Evander king of the Arcadians,

EVANDER. CARMENTAE, F. ABORIGINES
LITERAS. DOCVIT.

Under Demaratus the Corinthian,

DEMARATVS. CORINTHIVS.
HETRVSCARVM. LITERARVM. AVCTOR.

Under Claudius Cæfar, emperor of the Romans,

CLAVDIVS. IMP. TRES. NOVAS. LITERAS.
ADINVENIT.

Above him is painted an F, with this infcription,

RELIQVAE. DVAE. VSV. OBLITERATAE.
SVNT.

hich gives us to underftand, that the letter F was
ne of them, and that the other two are loft, or out
ufe; nor is it known what they were. But it does
ot feem probable that the emperor Claudius invented
iat letter; as Cicero, who lived long before him,
iakes mention of it in an epiftle to Atticus [13],
ho ufed, in joke, to call his friends Villa Formiana,
ic Digamma, becaufe it began with an F. The Di-
amma, amongft the Romans, being a charaƈter that
:prefented two capital Gammas, as the F does. Per-

* Schraderus adds H. P. Q.

[13] L. ix. Epift. 9. This paffage feems obfcure, and has
izzled many of the critics.

haps

haps Claudius might, in some measure, change either the shape or pronunciation of it, and from thence acquire the name and glory of being the inventor.

Under St. Chrysostom,

SANCT. IOHANNES. CHRYSOSTOMVS. ARMENIACARVM. LITERARVM. INVENTOR.

Under St. Jerome,

SANCT. HIERONYMVS. LITERARVM. ILLYRICARVM. INVENTOR,

Under St. Cyril,

S. CYRILLVS. ALIARVM. LITERARVM. ILLY. RICARVM. AVCTOR.

Under Ulphon, or Ulphilas [14],

VLPHILAS. EPISCOPVS. GOTHORVM. LITERAS, INVENIT.

Under that of our Saviour Jesus Christ,

EGO. SVM. ALPHA. ET. OMEGA. PRINCIPVM. ET. FINIS. IESVS. CHRISTVS. SVMMVS. MAGISTER. CAELESTIS. DOCTRINAE. AVCTOR.

The two last pieces are those of Sixtus and the Emperor.

Under the first is written,

CHRISTI. DOMINI. VICARIVS.

Under

[14] Ulphon, or Ulphilas, who lived in the fourth century, was the first that translated the bible into the Gothic language, and was hence called the inventor of their letters.

Under the other,
ECCLESIAE. DEFENSOR.

Thefe are all in the public library. In the other
'o rooms are painted the doctors of the church,
ith many of the faints, and feveral of the actions of
ktus, the particulars of which the reader perhaps,
ight think too great a trefpafs upon his patience;
r which reafon, we fhall only add what is infcribed
>on two fine marble tables, in the great library.

Upon the firft [15],

SIXTI. V. PONT. MAX.
PERPETVO. HOC. DECRETO.
DE. LIBRIS. VATICANAE. BIBLIOTHECAE.
CONSERVANDIS.
QVAE. INFRA. SVNT. SCRIPTA.
HVNC. IN. MODVM. SANCITA SVNTO.
INVIOLATEQVE. OBSERVANTOR.
NEMINI.
LIBROS. CODICES. VOLVMINA.
HVIVS. . VATICANEA. BIBLIOTHECAE.
X. EA. AVFERENDI. EXTRAHENDI. ALIO-
QVE. ASPORTANDI.
ON. BIBLIOTHECARIO. NEQVE. CVSTODI:
BVS. SCRIBISQVE.
EQVE. QVIBVSVIS. ALIIS. CVIVSVIS. ORDI-
NIS. ET. DIGNITATIS.

[15] Though it coft me much labour to reftore the true reading
the other infcriptions, thefe two were fo horribly mifprinted, that
hould never have been able to fet them right, if (after I had in
in enquired of moft of the bookfellers in London for Mutius Lan-
a very fcarce author, who gives an account of all the pictures
d infcriptions in the Vatican library) my worthy friend, the reve-
ad Mr. Fitzherbert, of Afhborne in Derbyfhire, had not procured
: a copy of them from Cambridge; for which, and many other
tances of his fingular kindnefs and humanity, I defire him to ac-
pt of my hearty thanks and acknowledgments.

NISI. DE; LICENTIA. SVMMI. ROM. PONT-
SCRIPTA. MANV.
FACVLTAS. ESTO:
SI. QVIS. SECVS. FECERIT.
LIBROS. PARTEMVE. ALIQVAM.
ABSTVLERIT. EXTRAXERIT. * CLEPSERIT.
CONCERPSERIT.
CORRVPERIT. DOLO. MALO.
ILLICO. A. FIDELVM. COMMVNIONE
EIECTVS MALEDICTUS.
ANATHEMATIS. VINCVLO. COLLIGATVS.
ESTO.
A. QVOQVAM. PRAETERQVAM. ROM. PONT.
NE. ABSOLVITOR.

Upon the fecond.

SIXTVS. V. PONT. MAX.
BIBLIBLIOTHECAM. APOSTOLICAM.
A. SANCTISSIMIS. PRIORIBVS. ILLIS. PONTI-
FICIBVS.
QVI. B. PETRI. VOCEM. AVDIVERVNT.
IN. IPSIS. ADHVC. SVRGENTIS. ECCLESIAE.
PRIMORDIIS. INCHOATAM.
PACE. ECCLESIAE. REDDITA. LATERANI. IN-
STITVTAM.
A. POSTERIORIBVS. DEINDE. IN. VATICANVM.
VT. AD. VSVS. PONTIFICIOS. PARATIOR.
ESSET.
TRANSLATAM.
IBIQVE. A. NICOLAO. V. AVCTAM.
A. SIXTO. IV. INSIGNITER. EXCVLTAM.
QVO. FIDEI. NOSTRAE.
ET. VETERVM. ECCLESIASTICAE. DISCIPLI-
NAE.
RITVVM. DOCVMENTA.
OMNIBVS. LINGVIS. EXPRESSA.

 * An old word ufed by Lucretius, from the Greek verb κλετ1o
or κλετw, to fteal.

ET.

ET. ALIORVM. MVLTIPLEX. SACRORVM.
COPIA. LIBRORVM.
CONSERVARENTVR.
AD. PVRAM. ET. INCORRVPTAM. FIDEI.
ET. DOCTRINAE. VERITATEM.
PERPETVA. SVCCESSIONE. IN. NOS. DERI-
VANDAM.
TOTO. TERRARVM. ORBE. CELEBERRIMAM.
CVM. LOCO. DEPRESSO. OBSCVRO. ET. IN-
SALVBRI. SITA. ESSET.
AVLA. PERAMPLA. VESTIBVLO.
CVBICVLIS. CIRCVM. ET. INFRA. SCALIS.
PORTICIBVS.
TOTOQVE. AEDIFICIO. A. FVNDAMENTIS.
EXTRVCTO.
SVBSELLIIS. PLVTEISQVE. ERECTIS. LIBRIS.
DISPOSITIS.
IN. HVNC. EDITVM. PERLVCIDVM.
SALVBREM. MAGISQVE. OPPORTVNVM. LO-
CVM. EXTVLIT.
PICTVRIS. ILLVSTRIBVS. VNDIQVE. ORNAVIT.
LIBERALIBVSQVE. DOCTRINIS.
ET. PVBLICAE. STVDIORVM. VTILITATI.
DICAVIT.
ANNO. MDLXXXVIII.
PONT. III.

This library may, without any exaggeration, be truly called the fineft in the univerfe; as it is ftocked with an infinite number of the choiceft manufcripts in the Hebrew, Arabick, Greek, Latin, and moft other languages; which Sixtus collected, with immenfe labour and expence, from all parts of the world. It was enriched with the fpoils of the Heidelbergh library (founded by the princes of the Palatinate, and reckoned the fineft collection then in Europe) which were fent to Rome, by count Tilly, when he took that city.

Near the library he built a large printing-houfe, that the world might have correct editions of fuch
books

books as the Proteſtants had unfairly and ungene-
rouſly corrupted.   He likewiſe cauſed the Holy Scrip-
tures to be printed in all the known languages of the
world, with the works of the fathers, and many
other books, proper, not only for the edification of
Chriſtians, but to inſtruct the moſt ignorant and ido-
latrous nations, in the way to ſalvation.

The management and ſuperintendance of it he
committed to Dominick Beſa *, a man of great learning and experience in this employment ; who ſo well
acquitted himſelf in the diſcharge of his duty, that
the preſs was very ſoon furniſhed with every thing
neceſſary, in a manner worthy of the founder, and
the whole conducted with all the accuracy, probity,
and good faith, that are requiſite in ſo uſeful and noble a profeſſion.

The year 1588 concluded with a moſt bloody tragedy, that was acted in France : the duke of Guiſe,
being declared head of the league, became ſo powerful, that he left little beſides the name of a king
to Henry III.   He wrote letters, formed leagues and
confederacies, entered into alliances with foreign
princes, without conſulting either the king, or his
council ; and depending upon the ſtrength of his
party, which indeed was very conſiderable, began to
grow moſt unſufferably inſolent and unreaſonable in
his demands : one of which was, to have the abſolute command of the army in his own hands, with the
title of *Lord High Conſtable of the Kingdom*, that ſo
he might be enabled to compel Henry to exclude the
K.. of Navarre from the ſucceſſion to the crown ;
which every body fully expected he would certainly
accompliſh, as two thirds of the kingdom were entirely at his devotion, and the other ſo intimidated,
that there was no likelihood of any oppoſition.

From theſe appearances, wiſe and diſcerning men
concluded, that before the breaking up of the ſtates,
then aſſembled at Blois, the king would have his
crown

* Fr. ſays Baza,

wn fhaved, and be fent to live in a cloyfter.
ɪny, indeed, did not fcruple to hint as much to his
jefty, and let him know the duke's faction made
:ir boafts, " That he was their prifoner, and they
would carry him to Paris in triumph, as the Romans ufed to do by the kings they had van-
quifhed, and there depofe him, allowing him a fmall
penfion to live upon."

Thefe infinuations were daggers in the king's
:aft ; and what made them ftill more poignant,
s, that they were but too well grounded, as hard-
any body was unacquainted with the defigns of
: league, upon his perfon and authority.   In fhort,
ngs were come to fuch a pafs, that there was no
ɪger any room for moderation ; either the king or
: duke muft fall : when the veffel itfelf is in
ɪger, no regard muft be had to the cargo ; the
ɔft defperate courfe muft be taken, and every
ng thrown overboard to keep it from finking.
ɪe king, perceiving the extremity he was driven to,
ɟ that he had nothing but the appearance of roy-
y left, took a refolution that furpiifed every body,
.t was acquainted with the gentlenefs and patience
his nature ; which was to deftroy the duke, let the
ɪfequence be what it would ; nay, though he was
e to perifh with him.

On the 23d of December, the king, being at Blois,
here he, two days before, to amufe the Guife
ɟion, had, in a very pathetic fpeech, recommend-
peace and unanimity to the ftates, as abfolutely
ɔeffary for the maintenance and prefervation of
: Catholick religion) pretended a defign to hunt
ɪt day, and fummoned the privy council to
:et very early in the morning.   The duke of
ɪife, whofe houfe was near the caftle, came firft to
: council-chamber, not in the leaft fufpecting any
ɟign of this kind [16].   The night before, the king
                                                    had

[16] Davilla, in the ninth book of his hiftory of the civil wars
                                                            of

had a fecret confultation with marfhal D'Aumont, De Retz, Rambouillet, and fome few others, in whom he repofed the greateft confidence, how to deliver himfelf out of the bondage and fubjection he was held in by the duke of Guife.

Some were of opinion, that to make any open attempt upon his perfon would end in the deftruction of the king; as his party, which was fo ftrong and numerous, would infallibly take the firft opportunity of revenging it. D'Aumont advifed to proceed againft him in a judiciary way, and bring him to trial as a rebel; but this was rejected, as too dangerous an expedient, if not impracticable: at laft, it was propofed that he fhould be affaffinated; which was approved of, and put in execution the next morning, when he came to the council, in the king's prefence.

A few hours after this, the king fent for cardinal Morofini, the Pope's legate, and told him, " He was abfolutely compelled to take fo violent a " refolution; that his eminence was no ftranger to " the innumerable confpiracies and intrigues of the " duke and his faction, which had reduced him to " the fatal neceffity of putting him to death after " that manner, in order to preferve his own life " and crown, which were both in extreme danger " whilft he was alive; and that as he had at laft " happily accomplifhed it, by the affiftance of God, " notwithftanding the almoft infuperable difficulties " that were to be furmounted, he thought it might " be juftified by the laws of God and man; that it " was notorious to all the world, how grievoufly " the royal majefty of kings had been wounded in " his perfon, by one that was his natural fubject, " without any reafon or provocation; that he had
" long

long borne it with incredible patience, for the
fake of preferving the peace and quiet of his kingdom, inclined thereto by his well-known difpofition
to gentlenefs and mercy ; that he defired his eminence would do him the juftice to reprefent this
matter in its true light to his holinefs, that he
might not fuffer in his efteem, through the calumnies
and mifreprefentation of his enemies."

Morofini, who was very well acquainted with the
uke's defigns, and the reports that had been fpread
broad, to the great difhonour of his majefty, was not
/illing to do any thing that might alienate the king's
ffections from the H. See, to which he feemed at
hat time fo well affected, and thought it more pru-
lent to confirm and encourage him, by mild and in-
lulgent methods, in the good refolution he was in
ɔ protect the Catholic religion; than to force him,
ɔy a contrary behaviour, into the arms of the Hu-
ʒonots.

For which purpofe, he put on a fhew of moderati-
ɔn, and faid, " He hoped and believed his holinefs,
' as the common and difinterefted father of all
' Chriftians, would give him a favourable hearing,
' and admit of his juftification, provided what he
' faid might be depended upon, of which he would
' beft convince his holinefs, by firmly perfevering
' in his refolution to fupport the Catholic religion,
' and extinguifh herefy." After a long conference,
his majefty promifed, and fwore folemnly, " That
" if his holinefs would join him heartily, he would
" exert all his force to the utter extirpation of here-
" tics;" and faid, " he was thoroughly determined
" to fuffer but one religion in France.

At the fame inftant that the D. of Guife was affaffinated, the marfhals D'Aumont and De Retz fecured
the perfons of cardinal Guife, the duke's brother,
and the archbifhop of Lyons, conveying them, under a ftrong guard, to a private prifon. They likewife arrefted cardinal Bourbon, who, being very old
and

and infirm, was not yet out of bed, and fent him prifoner to the caftle, with many others of their dependents, and followers.

The king's defign in fending for the legate was not in reality, to make any excufe or apology to him, for putting the duke to death, as he very well knew the Pope had no bufinefs to concern himfelf about an affair that did not in any wife prejudice the rights or interefts of the H. See; but to find how he was affected with the imprifonment of the cardinal and archbifhop.

When the legate found the king fo well difpofed to the H. See, and fo full of zeal for the Catholic religion, he declined entering into any converfation with him upon that fubject, as if he had not known any thing of the matter, and thought to take fome other more convenient opportunity of bringing it upon the carpet. He was fo far from feeming offended at what had happened, that he behaved with the fame, nay greater refpect than ufual, and waited upon his majefty that very morning, to hear mafs.

The king, feeing the legate did not much trouble his head about the imprifonment of the cardinals, refolved to follow his blow, and rid himfelf of cardinal Guife, a man of an ambitious and turbulent difpofition, and no lefs dangerous than his brother had been, thinking by thefe means, thoroughly to eradicate the evil, and extinguifh the hopes of the faction for ever.

For this purpofe he clofeted many of thofe that he thought he could moft depend upon, but could not meet with any one that would embrue his hands in the blood of the cardinal. With great promifes, he at laft prevailed upon Gas, captain of his guard, to undertake it; who went accordingly the next morning, which was the 24th of December, to the prifon (where the cardinal and archbifhop had paffed the night in great fear, confeffing each other, and watching in continual prayer) and told the
archbifhop

archbifhop, "he muft follow him, for the king
" had fomething to fay to him." The cardinal,
imagining they were conducting him to execution,
called out to him, " My lord archbifhop, think
" upon God:" But the archbifhop, who thought
the cardinal in full as much danger as himfelf, replied, " It behoves you to do fo too, my dear lord
cardinal." When Gas had taken the archbifhop into another room, he returned to the cardinal, and
told him, " He had his majefty's orders to put him
" to death." Upon which the cardinal defired,
" He would allow him a few moments to recom-
" mend his foul to God ;" which being granted,
he kneeled down and made a fhort prayer; after
which he covered his face with the lower part of his
robe, and undauntedly faid, " You may now exe-
" cute your mafter's commands;" at which inftant
four foldiers falling upon him, flew him with their
partizans, and carried his body to the place where
the duke's lay.

In the mean time the king was in great perplexity,
not knowing how to appeafe the pope, with whofe
fiery and impetuous temper he was fo well acquainted : For tho' the legate, who thoroughly knew the
affairs of France, rather inclined to his fide, and
feemed willing to reprefent thefe tranfactions in a favourable manner to his holinefs, he could not be
certain in what light the pope would look upon them,
as he was at fo great a diftance, and very likely
might have received bad impreffions, from the mifreprefentations of the league, and the ill offices of
the Spaniards. For this reafon, he determined to
fend an immediate account of it to the marquifs
Pifani, his ambaffador at Rome, that he might be
ready to refute any falfe reports that might be propagated to his difadvantage, and juftify his proceedings to the pope: As he had ordered Girolamo Gondi,
a Florentine, but a few days before, to hold himfelf
in readinefs to fet out for Rome, foon after Chrift

M m   mas-day

mas-day, to defire his Holinefs would be pleafed to confer the legation of Avignon upon the cardinal of Guife; the circumftances of affairs being now altered, he commanded him to fet out poft directly, that he might be ready to fecond Pifani in excufing the duke's death, and procure him abfolution, if neceffary; commanding him to take the fhorteft rout, and make all poffible hafte, left the news fhould arrive there before him, from fome other quarter. Gondi, after he had been with the king all night, to receive his inftructions, took horfe early the next morning, attended only by two domeftics, and two gentlemen, leaving orders for the reft of his train to follow him with all expedition.

End of the Ninth Book.

/

THE

THE
L I F E
OF
Pope SIXTUS the Fifth.

BOOK THE TENTH.

WHILST they were clebrating the beginning of the new year at Rome, a courier arrived there the fifth of January, at night, who had been difpatched by Morofini, immediately after his conference with the king upon the duke's death, with the news of that event: But as the cardinal was not put to death till after he was fet out, he could not bring any tidings of that.

The pope did not feem much affected, though he knew the duke was a ftrenuous defender of the Catholic religion, and was fenfible, that the league (of which he was the foul and firft mover) would foon diffolve and moulder away now he was dead; yet as a politician, and friend to refolute and fevere meafures, he rather feemed to approve of it; for he immediately fent for cardinal Joyeufe a Frenchman, and after fome difcourfe upon the duke's death, of his infolence, and the fubjection in which he had kept the king, he fhrugged up his fhoulders, and faid, " We fhould have done the fame, if we had been in " Henry's place." And when he had expatiated largely in praife of the king's courage and noble refolution, and the unfortunate end of the duke, he faid to the cardinal as he was going away, " Such, ge-

nerally,

" nerally, is the fate of inconfiderable and ambitious
" men; they rufh headlong into difficulties, out of
" which they have not the fenfe to extricate them-
" felves."

The next day, in the evening, Gondi arrived at
Rome, and finding the news of the cardinal's death,
and the archbifhop's imprifonment, had not yet reached
that court, he did not think fit to make it known to
any body but Pifani, the French ambaffador, with
whom he paffed the whole night, confidering how to
foften and prepare the pope to receive it with fome fort
of moderation.

But Sixtus, having received advice of it the fame
night, or early the next morning, fent for Gondi and
Pifani, and when he had acquainted them with it, he
flew into fuch a rage as is hardly poffible either to exprefs or conceive: He knit his brows, he bit his lips, he
ftamped and raved like a madman; and having beftowed plenty of harfh names upon them, upbraided
the K. of France in the fevereft terms, with having
violated, not only the Ecclefiaftical immunities, and the
privileges of the H. College, but all laws, human and
divine, by the murder of a cardinal and the imprifonment of an archbifhop (two of the moft confiderable
prelates of the church) with as little ceremony as if they
had been mere laymen.

The ambaffadors, with great modefty and refpect, but at the fame time with a proper degree
of fpirit, entered into a minute difcuffion and juftification of their mafter's proceedings, and having enlarged upon the enormity of the crimes which the
duke and thefe prelates had been guilty of, faid,
" The prodigious power and authority they had
" ufurped, not only exempted them from being pro-
" ceeded againft by his majefty, according to the
" ufual forms and courfe of juftice, but had embol-
" dened them to drive him forcibly out of his me-
" tropolis, which he was obliged to quit in difguife
" for the prefervation of his life; that all the difturb-
" ance

' ances and commotions in the kingdom, were en-
' tirely owing to their intrigues and cabals ; that his
' majefty being defirous of delivering himfelf out
' of a bondage fo fhameful and diſhonourable to
' a fovereign, and for the fecurity of his own life
' and crown, which he had too much reafon to
' imagine in the utmoft peril, (as their guilt was
' public and notorious to all the world) had a right
' to punifh their crimes in a manner that did not re-
' quire the tedioufnefs and formalities of judiciary
' proceedings; that, in fhort, they had fhewn them-
" felves unworthy of the pope's protection, by their
" facrilege, their contempt, and horrid profanation
" of the moft holy myfteries of the Chriftian faith,
" in fo often forfwearing themfelves, and abufing the
" honour and generofity of their mafter; that their
" zeal for the fupport of the Catholic religion, which
" was fincere and unaffected in his majefty, ferved
" only for a cloak and excufe for their ambition,
" which was the true and only caufe of all thofe con-
" vulfions that had fo miferably fhaken the kingdom
" of France, occafioned the effufion of fo much Chrif-
" tian blood, and the lofs of an infinite number of
" fouls; whilft they endeavoured, in the midft of
" thefe confufions, to open themfelves a way to the
" throne, by excluding the true and lawful heirs.
" They farther affured him, of the perfect and im-
" plicit fubmiffion of their mafter, as an obedient fon
" of the church; that he was ready to make any fatis-
' faction his Holinefs thought proper; and that he
' had fent Gondi to Rome for that purpofe; to defire
' he would be pleafed to give him his benediction,
' that he might be convinced he had forgiven what
' was paft."

This difcourfe had not much effect upon Sixtus;
ne told Pifani, " That he knew Gondi had been fent
' to Rome upon a quite different errand; that it was
' paft his comprehenfion, how the King of France
' could be faid to fhew any figns of fubmiffion, or

durft

" durſt preſume to aſk for abſolution, at the ſame
" time that he kept a cardinal and archbiſhop in
" priſon, who were ſubject to no other juriſdiction
" than that of the church; that if they had been guilty
" of any fault, the king ſhould have acquainted him
" with it, and he would have puniſhed them; as all
" the world knew he delighted in nothing ſo much as
" doing juſtice."

The ambaſſadors anſwered, " That their charac-
" ter ought to give them credit with his holineſs, as
" to what they had ſaid concerning the king's ſub-
" miſſion and deſire of abſolution." Sixtus replied,
" That as ambaſſadors, they had no power to treat of
" any thing but temporal affairs; that the queſtion
" at preſent was about things of a very different na-
" ture, and that in ſpiritual concerns, eſpecially ſuch
" as related to conſcience, it was neceſſary there ſhould
" be demonſtrations of contrition and repentance,
" before abſolution could be granted, or even hoped
" for; that the king ought to ſend an ambaſſador ex-
" traordinary to aſk pardon and to ſhew himſelf worthy
" of it, ſhould in the firſt place, ſet the prelates at
" liberty." Then beginning to grow warm again, he
raiſed his voice, and ſaid in a threatning manner,
" Both you and your maſter think to play tricks with
" me, and treat me as if I was a poor ignorant monk,
" that knew nothing of the world; but you are miſ-
" taken; I'll let you ſee you have a pope to deal with,
" that is ready to ſhed the laſt drop of his blood, if there
" ſhould be occaſion, to ſupport the honour and intereſts
" of the H. See."

Piſani, being a little nettled at laſt, ventured to
ſay, " What! Holy Father, ſhall not the king, my
" maſter, be allowed to rid himſelf of cardinal
" Guiſe his mortal enemy, when Pius IV, by his own
" authority, cauſed cardinal Caraffa to be ſtrangled,
" who had been one of his moſt intimate friends."
Which ſo provoked Sixtus, that he immediately diſmiſſed

miffed them in great wrath, with feveral fharp expreffions and threats of his difpleafure.

In the morning, he ordered a confiftory to be called,
and fent for Alberto Bedoarti, the Venetian ambaffador,
to whom he complained bitterly of Morofini's conduct,
calling him traitor and enemy to the H. See, and vowed he would make him feel the weight of his indignation.

The Venetian excufed his countryman in the beft manner he could, without faying any thing that he thought
might increafe the fury of Sixtus.

When the confiftory was affembled, he came into
it with a countenance that fhewed what humour he was
in, and began with railing at the behaviour of Morofini,
threatning to ftrip him of the purple, for being acceffary
to the death of the cardinal; and faid, " That if he had
" protefted againft his imprifonment, as he ought to
" have done, the king durft not have prefumed to have
" put him to death." He then related what had paffed betwixt him and the king's ambaffadors upon that
head, with the reafons why he had not granted him abfolution, and concluded in this manner; " There are
" fome cardinals, who are audacious enough to excufe
" and defend this murder, even in our prefence, at
" which we cannot fufficiently exprefs our aftonifhment,
" as it feems to betray forgetfulnefs of their own rank
" and dignity, not confidering how grievoufly they
" themfelves and the whole Sacred College are
" wounded by this outrage, committed upon the per-
" fon of cardinal Guife : For our own part, we are
" determined not to abandon the interefts of that
" venerable and auguft body, in fo bafe and coward
" ly a manner; and declare to you upon the faith
" of a fovereign pontiff, that, from henceforth we
" will never make any promotion at the inftance of
" crowned heads. Princes fhall fue for that honour
" in vain. Ye ought to reflect upon the prejudice ye
" do to your own character ; and what will now be-
" come

" come of the privileges ye have hitherto enjoyed.
" But why fhould we be concerned for the ftorms that
" threaten you on every fide, if you yourfelves are
" fo unaffected with them? We forefee that you
" will foon be expofed to contempt, and become a
" prey to the fury and revenge of temporal princes,
" who will have but little regard either to your ho-
" nour or blood, if the murder of your brother goes
" unpunifhed: Your infenfibility and unconcern,
" however, ought not to be a rule for our conduct;
" the high ftation that Providence has called us to,
" obliges us to avenge this crying fin: It avails not
" to deafen us with the ill confequences that may en-
" fue, and the miferies it may bring upon France;
" when it is neceffary to execute juftice and judg-
" ment, we ought only to regard our duty, and fear
" nothing but the difpleafure of God." As he fpoke
in Latin, and this was the laft fpeech he ever made
in that language, we fhall give it our readers at
large [1].

" INFANDUM fane dolorem explicare cogimur, et
" vere hodie nefandum, tum quia, nec parem
" exprimere poffumus, nec tale fcelus ex memoriâ
" hominum eft auditum. Occifus eft Cardinalis
" Ghifius, occifus eft; occifus eft Prefbyter Cardi-
" nalis, qui erat Archiepifcopus Remenfis, fine pro-
" ceffu, fine judicio, fine lege, fine legitimâ potef-
" tate, cum armis fæcularium, abfque fententiâ,
" abfque auctoritate noftrâ, et hujus fanctæ fedis,
" cujus nobile membrum erat : tanquam nos non ef-
" femus in mundo, tanquam non effet Deus in cœlo,
" et in terrâ et denique non effet fedes apoftolica;
" lex divina obligat omnes homines, et nemo ab eâ
" eft exemptus; lex divina mandat, non occides.
" Alicuine liceat occidere? certe nemini, etiamfi

[1] As it was the laft, we. hope it was the worft Latin fpeech he
ever made ; for it is not poffible to read it without thinking of Ig-
noramus, or the epiftolæ obfcurorum virorum. Perhaps it might
be owing to extreme grief, or anger.

" fit

" fit rex vel princeps. Princeps eft judex qui,
" mandante lege aliquem mori, non dicitur occidere,
" fed punire, caftigare, et coercere, juris et judicii
" fervato ordine: fed occifus eft, non judicatus, aut
" damnatus præcepto legis, aut mandato, vel per-
" miffione fui fuperioris, qui fumus nos : occifus eft
" tanquam vilis et plebeius quifquam, nullâ juris, nullâ
" gradûs, aut pontificalis ordinis, nullâ dignitatis aut
" honoris cardinalatûs habitâ ratione. Nec dicatur
" quod machinatus effet, vel quod aliquid dixerit, vel
" fecerit, contra legem, contra regem, et contra coro-
" nam : nam non videtur verum, aut verifimile, quia
" nuper rex fcripfit ad nos in ejus commendationem
" per oratorem fuum Gundum, rogans ut ei daremus,
" legationem avenionenfem, vacantem per ceffionem
" cardinalis Borboni, ac in fuis literis mirific è u m
" laudabat. Teftes funt ambo oratores regis, orator
" ordinarius, et dictus orator Gundus, qui paucis ante
" diebus, eafdem literas regis fuper eâ re, nobis fimul
" reddiderant, et nomine regis rogaverant, et infti-
" terant pro hujufmodi legatione, et aliis in favorem
" Ghifi: denuo nihil deinde factum eft vel occurrit
" per quod dici poffit illum contra regem, aliquid
" commififfe : fed efto, quod feciffet aliquid contra
" regem, quod prætenfa crimina ; nonne debebat
" ab hujufmodi facrilegio, et parricidio defiftere ? et
" cum fciret nos graviter animadvertere in facino-
" rofos et malos homines, nonne poterat eos nobis
" remittere puniendos ? Nonne poterat illum inte-
" rim detineri et cuftodiri facere, et deinde nobis
" fcribere, et fcire quid defuper agendum effet, et
" expectare mandatum noftrum ? Vel fi nolebat ex-
" pectare, nonne poterat confulere cardinalem Mau-
" rocenum, legatum noftrum, vel cum eo agere de
" perfonâ cardinalis Ghifii ? vel illi carceratum, fi
" de fugâ timebat, confignare, aut a fuis militibus
" interea cuftodiendum curare ? Eft cardinalis le-
" gatus ejus confidens, fuit a nobis factus cardinalis
" ad

" ad ejus preces, et inftantiam, et propter ipfum factus
" legatus de latere cum poteftate, quod alias non
" feciffemus, nifi ipfo inftante.

" Gratias autem agimus Deo, quod ita feciffemus,
" ut nobis vitio verti non poffet, quod nos non fa-
" tis feciffemus; nam fi non regi fatis feciffemus,
" nunc diceret nos fuiffe in caufâ hujus finiftri fuc-
" ceffûs; et fi non feciffemus nuntium cardinalem
" et legatum, ut rex poftulabat, id non fucceffiffet:
" fed nos fecimus, et cum injuria hujus Sacri Colle-
" gii, cum in eo effent viri fcientiâ, doctrinâ, et ex-
" perientiâ infignes, et ætate graves, ex quibus ali-
" quem Legatum de Latere noftro, ut par erat, mit-
" tere poteramus, et tunc non mifimus: et nos fcie-
" bamus injuriam irrogare cardinalibus præfentibus,
" ut fatisfaceremus regis voluntati, et fecimus car-
" dinalem abfentem, et illum creavimus, etiam le-
" gatum noftrum, ut ipfi regi omnem gratiam fa-
" ceremus. Ipfe tamen rex nullam hujus rationem
" habuit, nec ipfum fuper hujufmodi facto confu-
" luit, nec aliquid detulit authoritati aut dignitati
" ejus, et ille cardinalis attrociter occifus eft potef-
" tate laicali, fine fedis apoftolicæ auctoritate et per-
" miffione.

Here he ftopped a little, as if over-powered with grief,
and then proceeded as follows:

" Gratias agimus Deo quod hujufmodi factum,
" hic cafus, hoc malum, noftro tempore accidit,
" quia fic illi placuit; nos autem fperamus in ejus
" divinâ bonitate, quæ nobis a pueritiâ aftitit, et in
" futurum affiftet, et nos proteget, et fubminiftra-
" bit confilium et auxilium, ut tantis malis providere
" valeamus.

Here he made another ftop, and then proceeded in
this manner:

" Certe

" Certe tanto animi dolore afficimur, ut factum
" explicare nequeamus: Hesterna die venit ad nos
" orator regis, et supplex et prostratus cum alio
" oratore gundo pretebat, et postulabat a nobis ve-
" niam et absolutionem regis, et tantâ cum instant-
" tiâ, ut dicerent se inde non surrecturos, nec dis-
" cessuros, nisi ipsam illis impertiremur, et quasi no-
" bis vim inferebant: nos autem illis respondimus,
" quod si rex cuperat absolutionem, eam petiisset
" in literis, quas ipsi biduo ante nobis reddiderant ;
" sed tantum aberat, ut se poeniteret, et dolorem
" ostenderet, et errorem agnosceret, ut nihil omni-
" no de absolutione meminerit: Et cum orator ex-
" plicâsset se regis personam sustinere, et sibi cre-
" dendum esse, quia rex id sibi scripserat ; nos respon-
" dimus, quod ipse refert personam, et nomen re-
" gis, quantum ad negotia nomine regis tractanda
" pertinet, non autem quantum ad ejus peccata con-
" fitenda, et ad poenitentiam peragendam, quae a
" propriâ ipsius personâ exigatur, cum pars poeni-
" tentiae sit oris confessio : alium enim est negotia age-
" re et tractare, aliud peccatum agnoscere et confi-
" teri, et de eo veniam a Deo, et a nobis petere
" poenitentiam, cum ore proprio fassus esset ; et ideo
" dimissimus illos, cum nec literas nec mandatum ul-
" lum haberent ad impetrandam hujusmodi absoluti-
" onem a tanto facinore.

" Henricus Secundus, Angliae rex, infamatus fu-
" it quod occidi fecisset beatum Thomam Archiepis-
" copum Cantuariensem ; non quod rex occidi man-
" dasset, sed quod, cum haberet controversiam de
" libertate ecclesiae cum eo, neci ejus consensisse vi-
" deretur ; nam occiderent illum re verâ, non man-
" dato regis, sed putantes rem gratam facere, ut
" in ejus passione legitur, et deinde coopertum fuit.
" Veruntatem papa tunc commisit causam et pro-
" cessum adversus regem nonnullus praelatis et car-
" dinalibus quos suos legatos destinavit, et fuit fac-
" tus processus solemnitur, et tractata causa apud

" Sedem

" fedem apoſtolicam, et ſe expurgavit de prætenſo
" expreſſo mandato necis, et de verbis prolatis, qui-
" bus viſus fuerat illam deſiderare, culpam ſuam ag-
" novit, et confeſſus eſt, et humiliter pœnitentiam
" ſuſcepit, et peregit, cum omnibus qui illud ſacri-
" legium commiſerant, ſciverant, aut quovis modo
" participes fuerant: et tamen ille non erat cardina-
" lis, ſed archiepiſcopus tantum. Si dicatur quod
" ille erat ſanctus, dicimus quod tunc, dum vive-
" ret, non dicebatur ſanctus, ſed deinde ab eccle-
" ſiâ relatus eſt in catalogum ſanctorum. Theodo-
" ſius imperatur Auguſtus, ob cædem Theſſalonicen-
" ſium a Sancto Ambroſio Mediolanenſi ab Eccleſiæ
" limnibus repulſus et excluſus fuit, et ille humili-
" ter obedivit; et Theodoſius quidem non erat vilis
" perſona, vel plebeia, ſed vir magnus et inſignis,
" et erat clariſſimus imperator, qui nullus de tyran-
" nide victorias, ſed divinitus paratus reportaverat,
" de quo et Claudianus, tametſi gentilis cecinit,

  O nimium dilecte Deo, cui militat æther,
  Et conjurati veniunt ad claſſica venti.

" Erat Theodoſius imperator univerſi orbis: Non
" unius, vel alterius regni, veluti rex Franciæ; ſed
" obtinebat univerſum imperium, et omnia illius
" regna talia habebat. Habebat enim et Galliam
" ſue Franciam, et Hiſpaniam, Hungariam, Dalma-
" tiam, Græciam, Aſiam, cum tot regnis, et pro-
" vinciis, Syriam, Ægyptum et Africam itaque non
" unius regni rex, ſed multa tenebat regna, et im-
" peria; et nihilominus lachyrmis et magno dolore
" animi, facinus et peccatum ſuum confeſſus, pœni-
" tentiam a Sancto Ambroſio ſuſcepit, et ingenti
" cum humilitate peregit, paratiſſimum ſe exhibens
" ad mandatum, non papæ, ſed archiepiſcopi tan-
" tum, ac ita in eccleſiam et ad ſacramenta admiſ-
" ſus fuit. Dicit aliquis, Ambroſius erat Sanctus,
" et nos reſpondebimus, quod adhuc vivebat in car-
" ne, et non erat relatus apud Sanctos, et erat ar-
                                        " chiepiſcopus,

" chiepifcopus, et fortè epifcopus tantum, quia me-
" diolanenfis ecclefia nondum forfan habebat archie-
" pifcopum. Quo factum eft ut Deus illi deinde
" femper affifteret et faveret, ac præterea cum ita
" res fuccederent et filios et nepotes imperatores Au-
" guftos relinqueret. Si igitur ad mandatum epif-
" copi, non vilis aut humilis perfona, fed tantus im-
" perator humillime paruit, et obedivit, pœnitenti-
" am fufcepit implevitque, quanto magis et alii et
" reges facere debent?

" Fuerunt aliqui cardinales, qui etiam in præfen-
" tiâ noftrâ aufi funt hujufmodi facinus excufare;
" de quo nos valde mirati fumus, quod fui gradûs
" immemores approbare velint, quod in ipforum re-
" dundat injuriam, periculum, et difcrimen: Nos
" quidem certe affirmamus vobis certiffimofque faci-
" mus; quod non volumus fieri cardinales, nec age-
" mus cum aliquo principe aut rege, ut procuret
" effe cardinales: Nolumus amplius effe cardinales;
" ideoque quoad perfonam noftram parum hoc re-
" fert, fed quoad perfonas veftras multum quidem.
" Si ergo vultis ut nos privemur et fpoliemur immu-
" nitate, libertate, prærogativis, præeminentiis, ali-
" ifque privilegiis quibus ornati et decorati eftis,
" veftrum erit, nofque faciemus, ut deindè honore,
" reverentiâ, et dignitate deftituti fitis, et regibus
" et principibus contemptui, defpectui, vilipendio,
" præde et cædi. Profecto fi cardinalium cædes et
" injuriæ diffimulentur, hæ cædes cardinalibus reli-
" quis facile contingere poterant.

" Nos igitur faciemus juftitiam, et quod Deo pla-
" cuerit, et quod juftum fuerit: Sed fi dicatur quod
" mala multa ventura et timenda fint, nos dice-
" mus quod nihil timendum, cum fit juftitia: et ip-
" fe facit juftitiam et judicium, et juftus eft Domi-
" nus, et juftitiam diligit, ac propterea nihil timen-
" dum fit præter peccatum. Peccatum quidem per-
" timefcendum eft, non autum juftitia.

Here

Here he ſtopped a third time, and then concluded.

" Non poſſumus præ anguſtiâ doloris aliquid am-
" plius dicere vel loqui, cum nonnulla dicenda eſſent:
" Sed deinde faciemus deputationem aliquorum car-
" dinalium quibuſcum de hâc retractabitur; pre-
" camur autem Deum interim ùt ecclesiæ suæ et il-
" lius neceſſitatibus providere et ocurrere dignetur."

When he had done ſpeaking, he waited a while to
ſee if the cardinals had any thing to reply; but perceiving they were all ſilent, and in a ſort of conſternation, he ſaid, " He was ſo overpowered with grief
" that he could not proceed, tho' he had much more to
" ſay; but that the world might not have occaſion
" to reflect upon him, for acting raſhly and unadvi-
" ſedly in ſo important an affair, he would appoint
" a congregation to deliberate upon the ſtate of France
" and make a ſtrict inquiſition into the death of the
" cardinal." The members that compoſed this
congregation were Sorbelloni, a Milaneſe; Santorius,
archbiſhop of St. Severina, Fachinetto, a Bologneſe;
Lancelotto, a Roman; Caſtagna, and ſeveral other cardinals of the firſt rank and conſideration: The eyes
of all Europe were fixed upon them, and the reſult of
their deliberations expected with the utmoſt impatience.

When the Pariſians heard of the duke of Guiſe's
death, and the impriſonment of the prelates, they
were enraged to ſuch a degree, that they took up
arms, and ran in a tumultuos manner to the Lou-
vre, pulled down the king's ſtatue, and every thing
that had his arms upon it; plundered the royal apartments, impriſoned the officers, and then immediately
ſent four deputies to Rome, with a melancholy account of the whole affair, who were admitted to an
audience very ſoon after their arrival, and addreſſed
themſelves to the Pope in the following manner:

" T H E

" THE hope we had. vainly conceived fome
" days ago, holy father, of feeing France once
" more in tranquillity, after having been thirty
" years fo miferably diftracted, and almoft over-
" whelmed with civil difcord, and of being the mef-
" fengers of that joyful news to your holinefs, is
" now turned into mourning and bitter lamentation,
" by the barbarous murder of the moft valiant and
" religious duke of Guife, and his illuftrious brother
" the cardinal; which is fo much the more grie-
" vous and infupportable to us, as we are deprived
" of a champion in fo perilous a conjuncture, when
" the fury of the war is at the higheft, to whom
" we are obliged for our lives and liberty, and what
" little of the true religion is left, and by whofe
" death we have great reafon to fear we fhall now be-
" come a facrifice to that all-devouring herefy, that
" has fo long preyed upon the vitals of our wretched
" country; but fince it is the will of Heaven to put
" an end to the labours of that heroic prince, by
" a glorious death, and to make known that in-
" veterate rancour, that diabolical malice, that
" myftery of iniquity, that has been fo long and
" fo carefully concealed, at the expence of fo va-
" luable a life, we filently adore and reverence the
" wonderful judgments of the Almighty God, and
" here proftrate ourfelves at your feet, moft holy
" father, humbly imploring your patience and at-
" tention, by the mercies of Jefus Chrift, whilft
" we briefly recount the hidden caufes and mo-
" tives of fhedding that blood which cries day and
" night for vengeance, and that we may obtain
" fuccours from your holinefs fufficient to chaftife
" the perpetrators of fo cruel and deteftable a
" murder.

" In the firft place, nothing can be more falfe
" than that infatiable ambition (as it is artfully
" given out by the murderers) had made the
" duke forget his duty, and tranfgrefs thofe bounds
" of

" of modefty, that ought never to be exceeded by
" a loyal and obedient fubject; and that he fought,
" by putting the king to death, and the exclu-
" fion of the lawful heirs, to fet the crown upon
" his own head; as it is well known he often had
" the king in his power, and was blamed by ma-
" ny, for not doing what they faid was abfolutely
" neceffary for his own fafety, and the preferva-
" tion of the Catholic religion. But he, whofe
" foul abhorred the thoughts of embruing his hands
" in royal blood, full of that noble confidence
" and generofity which flows from innocence, and
" an unfpotted confcience, not in the leaft fufpect-
" ing that bafenefs and perfidy in others, which
" he was a ftranger to himfelf, defpifed the dan-
" gers he was forewarned of, and by that means
" fell a facrifice to the mean jealoufy of that
" blood-thirfty tyrant, who had fo long and fo ea-
" gerly fought his life, to the irreparable lofs of
" true religion and the church of Chrift.

" We may with much more truth affirm, that
" the caufe of his being murdered, was that (when
" he faw the king entirely governed by the coun-
" fels of Heretics and that upon the deceafe of
" his brother, he openly favoured the K. of Na-
" varre's pretenfions to the crown) being encouraged
" firft by the illuftrious cardinal of Bourbon, and
" then by Pope Gregory XIII, of happy memory,
" to exert himfelf in the fupport of the Catholics
" in France, he ufed his utmoft endeavours, em-
" ployed all his addrefs, patience, affiduity, perfua
" fion and intereft, with the king to eftablifh the
" true Religion, and extirpate Herefy; that he ever
" behaved like a faithful fubject, both in peace
" and war; that he neglected nothing that he
" thought might tend to preferve peace betwixt
" the king and his people, to conciliate the affec-
" tion of the nation to his majefty, and to fupport
" and defend the ancient dignity and prerogatives
" of

" of his crown, that when thefe things were debated
" in an affembly of the ftates, without fear or regard
" to the drawing upon himfelf the odium and male-
" volence of the king's enemies, he gave him fuch
" counfels as he thought highly neceffary for the good
" of the kingdom; that he had, in all refpects (as his
" greateft enemies were obliged to confefs) difcharged
" the office of a wife, good man, and a valiant fol-
" dier; that in return for thefe fervices (fo it pleafed
" God) the king, upon fome flight difguft, thought
" proper to accufe him of high treafon, after many
" reiterated profeffions of reconciliation, after receiv-
" ing the holy facrament, and calling upon God, in
" the moft folemn manner, to witnefs the fincerity of
" his friendfhip : Not to mention the many artifices
" he made ufe of to gain credit to his affeverations, as
" giving him the higheft poft in the army, appointing
" an ambaffador to intreat your Holinefs to beftow
" the legation of Avignon upon his brother the cardi-
" nal; as if all the reft of his wicked actions were not
" complete, and wanted confummation, except he made
" a dupe of the vicar of Jefus Chrift ; that he had
" wounded the majefty of kings by fo flagrant a vio-
" lation of his faith, deferved the name of murderer
" and affaffin, and had polluted his very palace (which
" furely, if any place, ought to be held faered) with
" innocent blood ; that he had, without any regard
" to decency, or even humanity, barbaroufly and
" meanly trampled upon the afhes of the dead, as if
" they had been of bafe blood, without the leaft re-
" fpect to the fplendor and nobility of their birth ; and
" after he had made his kingdom one continued fcene
" of confufion, bloodfhed, and defolation, he pretends
" that he is accountable for his actions to none but
" God alone.

" We cannot forbear expreffing our aftonifhment,
" as well as deteftation of his unparalleled infolence,
" and the heinous nature of the indignity offered to

" your

" your Holinefs and the Apoftolic See, in audacioufly
" committing a murder, almoft in the prefence of your
" legate ; a murder fufficient to make the whole church
" tremble, for it cannot be expected that he will
" treat the members with any fort of decency,
" when he has fhewn fo little refpect to one of the
" heads."

" He has endeavoured, to the utmoft of his pow-
" er to deftroy that holy religion, which he fo folemn-
" ly promifed. and fwore at his coronation to fupport
" and defend, and barbaroufly put to death that vener-
" able father of the church, who anointed him with
" the holy oil [2]. What comfort then, or fecurity,
" can any devout Chriftian enjoy under the tyranny of
" fuch a monfter ? Or in what part of his dominions is
" there any afylum for piety and virtue, ·whilft he is fo
" intent to extirpate both ; thcfe confiderations have de-
" termined the wife and virtuous part of the nation to
" lay down their lives, rather than groan and linger
" them away, under fo infupportable a domination,
" which threatens, not only deftruction to the kingdom,
" but confequentially the utter extinction of the Catho-
" lic religion.

" Things are now come to that pafs, that it is highly
" neceffary to exert , the antient valour and uncor-
" rupted piety of the French nation ; wherefore,
" moft Holy father, we humbly implore your pa-
" ternal aid and affiftance in three things of the grea-
" teft confequence. Firft, that your Holinefs will
" be pleafed to abfolve us from our allegiance, and
" the obligation of the oath we took to Henry lll.
" Secondly, that the war which we are going to en-
" gage in with the public enemy of our peace and

[2] In the church of Rheims (a city that gives title to the firft
duke and peer of France, who is the archbifhop of that fee) is preferved the oil or balfam made ufe of at the coronation of the king's
of France, is a little veffel called Sancta Ampulla, fent, as they pretend, by an angel from Heaven, at the coronation and anointing of
Clovis.

" religion,

" religion, may be declared juſt and neceſſary.
" Thirdly, that your Holineſs will be pleaſed to
" grant a plenary indulgence to all princes and other
" perſons, who ſhall aſſiſt us with their forces, or
" prayers, or any other way to carry on this great
" and important undertaking. And we preſume to
" hope we ſhall not meet with a denial in theſe re-
" queſts, ſince it is abſurd· and prepoſterous that
" true Catholics ſhould live under the government
" of one who is not only a notorious Heretic him-
" ſelf, but an open abettor of all others that are ſo,
" and by the enormity of the crimes which he has al-
" ready committed, beſides what he daily meditates,
" has incurred the penalties of extreme malediction
" and excommunication, as there have been exam-
" ples in former times of the French nation being able
" by the aſſiſtance of your Holineſs's predeceſſors to
" dethrone kings that were bad indeed, but righteous
" men when compared with the preſent. And we
" conceive we have the more reaſon to expect this in-
" dulgence from your Holineſs, ſince he himſelf has
" often publicly declared, that whenever he ſhould
" violate his oaths and engagements, he would freely
" abſolve us from our oath of allegiance : As the na-
" ture of the affair was ſo preſſing that it would not
" ſuffer us to wait for an anſwer from your Holineſs,
" and that we might not do any thing inconſiſtent with
" the peace of our conſciences, we conſulted the moſt
" reverend divines of the Sorbonne [3], who, at our
" repeated and moſt preſſing ſolicitations, aſſembled to
" the number of 70, and having with great maturity

[3] The Sorbonne is the principal college of the Univerſity of
Paris, and was rebuilt with extraordinary magnificence at the charge
of cardinal Richlieu, with lodgings for a great number of doctors,
who are called the Society of the Sorbonne ; they that are received
amongſt them before they have taken their doctor's degree, are
called, the Hoſpitallers of the Sorbonne. Claud. Hemeræus.

N n 2   " and

" and deliberation fully confidered this important point,
" unanimoufly gave it as their opinion, that he had
" forfeited his crown, that we ought for that reafon to
" apply to your Holinefs, and had the higheft reafon
" to expect a favourable anfwer [4] : And we have a
" commiffion from that learned body, to affure your
" Holinefs, that they intend very foon to publifh the
" reafons that determined them in their opinion. We
" therefore moft earneftly intreat you holy father, to
" be a fhield and defence to us, againft the open and
" fecret machinations of our enemies, to give credit
" to the truth of our remonftrances ; and that if our
" enemies, by mifreprefentations, and fetting things
" in a falfe light, fhould have already obtained any
" thing from your Holinefs (which God avert) that
" may be prejudicial to the kingdom of France, and
" the holy church, your Holinefs will be pleafed graci-
" oufly to abrogate it by your Apoftolic authority ;
" humbly begging pardon for this our importunity
" which nothing could have excufed or prevailed upon
" us to make ufe of, but our concern for the extreme
" danger in which we behold the Catholic religion,
" and the defire we have to prevent the king of France,
" as far as we are able, from adding to his other wick-
" ednefs, in having abufed your Holinefs, the further
" crime of glorying in it."

[4] " The king's ambaffadors infifted, that this decree of the
" Sorbonne ought to be revoked and nullified, as it was not only
" exorbitant and unjuft, but infolent and prejudicial to the H. See;
" of which thofe divines made fo little account, that they had dared
" to determine a point of fo great confequence as the depofing a
" king. A thing, which though it fhould be granted to belong to
" the ecclefiaftical power, yet it would furely be fimply to the
" higheft power, which is the vicar of Chrift ; and not a petulant
" college, confifting of a few paffionate and corrupted perfons."
But neither could this be obtained ; for the pope confeffing the decree was prefumptuous and worthy of cenfure, faid, " he would
" proceed to that, when the king had given him full fatisfaction."
Davila.

Sixtus

Sixtus liftened to their difcourfe with great attention,
but anfwered in ambiguous and general terms, " That
" he was well pleafed with the zeal they expreffed
" for the Catholic religion, and would endeavour to
" fhew he had the good of the kingdom of France
" at heart: Exhorting them to behave in the fame
" manner."

The king thought proper in the mean time to redouble his application at the court of Rome ; for
which purpofe he fent his favourite Claude d' Augennes,
bifhop of Mans, of the family of Rambouillet, a prelate of great learning and fingular eloquence, fully
inftructed and furnifhed with every argument that was
neceffary to be made ufe of in his juftification, to
folicit afrefh for his abfolution, and to make his peace
with the pope, to whom he was ready to make any
fort of fubmiffion that was confiftent with his honour
and fafety.

When he arrived at Rome, having conferred with
the other two ambaffadors, he went with them to
defire an audience of his Holinefs; in which, after
the firft compliments were over, they reprefented to
him with great fubmiffion, " That they conceived the
" king their mafter could not be faid to have incurred
" any cenfure, as he had violated no ecclefiaftical
" immunity ; the cardinal being guilty of the crime
" of rebellion, in which cafe the clergy of France,
" even of the higheft rank, are always fubject to the
" fecular jurifdiction, and as he was a peer of the realm,
" his caufe ought naturally to have come before the
" High Court of Peers, in which all the princes and
" great officers of the kingdom were affembled ; fo
" that if the king had infringed any jurifdiction,
" it was that of the peers, and no other, as the eccle-
" fiaftical tribunal had nothing at all to do with the
" peers of France."

Sixtus, inftead of being fatisfied with thefe reafons,
feemed to be much offended at them, and faid,
" That

" That the cardinals were immediately fubject to the
" pontifical jurifdiction, and had no judge upon earth
" but the vicar of Jefus Chrift." The ambaffadors,
feeing his choler began to rife, boldly faid, " The king
" of France could not be excommunicated ;" and alledged the privileges of the Gallican church.   This fo
exceedingly enraged him, that he warned them, " To
" take care how they advanced any thing that favoured
" of herefy; for if they did, he would make them re-
" pent it.   To which Pifani couragioufly replied,
" That the character of ambaffadors protected them
" from outrage ; and that neither fear nor any other
" confideration fhould ever prevail upon him to give
" up the rights of his mafter." But as their inftructions were rather to footh and appeafe than exafperate
the pope, they proceeded to acquaint him, " That his
" majefty had obtained abfolution by virtue of a brief
" granted fome months before, in which his Holinefs
" had given him leave to be abfolved in all referved
" cafes, by his own confeffor, which they entreated
" his Holinefs to ratify, at leaft not to revoke." But
he anfwered, " That the brief was granted for things
" paft, and did not extend to future offences, the
" abfolution of which could not be anticipated ; that
" fuch a cafe as this, in which the H. See was fo openly
" infulted, to the great fcandal of all Chriftendom,
" was not comprehended in it ; that the explanation
" properly belonged to him that granted it ; and that
" he never defigned to give the king a power to be ab-
" folved from his future fins."

In this fituation things continued for five months
after the death of the duke of Guife; at laft, the
pope, after feveral monitions, declared, " That if the
" king did not fet the cardinal of Bourbon, and the
" archbifhop of Lyons at liberty in a certain time,
" and give advi e of it to the court of Rome within
" 60 days after, by letters under his own hand and
" feal, he would actually excommunicate him with-

" out

" out further ceremony, and all thofe that adhered to, " and with their counfels or any other way affifted him." He likewife cited the king to appear before him either peifonally or by proxy, in fixty days from the time the citation was notified to him, to give an account of the murder of the duke and cardinal of Guife, and the imprifonment of the other two prelates; and to fhew caufe why fentence of excommunication fhould not pafs upon him. All thofe that had any part, or had been in the leaft acceffary to this murder, were likewife cited in the fame manner.

He further declared, " That none of them, not " even the king, fhould receive abfolution from any " perfon, but the pope himfelf, except in the arti- " cle of death; and not even then, without they " would give fecurity to fubmit themfelves to the " church, and voluntarily undergo the penances " that fhould be enjoined them; that if he and they " did not comply with this, they fhould receive no " benefit from the general abfolutions that are grant- " ed at jubilees and crufades, any faculty or promife " made to the faid king, his predeceffors, or others, " at any time, or in any form to the contrary, not- " withftanding [5]."

As

[5] " This feeming very ftrange to the ambaffadors, and fee- " ing that they had propofed all thofe fpiritual fatisfactions, which " they (even to the prejudice of the crown) could offer; and with " fo great hnmiliation, that more could not he defired from a king: " They intended to try another way; and the marquis, whofe wife " was a Roman lady, began, by means of that alliance, to treat " with Donna Camilla, the pope's fifter; offering, amongft other " rewards, which the pope's kindred fhould have (if by their means " abfolution was obtained) to give the marquifate of Saluzzo, in " in fee-farm to his nephew, Don Michael; which the king pro- " fered (when he had made peace with the Catholics of his king- " dom) to recover out of the hands of the duke of Savoy. But " neither could this prevail on the obduracy of the pope: partly " becaufe the marquifiate was now in the power of another, nor " could be regained without a tedious war; and partly becaufe he
faw

As soon as the pope had made known his resolution by this citation, cardinal Joyeuse, the bishop of
Mans, and Pisani, left Rome, after having a long time
in vain endeavoured to hinder the publication of the
monitory, and obtain absolution for the king. Joyeuse
who was protector of the French nation, retired to
Venice, where he was kindly received : the other two
embarked for Marseilles. They made heavy complaints
of the pope's ill usage and injustice to their master, in
all the places they passed through, bitterly complaining of his " wrong-headed and obstinate manner of
" proceeding, who, to humour the Spaniards, and
" countenance their ambitious designs upon France,
" ran the hazard of losing that kingdom, as one of his
" predecessors had done England, by complying with
" their request, and refusing to divorce Henry VIII.
" from his queen Catharine." They likewise published many anonymous writings in vindication of the
king's conduct, to justify the course he had taken with
the Guises, and to expose the perverseness and absurdity of the pope's measures.

Two months and a few days after the citation was
issued out, the K of France was stabbed in the belly with
a two edged knife, at St. Cloud, a village about two
leagues from Paris, whilst he was besieging that city,
by James Clement, a Jacobin friar, of which wound
he died that night [6].

After

" saw the kingdom involved in such distraction, and the Catholic
" party so strong, that he doubted whether his absolution would
" be able to restore its peace." Davila, lib. x.

[6] The character of this prince is finely drawn by Davila, in the
tenth book of his history ; which I shall here subjoin for the satisfaction of the reader.

" It is indeed a thing worthy (says he) of very great considera-
" tion, to think how the singular virtues of so brave a prince,
" should bring him to so cruel and unfortunate an end : From
" whence we may learn this excellent lesson, that the skilfulness of
" the pilot avails but little, if the wind of Divine Favour, with
" which

After the death of Henry III, there followed a long
and bloody war betwixt the league and the K. of Navarre; many battles were fought with various fuccefs: At laft the fortune of that prince prevailed at
the battle of Yvry, where, after both fides had fought
with the higheft valour and bravery, Henry got the
victory; but with the lofs of the greateft part of the
nobility of France, who had followed his ftandard
that day.

After this battle, a report prevailed at Rome, for
three months, that the K. of Navarre was dead of
his wounds; which, tho' falfe, was believed, not only by the lower fort of people, but thofe of rank and
underftanding.   When it came to the pope's ears,
he faid, "If he is dead, the world has loft a great
" prince."   Count Olivarez, happening to come to

" which Eternal Providence, governs mortal affairs, help not to
" bring our actions to the defired port. For in Henry III. were
" all amiable qualities ; which, in the beginning of his life, were
" exceedingly reverenced and admired : Singular prudence, royal
" magnanimity, and inexhauftible munificence, profound piety,
" ardent zeal for religion, perpetual love to the good, implacable
" hatred to the bad, infinite defire of doing good to all : Popular
" eloquence, affability becoming a prince, generous courage, un-
" daunted valour, and wonderful dexterity in arms ; for which
" virtues, during the reign of his brother, he was more admired
" and efteemed than the king himfelf. He was a general before
" he was a foldier ; and a great ftatefman before he came to what
" are commonly reckoned years of maturity. He made war with*
" fpirit, eluded the experience of the moft able commanders, won
" many bloody battles, and took fortreffes that were held impreg-
" nable, gained the hearts of people far remote, was renowned
" and glorious in the mouths of all men. Yet when he came to
" the crown, and fought by fubtle devices to free himfelf from
" the yoke and fervitude of faction, both parties conceived fuch a
" hatred againft him, that his religion was counted hypocrify ;
" his prudence, low cunning ; his policy, meannefs of fpirit ; his
" liberality, licentious and unbridled prodigality ; his affability
" was contemned, his gravity hated, his name detefted, his pri-
" vate converfations imputed to enormous vices ; and his death
" being extremely rejoiced at by factious men, and the vulgar,
" was rafhly judged to be a ftroke of Divine Juftice."

* Con fortezza.

court

court the next day, Sixtus told him, "he heard the
" K. of Navarre was dead." " Dead! Holy Father,
" replied the count, I have juft received a letter
" from him." We mean Henry K. of Navarre."
faid the Pope; and I mean my mafter K. Philip II.
of Spain," returned the ambaffador; " for I know
" no other K. of Navarre; I fhall never acknowledge
" Henry of Bourbon, as any thing more than the
" prince of Bearn."

Notwithftanding the vehement folicitations of the
league, and the perilous condition they faid the R.
Catholic Religion was reduced to in France, the
pope would never fend them any affiftance, as his
legate had given them reafon to expect.

Some were of opinion that his motives for it were,
that he thought if the other fide got the better of the
K. of Navarre, the Spaniard would grow too powerful by their giving up fome part of the French monarchy to him for the fervices he had done them, as,
according to Cicero, " Bellorum civilium ii femper
" funt exitus, ut non ea folum fiant quæ velit vic-
" tor, fed etiam uti iis mos gerendus fit quibus ad-
" jutoribus parta fit victoria." At the end of a civil
war, it generally happens, that not only the con-
queror muft be fatisfied, but his friends and auxilia-
ries rewarded for the affiftance they have given him.

This reafoning was not ill-grounded; for as he,
from the beginning of his pontificate, had formed a
defign of attacking fome part of that monarchy, he
was in the right to prevent its growing ftronger
by any new acquifition. Others imagined he hoped
that the K. of Navarre, being acknowledged the
lawful fovereign of France, and promifing to turn
R. Catholic, might eafily prevail upon his followers
to abandon their new opinions, and return into
the bofom of the church. This was infinuated
to him by the duke of Luxembourg, ambaffador
at Rome, from the nobility of France, and confirmed
by feveral letters that he daily received from the
                                                    K. of

K. of Navarre's friends: But it was generally fuppofed, that the true reafon why he would not give
the league any ailiftance was that the D. of Luxembourg had affured him, " It was in vain to oppofe
" the K. of Navarre's juft claim to the crown;
" that it was abfolutely throwing men and money
" away to no purpofe; that he had fo ftrong a par-
" ty in the kingdom, encouraged and fupported by
" a powerful army, that he would infallibly bear
" down all oppofition before him; that it would be
" a wrong meafure to irritate him ftill more againft
" the Catholics, by fiding with his enemies, as he
" would be acknowledged in fpite of them, and
" acting unlike a wife man, to run the hazard of
" lofing when there was nothing to win." Whatever were his reafons, the inftances of the league
made fo little impreffion upon him, that he only
furnifhed them with 50,000 crowns, and that with
a very ill will. Some thought that his backward-
nefs to fend them any affiftance proceeded from the
great efteem he had conceived for the K. of Navarre,
ever fince he caufed his protefts to be ftuck up at
the Vatican. The generofity and fpirit of that action, followed by many other demonftrations of his
courage and noble refolution, made Sixtus think him
worthy of a crown, and that he ought not in juftice
to oppofe him in the means he took to get poffeffion of it; for when any body fpoke of him, he ufed
to fay, " his head was made on purpofe for a
" crown."

The K. of Spain was exceedingly difgufted that
the pope would neither do any thing to affift the
league, nor excommunicate the princes and prelates that adhered to the K. of Navarre. This
occafioned an infinite number of libels and pafquinades, in which Sixtus was feverely reflected upon,
and even treated as an Heretic. Olivarez was ordered to proteft againft his proceedings, and accufe
him of breaking his word: which he did in the confiftory

fiftory. But he eafily juftified himfelf to the cardinals, and acquainted them with the reafons of his conduct, in regard to the affairs of France; and fome of them interfering, prevented the proteft from being made public.

In the mean time an account arrived at Rome (which was not a little exaggerated by the Spaniards) that not only the league, but almoft all the kingdom, had acknowledged the cardinal of Bourbon as king, by the name of Charles the tenth, and that the affairs of the king of Navarre were defperate. This determined Sixtus to fend a legate into France, that he might feem to have a hand in fo great a revolution, to ufe all poffible means to unite the fubjects of that kingdom in their fidelity and obedience to this new king, for whofe releafe he had laboured with fo much diligence, as he thought it was a point that nearly concerned the honour and interefts, not only of the Sacred College, but the Holy See itfelf.

For a legation of fuch confequence, he chofe Henry Caietan, a perfon of very illuftrious birth, and confummate experience in ftate affairs. There were feveral other prelates appointed to attend him in this negociation, all men of great addrefs in fuch matters; amongft them were Lorenzo Bianchetti, and Philip Lega, afterwards cardinals; Mark Anthony Mocenigo, bifhop of Ceneda, who was a great favourite with the pope, and had been often employed by him as nuncio in foreign courts; Francis Panigarolo, a celebrated preacher, and Robert Bellarmine, a Jefuit, one of the moft learned men of the age. He furnifhed him with letters of exchange for 100,000 crowns [7] upon the bankers of Lyons, with orders to lay out this money in fuch a manner as he thought

[7] *Davila* fays 300,000.

moft

moft neceffary for the honour of the H. See, and particularly to procure the liberty of cardinal Bourbon.

But his zeal began to abate, and he was ftrangely embarraffed when he received certain advice from the duke of Luxembourg, that the K. of Navarre was declared true and lawful heir to the crown, with a particular account of this important event; and that the nobility of France had deputed him to come and acquaint his Holinefs with the reafons that moved that illuftrious body to acknowledge him; and to befeech him, as the common father of all Chriftians, to contribute his endeavours, to eftablifh a firm and lafting peace amongft his children. By this he perceived he had been impofed upon by the deputies of the league, who affured him, " That the great-
" eft part of the nation had declared againft the
" K. of Navarre, and that he was only followed
" by fome few people of defperate fortunes." Upon which he fent word to the duke of Luxembourg, that he fhould be glad if he would come to Rome (which he did foon after) and wrote at the fame itime, to the nobility that were in the king's army, in terms of the greateft affection, conjuring them,
" to continue fteady in the Catholic faith; pro-
" tefting that he had no other view or intereft in
" fending a legate, than to procure them a king
" of the fame Religion with them and their ancef-
" tors; that he was indifferent about the perfon,
" provided he was not a Heretic, or one whom he
" could not acknowledge as a fon of the church;
" that if they would take care of that, they might
" appoint whom they thought proper, and he would
" willingly confent to their choice; and giving them
" his benediction, he wifhed them all manner of
" happinefs and profperity."

Thefe letters were fhewn to the K. of Navarre,
who

who perceived from thence that Sixtus had no particular exception to him : When he read them, he finiled, and faid, " The pope was a very great man ; " and that he would turn Catholic, if it was only " to have the honour of being one of his fons."

The deputies of the league being informed of what had paffed, were very urgent with the pope to fend away the legate immediately, alledging, " That thefe reports were artfully propagated by " the K. of Navarre, to amufe his Holinefs, and " to gain time, which would be of the utmoft fer- " vice to his affairs." Sixtus, that he might in fome meafure feem to comply with them, and free himfelf from their importunities, ordered Caietan to fet cut for France as foon as poffible, but with very different inftructions from what he had given him before : For as he had then enjoined him to ufe his utmoft efforts to confirm the election of cardinal Bourbon, and procure his liberty, he now commanded him to make it his chief care to reunite the Catholics in the election of a king of their own communion, and fuch a one as would be agreeable to the nation in general, without fpecifying any perfon ; enjoining him not to declare openly, upon any account, againtft the K. of Navarre, as long as there was any hope of his return to the R. Catholic religion ; but if that prince fhould fhew any figns of converfion, then publicly to efpoufe his intereft.

The legate, however, was not very punctual in obeying thefe orders : The Spaniards had fo entirely got poffeffion of him, that upon his arrival at Paris, he immediately joined himfelf to the league, and declared againft the K. of Navarre ; which fo provoked the Pope, that he inftantly countermanded his letters of credit upon the merchants of Lyons, and, by that means, put it out of his power to do the league much fervice, efpecially as he further made it known, that he did by no means approve of his

conduct

conduct [8]. On the other hand, the K. of Navarre complained bitterly of the legate to the bifhop of Ceneda, who came to propofe a truce to him ; and faid, "He fhewed more regard to the interefts of " Spain, than of the true religion ; that he had as " much reafon to be offended at his behaviour, as " to acknowledge the favourable intentions of his " Holinefs ; that it feemed very ftrange to him, that, " contrary to the duty of a legate, he began with " giving manifeft demonftrations of partiality, by " taking up his refidence at Paris which city the " league had made their head quarters ; that as " he reprefented the common father of all Chriftians, " he fhould have chofen a neutral place, to avoid " all fufpicion and obloquy, and that he might the " better take proper meafures to eftablifh peace, the " great end for which he was fent by his Holinefs in- " to that kingdom."

The fenate of Venice had deliberated fome time whether they fhould fuffer their ambaffador to continue in France with the K. of Navarre, as it would be, in effect, to acknowledge him in lawful poffeffi- on of the crown ; and having weighed the matter with that prudence and maturity of judgment, which they obferve in their actions, were of opinion it would be more for the advantage of Chriftendom in general, that the kingdom fhould remain in poffef- fion of the lawful heir, than be difmembered or parcelled out betwixt the league and the Spaniards, or given to fome foreign prince. Befides the K. of Navarre being acknowledged by the greateft part of

[8] Ibi rex literas a Lucemburgo, qui Romæ erat, accepit, quibus certior fiebat de Pontificis voluntate, multum a fœde- ratis alienatâ, ut qui, de rebus noftris per ipfum Lucemburgum in- ftructior promiffa auxilia fumminiftrare prorfus recufaret, et Caie- tano legato graviter fuccenferet, quod factiofis in urbe fe ad- junxiffet, et non potius, ficuti juffus erat, cum Carolo Vindoci- no, et Philippo Lenoncurio, Cardinalibus, qui regias partes fe- quebantur, concilia communicaffet. *Thuan.* lib. xcviii.

· the

the French nobility, in whom the ftrength of that
nation principally confifts, would certainly eftablifh
himfelf in the throne, in fpight of all the endeavours of his enemies to the contrary. Thefe reafons determined the republic to let their ambaffador remain with the K. Navarre, as K. of France,
with orders to make him a tender of all the affiftance
they had at any time given to his predeceffors, in
their greateft and moft prefling neceffities.

Henry the great (as he was afterwards called) fpoke
of thefe good offices of the Venetians with the higheft gratitude, and remembered them to the laft day
of his life: As feveral other ftates and princes foon
followed their example, and acknowledged him for
the true and lawful K. of France.

Jerome Mattenci, who was then nuncio at Venice,
and the Spanifh ambaffador, made loud complaints,
in full fenate, that the republic had acknowledged a perfon for K. of France, who was a contumacious Heretic, and a rebel, and had been
excommunicated by the pope. But the fenate, who
knew how Sixtus ftood affected to him, anfwered
" That they did not pretend to determine con-
" cerning matters of faith, that properly belonging
" to no body but his holinefs; but as they were
" fully convinced that Henry of Bourbon was true
" heir to the crown of France, they were obliged to
" treat with him about fome temporal affairs, in
" which both France and the republic were mu-
" tually concerned, without any defign to prejudice
" the fpiritual power or authority of the H. See."

The nuncio was highly diffatisfied with this anfwer; and having made fome protefts, left Venice in
great hafte, and came poft to Rome, thinking he
had acted in a manner that would be very agreeable to the pope; but found himfelf grievoufly difappointed at his arrival; for his holinefs would not
fo

fo much as admit him to an audience, but commanded him to mount the fame horfe, and return
inftantly to Venice, which he was obliged to comply with, to his great mortification, and the infinite
laughter of the Venetians.

It was commonly reported at that time, that
there was a fecret correfpondence betwixt the
fenate and the pope; and that their ambaffador at
Rome had privately confulted him about acknowledging the K. of Navarre, before they publicly
deliberated upon it; who perceiving how well he
was difpofed towards that prince, acquainted the
fenate with it, which was the reafon of their acting
as they did. It is certain that Henry IV, in a great
meafure, owed his eftablifhment upon the throne of
France to Sixtus. For if he had openly declared a-
gainft him, and fupported the interefts of the league,
they would have acted with as much vigour as ever,
and the republic of Venice would hardly have been
fo forward to acknowledge him. Many other ftates
could not well tell which fide to favour, as they did
not know with any certainty, what part the pope
intended to act; tho' it is paft doubt that he was
fecretly inclined to favour the juft and generous attempts of Henry. But when they faw fo fage and
powerful a body as the Venetian fenate take this ftep,
it foon determined them; and as it added great
ftrength and reputation to the K. of Navarre's
caufe, it of confequence proportionably diminifhed
the power and credit of the league. King Henry
wrote letters to the fenate with his own hand, in
which he thanked them for fo fignal a piece of fervice, in the moft refpectful terms; and ordered his
ambaffador at Venice to affure them of his perpetual
efteem and regard. The D. of Luxembourg fpoke
in the fame ftrain to the pope, and faid, "That
"the king his mafter would ever remember his
"good offices, as he had fhewn himfelf truly wor-
"thy of the name of a good fhepherd."

O o   Of

Of all the ambaſſadors that reſided at Rome,
there was not any that had been ſo often and ſo
remarkably affronted by the pope, as count Olivarez; yet nobody ſpoke with more freedom and boldneſs, tho' he was ſometimes obliged to lower his
topſails a little, when Sixtus was in his frantic
moods. Towards the latter end of this year, he
happened unluckily, to have two or three diſputes
with his Holineſs, in which he was treated by him
in ſuch a manner as perhaps no ambaſſador ever
was before or ſince his time [9].

The firſt diſlike he took to him, was for ſo conſtantly teazing him to ſend aſſiſtance to the league,
which he was very unwilling to have done, but
was, in the end, compelled to it, by his everlaſting
importunities (and to make ſome ſhew of zeal for
the R. C. Religion) which he could never forgive,
and was reſolved to take the firſt opportunity of revenge that offered.

He had cauſed the vulgate Latin edition of the
bible to be publiſhed the laſt year, which occaſioned
a good deal of clamour in the world; but nothing
like what there was this year, upon his printing an
Italian verſion of it. This ſet all the Roman Catholic part of Chriſtendom in an uproar. Count Olivarez, and ſome of the cardinals, ventured to expoſtu-
late with him pretty freely upon it, and ſaid, "It
" was a ſcandalous, as well as a dangerous thing,
" and bordered very nearly upon hereſy." But
he treated them with contempt, and only ſaid,
" We do it for the benefit of you that don't under-
" ſtand

[9] Non mediocriter regis animum recrearunt literæ ad Caie-
tanum a Româ ſcriptæ, quibus ſignificabatur, Comitem Olivarem
Philippi Oratorem cum Pontifice, magrâ verborum acerbitate,
contendiſſe, ut Lucemburgum a ſe dimitteret, et proceres alioſ-
que omnes, qui pro rege militabant, diris devoveret;
alioqui fore ut deinceps Philippus minime ipſum pro Pontifice colituros fit: Pontificem autem, hominis arrogantiam non
ferentem, congregatione cardinalium factâ de ipſo Olivare Româ pellendo deliberâſſe, parumque rem ab'exitu abfuiſſe. Thuan. lib. xcviii.

" ſtand Latin." The moſt zealous of the cardinals wrote to the K. of Spain, intreating him, " To " interpoſe and think of ſome remedy for this evil, " as he was more intereſted in it than any one elſe, " with regard to the kingdoms of Naples and Sicily, " and the duchy of Milan; for if the bible ſhould " come to be publicly read there, in the vulgar " tongue, it might raiſe ſcruples and uneaſineſſes in " the conſciences of thoſe people : As it was, beſides, " one of the firſt principles of heretics, to read " the ſcriptures in the common tongue."

Philip, who was a furious bigot, ordered his ambaſſador, " To uſe his utmoſt endeavours with the " pope, to ſuppreſs this edition, as it would give " infinite offence ; and ſaid, if he did not, he ſhould " be obliged to make uſe of ſuch means to prevent " its being read in his kingdoms, as his zeal for " true religion ſuggeſted, and the Almighty had " put in his hands." Olivarez, having received theſe orders, immediately demanded an audience of the Pope, and repreſented to him with much warmth, " How diſagreeable this new verſion was to his " maſter, and what ſcandal it gave to his whole " court." Sixtus ſuffered him to harangue, with great vehemence, for above an hour, and when he was come to the end of his career, made no anſwer. Upon which the count ſaid, " Won't your " Holineſs be pleaſed to let me know your thoughts " upon this matter." " I am thinking, ſays Sixtus, " to have you thrown out of the window, to teach " other people how to behave when they addreſs " themſelves to the pontiff." And immediately withdrew into another apartment.

The poor ambaſſador, who was ſufficiently acquainted with the temper of Sixtus, made haſte out of the Vatican, expecting he would have been as good as his word ; and when he got home, and had recovered his ſpirits a little, ſaid, " Thank " God, I have had a great eſcape to day."

Some authors have ventured to affert that Sixtus
never published any fuch edition; which is moft no-
torioufly falfe, as may eafily be proved, not only
from the authentic teftimony of many writers of
that time, but from feveral copies that are now actually to be feen in the grand duke of Tufcany's library, that of St. Lawrence, the Ambrofian at Milan
[10], not to mention two in the public library
at Geneva, and feveral others. Philip Brietius, a
learned Jefuit, fays, in the 247th page of the fecond part of his annals, printed at Paris, in the
year 1663, "Inter hæc mortuus eft Romæ Sixtus
" V. editis bibliis facris in linguâ Italiçâ, quæ tan-
" tum negotii nobis exhibuerunt; quibus et præ-
" fixerat bullam, quam reverâ bullam non fuiffe,
" poftea compertum eft, nec adhibitos in confilium
" peritos viros, ut perperam in eâ ipfe profitebatur,
" &c. Sed cum huic contradicere audebat nemo,
" et fertur Hifpanico legato conftantius refiftenti
" perniciem parâffe." And befides the common report that was in every body's mouth at Rome, I
remember myfelf to have feen in a manufcript,
giving an account of the tranfactions of thofe times,
that the cardinal of Toledo who moft violently oppofed this meafure, when he found the pope refolved to perfift in it, contrary to the advice of the
wifeft and moft learned cardinals, as well as the
repeated inftances of count Olivarez, faid, " How
" has God abandoned his church! may he be
" pleafed to deliver us foon from this wicked pope."

The K. of Spain, thinking himfelf highly affronted by the ill ufage and contempt fhewn to his ambaffador, by his unwillingnefs to affift the league,
by his countenancing the K. of Navarre, and his
party, by the publication of the bible in the Italian
tongue, contrary to his remonftrances, by the little
care he took to fupport the Catholic interefts in

[10] Founded by Ambrofe, bifhop of that place, a very good
man, who went by the name of doctor Mellifluus, upon the account of his great elcquence.

England

England, and the defigns which he knew, he harboured upon the kingdom of Naples ; notwithftanding his great zeal for religion, and the refpect he
had always profeffed for the H. See, called together
his council of confcience, and demanded of them,
" What methods were moft proper to be taken with
" fuch a pope ? They told his majefty, " That
" he both might and ought in confcience to convoke
" a general council in his dominions, firft ac-
" quainting the pope with his defign, and (if he
" oppofed it) to cite him to appear before it, where
" he would certainly be depofed, and another elect-
" ed, as he had prefumed, 'on his own head, to do
" things that approached very near to herefy."
When they had delivered this as their opinion,
the king ordered letters to be written to his ambaffador at Rome, to confult the cardinal of Toledo
(whom he looked upon as a faint) with all the o-
ther cardinals that were moft zealous for the honour of the Spanifh nation, and commanded him,
if they approved of it, to take the opportunity of
fome folemn feftival (where the pope fhould be prefent) to notify to him in public " his refolution of
" affembling fuch a council at Sevil, to confider
" what was fitteft to be done for the fervice of God,
" and the glory of his holy religion, fince he took
" upon him to do every thing without the advice,
" and often contrary to the opinion of his confi-
" ftory, and had prepofteroufly caufed a bible to
" be publifhed that had given offence to all Chri-
" ftendom."
Tho' Olivarez had already received fufficient proof
of the roughnefs of the pope's difpofition, and was
pretty well affured he would not fuffer his authority
to be called in queftion ; yet, in obedience to his
mafter's commands, he prepared a writing, by way
of notification of the council, which he intended to deliver to the pope foon after, at a folemn cavalcade that
he had appointed, upon his going to refide, for the firft
time, at the palace lately built near St. John de Lateran.

Sixtus

Sixtus was informed of this by his fpies, the night before it was to be put into execution, and of the time and place where the writings was to be prefented to him; upon which he fent in all hafte for the governor, and two mafters of the ceremonies, and underftanding from them, that every thing was in readinefs for the cavalcade the next day, he told them, "He had altered his mind as to the order "that was to be obferved in the proceffion; that it "was his pleafure they themfelves fhould immedi-" "ately precede his perfon, the common hangman "going next before them, with a halter in his hand, "and before him 200 of the guards, four and four; "and that if any perfon fhould dare to offer a pa-" "per or writing to him, they fhould order the "hangman to fall upon him that moment and ftran-" "gle him, without further ceremony, tho' he were "an ambaffador, cardinal, king, or emperor." Thefe orders were repeated the next morning, to the great furprize of the governor, who, tho' he was not acquainted with the reafons, took care however to marfhal the cavalcade exactly as he was commanded.

The ambaffador was acquainted with this dif-pofition (as it was fuppofed) by the pope's private directions, juft as he was going out of his houfe to deliver the writing, and was fo terrified with it, that he once defigned to have left the city immedi-ately, and retire to Naples; but his pride at laft got the better of that refolution, as he thought fuch a ftep would be a blot upon his character: For which reafon he ventured to ftay in his palace, and barring all the gates and doors, threw the writing into the fire, and went to his prayers, recommend-ing himfelf to God, and expecting to be ftrangled as foon as ever the cavalcade was over: tho' we may take it for granted, that Sixtus only defigned to fright-en him, and make him defift from his undertaking.

As the reafons of the pope's ordering fo vile and ignominious a fellow as the common hangman to

attend

attend at the cavalcade, in which nobody ufed to
be feen but cardinals, prelates, and perfons of the
firft quality, were not yet made public, it occafioned a great terror in the city, as they imagined
he was going to put fome cruel defign in execution;
but when his motives were known, and the people freed from their apprehenfions, every one highly
applauded his refolution.

" * Violent remedies are never to be adminiftered,
" either in bodies natural or politic, except in
" defperate cafes; and the fuccefs of them depends
" entirely upon what the Heathens called Fortune,
" and the Chriftians Providence. It is certain the
" appearance of rigour in a prince, rightly timed,
" has been the prefervation of many a ftate." And
it is very probable, that Sixtus by this fpirited
manner of proceeding, crufhed a fchifm in the em-
bryo, that might have long difturbed the peace of
Chriftendom: For when K. Philip faw how difficult
it would be to deliver the writing that was neceffary
for that purpofe, and what tumults and diftractions
might be occafioned by a council, he dropped his
defign, and thought it would be better to revenge
himfelf upon the pope fome other way, that might
not be prejudicial to the church.

Soon after, Pafquin appeared in the drefs of a
courier, with a letter in his hand, directed, to
fignior Gigolo (that was the hangman's name) common
hangman of Rome, and one of his Holinefs's train;
alluding to the ftation he was in at the cavalcade.

When the ftorm was pretty well blown over,
count Olivarez called feveral of the Spanifh cardinals
together, to confult what was proper to be done in
an affair, wherein not only his own reputation, but
that of his mafter was fo highly concerned; after
much deliberation it was thought the beft way, " to
" take no notice, and pretend not to be informed of
" it, as the pope had only given his orders to the go-
" vernor in general terms, without fpecifying any per-

* Machiavel.

fon;

" fon ; for by taking upon himfelf to refent an affront
" that was not offered to any body in particular, he
" would involve himfelf in frefh quarrels with the pope,
" and make two evils of one ; that it was therefore
" more prudent to put it up, for the prefent, however,
" and go to court with the fame freedom as
" ufual."

Not much unlike this was his behaviour to the
marquis Polagni, ambaffador from Alphonfo, duke
of Ferrara; tho' he was much efteemed by the pope
upon the account of his great learning.   It happened that this prince had fome difpute with the
pope about the right to a village upon his frontiers,
which (as the lawyers pretended to have found out)
did not belong to the duke but to the ecclefiaftical
ftate, as part of a dependance upon Bologna ; upon which the pope took poffeffion of it immediately,
without any ceremony or formality.

This occafioned the duke to reprefent to his Holinefs, by his ambaffador, the manifeft injuftice
that was done to him, with the reafons upon which
he founded his title to the place in difpute; which
he endeavoured to do, and at the fame time to
prefent feveral writings and memorials to him,
drawn up by lawyers, relating to the affair.   But
Sixtus, to ftrengthen his poffeffion by length of time,
would not admit him to an audience, putting him
off from day to day, with varicus excufes: Till at
laft the ambaffador grew fo impatient, that he went
one day into the pope's ante-chamber, and protefted
" he would not ftir frcm thence till he had obtained an audience."

When Sixtus was informed of this, he fent him
word, " That if he did not get out of the palace in
" half an hour, he would have him thrown headlong
" out of a window ; and if he did not leave the city
" in two days, he fhould be fet upon the back of an
" afs, and whipped out of it." Upon which the
                                          ambaffador,

ambaffador, who had heard fome of his Holinefs's feats of this kind, foon altered his refolution of ftaying in the ante-chamber; and made what hafte he could out of Rome. This was all the fatisfaction the duke was ever able to obtain; for the pope kept poffeffion of the place, and united it to his dominions.

We fhall here recite. fome other particulars which happened this year, that may ferve to give us a further idea of his humour and government.

He had appointed one Marcus Octavius, a Bolognefe, fecretary to his nephew cardinal Montalto. This perfon had refided in Rome above 20 years and been in feveral employments during· the reigns of Pius V. and Gregory XIII. in all which he had behaved with great prudence and fidelity; and as he had much experience in worldly affairs, and was of a mature age (being about 57 years old) the pope thought he might be very ufeful to his nephew·; for which reafon, and to induce him to ferve, him the more affiduoufly, he had him ordained and gave him a good canonry, with other handfome appointments. In a fhort time he obtained fo high a degree of confidence, both with Sixtus and his nephew, that he was often entrufted to carry meffages concerning things of the greateft importance, from one to the other, when either of them was indifpofed, or any thing happened that prevented their coming together. Now as Sixtus had really a defign upon Naples, and was making fecret preparations for it, he wanted to eftablifh an intereft in that kingdom; for which purpofe he employed Octavius, of whofe fidelity he had the higheft opinion, to invite fome Neapolitan gentlemen, of good families, to come and live in the ecclefiaftical dominions, with a promife of honourable and profitable employments; that he might by their means, acquaint himfelf with the ftate and affections of the Neapolitans, and drew over their relations to his interefts. But thefe practices coming to the knowledge of count Olivarez, he complained of them to cardinal Montalto; from whence both the pope and he, concluding that Octa-

vius

vius had betrayed them, as they had not trufted any other perfon with the fecret, Sixtus was determined to punifh him in the fevereft manner; but was a little perplexed how to proceed, as there was no evidence fufficient to put him to the torture, and bare fufpicion was not enough to juftify the imprifonment of one in holy orders: he condemned him however to the gallies; but his nephew, who had a great affection for the man, prevailed upon him, fome time after, to mitigate his punifhment; and he contented himfelf with depriving him of his benefice, and banifhing him for ever from the ecclefiaftical ftate without any form of procefs.

As every body thought Octavius was in the high road to preferment, and would foon be made a bifhop, if not a cardinal, they were ftrangely furprized at this fudden difgrace: The punifhment was heavy and vifible; but nobody knew his crime, fome fufpecting one thing, fome another: And indeed after all it is not improbable that Octavius was innocent, and that Olivarez had no other reafon but fufpicion to ground his complaint upon. However it was, the poor man was fo affected with it, that not being admitted to juftify himfelf, he left Rome to go to his own country, and arriving at Loretto, died there at an inn, about three days after.

No lefs remarkable and fevere was the deftiny of Camillus Lana, majordomo to cardinal Montalto: He had been promifed the firft canonry that became vacant in the church of St. Maria Maggiore, in lieu of a bifhopric, which he had refufed; and was talking one day with the chamberlain of an old canon belonging to that church, who was brother to a perfon that had married his niece: Amongft other things that paffed in converfation, Lana afked him, "How "his mafter did?" The fervant anfwered, "Pretty "well confidering he was 70 years of age: Upon which Lana faid in a jocofe manner, "Could not "you give him a dofe, do you think, and fend him "into

" into another world, to do a friend and a relation of
" yours a service? The chamberlain answered, in
the same manner, " Such a thing may be done;
" there's no impossibili.y in it." It happened very
unfortunately for both, that this discourse was over-
heard, thro' a hole in the wainscot, by a domestic
of the same cardinal, who owing Lana a grudge, and
thinking this a good opportunity to take his revenge,
went immediately to the governors and related this
conversation to him, with some additions not at all to
Lana's advantage.

The governor could not tell how to proceed in the
affair: It appeared to him only a piece of common
chat, *loquendi gratia*; but then he knew the boister-
ous temper of Sixtus, and was afraid, when he came
to be acquainted that he was informed of it, and had
not communicated it to him, he would fly into one of
his passions, and perhaps turn him out of his office;
for which reason he went and told him the whole; representing it as " an idle trifling story, and not worth
" notice if it was true."

Whilst the governor was making this report to the
pope, cardinal Montalto came in, and not knowing
any thing of the matter, seemed surprized at it, but
much more so, when he heard his uncle order the governor to send Lana, the chamberlain, and Coccia the
informer, instantly to prison; and though both the cardinal and the governor endeavoured all they could to
dissuade him from it, it had no effect: He answered,
" Such conversations are of dangerous consequence,
" and may do a great deal of mischief, if they are not
" discouraged in time by an exemplary severity; we
" command you therefore, to imprison, examine and
" proceed against them directly." They were accordingly, all three carried to prison the same day, without
knowing the reason of it; especially the two first, who
had quite forgot a thing that had been spoke only for
the sake of a little conversation. When they were examined separately, they readily confessed they had spoke
the

the words that were laid to their charge, protesting, it was without the least intention to prejudice any body. But, Sixtus would not admit of such excuses, and had them all condemned to the gallies; Lana and the chamberlain for the conversation above mentioned, which he said must proceed from some wicked design; and the other because his information was not owing to any zeal or regard for justice, and the public good, but out of private pique, and a desire to revenge himself upon Lana, who a few days before had given him a box on the ear. He ordered them, however, to be set at liberty, after they had been in the gallies about a month.

The next instance of his severity was in the case of a poor barber, who happening to have a quarrel with another man in the street, after having called him many reproachful names, shook his fist at him in a threatning manner, and said, " if ever you come " under my hands, I'll do your business for you." This being reported to Sixtus by one of his spies, he ordered him to be immediately sent to prison, and a process commenced against him. But hearing no more of it for some days, he sent for the governor, and asking him the reason of it, the governor answered, " He did not know how he could be punished for a few " indiscreet words spoken in a passion; that according " to the forms of the law, he ought to be set at liber- " ty; and thought the imprisonmet he had suffered was " sufficient punishment."

When the pope heard him mention the setting him at liberty, he flew into a most violent passion; and looking at the governor, as if he would tear him in pieces, said, " Pray, sir, what sort of justice is this? " Don't you know that a barber's threatning to cut " a man's throat is a very great crime? But we shall " endeavour to prevent such things for the future, by " making an example of him. It is our pleasure that " he be soundly whipped in the presence of all the " barbers of the city, and then sent to the gallies for " three years."

On

On the day appointed for this piece of difcipline, the governor ordered all the barbers in Rome to appear, with their apprentices (on penalty of being fined 100 crowns, and banifhed the city) in a large area called the Piazza del Compidoglio, where they were to ftand in two rows, through which he was to be whipped three times. This was accordingly performed, in the fight of an infinite concourfe of people, who were drawn together by the novelty of the fpectacle. But at the earneft folicitation of feveral magiftrates and perfons of great diftinction, he was fo merciful as to excufe him from the going to the gallies.

The next day he publifhed an edict, by found of trumpet, as ufual, forbidding every one on pain of whipping and the gallies, to make ufe of fuch threats, as the nature of their profeffion or occupation furnifhed them with means of putting in execution : For example, a phyfician or apothecary to poifon; a furgeon to lame by bleeding; a barber to cut one's throat, &c.

It was thought this edict would have had a good effect, and made people of thofe profeffions afraid to commit the action, when they faw how feverely he punifhed thofe that only threatened it. But no law or punifhment is fufficient to reftrain *the fons of men, when their hearts are fully fet in them to do evil.*

John Baptift Marchefini, a very rich citizen of Rome, had been married feveral years without having any children; and his eftate, for want of fons, was to defcend to a nephew, who was a phyfician, of good reputation, and of the fame name. It happened that Marchefini's wife was taken dangeroufly ill, and the phyfician fearing if fhe died his uncle might marry again, and have children, which would difappoint him of the eftate, applied to an apothecary whofe name was Marcus Vita, his intimate friend and acquaintance, and offered him 200 crowns to give his uncle, who was ill bed of the cholic fome medicines that he fhould prefcribe.

scribe. The apothecary readily accepted the offer, and promised to do it as soon as possible. But when Providence is disposed to save or destroy, it often makes use of means dark and mysterious to human sight. The apothecary's 'prentice had a mistress whom he used to convey secretly to his chamber, whenever he had an opportunity; and had concealed her one day in the closet of a room, where the physician and apothecary came to talk about the poison, which, was to be administered that day, in a clyster. As soon as they were gone, the young woman, who had over-heard all their conversation, came out of the closet; and knowing with what rigour Sixtus treated those that were privy to the crimes of others, and did not reveal them, went directly to the Vatican, and gave him an account of the whole.

As there was no time to be lost, he immediately sent for the governor, and ordered him to arrest the physician, apothecary, and apprentice, and send them to prison, which was done without delay. The young woman was likewise secured, that she might be an evidence if there was occasion. When Sixtus heard they were in prison, he told the governor, " That the in-
" tention to do evil was as great a crime as actually
" committing it, and that the will ought to be taken for
" the deed; that if these wretches had not been pre-
" vented they had before that time executed their
" wicked design; that with regard to them, Marchesini
" ought to be looked upon as actually dead, and their
" attempt to poison him fully accomplished; that there
" could not well be conceived a crime of a deeper dye,
" or a greater contempt manifested of the edict, pub-
" lished but a few days before; that he had a fine op-
" portunity of shewing a strict regard to justice, of
" signalizing himself, and doing an honour to his pon-
" tificate."

These hints were perfectly understood by the governor, who immediately sent for the parties, to be
examined by himself, where the young woman confirmed

firmed what fhe had before depofed, in the prefence
of the phyfician and the apothecary; and the 'prentice
confeffed he had concealed her in that clofet; that he
faw them go into the room next to it, and ftay there
about half an hour, with the door fhut contrary to
cuftom. After this examination they were both fet
at liberty; the fhop and principal rooms, both in the
phyfician's and apothecary's houfe, locked up, with
feals upon the doors, and centinels placed to prevent
any thing being taken out of them. As this is never
done but in crimes of the higheft nature, or where
the inquifition is concerned, it occafioned much fpe-
culation amongft the people, who were yet ignorant
of the caufe. The phyfician and apothecary being
feparately examined pofitively denied what was laid to
their charge; infifting that no regard ought to be had
to what was depofed by a woman of her character.
Upon this, the torture being ordered, the apothecary
fuffered himfelf to be ftripped and bound; but when
he faw they were in earneft, he confeffed the whole.
The phyfician ftill continued to deny it, and bore the
torture half an hour; at laft, not being able to fupport
it any longer he likewife confeffed.

They had agreed, it feems, to give him a poi-
fonous clyfter and potion, and to file a very different
prefcription in the apothecary's fhop, to ftop people's mouths, in cafe there fhould be any talk or fufpicion of foul play after his death, and were preparing it at the time they were taken up. When the
governor made a report of this to Sixtus, he faid,
" The delinquents have done well to exonerate their
" confciences, by the confeffion of fo henious a crime;
" it now remains that you worthily difcharge your
" duty, by paffing a proper fentence upon them: It
" high time that fatisfaction be made to our laws."
The judges were of opinion, when it came before
them, that they could not with a fafe confcience pafs
fentence of death upon them, as there had been no
life loft, nor their defign actually accomplifhed; and
thought

thought condemning them to the gallies for ten years,
was a puniſhment ſufficiently rigorous. But the governor, who had been ſpoken to twice by his Holineſs, upon this ſubject, told them, how neceſſary it was, in
" ſuch caſes, to accommodate. themſelves to his hu-
" mour, who did not ſeem much inclined to practice
" the ſacred leſſon, *I have no pleaſure in the death of the*
" *wicked, but that he turn from his way and live* ; and
" and that he had already declared, the intention con-
" ſtituted the ſin ; as God not only enjoined us in his
" holy commandments, not to ſteal, but not even ſo
" much as to covet or deſire our neighbour's goods:
" From whence it appeared, that he looked upon the
" deſign to ſteal, and the actual commiſſion of theft
" as the ſame ; ſo that theſe people had been really,
" to all intents and purpoſes, guilty of poiſoning and
" murder, by forming the deſign, and making pre-
" parations to put it in execution." He ſaid ſo much
to the judges that they altered their opinion, and condemned them to be beheaded, giving their friends and
relations time to apply for a pardon.

When Sixtus heard of this he was exceeding angry,
and ſaid, " he ſuppoſed the governor and his tri-
" bunal deſigned to make a joke of him ; but they
" ſhould find themſelves miſtaken :" And gave orders to have the ſentence changed into hanging and
confiſcation of goods. Though this was a very ſevere
one, it did not occaſion ſo much murmuring as ſome
others had done ; as it was, without doubt, a very
wicked deſign and worthy of death. Many of the
cardinals endeavoured to get it changed for the gallies ; but he would not conſent to it, and treated thoſe
in a very rough manner that had ventured to aſk that
favour of him. They were executed ſoon after, and
ſhewed but little remorſe for their crime, inſiſting to
the laſt, that they ſuffered unjuſtly ; for which reaſon their bodies were not permitted to be buried.
What happened afterwards occaſioned more noiſe than
the ſentence that was paſſed upon them.

When

When Marchefini, the uncle of the phyfician that was hanged, firft heard of his nephew's crime and condemnation, he was prodigioufly affected with it, and offered 20,000 crowns to have his fentence changed into that of the gallies; but Sixtus found means to come at the money without ftopping the courfe of juftice.

As he was very ill of the cholic when this event happened, his concern for the death of his nephew, and the difgrace it brought upon the family, fo increafed the diftemper, that he died foon after, leaving above 50,000 crowns in legacies to feveral different people.

When Sixtus heard of his death, he pretended that his effects belonged to the nephew that was hanged (as an eftate in truft) and for furenefs ordered the officers of the Apoftolic Chamber to feize upon it, and keep poffeffion till that point was fettled with the legatees, as it foon was by the Ruota, in favour of the Apoftolic Chamber. Indeed the pope, not long after this determination, ordered one half of it to be given (as a favour) to the legatees, which in fome degree abated the murmurs, of the people, who looked upon it as a moft unjuft and rapacious action.

Whilft Sixtus was thus induftrious in accumulating wealth for the neceffities of the public, he was not forgetful of his own family: Nay, it is certain he may be numbered amongft thofe popes that have fhewn the greateft affection and partiality to their relations, as he neglected no opportunity to aggrandife them by riches, or honours, or noble and powerful alliances.

But he behaved in this, as in every thing elfe, with great prudence and circumfpection; for except in the inftance of bringing them to Rome, and creating his nephew a cardinal in the firft month of his pontificate, he proceeded but flowly in conferring favours upon them. His firft endeavour was to acquire the reputation of juft and zealous; when he faw this pretty well eftablifhed, and that he was revered and looked

upon

upon with a fort of admiration, by all the world, and
that it was matter of aftonifhment to every body,
how he raifed money to accomplifh his vaft defigns,
and perform fuch things as furpaffed the grandeur
and magnificence of the ancient Romans ; he then began to think of his family, and fettled an income of
100,000 crowns per annum, in eftate, and ecclefiaftical benefices, befides 250,000 crowns in houfes,
rich furniture, plate and jewels, upon his nephew
the cardinal ; heaping upon him the moft honourable
and lucrative employments in his difpofal, as chancellor of the church, arch-prieft of St Maria Maggiore, protector of the kingdom of Poland, &c. In
fhort he was not only the richeft and moft powerful
cardinal of his time, but the moft careffed and beloved ; to which his princely manner of behaviour
did not a little contribute.

After he had fufficiently taken care of him, he
made fuch a provifion for his nieces, that they were
envied by ladies of the greateft families in Rome.
They were both of a difpofition that would have done
honour to the moft exalted birth. As one of them
was only 12, and the other but 10 years old when
they came to Rome, his Holinefs committed them to
the care of two noble matrons, as governeffes, by
whofe example and inftructions they learned to behave themfelves in a manner that would have fhamed
many who were born princeffes.

They were afked in marriage by feveral of the firft
quality, and the eldeft, Donna Orfina, was given to
Mark Anthony Colonna, prince of Sonnino and Manu-
pelli, duke of Tagliccizza and Paliano, marquis of Al-
tezza, count of Albi, high conftable of the kingdom of Naples, knight of the Golden Fleece, and
grandee of Spain. The eftates of this prince being
much impaired by living in a manner fuitable to his
quality, and the great fums which his father and
grand-father had fpent in the fervice of Charles V.
and Philip II. he thought fo accomplifhed a woman,
with the immenfe fortune fhe was certain to have,
would

would reftore his family, which was one of the beft in Italy, to its ancient fplendor and magnificence.

There were many other advantages likely to accrue from this match, which made him defire it the more eagerly. It was no lefs agreeable to Sixtus, upon account of the great honour it reflected upon his family, the fupport and protection they might expect from an alliance with a houfe of fo great credit and authority, not only in Italy but in Spain, and indeed all over Europe, as it likewife furnifhed him with an opportunity of fhewing his gratitude to a family, which, as he acknowledged, had conferred many great obligations upon him. The pope gave her for dower 100,000 crowns, befides 2000 piftoles to defray the expence of the wedding. The cardinal and her mother each 10,000, her brother 6000. When he gave them his benediction, he could fcarce refrain from fhedding tears of joy. The nuptials were celebrated with a royal pomp and magnificence, in the prefence of fixteen cardinals, fix ambaffadors, an infinite number of nobility, and perfons of the higheft diftinction. Befides balls, mafquerades, bonfires, illuminations, and other demonftrations of joy thro' the whole city, upon this occafion, the conduits were made to run with wine for eight days.

The K. of Spain, either out of compliment to Colonna, as his high conftable of Naples, or to ingratiate himfelf with Sixtus, fent the bride a jewel worth 8000 crowns.

Befides the large dower which the pope had already given her, he made her hufband a prefent of the Jus patronatûs of feveral abbies, and abolifhed, by a fpecial bull, the cuftom of folemnly excommunicating [11] that family every Holy Thurfday, which had prevailed ever fince the time of Boniface VIII; a circumftance of great honour, which they were never able to obtain before (tho' they had often earneftly folicited it) notwithstanding the many fignal fervices they had done to the crown of Spain, the empire, the church, the H. See, and all Chriftendom.

[11] I cannot find any clear account of this matter.

P p 2   That

That he might likewife be in a capacity to pay his debts, which were large and numerous, and buy fuch eftates and lordfhips as lay convenient for him, he lent him 400,000 crowns out of the Apoftolic Chamber, for ten years, without intereft. Certain it is, that this match preferved the family of Colonna from abfolute ruin and deftruction.

As he had fucceeded fo well in marrying one of his nieces, he thought he had as much reafon to hope he might difpofe of the other, whofe name was Flavia, in a manner equally advantageous; efpecially as it was an honour afpired to by many of the principal nobility. The only difficulty refulting from the number of fuitors. Gregory Buon Compagnon, duke of Sora, nephew to Gregory XIII, demanded her for his eldeft fon: But Sixtus would not liften to his propofals, as he had no refpect for that family, fince the ill ufage he met with, both from Gregory himfelf and cardinal St. Sixtus, whilft he was at the head of affairs in his uncle's pontificate.

The next that offered himfelf was Frederick Savelli, to whofe perfonal merit and family there could be no objection; but when his eftate came to be examined, it was found to be much incumbered, and his debts fo large that her dower was not fufficient to pay them off.

At laft Virginius Orfino was fixed upon, who had a yearly eftate of 100,000 crowns, free from all manner of debt, and of a family that none could ftand in competition with, except that of Colonna: As it was thought fuch an alliance betwixt thofe two great houfes would ftrengthen and aggrandize them both, to him fhe was given, with a dower equal to that of her fifter, and the marriage celebrated with no lefs fplendor, to the infinite fatisfaction of the pope, and Donna Camilla.

If he was thus generous to his nieces, he was much more fo to his nephew Michael Peretti, the only male heir that was left to propagate his name

and

and family: As he had already fufficiently enriched
the cardinal, with large benefices and other honourable appointments, he now purchafed the principality
of Venetro, the marquifate of Lamentada, and the *
county, or countfhip, of Celano for his brother, and
gave him an eftate of 60,000 crowns per annum,
with two fuperb palaces, one in the country and the
other at Rome, both furnifhed in a regal manner:
And it was computed, that at the death of his
uncle, he was worth in ready money and jewels,
above 300,000 crowns. He was married very
young to a princefs of the Colonna family, of great
beauty and accomplifhments. The iffue of this marriage, that lived, was only a fon, and a daughter,
who married prince Savelli, hereditary grand marfhal of the church; luckily for that family, as fhe
lived to be fole heir to her own.

The fon, Francis Peretti, lived as a layman till
the death of his uncle the cardinal, who enjoyed an
annual revenue of above 40,000 crowns, from fome
abbies that Sixtus had given him, which were to
defcend at his death to the next heir of the Peretti
family that was qualified to hold them. When that
happened, he went into orders, and took upon him
the ecclefiaftical habit, for the fake of keeping fo
much preferment in the family, and affumed the
title of abbot Peretti. His uncle left him above
400,000 crowns more in money, &c. When the
prince his father died, he became the richeft prelate that ever was in the church. He was a great
partifan of Spain, from which crown he received,
in penfions and benefices, 50,000 crowns per annum.
It was computed, that the whole of his income a-
mounted to the yearly fum of 180,000 crowns.
Tho' he was but an abbot, he had a court like a
prince, and was much more followed and efteemed
than any prelate or cardinal in Rome. Some thought
he would have quitted the ecclefiaftical habit to
keep up the name of Peretti, and put on the mi-

* Contado.

litary

litary; but he did not much trouble himfelf about pofterity, and feemed rather to aim at the purple.

The K. of Spain created him fuperintendant general of all his affairs in Italy; fo that the governor of Milan, the viceroys of Sicily, Naples, and Sardinia, and the ambaffadors at the court of Rome, in a manner, depended upon him: He was afterwards named by that king for a hat; but the two Barbarini's did not care to have one in the college, that would have fo much outfhined them; and as Peretti did not fhew them a great deal of refpect, whilft he was only an abbot, they concluded he would fhew them ftill lefs when he came to be cardinal. This hindered his promotion above fix years, as Urban would not create any upon that account, tho' he was moft earneftly folicited by the K. of Spain: His holinefs, however, was forced to comply at laft, and he was made cardinal-prieft by that pontiff retaining the name of Peretti; and without doubt, if he had lived, would have been one of the greateft and moft powerful cardinals that Rome ever faw; but he died within two years after his exaltation to the purple, poifoned, as it was fuppofed by thofe that envied him. He made his fifter, that was married to prince Savelli, his heir, without which acquifition of fortune, that family muft inevitably have been ruined, their debts amounting to above a million of crowns. In him ended the name of Peretti: Such was the rife, progrefs, and extinction of that family.

End of the TENTH BOOK.

THE

L I F E

O F

Pope SIXTUS the Fifth.

BOOK THE ELEVENTH.

SIXTUS began the laft year of his pontificate, with a piece of very rough behaviour to
count Olivarez, without the leaft regard to the law
of nations, or thofe privileges, of which he himfelf
was fo ftrenuous an affertor, when his own minifters were infulted by any other power. As the
count grew every day more difagreeable to him,
and he had a mind to put a flight upon the K. of
Spain, in the perfon of his ambaffador, and let him
fee that he neither feared nor refpected him, he
fent an exprefs to the court of Spain the firft day
of the new year, and the next day a mafter of
the ceremonies, to acquaint the count, " That he
" did not intend to acknowledge him, for the fu-
" ture, as ambaffador, and defired he would not
" appear at court in any other character than
" that of a private perfon, much lefs prefume to
" concern himfelf in public affairs; and that he
" had wrote to the king his mafter to let him
" know of it, and defire he would fend another
" ambaffador to the court of Rome in his ftead."
This arbitrary way of proceeding occafioned much
whifpering at court; and the next day Pafquin appeared with a pair of boots and fpurs, and a whip
in his hand; and being afked by Marforio, " Whither

" ther he was going," anfwered, " To carry this
" new year's gift from his Holinefs to count Oliva-
" rez ;" and the day after, with a letter directed " to
" count Olivarez late ambaffador from the K. of
" Spain at the court of Rome." It is remarkable,
that in lefs than five years, he banifhed the French
king's ambaffador from his court, and deprived
the K. of Spain's of his character; two events that
hardly ever happened before or fince at any any other
court.

K. Phillip bore this affront without the leaft feeming refentment ; either becaufe he was confcious he
had been to blame in threatning to fummon a
council in Spain, or had not a mind to have any
more quarrels with the pope ; or thought the count
was not a fit perfon to refide there ; or was willing to comply with his defire of being recalled:
Whatever was the reafon, he ordered him to come
away, and fent the duke of Seffa in his room, a
nobleman of great abilities, mature judgment, and
far advanced in years.

When Sixtus heard of it, he faid, " The K. of
" Spain was pleafed to fend us a beardlefs ambaf-
" fador in the firft year of our pontificate, but now
" he has fent us one with beard enough." To underftand the humour of this, it is neceffary to inform the reader, that upon the affumption of Sixtus, the king fent the high conftable of Caftile,
the firft nobleman in his kingdom, but very young,
as ambaffador extraordinary, to congratulate his
holinefs upon that occafion. Sixtus either being affronted at his fending fo young a perfon, or defirous to do fomething that would make himfelf
talked of, faid to the conftable, when he was introduced to his firft audience, " Are the dominions
" of your mafter fo thin of fubjects, that he can-
" not find a perfon fit for an ambaffador, with a
" beard fomething larger than this?" And (as he
fpoke) took him gently by the chin.

The

The conftable not at all difconcerted, fmartly anfwered, "If the king my mafter had been a-" ware, holy father, that merit confifted in a great "beard, as your Holinefs feems to think, he "would have fent 'you a ram-goat for his am-" baffador, and not a nobleman of my quality "and diftinction." With which repartee he was fo well pleafed, that he grew very fond of the conftable, and fhewed him great honour all the while he ftayed at Rome.

The K. of Spain was at this time fo entangled in the affairs of France, and the Low Countries, that he had not leifure to attend to any thing elfe, which we may look upon as another reafon why he bore the repeated provocations and affronts he met with from the court of Rome, fo patiently. And Sixtus, for his part always attentive to his own intereft, was not a little glad to fee his hands fo full, to the great confumption of his treafure and forces.

The world imagined it was by his fecret infti-gation, that Queen Elizabeth of England fent a ftrong fquadron to Lifbon, in favour of Anthony K. of Portugal (tho' it did not anfwer) to find him employment in feveral places at once, as he thought that would prevent him from fending any troops to oppofe him in his defigns upon Naples, which he had exceedingly fet his heart upon, and was daily taking meafures to put in execution, mak-ing all manner of preparations for that purpofe, with as much fecrefy as poffible, at Civita Vechia, fill-ing his arfenals and magazines with every kind of provifions, arms, and ammunitions; and raifing im-menfe fums of money by various expedients, with incredible diligence, often faying, "That all enter-" prizes ought to be built upon foundations of "gold."

The duke of Savoy marched this year, with the greateft part of his army, into Provence, being called thither by the parliament of that place to defend them

them againſt K. Henry, and was acknowledged by them, not only as a governor, but as their ſovereign. In the mean time the Genevefe, under the command of Lubrigni, whom K. Henry had ſent to be their general, made terrible inroads into the duke's territories, having beat the Savoyards, facked the city of Monthoufe, demolifhed the caſtle of Baſtia, taken the ſtrong fortreſs of Cluſa, and laid waſte the country for many miles round.

The ducheſs Catharine, who was daughter to K. Philip, though ſhe was much rejoiced to hear of the duke her huſband's extraordinary ſucceſs in Provence could not help being ſenſibly mortified at the cruel devaſtation the Genevefe had made in Savoy, and the ſtill greater dangers ſhe was threatened with : She therefore, as regent of ſtate, in her huſband's abſence, wrote to Sixtus, and repreſented to him, " the abſolute ne- " ceſſity there was to exert himſelf vigorouſly in the " common cauſe of religion; as the Proteſtants, not " content with the terrible havoc they were making, " had ſcattered the feeds of hereſy quite through her " dominions : So that if his Holineſs did not ſend her " ſpeedy and effectual aſſiſtance, he might very ſoon " expect to receive further accounts of their ſucceſs, " nay, perhaps, of their paſſing the Alps."

Sixtus was not very well pleaſed at the duke's going into Provence, with a deſign to make himſelf maſter of it, without having communicated any part of his ſcheme to him, ſo that he gave but little attention to the remonſtrances of the ducheſs, and anſwered coolly, " That if her father, who had ſo many kingdoms, " abandoned her, how could ſhe expect any aſſiſtance " from him that had only one, and that hardly ſufficient " to ſupport his own dignity; that the duke her huſ- " band was too ambitious and enterprizing, and did " not ſeem to remember the old proverb, * He that " covets all, generally loſes all.

But

* Chi tutto vuol, tutto perdo.

But what perplexed Sixtus the moſt, and gave him the greateſt uneaſineſs, was the conduct of the league in France: As he clearly ſaw the king of Spain's deſign in intereſting himſelf ſo much in the diſturbances of that kingdom, was (when he had deſtroyed the K. of Navarre) to make himſelf maſter of it, either by ſome marriage or election, or downright force of arms: For which purpoſe he had cauſed Farneſe, with infinite peril and fatigue, to march out of the Low Countries to the aſſiſtance of the Pariſians. This made him ſtill more unwilling to eſpouſe the cauſe of the league, as it was, in fact, only carrying on the deſigns of K. Philip: On the other hand, it galled him to be railed at by all the Catholics in Europe, who could not penetrate into the ſecret ſprings of his actions, as negligent and unconcerned in the intereſts of their religion in France.

But the heads of the league were the loudeſt in their complaints, as we may ſee in the following letter, from the duke of Main, ſent by an expreſs to the pope, which he at firſt intended to have communicated to the cardinals, in conſiſtory, but afterwards altered his reſolution, as he knew many of them were ſtrongly attached to the Spaniſh intereſt.

Most Holy Father,

"IT is with the deepeſt concern, we are informed
" from ſeveral hands, that your Holineſs has
" changed the reſolution you had once ſo piouſly taken,
" of ſending a ſupply of men and money to the aſſiſt-
" ance of the Catholic arms in this kingdom, and the
" ſupport of cardinal Bourbon, our true and lawful ſo-
" vereign. We are utterly at a loſs to know what
" can have diverted your Holineſs from ſo righteous
" and ſalutary a meaſure, as our intentions have always
" been pure and void of all manner of guile and hy-
" pocriſy: Nor can any one pretend to ſay we ever
" had any other deſign in our actions, than the glory
" of God, the welfare of the kingdom, and the preſervation

" fervation of our holy religion. The Almighty God,
" that omnifcient Being, to whom all hearts are open,
" knows that I never fought any other glory or rewaid,
" than to difcharge my confcience in that refpect, and
" to be inftrumental in bringing about fo defirable an
" event.

" But when the intention and actions of our ene-
" mies, the K. of Navarre and his adherents, fhall be
" truly reprefented to your Holinefs, you will eafily
" perceive (as indeed it is not poffible to conceal it)
" that his immutable refolution is to extirpate the Ro-
" man Catholic religion, and eftablifh the abominable
" herefy, in which he has been brought up from his
" infancy. And we think it is fufficiently manifeft to
" all the world, from his way of proceeding, fome-
" times by force, at others, by artifice, endeavouring
" to gain time and amufe us, by fpecious pretences,
" whilft he is affifted (to their eternal fhame and infamy
" be it fpoken) by thofe who vilely betray the caufe of
" the religion which they profefs, that he intends,
" when he is firmly feated on the throne, to make an
" open and public declaration of his wicked purpofe,
" and compel us to obedience.

" As to the fuccours we had fo juft reafon to expect,
" if your Holinefs at any time judged them neceffary,
" they certainly were never more fo than at prefent :
" Which infpires us with hope, that your inclination
" to affift us will increafe in proportion to the number
" and greatnefs of our diftreffes; when your Holinefs
" recollects that you formerly approved of our caufe as
" good and juft, when we took up arms againft a king,
" apparently Catholic, and to whom nothing could
" be objected but conjectures and fufpicion of his evil
" intentions, before the murder at Blois, you will cer-
" tainly think yourfelf under much ftronger obligations
" to countenance us at this time, as the perfon who
" now pretends to the crown is a pofeffed Heretic,
" whom your Holinefs has long declared excommuni-
" cate and incapable of fucceeding to it, to encourage
all

" all true Catholics to oppofe him, and quiet their fcru-
" ples, with the affurance that they have acted as be-
" came good Chriftians, when they took up arms a-
" gainft him, as we have done, bravely expofing our
" lives and fortunes to maintain a good confcience.
" We cannot therefore fuffer ourfelves to entertain the
" leaft doubt, that your Holinefs can think of chang-
" ing a meafure fo deliberately weighed, fo mature-
" ly digefted by yourfelf and the whole college of
" cardinals; and that you will abandon us after the
" many folemn and reiterated promifes to the con-
" trary.

" We humbly intreat your Holinefs to recall to your
" memory the great fervices done by this kingdom to
" the H. See, how well it has deferved, and of what
" fatal confequences the abolition of the true religion
" here, of fo many noble foundations and other il-
" luftrious monuments of piety, with which it abounds,
" would be to Chriftianity; which muft infallibly be
" the cafe, if we are not very foon and very effectually
" affifted; and hope you will be pleafed to confider,
" that a fmall part of the immenfe treafure, which the
" world fays your Holinefs has accumulated, cannot
" be laid out in any thing that will make your name
" more glorious to pofterity, than affording us your
" fatherly aid and protection in this perilous conjunc-
" ture.

" There are fome, we doubt not, who will endea-
" vour to make your Holinefs believe, the king of
" Navarre is well affected to our holy religion, and
" will turn Catholic : But what has he done to induce
" us ever to expect fo bleffed a change ? Has he not
" deluded the hope of the Catholics, by various pre-
" tences, of conforming at a ftated time, fixed by him-
" felf, and, after that had elapfed, ftill appointed ano-
" ther and another? taking all methods, in thofe in-
" tervals, to ftrengthen himfelf and eftablifh his affairs,
" as he does every day, whilft our friends ftand at a
" diftance looking at us with unconcern, and your
" Holinefs thinks it fufficient to be only a fpectator of
our

" our calamities, without offering to adminifter any
" remedy.

" But admitting he fhould make a fhew of returning
" into the bofom of the church; what can we expect
" from fuch a pretended converfion, but that he will
" make ufe of it as a means to promote his deftructive
" fchemes, and bring about the total change of. re-
" ligion he has fo long meditated ? The legate, whom
" your Holinefs has fent into France, we acknowl dge
" as a man of great zeal and piety, as well as pru-
" dence, and has had fufficient time to inform himfelf
" of the evil cafe we are reduced to, and the nature
" of the remedies that are proper to be applied to our
" wounds, if he pleafes to acquaint your Holinefs with
" them.

" However, that we may not be wanting to our-
" felves, and in order to clear our confciences before
" God and man, humbly befeeching your Holinefs
" will not be offended, as it is our duty, and to dif-
" charge the laft part of our obligation, we folemnly
" and publicly proteft in the face of Chriftendom, that
" apprehending ourfelves to be deferted by all other
" friends, we make this our final application to your
" Holinefs, that it may be remembered in future times,
" and teach pofterity to lay the blame where it is
" properly due, without accufing us who deferve it
" not.

" We are informed, H. father, that the K. of Na-
" varre's forces have been fo magnified, that your
" Holinefs is apprehenfive whatever fuccour you fend
" us will be ufelefs and infignificant, and that it
" would be better to give way to the neceffity of the
" times, than to provoke him to no purpofe. But
" thefe advices came from fuch as are either ill affect-
" ed to us, or unacquainted with the ftate and con-
" dition of our affairs. It is true he met with fome
" little fuccefs about eight days ago (which God per-
" mitted as a punifhment of our fins) and that he
" has gained one battle in which we loft many men.
" We have fent a memorial by our ambaffador, to
be

" be prefented to your Holinefs, in which you will
" fee the reafons that moved us to come to an en-
" gagement, with the advice and opinion of all our
" principal officers, the meafures whereby we hope
" to retrieve our affairs, and to convince your Holi-
" nefs, that we have left nothing unattempted, that
" could be expected or defired from good and con-
" fcientious men; humbly thanking God that there
" is no room to reproach us with omitting any thing
" that we thought could tend to his glory.

" We are not without apprehenfions, H. Fa-
" ther, that the lofs of this battle may be at-
" tended with fome further ill confequences, and
" afraid the ill grounded report of the K. of Na-
" varre's ftrength and our weaknefs, which before
" prevented your Holinefs from fending us any affif-
" tance may now have a greater weight with you. But
" we can affure you and (humbly entreat your Holi-
" nefs fo believe what we fay) that there are fo ma-
" ny worthy men of every quality and degree,
" ecclefiaftics, nobility, and gentry, fo many ci-
" ties and provinces refolved to live and die to-
" gether in this caufe, and whofe courage is rather
" increafed than abated, by the late inconfiderable
" defeat; that our enemy cannot yet boaft of an
" equality with us, if we are countenanced by your
" holinefs, and you will fhew us that you are
" in earneft in your endeavours to root out and ex-
" tinguifh all Heretics and their followers, to which
" you are more particularly obliged than any other
" perfon, as head of the church; and ought not to be
" carried away by the too refined reafonings of thofe
" weakfighted politicians, who would perfuade you
" that our fuccefs will be ftill throwing weight in-
" to the fcale of Spain, already too powerful. The
" care of religion ought to prevail over all word-
" ly confiderations, and we folemnly declare our-
" felves ftrangers to any other view of the K. of
" Spain, but that of preferving the Holy Catho-
" lic Faith pure and uncorrupted in this kingdom.
" If

" If we pretend therefore to any fort of goodnefs
" or virtue, to the character of religious men, and
" Chriftians, he ought to be for ever dear to us and
" our pofterity, and we fhould reflect, with tears of
" gratitude in our eyes, on his unwearied endeavours
" for the prefervation of our religion, the laws and
" liberties of our country.

" But if this fufpicion has had fo fatal an influence,
" as to prevail upon your Holinefs, to forfake us in
" the midft of the difafters and calamities that gather
" round us on every fide, at a time when we moft of
" all ftand in need of your protection, and make us
" acknowledge ourfelves obliged to that monarch for
" our lives and fortunes, and our altars, we know
" very well it is the only one that has been inftilled
" into your Holinefs, and that I in particular have
" been reprefented as an ambitious man, feeking my
" own intereft and advancement in the confufions of
" the public, which I foment under the facred name of
" patriotifm, and concern for religion. But I folemn-
" ly proteft to your Holinefs, I fhall at any time moft
" willingly refign my command, and retire to the
" condition of a private fubject, whenever you pleafe
" to order me, and the public good requires it; and be
" ever ready to fhew a chearful obedience to any per-
" fon that will protect and maintain the Catholic
" faith.

" Let our entreaties and fupplications, therefore,
" Holy father, have their due weight, and prevail
" upon you to follow your firft refolution of fuc-
" couring us with fuch a fupply of men and money
" as fhall feem moft proper to your confummate wif-
" dom and affection; for which we are ready to give
" you any fecurity that you can expect. If your Holi-
" nefs will be pleafed to grant this, it will excite other
" Catholic princes to follow your noble example, to the
" common advantage of all Chriftendom, the utter
" confufion of Heretics, and the eternal glory of our
                                        pontificate.

" pontificate. But if you deny it, the tears and la-
" mentations of so many millions of perfecuted Ca-
" tholics will pierce Heaven, and cry day and night
" against thofe that have been the occafion of their
" misfortunes.

" We, for our parts, however, fhall continue to
" exert ourfelves to the laft drop of our deareft heart's
" blood, in the fupport of this righteous caufe, in
" which, if it fhall pleafe God that we lofe our lives,
" we fhall die at leaft with the comfortable reflection
" of having preferved our confciences pure and im-
" maculate.

" So kiffing your Holinefs's feet with all humility,
" we fhall never ceafe to pray the Almighty to blefs
" your days with peace and profperity, for the good of
" his church and this poor diftracted kingdom.

" I am, Holy Father,
        " (in the name of the confederate
            " Catholics of France)
Soiffons, March 20,   " Your moft humble, moft
        1590.   " obedient and moft dutiful
                    " Son and Servant,
    "CHARLES of LORRAIN, Duke of Main."

Sixtus returned a very affectionate anfwer to this
letter, but in general terms and made them fome
promifes, which it is thought he never intended to
perform ; for though his zeal was great in the propagation of the Catholic religion, yet was he, for the
moft part, governed by maxims of ftate and political confiderations : He was highly difpleafed at Philip,
for ordering his clergy to preach up, every where,
the neceffity of fuccouring the league againft king
Henry, and to animadvert upon the unwillingnefs he
himfelf fhewed to give them any affiftance ; and being informed that Panigarola, the moft eloquent
preacher of thofe times, who attended cardinal Caietan into France, had been fet on to enflame the
minds of the people, by declaiming very feverely
            Qq   againft

againſt Henry wherever he came [1], he ordered him back to Rome, pretending a deſire to have him for his own preacher.

Sixtus ſaw very plainly that the Proteſtants in gene-ral, both in France and elſewhere, intereſted themſelves warmly in the cauſe of Henry, and ſent him large ſup-plies, that the Catholics were divided, and that ſuch as were averſe to the Spaniſh dominion, and could not bear the thoughts of ſeeing their own kingdom diſmembered, entirely leaned on his ſide; and as he was well convinced of the valour and prudence of Henry, he had little hope from the league, and rightly judged, it could not ſubſiſt long, but muſt moulder away, notwithſtanding any ſuccour that might be gi-ven to it.

That he might not therefore be teazed any longer, by the Spaniards and heads of the league, he at laſt took off the maſk, and declared publicly, " That the more he conſidered the affairs of France, " the more reaſon he ſaw every day to change the " reſolution he had once formed of favouring the " league; that Henry was too wiſe and powerful a " prince not to maintain his right, and the laws of " the kingdom, which were clearly on his ſide; that " indeed it was his misfortune more than any body's " elſe to be a Heretic, but that his converſion was " not to be deſpaired of; that the ſeeing himſelf in

[1] Præcipua vero concionatorum intemperies fuit, qui, omiſſa verbi dominici, interpretatione, bacchantibus ſimiles, conviciorum plauſtra in regem evomebant dicenda, tacenda, blaterantes; tyrannum, hypocritam, perfidum, crudelem, vocitantes, ad rau-cedinem uſque clamoſi : quorum exemplo etiam pædagogi, et hujuſmodi rancida ſcholaſtici pulveris purgamenta, miſeros ac ridiculos verſus, ſeu rhythmos balbutiebant, five in regis oppro-brium, five in defunctorum laudes. His accedebant libelli inep-tiſſimi de martyrio fratrum, cum imaginibus eorum inſcitè pictis. Nec contenti libris, eorundem effigies, juſtâ hominis menſurâ, ad pulvinaria templorum quotidie fiſtebant, ſan guinolentas et pallore violentæ mortis horridas, additi et libelli nugamentis calumnioſe confictis ad faſtidium in regem referti quibus iram plebis credulæ ad rabiem acuebant. Thuan. lib. xciv.

" poſſeſſion

" poffeffion of a kingdom that had always been the
" great fupport and bulwark of the Catholic faith,
" might prevail upon him to return to the religion of
" his anceftors; that, upon the whole, he thought it
" was more prudent and Chriftian like, to endeavour
" to win him over by mild and gentle meafures, than
" to drive him from the fold, perhaps for ever, by
" fuch as were violent and compulfory."

At the end of the laft year, and the beginning of
this, the rains were fo violent that every one began
to think there would be a fecond deluge; the Tiber
twice overflowed its banks with fuch impetuofity, that
moft part of the city lay under water; the people were
forced to pafs from one houfe to another in boats: The
damage that was done to churches, palaces, and reli-
gious-houfes, exceeded computation.

This calamity was not peculiar to Rome, there was
not a river in Italy that did not flood the adjacent
country, to the immenfe lofs and almoft ruin of the
inhabitants: What added to the misfortune was,
that thefe exceffive rains were attended with very boi-
fterous and tempeftuous winds, which blew down feveral public buildings, and fo damaged the lands, that
they were fowed three or four times with corn before
they produced any crop. After this, the wind fetting
in from the South, for a confiderable time occafioned the
moft unhealthful feafon, and the fevereft famine that
had ever been known in the memory of man. Tho'
it raged all over Italy, Rome and the adjacent country
fuffered the moft, as Sixtus had been more intent upon
filling the treafury, than the magazines. It feems hard
to believe, tho' nothing is more true, that a pound of
coarfe bread was fold for 13 * Julios, and difficult to be
got at that price. Many were found ftarved in the high-
ways and fields, with herbs and roots in their mouths:
there were nothing fo bad but it was eat: The flefh
of affes, dogs, cats, and mice, was reckoned a de-
licacy.

* About 6s 6d.

Tho'

Tho' the famine was fo fevere, it is remarkable there was not the leaft theft or robbery committed in the city; people chufing rather to die of hunger, than end their days upon a gallows, as they were fure to do if they were detected: So great an awe had the rigour of Sixtus impreffed upon their minds.

To make a trial of their honefty, he caufed a waggon-load of bread to be brought to Rome, from a place that was a good diftance off; and tho' it was met by thoufands of poor people that were ready to perifh, upon the road, not one of them offered to ftop the cart, or touch the bread: Whereas, if it had happened in the late pontificate, they would very likely have eat the bread and horfes too. He was much affected with this terrible judgment as it obliged him not only to excufe the people their taxes, but to lend them money, which he did, very fparingly however, tho' he had already depofited five millions of crowns in his treafury at St. Angelo, of which he lent the † city chamber 500,000, for the ufe of the poor, to be repaid in three years.

Notwithftanding the affairs of France had taken up fo much of his attention, he was not, in the mean time, forgetful or remifs in doing any thing that might conduce to the welfare and good government of his own fubjects, continually either amending the old laws, or making new ones for that purpofe.

As he had taken notice of the prodigious degree of luxury and extravagance that reigned at that time in Rome, he ordered cardinal Aldobrandino to confider of proper means to reftrain all exceffes of that kind, and publifhed a fumptuary law, with fevere penalties againft fuch as fhould dare to tranfgrefs it. It was thought, his intention in making this law, was only to raife money by fines upon the offenders: But it was fo well obeyed, that during the fpace of fome months, which he lived after the

† *Communita dello flato.*

publication

publication of it, nobody incurred the penalty, every one obferving the greateft decency and modefty in their dreſs.

He gave the reformation of the Conventuals in charge to the fame cardinal, with ftrict orders to inform him of all the abuſes that had crept into' the religious houſes, and to think of neceſſary remedies. His intention was to fupprefs feveral orders, and keep up only thoſe that ſtood upon great and ancient foundations, or had maintained their original purity, and lived up to the defign of the founder. For which purpoſe he had fevcral confe-.rences with him; but death feized him in the midſt of his great undertakings, and prevented this good defign.

So exactly and impartially had. he adminiftered juftice to his fubjects, that there is hardly an inſtance of his pardoning a criminal of any degree. It gave him a particular pleafure to bring hidden crimes to light, and punifh fuch as were thought long ago forgot, with the utmoſt feverity. On the other hand, he ftrenuoufly defended the rights of the poor, the deftitute, the widow and fatherlefs, nobly fupporting the majefty of the tribunals. In fhort, he had wrought fuch a reformation in Rome, that the governor told him one day, "The place of a judge " was now become a perfect fineeure." To which he anfwered, " That if he thought the people would " relapfe into their former licentioufnefs, after he " was dead, he would hang them all whilft he was " alive."

He was very eafy of accefs, and refuſed audience to nobody, ordering his mafters of the ceremonies .to introduce the pooreft to him fiift : But was more particularly ready to hear fuch as brought any accuſation againft their magiftrates or governors, and made them explain every minute particular of their complaint. The fame conduct he obferved betwixt the clergy and their fuperiors, always applying quick and effectual, tho' moſtly very fevere remedies.

dies. But he never liftened to any one that complained of taxes and duties, which amounted to 40
in number, as he himfelf had impofed them. Thefe
were collected by officers appointed for that purpofe,
with fo much vigour and exactnefs, that there was
not a day, beyond the time fixed, allowed for the
payment of them, to the great impoverifhment of
the ecclefiaftical ftate.

He indulged his fubjects in a great deal of liberty
at the time of the Carnival [2], permitting them to
divert themfelves with feafts, balls, comedies, mafquerades, and public fpectacles: And this not only in Rome, but quite thro' his dominions, giving
orders to all the governors of cities and provinces
to do the fame. Some have faid that his defign in
this was to lay a temptation in people's way of tranf-
greffing his edicts (as it was natural enough to expect) amidft the revelling and diffipation of thought
that is ufual at fuch times. But this is doing him
great injuftice, and accufing him of a mean defign
that never entered into his heart, as plainly appears
from his ordering whipping pofts in the * ftreet
where the races are run, and moft of the fhews ex-
hibited, for the punifhment of thofe who fhould dare
to interrupt the public diverfions, or occafion any
difturbance. He condemned a poor taylor to the
gallies, only for giving a box on the ear to another
perfon of the fame occupation, tho' he was employed
in the fervice of his houfhold; and a footman belonging to cardinal Sorbelloni to be whipped, for

[2] Carnival or Carnaval, is a feafon of mirth and rejoicing,
obferved with great folemnity all over Italy, particularly by the
Venetians. The Italian word is Carnavale, which Du Cange
derives from Carn a val, i. e. from the flefh then going plentifully
to the pot, to make amends for the enfuing feafon of abftinence.
He obferves that in the corrupt Latin, it was called Carne leva-
men, and Carnis fprivium; and the Spaniards ftill call it Car-
nes tollendas. It commences from the twelfth day, and continues
till lent, during which time there is nothing to be feen or heard
of, but feafts, balls, operas, mafquerades, concerts of mufic, intrigues, marriages, &c.

having

having faid fomething obfcene to a woman, tho' fhe
did not make any complaint of it herfelf. As foon
as Sorbelloni heard of the fentence, he went to intercede for his fervant, but came too late, for he had
already undergone the punifhment.

It was owing to fuch neceffary feverities, that in
the five Carnivals that were celebrated, whilft Sixtus was pope, there was not the leaft riot or difturbance, but every thing carried on with the higheft
decorum, to the infinite fatisfaction of all the people.

Others were of opinion, and certainly had a greater degree of probability on their fide; that having
loaded his fubjects fo heavily with taxes and impofitions, he thought, in fome meafure, to take off
their fting, by allowing them a proper indulgence
in pleafures of this kind; a piece of policy not unworthy of imitation.

Whilft cardinal, he was remarkably temperate
and abftemious in his diet (if he did not regale
himfelf in private) making a great fhew of fafting
and mortification; but when he came to be pope,
he took more liberty in that refpect, and made
hearty meals, tho' he did not keep a very expenfive
table, or fuffer it to be fpread with much variety.
He had many different forts of the moft exquifite
wines, of which he would drink pretty freely at dinner [3], but never fo as to be intoxicated, tho' he
called for a glafs betwixt almoft every mouthful.

In bufinefs he was indefatigable, and took the management of every thing, even affairs of the minuteft confequence, wholly into his own hands. It was
thought that being exhaufted by this inceffant labour,
was the occafion of his eating fo plentifully, as fuch a
confumption of fpirits muft naturally require a proportionable fupply of food and nutriment; efpecially
as he was obferved to be fo moderate whilft he was a

[3] *Vino nivem femper infundens*; " Always putting fnow into
his wine." *Thuan.* lib. c.

cardinal

cardinal, and led a fedentary, inactive life; tho' fome think (as he diffembled in almoft every thing elfe) this was all hypocrify and grimace.

His brain was fo conftantly employed that it was never at reft, except it may be' faid to be fo in the few hours that he allowed himfelf for fleep. He talked much, particularly at his meals, where he would fit fometimes two hours or more, unlefs he had any af- fairs of great importance upon his hands; for then he eat his meat ftanding, and in a hafty manner; or if he had fat down to the table, it was but for a few minutes. He flept little, and had no ftated time of going to bed. When he had any very urgent bufi- nefs, he fat up all night, without ever clofing his eyes, or taking the leaft repofe: At other times, when there was nothing to be done, he would lie till late in the morning: But always gave orders, that if any thing unforfeen happened, or any courier extra- ordinary arrived in the night, he fhould be immedi- ately called, tho' he was but juft gone to fleep; and was once very angry with his chamberlain for not in- forming him of the arrival of a courier in the night, with letters from his legate at Bologna; and faid, " We were not made for fleep, but fleep for us."

It was his cuftom to rebuke thofe feverely that had difobeyed his orders, or otherwife difpleafed him in their conduct. However, when he reprimanded a perfon of any account, he would fuffer him to de- fend himfelf; and was pleafed if he did it in fuch a manner as did not border either upon meannefs or impudence : for tho' he defpifed fuch as had not fpi- rit enough to vindicate themfelves modeftly, when they were accufed, he would not bear with thofe that were guilty of the leaft infolence or difrefpect.

He often flew into paffions with his officers and de- meftics, and would fometimes rate them, even in the prefence of ambaffadors and cardinals; but was very kind to them in the main; tho' he ftrictly or- dered them never to afk any favour to the prejudice

of

of juſtice, or injury of any other perſon; declaring, "He would take care to reward their ſervices him-ſelf, in a proper manner." And indeed he was very liberal and munificent in this reſpect, making ſome biſhops, and others archbiſhops: Three of them he promoted to the purple, of which number was John Baptiſt Caſtruccio, of Lucca, whom he had often treated very harſhly, and in a rough manner, tho' he had ſerved him many years with great fidelity.

But if he was kind to, and rewarded thoſe, that had behaved themſelves well, in an extraordinary manner, he puniſhed ſuch as were guilty of any miſdemeanor very ſeverely, and without the leaſt regard to their paſt ſervices, which made them exceedingly cautious how they offended him.

His affection to Donna Camilla, and his other relations, was very great, and he enriched them all, as we have before related; in ſuch a manner however, that the world could not upbraid him with having plundered the church, as many of his predeceſſors had done.

The ſelling of places, which uſed before to be given away by the popes to their dependents and followers, was firſt introduced by him; ſuch as the commiſſaries and treaſurers of the Apoſtolic Chamber, and that of the vice-chamberlain, which are the moſt important, with many others.

Cardinal Caſtagna, who was in great favour with the pope, thinking this cuſtom would bring a ſcandal upon the H. See, gave him his opinion of it very freely, and in a few words. Upon which Sixtus ſaid, "Is it reaſonable that we ſhould pay our ſervants "before-hand? I ſhall put an end to that ridiculous "practice, and make thoſe people pay for it that "are ambitious of ſerving us; and we ſhould adviſe "you to do the ſame when you fill our place." for he ſeemed to be perſuaded, from the beginning of his pontificate, that Caſtagna would ſucceed him; and upon that account always treated him with great

reſpect,

refpect, confulting him in the moft important affairs. He appointed him commiffary of three congregations, viz. that of the H. Office, that which determines the difputes betwixt bifhops and regulars, and that which was inftituted for the redrefs of grievances, endeavouring by this to give him all the proofs he could of the fincerity of his efteem, and to induce him to take his nephews and relations under his protection when he was dead. He told him feveral times he was fure he would be his fucceffor; and faid to him one time, when they were talking of the ftreet he was building, which begins at the church di Sante Croce, and paffing by St. Maria Maggiore, ends at that of Trinità de' Monti, " I leave that for you to finifh." A few days before he died, there being fome fruit upon the table after dinner, he took a pear, but finding it rotten within, he cut another that was not much better, upon which he threw it down, and faid, with fome emotion, " I Romani fano fatii delle pere, " onde bifognerà dargli caftagne." If pears will go " down no longer with the Romans, they muft e'en " have chefnuts," punning upon his own name Peretti, and Caftagna, that of the cardinal; the former of which words fignifies pears, the latter a chefnut, in the Italian tongue. Another time joking with him, he faid, "Lord cardinal, when pears go out, " chefnuts come in."

In his drefs he was fo frugal, that he fometimes wore fhirts that were patched and darned, not only whilft he was cardinal, but afterwards when he came to be pope: His fifter finding fault with him one day for it, and telling him how much it was below the dignity of a fovereign pontiff to wear fuch fhabby linen, he anfwered, " Tho' we are exalted, thro' " the favour of Providence, to this high ftation, we " ought never to forget the meannefs of our birth, " and that fhreds and patches are the only coat of " arms our family has any title to." Without doubt he judged very rightly in being thus parfimonious: There was great reafon for it, as he well knew how

neceffary

neceffary money was to carry on any enterprize with fuccefs, and how vaft a fum he fhould have occafion for to accomplifh his great defigns; upon which account he fet himfelf to invent every poffible way of both faving and getting it, from the very firft day that he entered the Vatican.

Hé depofited in the caftle of St. Angelo whatever he could lay up out of his revenue, for the exigencies of ftate, and never gave a fingle farthing of the church's eftate to any of his relations, having it in his power to enrich them fufficiently with eccleliaftical benefices, and other emoluments that are entirely at the pope's difpofal.

It ufed to coft the Apoftolic Chamber 600,000 crowns, communibus annis, in penfions and gratuities, which he entirely cut off: Indeed it caufed great murmuring amongft the courtiers, and could not have been effected by any pope lefs abfolute and peremptory than Sixtus.

He erected feveral banks to lend money at a large intereft, and by that method at the fame time confiderably increafed the revenue of the exchequer. He fplit the offices of chamberlain and auditor of the chamber, to put them in commiffion, and create a new one, called keeper of the archives of the ecclefiaftical ftate, which he immediately fold for a large fum of money.

In the firft year of his pontificate he laid up a million of gold in his treafury at St. Angelo, and made a conftitution which he caufed to be figned by all the cardinals; wherein they were ftrictly forbid to touch it, except upon the following occafions, and not even then, unlefs there was the utmoft neceffity; firft, to encourage a crufade for the recovery of the Holy Land; in which cafe however they are forbid to difburfe any money, till they have certain advice of the Chriftian army being landed in the country of the Infidels, fecondly, to relieve the people of Rome in the time of fevere famine, or peftilence; thirdly, to fuccour and protect any Chriftian city or province, in

cafe

cafe of imminent danger, againft the attempts of the
common enemy; fourthly, to defend the H. See, if
attacked by any power, either Chriftian or Infidel,
but not till the enemy draws near to the confines of
the ecclefiaftical ftate; and laftly, to recover any
territory that had been taken, or fallen from its obedience to the church.

The pope fwore folemnly to obferve this conftitution himfelf in all refpects, and caufed his oath to
be recorded, enjoining all his fucceffors to take the
fame, as foon as they fhould be elected, and drew
up a large decree for the fame purpofe, which was
figned by him and all the cardinals in a full confiftory.

In the third year of his pontificate he added another million to it, with the like formalities, and to
be employed in the fame ufes, with this alteration,
that if any part of the Holy Land was recovered out
of the hands of the Infidels by the affiftance of this
money, it fhould for the future belong to the church,
or be exchanged for fuch other dominions as lay more
convenient for the Holy See. Cardinal Caftagna, talking to him one day with his ufual freedom, concerning the ufes to which this money was deftined, afked
him, " If it would not be proper to add another
" claufe to the conftitution, allowing the money to
" be applied to the extirpation of Heretics, efpeci-
" ally in France." Sixtus anfwered, " In our ponti-
" ficate, we will lay up money for the prefervation
" of Catholics, which is no inconfiderable point;
" when you come to be pope, let it be your care to
" provide money for the extinction of Herefy, an
" undertaking highly worthy of you, as we can't at-
" tend to two fuch confiderable enterprizes at one
" time."

He made large additions to this treafure every
year, continually renewing the conftitution, and making fuch alterations in it as he thought neceffary;
fo that when he died, there were found five millions
in the cheft, to which he had caufed new bolts and

locks

locks to be made, and ordered, by a fresh decree, that there should be three keys to it, one of them to be kept by the pope, another by the cardinal-dean, and the third by the chamberlain.

It is certain the church had great obligations to this pontiff upon many accounts ; not only for having embellished the city with so many noble edifices, to the great service and glory of the H. See, but for accumulating this treasure, so necessary to the preservation and grandeur of the state. How shameful was it that the common mother of all Christans should be so indigent and necessitous, that she never, till his time, had wherewith to relieve the necessities of her chil dren in their most pressing wants? Instead of complaining of him for loading his people with taxes, for selling offices that had always been given away, and being so great an œconomist in the Vatican, a festival ought yearly to be celebrated to his memory throughout Christendom ; particularly the ecclesiastical state, to the aggrandizing of which he sacrificed all his cares, and made it so puissant and formidable by the immense treasures he left in his coffers, that the subjects of it ought for ever to remember him with gratitude and veneration.

Besides all the great things which we have already mentioned, he likewise established a fund of 200,000 crowns to maintain perpetual plenty in Rome, which he saved out of his own domestic expences, " being " content to live in a penurious manner himself, " that his subjects might enjoy abundance," as it is expressed in one of his bulls, where he exhorts his successors rather to increase than diminish this fund, so highly necessary to the welfare of the people.

It seems incredible, and indeed almost miraculous, that he was able to amass such immense sums of money, considering the circumstances of the times. For in the first place, the people, during his reign, suffered extremely by famine and pestilence : The dominions of the church were not near so large as they are at present ; the two fertile and opulent duchies

of

of Urbino and Ferrara, having been fince added to
them. The French were fo far from being in a condition to furnifh the contributions which the popes
ufed to draw from them that they were continually
importu ing him for affiftance; that kingdom being
involved in civil diftraðions, and full of Proteftants
who did not care a ftraw for the pope, or make the
leaft account of his indulgences and difpenfations.
Germany and Poland were in confufion; the K. of
Spain exhaufted by the lofs of his Armada (not to
mention his continual wars in the low countries) and
England irrecoverably loft.

Thefe are fome of the glories of his reign: When
thefe are recited, they feem to caft a blemifh upon
the conduct of all the pontiffs that have fucceeded
him: For tho' the revenues of the church have been
fince confiderably augmented, and the ecclefiaftical
dominions greatly enlarged by the acceffion of the
two above-mentioned duchies, the offices and places
fold for twice as much, and the taxes full as heavy
as they were in his pontificate, Spain and Portugal
entirely at the devotion of the church, France in a
flourifhing condition, and the Hugonots, then fo numerous in that kingdom, almoft totally extirpated;
And tho' fome of the popes have lived ten, fifteen,
and twenty years, it may be truly affirmed, that all of
them together have not done fo great things, nor
contributed fo much to the power and grandeur of
the Holy See as Sixtus alone in the five years that he
reigned.

The Proteftants reckon it amongft the greateft and
moft remarkable mercies of God towards them, that
he permits the popes to fpoil the church of its treafure, and divide it amongft their nephews and relations, which makes them incapable of attempting
any enterprize of confequence: Whereas, if they
would imitate Sixtus, and lay up five, or four, or if
it was but two millions, in every pontificate, they
might exert themfelves with vigour, to the utter ex-
tinðion of both Infidels and Heretics.

In

In order to give all the luftre and dignity that was poffible to the Holy College, he reformed feveral abu-fes that had crept into it by the favour of certain de-crees and bulls granted by his predeceffors, fome of which he new modelled, totally abolifhing others, as ufelefs and fuperfluous.

He ordained that the number of cardinals fhould not exceed feventy, and this for feveral reafons: Firft, becaufe fome popes had defigned to have made them up a hundred, in imitation of the ancient Ro-mans, whofe fenate confifted of that number, called the centum patres: A conceit which Sixtus defpifed, efpecially as he faw it impoffible to keep up the re-fpect due to that illuftrious body, if they were fo nu-merous. Another reafon was, that he thought when the number was fixed, it would prevent the popes making fo frequent promotions, as they ufed to do, to the great difhonour and reproach of the H. College, by exalting perfons of no merit or character, and thereby making the purple cheap, and of no account in the eyes of the world; as they could not difpofe of a hat, till there was a vacancy by death, or other-ways, amongft the cardinals. At firft he defigned to have reduced the number to fixty, but afterwards altered his refolution; confidering that the number feventy equalled that of the difciples, whom they re-prefented, as he himfelf reprefented Jefus Chrift; which is the principal reafon he affigned in a bull pub-lifhed for their eftablifhment.

He decreed that there fhould always be in the col-lege four doctors in divinity taken out of the Regu-lars and Mendicants, which was but reafonable, as it is well known the Regulars had propagated the Chrif-tian Religion in every part of the globe, and often generoufly laid down their lives to eftablifh the true faith amongft Infidels and Idolaters. Sixtus, who valued himfelf upon rewarding merit of any kind, particularly fervices done to the church, thought himfelf obliged to fhew this teftimony of his gratitude to the religious Mendicants; more efpecially as he
judged

judged it neceffary for the reputation of the H. College to have always fome learned and eminent divines amongft them : His fuccefſois, however, have
ſhewn but little regard to thoſe wiſe inſtitutions, un-
gratefully neglecting and over-looking the poor orders, who are the firmeſt pillars and ſupport of the
Romiſh Church, to ſuch a degree, that at preſent,
there is not one of them honoured with a cardinal's
hat.

He further ordained, that no promotions ſhould be
made at any time but in the ember-week of December:
This cuſtom, eſtabliſhed by Pope Clement I, and obſerved for above 600 years, was renewed by Sixtus,
tho' he broke in upon it twice himſelf, the firſt time
in the creation of cardinal Moroſini, the ſecond by
the promotion of his nephew Montalto, which was in
May. He likewiſe confirmed the decrees of Julius
II, in which it is forbidden to give the hat to two
brothers, and extended the prohibition to a more remote degree of conſanguinity, which, with his reaſons for it, is ſpecified in the bull.

It was a maxim with him always to keep ſome va-
cancies in the college, to be filled upon any emergency ; and in the ſame bull he exhorts his ſuccef-
ſors to do the ſame, that they may at all times have
it in their power to reward particular merit, or eminent ſervices done to the church, or oblige France
or Spain, or other powers, with the nomination to a
hat, in caſe they ſhould have any favour to aſk, or
it ſhould be dangerous to deny them.

During his pontificate he created thirty-three cardinals, at eight different promotions, in the laſt of
which he had ſome thoughts of filling up all the vacan-
cies ; and very likely would have done it, if he had
expected to die ſo ſoon.

As it had been a cuſtom, tho' a ſcandalous one,
amongſt the clergy, and even ſuch as had good benefices, to wear lay-habits, he publiſhed an edict,
commanding all whoſe revenue exceeded 60 crowns
per annum to wear the eccleſiaſtical habit, except
the

the * knights of Loretto, on penalty of being deprived of their revenues ; a reform with which the whole
court and city were much pleafed.

Towards the latter end of his pontificate he marched
a confiderable body of troops to that part of his dominions that borders upon Naples, giving out that
it was to prevent the incurfions of the Banditi, of
whom great numbers had fled into that kingdom, and
daily infefted the ecclefiaftical ftate with their robberies and murders : He went himfelf to Terracina, to
fee, as he pretended, the fens and marfhes of that
country laid dry [4]: But his true defign was to
make a fudden defcent upon the kingdom of Naples.

When the Spaniards, who were apprehenfive of it
for fome time before, had certain intelligence of this
ftep, they fent 4000 of their beft troops towards
their frontiers, commanded by count Spinelli, as they
faid, to drive the Banditi out of their dominions,
but in reality to obferve the motions of the pope,
whom they had much more reafon to be afraid of ;
efpecially as it was commonly reported that his army
was to be joined by a great number of the Banditi,
as foon as he entered the kingdom. But whether he
found his defign was difcovered, or all things were not
yet ripe for the execution of it, after he had received
the compliments of the viceroy, by his fon, whom
he fent on purpofe to Terracina, he fuddenly returned to Rome, where he died foon after, to the great
joy of the Spaniards, and the infinite concern of Henry the Great.

As this event occafioned various reports and fpeculations, we fhall here take notice of fuch circumftances relating to it as have come to our knowledge.
Some months before he died he was troubled with
an intenfe pain in his head, which he imputed to his

* Ital. *I Cavalleri Lauretani.* French. *Les Chevaliers de Notre
Dame de Loretto.*

[4] Pomptinas paludes, opus a multis fruftra tentatum, juxta
Terracinam, deficcare, nec non et Clanianas in Etruria eodem
tempore inftitit, et tantos conatus exitu non carituros, initio fpes
fuit. *Thuan. lib. c.*

too great application to bufinefs; and being one day
at a public fignature, he entered into a long difcourfe
concerning the quality of his diforder, the nature of
his conftitution, the common regimen, and the remedies that were proper to be made ufe of; often
quoting Galen and Hippocrates with as much readinefs as if he had been educated a phyfician.

Notwithftanding he perceived this malady daily
grow upon him, he would not refrain from bufinefs,
as he faid it was a relief and amufement to him, indulging himfelf but little in repofe, tho' his nephew
and fifter were very urgent with him to take more
care of his health, and fpare himfelf fometimes; but
he did not fhew much regard to their advice, or the
prefcriptions of his phyficians, feeming rather to make
a joke of their confultations; tho' he would often
fend for and order them to difcourfe of the nature of
his difeafe before him.

He went much abroad, fometimes on horfeback,
tho' oftner on foot, for he was very fond of walking,
and never entered into converfation about bufinefs,
with ambaffadors, as other popes ufed to do at thofe
times, but admitted them to an audience, generally
leaning upon a table, his indifpofition not permitting
him to act with his ufual fpirit and vivacity. He had
the faying of Vefpafian frequently in his mouth,
" That a prince ought to die ftanding;" that is labouring to the very laft moment of his life for the
good of his country: A maxim which he ftrictly followed, giving audience and doing bufinefs, even upon thofe days that he found himfelf the worft, and
being angry at fuch as would have diffuaded him
from it.

On Saturday the 18th of Auguft, he went with a
numerous attendance to St. Maria di Tedefchi, a German church, at the particular defire of the protector
of that nation, to return God thanks for the converfion of a German prince, which was effected by the
labours of fome fathers of the Francifcan order : And

to

to give the greater proof of his devotion, he both
went thither and returned on foot.

On Monday he was feized with a high fever, which
began with a fhivering; and notwithftanding the moft
earneft folicitations of his phyficians and relations to
the contrary, he got up, gave audience, and difpatched fome affairs that might very well have been
let alone till another time, as they did not require
much expedition. After that, he fent for the governor, and commanded him to condemn all the prifoners, that were convicted of any crime, to the gallies, and fend them away directly to Civita Vecchia.

On Wednefday he had a more violent return of his
fever: The next morning (being the day of intermiffion) he afifted at a congregation of the H. Office,
and caufed feveral affairs of great importance to be
difcuffed in his prefence, feeming to take it ill, that
fome cardinals, at the defire of the phyficians, endeavoured to hurry things over in a perfunctory manner, and called for a lift of fuch as were in the prifons of the Inquifition. Tho' his fever returned every time with greater fury, he never would eat in bed,
but always rofe, and fat down with company to the
table, and feemed particularly fond of raw fruit.

On Sunday they gave him fome Caffia and Manna,
which had no great effect upon him, as he did not
take the whole dofe; after which his fever increafed
to fuch a degree, that, thinking himfelf in great danger, he heard mafs and received the facrament; but
growing weaker and weaker, they made all hafte to
give him the extreme unction, before which he fent
for Caftagna, whom he always looked upon as his fucceffor, and recommending to him the difpatch of certain affairs that were then depending before fome of
the congregations, he faid to his nephew, who was
prefent, "This is the moft worthy cardinal in the
" whole college."

On Monday the 27th of Auguft 1590, in the dufk
of the evening, he expired in the arms of the above-
mentioned

mentioned cardinal, his nephew and other relations weeping bitterly by his bedſide.

This is the account of his death that was publiſhed amongſt the people, and confirmed by the eccleſiaſtics, to prevent all occaſion of ſcandal; but people of penetration ſeemed to be thoroughly convinced, from all appearances, that he died by a ſlow, lingering poiſon; and this opinion was countenanced by the report of the phyſicians, who, upon opening him, found his brain tainted and diſcoloured by the malignity of the poiſon, which was the occaſion of that continual pain in his head that he was afflicted with all the time of his illneſs. Indeed he ſeemed to ſuſpect ſomething of this kind himſelf; for he ſaid one day to the doctors, " I perceive the Spaniards are " tired of my pontificate; it is well if they don't con- " trive ſome method to ſhorten my days." Some ſay there were freſh poiſon given him in the Manna which he took the day before he died. Every one that durſt ſpeak out, made no ſcruple of ſaying the Spaniards did him this kindneſs, as there was but too much reaſon indeed to ſuſpect it. In the firſt place it was well known what mortal jealouſy and inquietude he gave them upon the account of Naples, and the continual alarms he occaſioned by the warlike preparations he was daily making upon the frontiers of that kingdom. To this we may add the diſguſt they took from his unwillingneſs to declare for the league againſt the K. of Navarre, to the utter diſappointment of the deſigns they had formed upon the crown of France: Not to mention his ill uſage to their ambaſſador and refuſing to ſuccour the duke of Savoy, whom they had ſtirred up to the enterprize upon Geneva, which we have taken notice of before. It is ſaid the duke had proceeded ſo far as to build forts all round that city, and made himſelf ſure of carrying it, but was obliged to raiſe the ſiege in a diſgraceful manner, for want of the aid that he expected from Sixtus; which occaſioned the Spaniards to publiſh every

ry where, " That it was entirely owing to Sixtus that
" the duke did not take Geneva."

All thefe reafons put together, with the remembrance of the manner in wiiich he had behaved, in
relation to the affairs of England, provoked the Spaniards to fuch a degree, as it was reported, that they
determined to rid themfelves of him as foon as poffible, and get another chofen that was fitter for their
purpofe, who would favour the league, and give no
quarter to Heretics.

Such were the reports and furmifes that prevailed
at that time in Italy : But it muft be confidered on the
other hand, that thefe were chiefly propagated by the
enemies and ill-wifhers to the Spaniards, with a view
to ruin their intereft at Rome, and make them infamous thro' Chriftendom.   For how fubtle and malicious foever that nation may be reckoned, it is certain
the poifoning of a pope could not be effected by any
one perfon ; and the communication of fo horrid an
undertaking to feveral accomplices would be very
dangerous, and inconfiftent with their ufual circumfpection, as they could not but know the great number of fpies he conftantly kept in pay.

When Henry IV. heard of it, he faid, " This is
" a ftroke of Spanifh politics; Heaven has no fhare
" in it:" And foon after, "I have loft a pope after
" my own heart, may God fend us another like him."

As he died in the palace at Monte Cavallo, his body was carried in a litter to St. Peter's, and there interred with the ufual ceremonies : His nephew cardinal Montalto (a perfon of extraordinary virtue) removed it the year after with great pomp to a chapel
which he had built in St. Maria Maggiore, where he
celebrated his obfequies with a magnificence due to fo
great a pontiff.

During the vacancy of the See, which continued
18 days, fome Spaniards, and other difaffected people, took it into their heads to pull down his ftatue
in the capitol :, When the fenate heard of it, they
publifhed a decree, in which it was forbid, for the future

ture, to erect a statue to any pope in his life-time, and had it engraved on a marble pillar in the capitol; the words are as follow:

SI. QVIS.
SIVE. PRIVATVS. SIVE. MAGISTRATVM.
GERENS.
DE. COLLOCANDA. VIVO. PONTIFICI.
STATVA.
MENTIONEM. FACERE. AVSIT.
LEGITIMO. S. P. Q. R. DECRETO. IN. PER-
PETVVM. INFAMIS.
ET. PVBLICORVM. MVNERVM. EXPERS.
ESTO.
M. D. X. C. MENS. AVG.

It may not be amiss, by way of conclusion, to inform the reader in what condition Sixtus left the revenues of the Apostolic Chamber, after he had introduced an infinity of taxes and imposts, never thought of by former popes, although their necessities had often been very great. It is true, indeed, none of them had ever expended a tenth part of the money, nor left any thing like what he did behind them: Nay it may be affirmed with strict truth, that all the popes together, that had reigned during the two last centuries, had not laid out so much in public buildings, or deposited half the sum that he did in the treasury, which things to be sure could not have been effected without laying very heavy loads upon the people.

It cannot be denied that the city was very much obliged to him for the great variety of noble fabrics, &c. with which he adorned it; the treasury, for not only leaving it clear and out of debt, but with five millions of gold in it; and the ecclesiastical state, in general, for the speedy and impartial administration of justice, which had been so shamefully neglected, and indeed almost laid aside, in the reign of his predecessor: But he left the people so thoroughly drained and exhausted, that, for many years after, (except amongst families that were enriched

riched by being a-kin to the succeeding popes, or such
as enjoyed places of great profit) there was nothing
to be heard but murmurs, and complaints of poverty and desolation.

He used to say, that "Christians ought to be let
" blood in the neck, for an example to the Jews,
" and the Jews in the pocket, to save the purses
" of Christians;" and indeed he put only one Jew
to death all the while he was pope, but often used
to punish them by large fines and commutations;
notwithstanding which there was an increase of 200
Jewish families in his time drawn to Rome by the
great security they enjoyed there: A consideration
that weighs much with that people. In the reign
of Gregory XIII. great numbers of them had retired
into other states, to avoid the insupportable insolence
and cruelties that were exercised upon them by the
Christians. But after his death they returned to
Rome with additional numbers, encouraged by the
protection of Sixtus, who would not suffer them to
be insulted or abused by any person whatsoever.

He ordered a servant, belonging to a house of
Conti, to be severely whipped for pulling off a Jew's
hat, as he passed by, and throwing it into the Tiber; which example had so good an effect, that they
afterwards lived without any disturbance or molesta-
tion, nobody daring to offer them the least affront:
It is true, Sixtus made them pay very handsomely,
upon particular occasions, for this indulgence.

We have, in the former part of this work, given
an account of the nature and value of the pontifical revenue, when Sixtus ascended the throne, and
of the augmentation he made to it: But if we include both ordinary and extraordinary, it is not sufficient to account for his vast expences, and the
treasure he left behind him. It is certain, no prince
was ever more industrious in searching out ways and
means of raising money; and tho' we have already
taken notice of the custom, which he introduced,
of selling offices and places of profit, and the great
                                                    sums

fums he amaffed that way, as we have received
fome frefh informations relating to this particular,
fince thofe fheets were printed off, we beg leave to
acquaint the reader, that the number of places which
he fold was 36,550, and that the fum given for them
amounted to 5,547, 630 crowns.

From this we may form fome idea of the infinity of
bufinefs that is tranfacted at Rome, and the grandeur
of that court. It may be wondered where purchafers
could be found for fuch a number of employments :
But this difficulty is eafily folved, when we inform
him that they are fold in reverfion, and yield a profit
of 7, 10, nay, fome of 14 per cent. per annum : So
that, befides the honour, the buyer receives very
confiderable intereft for his money. In the next
place, they that purchafe them are not obliged to
be Romans, but may be natives of any other country,
and refide elfewhere, if the pope pleafes.

Many of them were inftituted de novo by Sixtus,
others divided, and put into commiffion; and they
that were already in poffeffion, obliged to pay large
fums to be continued in it. In this he made no diftinction of perfons; the cardinals themfelves were
not excepted; for when he preferred his nephew
Montalto to the vice-chancellorfhip of the church, he
gave him 23,000 crowns to pay into the Apoftolic
Chamber for that high dignity. But when Aldobrandino came afterwards to be pope, with the name
of Clement VIII, he publifhed a bull, declaring that
the vice-chancellorfhip, the offices of chamberlain, datary, grand penetentiary, with five or fix others that
ufed to be enjoyed by cardinals, fhould be given
away gratis, for the honour and reputation of the H.
College : And indeed it muft be acknowledged, it
was rather fcandalous and unjuft in Sixtus to oblige
thofe to pay for their offices, that were his brothers
and affeffors in the adminiftration of government.

This, in fome meafure, points out the fource from
whence he was enabled to perform fuch wonders
whilft he lived, and leave his coffers fo full when he
died,

died, tho' it occafioned endlefs fcandal and murmurs, not only amongft the Catholics, but Proteftants, quite thro' Chriftendom, and gave the latter a handle to fay, by way of reproach, " That Rome was be- " come a fink of venality and proftitution," when they faw all offices, both facred and profane, expofed to fale in fo fhamelefs and barefaced a manner. An example that was foon imitated by other Chriftian princes, when they had fo good an authority.

Tho' Sixtus was duly informed by his fpies of the complaints that fuch a manner of proceeding raifed amongft his fubjects, and tho' his nephew reprefent- ed to him, that all the odium would fall upon him after his death, he only anfwered, " My dear ne- " phew, the difcontent of the people is like fnow in " fummer, which foon melts away : If they pay " well, let them have their fill of murmuring ; com- " plaints are the food of the populace, they cannot " live without them ; but money is the foundation " of the prince's greatnefs : Don't be afraid of any " odium falling upon you after my death ; when I " am gone, their murmurs and complaints will be " turned into reverence and admiration."

The number of vendible places has been much increafed by the fucceeding popes ; amongft the reft there are now twelve clerks of the Apoftolic Cham- ber, every one of whofe offices is fold for 42,000 crowns : So that, at prefent there are above 40,000 to be difpofed of in the court of Rome, fome of which are prodigioufly rifen in their value ; as the office of treafurer, which is fold for 70,000 crowns, and that of the auditor of the exchequer for as much.

This is a fine harveft for the pope's nephews, it having been computed by the people who were ac- quainted with the affairs of thofe times, that the Bar- berini's, during the pontificate of Urban VIII, which lafted 23 years, made 18 millions of crowns by the fale of offices.

It is now become a cuftom, when the popes want money for their relations, to make thofe perfons

cardinals

cardinals who poffefs the moft lucrative pofts, and then to fell them to others : So that there is feldom a promotion made in thefe times, but the treafurer, the auditor, and perhaps one of the cleks, are of the number. It is reckoned, that, at an average, the popes make 300,000 crowns per annum by the fale of places, which is accounted part of their extraordinary revenue.

We have faid that Sixtus was very rigorous and exact in the collection of his taxes, that his collectors would not allow the people a day beyond the time appointed for the payment of them, and fometimes compelled them to fell all they had to raife the money : The reafon he gave for this was, that it obliged his fubjects to be frugal and diligent, which otherwife they would not be, and occafioned a fpirit of induftry amongft them ; it being very true, that when a man knows he is obliged to pay a fum of money at a fixed time, on fevere penalties, to a furly and unmerciful creditor, it will make him take unufual pains, and exert his faculties, if he has any, to difcharge the debt.

Tho' Sixtus had reduced the ordinary expences of government to a third part of what they ufed to be, and his revenues were gathered to the uttermoft farthing, the extraordinary, however, amounted to 600,000 crowns per annum, which he raifed from the firft fruits of vacant benefices, the contributions of Spain, Naples, Portugal, and many other fountains, leaving no method un-attempted that he thought would bring in money : So that his projectors, who knew his temper, racked their brains day and night to gain his favour, by finding out fome new way to increafe his income. There furely never was any prince more attentive and indefatigable in his application to this point.

The French ambaffador, afking him fome queftions one day, concerning his revenue, for the fatisfaction of a perfon, who, as he told him, was going
to

to write a hiftory of the court of Rome, he faid,
" Pray tell your hiftorian, that if the pope has but
" a farthing in his pocket to buy a pen, he may
" make his revenue as large as he pleafes." It is certain he did wonderful things with that fmall engine;
fome of which, it is true, wear the afpect of extorti-
on. I remember to have feen the following obfervation in the margin of a little manufcript, fent me
by a friend out of Italy, which gives an account of the
treafure that Sixtus left in the caftle of St. Angelo,
" A million and a half of this money was raifed by
" the confifcation of the goods of fuch as were con-
" victed of maintaining a correfpondence with the
" Banditi:" And there is no manner of doubt, if we
may judge from the number of thofe that were condemned, but the fums which he drew from fines,
commutations, &c. were immenfe, as he did not
forgive the flighteft offence without fome pecuniary
confideration. In the firft year of his pontificate he
- filled Rome, and the ecclefiaftical ftate, with execu-
tions; but when once the fame of his juftice was
eftablifhed, he punifhed the rich by fines and confif-
cations, and the poor, who could not redeem themfelves, with death.

He likewife reduced the expences of the Apoftolic
Chamber to lefs than half of what they were when
he came to the pontificate, that is, to about 313,000
crowns, retrenching, or entirely cutting off, the falaries of feveral officers that he thought ufelefs, of
which (tho' it occafioned great difcontent) only two
or three perfons had the courage to complain, praying his Holinefs " to confider that, as they had en-
" joyed them feveral years, the taking them away
" in fo fudden a manner, muft of courfe be a very
" great inconvenience as well as furprize to them."
To which he anfwered, in a few words, " That they
" ought to follow his example, who, when Gregory
" XIII. had taken away the penfion that had been
" allowed him by Pius V. made no remonftrance,
" but bore it patiently and without murmuring."

As for the extraordinary expences of the popes, which were ufually every year about 146,000 crowns, he not only did not reduce but confiderably increafed them, as he was very oftentatious, and affected much ftate and magnificence, upon public occafions: But his greateft ambition and expence feemed to confift in erecting obelifks, hofpitals, palaces, churches, and other public buildings, in which it is computed that he yearly expended the fum of 340,000 crowns for the ufe and ornament of the city, and to perpetuate his memory, which in all likelihood will be revered and held in admiration by the lateft pofterity.

End of the ELEVENTH *and* LAST BOOK.

THE

THE

CONTENTS.

BOOK I.

CONTENTS.

CONTENTS.

BOOK II.

CONTENTS.

CONTENTS.

BOOK III.

S

CONTENTS.

CONTENTS.

BOOK IV.

Farnefe

CONTENTS.

BOOK, V.

CONTENTS.

BOOK VI.

CONTENTS.

BOOK VII.

BOOK VIII.

tail

CONTENTS.

BOOK IX.

BOOK X.

C-ONTENTS.

BOOK XI.

FINIS.

Printed in the USA
CPSIA information can be obtained
at www.ICGtesting.com
LVHW051535151023
761145LV00011B/302